CURTAIN

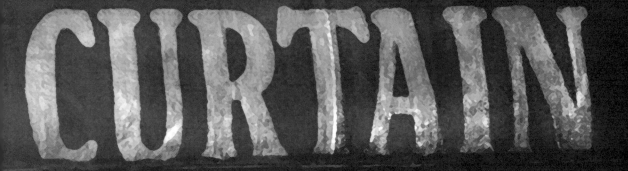

ALICE IN SUNDERLAND
BY
BRYAN TALBOT

For Tabitha

Dark Horse Books™

publication design
BRYAN TALBOT

publisher
MIKE RICHARDSON

editor
CHRIS WARNER

ALICE IN SUNDERLAND

Dark Horse Books™
A division of Dark Horse Comics, Inc.
10956 SE Main Street
Milwaukie OR 97222

darkhorse.com

To find a comics shop in your area,
call the Comic Shop Locator Service toll-free at 1-888-266-4226

First edition: April 2007
ISBN-10: 1-59307-673-8
ISBN-13: 978-1-59307-673-3

3 5 7 9 10 8 6 4 2
Printed in China

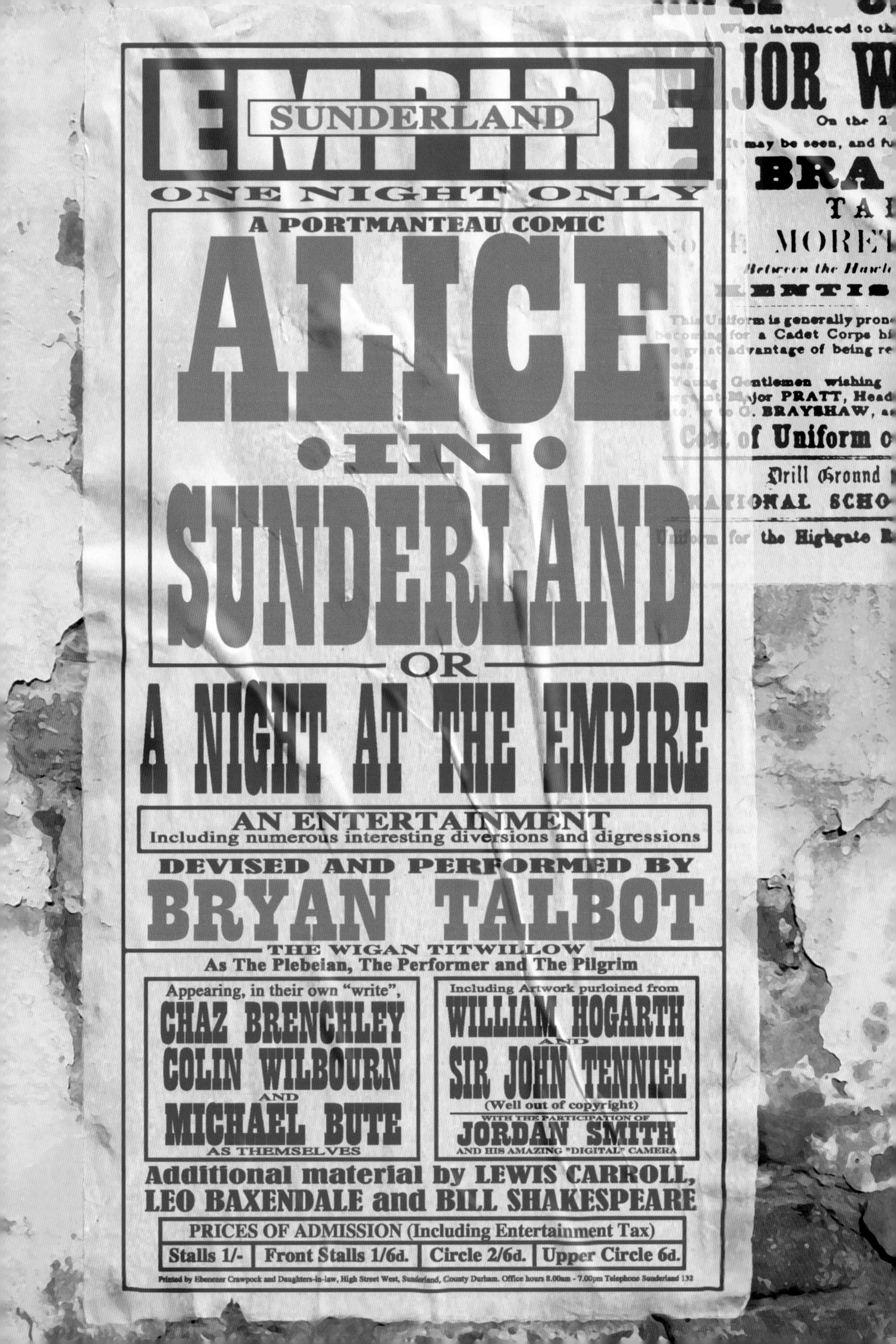

EMPIRE
SUNDERLAND

ONE NIGHT ONLY

A PORTMANTEAU COMIC

ALICE
· IN ·
SUNDERLAND
— OR —
A NIGHT AT THE EMPIRE

AN ENTERTAINMENT
Including numerous interesting diversions and digressions

DEVISED AND PERFORMED BY
BRYAN TALBOT

THE WIGAN TITWILLOW
As The Plebeian, The Performer and The Pilgrim

Appearing, in their own "write",
CHAZ BRENCHLEY
COLIN WILBOURN
AND
MICHAEL BUTE
AS THEMSELVES

Including Artwork purloined from
WILLIAM HOGARTH
AND
SIR JOHN TENNIEL
(Well out of copyright)
WITH THE PARTICIPATION OF
JORDAN SMITH
AND HIS AMAZING "DIGITAL" CAMERA

Additional material by LEWIS CARROLL, LEO BAXENDALE and BILL SHAKESPEARE

PRICES OF ADMISSION (Including Entertainment Tax)

Stalls 1/-	Front Stalls 1/6d.	Circle 2/6d.	Upper Circle 6d.

Printed by Ebenezer Crawpock and Daughters-in-law, High Street West, Sunderland, County Durham. Office hours 8.00am - 7.00pm Telephone Sunderland 132

"Reality is not enough; we need nonsense too. Drifting into a world of fantasy is not an escape from reality but a significant education about the nature of life. And reality is not an escape from nonsense. Our education goes on everywhere."

Edmund Miller
Lewis Carroll Observed

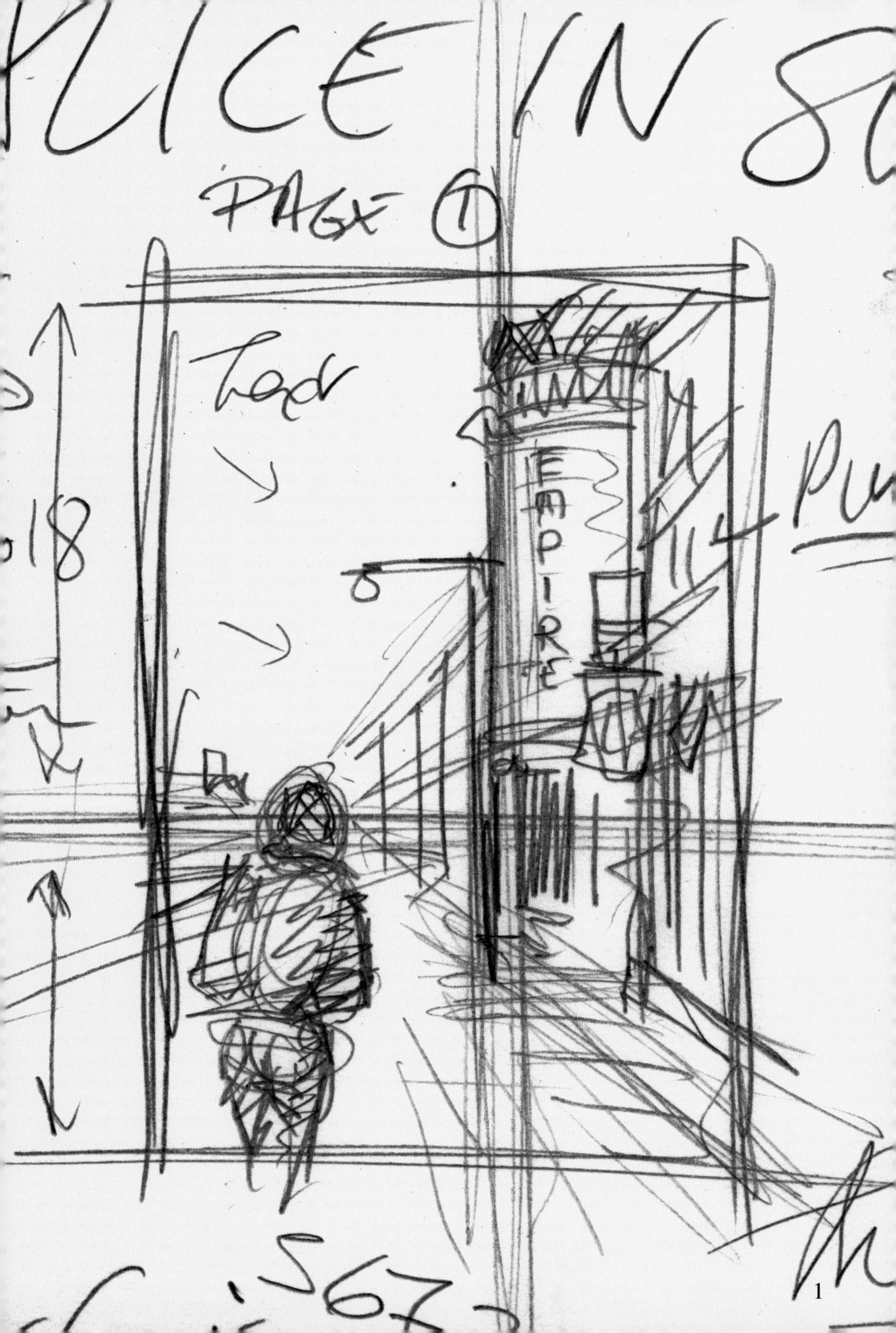
PAGE ①
EMPIRE

Well, there's this guy, right...

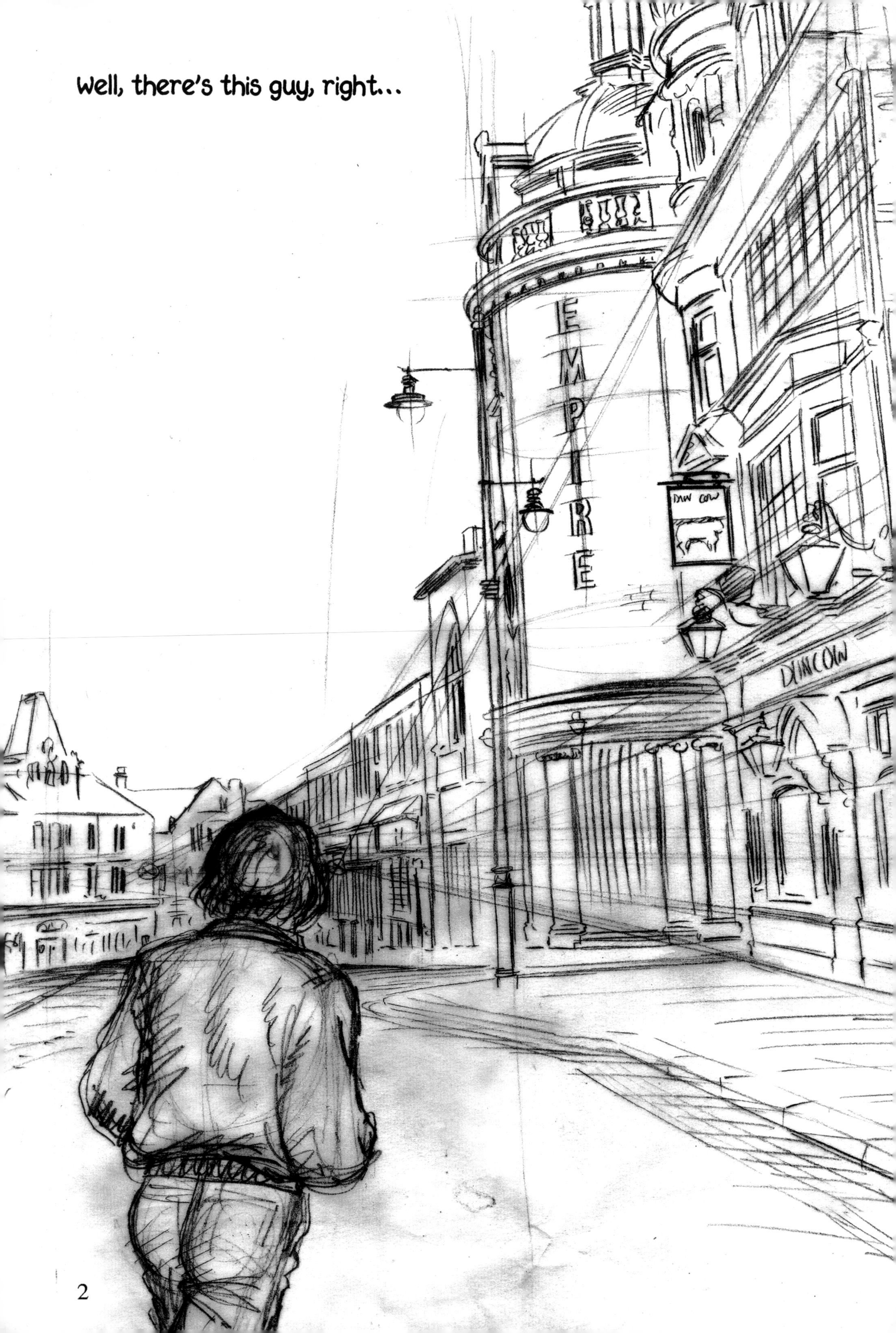
EMPIRE
DUN COW
DUN COW

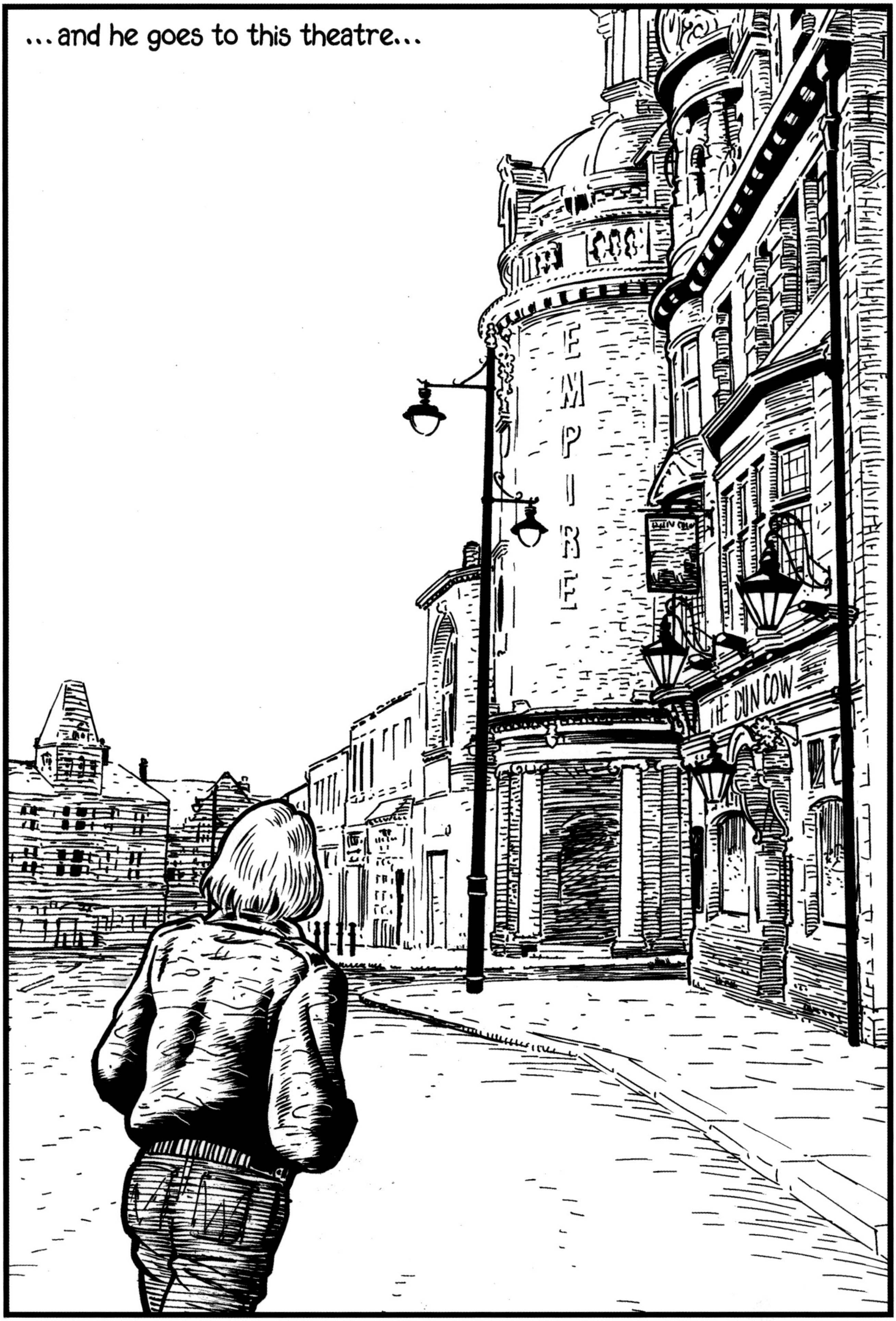
...and he goes to this theatre...
EMPIRE
THE DUN COW

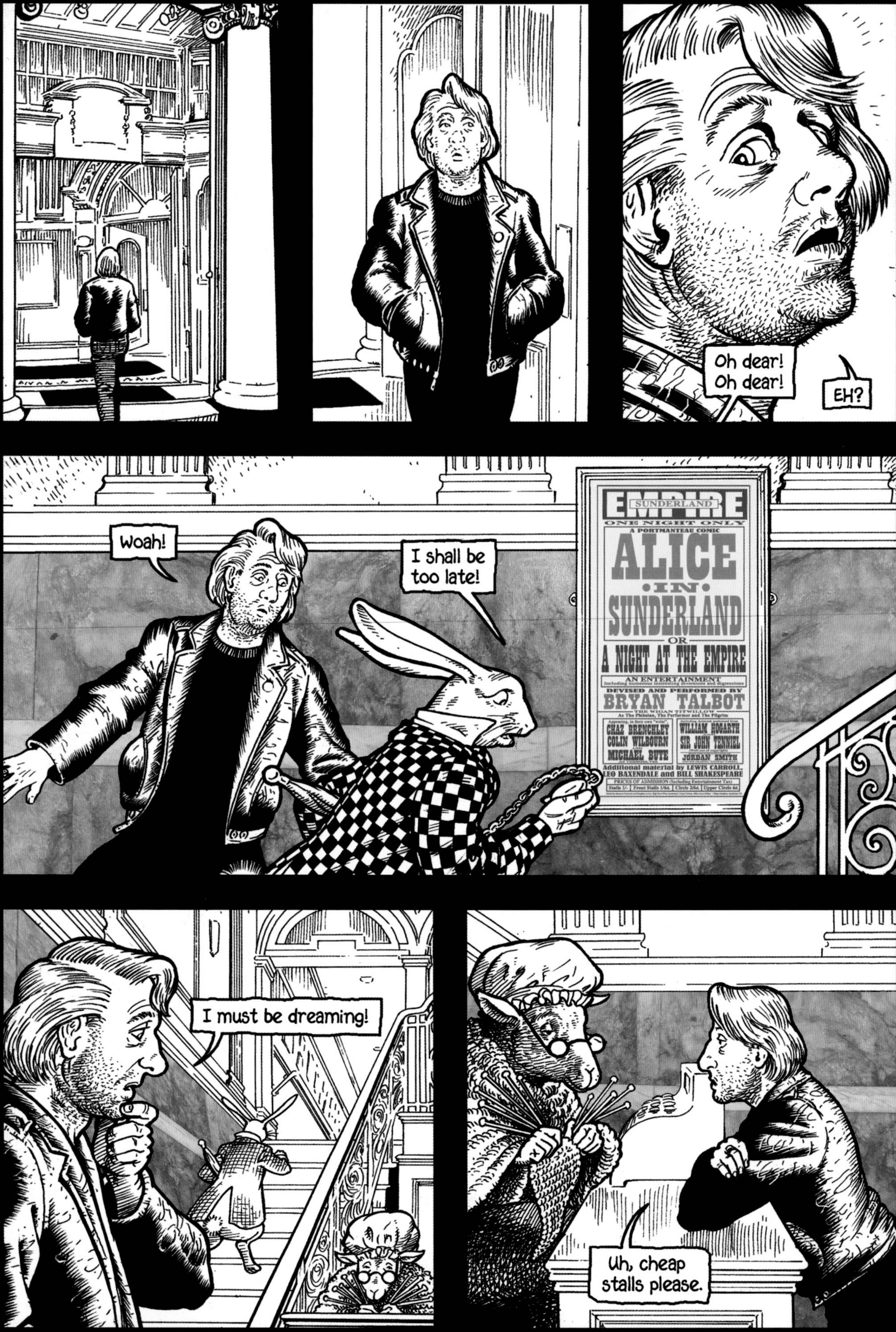
Oh dear! Oh dear!
EH?
Woah!
I shall be too late!
EMPIRE
SUNDERLAND
ONE NIGHT ONLY
A PORTMANTEAU COMIC
ALICE
•IN•
SUNDERLAND
OR
A NIGHT AT THE EMPIRE
AN ENTERTAINMENT
Including numerous interesting diversions and digressions
DEVISED AND PERFORMED BY
BRYAN TALBOT
THE WIGAN TITWILLOW
As The Plebeian, The Performer and The Pilgrim
Appearing, in their own "write",
CHAZ BRENCHLEY
COLIN WILBOURN
AND
MICHAEL BUTE
WILLIAM HOGARTH
SIR JOHN TENNIEL
(Well out of copyright)
JORDAN SMITH
Additional material by LEWIS CARROLL, LEO BAXENDALE and BILL SHAKESPEARE
PRICES OF ADMISSION (Including Entertainment Tax)
Stalls 1/- | Front Stalls 1/6d. | Circle 2/6d. | Upper Circle 6d.
I must be dreaming!
Uh, cheap stalls please.

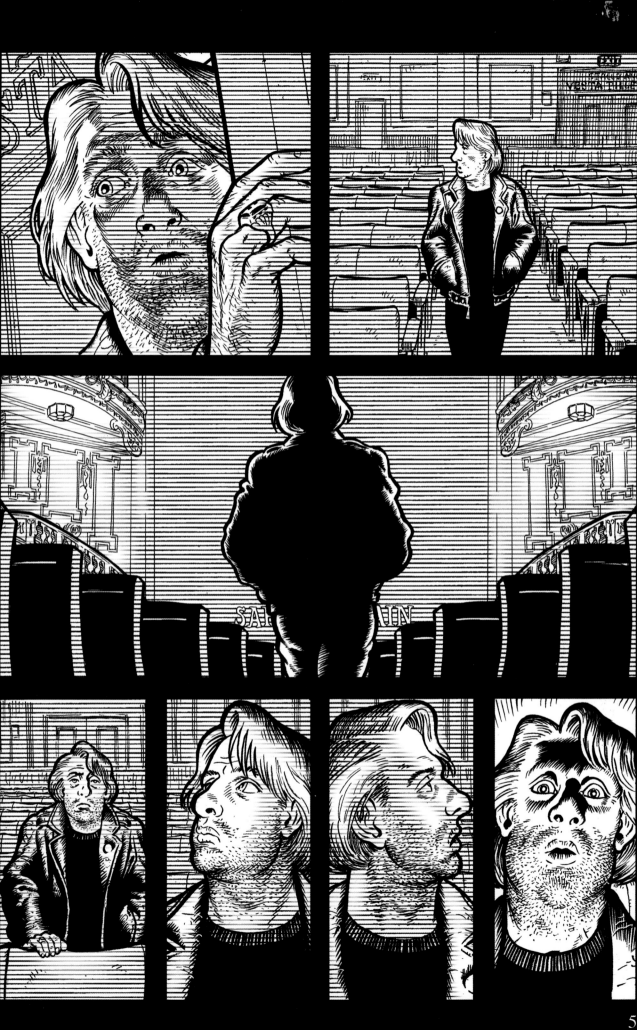

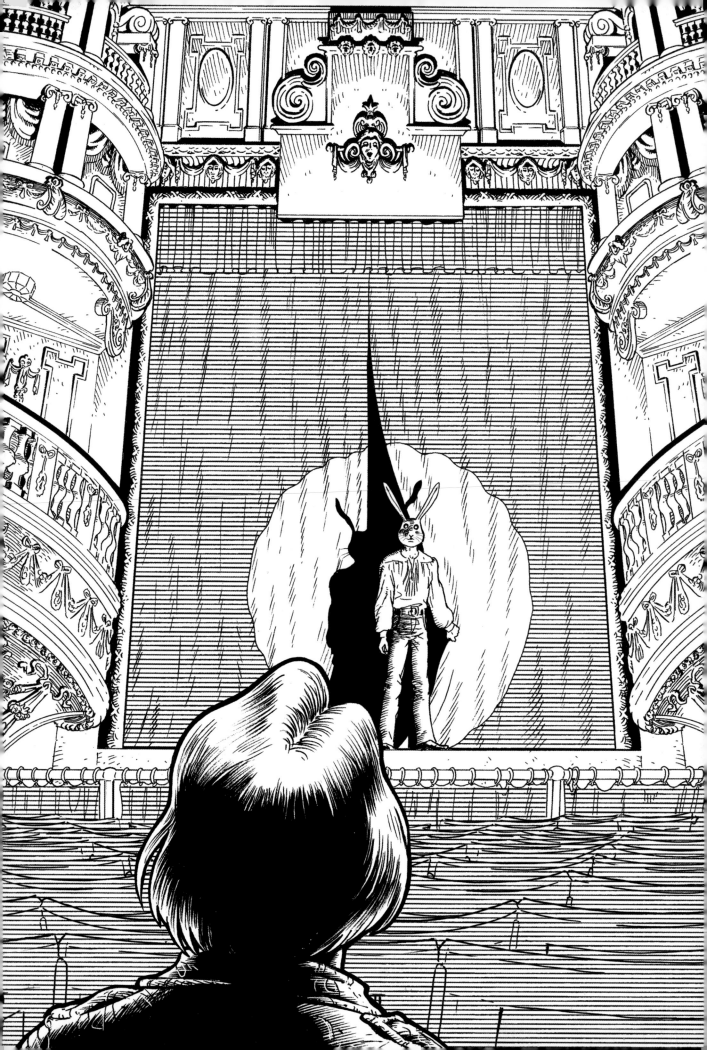

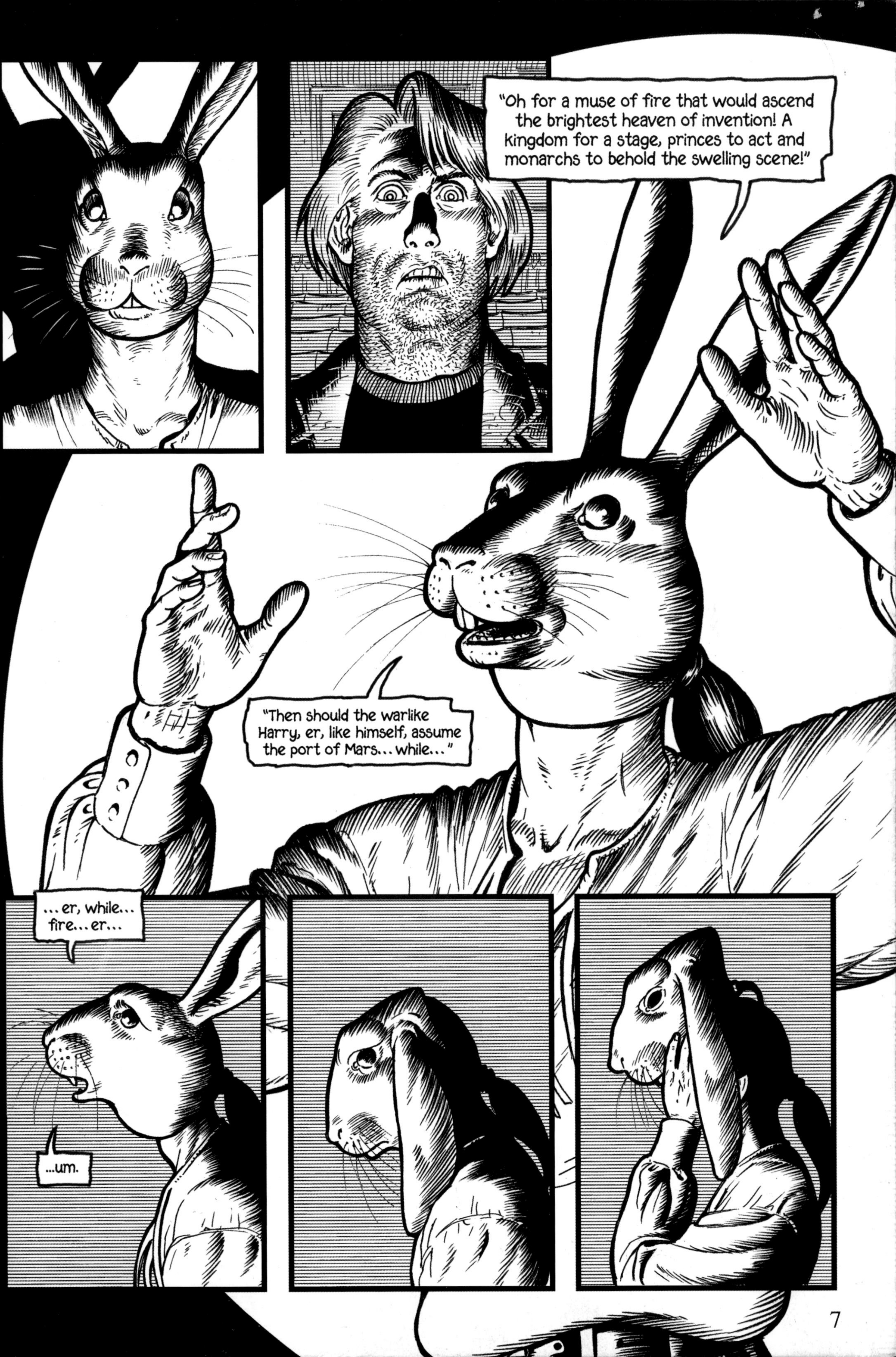
"Oh for a muse of fire that would ascend the brightest heaven of invention! A kingdom for a stage, princes to act and monarchs to behold the swelling scene!"
"Then should the warlike Harry, er, like himself, assume the port of Mars... while..."
...er, while... fire...er...
...um.

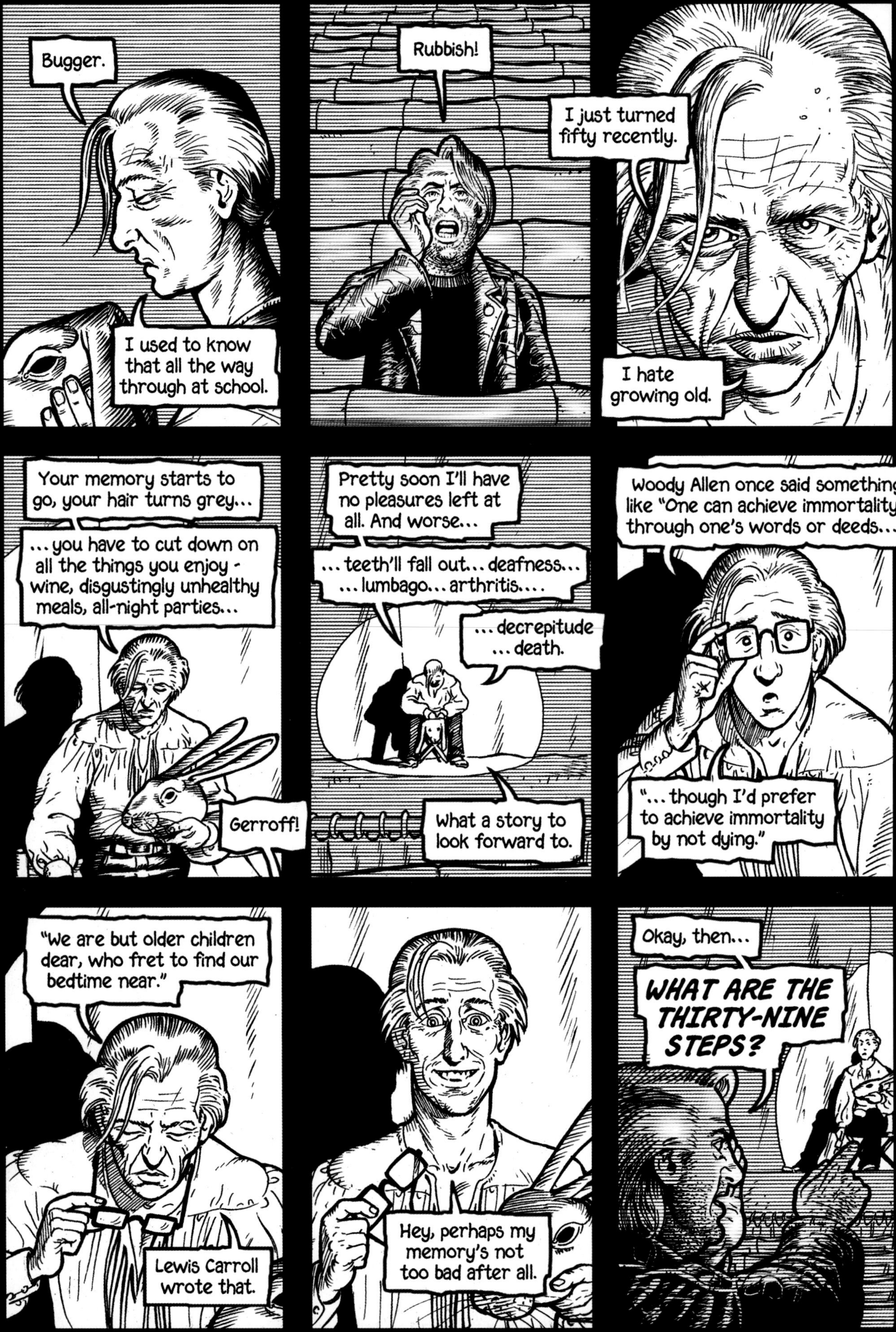
Bugger.
I used to know that all the way through at school.
Rubbish!
I just turned fifty recently.
I hate growing old.
Your memory starts to go, your hair turns grey...
...you have to cut down on all the things you enjoy - wine, disgustingly unhealthy meals, all-night parties...
Gerroff!
Pretty soon I'll have no pleasures left at all. And worse...
...teeth'll fall out...deafness... ...lumbago...arthritis....
...decrepitude ...death.
What a story to look forward to.
Woody Allen once said something like "One can achieve immortality through one's words or deeds..."
"...though I'd prefer to achieve immortality by not dying."
"We are but older children dear, who fret to find our bedtime near."
Lewis Carroll wrote that.
Hey, perhaps my memory's not too bad after all.
Okay, then...
WHAT ARE THE THIRTY-NINE STEPS?

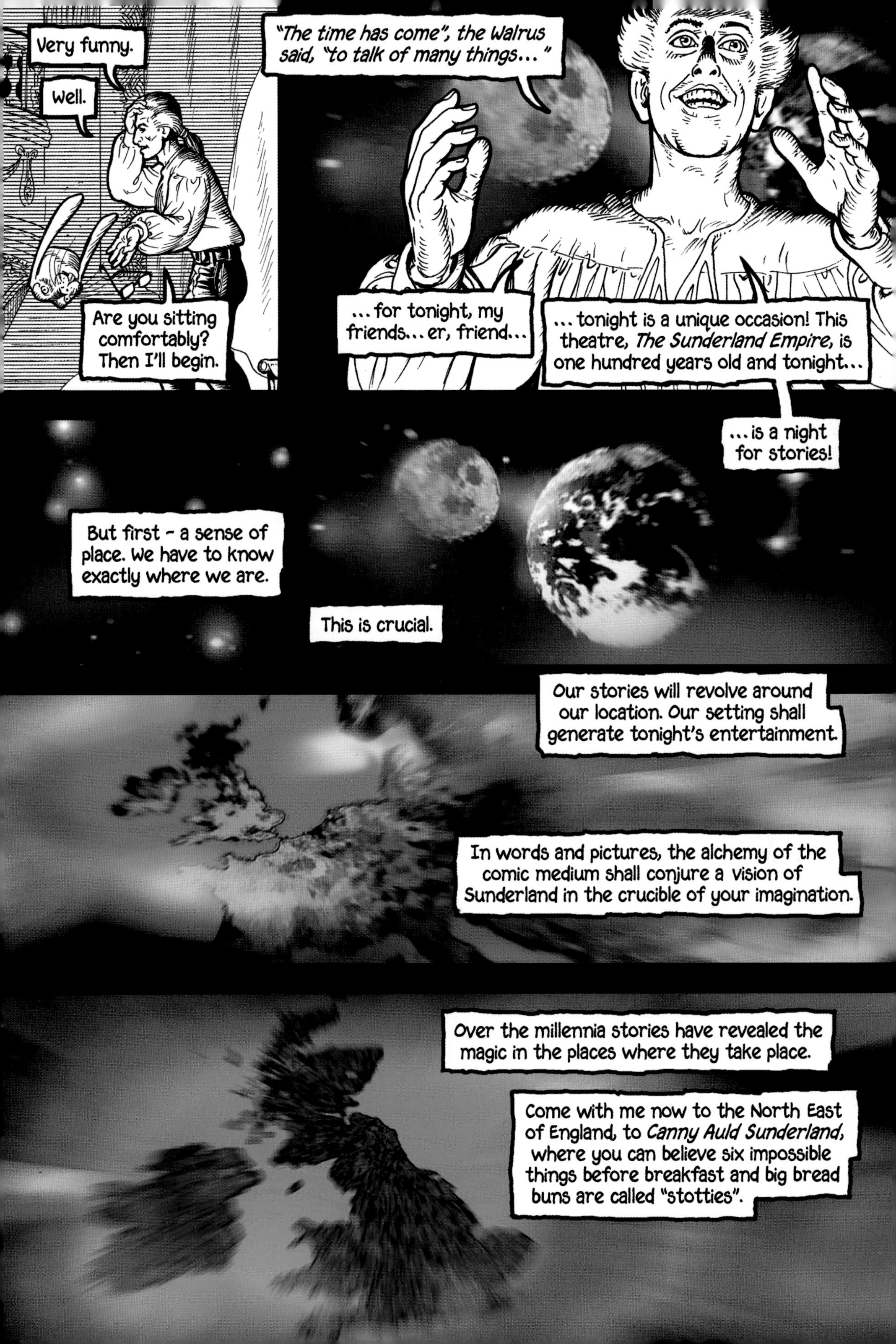
Very funny.
Well.
Are you sitting comfortably? Then I'll begin.
"The time has come", the Walrus said, "to talk of many things..."
...for tonight, my friends... er, friend...
...tonight is a unique occasion! This theatre, *The Sunderland Empire,* is one hundred years old and tonight...
...is a night for stories!
But first - a sense of place. We have to know exactly where we are.
This is crucial.
Our stories will revolve around our location. Our setting shall generate tonight's entertainment.
In words and pictures, the alchemy of the comic medium shall conjure a vision of Sunderland in the crucible of your imagination.
Over the millennia stories have revealed the magic in the places where they take place.
Come with me now to the North East of England, to *Canny Auld Sunderland,* where you can believe six impossible things before breakfast and big bread buns are called "stotties".

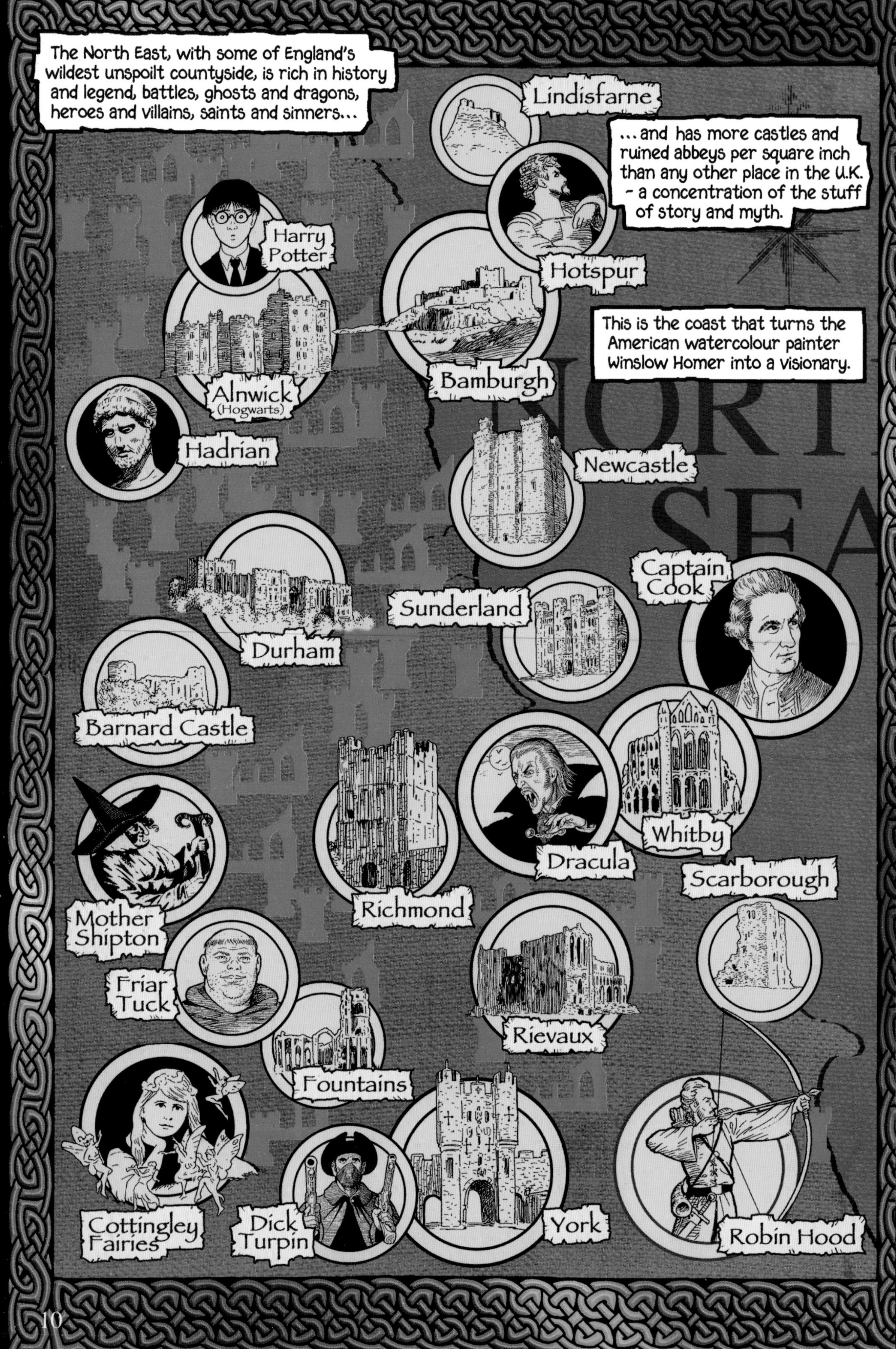

The North East, with some of England's wildest unspoilt countyside, is rich in history and legend, battles, ghosts and dragons, heroes and villains, saints and sinners...
Lindisfarne
...and has more castles and ruined abbeys per square inch than any other place in the U.K. - a concentration of the stuff of story and myth.
Harry Potter
Hotspur
This is the coast that turns the American watercolour painter Winslow Homer into a visionary.
Bamburgh
Alnwick (Hogwarts)
NORT
SEA
Hadrian
Newcastle
Captain Cook
Sunderland
Durham
Barnard Castle
Whitby
Dracula
Scarborough
Richmond
Mother Shipton
Friar Tuck
Rievaux
Fountains
Cottingley Fairies
Dick Turpin
York
Robin Hood

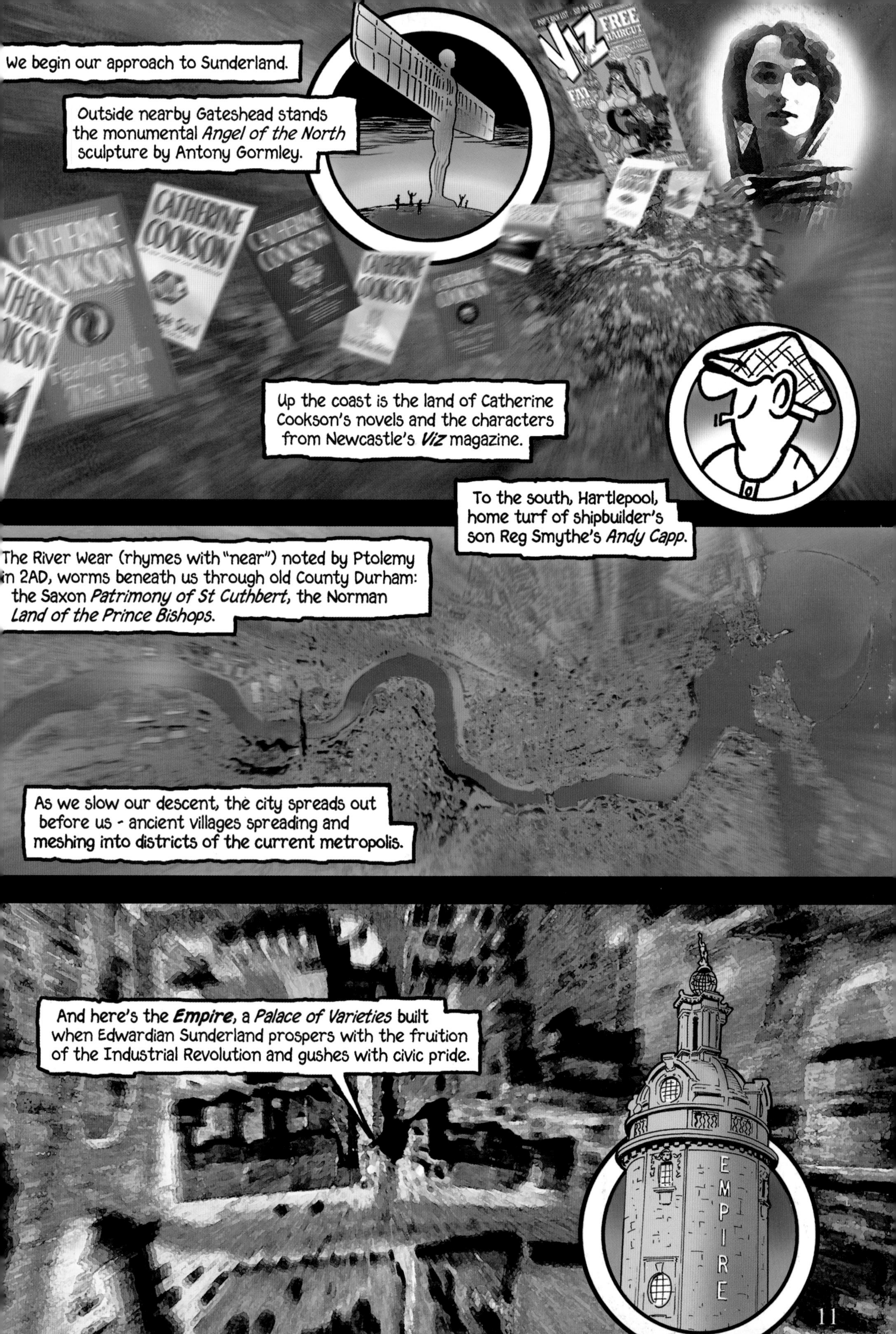
We begin our approach to Sunderland.
Outside nearby Gateshead stands the monumental *Angel of the North* sculpture by Antony Gormley.
VIZ
FREE HAIRCUT
CATHERINE COOKSON
Feathers In The Fire
Up the coast is the land of Catherine Cookson's novels and the characters from Newcastle's *Viz* magazine.
To the south, Hartlepool, home turf of shipbuilder's son Reg Smythe's *Andy Capp*.
The River Wear (rhymes with "near") noted by Ptolemy in 2AD, worms beneath us through old County Durham: the Saxon *Patrimony of St Cuthbert*, the Norman *Land of the Prince Bishops*.
As we slow our descent, the city spreads out before us - ancient villages spreading and meshing into districts of the current metropolis.
And here's the ***Empire***, a *Palace of Varieties* built when Edwardian Sunderland prospers with the fruition of the Industrial Revolution and gushes with civic pride.
EMPIRE

Crowning the tower with its marble and alabaster lobby, the seven foot high statue of *Terpsichore*, the Greek muse of Dance, the Dramatic Chorus and Lyric Poetry, gazes across at *St Michael's and All The Angels*, *Sunderland Minster*, built on the site of a temple to the Norse God *Thor*.

This theatre, the largest in the North East, is the dream of **Richard Thornton**, a poor pit-boy who learns the violin and works his way up to orchestra leader and impresario.

In partnership with Edward Moss and Oswald Stoll, his chain of *Empire Theatres* eventually spreads over England.

1906: The international stage superstar, male impersonator **Vesta Tilley** lays the foundation stone and returns for the opening night to a packed auditorium and a rapturous standing ovation.

THIS STONE WAS PLACED BY MISS VESTA TILLEY SEPT 29ᵀᴴ 1906

The *Empire* is a resounding success...

SUNDERLAND EMPIR
The Place to Spend a Pleasant Eveni
GRAND OPENING NIGHT
MONDAY, JULY 1st, 1907,
And TWICE NIGHTLY during the Week at 6·45 and 9 o'clock.
Matinee Every Saturday at 2·30. Doors open at

VESTA
TILLEY
DORA MARTINI, THE BIOSCO
ASTRONOMY
THE SOUSLOFFS
WILL VAN-ALLEN
THORPE AND C
MAUDIE FRANCIS, GEORGE
Lilian
PRICES TO SUIT EVERYONE.

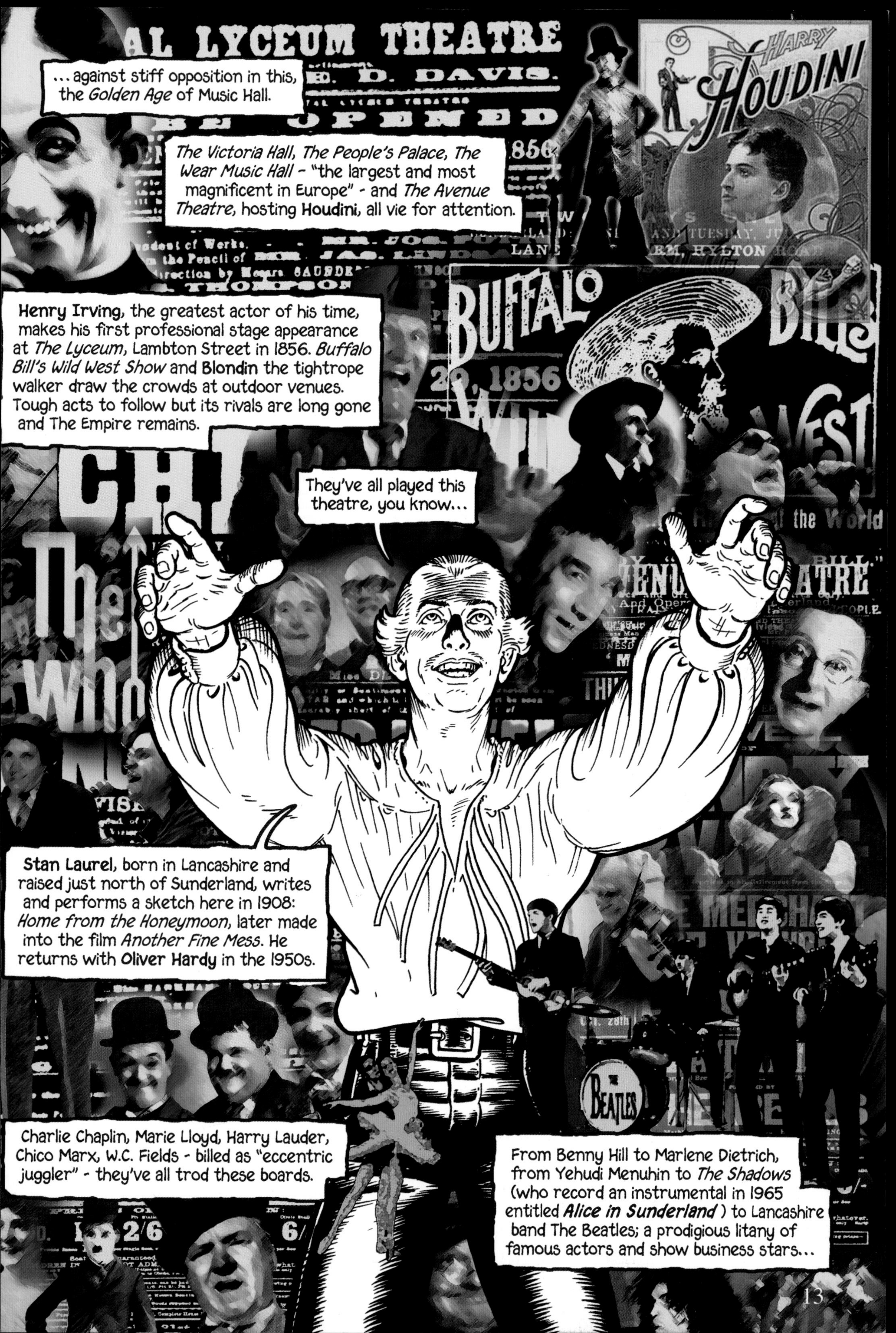
AL LYCEUM THEATRE
E. D. DAVIS.
...against stiff opposition in this, the *Golden Age* of Music Hall.
HARRY HOUDINI
The Victoria Hall, The People's Palace, The Wear Music Hall - "the largest and most magnificent in Europe" - and *The Avenue Theatre*, hosting **Houdini**, all vie for attention.
BUFFALO BILL
WILD WEST
Henry Irving, the greatest actor of his time, makes his first professional stage appearance at *The Lyceum*, Lambton Street in 1856. *Buffalo Bill's Wild West Show* and **Blondin** the tightrope walker draw the crowds at outdoor venues. Tough acts to follow but its rivals are long gone and The Empire remains.
They've all played this theatre, you know...
Stan Laurel, born in Lancashire and raised just north of Sunderland, writes and performs a sketch here in 1908: *Home from the Honeymoon*, later made into the film *Another Fine Mess*. He returns with **Oliver Hardy** in the 1950s.
THE BEATLES
Charlie Chaplin, Marie Lloyd, Harry Lauder, Chico Marx, W.C. Fields - billed as "eccentric juggler" - they've all trod these boards.
From Benny Hill to Marlene Dietrich, from Yehudi Menuhin to *The Shadows* (who record an instrumental in 1965 entitled ***Alice in Sunderland***) to Lancashire band The Beatles; a prodigious litany of famous actors and show business stars...

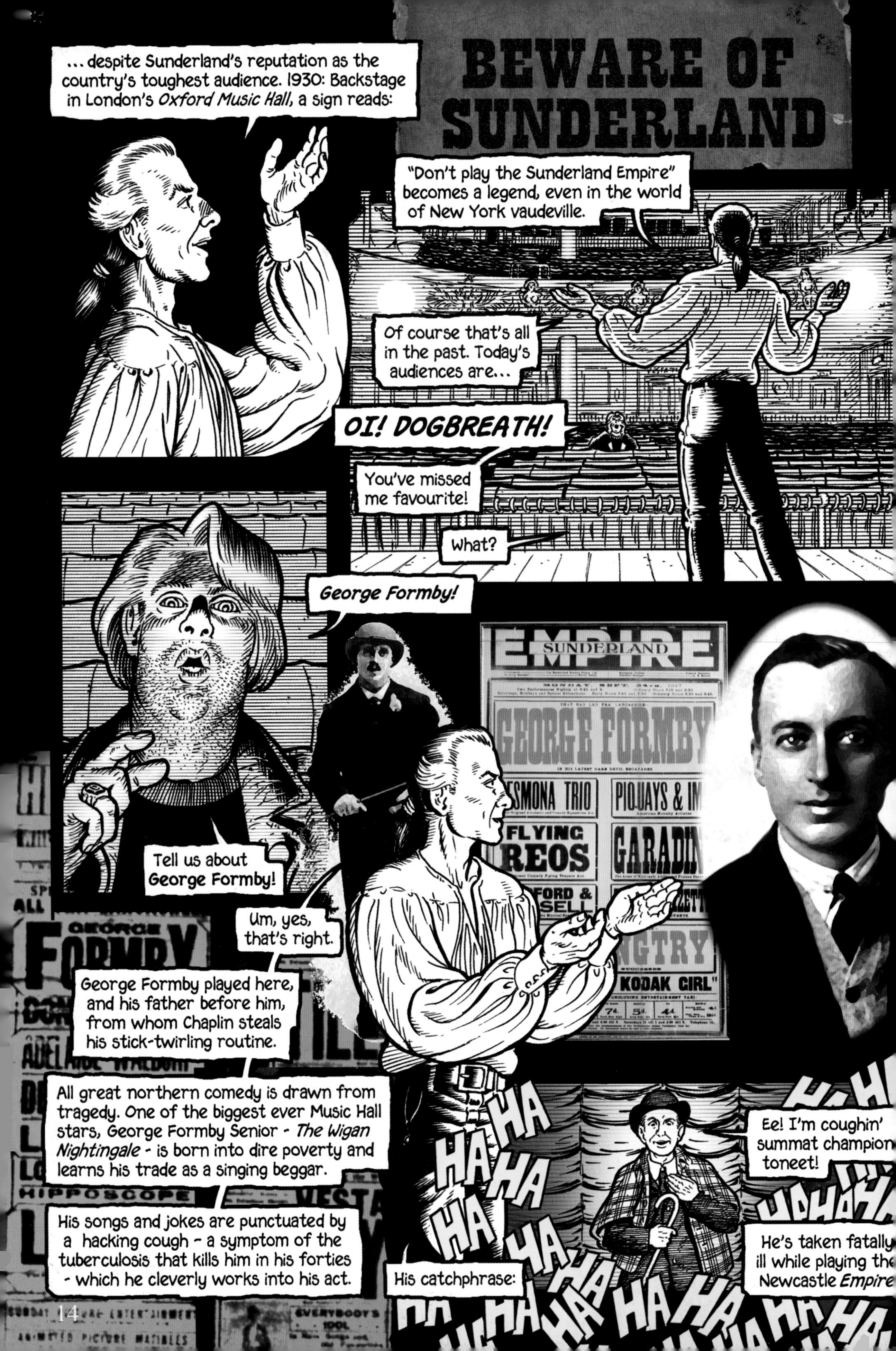

...despite Sunderland's reputation as the country's toughest audience. 1930: Backstage in London's *Oxford Music Hall*, a sign reads:
BEWARE OF SUNDERLAND
"Don't play the Sunderland Empire" becomes a legend, even in the world of New York vaudeville.
Of course that's all in the past. Today's audiences are...
OI! DOGBREATH!
You've missed me favourite!
What?
George Formby!
Tell us about George Formby!
Um, yes, that's right.
George Formby played here, and his father before him, from whom Chaplin steals his stick-twirling routine.
EMPIRE
SUNDERLAND
GEORGE FORMBY
FLYING
REOS
GARADIN
KODAK GIRL"
All great northern comedy is drawn from tragedy. One of the biggest ever Music Hall stars, George Formby Senior - *The Wigan Nightingale* - is born into dire poverty and learns his trade as a singing beggar.
His songs and jokes are punctuated by a hacking cough - a symptom of the tuberculosis that kills him in his forties - which he cleverly works into his act.
His catchphrase:
Ee! I'm coughin' summat champion toneet!
HA HA HA HA HA HA HA HA HA
He's taken fatally ill while playing the Newcastle *Empire*

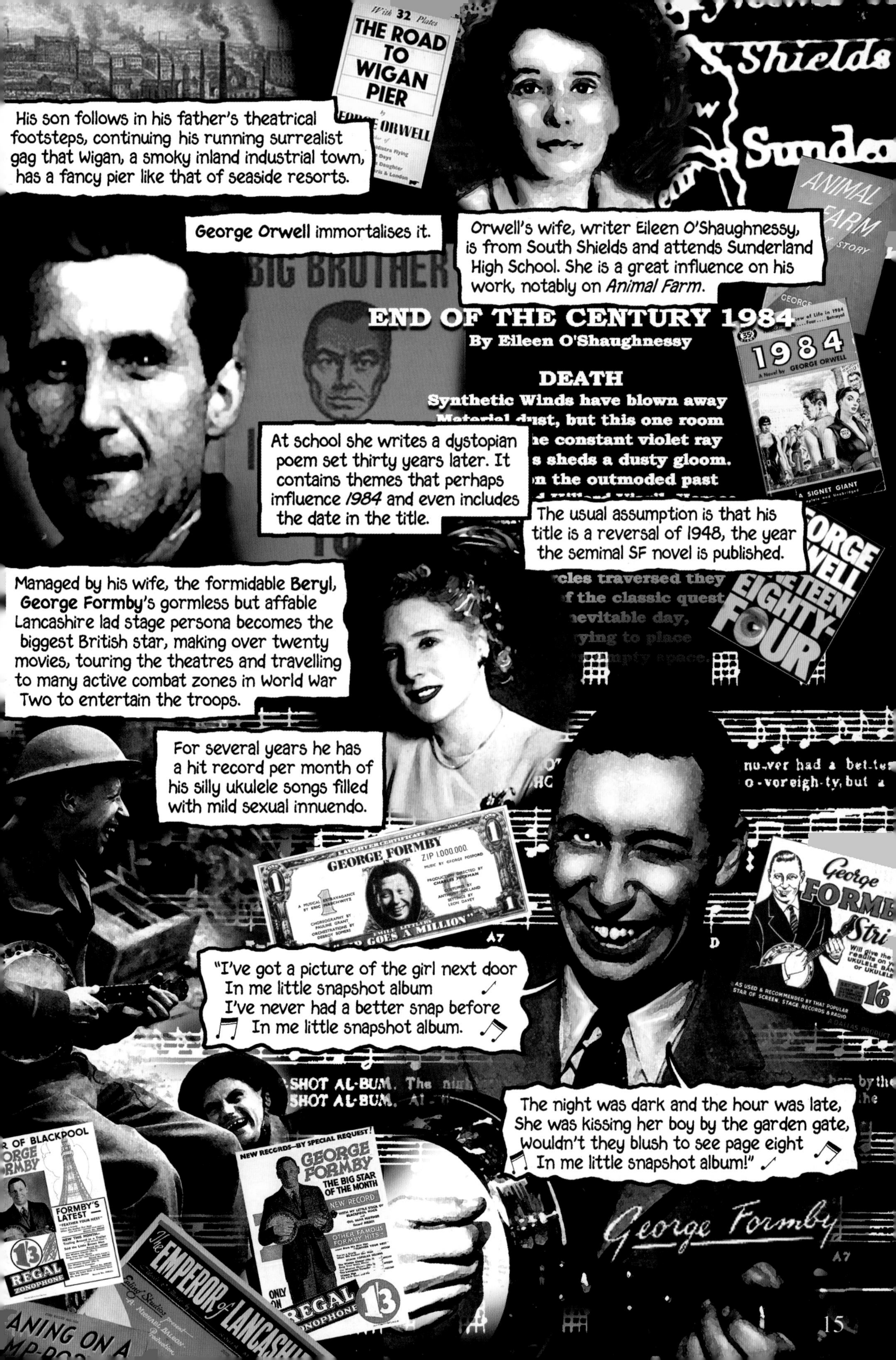
With 32 Plates
THE ROAD TO WIGAN PIER
GEORGE ORWELL
His son follows in his father's theatrical footsteps, continuing his running surrealist gag that Wigan, a smoky inland industrial town, has a fancy pier like that of seaside resorts.
S. Shields
ANIMAL FARM
George Orwell immortalises it.
Orwell's wife, writer Eileen O'Shaughnessy, is from South Shields and attends Sunderland High School. She is a great influence on his work, notably on *Animal Farm*.
BIG BROTHER
END OF THE CENTURY 1984
By Eileen O'Shaughnessy
DEATH
Synthetic Winds have blown away
1984
A Novel by GEORGE ORWELL
A SIGNET GIANT
At school she writes a dystopian poem set thirty years later. It contains themes that perhaps influence *1984* and even includes the date in the title.
The usual assumption is that his title is a reversal of 1948, the year the seminal SF novel is published.
NINETEEN EIGHTY-FOUR
Managed by his wife, the formidable **Beryl**, **George Formby**'s gormless but affable Lancashire lad stage persona becomes the biggest British star, making over twenty movies, touring the theatres and travelling to many active combat zones in World War Two to entertain the troops.
For several years he has a hit record per month of his silly ukulele songs filled with mild sexual innuendo.
GEORGE FORMBY
ZIP GOES A MILLION
"I've got a picture of the girl next door
In me little snapshot album
I've never had a better snap before
In me little snapshot album.
SHOT AL-BUM.
The night was dark and the hour was late,
She was kissing her boy by the garden gate,
Wouldn't they blush to see page eight
In me little snapshot album!"
George FORMBY
George Formby
NEW RECORDS—BY SPECIAL REQUEST!
GEORGE FORMBY
THE BIG STAR OF THE MONTH
NEW RECORD
REGAL ZONOPHONE
FORMBY'S LATEST
The EMPEROR of LANCASHIRE

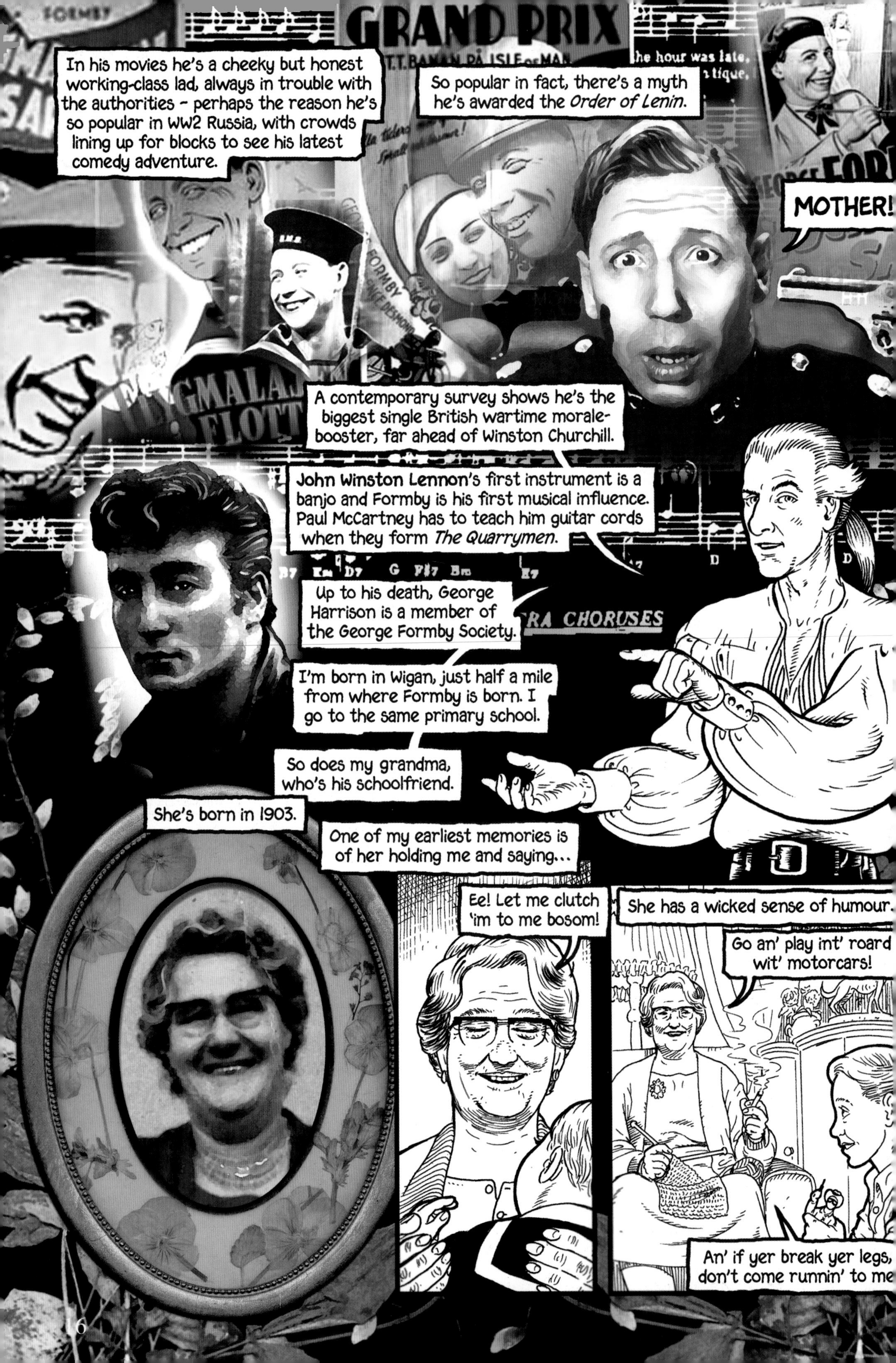

GRAND PRIX
In his movies he's a cheeky but honest working-class lad, always in trouble with the authorities - perhaps the reason he's so popular in WW2 Russia, with crowds lining up for blocks to see his latest comedy adventure.
So popular in fact, there's a myth he's awarded the *Order of Lenin*.
MOTHER!
A contemporary survey shows he's the biggest single British wartime morale-booster, far ahead of Winston Churchill.
John Winston Lennon's first instrument is a banjo and Formby is his first musical influence. Paul McCartney has to teach him guitar cords when they form *The Quarrymen*.
Up to his death, George Harrison is a member of the George Formby Society.
I'm born in Wigan, just half a mile from where Formby is born. I go to the same primary school.
So does my grandma, who's his schoolfriend.
She's born in 1903.
One of my earliest memories is of her holding me and saying...
Ee! Let me clutch 'im to me bosom!
She has a wicked sense of humour.
Go an' play int' roard wit' motorcars!
An' if yer break yer legs, don't come runnin' to me

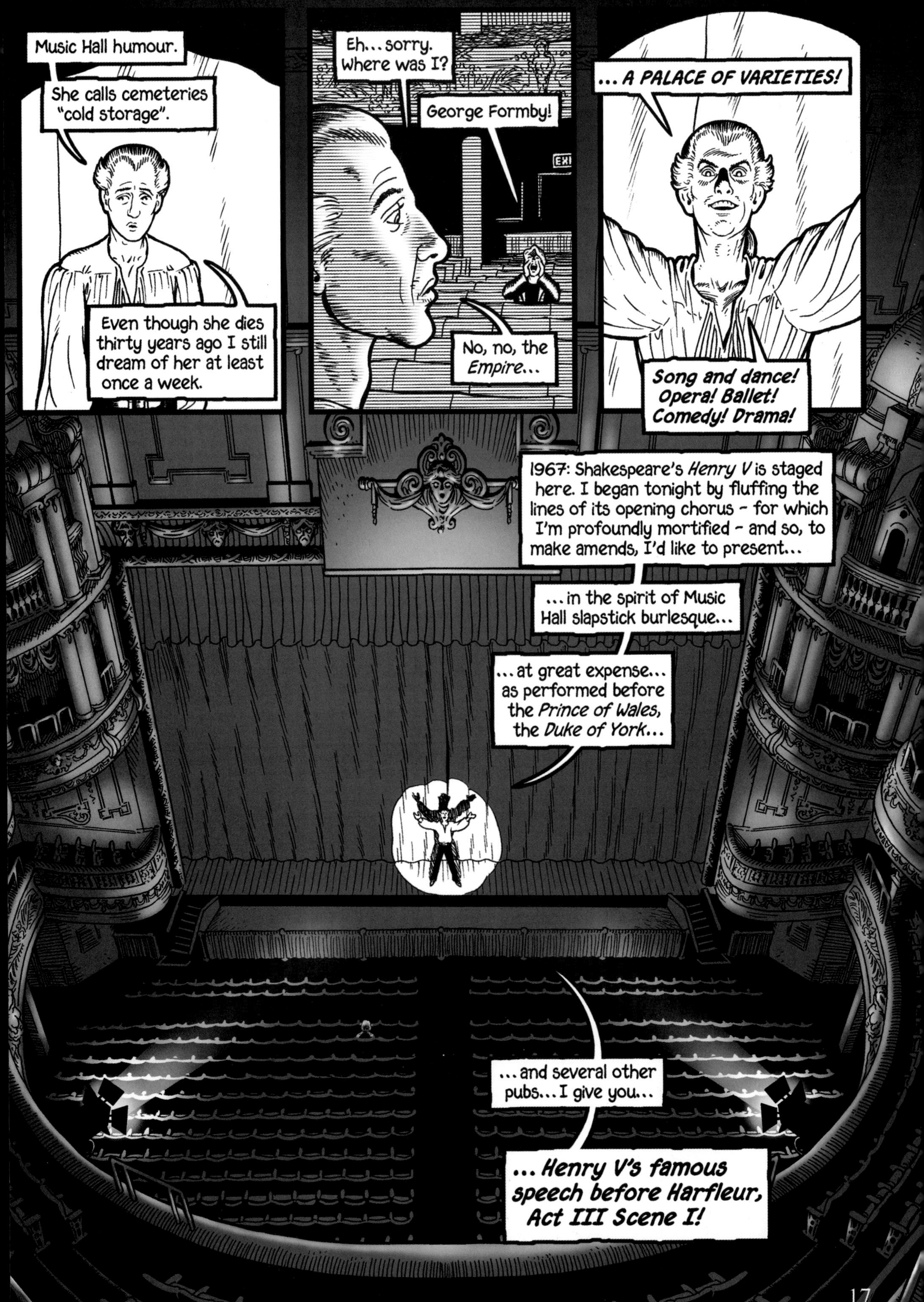
Music Hall humour.
She calls cemeteries "cold storage".
Even though she dies thirty years ago I still dream of her at least once a week.
Eh... sorry. Where was I?
George Formby!
EXI
No, no, the *Empire*...
... A PALACE OF VARIETIES!
Song and dance! Opera! Ballet! Comedy! Drama!
1967: Shakespeare's *Henry V* is staged here. I began tonight by fluffing the lines of its opening chorus – for which I'm profoundly mortified – and so, to make amends, I'd like to present...
... in the spirit of Music Hall slapstick burlesque...
... at great expense... as performed before the *Prince of Wales*, the *Duke of York*...
... and several other pubs... I give you...
... Henry V's famous speech before Harfleur, Act III Scene I!

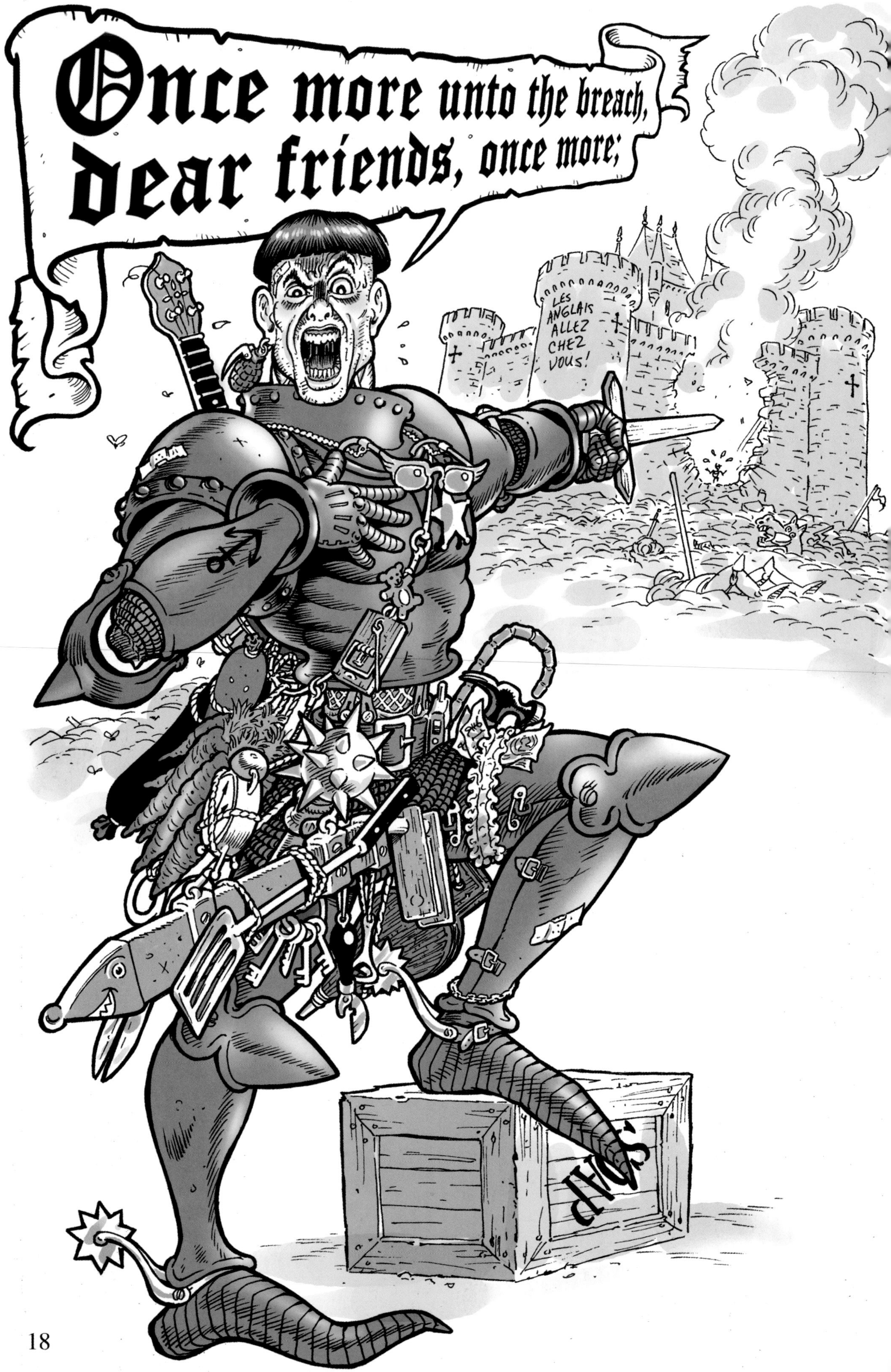
Once more unto the breach, dear friends, once more;
LES ANGLAIS ALLEZ CHEZ VOUS!

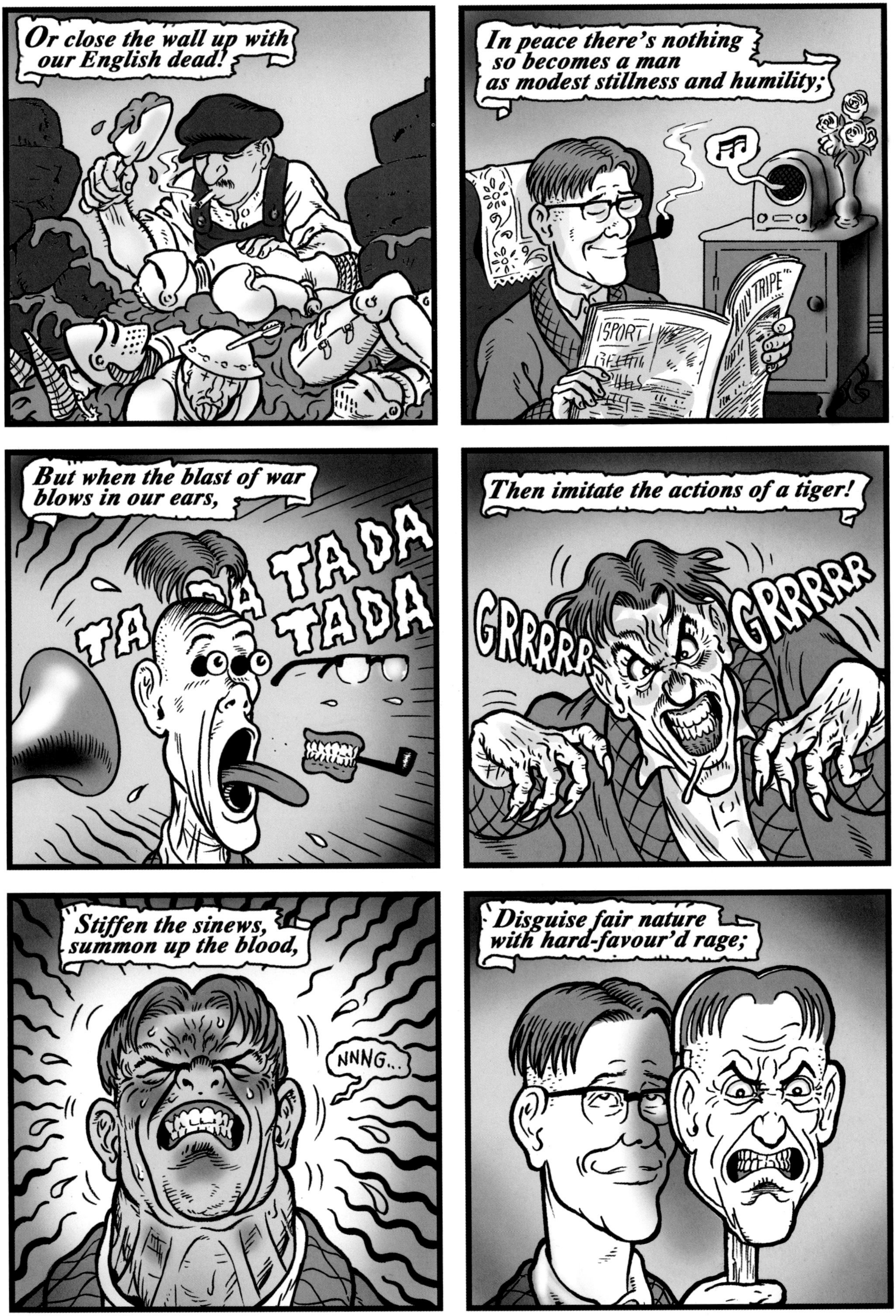
Or close the wall up with our English dead!
In peace there's nothing so becomes a man as modest stillness and humility;
"TRIPE"
SPORT
But when the blast of war blows in our ears,
TA
TA DA
TADA
Then imitate the actions of a tiger!
GRRRRR
GRRRRR
Stiffen the sinews, summon up the blood,
NNNG...
Disguise fair nature with hard-favour'd rage;

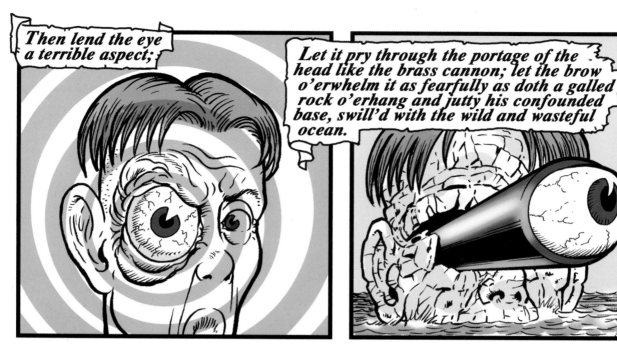

Then lend the eye a terrible aspect;

Let it pry through the portage of the head like the brass cannon; let the brow o'erwhelm it as fearfully as doth a galled rock o'erhang and jutty his confounded base, swill'd with the wild and wasteful ocean.

Now set the teeth and stretch the nostril wide;

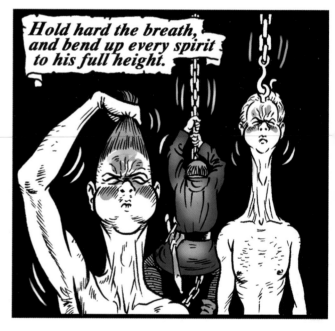

Hold hard the breath, and bend up every spirit to his full height.

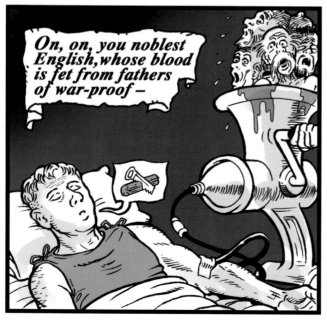

On, on, you noblest English, whose blood is fet from fathers of war-proof –

BAH!

Fathers that like so many Alexanders have in these parts from morn till even fought, and sheath'd their swords for lack of argument.

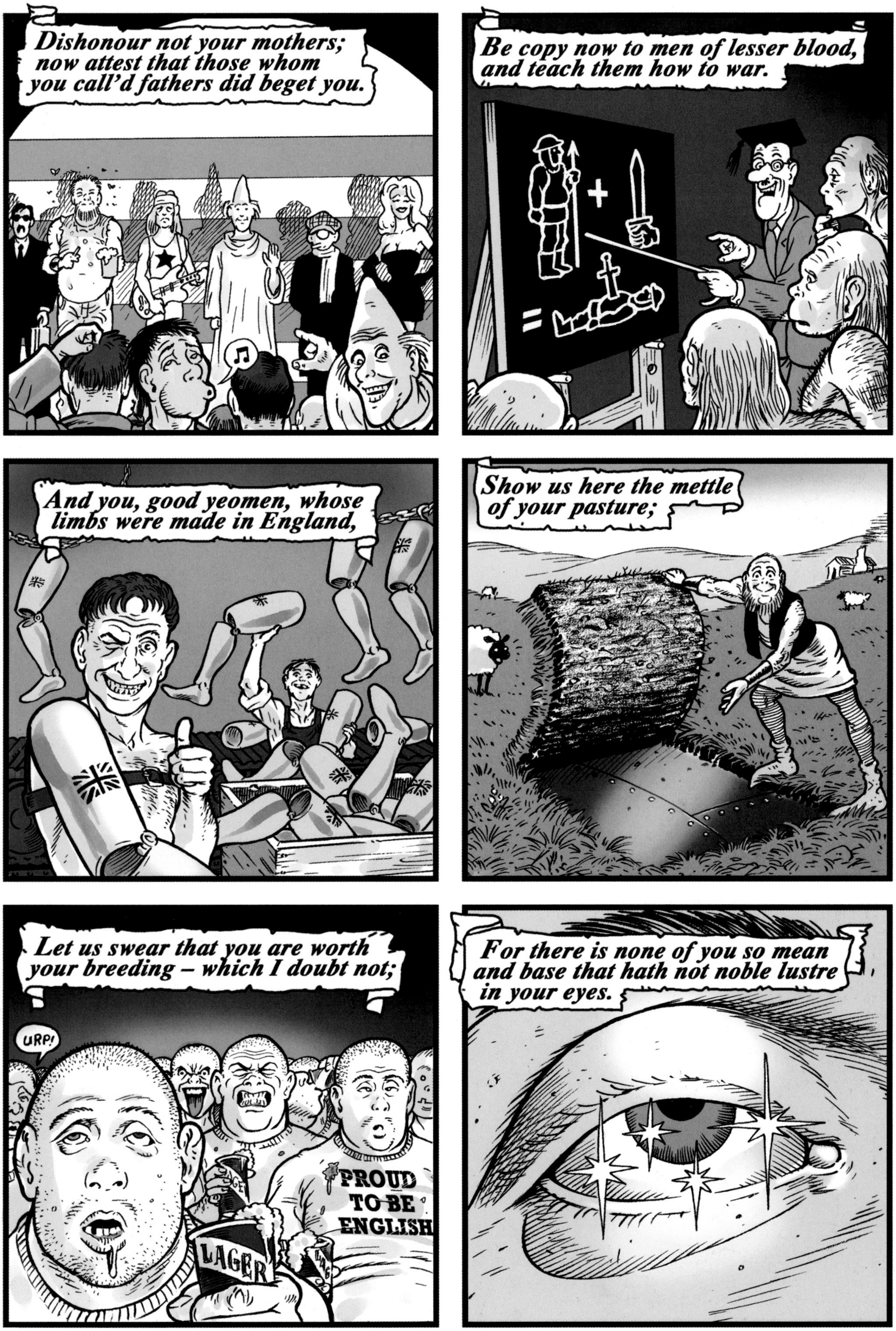
Dishonour not your mothers; now attest that those whom you call'd fathers did beget you.
Be copy now to men of lesser blood, and teach them how to war.
And you, good yeomen, whose limbs were made in England,
Show us here the mettle of your pasture;
Let us swear that you are worth your breeding – which I doubt not;
URP!
PROUD TO BE ENGLISH
LAGER
For there is none of you so mean and base that hath not noble lustre in your eyes.

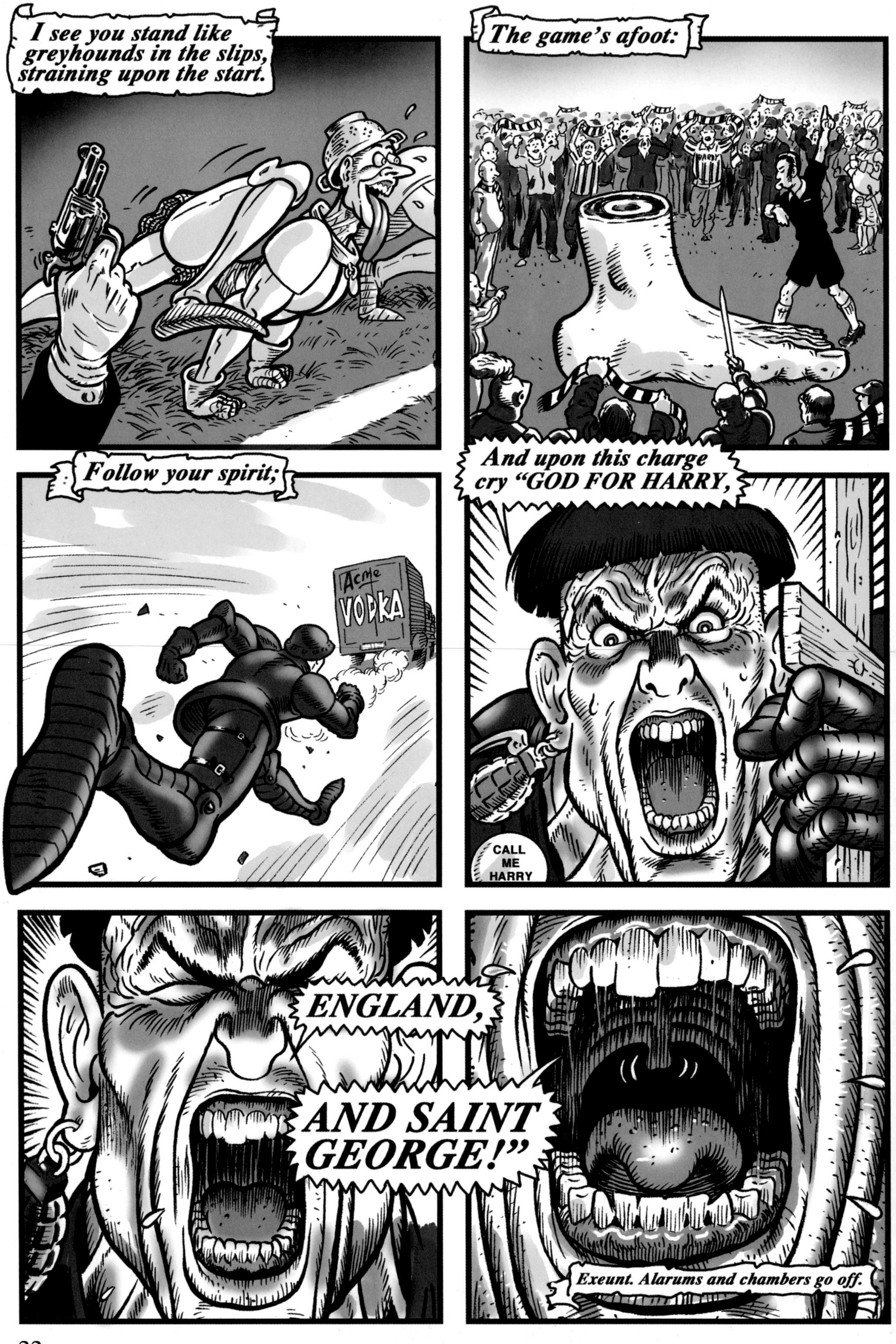
I see you stand like greyhounds in the slips, straining upon the start.
The game's afoot:
Follow your spirit;
Acme
VODKA
And upon this charge cry "GOD FOR HARRY,
CALL ME HARRY
ENGLAND,
AND SAINT GEORGE!"
Exeunt. Alarums and chambers go off.

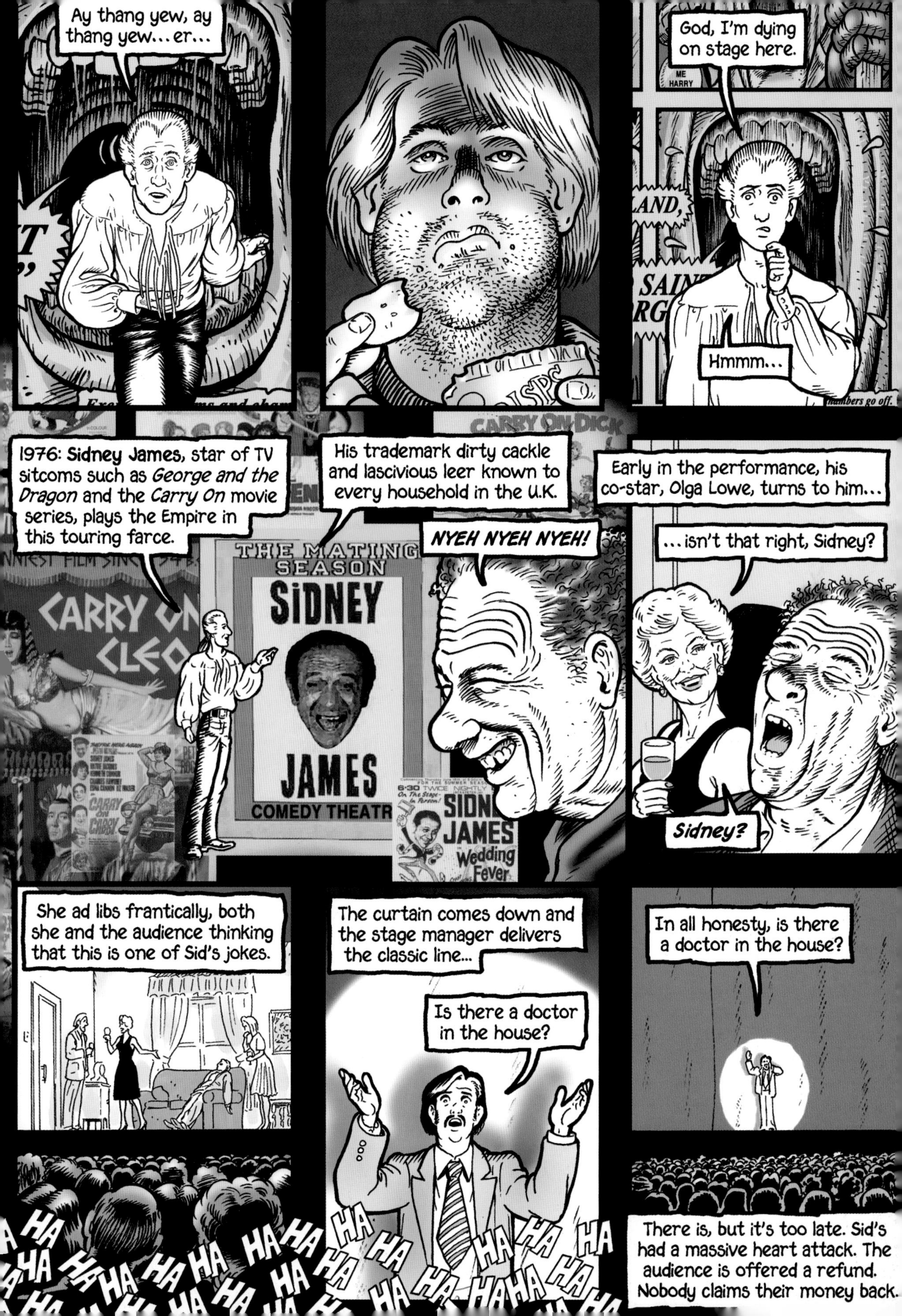
Ay thang yew, ay thang yew... er...
God, I'm dying on stage here.
Hmmm...
1976: Sidney James, star of TV sitcoms such as George and the Dragon and the Carry On movie series, plays the Empire in this touring farce.
CARRY ON CLEO
THE MATING SEASON
SIDNEY JAMES
COMEDY THEATR
SIDNEY JAMES
Wedding Fever
His trademark dirty cackle and lascivious leer known to every household in the U.K.
NYEH NYEH NYEH!
Early in the performance, his co-star, Olga Lowe, turns to him...
...isn't that right, Sidney?
Sidney?
She ad libs frantically, both she and the audience thinking that this is one of Sid's jokes.
HA HA HA HA HA HA HA HA HA
The curtain comes down and the stage manager delivers the classic line...
Is there a doctor in the house?
HA HA HA HA HA HA HA HA HA HA HA HA HA
In all honesty, is there a doctor in the house?
There is, but it's too late. Sid's had a massive heart attack. The audience is offered a refund. Nobody claims their money back.

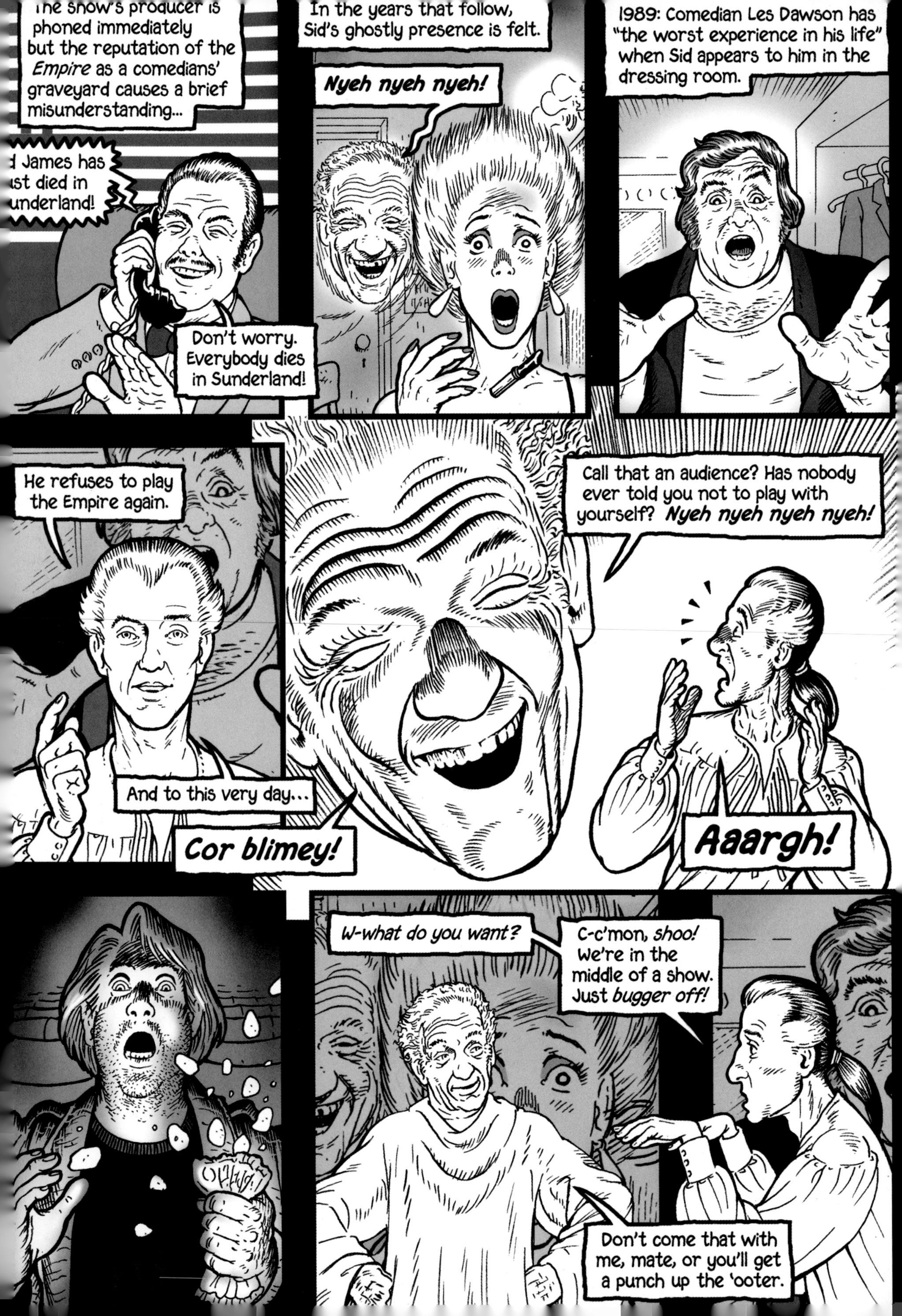

The show's producer is phoned immediately but the reputation of the *Empire* as a comedians' graveyard causes a brief misunderstanding...
d James has ust died in underland!
Don't worry. Everybody dies in Sunderland!
In the years that follow, Sid's ghostly presence is felt.
Nyeh nyeh nyeh!
1989: Comedian Les Dawson has "the worst experience in his life" when Sid appears to him in the dressing room.
He refuses to play the Empire again.
And to this very day...
Cor blimey!
Call that an audience? Has nobody ever told you not to play with yourself? *Nyeh nyeh nyeh nyeh!*
Aaargh!
W-what do you want?
C-c'mon, *shoo!* We're in the middle of a show. Just *bugger off!*
Don't come that with me, mate, or you'll get a punch up the 'ooter.

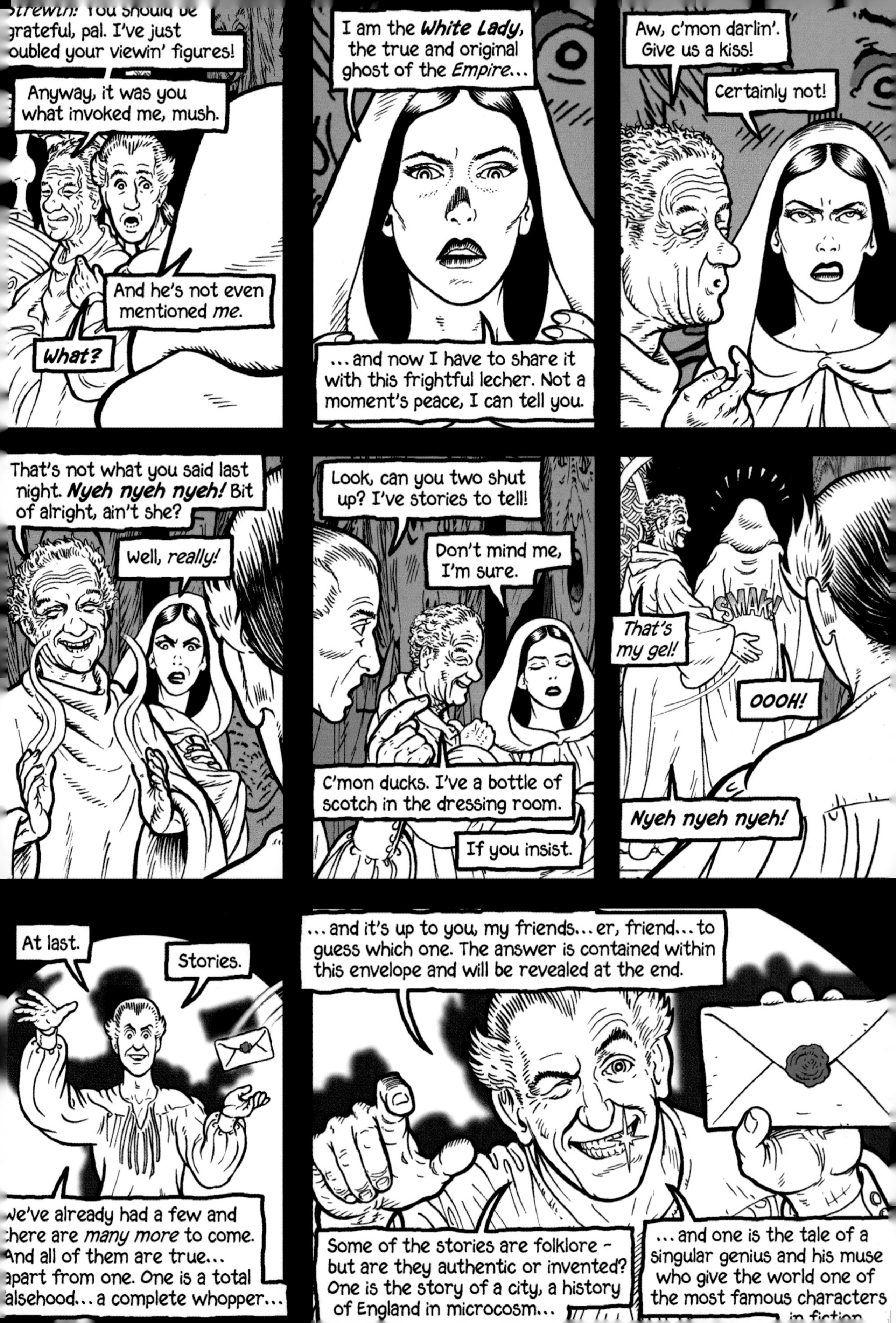

Strewth! You should be grateful, pal. I've just oubled your viewin' figures!
Anyway, it was you what invoked me, mush.
And he's not even mentioned *me*.
What?
I am the ***White Lady***, the true and original ghost of the *Empire*...
...and now I have to share it with this frightful lecher. Not a moment's peace, I can tell you.
Aw, c'mon darlin'. Give us a kiss!
Certainly not!
That's not what you said last night. ***Nyeh nyeh nyeh!*** Bit of alright, ain't she?
Well, *really!*
Look, can you two shut up? I've stories to tell!
Don't mind me, I'm sure.
C'mon ducks. I've a bottle of scotch in the dressing room.
If you insist.
SMAK!
That's my gel!
OOOH!
Nyeh nyeh nyeh!
At last.
Stories.
We've already had a few and there are *many more* to come. And all of them are true... apart from one. One is a total falsehood... a complete whopper...
...and it's up to you, my friends... er, friend... to guess which one. The answer is contained within this envelope and will be revealed at the end.
Some of the stories are folklore – but are they authentic or invented? One is the story of a city, a history of England in microcosm...
...and one is the tale of a singular genius and his muse who give the world one of the most famous characters in fiction

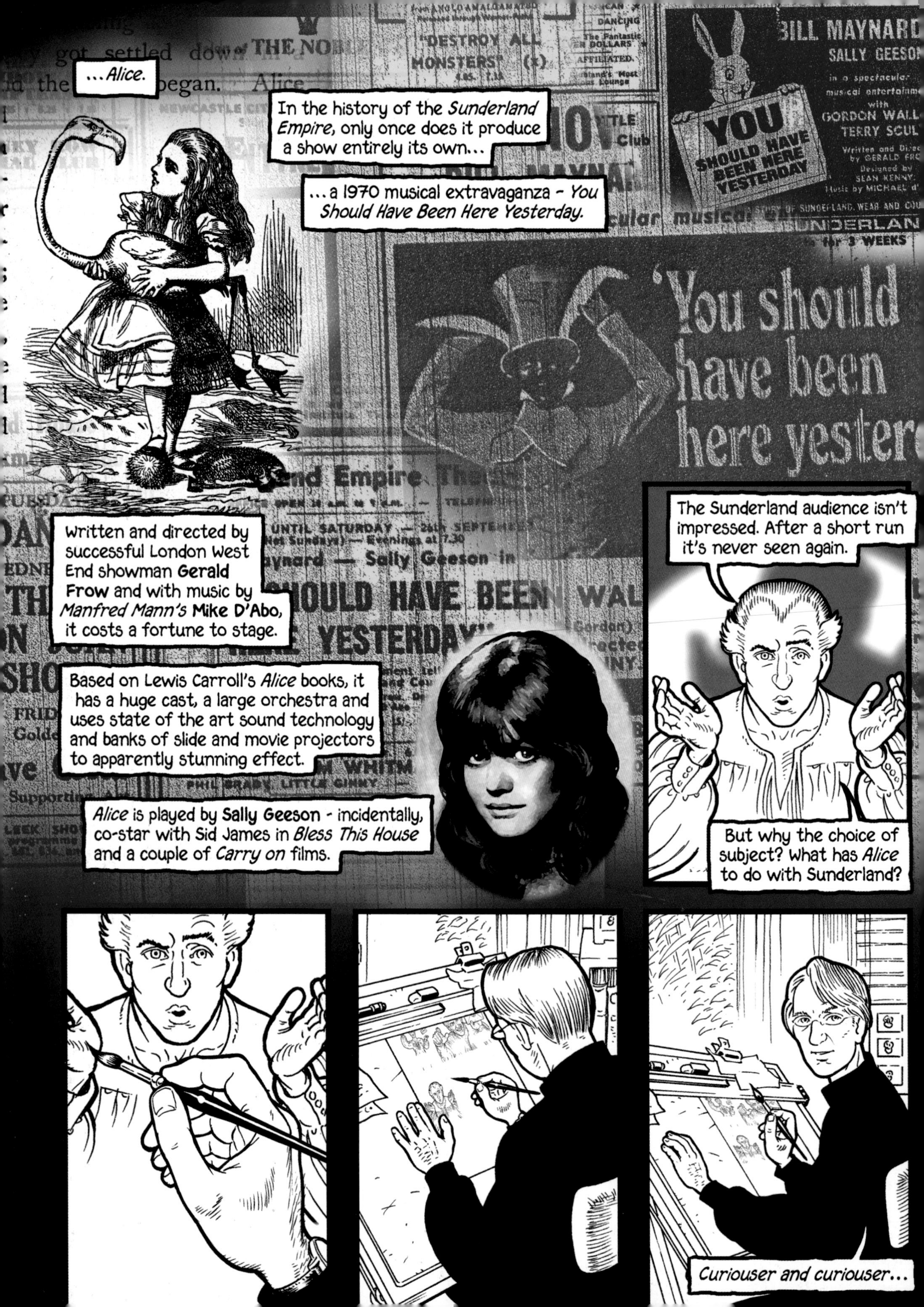

...Alice.
In the history of the Sunderland Empire, only once does it produce a show entirely its own...
...a 1970 musical extravaganza - You Should Have Been Here Yesterday.
Written and directed by successful London West End showman Gerald Frow and with music by Manfred Mann's Mike D'Abo, it costs a fortune to stage.
Based on Lewis Carroll's Alice books, it has a huge cast, a large orchestra and uses state of the art sound technology and banks of slide and movie projectors to apparently stunning effect.
Alice is played by Sally Geeson - incidentally, co-star with Sid James in Bless This House and a couple of Carry on films.
The Sunderland audience isn't impressed. After a short run it's never seen again.
But why the choice of subject? What has Alice to do with Sunderland?
Curiouser and curiouser...

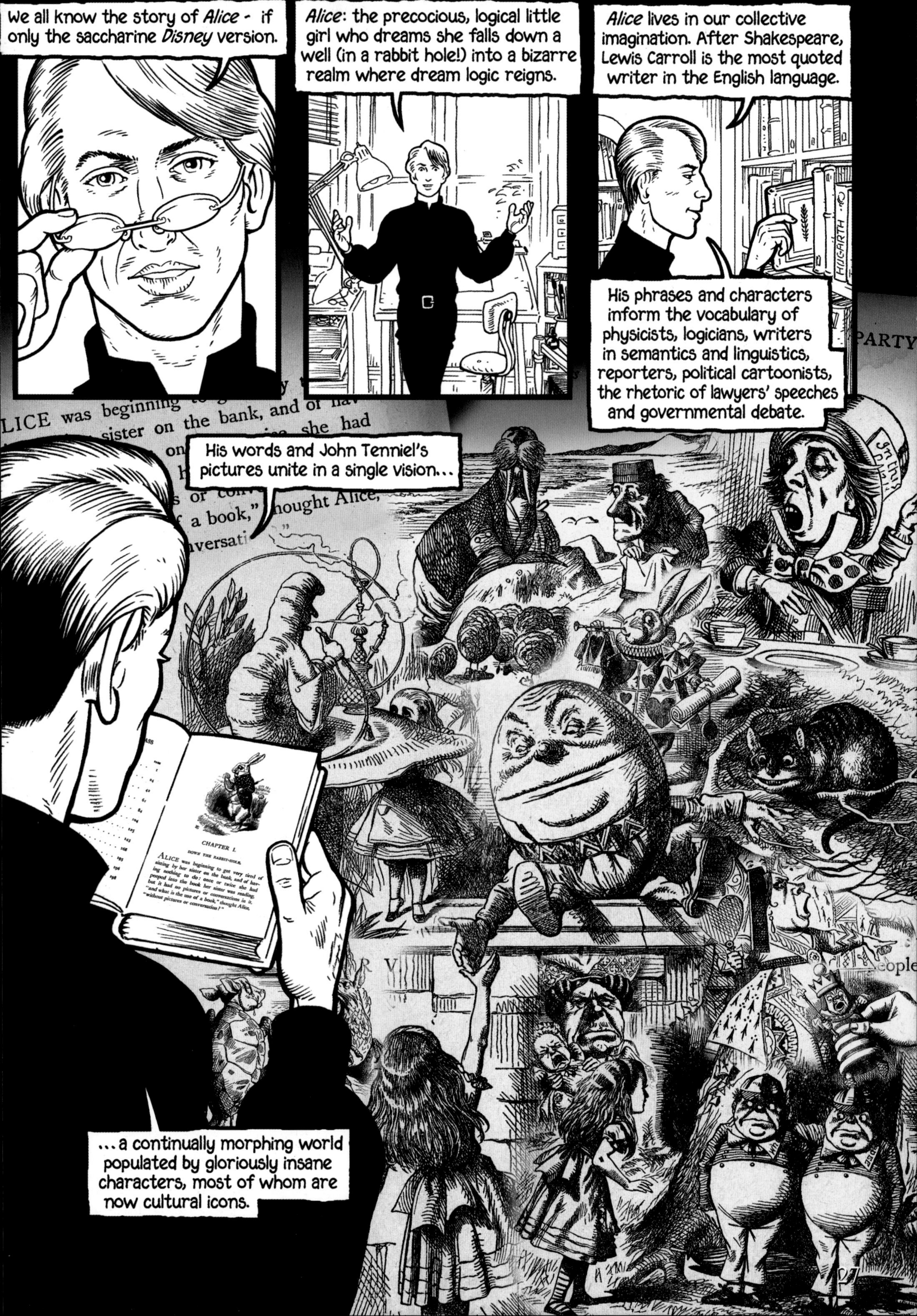
We all know the story of *Alice* - if only the saccharine *Disney* version.
Alice: the precocious, logical little girl who dreams she falls down a well (in a rabbit hole!) into a bizarre realm where dream logic reigns.
Alice lives in our collective imagination. After Shakespeare, Lewis Carroll is the most quoted writer in the English language.
His phrases and characters inform the vocabulary of physicists, logicians, writers in semantics and linguistics, reporters, political cartoonists, the rhetoric of lawyers' speeches and governmental debate.
His words and John Tenniel's pictures unite in a single vision...
...a continually morphing world populated by gloriously insane characters, most of whom are now cultural icons.
CHAPTER I.
DOWN THE RABBIT-HOLE.
ALICE was beginning to get very tired of sitting by her sister on the bank, and of having nothing to do: once or twice she had peeped into the book her sister was reading, but it had no pictures or conversations in it, "and what is the use of a book," thought Alice, "without pictures or conversation?"

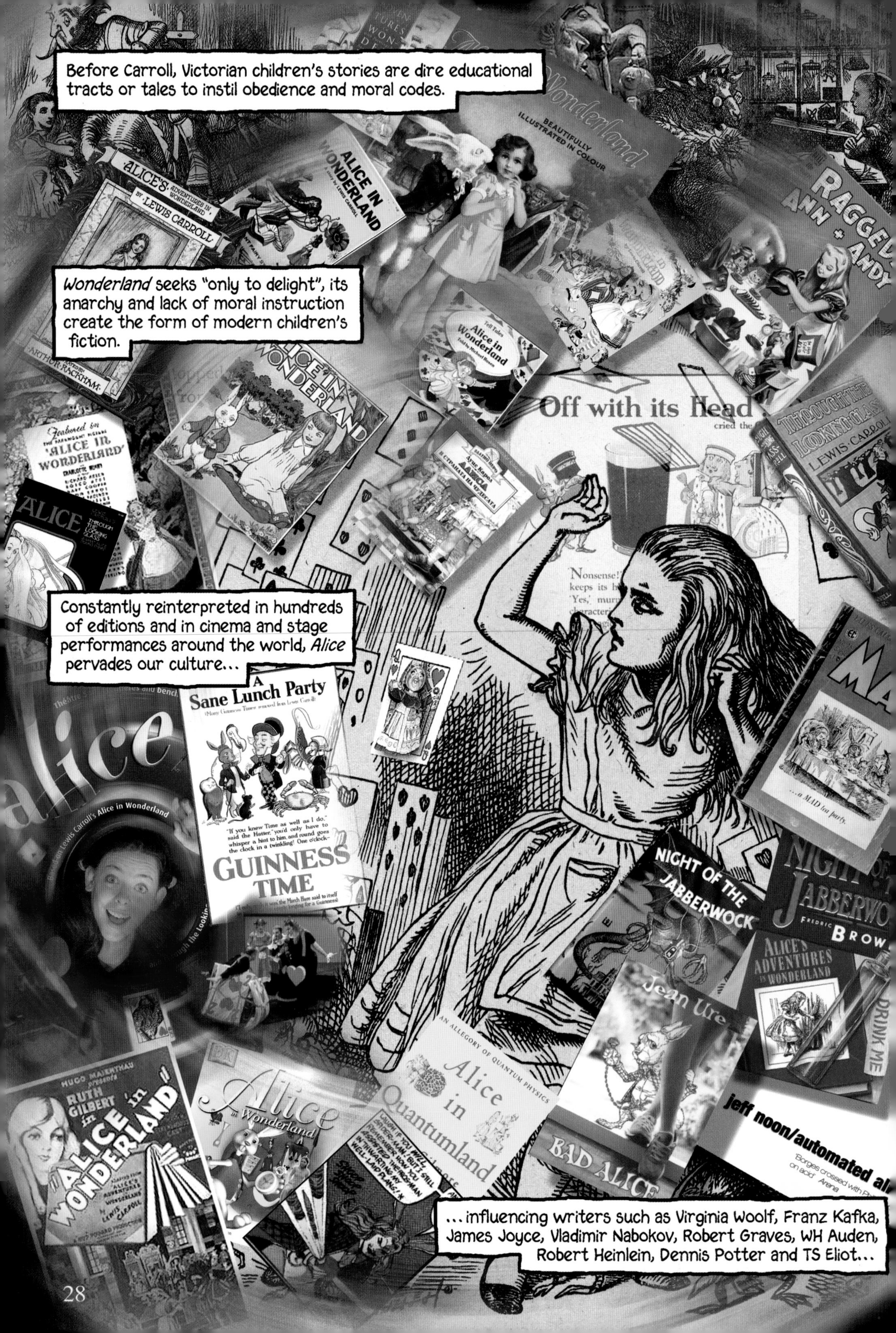
Before Carroll, Victorian children's stories are dire educational tracts or tales to instil obedience and moral codes.
Wonderland seeks "only to delight", its anarchy and lack of moral instruction create the form of modern children's fiction.
Constantly reinterpreted in hundreds of editions and in cinema and stage performances around the world, *Alice* pervades our culture...
...influencing writers such as Virginia Woolf, Franz Kafka, James Joyce, Vladimir Nabokov, Robert Graves, WH Auden, Robert Heinlein, Dennis Potter and TS Eliot...

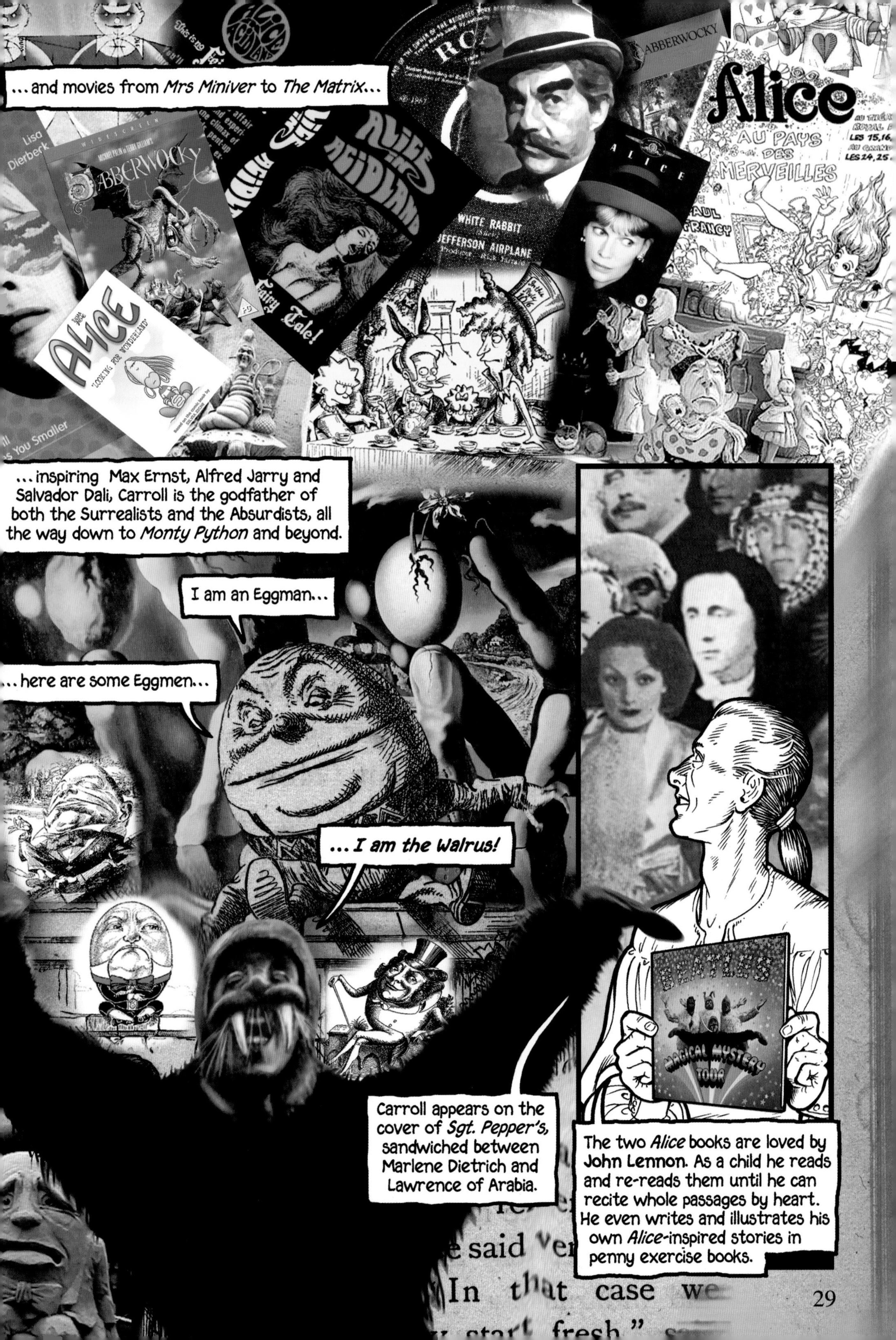

...and movies from *Mrs Miniver* to *The Matrix*...
...inspiring Max Ernst, Alfred Jarry and Salvador Dali, Carroll is the godfather of both the Surrealists and the Absurdists, all the way down to *Monty Python* and beyond.
I am an Eggman...
...here are some Eggmen...
...*I am the Walrus!*
Carroll appears on the cover of *Sgt. Pepper's*, sandwiched between Marlene Dietrich and Lawrence of Arabia.
The two *Alice* books are loved by John Lennon. As a child he reads and re-reads them until he can recite whole passages by heart. He even writes and illustrates his own *Alice*-inspired stories in penny exercise books.
JABBERWOCKY
ALICE IN ACIDLAND
WHITE RABBIT
JEFFERSON AIRPLANE
Alice
AU PAYS DES MERVEILLES
BEATLES
MAGICAL MYSTERY TOUR

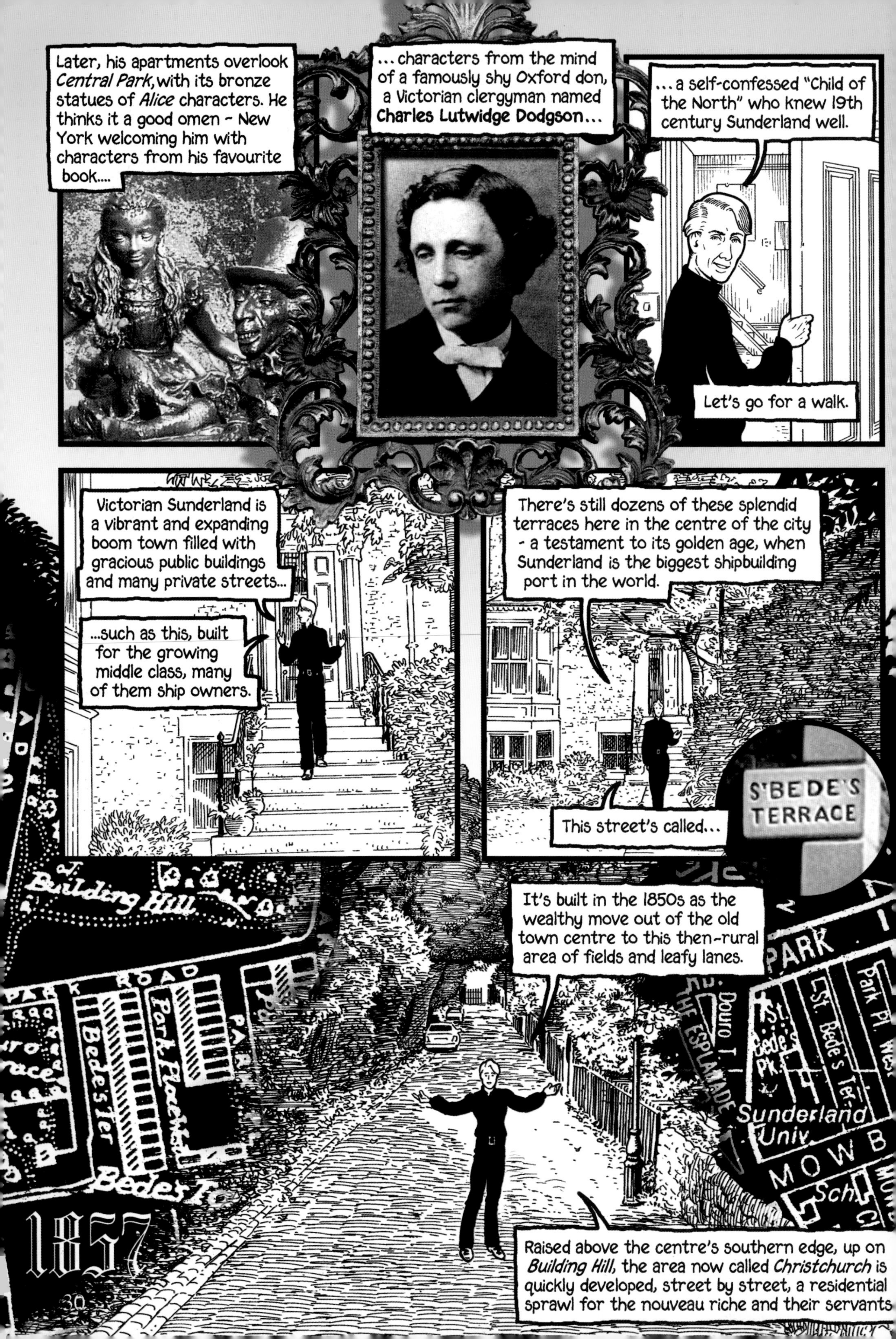

Later, his apartments overlook *Central Park*, with its bronze statues of *Alice* characters. He thinks it a good omen – New York welcoming him with characters from his favourite book....
...characters from the mind of a famously shy Oxford don, a Victorian clergyman named **Charles Lutwidge Dodgson**...
...a self-confessed "Child of the North" who knew 19th century Sunderland well.
Let's go for a walk.
Victorian Sunderland is a vibrant and expanding boom town filled with gracious public buildings and many private streets...
...such as this, built for the growing middle class, many of them ship owners.
There's still dozens of these splendid terraces here in the centre of the city – a testament to its golden age, when Sunderland is the biggest shipbuilding port in the world.
This street's called...
S'BEDE'S TERRACE
It's built in the 1850s as the wealthy move out of the old town centre to this then-rural area of fields and leafy lanes.
Building Hill
PARK ROAD
Park Place
Bedes Ter
PARK
St. Bede's Ter.
THE ESPLANADE
Sunderland Univ.
MOWB
1857
Raised above the centre's southern edge, up on *Building Hill*, the area now called *Christchurch* is quickly developed, street by street, a residential sprawl for the nouveau riche and their servants

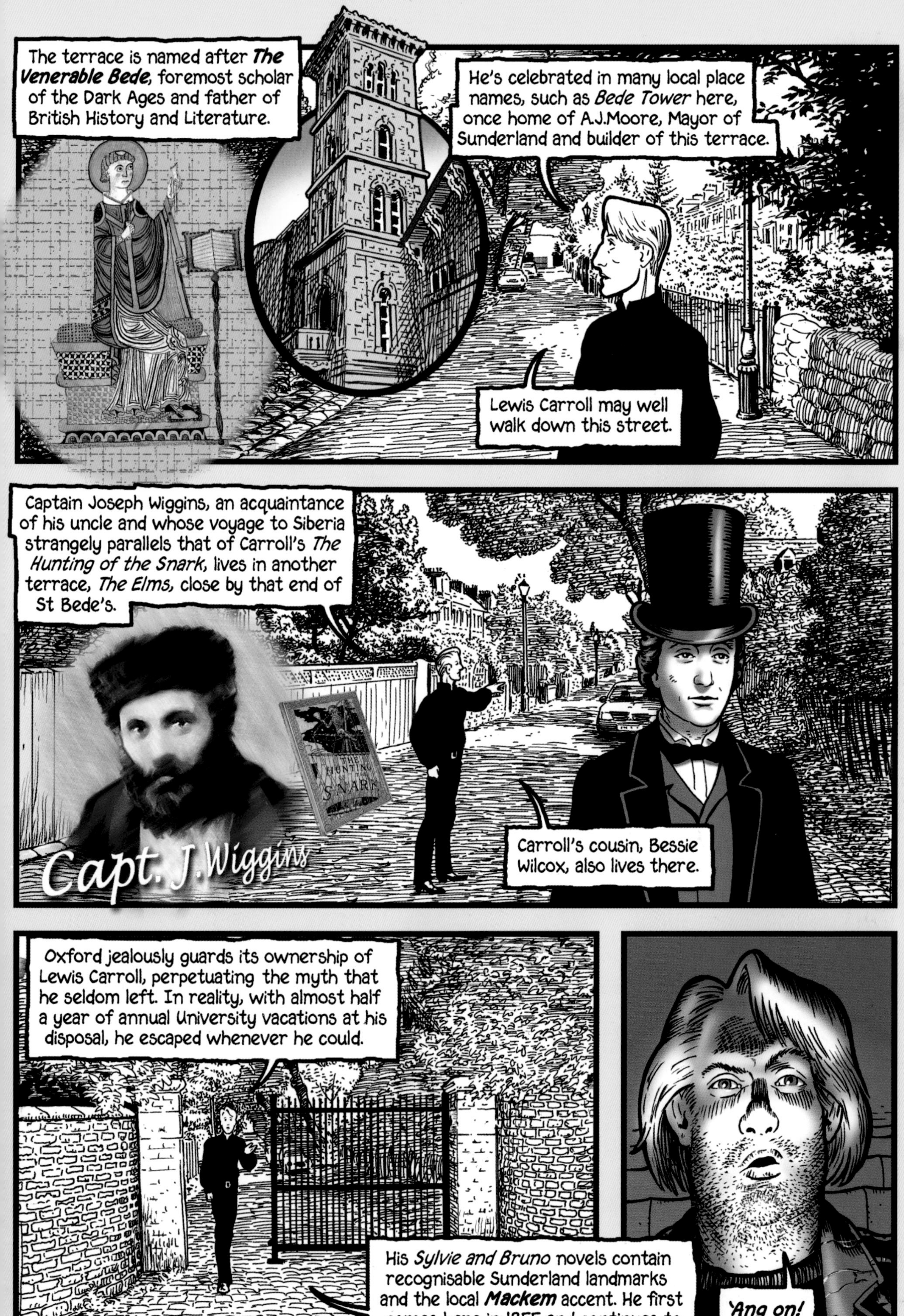
The terrace is named after ***The Venerable Bede***, foremost scholar of the Dark Ages and father of British History and Literature.
He's celebrated in many local place names, such as *Bede Tower* here, once home of A.J.Moore, Mayor of Sunderland and builder of this terrace.
Lewis Carroll may well walk down this street.
Captain Joseph Wiggins, an acquaintance of his uncle and whose voyage to Siberia strangely parallels that of Carroll's *The Hunting of the Snark*, lives in another terrace, *The Elms*, close by that end of St Bede's.
Capt. J.Wiggins
THE HUNTING OF THE SNARK
Carroll's cousin, Bessie Wilcox, also lives there.
Oxford jealously guards its ownership of Lewis Carroll, perpetuating the myth that he seldom left. In reality, with almost half a year of annual University vacations at his disposal, he escaped whenever he could.
His *Sylvie and Bruno* novels contain recognisable Sunderland landmarks and the local ***Mackem*** accent. He first comes here in 1855 and continues to visit the area for over thirty years...
'Ang on!

the myth that ... ... with a ...versity vacat... whenever he could.

...

Yes?

Who's this **Charlie Dodgson** bloke then?

Lewis Carroll is his pen name...

...taken from his first two names - Charles latinized to *Carolus* and Lutwidge, from the latin *Ludovici*, being German for *Louis*.

Charles
Lutwidge
Dodgson
Louis
Carolus
Lewis Carroll

I *was* going to tell you later. Just be patient.

At the end of the terrace is *Mowbray Park*, much admired by Carroll's Mackem brother-in-law, the **Rev CS Collingwood**...

HAVELOCK

...and, on the crest of Building Hill, a statue commemorating Sunderland's Sir Henry Havelock, shipbuilder's son and hero of the battle that relieved the *Siege of Lucknow*...

...renowned in Victorian England for his relentless hunting down and slaughter of the rebels of the *Indian Mutiny*.

A very religious man.

Another statue of him stands in London's *Trafalgar Square*.

Two Russian cannon, known as *Joshua* and *Caleb*, captured at the *Siege of Sebastopol*, are donated to Sunderland in 1857. These are replicas, the originals melted down for the *War Effort* in 1940.

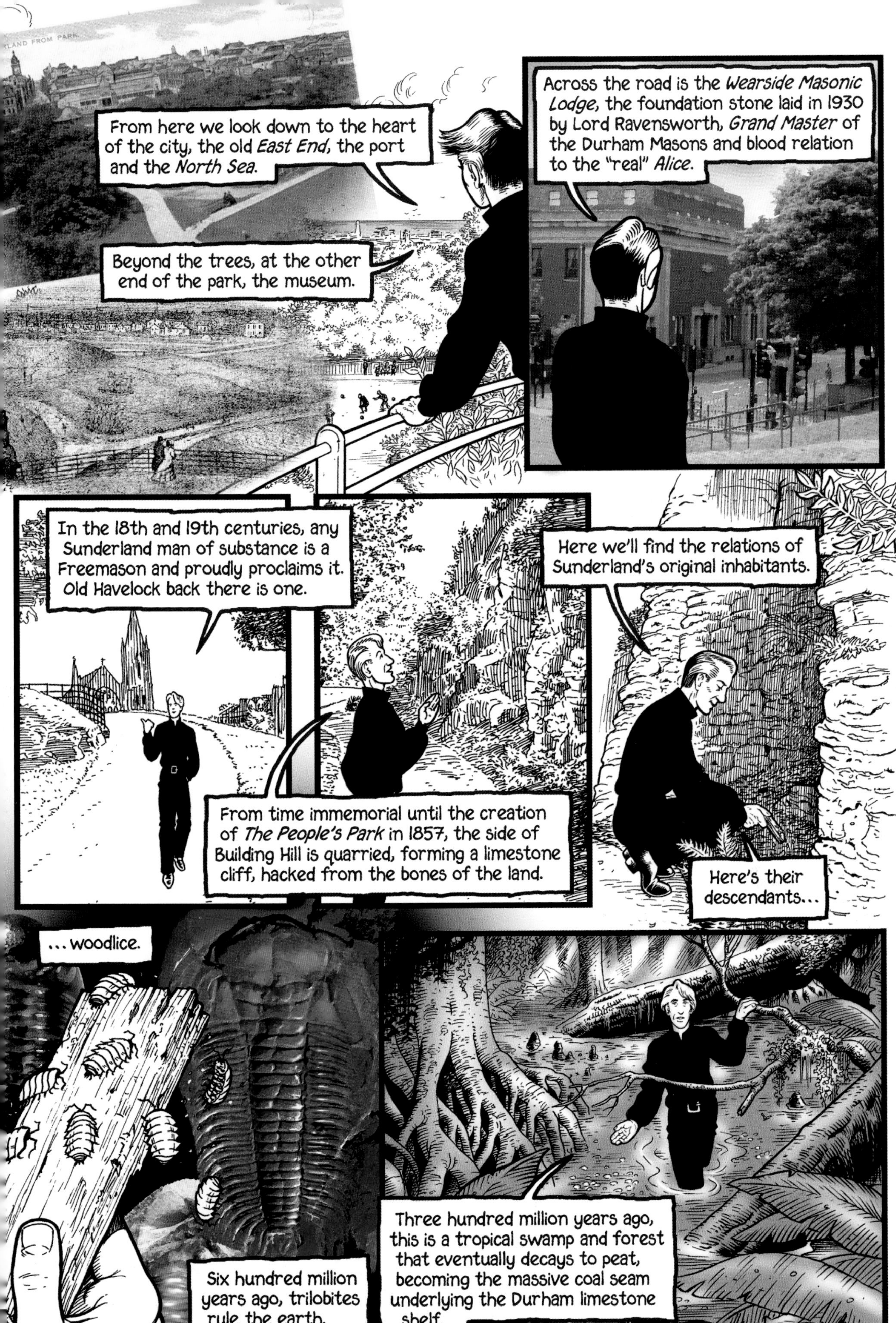
From here we look down to the heart of the city, the old *East End*, the port and the *North Sea*.
Beyond the trees, at the other end of the park, the museum.
Across the road is the *Wearside Masonic Lodge*, the foundation stone laid in 1930 by Lord Ravensworth, *Grand Master* of the Durham Masons and blood relation to the "real" *Alice*.
In the 18th and 19th centuries, any Sunderland man of substance is a Freemason and proudly proclaims it. Old Havelock back there is one.
From time immemorial until the creation of *The People's Park* in 1857, the side of Building Hill is quarried, forming a limestone cliff, hacked from the bones of the land.
Here we'll find the relations of Sunderland's original inhabitants.
Here's their descendants...
...woodlice.
Six hundred million years ago, trilobites rule the earth.
Three hundred million years ago, this is a tropical swamp and forest that eventually decays to peat, becoming the massive coal seam underlying the Durham limestone shelf.

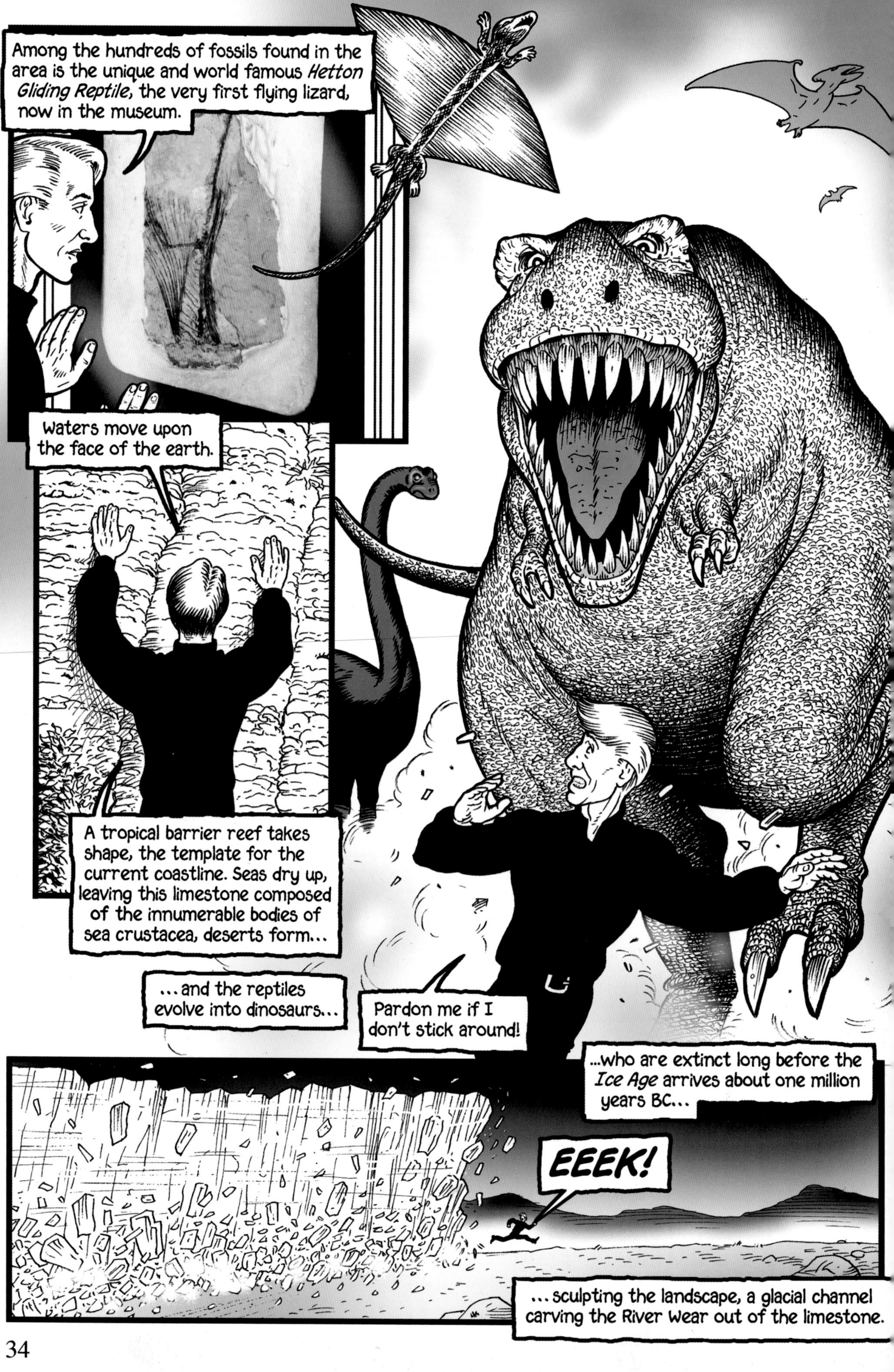

Among the hundreds of fossils found in the area is the unique and world famous *Hetton Gliding Reptile*, the very first flying lizard, now in the museum.
Waters move upon the face of the earth.
A tropical barrier reef takes shape, the template for the current coastline. Seas dry up, leaving this limestone composed of the innumerable bodies of sea crustacea, deserts form...
...and the reptiles evolve into dinosaurs...
Pardon me if I don't stick around!
...who are extinct long before the *Ice Age* arrives about one million years BC...
EEEK!
...sculpting the landscape, a glacial channel carving the River Wear out of the limestone.

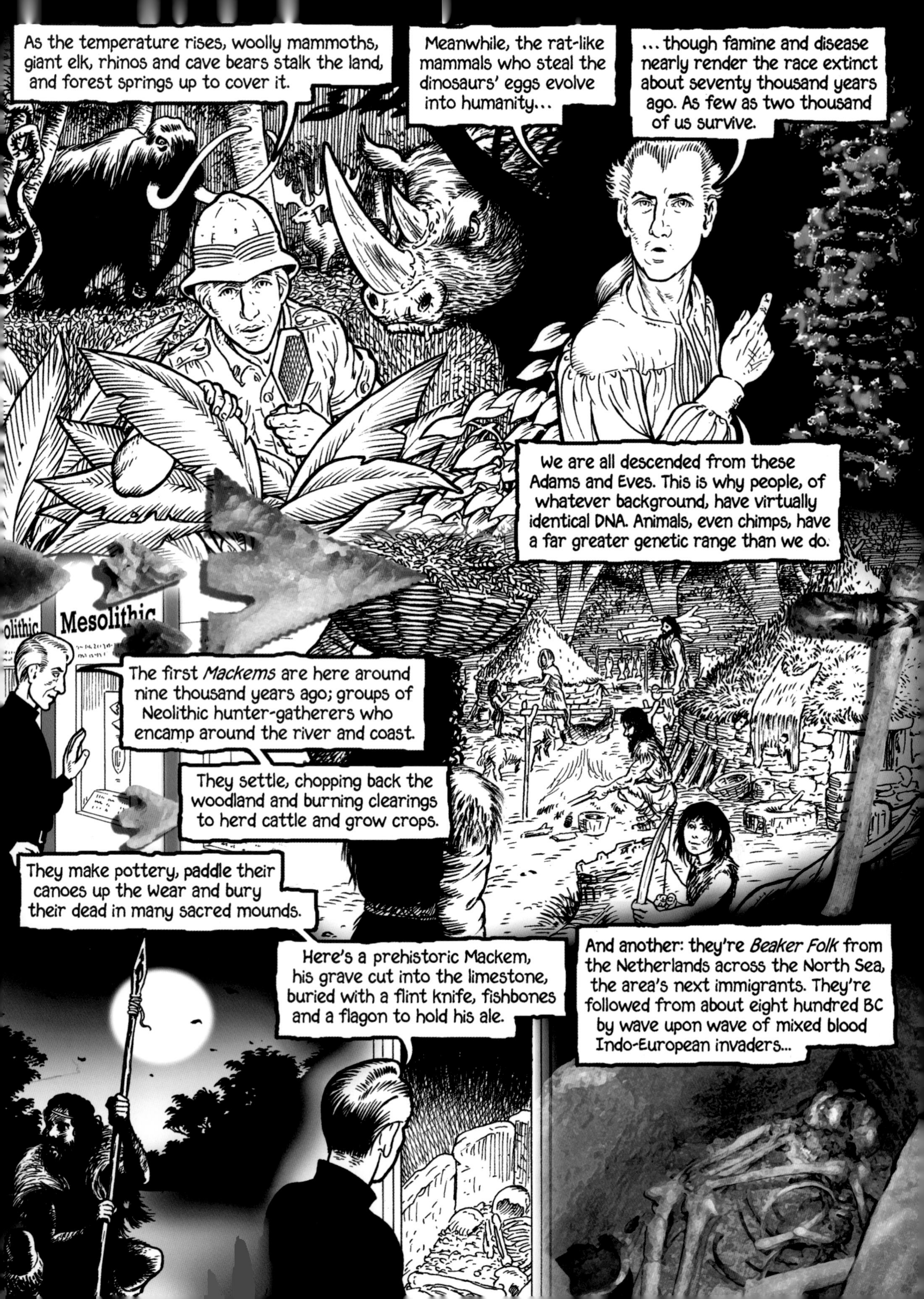
As the temperature rises, woolly mammoths, giant elk, rhinos and cave bears stalk the land, and forest springs up to cover it.
Meanwhile, the rat-like mammals who steal the dinosaurs' eggs evolve into humanity...
... though famine and disease nearly render the race extinct about seventy thousand years ago. As few as two thousand of us survive.
We are all descended from these Adams and Eves. This is why people, of whatever background, have virtually identical DNA. Animals, even chimps, have a far greater genetic range than we do.
olithic
Mesolithic
The first *Mackems* are here around nine thousand years ago; groups of Neolithic hunter-gatherers who encamp around the river and coast.
They settle, chopping back the woodland and burning clearings to herd cattle and grow crops.
They make pottery, paddle their canoes up the Wear and bury their dead in many sacred mounds.
Here's a prehistoric Mackem, his grave cut into the limestone, buried with a flint knife, fishbones and a flagon to hold his ale.
And another: they're *Beaker Folk* from the Netherlands across the North Sea, the area's next immigrants. They're followed from about eight hundred BC by wave upon wave of mixed blood Indo-European invaders...

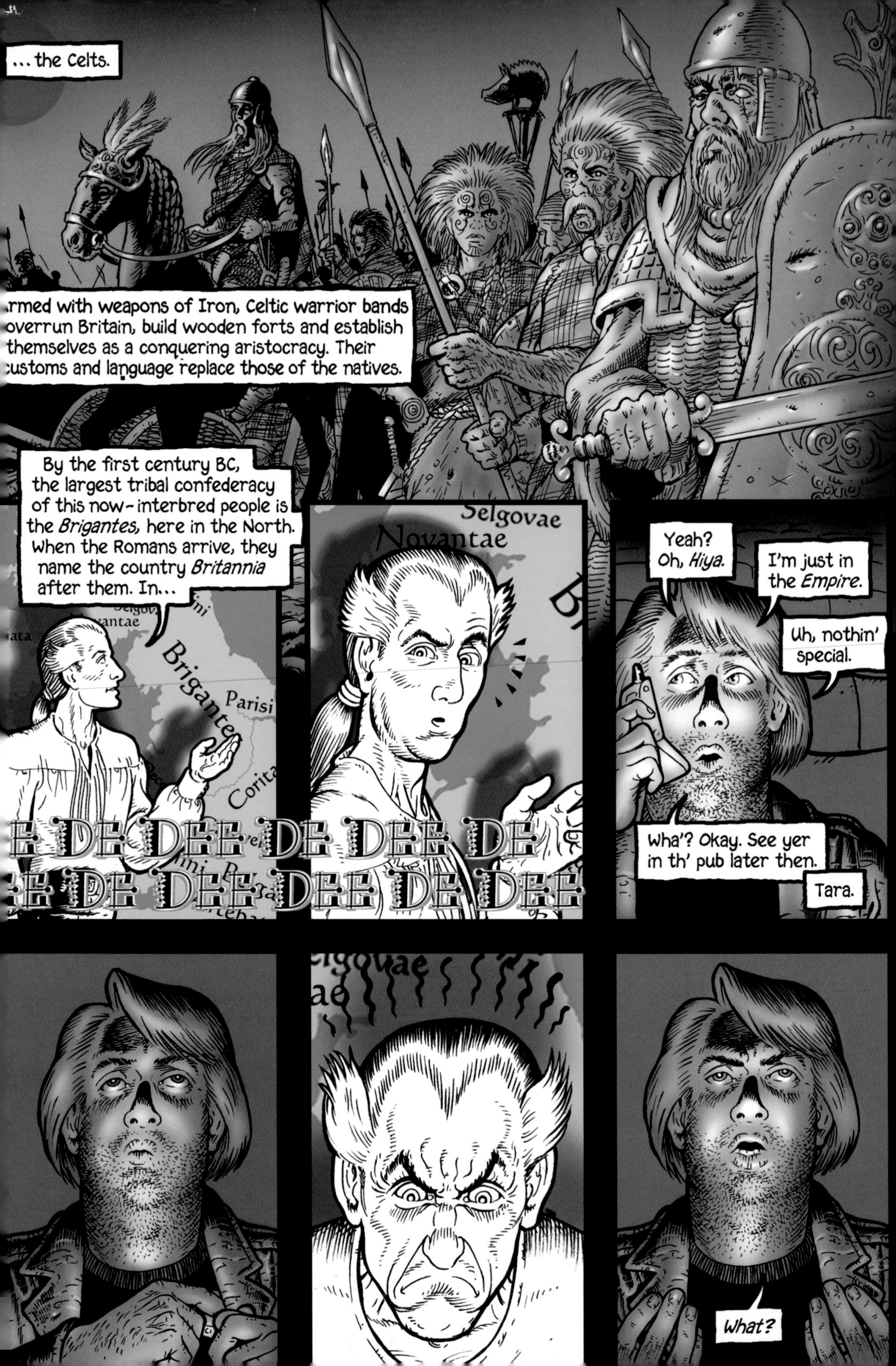

… the Celts.
rmed with weapons of Iron, Celtic warrior bands overrun Britain, build wooden forts and establish themselves as a conquering aristocracy. Their customs and language replace those of the natives.
By the first century BC, the largest tribal confederacy of this now-interbred people is the *Brigantes,* here in the North. When the Romans arrive, they name the country *Britannia* after them. In…
Parisi
DE DEE DE DEE DE
DE DEE DEE DE DEE
Selgovae
Novantae
Yeah? Oh, *Hiya.*
I'm just in the *Empire.*
Uh, nothin' special.
Wha'? Okay. See yer in th' pub later then.
Tara.
What?

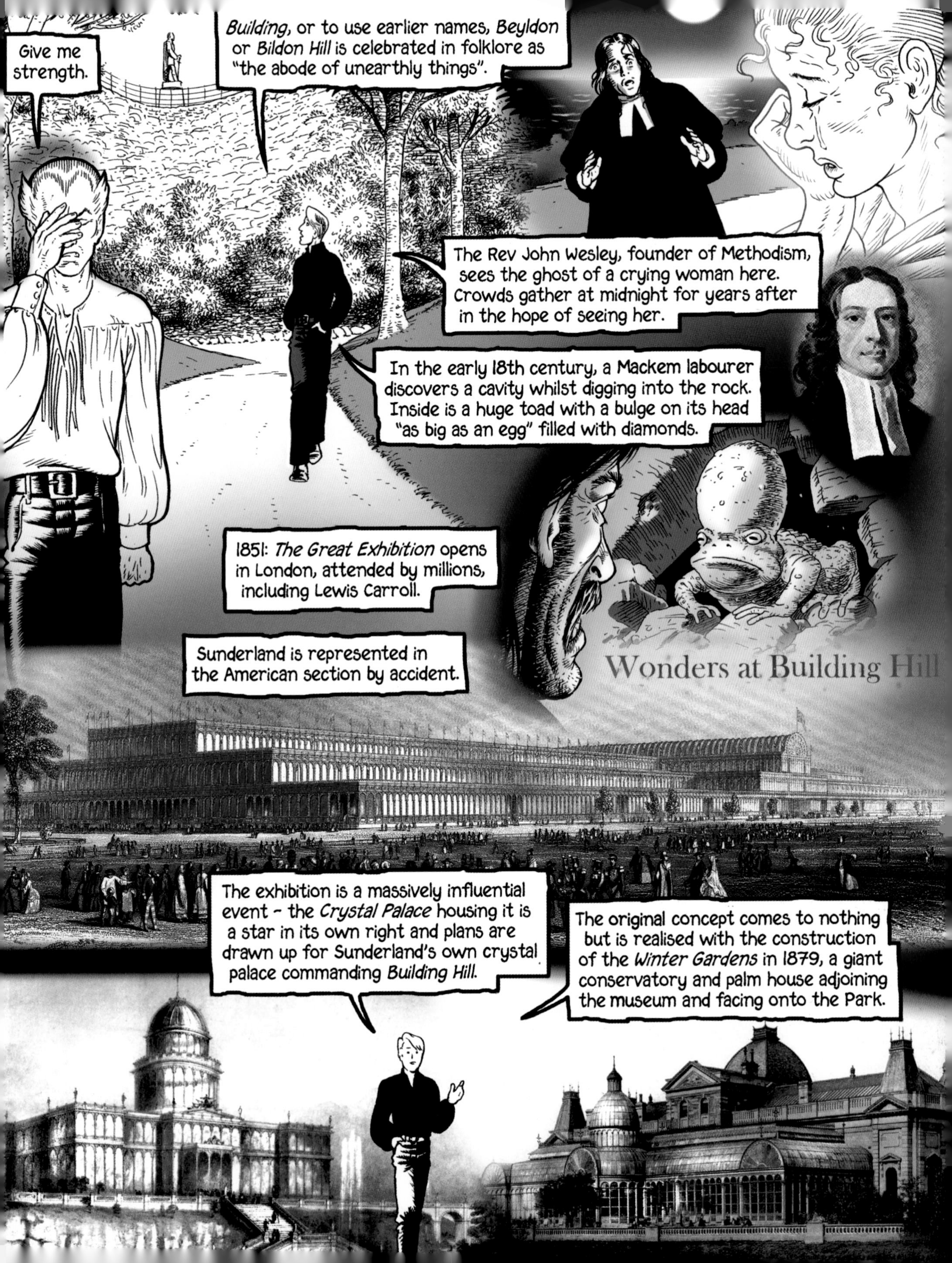
Give me strength.
Building, or to use earlier names, Beyldon or Bildon Hill is celebrated in folklore as "the abode of unearthly things".
The Rev John Wesley, founder of Methodism, sees the ghost of a crying woman here. Crowds gather at midnight for years after in the hope of seeing her.
In the early 18th century, a Mackem labourer discovers a cavity whilst digging into the rock. Inside is a huge toad with a bulge on its head "as big as an egg" filled with diamonds.
Wonders at Building Hill
1851: The Great Exhibition opens in London, attended by millions, including Lewis Carroll.
Sunderland is represented in the American section by accident.
The exhibition is a massively influential event – the Crystal Palace housing it is a star in its own right and plans are drawn up for Sunderland's own crystal palace commanding Building Hill.
The original concept comes to nothing but is realised with the construction of the Winter Gardens in 1879, a giant conservatory and palm house adjoining the museum and facing onto the Park.

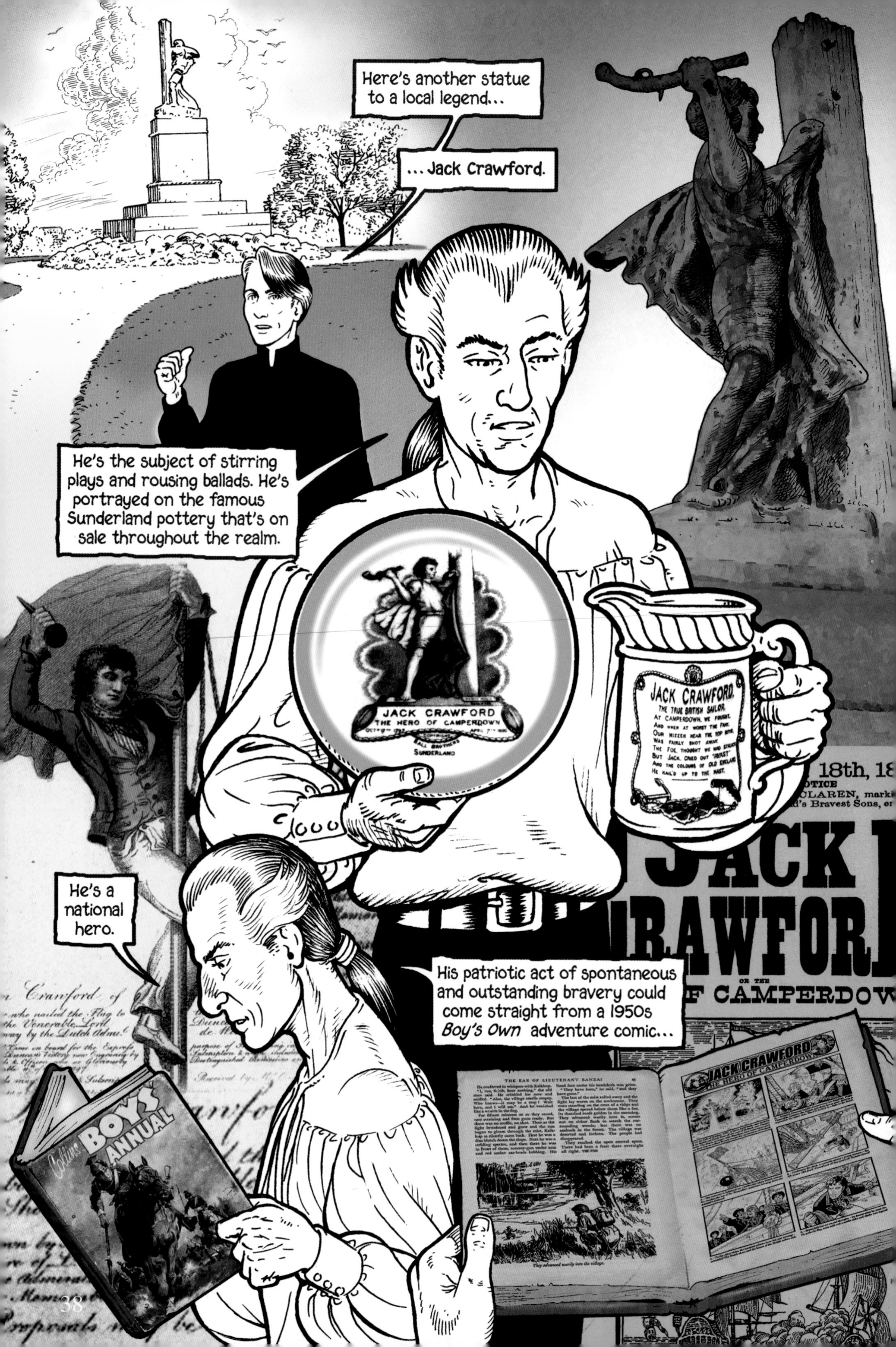
Here's another statue to a local legend...
... Jack Crawford.
He's the subject of stirring plays and rousing ballads. He's portrayed on the famous Sunderland pottery that's on sale throughout the realm.
JACK CRAWFORD
THE HERO OF CAMPERDOWN
SUNDERLAND
JACK CRAWFORD.
THE TRUE BRITISH SAILOR.
He's a national hero.
His patriotic act of spontaneous and outstanding bravery could come straight from a 1950s *Boy's Own* adventure comic...
BOYS ANNUAL
JACK CRAWFORD
THE HERO OF CAMPERDOWN

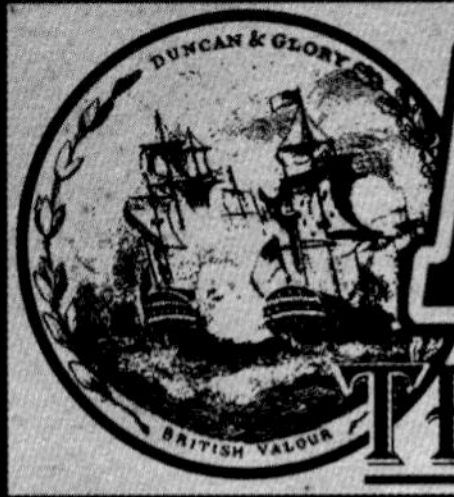
DUNCAN & GLORY
BRITISH VALOUR

JACK CRAWFORD

THE HERO OF CAMPERDOWN

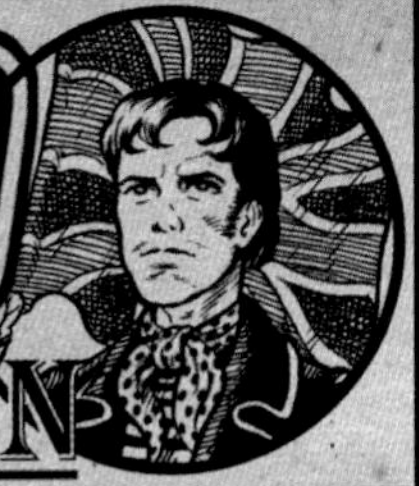

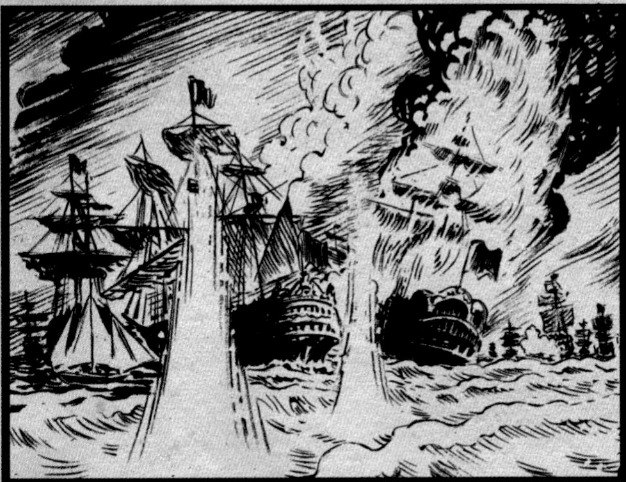

It is the 11th of October, 1797. A fierce naval battle rages between the British and Dutch fleets off the coast of Holland, near *Camperdown.* The Dutch, in league with *Napoleon,* have been intercepted on their way to collect French troops for an invasion of Ireland.

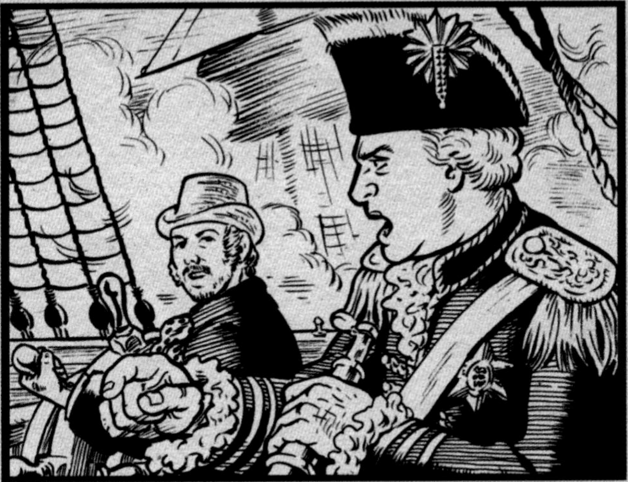

2. - Admiral Duncan boldly manoeuvres his flagship, the *HMS Venerable,* between the Dutch and their home port. Retreat is impossible for either side. They're locked in a fight to the finish. This day shall see brave deeds and gallant action second to none!

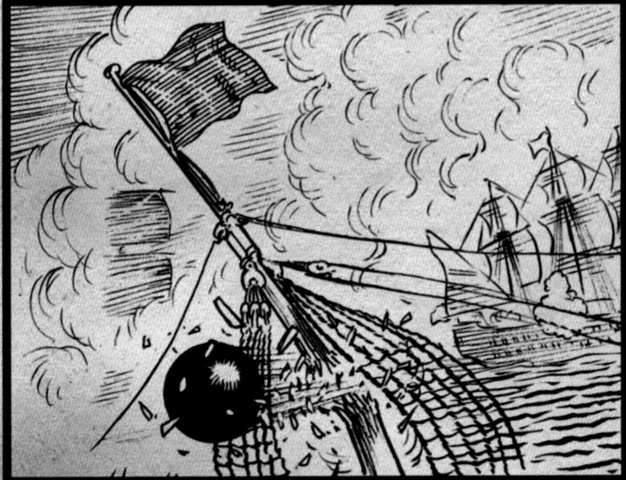

3. - The sailors shout defiance in the heat of battle. The outcome is balanced on a knife-edge when Dutch cannonfire smashes the top of the *Venerable*'s noble mainmast, bringing down the Admiral's *Colours!*

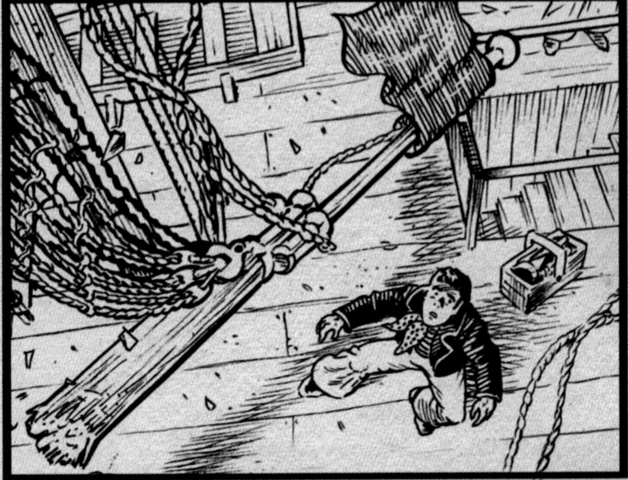

4. - Crashing noisily to the deck, the heavy mast narrowly misses a young seaman – the twenty-three year old *Jack Crawford* of the port of *Sunderland!* This is a day that he shall remember for the rest of his life.

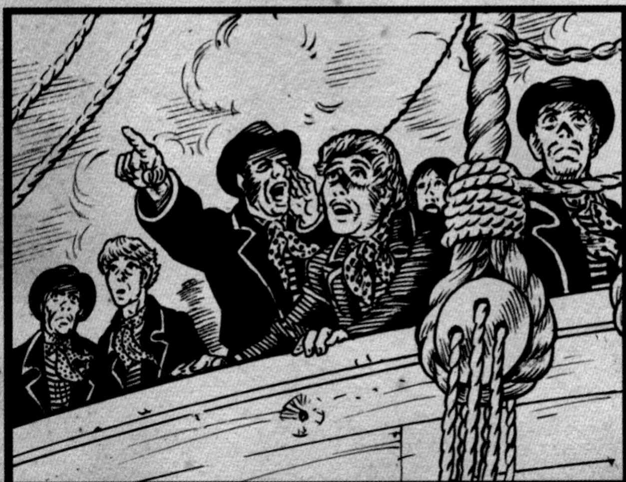

5. - To the other ships, the lowered colours have but one message - *surrender!* The Dutch cheer and the hearts of the British sailors sink.

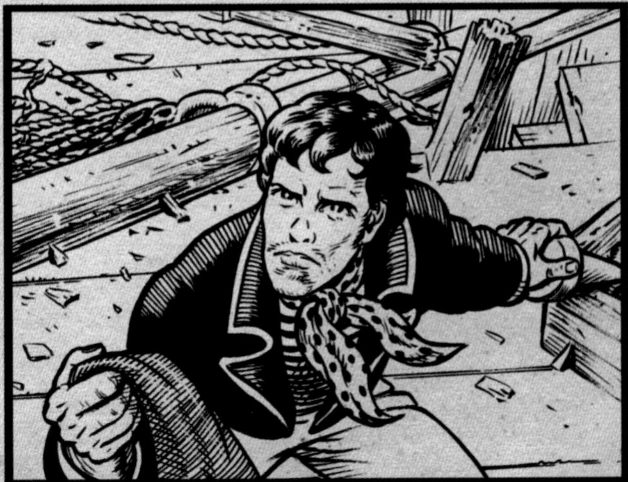

6. - *Brave Jack* has no second thoughts - he *knows* what he must do. He grabs the flag, some nails and a marlinspike and climbs into *legend!*

ABOVE AND BEYOND THE CALL OF DUTY

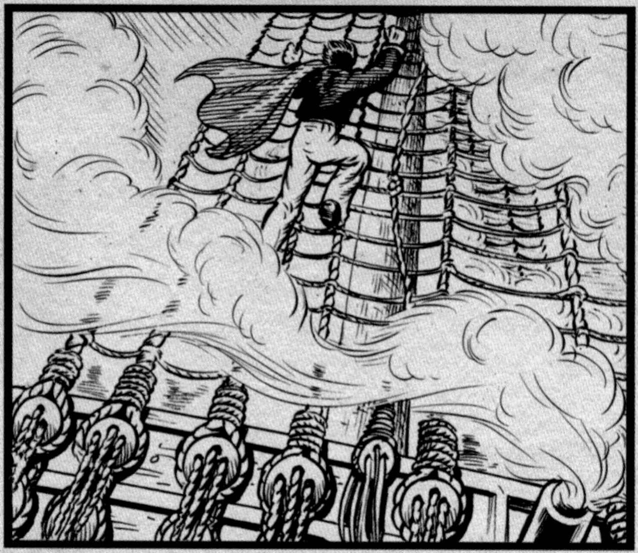

7. - With the flag between his teeth he scales the rigging, oblivious to the grapeshot and musket balls screaming past his head.

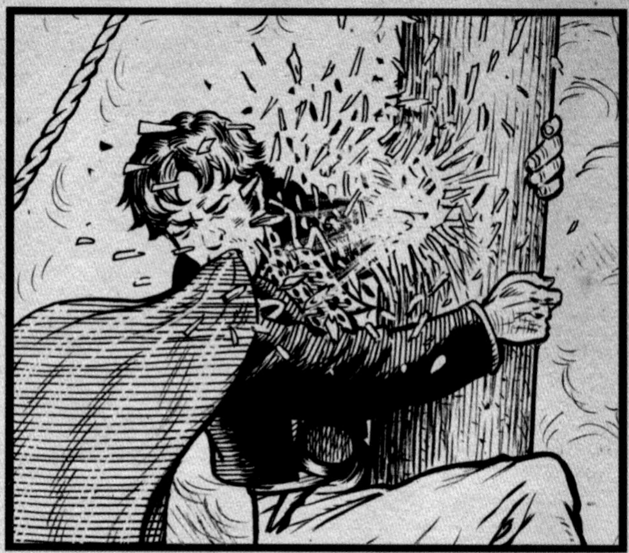

8. - Jack reaches the mainmast platform and hauls himself up the mast. Suddenly it is struck, the wood *erupting* in an explosion of splinters!

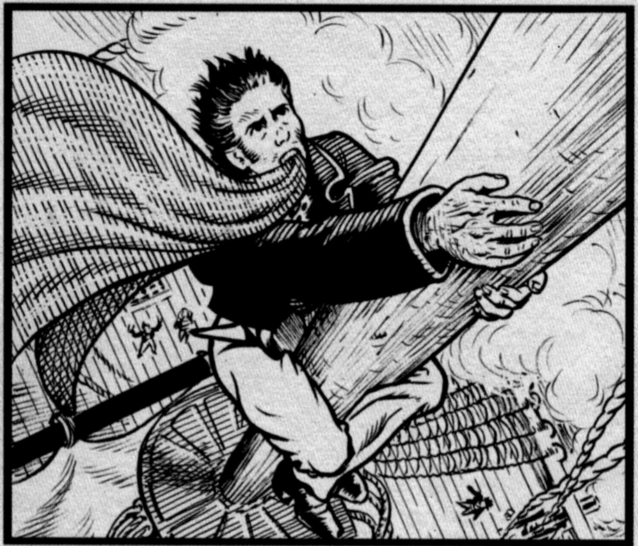

9. - His cheek is ripped wide open but Jack remains steadfast in the face of danger and continues undeterred, cheered on by his shipmates.

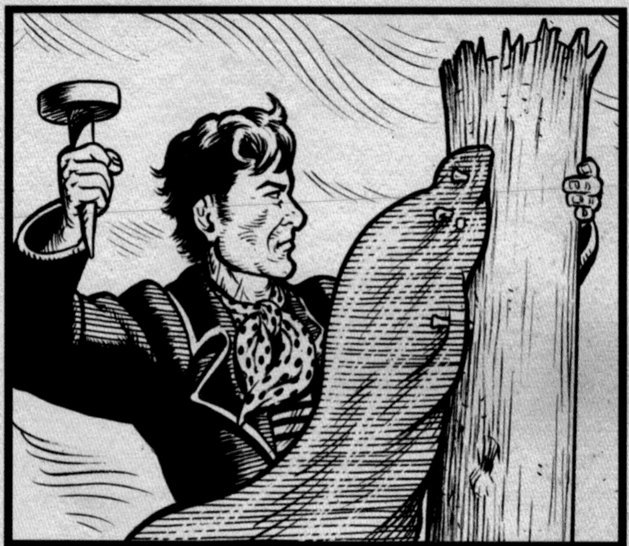

10. - Nearing the top of the shattered *topgallant*, Jack firmly fixes the blue flag of Duncan in place, signalling to the other ships "no surrender".

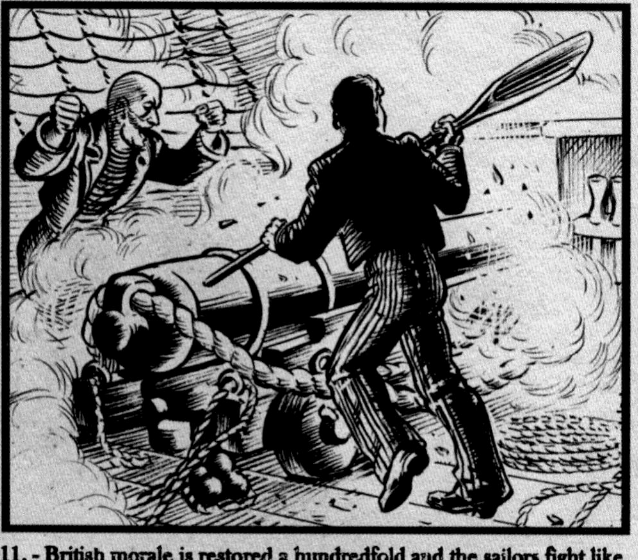

11. - British morale is restored a hundredfold and the sailors fight like demons! *Captain William Bligh* (later of *The Bounty*) captures the enemy flagship. Thanks to Jack Crawford, the British navy is victorious!

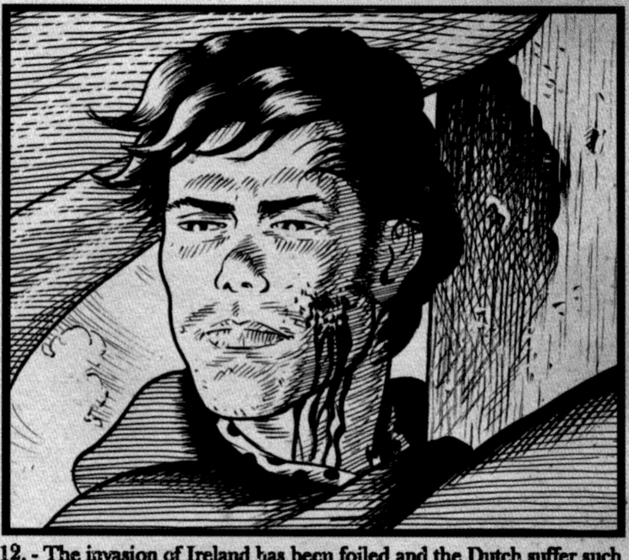

12. - The invasion of Ireland has been foiled and the Dutch suffer such a crushing defeat that Holland ceases to be a maritime power. By turning the tide of battle, Jack has changed the course of history.

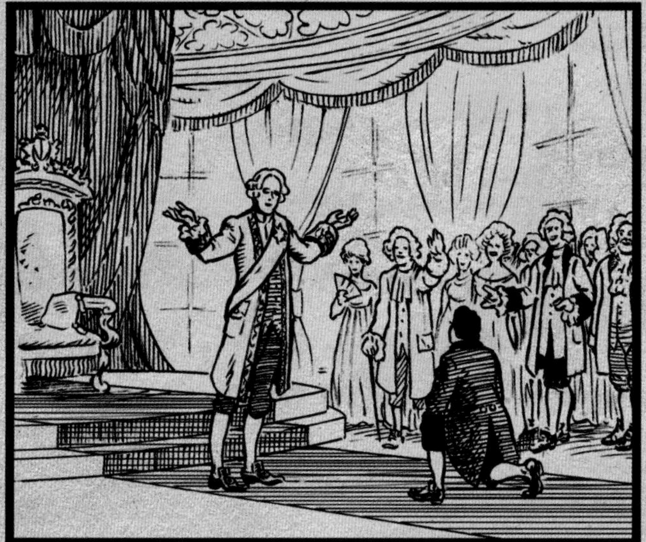

13. - For the government, during an unpopular war, this common man is a God-given patriotic champion, a ***national idol***, loved by the mob and fêted by high society and His Royal Highness ***King George III***.

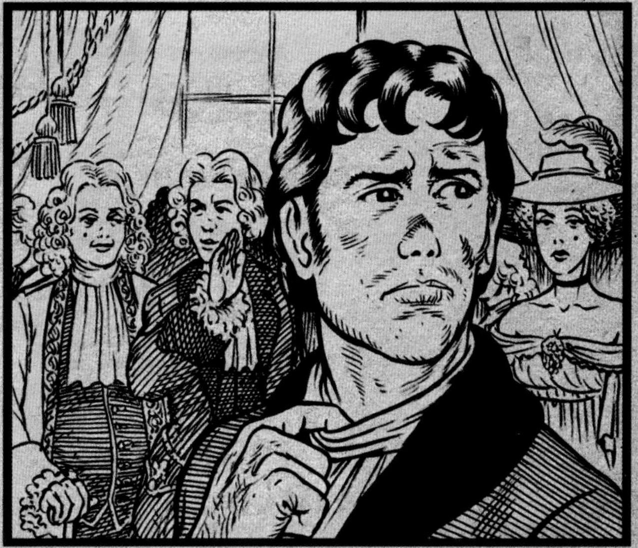

14. - Uncomfortable in the presence of aristocrats and reticent of public engagements, he refuses to play the hero, even avoiding his official parade of honour through the thronged London streets.

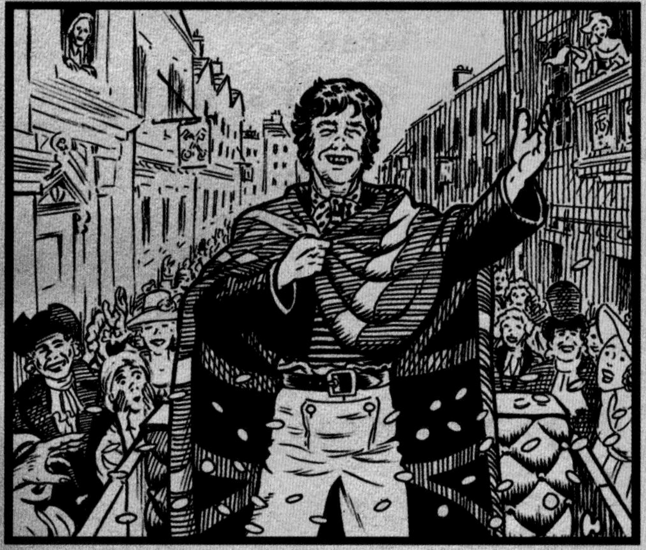

15. - An official stand-in, a sailor of the same age and build, draped with the ***Union Flag*** has so much money thrown into his carriage by an adoring public that he never has to work again.

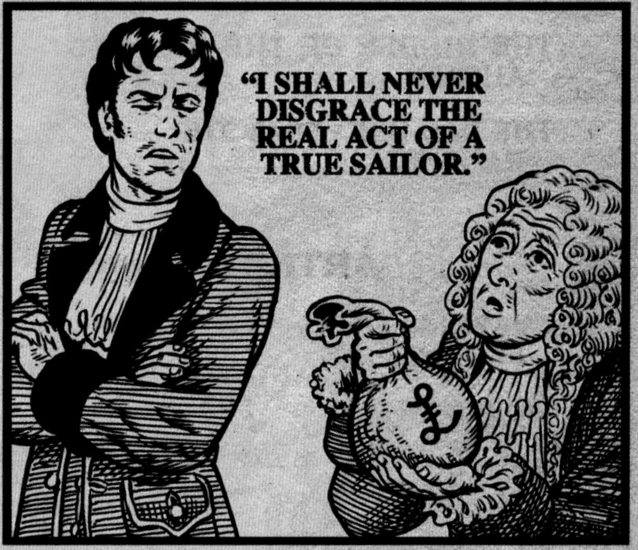
"I SHALL NEVER DISGRACE THE REAL ACT OF A TRUE SAILOR."

16 . - Jack also refuses an offer of one hundred pounds a week (then a small fortune) to appear in re-enactments of the ***Battle of Camperdown*** at the ***Vauxhall Pleasure Gardens***.

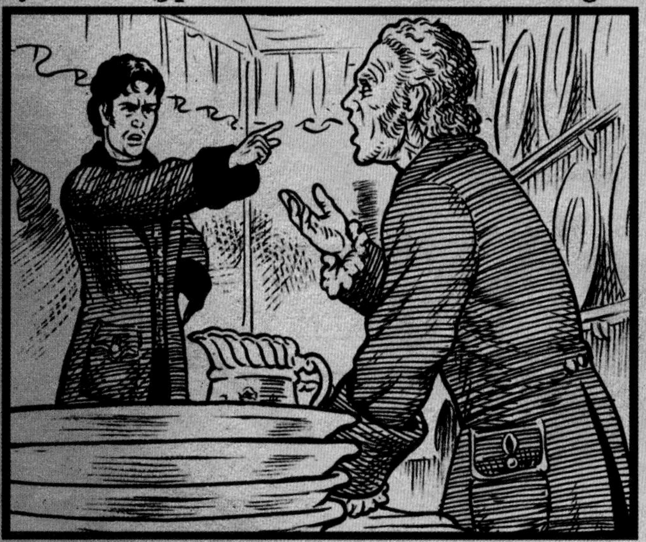

17. - Even critical of the merchandising of the popular ***Sunderland Pottery*** illustrated with depictions of his famous feat of bravery and sold all over the world, modest Jack shuns his unasked-for fame.

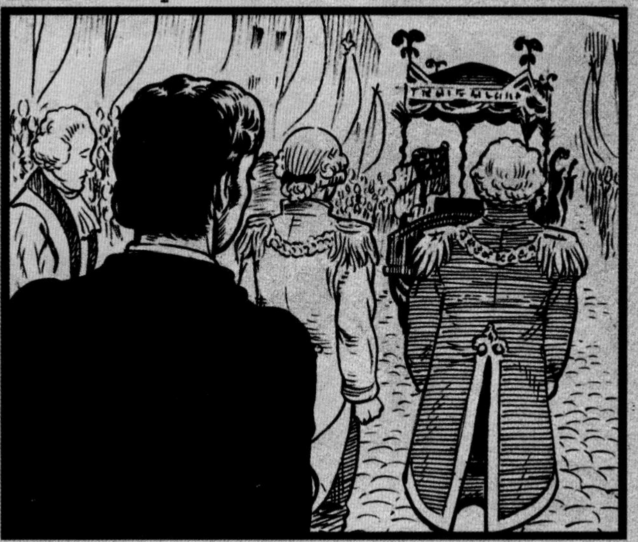

18. - Although he does accept the honour of being invited to walk in the funeral procession of ***Admiral Horatio Nelson*** and receives a ***Medal for Gallantry*** from the people of Sunderland. ***The end.***

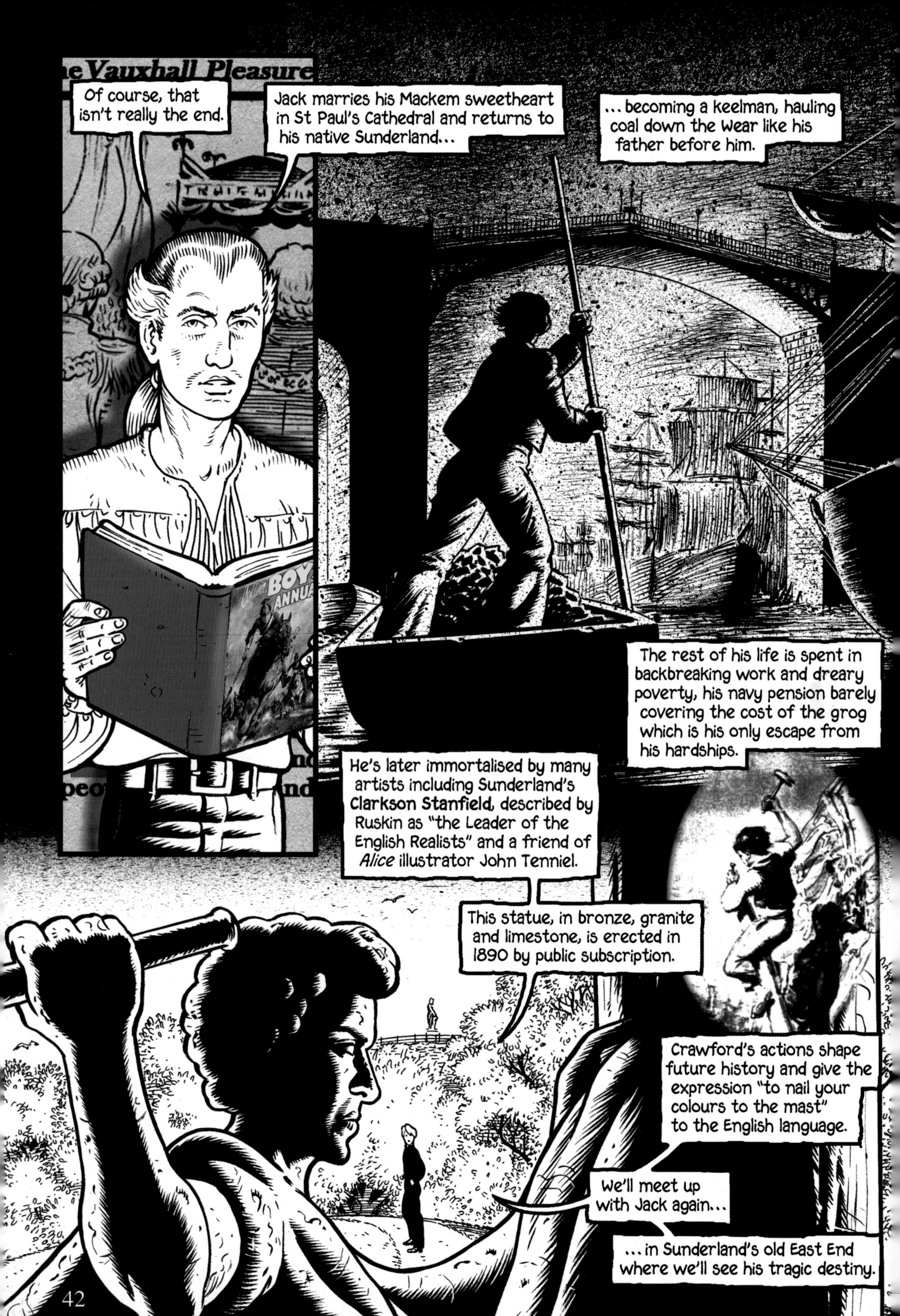

Vauxhall Pleasure
Of course, that isn't really the end.
Jack marries his Mackem sweetheart in St Paul's Cathedral and returns to his native Sunderland...
... becoming a keelman, hauling coal down the Wear like his father before him.
The rest of his life is spent in backbreaking work and dreary poverty, his navy pension barely covering the cost of the grog which is his only escape from his hardships.
He's later immortalised by many artists including Sunderland's **Clarkson Stanfield**, described by Ruskin as "the Leader of the English Realists" and a friend of *Alice* illustrator John Tenniel.
This statue, in bronze, granite and limestone, is erected in 1890 by public subscription.
Crawford's actions shape future history and give the expression "to nail your colours to the mast" to the English language.
We'll meet up with Jack again...
... in Sunderland's old East End where we'll see his tragic destiny.

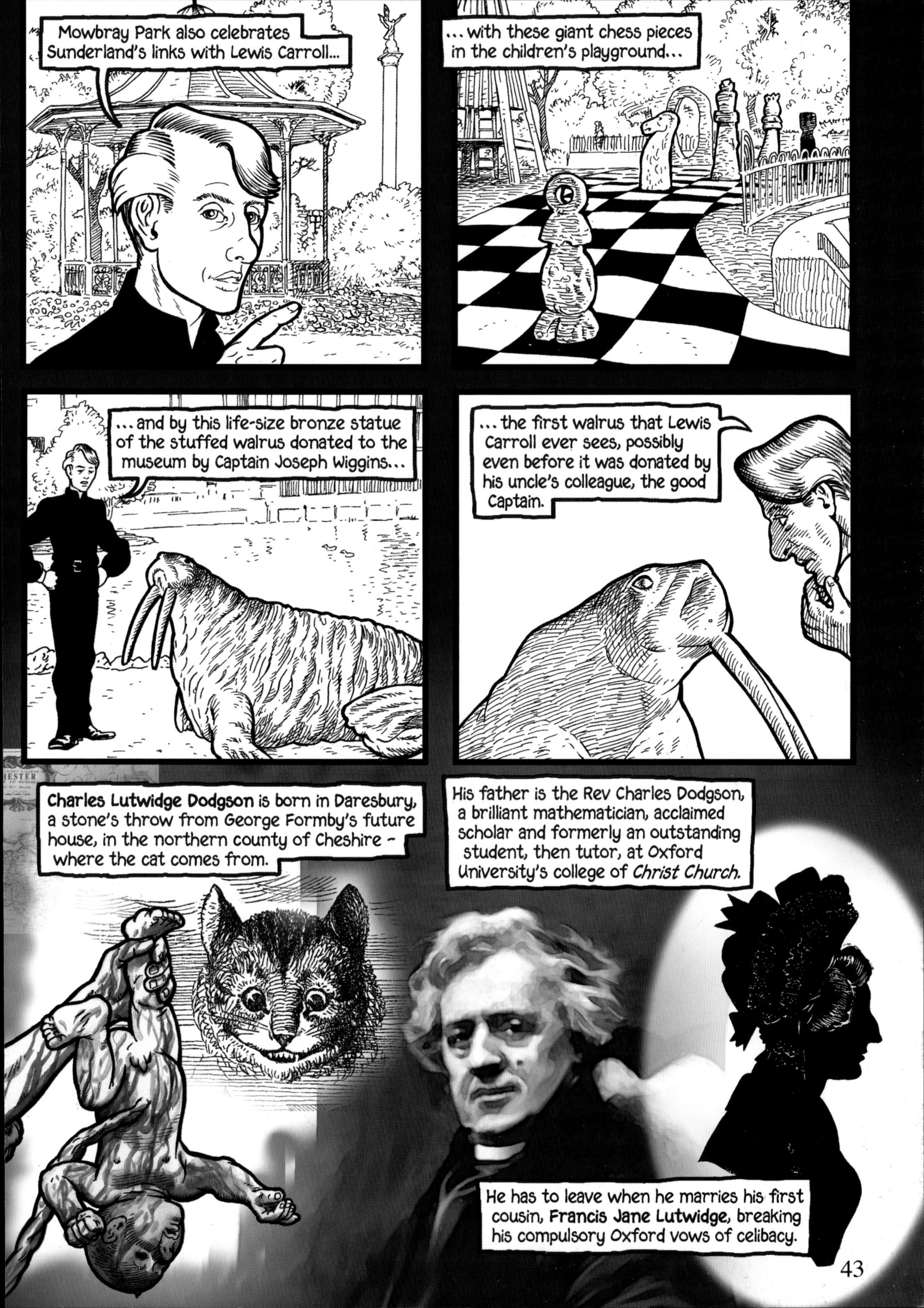
Mowbray Park also celebrates Sunderland's links with Lewis Carroll...
... with these giant chess pieces in the children's playground...
... and by this life-size bronze statue of the stuffed walrus donated to the museum by Captain Joseph Wiggins...
... the first walrus that Lewis Carroll ever sees, possibly even before it was donated by his uncle's colleague, the good Captain.
Charles Lutwidge Dodgson is born in Daresbury, a stone's throw from George Formby's future house, in the northern county of Cheshire - where the cat comes from.
His father is the Rev Charles Dodgson, a brilliant mathematician, acclaimed scholar and formerly an outstanding student, then tutor, at Oxford University's college of *Christ Church.*
He has to leave when he marries his first cousin, **Francis Jane Lutwidge**, breaking his compulsory Oxford vows of celibacy.

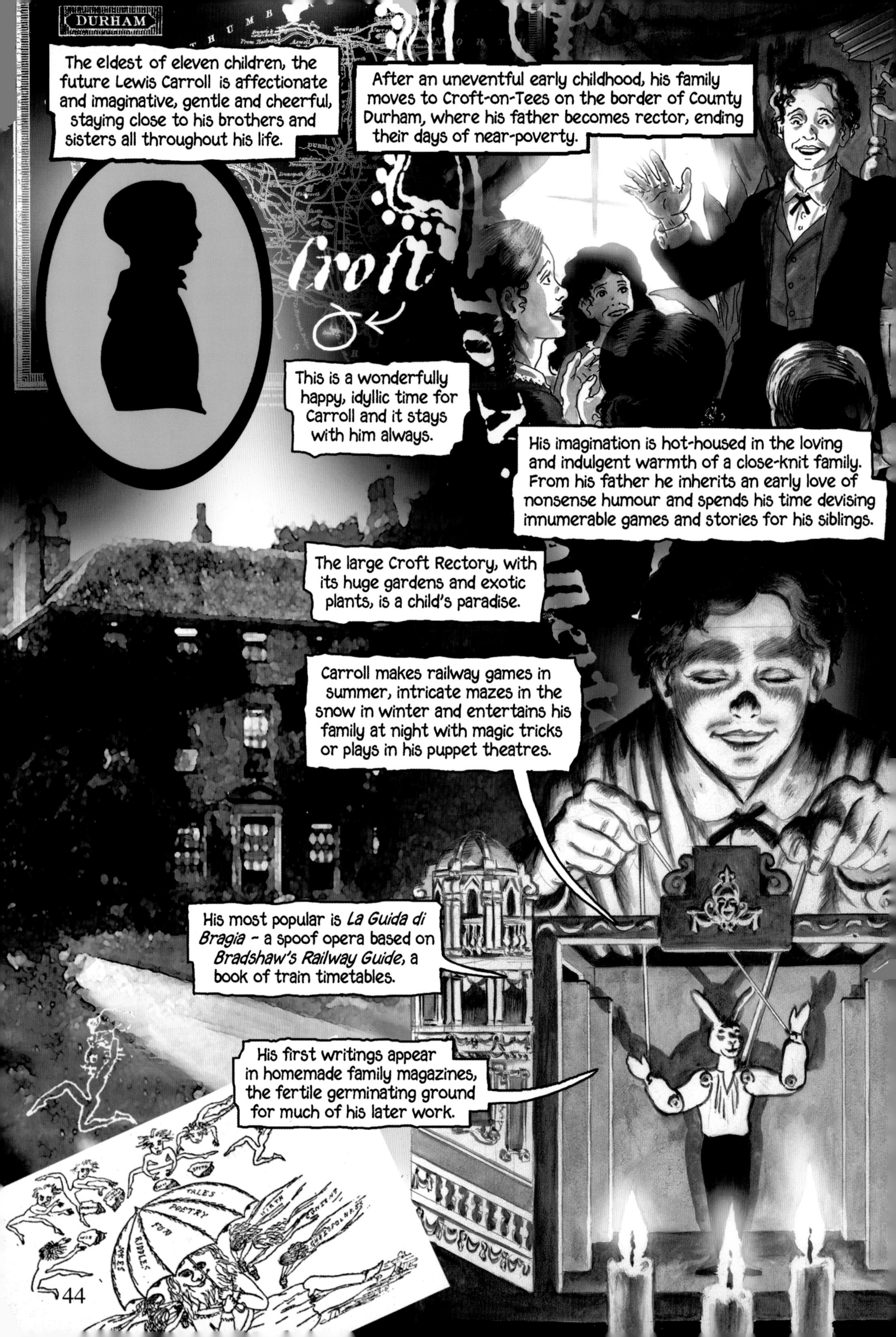
DURHAM
The eldest of eleven children, the future Lewis Carroll is affectionate and imaginative, gentle and cheerful, staying close to his brothers and sisters all throughout his life.
After an uneventful early childhood, his family moves to Croft-on-Tees on the border of County Durham, where his father becomes rector, ending their days of near-poverty.
Croft
This is a wonderfully happy, idyllic time for Carroll and it stays with him always.
His imagination is hot-housed in the loving and indulgent warmth of a close-knit family. From his father he inherits an early love of nonsense humour and spends his time devising innumerable games and stories for his siblings.
The large Croft Rectory, with its huge gardens and exotic plants, is a child's paradise.
Carroll makes railway games in summer, intricate mazes in the snow in winter and entertains his family at night with magic tricks or plays in his puppet theatres.
His most popular is *La Guida di Bragia* – a spoof opera based on *Bradshaw's Railway Guide*, a book of train timetables.
His first writings appear in homemade family magazines, the fertile germinating ground for much of his later work.
TALES
POETRY
FUN
RIDDLES
JOKES
MIRTH

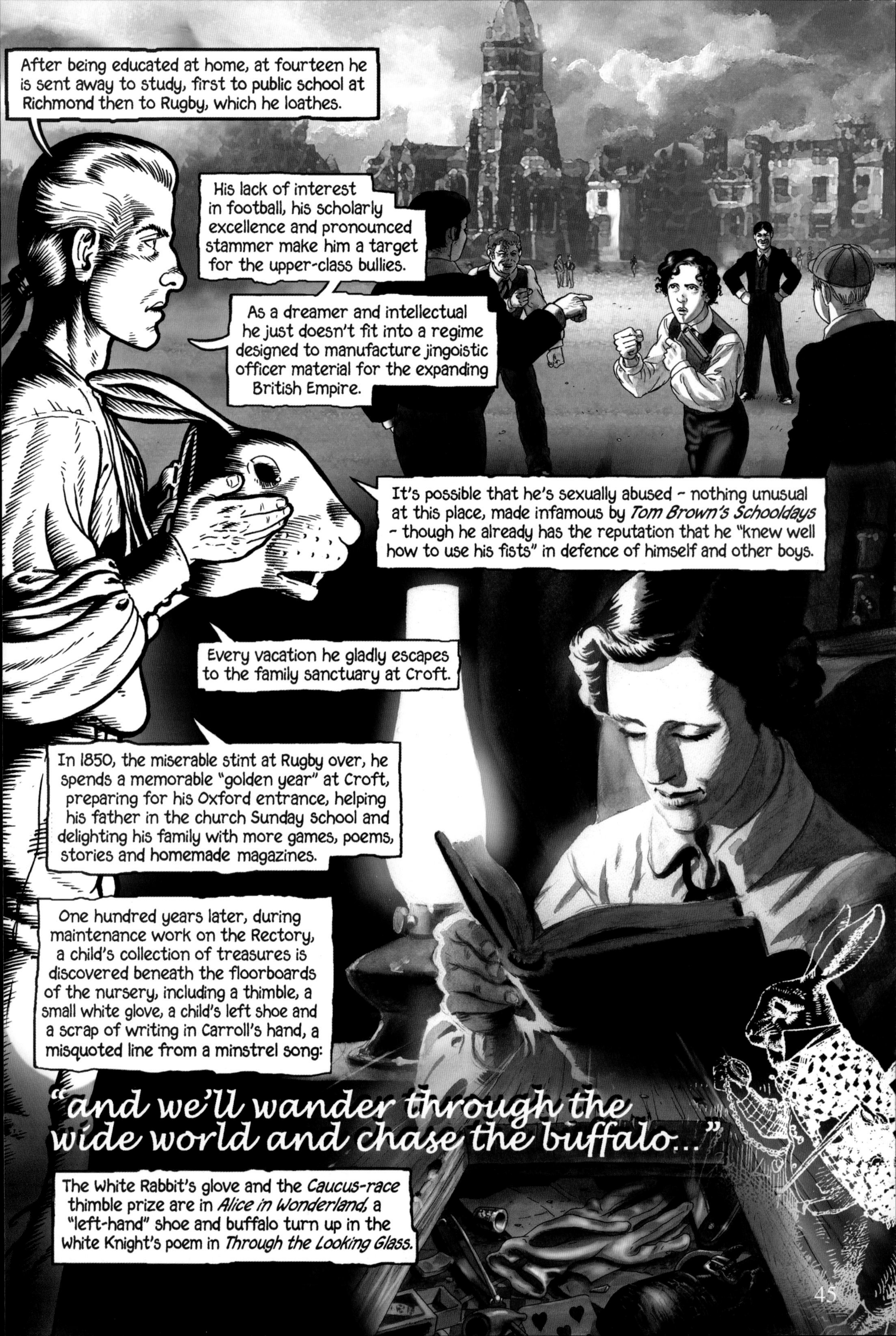

After being educated at home, at fourteen he is sent away to study, first to public school at Richmond then to Rugby, which he loathes.
His lack of interest in football, his scholarly excellence and pronounced stammer make him a target for the upper-class bullies.
As a dreamer and intellectual he just doesn't fit into a regime designed to manufacture jingoistic officer material for the expanding British Empire.
It's possible that he's sexually abused – nothing unusual at this place, made infamous by *Tom Brown's Schooldays* – though he already has the reputation that he "knew well how to use his fists" in defence of himself and other boys.
Every vacation he gladly escapes to the family sanctuary at Croft.
In 1850, the miserable stint at Rugby over, he spends a memorable "golden year" at Croft, preparing for his Oxford entrance, helping his father in the church Sunday school and delighting his family with more games, poems, stories and homemade magazines.
One hundred years later, during maintenance work on the Rectory, a child's collection of treasures is discovered beneath the floorboards of the nursery, including a thimble, a small white glove, a child's left shoe and a scrap of writing in Carroll's hand, a misquoted line from a minstrel song:
"and we'll wander through the wide world and chase the buffalo..."
The White Rabbit's glove and the *Caucus-race* thimble prize are in *Alice in Wonderland*, a "left-hand" shoe and buffalo turn up in the White Knight's poem in *Through the Looking Glass.*

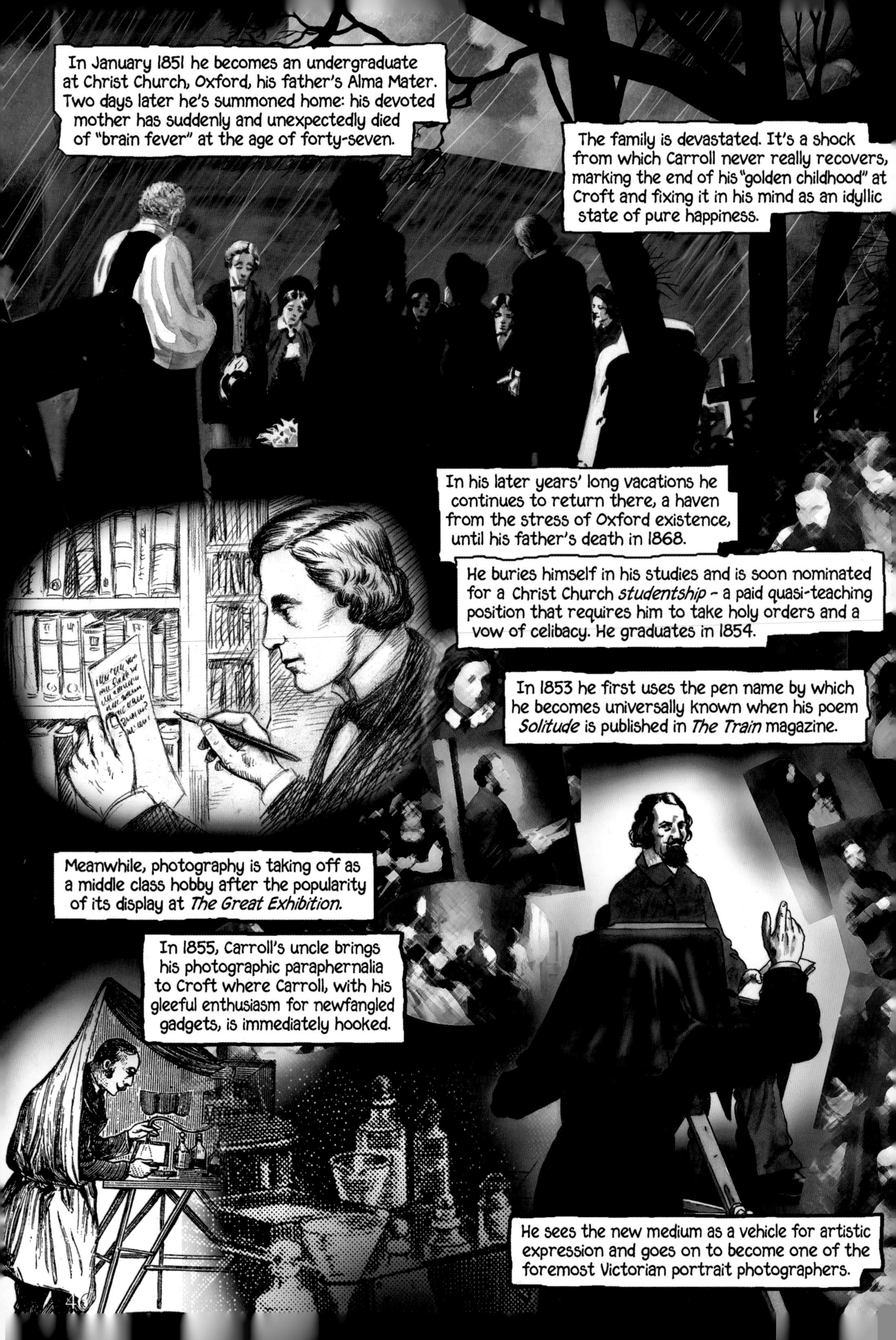
In January 1851 he becomes an undergraduate at Christ Church, Oxford, his father's Alma Mater. Two days later he's summoned home: his devoted mother has suddenly and unexpectedly died of "brain fever" at the age of forty-seven.
The family is devastated. It's a shock from which Carroll never really recovers, marking the end of his "golden childhood" at Croft and fixing it in his mind as an idyllic state of pure happiness.
In his later years' long vacations he continues to return there, a haven from the stress of Oxford existence, until his father's death in 1868.
He buries himself in his studies and is soon nominated for a Christ Church *studentship* – a paid quasi-teaching position that requires him to take holy orders and a vow of celibacy. He graduates in 1854.
In 1853 he first uses the pen name by which he becomes universally known when his poem *Solitude* is published in *The Train* magazine.
Meanwhile, photography is taking off as a middle class hobby after the popularity of its display at *The Great Exhibition.*
In 1855, Carroll's uncle brings his photographic paraphernalia to Croft where Carroll, with his gleeful enthusiasm for newfangled gadgets, is immediately hooked.
He sees the new medium as a vehicle for artistic expression and goes on to become one of the foremost Victorian portrait photographers.

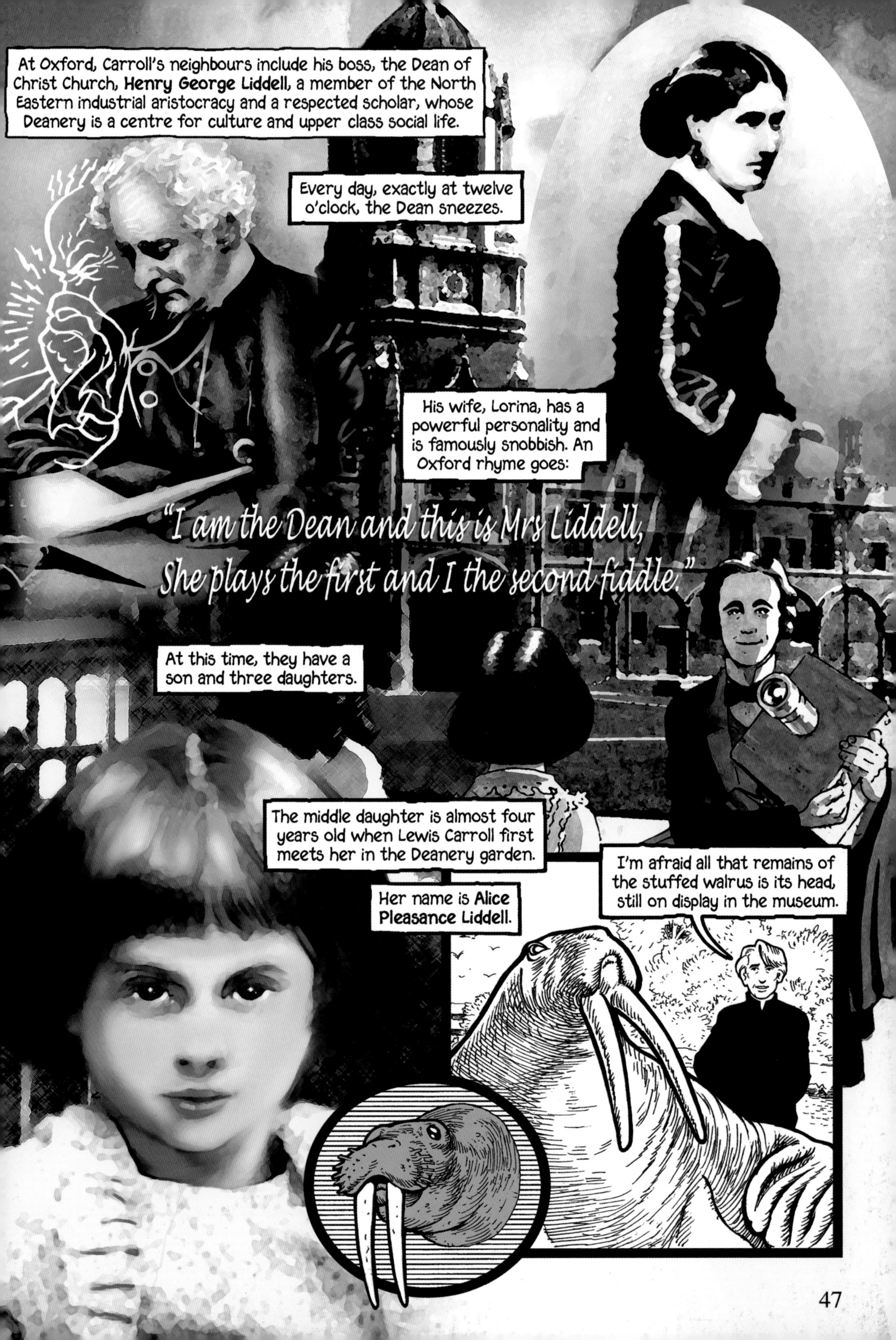
At Oxford, Carroll's neighbours include his boss, the Dean of Christ Church, **Henry George Liddell**, a member of the North Eastern industrial aristocracy and a respected scholar, whose Deanery is a centre for culture and upper class social life.
Every day, exactly at twelve o'clock, the Dean sneezes.
His wife, Lorina, has a powerful personality and is famously snobbish. An Oxford rhyme goes:
"I am the Dean and this is Mrs Liddell,
She plays the first and I the second fiddle."
At this time, they have a son and three daughters.
The middle daughter is almost four years old when Lewis Carroll first meets her in the Deanery garden.
Her name is **Alice Pleasance Liddell**.
I'm afraid all that remains of the stuffed walrus is its head, still on display in the museum.

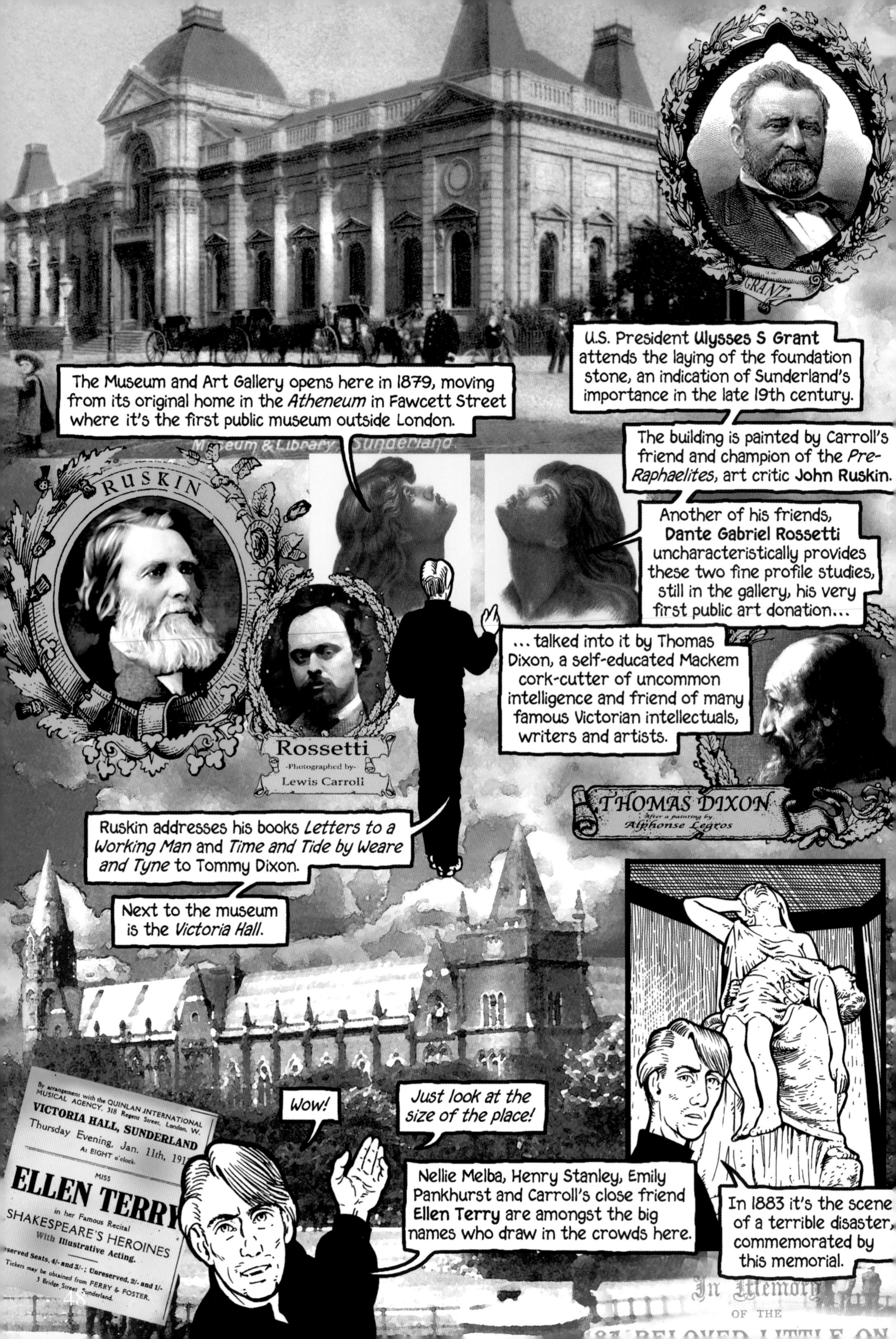

GRANT
U.S. President Ulysses S Grant attends the laying of the foundation stone, an indication of Sunderland's importance in the late 19th century.
The Museum and Art Gallery opens here in 1879, moving from its original home in the Atheneum in Fawcett Street where it's the first public museum outside London.
Museum & Library, Sunderland
The building is painted by Carroll's friend and champion of the Pre-Raphaelites, art critic John Ruskin.
RUSKIN
Another of his friends, Dante Gabriel Rossetti uncharacteristically provides these two fine profile studies, still in the gallery, his very first public art donation...
...talked into it by Thomas Dixon, a self-educated Mackem cork-cutter of uncommon intelligence and friend of many famous Victorian intellectuals, writers and artists.
Rossetti
-Photographed by-
Lewis Carroll
THOMAS DIXON
After a painting by
Alphonse Legros
Ruskin addresses his books Letters to a Working Man and Time and Tide by Weare and Tyne to Tommy Dixon.
Next to the museum is the Victoria Hall.
By arrangement with the QUINLAN INTERNATIONAL MUSICAL AGENCY, 318 Regent Street, London, W.
VICTORIA HALL, SUNDERLAND
Thursday Evening, Jan. 11th, 191
At EIGHT o'clock.
MISS
ELLEN TERRY
in her Famous Recital
SHAKESPEARE'S HEROINES
With Illustrative Acting.
served Seats, 4/- and 3/-; Unreserved, 2/- and 1/-
Tickets may be obtained from FERRY & FOSTER, 3 Bridge Street, Sunderland.
Wow!
Just look at the size of the place!
Nellie Melba, Henry Stanley, Emily Pankhurst and Carroll's close friend Ellen Terry are amongst the big names who draw in the crowds here.
In 1883 it's the scene of a terrible disaster, commemorated by this memorial.
In Memory
OF THE

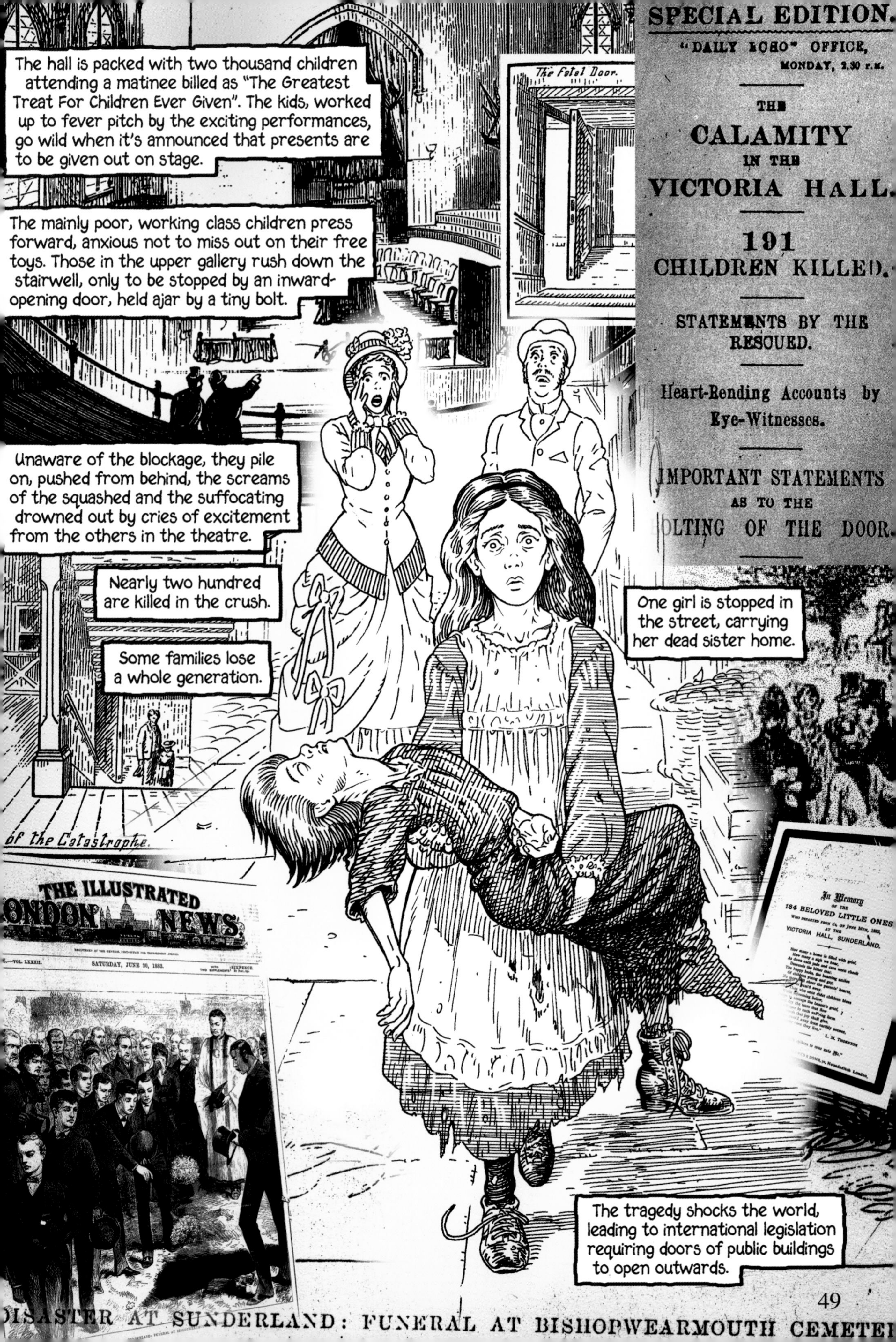

SPECIAL EDITION.
"DAILY ECHO" OFFICE,
MONDAY, 2.30 P.M.
THE
CALAMITY
IN THE
VICTORIA HALL.
191
CHILDREN KILLED.
STATEMENTS BY THE
RESCUED.
Heart-Rending Accounts by
Eye-Witnesses.
IMPORTANT STATEMENTS
AS TO THE
OLTING OF THE DOOR.
The hall is packed with two thousand children attending a matinee billed as "The Greatest Treat For Children Ever Given". The kids, worked up to fever pitch by the exciting performances, go wild when it's announced that presents are to be given out on stage.
The Fatal Door.
The mainly poor, working class children press forward, anxious not to miss out on their free toys. Those in the upper gallery rush down the stairwell, only to be stopped by an inward-opening door, held ajar by a tiny bolt.
Unaware of the blockage, they pile on, pushed from behind, the screams of the squashed and the suffocating drowned out by cries of excitement from the others in the theatre.
Nearly two hundred are killed in the crush.
Some families lose a whole generation.
One girl is stopped in the street, carrying her dead sister home.
of the Catastrophe.
THE ILLUSTRATED LONDON NEWS
—VOL. LXXXII.
SATURDAY, JUNE 30, 1883.
SIXPENCE
In Memory
OF THE
184 BELOVED LITTLE ONES
WHO DEPARTED FROM US, ON JUNE 16TH, 1883,
AT THE
VICTORIA HALL, SUNDERLAND.
L. M. THORNTON
The tragedy shocks the world, leading to international legislation requiring doors of public buildings to open outwards.
DISASTER AT SUNDERLAND: FUNERAL AT BISHOPWEARMOUTH CEMETE

And William McGonagall is inspired to create a piece of authentic doggerel.

It begins...

"'Twas in the town of Sunderland in the year of 1883, That about two hundred children were launched into Eternity..."

It deteriorates from there on in.

High House Ireshopeburn

It's strange to think that the Victoria Hall's Sunderland-built pipe organ is still used every week in a chapel in Weardale.

The hall itself is wrecked by a parachute mine during a six hour bombing raid in 1941.

Being a major shipbuilding port makes Sunderland a prime target. In World War One it's bombed by zeppelins on two occasions.

This concrete *acoustic mirror* zeppelin early-warning station remains, a stark reminder of the threat of death from the sky.

World War Two is much worse.

Sunderland is one of the most heavily bombed places in Britain. Ninety per cent of its buildings are in some way damaged.

"The town bore the scars in its flattened heart for more than two decades." T. Corfe

A bomb lands in the back lane at St Bede's Terrace, but causes little damage.

The last bombardment - the horrific *Night of Hell* in 1943 - leaves thirty-five hundred people homeless.

LE SOI
SALLE DE DÉPÊCH
ROYALE. 124
(20 lignes)
Des Stukas, en vagues succe
attaquent le port de Sunde

50

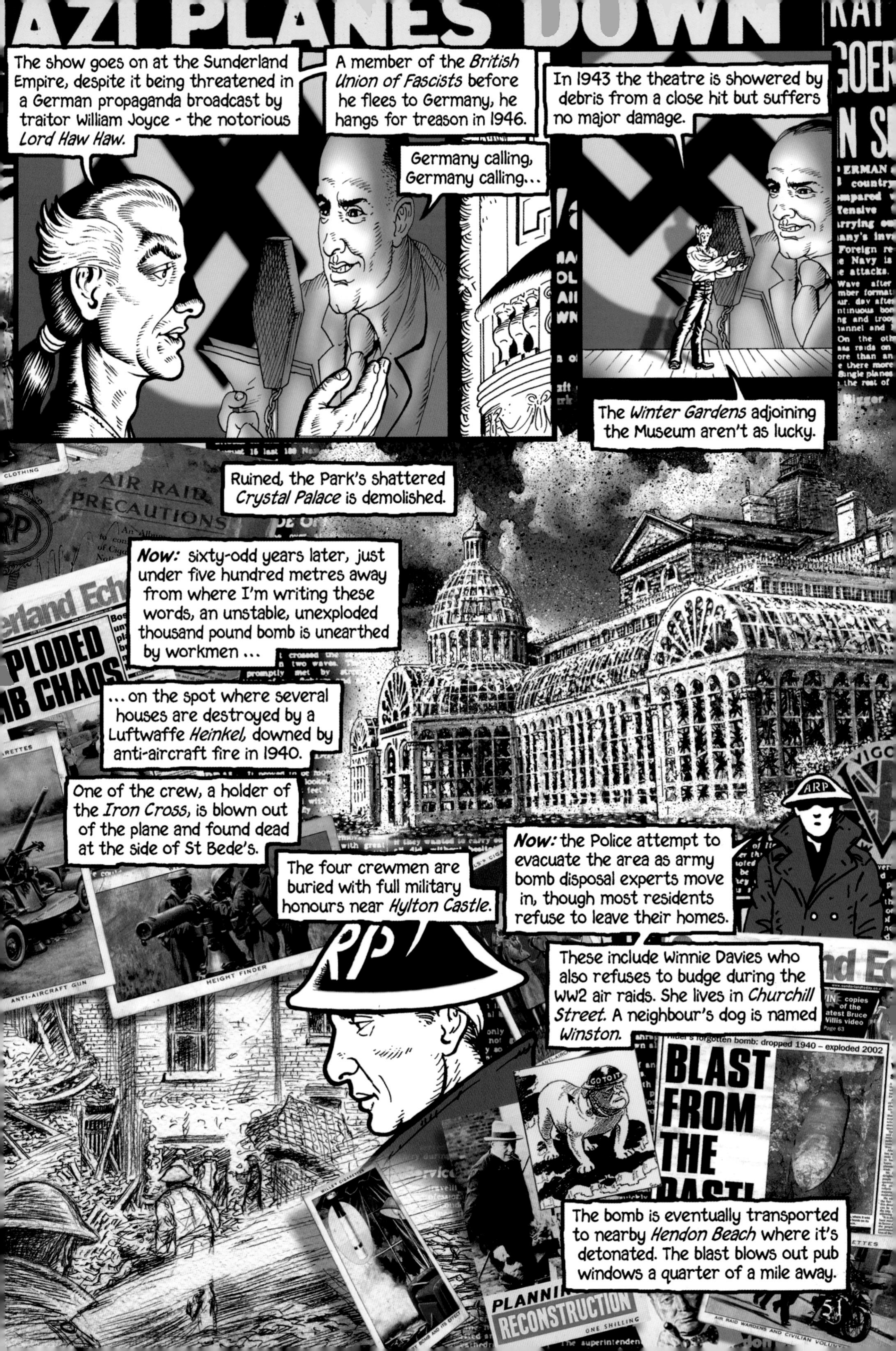
AZI PLANES DOWN
The show goes on at the Sunderland Empire, despite it being threatened in a German propaganda broadcast by traitor William Joyce - the notorious *Lord Haw Haw.*
A member of the *British Union of Fascists* before he flees to Germany, he hangs for treason in 1946.
Germany calling, Germany calling...
In 1943 the theatre is showered by debris from a close hit but suffers no major damage.
The *Winter Gardens* adjoining the Museum aren't as lucky.
Ruined, the Park's shattered *Crystal Palace* is demolished.
AIR RAID PRECAUTIONS
Now: sixty-odd years later, just under five hundred metres away from where I'm writing these words, an unstable, unexploded thousand pound bomb is unearthed by workmen ...
PLODED
MB CHAOS
...on the spot where several houses are destroyed by a Luftwaffe *Heinkel,* downed by anti-aircraft fire in 1940.
One of the crew, a holder of the *Iron Cross,* is blown out of the plane and found dead at the side of St Bede's.
The four crewmen are buried with full military honours near *Hylton Castle.*
Now: the Police attempt to evacuate the area as army bomb disposal experts move in, though most residents refuse to leave their homes.
These include Winnie Davies who also refuses to budge during the WW2 air raids. She lives in *Churchill Street.* A neighbour's dog is named *Winston.*
ANTI-AIRCRAFT GUN
HEIGHT FINDER
GO TO IT
Hitler's forgotten bomb: dropped 1940 – exploded 2002
BLAST FROM THE
The bomb is eventually transported to nearby *Hendon Beach* where it's detonated. The blast blows out pub windows a quarter of a mile away.
PLANNING
RECONSTRUCTION
ONE SHILLING

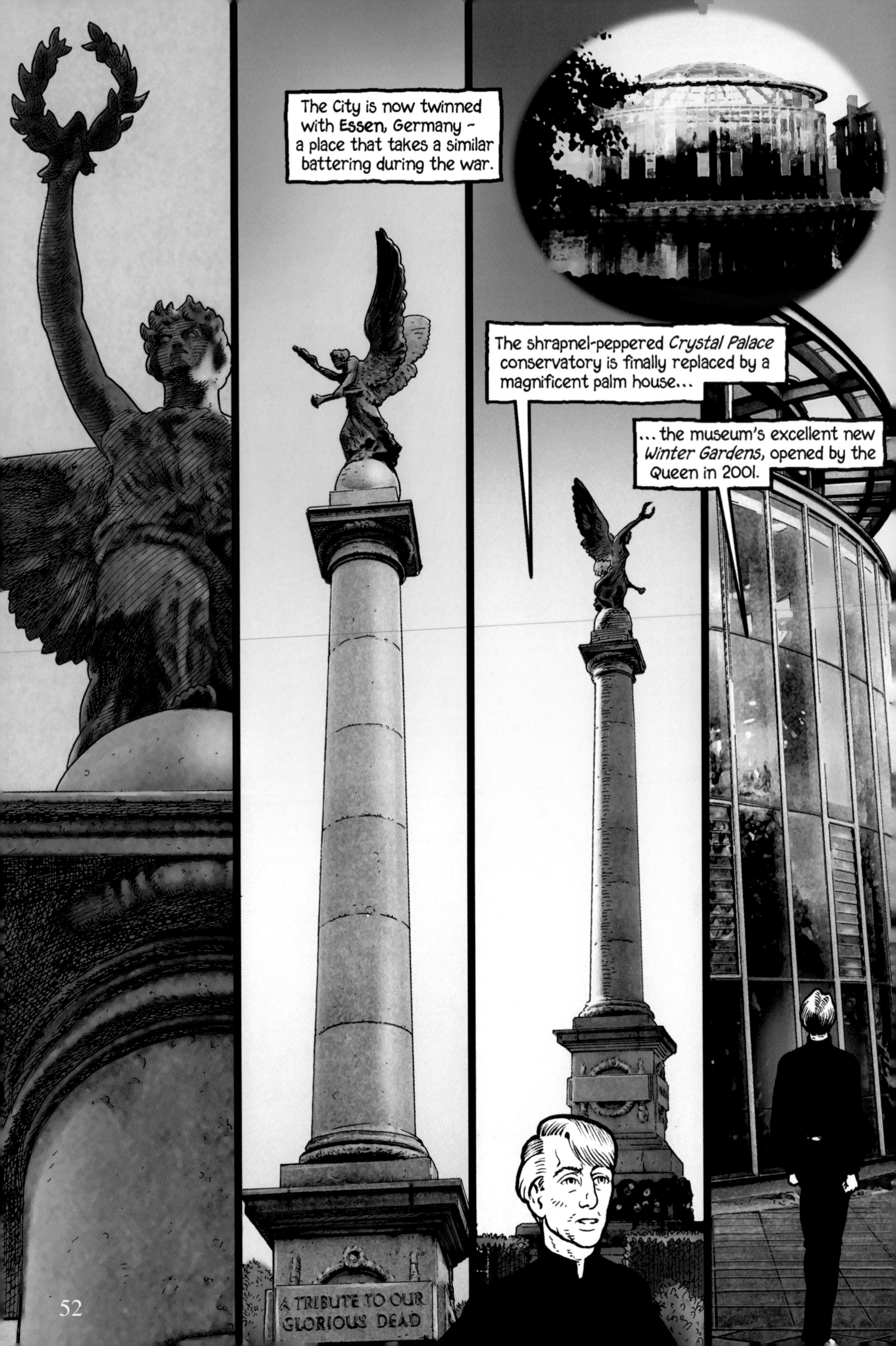
The City is now twinned with Essen, Germany - a place that takes a similar battering during the war.
A TRIBUTE TO OUR GLORIOUS DEAD
The shrapnel-peppered *Crystal Palace* conservatory is finally replaced by a magnificent palm house...
...the museum's excellent new *Winter Gardens*, opened by the Queen in 2001.

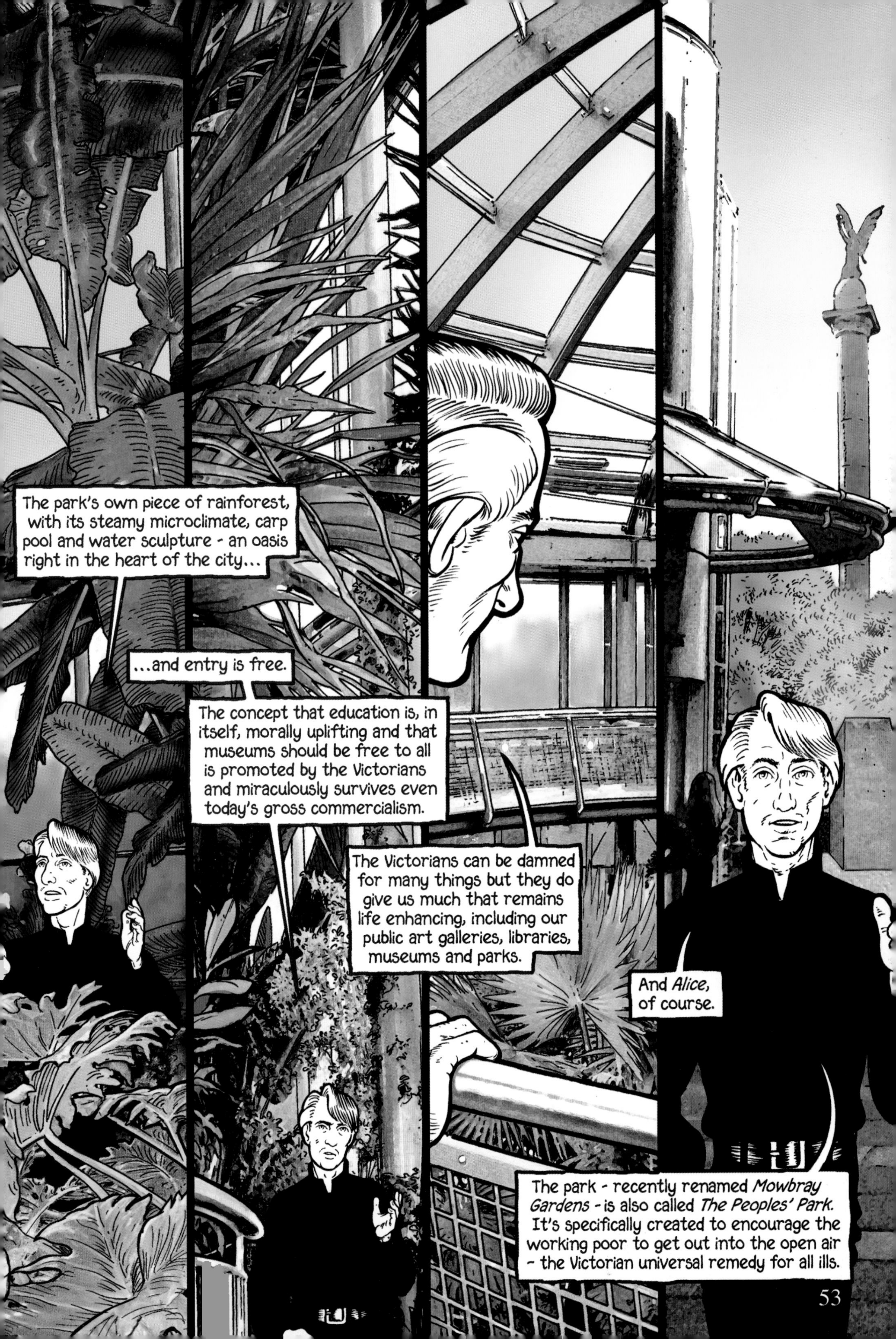
The park's own piece of rainforest, with its steamy microclimate, carp pool and water sculpture - an oasis right in the heart of the city...
...and entry is free.
The concept that education is, in itself, morally uplifting and that museums should be free to all is promoted by the Victorians and miraculously survives even today's gross commercialism.
The Victorians can be damned for many things but they do give us much that remains life enhancing, including our public art galleries, libraries, museums and parks.
And *Alice*, of course.
The park - recently renamed *Mowbray Gardens* - is also called *The Peoples' Park*. It's specifically created to encourage the working poor to get out into the open air - the Victorian universal remedy for all ills.

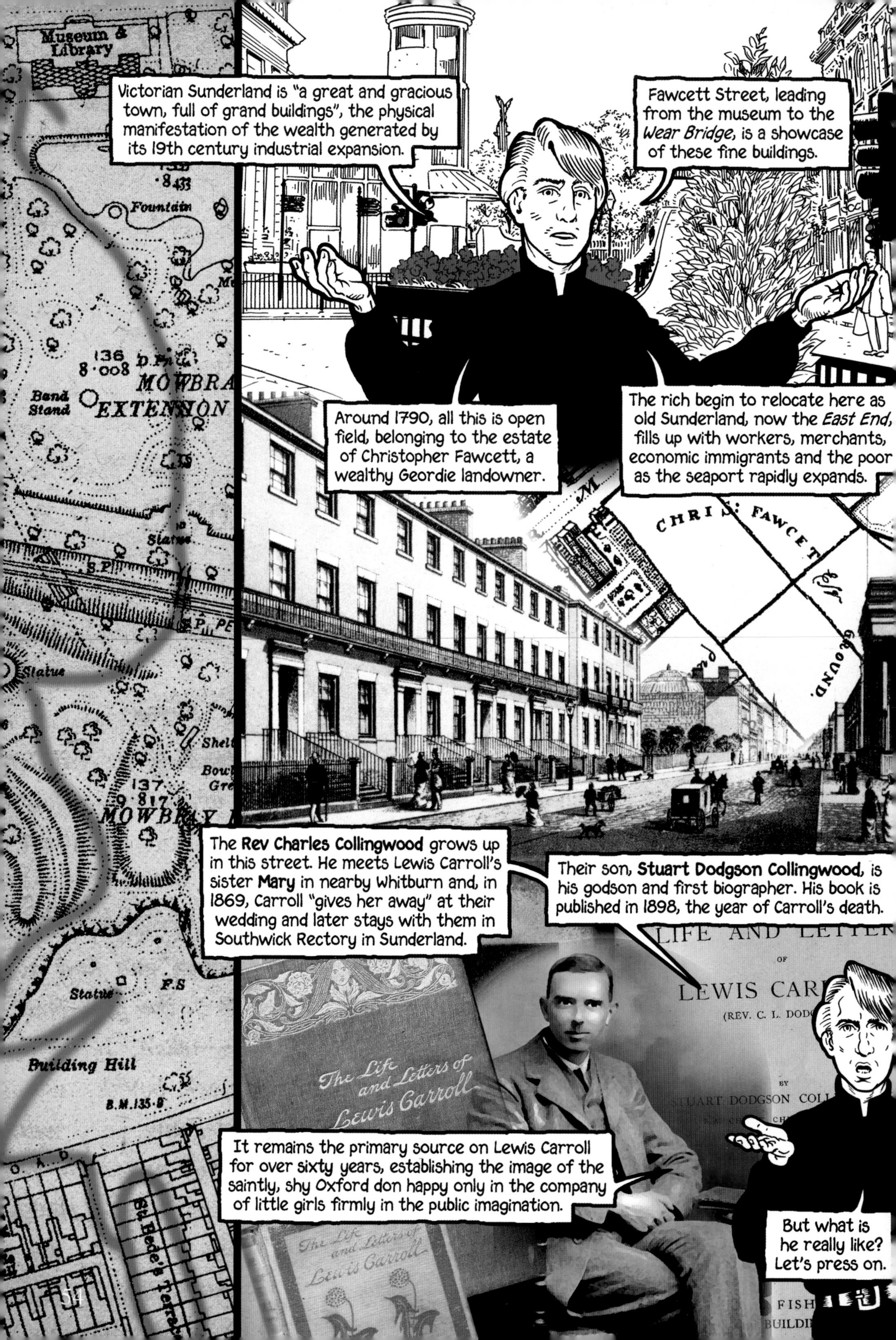

Museum & Library
Fountain
MOWBRA
EXTENSION
Band Stand
Statue
Building Hill
St Bede's Terrace
Victorian Sunderland is "a great and gracious town, full of grand buildings", the physical manifestation of the wealth generated by its 19th century industrial expansion.
Fawcett Street, leading from the museum to the *Wear Bridge,* is a showcase of these fine buildings.
Around 1790, all this is open field, belonging to the estate of Christopher Fawcett, a wealthy Geordie landowner.
The rich begin to relocate here as old Sunderland, now the *East End,* fills up with workers, merchants, economic immigrants and the poor as the seaport rapidly expands.
GROUND.
The **Rev Charles Collingwood** grows up in this street. He meets Lewis Carroll's sister **Mary** in nearby Whitburn and, in 1869, Carroll "gives her away" at their wedding and later stays with them in Southwick Rectory in Sunderland.
Their son, **Stuart Dodgson Collingwood,** is his godson and first biographer. His book is published in 1898, the year of Carroll's death.
The Life and Letters of Lewis Carroll
It remains the primary source on Lewis Carroll for over sixty years, establishing the image of the saintly, shy Oxford don happy only in the company of little girls firmly in the public imagination.
But what is he really like? Let's press on.

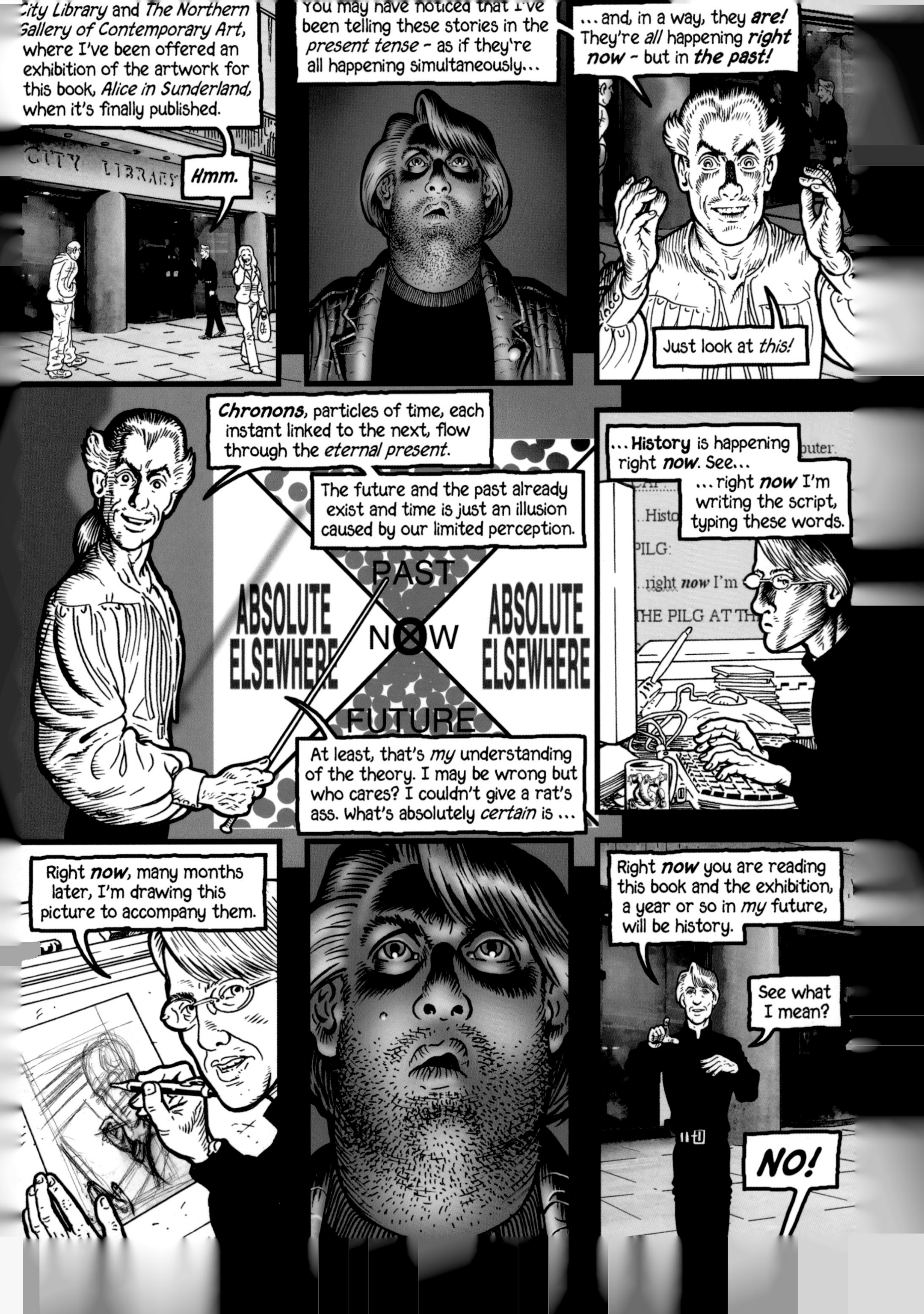
City Library and The Northern Gallery of Contemporary Art, where I've been offered an exhibition of the artwork for this book, Alice in Sunderland, when it's finally published.
CITY LIBRARY
Hmm.
You may have noticed that I've been telling these stories in the present tense - as if they're all happening simultaneously...
... and, in a way, they are! They're all happening right now - but in the past!
Just look at this!
Chronons, particles of time, each instant linked to the next, flow through the eternal present.
The future and the past already exist and time is just an illusion caused by our limited perception.
PAST
ABSOLUTE ELSEWHERE
NOW
ABSOLUTE ELSEWHERE
FUTURE
At least, that's my understanding of the theory. I may be wrong but who cares? I couldn't give a rat's ass. What's absolutely certain is ...
... History is happening right now. See...
... right now I'm writing the script, typing these words.
Right now, many months later, I'm drawing this picture to accompany them.
Right now you are reading this book and the exhibition, a year or so in my future, will be history.
See what I mean?
NO!

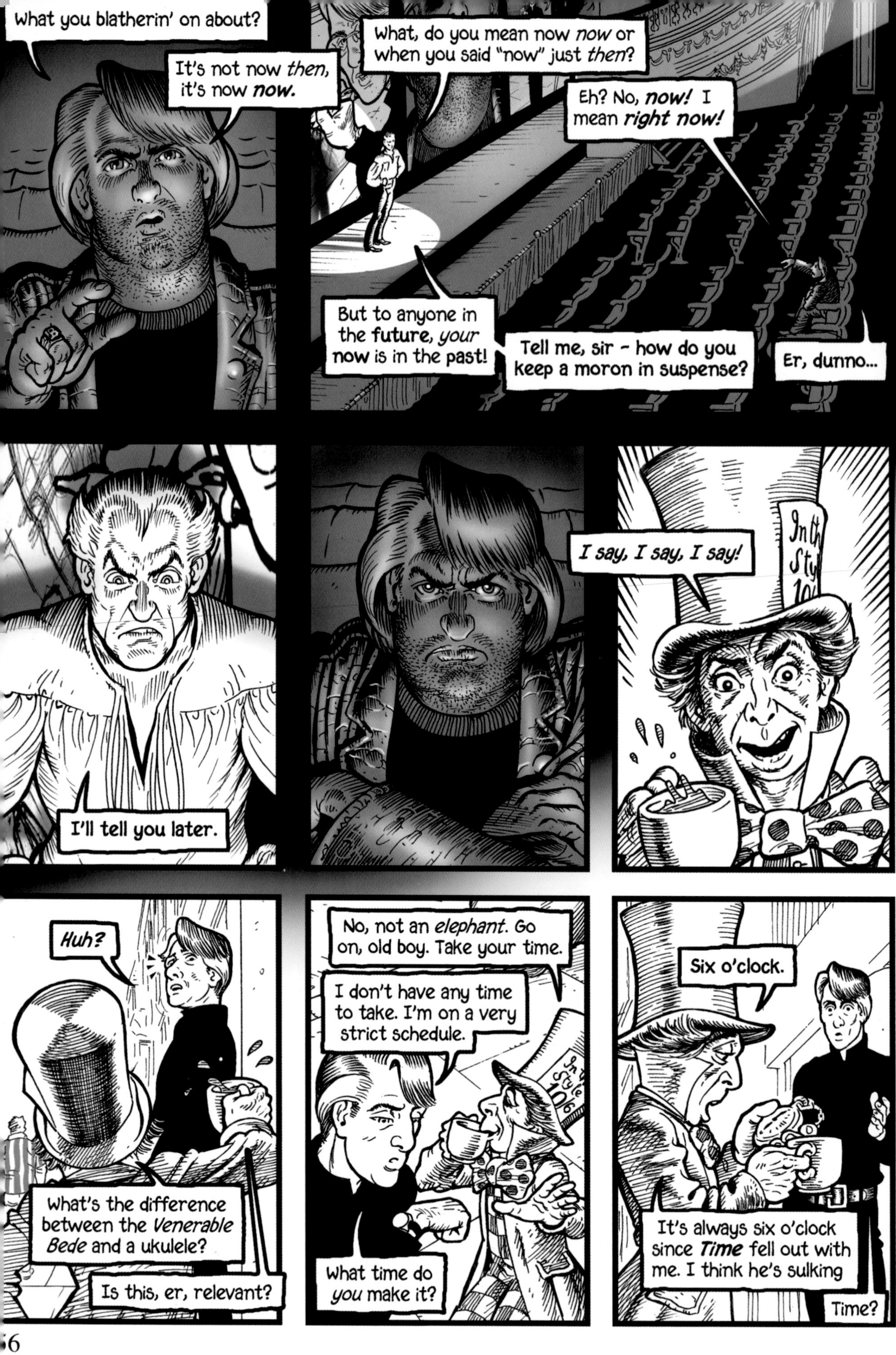
What you blatherin' on about?
It's not now *then*, it's now ***now.***
What, do you mean now *now* or when you said "now" just *then*?
Eh? No, ***now!*** I mean ***right now!***
But to anyone in the **future**, *your* **now** is in the past!
Tell me, sir - how do you keep a moron in suspense?
Er, dunno...
I'll tell you later.
I say, I say, I say!
Huh?
What's the difference between the *Venerable Bede* and a ukulele?
Is this, er, relevant?
No, not an *elephant*. Go on, old boy. Take your time.
I don't have any time to take. I'm on a very strict schedule.
What time do *you* make it?
Six o'clock.
It's always six o'clock since ***Time*** fell out with me. I think he's sulking
Time?

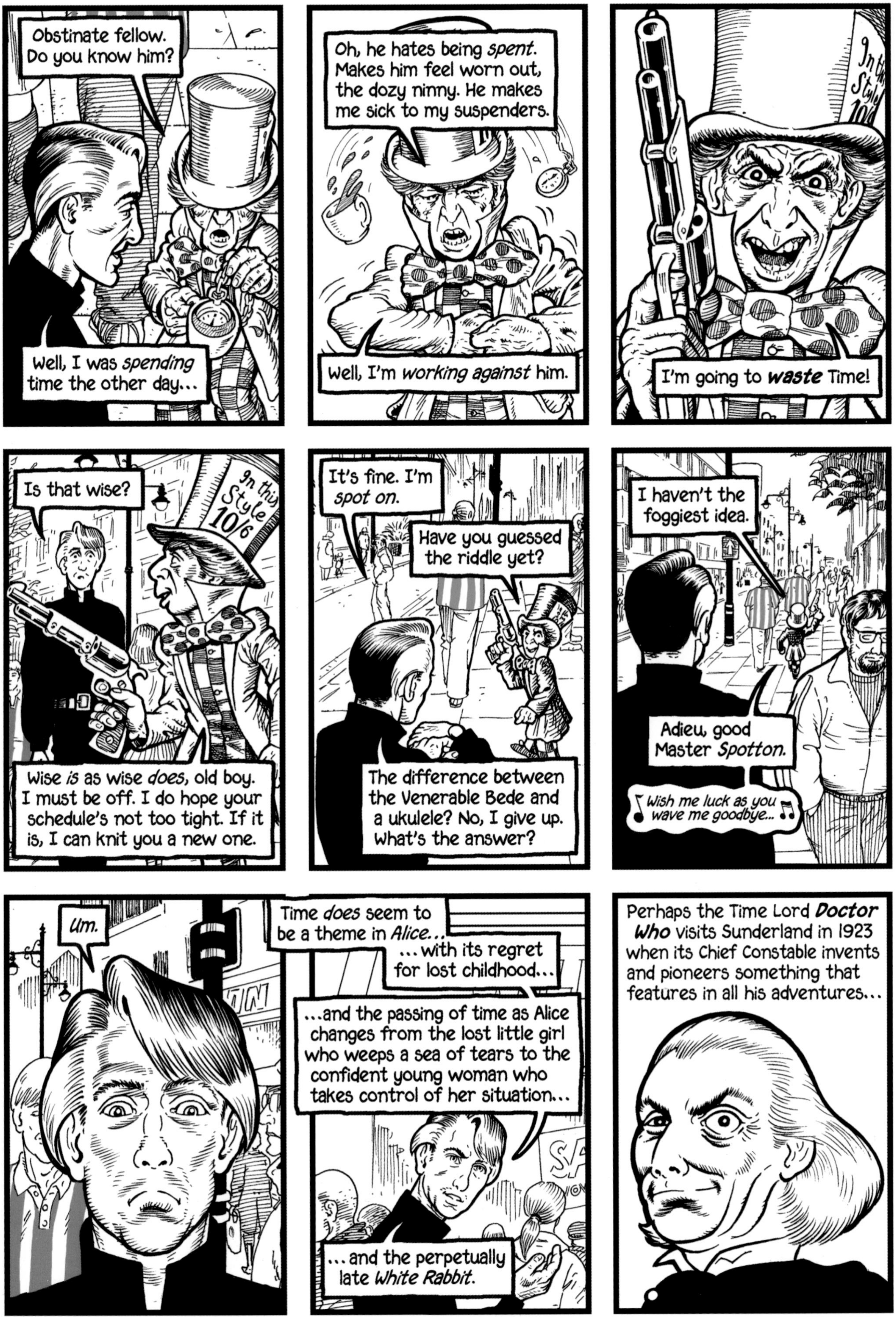
Obstinate fellow. Do you know him?
Well, I was *spending* time the other day...
Oh, he hates being *spent*. Makes him feel worn out, the dozy ninny. He makes me sick to my suspenders.
Well, I'm *working against* him.
I'm going to ***waste*** Time!
Is that wise?
In this Style 10/6
Wise *is* as wise *does*, old boy. I must be off. I do hope your schedule's not too tight. If it is, I can knit you a new one.
It's fine. I'm *spot on.*
Have you guessed the riddle yet?
The difference between the Venerable Bede and a ukulele? No, I give up. What's the answer?
I haven't the foggiest idea.
Adieu, good Master *Spotton.*
♪ *Wish me luck as you wave me goodbye...* ♫
Um.
Time *does* seem to be a theme in *Alice...*
...with its regret for lost childhood...
...and the passing of time as Alice changes from the lost little girl who weeps a sea of tears to the confident young woman who takes control of her situation...
...and the perpetually late *White Rabbit.*
Perhaps the Time Lord ***Doctor Who*** visits Sunderland in 1923 when its Chief Constable invents and pioneers something that features in all his adventures...

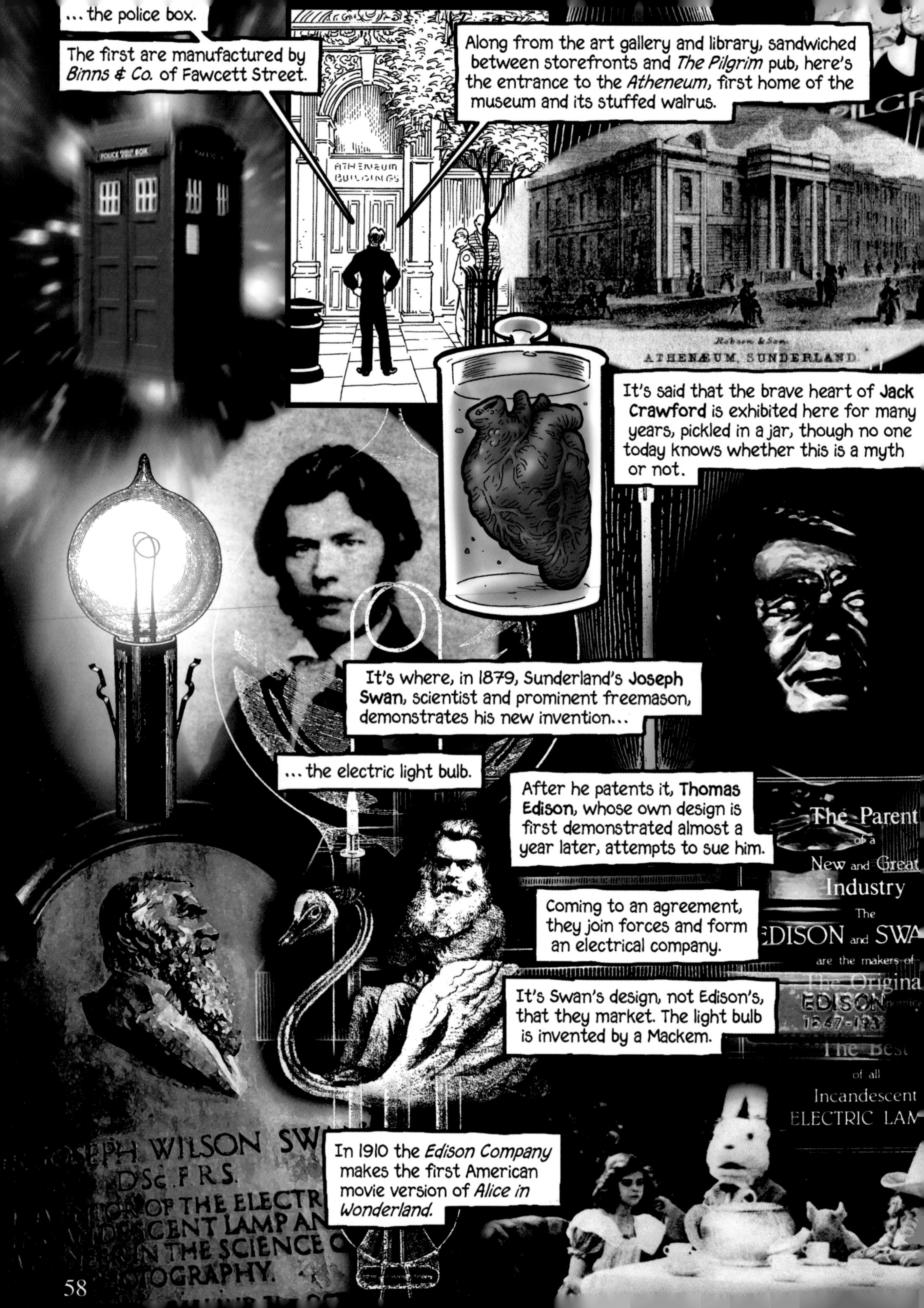

... the police box.
The first are manufactured by *Binns & Co.* of Fawcett Street.
Along from the art gallery and library, sandwiched between storefronts and *The Pilgrim* pub, here's the entrance to the *Atheneum*, first home of the museum and its stuffed walrus.
ATHENÆUM BUILDINGS
ATHENÆUM, SUNDERLAND
It's said that the brave heart of **Jack Crawford** is exhibited here for many years, pickled in a jar, though no one today knows whether this is a myth or not.
It's where, in 1879, Sunderland's **Joseph Swan**, scientist and prominent freemason, demonstrates his new invention...
... the electric light bulb.
After he patents it, **Thomas Edison**, whose own design is first demonstrated almost a year later, attempts to sue him.
The Parent of a New and Great Industry
Coming to an agreement, they join forces and form an electrical company.
It's Swan's design, not Edison's, that they market. The light bulb is invented by a Mackem.
of all Incandescent
In 1910 the *Edison Company* makes the first American movie version of *Alice in Wonderland*.
DSc F.R.S.

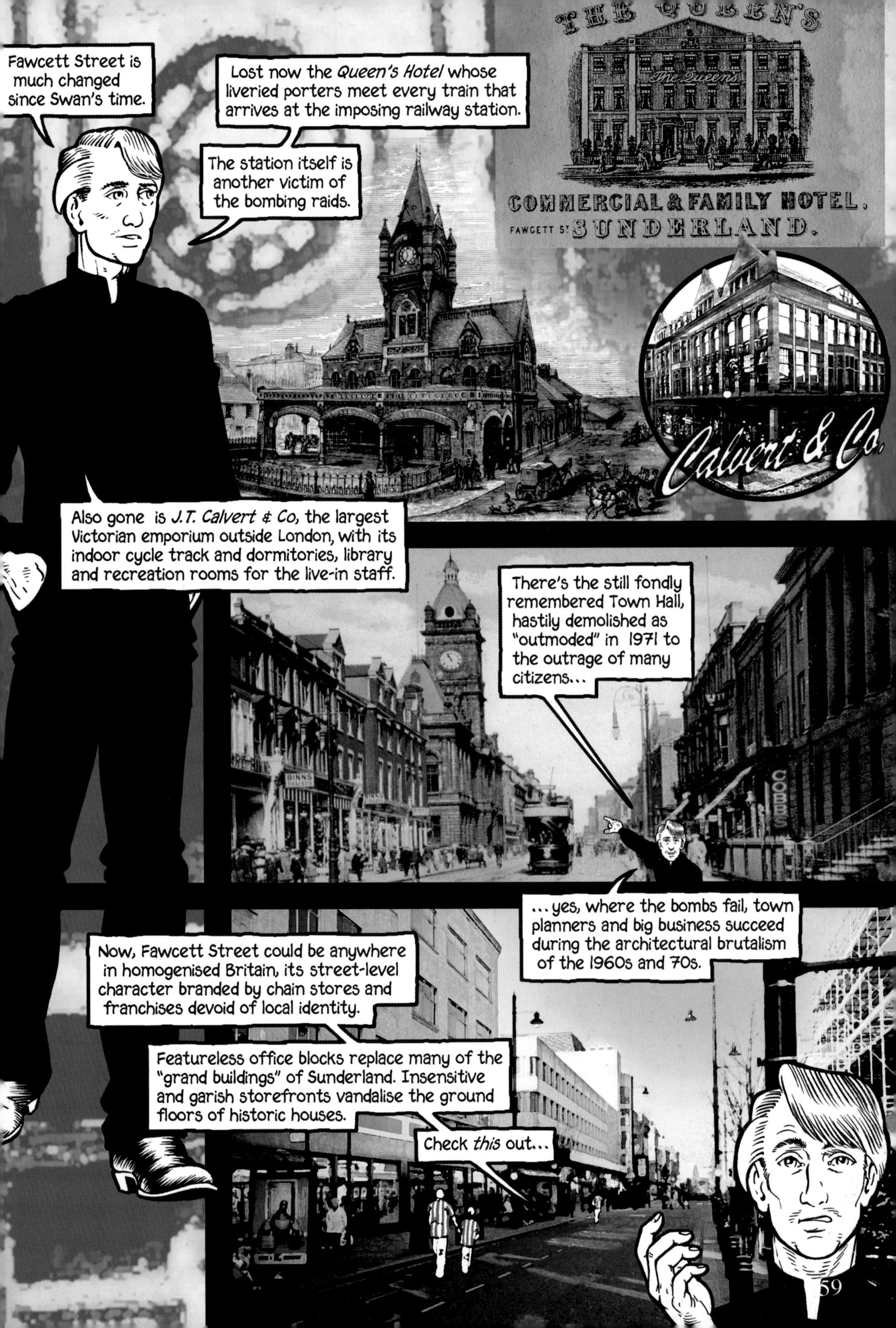
Fawcett Street is much changed since Swan's time.
Lost now the *Queen's Hotel* whose liveried porters meet every train that arrives at the imposing railway station.
The station itself is another victim of the bombing raids.
THE QUEEN'S
The Queen's
COMMERCIAL & FAMILY HOTEL,
FAWCETT ST. SUNDERLAND.
Calvert & Co.
Also gone is *J.T. Calvert & Co*, the largest Victorian emporium outside London, with its indoor cycle track and dormitories, library and recreation rooms for the live-in staff.
There's the still fondly remembered Town Hall, hastily demolished as "outmoded" in 1971 to the outrage of many citizens...
BINNS
COBBS
...yes, where the bombs fail, town planners and big business succeed during the architectural brutalism of the 1960s and 70s.
Now, Fawcett Street could be anywhere in homogenised Britain, its street-level character branded by chain stores and franchises devoid of local identity.
Featureless office blocks replace many of the "grand buildings" of Sunderland. Insensitive and garish storefronts vandalise the ground floors of historic houses.
Check *this* out...

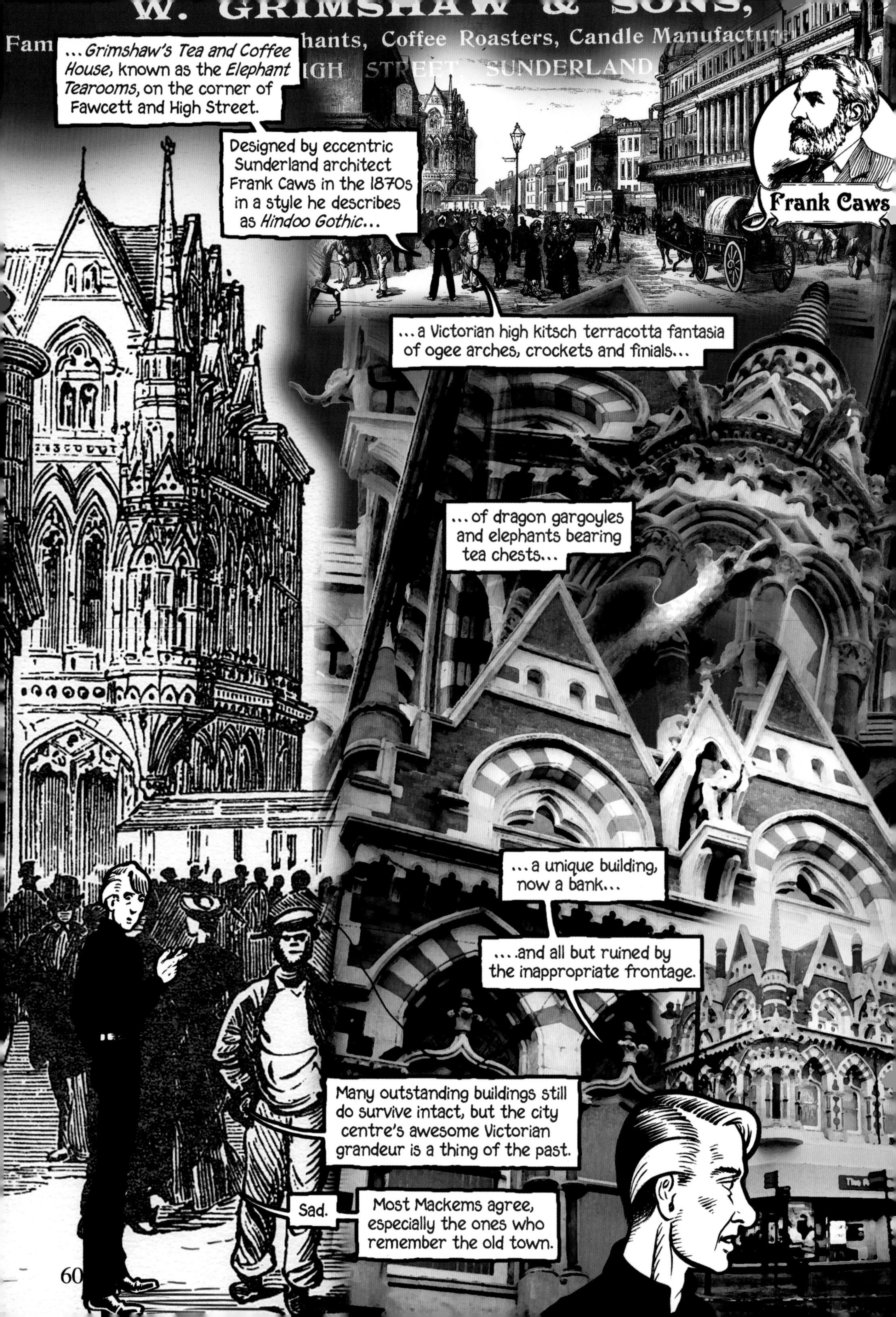

W. GRIMSHAW & SONS,
Fam... hants, Coffee Roasters, Candle Manufactur...
...IGH STREET, SUNDERLAND.
...*Grimshaw's Tea and Coffee House*, known as the *Elephant Tearooms*, on the corner of Fawcett and High Street.
Designed by eccentric Sunderland architect Frank Caws in the 1870s in a style he describes as *Hindoo Gothic*...
Frank Caws
...a Victorian high kitsch terracotta fantasia of ogee arches, crockets and finials...
...of dragon gargoyles and elephants bearing tea chests...
...a unique building, now a bank...
...and all but ruined by the inappropriate frontage.
Many outstanding buildings still do survive intact, but the city centre's awesome Victorian grandeur is a thing of the past.
Sad.
Most Mackems agree, especially the ones who remember the old town.

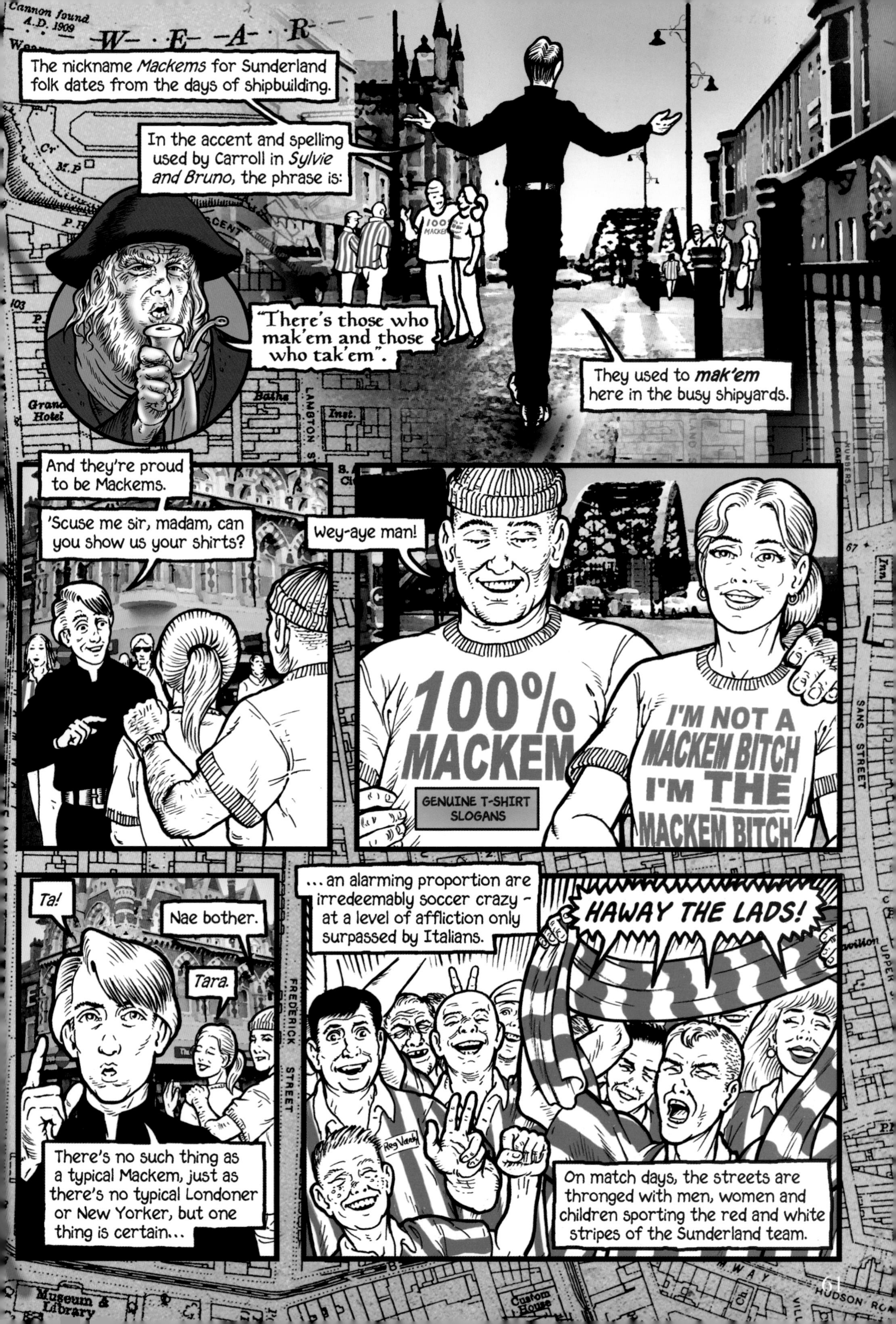

The nickname *Mackems* for Sunderland folk dates from the days of shipbuilding.
In the accent and spelling used by Carroll in *Sylvie and Bruno*, the phrase is:
"There's those who mak'em and those who tak'em".
They used to **mak'em** here in the busy shipyards.
And they're proud to be Mackems.
'Scuse me sir, madam, can you show us your shirts?
Wey-aye man!
100% MACKEM
I'M NOT A MACKEM BITCH I'M THE MACKEM BITCH
GENUINE T-SHIRT SLOGANS
Ta!
Nae bother.
Tara.
There's no such thing as a typical Mackem, just as there's no typical Londoner or New Yorker, but one thing is certain...
...an alarming proportion are irredeemably soccer crazy – at a level of affliction only surpassed by Italians.
HAWAY THE LADS!
On match days, the streets are thronged with men, women and children sporting the red and white stripes of the Sunderland team.

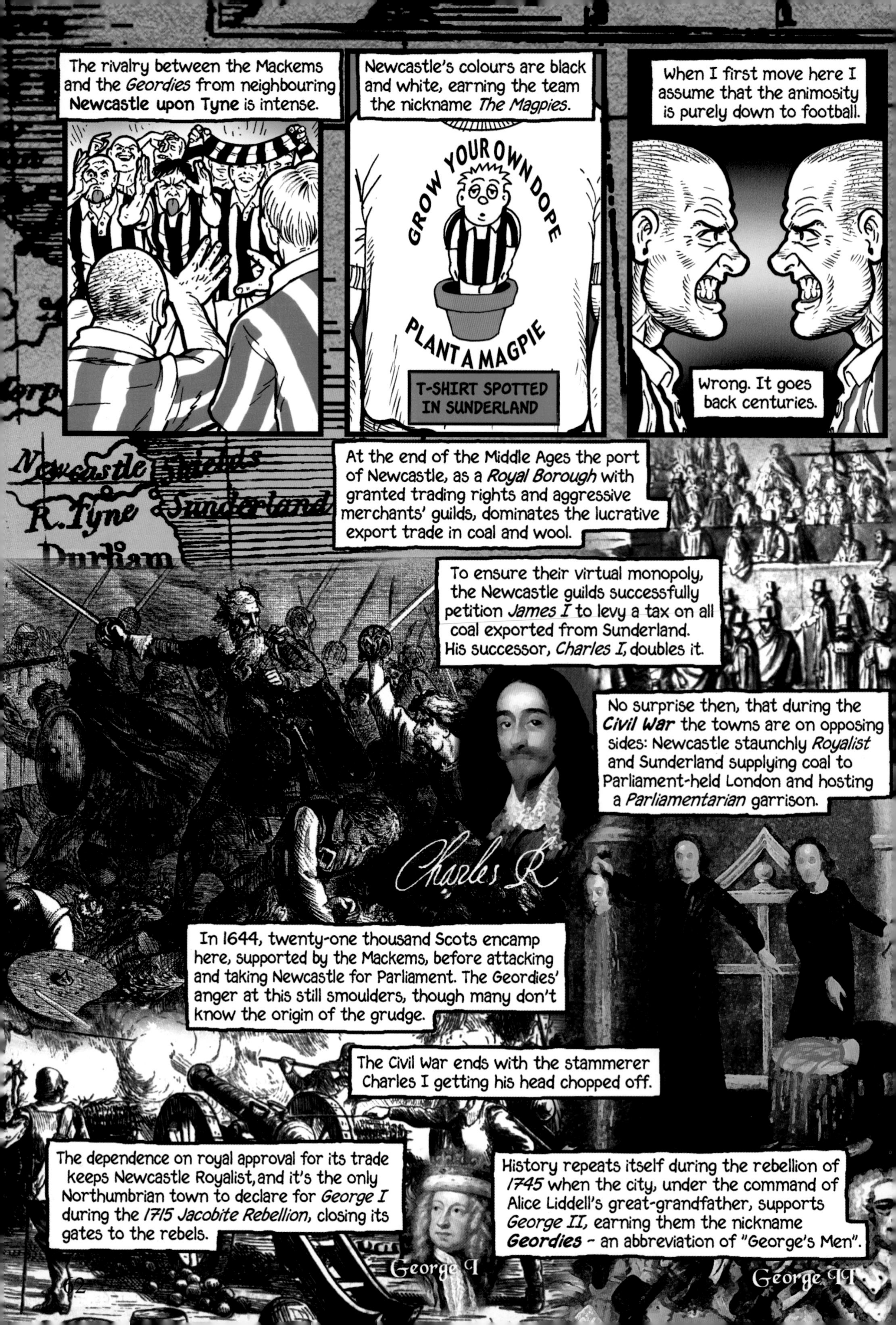

The rivalry between the Mackems and the *Geordies* from neighbouring **Newcastle upon Tyne** is intense.
Newcastle's colours are black and white, earning the team the nickname *The Magpies*.
GROW YOUR OWN DOPE
PLANT A MAGPIE
T-SHIRT SPOTTED IN SUNDERLAND
When I first move here I assume that the animosity is purely down to football.
Wrong. It goes back centuries.
Newcastle
Shields
R. Tyne
Sunderland
Durham
At the end of the Middle Ages the port of Newcastle, as a *Royal Borough* with granted trading rights and aggressive merchants' guilds, dominates the lucrative export trade in coal and wool.
To ensure their virtual monopoly, the Newcastle guilds successfully petition *James I* to levy a tax on all coal exported from Sunderland. His successor, *Charles I*, doubles it.
No surprise then, that during the ***Civil War*** the towns are on opposing sides: Newcastle staunchly *Royalist* and Sunderland supplying coal to Parliament-held London and hosting a *Parliamentarian* garrison.
Charles R
In 1644, twenty-one thousand Scots encamp here, supported by the Mackems, before attacking and taking Newcastle for Parliament. The Geordies' anger at this still smoulders, though many don't know the origin of the grudge.
The Civil War ends with the stammerer Charles I getting his head chopped off.
The dependence on royal approval for its trade keeps Newcastle Royalist, and it's the only Northumbrian town to declare for *George I* during the *1715 Jacobite Rebellion*, closing its gates to the rebels.
George I
History repeats itself during the rebellion of *1745* when the city, under the command of Alice Liddell's great-grandfather, supports *George II*, earning them the nickname ***Geordies*** – an abbreviation of "George's Men".
George II

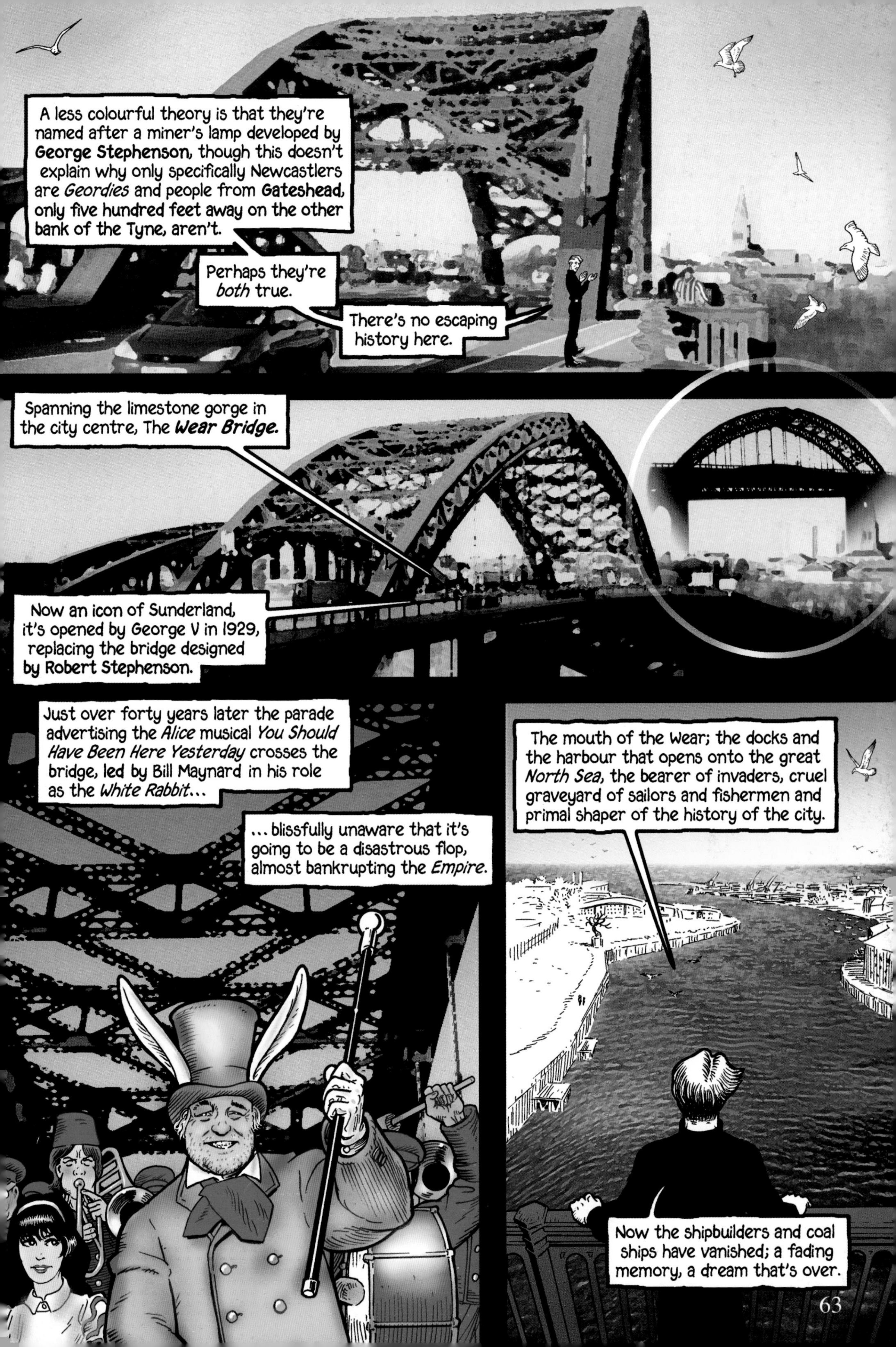
A less colourful theory is that they're named after a miner's lamp developed by George Stephenson, though this doesn't explain why only specifically Newcastlers are Geordies and people from Gateshead, only five hundred feet away on the other bank of the Tyne, aren't.
Perhaps they're both true.
There's no escaping history here.
Spanning the limestone gorge in the city centre, The Wear Bridge.
Now an icon of Sunderland, it's opened by George V in 1929, replacing the bridge designed by Robert Stephenson.
Just over forty years later the parade advertising the Alice musical You Should Have Been Here Yesterday crosses the bridge, led by Bill Maynard in his role as the White Rabbit...
...blissfully unaware that it's going to be a disastrous flop, almost bankrupting the Empire.
The mouth of the Wear; the docks and the harbour that opens onto the great North Sea, the bearer of invaders, cruel graveyard of sailors and fishermen and primal shaper of the history of the city.
Now the shipbuilders and coal ships have vanished; a fading memory, a dream that's over.

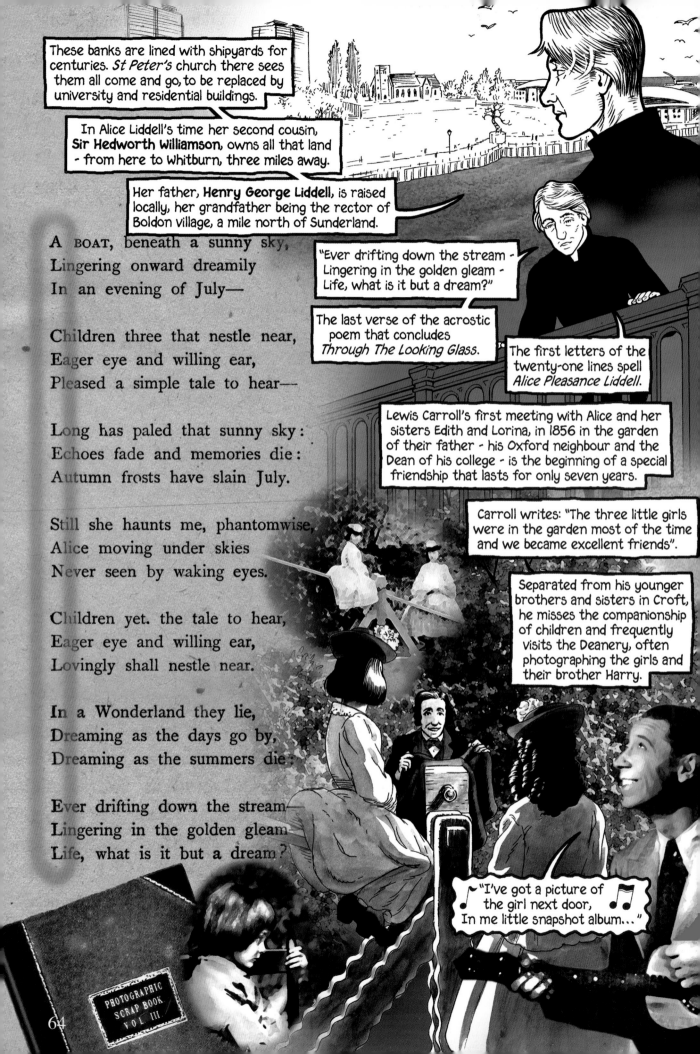

These banks are lined with shipyards for centuries. *St Peter's* church there sees them all come and go, to be replaced by university and residential buildings.

In Alice Liddell's time her second cousin, **Sir Hedworth Williamson**, owns all that land - from here to Whitburn, three miles away.

Her father, **Henry George Liddell**, is raised locally, her grandfather being the rector of Boldon village, a mile north of Sunderland.

A BOAT, beneath a sunny sky,
Lingering onward dreamily
In an evening of July—

Children three that nestle near,
Eager eye and willing ear,
Pleased a simple tale to hear—

Long has paled that sunny sky:
Echoes fade and memories die:
Autumn frosts have slain July.

Still she haunts me, phantomwise,
Alice moving under skies
Never seen by waking eyes.

Children yet. the tale to hear,
Eager eye and willing ear,
Lovingly shall nestle near.

In a Wonderland they lie,
Dreaming as the days go by,
Dreaming as the summers die:

Ever drifting down the stream—
Lingering in the golden gleam—
Life, what is it but a dream?

"Ever drifting down the stream - Lingering in the golden gleam - Life, what is it but a dream?"

The last verse of the acrostic poem that concludes *Through The Looking Glass.*

The first letters of the twenty-one lines spell *Alice Pleasance Liddell.*

Lewis Carroll's first meeting with Alice and her sisters Edith and Lorina, in 1856 in the garden of their father - his Oxford neighbour and the Dean of his college - is the beginning of a special friendship that lasts for only seven years.

Carroll writes: "The three little girls were in the garden most of the time and we became excellent friends".

Separated from his younger brothers and sisters in Croft, he misses the companionship of children and frequently visits the Deanery, often photographing the girls and their brother Harry.

"I've got a picture of the girl next door, In me little snapshot album...."

PHOTOGRAPHIC SCRAP BOOK VOL III

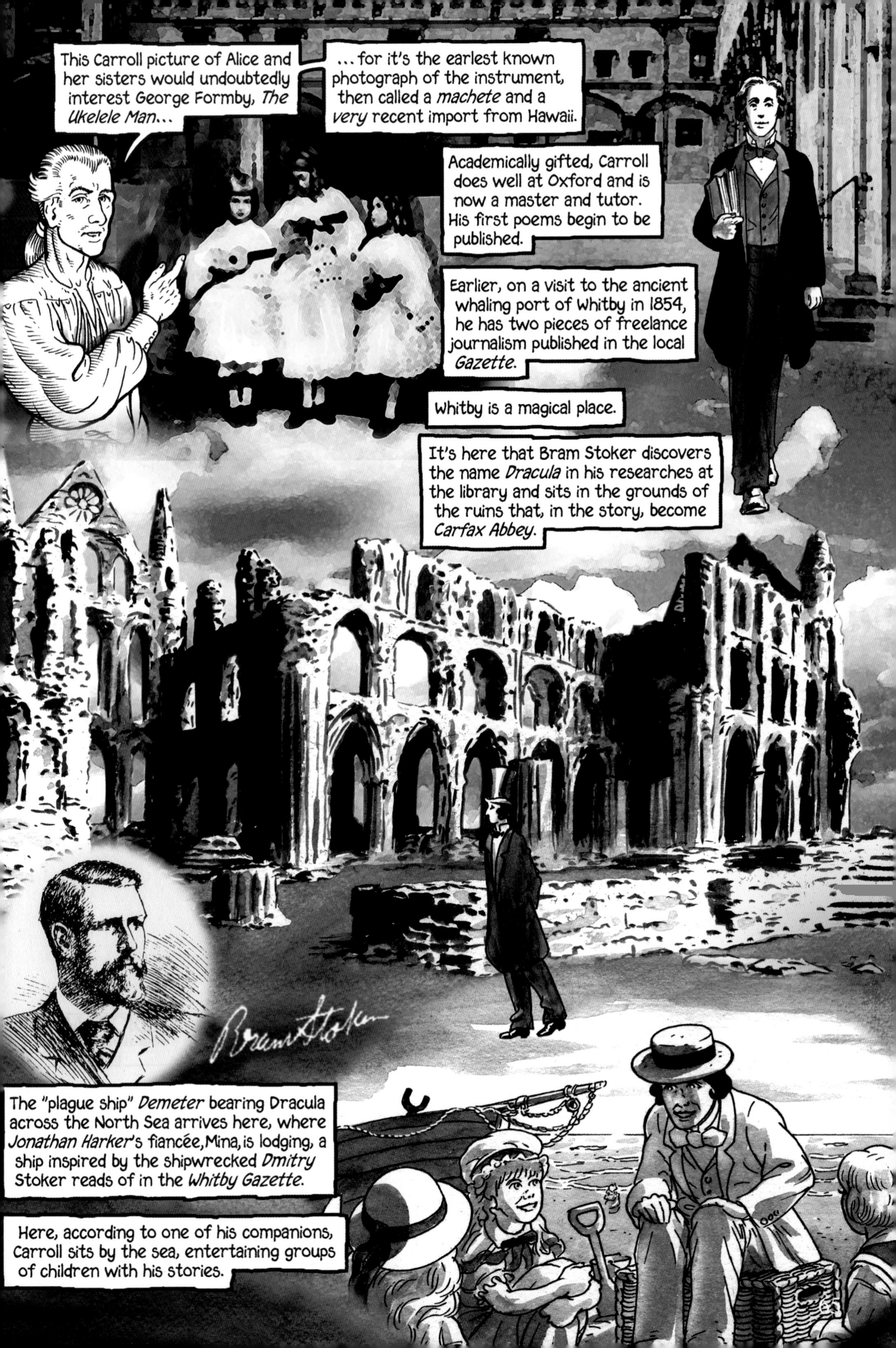
This Carroll picture of Alice and her sisters would undoubtedly interest George Formby, *The Ukelele Man*...
...for it's the earlest known photograph of the instrument, then called a *machete* and a *very* recent import from Hawaii.
Academically gifted, Carroll does well at Oxford and is now a master and tutor. His first poems begin to be published.
Earlier, on a visit to the ancient whaling port of Whitby in 1854, he has two pieces of freelance journalism published in the local *Gazette*.
Whitby is a magical place.
It's here that Bram Stoker discovers the name *Dracula* in his researches at the library and sits in the grounds of the ruins that, in the story, become *Carfax Abbey*.
Bram Stoker
The "plague ship" *Demeter* bearing Dracula across the North Sea arrives here, where *Jonathan Harker*'s fiancée, Mina, is lodging, a ship inspired by the shipwrecked *Dmitry* Stoker reads of in the *Whitby Gazette*.
Here, according to one of his companions, Carroll sits by the sea, entertaining groups of children with his stories.

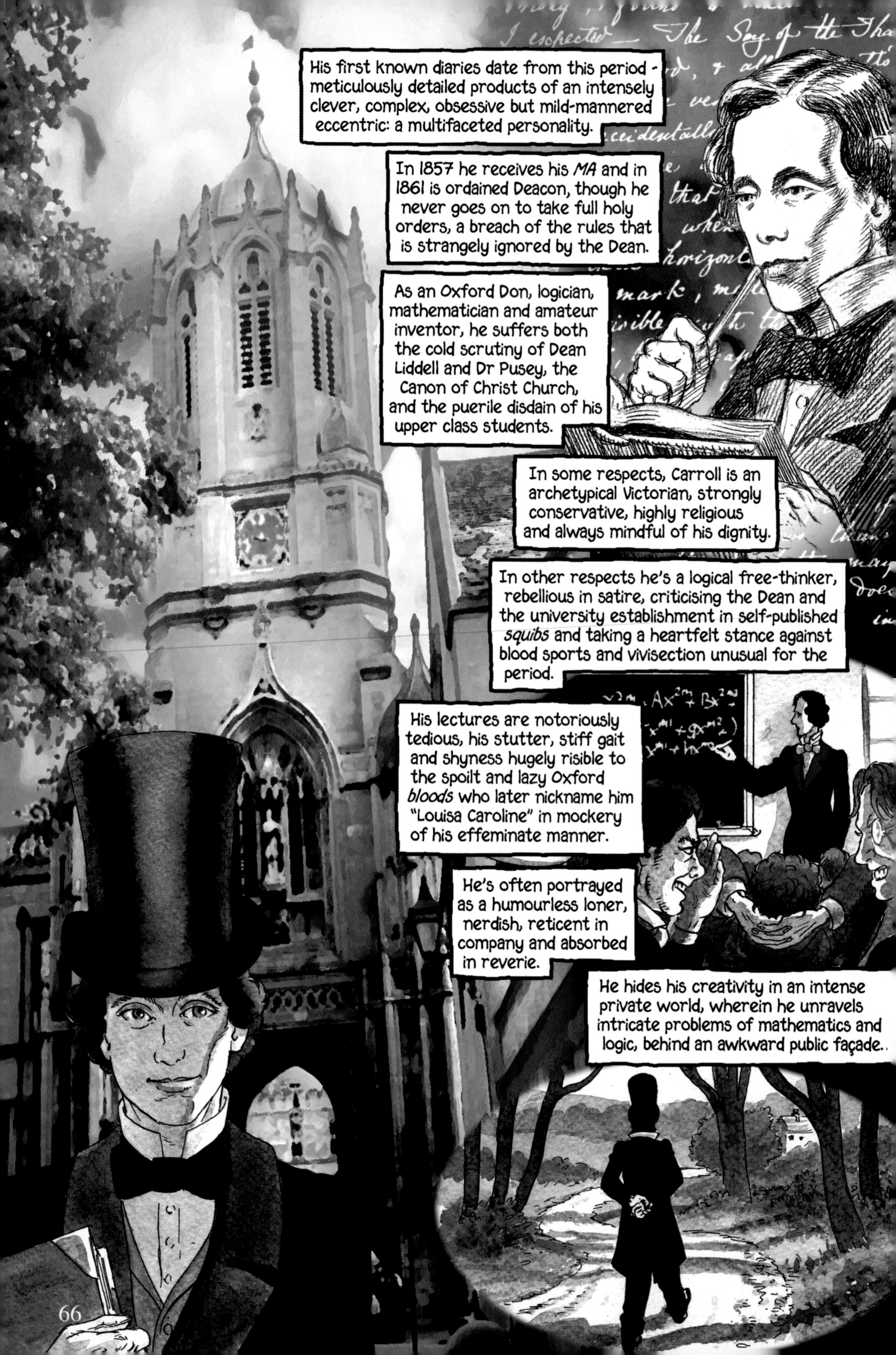
His first known diaries date from this period - meticulously detailed products of an intensely clever, complex, obsessive but mild-mannered eccentric: a multifaceted personality.
In 1857 he receives his *MA* and in 1861 is ordained Deacon, though he never goes on to take full holy orders, a breach of the rules that is strangely ignored by the Dean.
As an Oxford Don, logician, mathematician and amateur inventor, he suffers both the cold scrutiny of Dean Liddell and Dr Pusey, the Canon of Christ Church, and the puerile disdain of his upper class students.
In some respects, Carroll is an archetypical Victorian, strongly conservative, highly religious and always mindful of his dignity.
In other respects he's a logical free-thinker, rebellious in satire, criticising the Dean and the university establishment in self-published *squibs* and taking a heartfelt stance against blood sports and vivisection unusual for the period.
His lectures are notoriously tedious, his stutter, stiff gait and shyness hugely risible to the spoilt and lazy Oxford *bloods* who later nickname him "Louisa Caroline" in mockery of his effeminate manner.
He's often portrayed as a humourless loner, nerdish, reticent in company and absorbed in reverie.
He hides his creativity in an intense private world, wherein he unravels intricate problems of mathematics and logic, behind an awkward public façade..

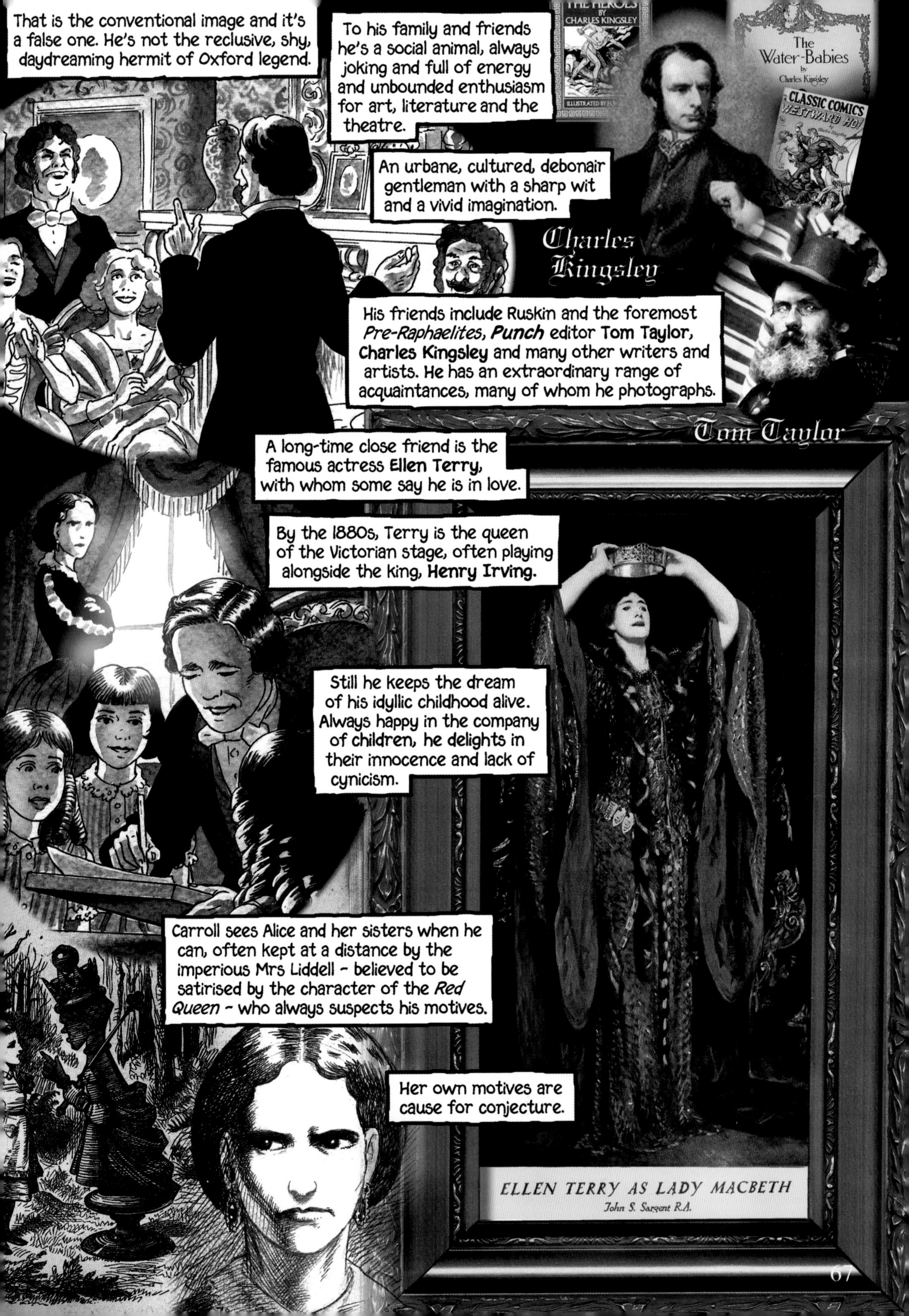

That is the conventional image and it's a false one. He's not the reclusive, shy, daydreaming hermit of Oxford legend.
To his family and friends he's a social animal, always joking and full of energy and unbounded enthusiasm for art, literature and the theatre.
THE HEROES BY CHARLES KINGSLEY
The Water-Babies by Charles Kingsley
CLASSIC COMICS WESTWARD HO!
An urbane, cultured, debonair gentleman with a sharp wit and a vivid imagination.
Charles Kingsley
His friends include Ruskin and the foremost *Pre-Raphaelites*, **Punch** editor **Tom Taylor**, **Charles Kingsley** and many other writers and artists. He has an extraordinary range of acquaintances, many of whom he photographs.
Tom Taylor
A long-time close friend is the famous actress **Ellen Terry**, with whom some say he is in love.
By the 1880s, Terry is the queen of the Victorian stage, often playing alongside the king, **Henry Irving**.
Still he keeps the dream of his idyllic childhood alive. Always happy in the company of children, he delights in their innocence and lack of cynicism.
Carroll sees Alice and her sisters when he can, often kept at a distance by the imperious Mrs Liddell – believed to be satirised by the character of the *Red Queen* – who always suspects his motives.
Her own motives are cause for conjecture.
ELLEN TERRY AS LADY MACBETH
John S. Sargent R.A.

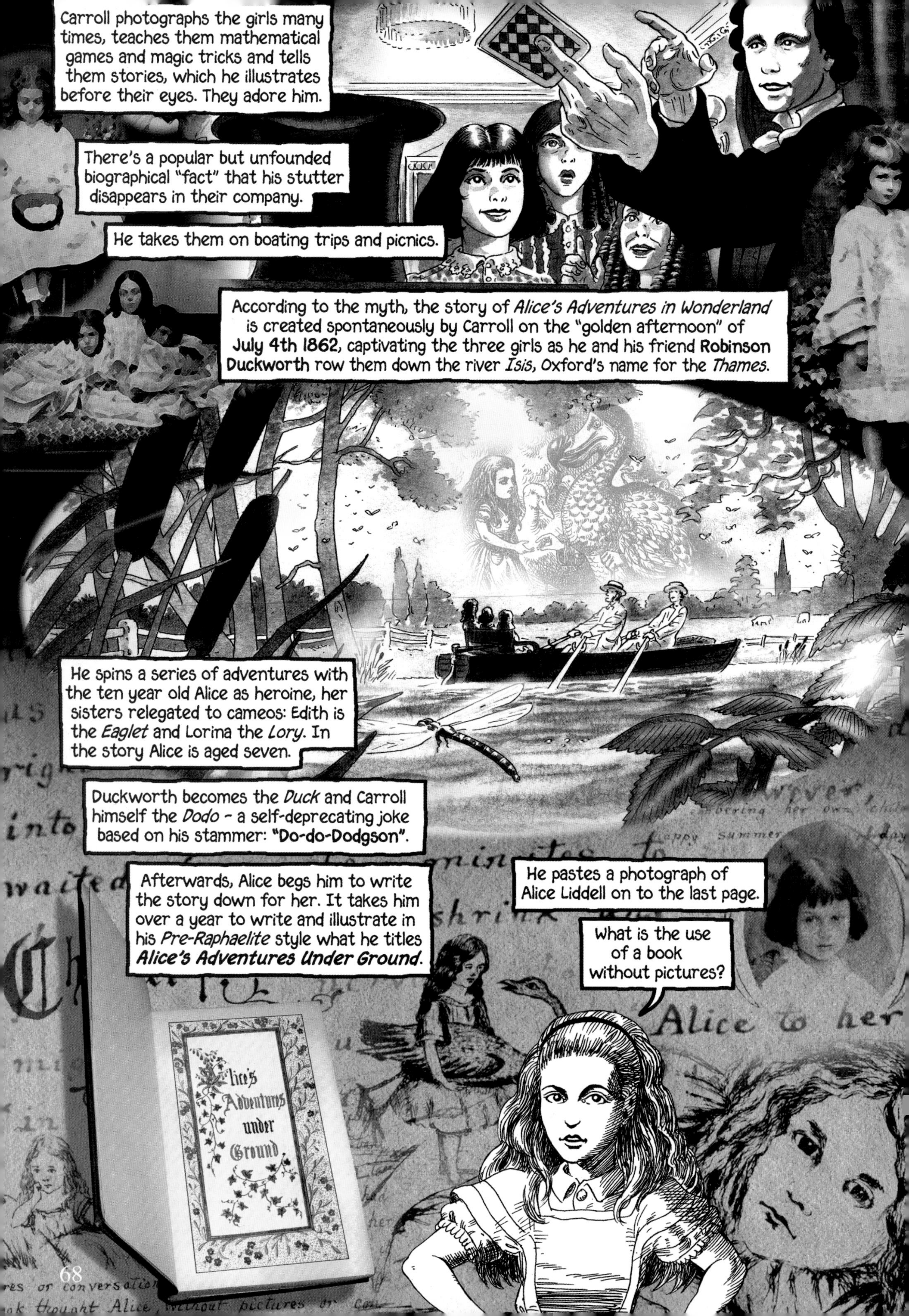

Carroll photographs the girls many times, teaches them mathematical games and magic tricks and tells them stories, which he illustrates before their eyes. They adore him.
There's a popular but unfounded biographical "fact" that his stutter disappears in their company.
He takes them on boating trips and picnics.
According to the myth, the story of *Alice's Adventures in Wonderland* is created spontaneously by Carroll on the "golden afternoon" of **July 4th 1862**, captivating the three girls as he and his friend **Robinson Duckworth** row them down the river *Isis*, Oxford's name for the *Thames*.
He spins a series of adventures with the ten year old Alice as heroine, her sisters relegated to cameos: Edith is the *Eaglet* and Lorina the *Lory*. In the story Alice is aged seven.
Duckworth becomes the *Duck* and Carroll himself the *Dodo* – a self-deprecating joke based on his stammer: **"Do-do-Dodgson"**.
Afterwards, Alice begs him to write the story down for her. It takes him over a year to write and illustrate in his *Pre-Raphaelite* style what he titles ***Alice's Adventures Under Ground***.
He pastes a photograph of Alice Liddell on to the last page.
What is the use of a book without pictures?
Alice's Adventures under Ground

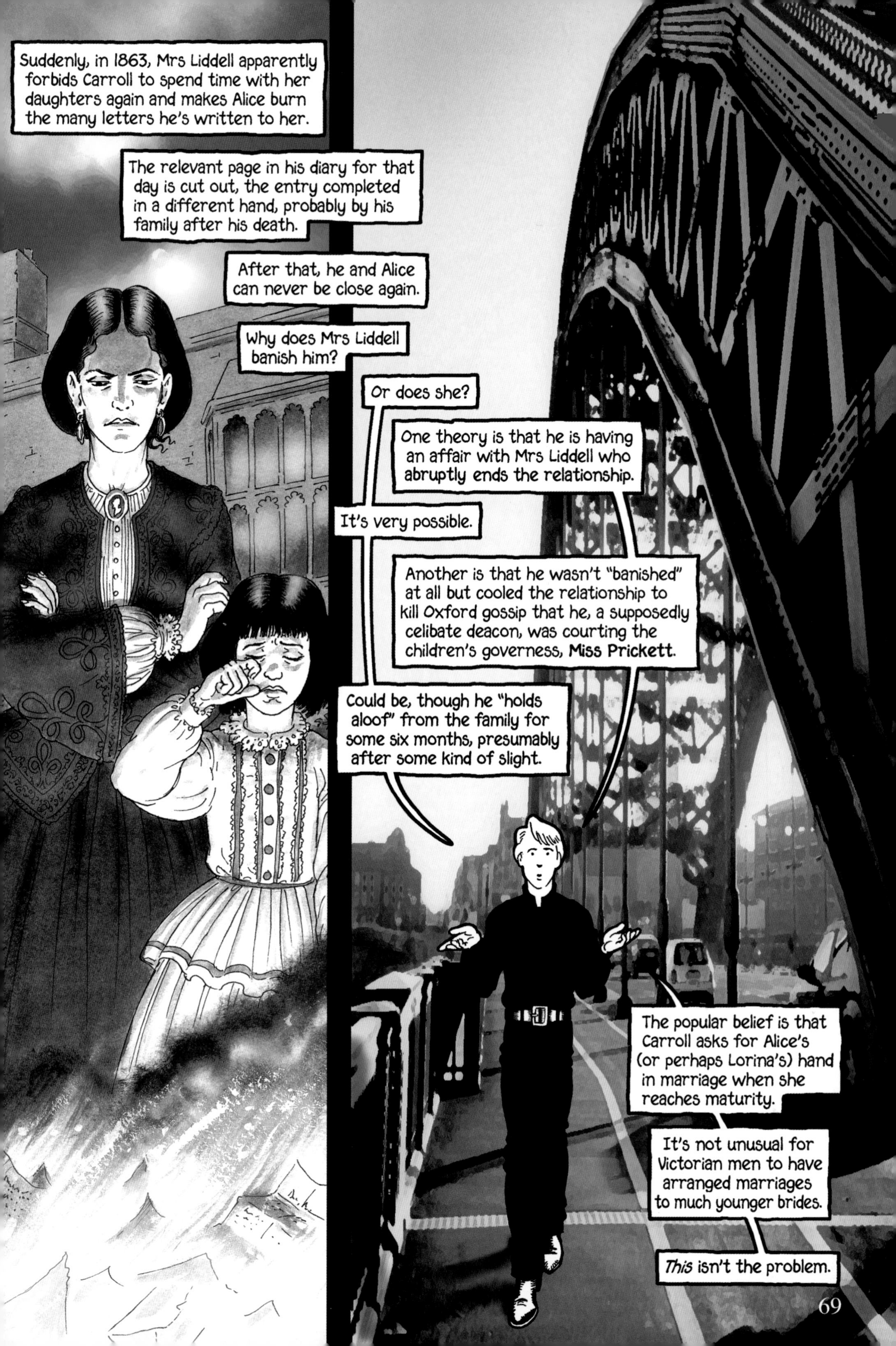

Suddenly, in 1863, Mrs Liddell apparently forbids Carroll to spend time with her daughters again and makes Alice burn the many letters he's written to her.
The relevant page in his diary for that day is cut out, the entry completed in a different hand, probably by his family after his death.
After that, he and Alice can never be close again.
Why does Mrs Liddell banish him?
Or does she?
One theory is that he is having an affair with Mrs Liddell who abruptly ends the relationship.
It's very possible.
Another is that he wasn't "banished" at all but cooled the relationship to kill Oxford gossip that he, a supposedly celibate deacon, was courting the children's governess, Miss Prickett.
Could be, though he "holds aloof" from the family for some six months, presumably after some kind of slight.
The popular belief is that Carroll asks for Alice's (or perhaps Lorina's) hand in marriage when she reaches maturity.
It's not unusual for Victorian men to have arranged marriages to much younger brides.
This isn't the problem.

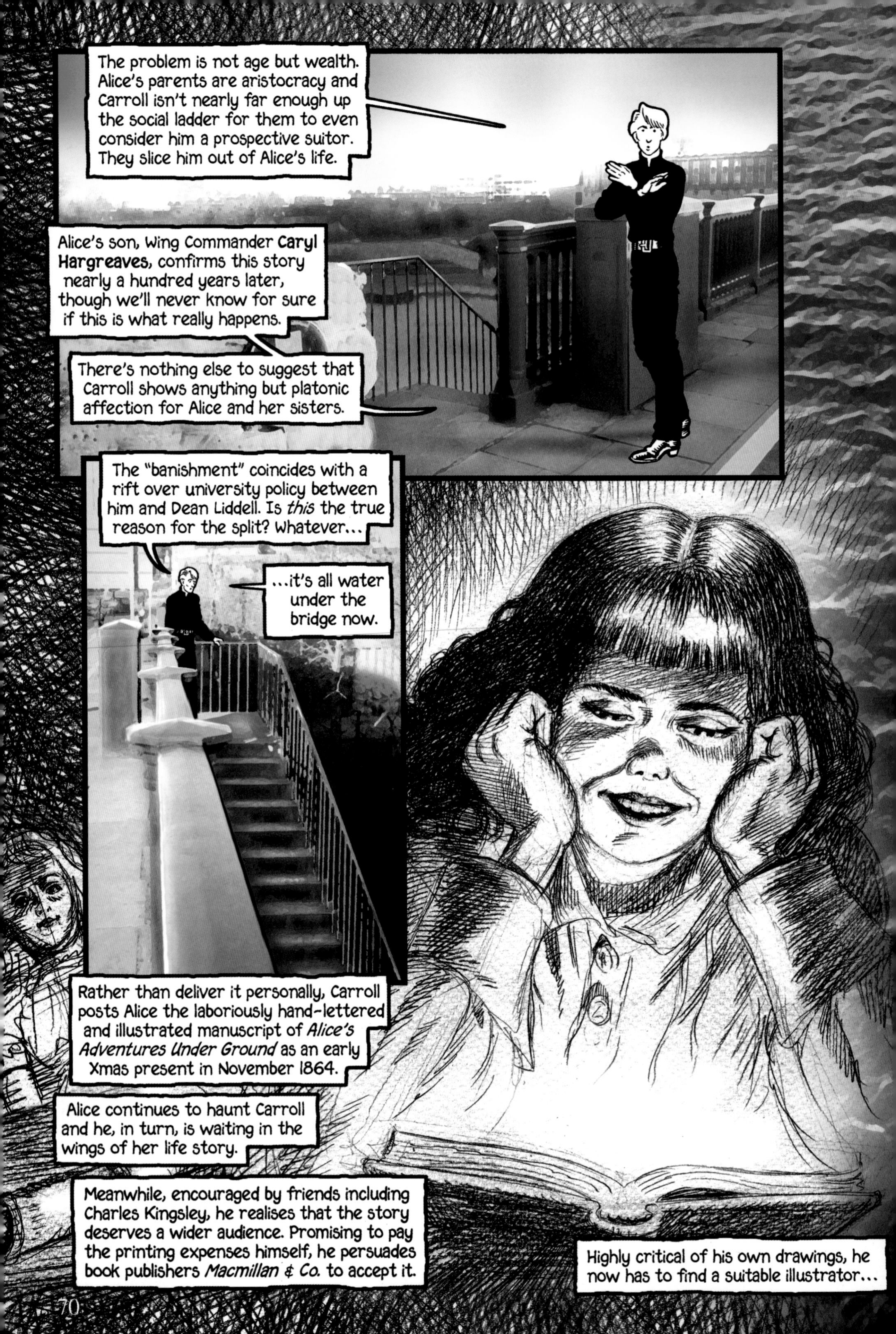

The problem is not age but wealth. Alice's parents are aristocracy and Carroll isn't nearly far enough up the social ladder for them to even consider him a prospective suitor. They slice him out of Alice's life.
Alice's son, Wing Commander **Caryl Hargreaves,** confirms this story nearly a hundred years later, though we'll never know for sure if this is what really happens.
There's nothing else to suggest that Carroll shows anything but platonic affection for Alice and her sisters.
The "banishment" coincides with a rift over university policy between him and Dean Liddell. Is *this* the true reason for the split? Whatever...
...it's all water under the bridge now.
Rather than deliver it personally, Carroll posts Alice the laboriously hand-lettered and illustrated manuscript of *Alice's Adventures Under Ground* as an early Xmas present in November 1864.
Alice continues to haunt Carroll and he, in turn, is waiting in the wings of her life story.
Meanwhile, encouraged by friends including Charles Kingsley, he realises that the story deserves a wider audience. Promising to pay the printing expenses himself, he persuades book publishers *Macmillan & Co.* to accept it.
Highly critical of his own drawings, he now has to find a suitable illustrator...

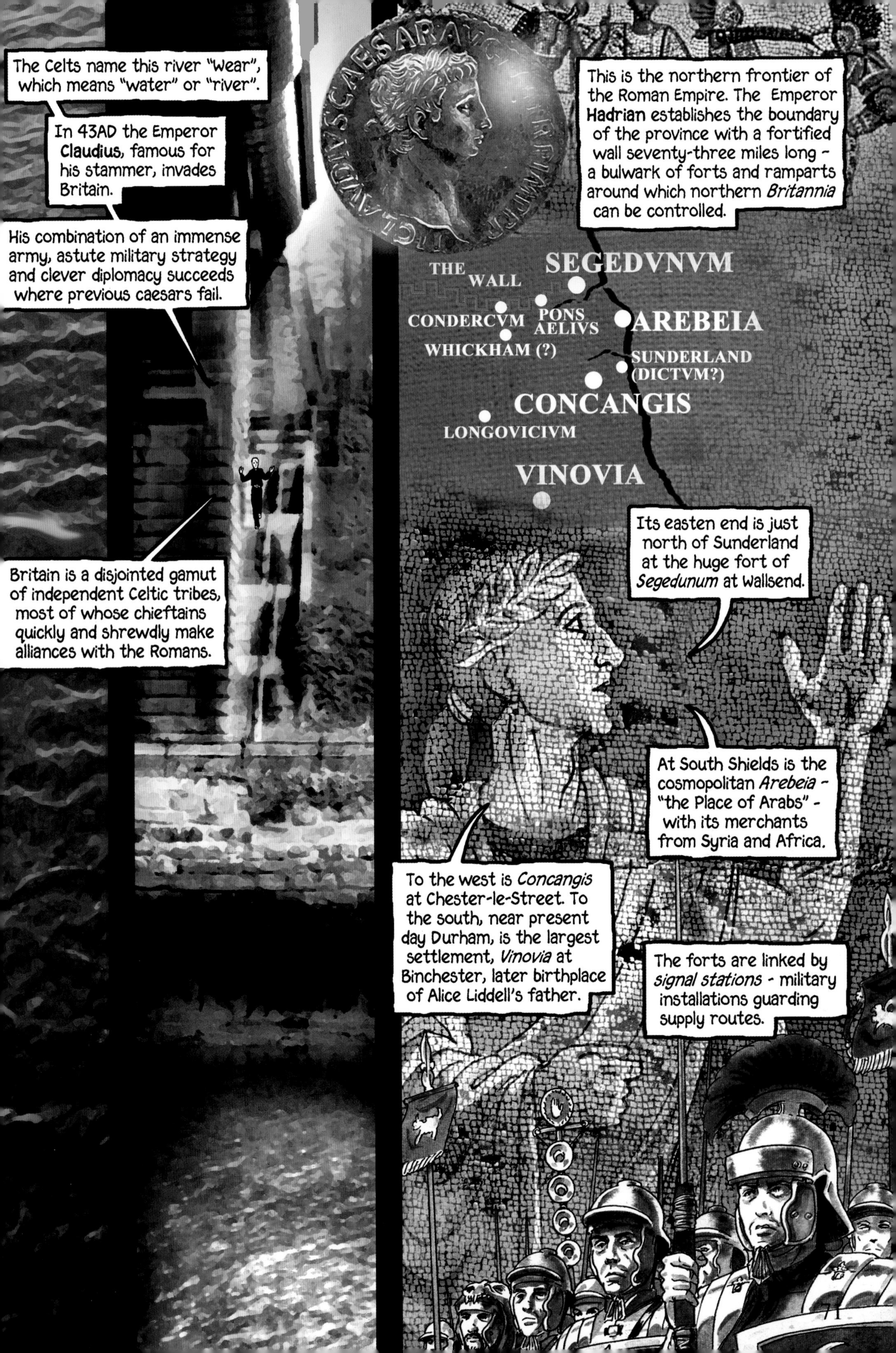
The Celts name this river "Wear", which means "water" or "river".
In 43AD the Emperor **Claudius**, famous for his stammer, invades Britain.
His combination of an immense army, astute military strategy and clever diplomacy succeeds where previous caesars fail.
Britain is a disjointed gamut of independent Celtic tribes, most of whose chieftains quickly and shrewdly make alliances with the Romans.
This is the northern frontier of the Roman Empire. The Emperor **Hadrian** establishes the boundary of the province with a fortified wall seventy-three miles long - a bulwark of forts and ramparts around which northern *Britannia* can be controlled.
THE WALL
SEGEDVNVM
CONDERCVM
PONS AELIVS
AREBEIA
WHICKHAM (?)
SUNDERLAND (DICTVM?)
CONCANGIS
LONGOVICIVM
VINOVIA
Its easten end is just north of Sunderland at the huge fort of *Segedunum* at Wallsend.
At South Shields is the cosmopolitan *Arebeia* - "the Place of Arabs" - with its merchants from Syria and Africa.
To the west is *Concangis* at Chester-le-Street. To the south, near present day Durham, is the largest settlement, *Vinovia* at Binchester, later birthplace of Alice Liddell's father.
The forts are linked by *signal stations* - military installations guarding supply routes.

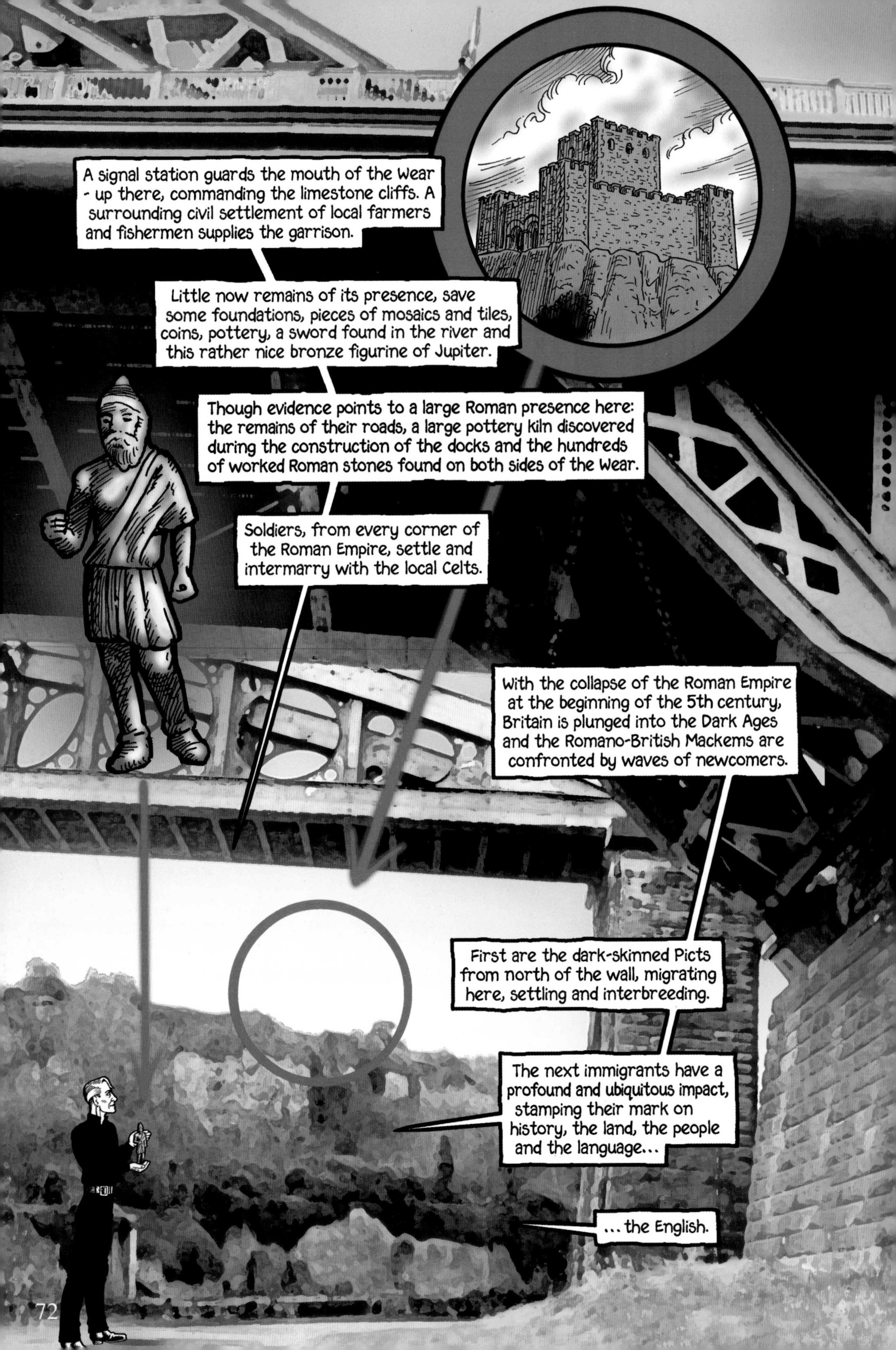
A signal station guards the mouth of the Wear - up there, commanding the limestone cliffs. A surrounding civil settlement of local farmers and fishermen supplies the garrison.
Little now remains of its presence, save some foundations, pieces of mosaics and tiles, coins, pottery, a sword found in the river and this rather nice bronze figurine of Jupiter.
Though evidence points to a large Roman presence here: the remains of their roads, a large pottery kiln discovered during the construction of the docks and the hundreds of worked Roman stones found on both sides of the Wear.
Soldiers, from every corner of the Roman Empire, settle and intermarry with the local Celts.
With the collapse of the Roman Empire at the beginning of the 5th century, Britain is plunged into the Dark Ages and the Romano-British Mackems are confronted by waves of newcomers.
First are the dark-skinned Picts from north of the wall, migrating here, settling and interbreeding.
The next immigrants have a profound and ubiquitous impact, stamping their mark on history, the land, the people and the language...
... the English.

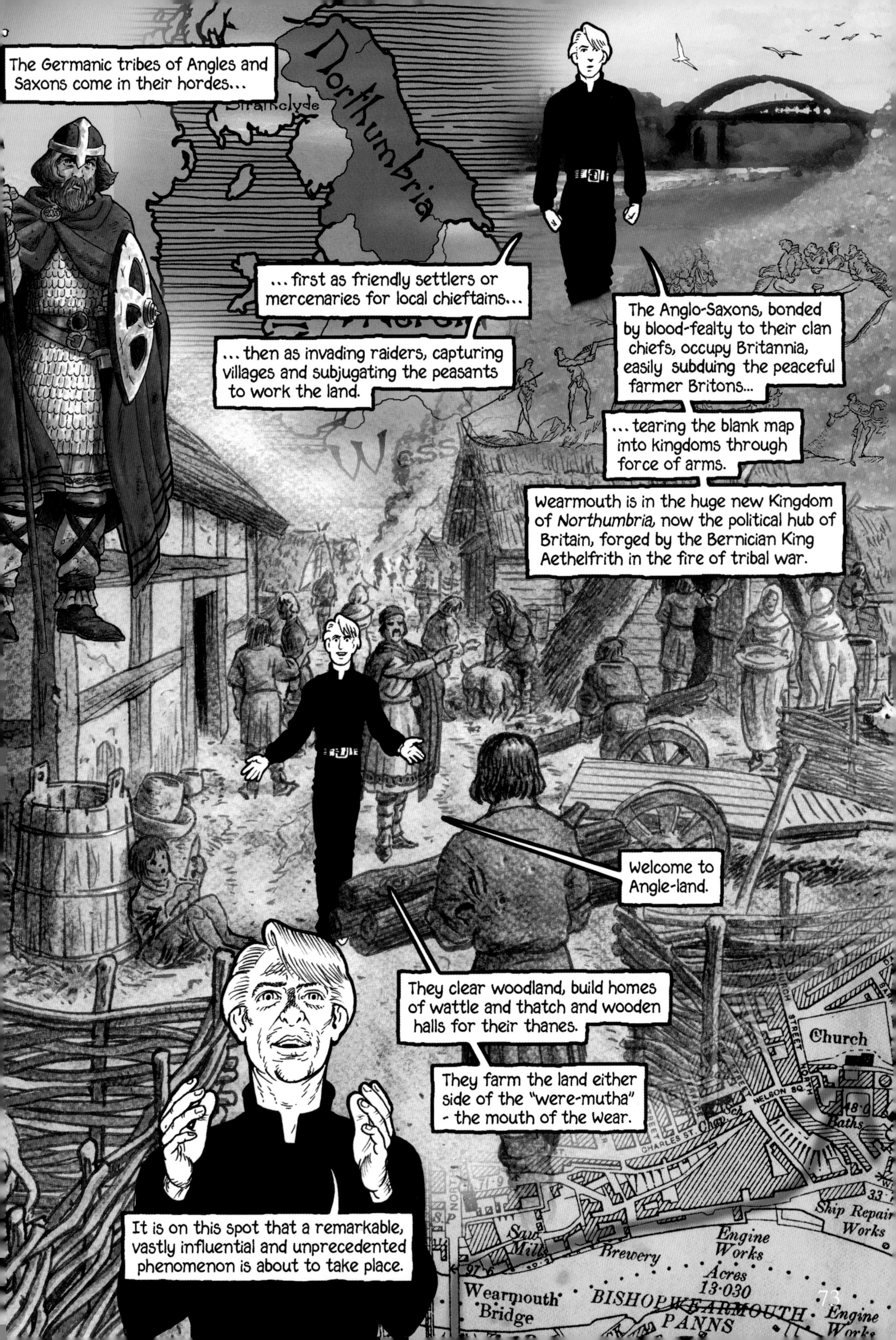

The Germanic tribes of Angles and Saxons come in their hordes...
Strathclyde
Northumbria
...first as friendly settlers or mercenaries for local chieftains...
...then as invading raiders, capturing villages and subjugating the peasants to work the land.
The Anglo-Saxons, bonded by blood-fealty to their clan chiefs, occupy Britannia, easily subduing the peaceful farmer Britons...
...tearing the blank map into kingdoms through force of arms.
Wearmouth is in the huge new Kingdom of *Northumbria*, now the political hub of Britain, forged by the Bernician King Aethelfrith in the fire of tribal war.
Welcome to Angle-land.
They clear woodland, build homes of wattle and thatch and wooden halls for their thanes.
They farm the land either side of the "were-mutha" - the mouth of the Wear.
It is on this spot that a remarkable, vastly influential and unprecedented phenomenon is about to take place.
Church
Baths
Ship Repair Works
Engine Works
Brewery
Acres 13·030
Wearmouth Bridge
BISHOPWEARMOUTH
PANNS

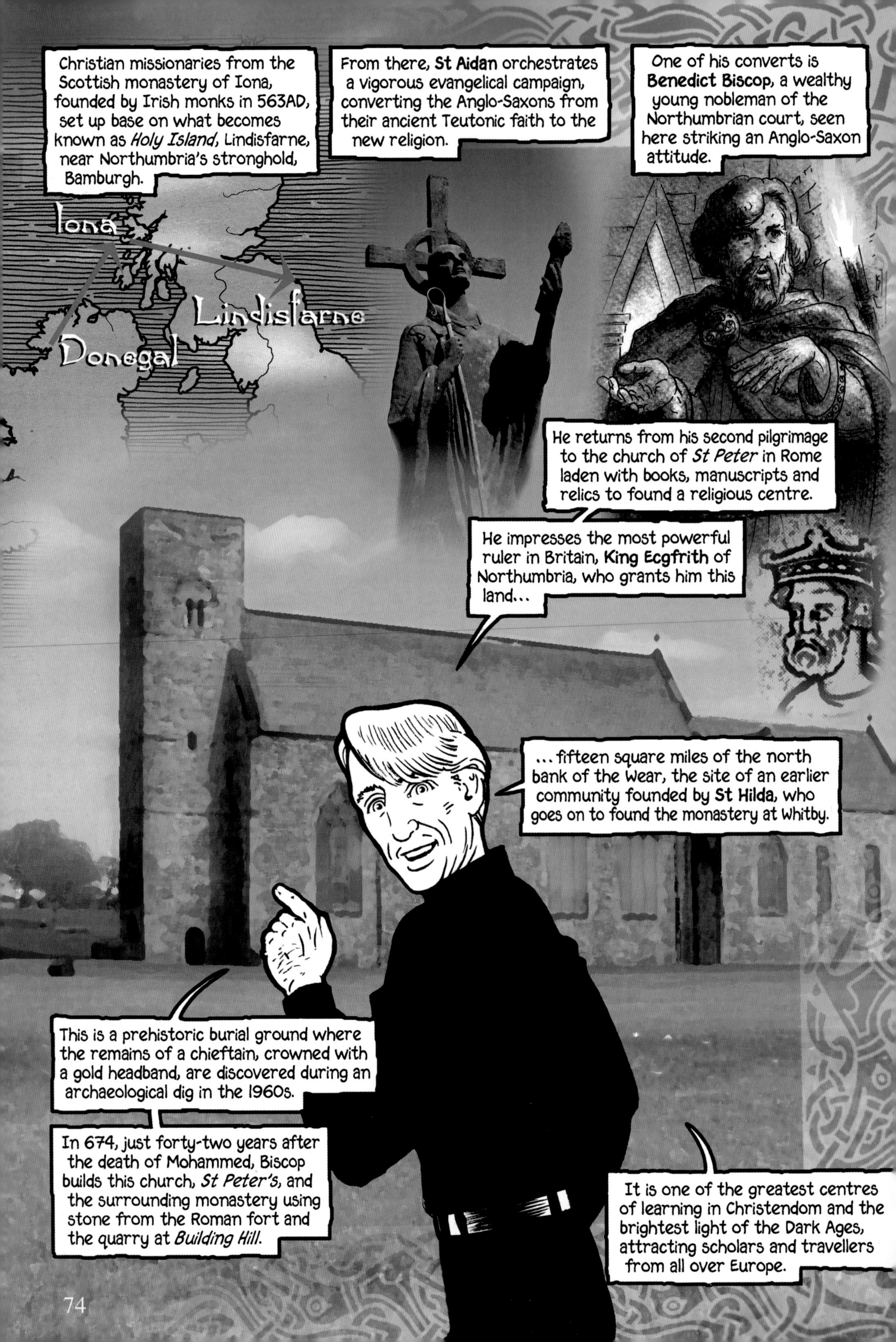
Christian missionaries from the Scottish monastery of Iona, founded by Irish monks in 563AD, set up base on what becomes known as *Holy Island*, Lindisfarne, near Northumbria's stronghold, Bamburgh.
Iona
Lindisfarne
Donegal
From there, **St Aidan** orchestrates a vigorous evangelical campaign, converting the Anglo-Saxons from their ancient Teutonic faith to the new religion.
One of his converts is **Benedict Biscop**, a wealthy young nobleman of the Northumbrian court, seen here striking an Anglo-Saxon attitude.
He returns from his second pilgrimage to the church of *St Peter* in Rome laden with books, manuscripts and relics to found a religious centre.
He impresses the most powerful ruler in Britain, **King Ecgfrith** of Northumbria, who grants him this land...
...fifteen square miles of the north bank of the Wear, the site of an earlier community founded by **St Hilda**, who goes on to found the monastery at Whitby.
This is a prehistoric burial ground where the remains of a chieftain, crowned with a gold headband, are discovered during an archaeological dig in the 1960s.
In 674, just forty-two years after the death of Mohammed, Biscop builds this church, *St Peter's*, and the surrounding monastery using stone from the Roman fort and the quarry at *Building Hill*.
It is one of the greatest centres of learning in Christendom and the brightest light of the Dark Ages, attracting scholars and travellers from all over Europe.

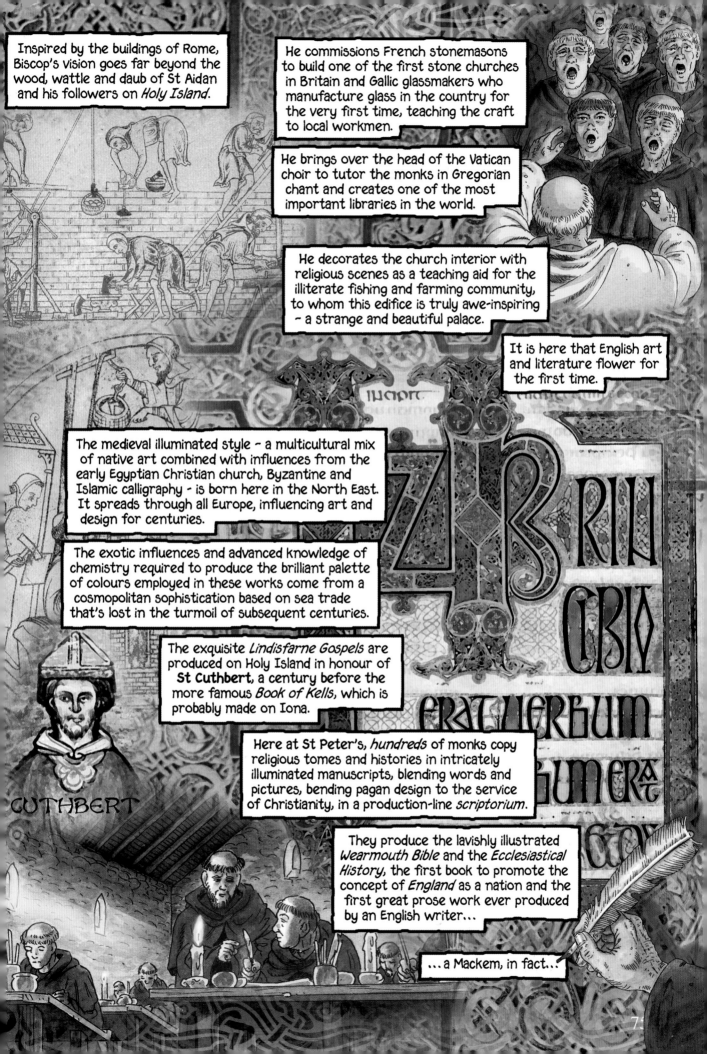

Inspired by the buildings of Rome, Biscop's vision goes far beyond the wood, wattle and daub of St Aidan and his followers on *Holy Island*.

He commissions French stonemasons to build one of the first stone churches in Britain and Gallic glassmakers who manufacture glass in the country for the very first time, teaching the craft to local workmen.

He brings over the head of the Vatican choir to tutor the monks in Gregorian chant and creates one of the most important libraries in the world.

He decorates the church interior with religious scenes as a teaching aid for the illiterate fishing and farming community, to whom this edifice is truly awe-inspiring ~ a strange and beautiful palace.

It is here that English art and literature flower for the first time.

The medieval illuminated style ~ a multicultural mix of native art combined with influences from the early Egyptian Christian church, Byzantine and Islamic calligraphy ~ is born here in the North East. It spreads through all Europe, influencing art and design for centuries.

The exotic influences and advanced knowledge of chemistry required to produce the brilliant palette of colours employed in these works come from a cosmopolitan sophistication based on sea trade that's lost in the turmoil of subsequent centuries.

The exquisite *Lindisfarne Gospels* are produced on Holy Island in honour of **St Cuthbert**, a century before the more famous *Book of Kells*, which is probably made on Iona.

CUTHBERT

Here at St Peter's, *hundreds* of monks copy religious tomes and histories in intricately illuminated manuscripts, blending words and pictures, bending pagan design to the service of Christianity, in a production-line *scriptorium*.

They produce the lavishly illustrated *Wearmouth Bible* and the *Ecclesiastical History*, the first book to promote the concept of *England* as a nation and the first great prose work ever produced by an English writer...

...a Mackem, in fact...

81

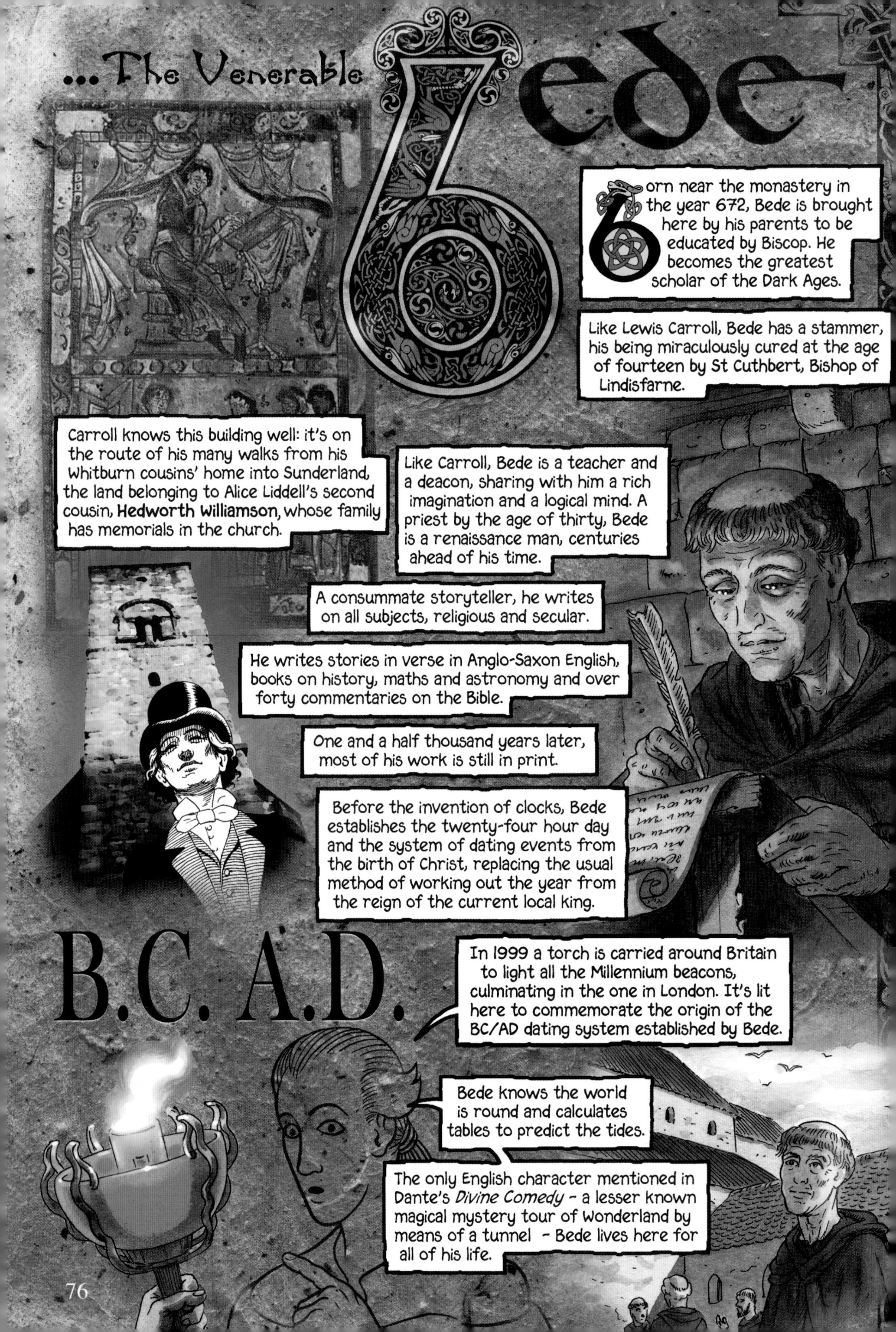

...The Venerable Bede
Born near the monastery in the year 672, Bede is brought here by his parents to be educated by Biscop. He becomes the greatest scholar of the Dark Ages.
Like Lewis Carroll, Bede has a stammer, his being miraculously cured at the age of fourteen by St Cuthbert, Bishop of Lindisfarne.
Carroll knows this building well: it's on the route of his many walks from his Whitburn cousins' home into Sunderland, the land belonging to Alice Liddell's second cousin, **Hedworth Williamson**, whose family has memorials in the church.
Like Carroll, Bede is a teacher and a deacon, sharing with him a rich imagination and a logical mind. A priest by the age of thirty, Bede is a renaissance man, centuries ahead of his time.
A consummate storyteller, he writes on all subjects, religious and secular.
He writes stories in verse in Anglo-Saxon English, books on history, maths and astronomy and over forty commentaries on the Bible.
One and a half thousand years later, most of his work is still in print.
Before the invention of clocks, Bede establishes the twenty-four hour day and the system of dating events from the birth of Christ, replacing the usual method of working out the year from the reign of the current local king.
B.C. A.D.
In 1999 a torch is carried around Britain to light all the Millennium beacons, culminating in the one in London. It's lit here to commemorate the origin of the BC/AD dating system established by Bede.
Bede knows the world is round and calculates tables to predict the tides.
The only English character mentioned in Dante's *Divine Comedy* – a lesser known magical mystery tour of Wonderland by means of a tunnel – Bede lives here for all of his life.

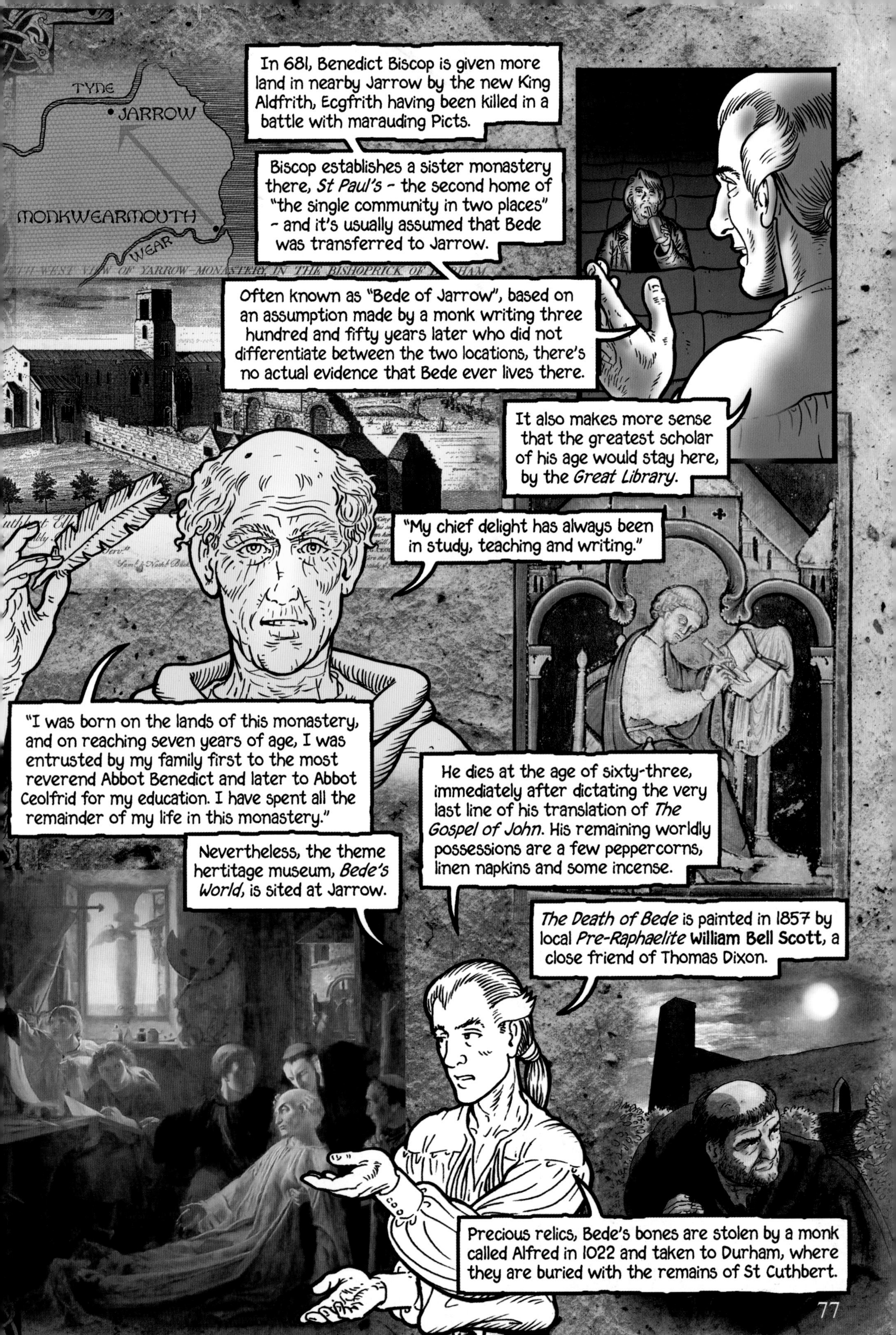
TYNE
JARROW
MONKWEARMOUTH
WEAR
In 681, Benedict Biscop is given more land in nearby Jarrow by the new King Aldfrith, Ecgfrith having been killed in a battle with marauding Picts.
Biscop establishes a sister monastery there, *St Paul's* – the second home of "the single community in two places" – and it's usually assumed that Bede was transferred to Jarrow.
Often known as "Bede of Jarrow", based on an assumption made by a monk writing three hundred and fifty years later who did not differentiate between the two locations, there's no actual evidence that Bede ever lives there.
It also makes more sense that the greatest scholar of his age would stay here, by the *Great Library*.
"My chief delight has always been in study, teaching and writing."
"I was born on the lands of this monastery, and on reaching seven years of age, I was entrusted by my family first to the most reverend Abbot Benedict and later to Abbot Ceolfrid for my education. I have spent all the remainder of my life in this monastery."
Nevertheless, the theme hertitage museum, *Bede's World*, is sited at Jarrow.
He dies at the age of sixty-three, immediately after dictating the very last line of his translation of *The Gospel of John*. His remaining worldly possessions are a few peppercorns, linen napkins and some incense.
The Death of Bede is painted in 1857 by local *Pre-Raphaelite* **William Bell Scott**, a close friend of Thomas Dixon.
Precious relics, Bede's bones are stolen by a monk called Alfred in 1022 and taken to Durham, where they are buried with the remains of St Cuthbert.

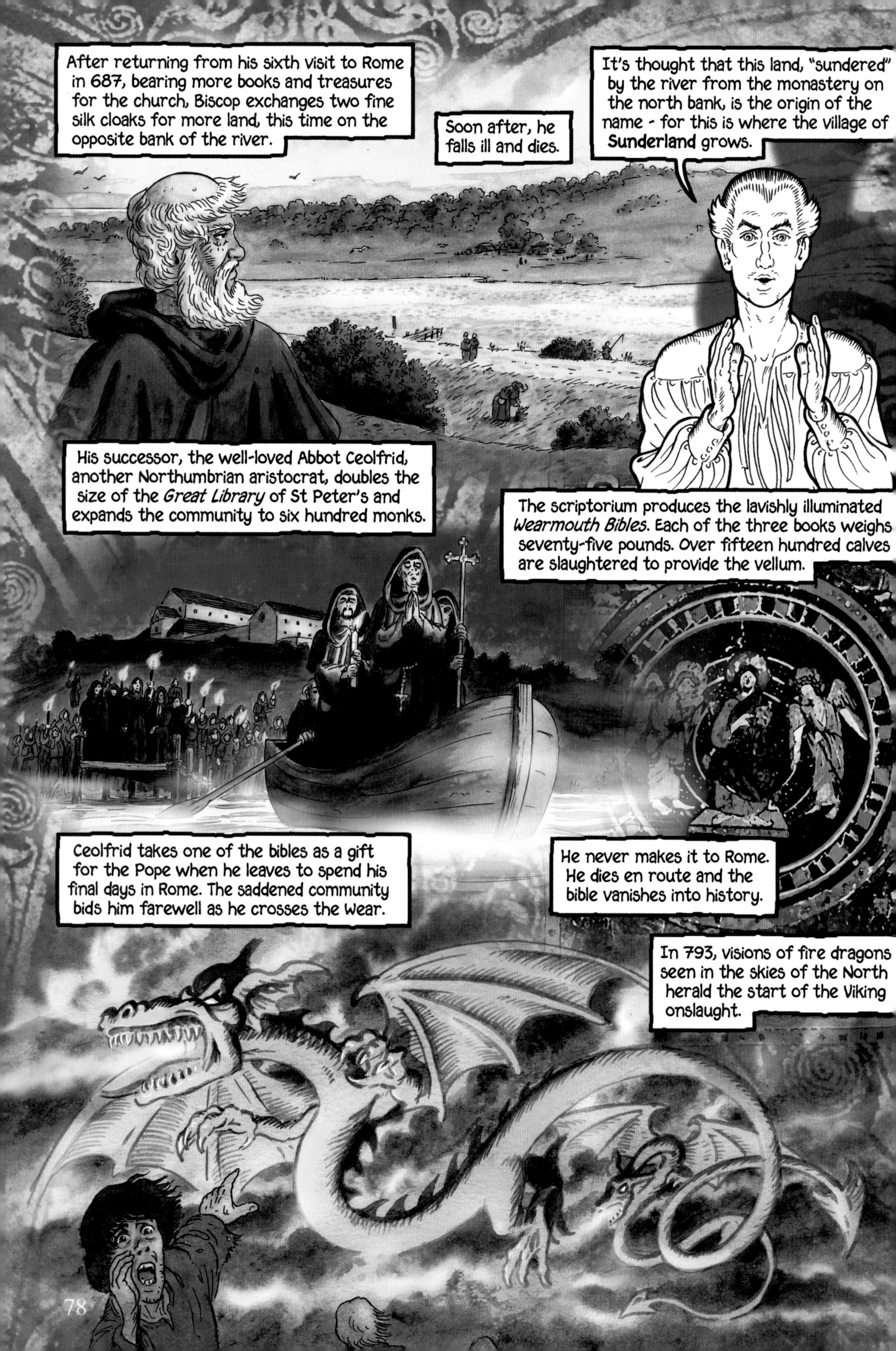
After returning from his sixth visit to Rome in 687, bearing more books and treasures for the church, Biscop exchanges two fine silk cloaks for more land, this time on the opposite bank of the river.
Soon after, he falls ill and dies.
It's thought that this land, "sundered" by the river from the monastery on the north bank, is the origin of the name - for this is where the village of Sunderland grows.
His successor, the well-loved Abbot Ceolfrid, another Northumbrian aristocrat, doubles the size of the Great Library of St Peter's and expands the community to six hundred monks.
The scriptorium produces the lavishly illuminated Wearmouth Bibles. Each of the three books weighs seventy-five pounds. Over fifteen hundred calves are slaughtered to provide the vellum.
Ceolfrid takes one of the bibles as a gift for the Pope when he leaves to spend his final days in Rome. The saddened community bids him farewell as he crosses the Wear.
He never makes it to Rome. He dies en route and the bible vanishes into history.
In 793, visions of fire dragons seen in the skies of the North herald the start of the Viking onslaught.

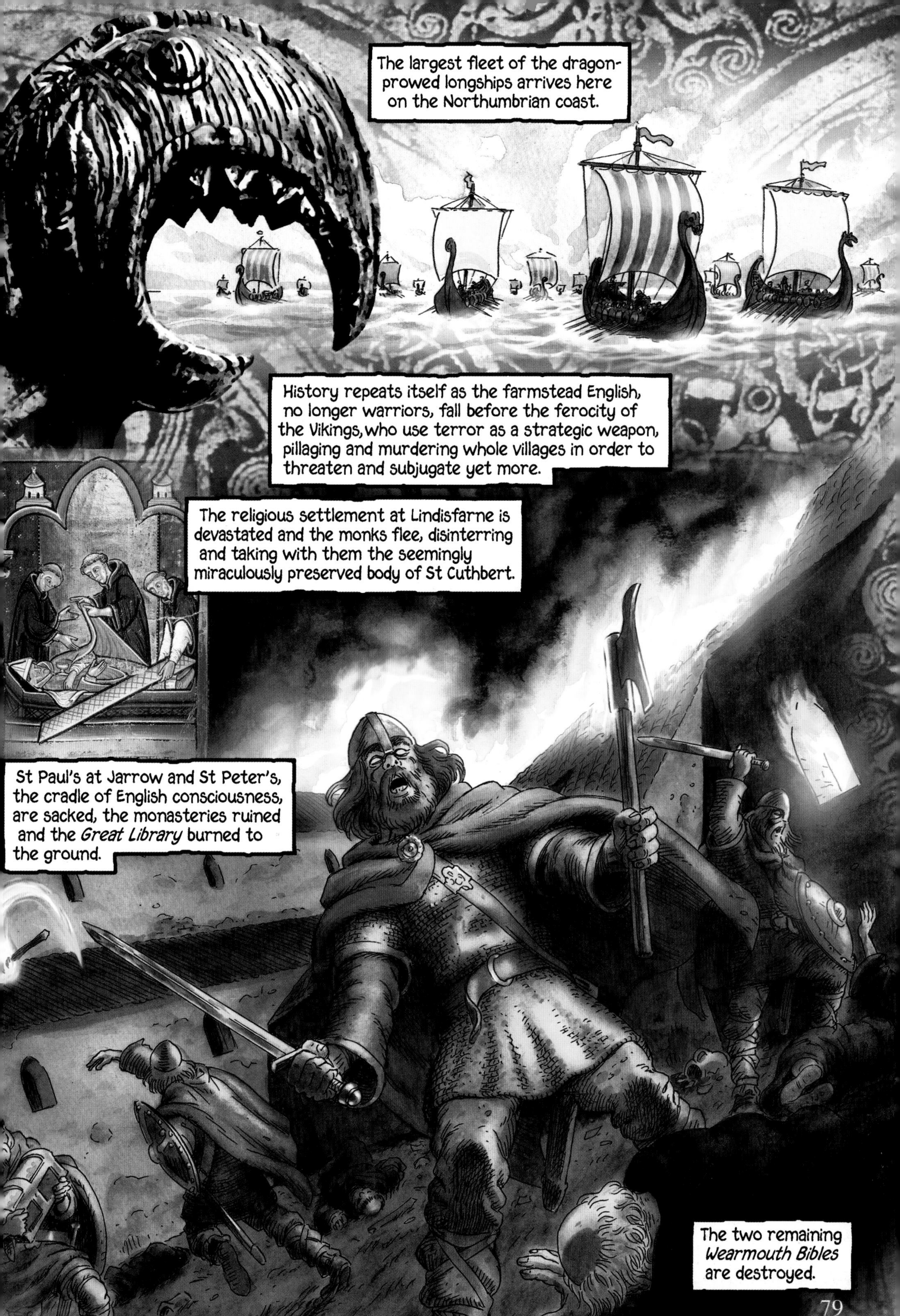
The largest fleet of the dragon-prowed longships arrives here on the Northumbrian coast.
History repeats itself as the farmstead English, no longer warriors, fall before the ferocity of the Vikings, who use terror as a strategic weapon, pillaging and murdering whole villages in order to threaten and subjugate yet more.
The religious settlement at Lindisfarne is devastated and the monks flee, disinterring and taking with them the seemingly miraculously preserved body of St Cuthbert.
St Paul's at Jarrow and St Peter's, the cradle of English consciousness, are sacked, the monasteries ruined and the *Great Library* burned to the ground.
The two remaining *Wearmouth Bibles* are destroyed.

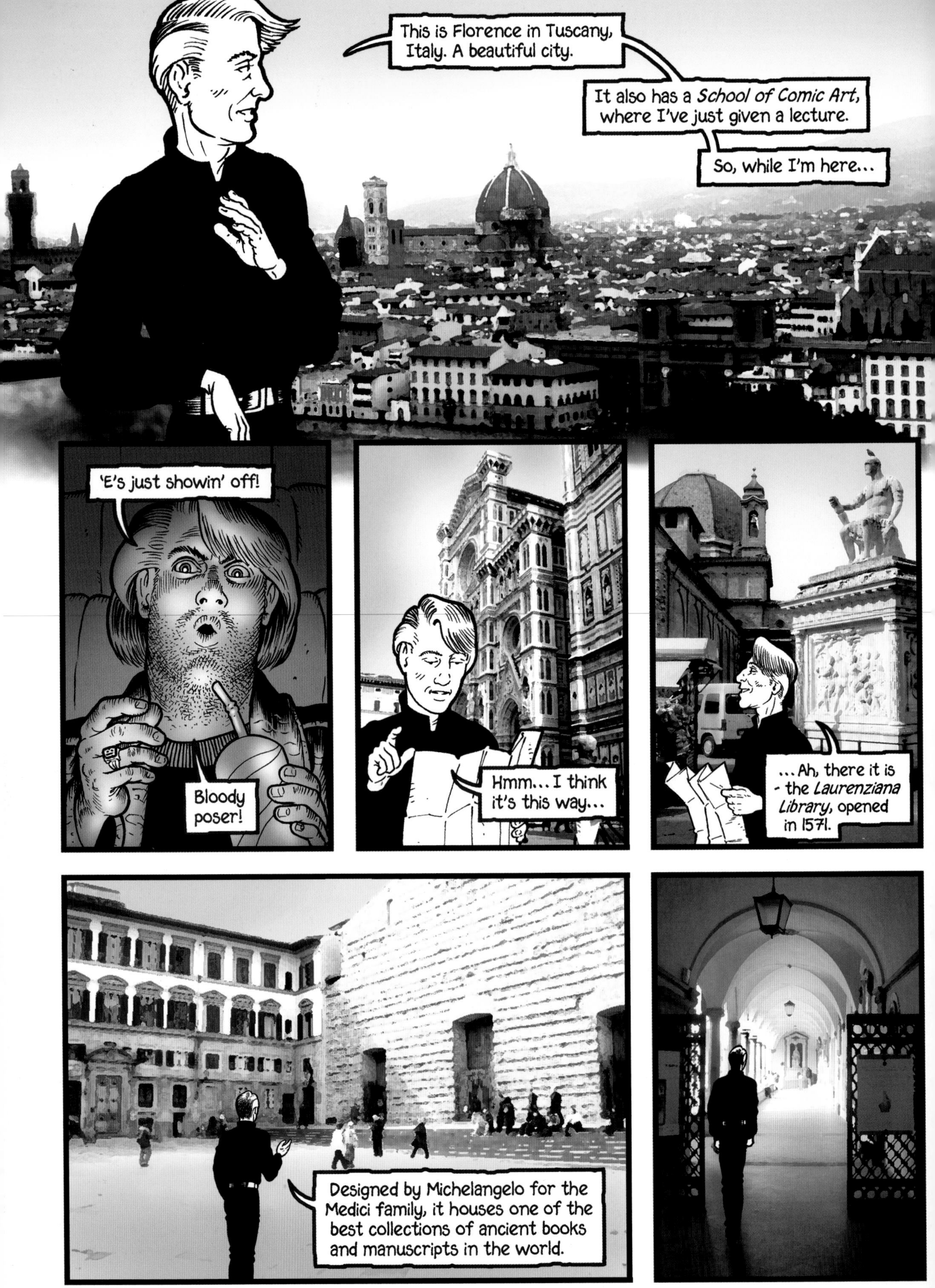
This is Florence in Tuscany, Italy. A beautiful city.
It also has a *School of Comic Art*, where I've just given a lecture.
So, while I'm here...
'E's just showin' off!
Bloody poser!
Hmm... I think it's this way...
...Ah, there it is - the *Laurenziana Library*, opened in 1571.
Designed by Michelangelo for the Medici family, it houses one of the best collections of ancient books and manuscripts in the world.

Lost for eleven centuries, Ceolfrid's copy of the *Wearmouth Bible* intended for the Pope is rediscovered here in the early 20th century.

Now known as the *Codex Amiatinus*, it's the oldest complete Latin bible in existence.

And it's just in there.

Michelangelo designed this vestibule to be a "dark prelude to the brightness of the Reading Room", where we find...

BONK!

...OW!

Bugger!

Unfortunately, the public isn't allowed to see it. It's kept under lock and key in the vaults.

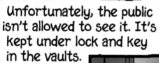

Still, with the magic of comics on our side, that doesn't stop us! C'mon!

Here it is!

Wonderful stuff!

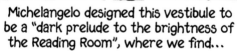

A triumph of Mackem art!

This is an illo of *Ezra the Scribe* - the scribbling monks of the Wearmouth scriptorium must have been his biggest fans.

Let's get back there - to St Peter's.

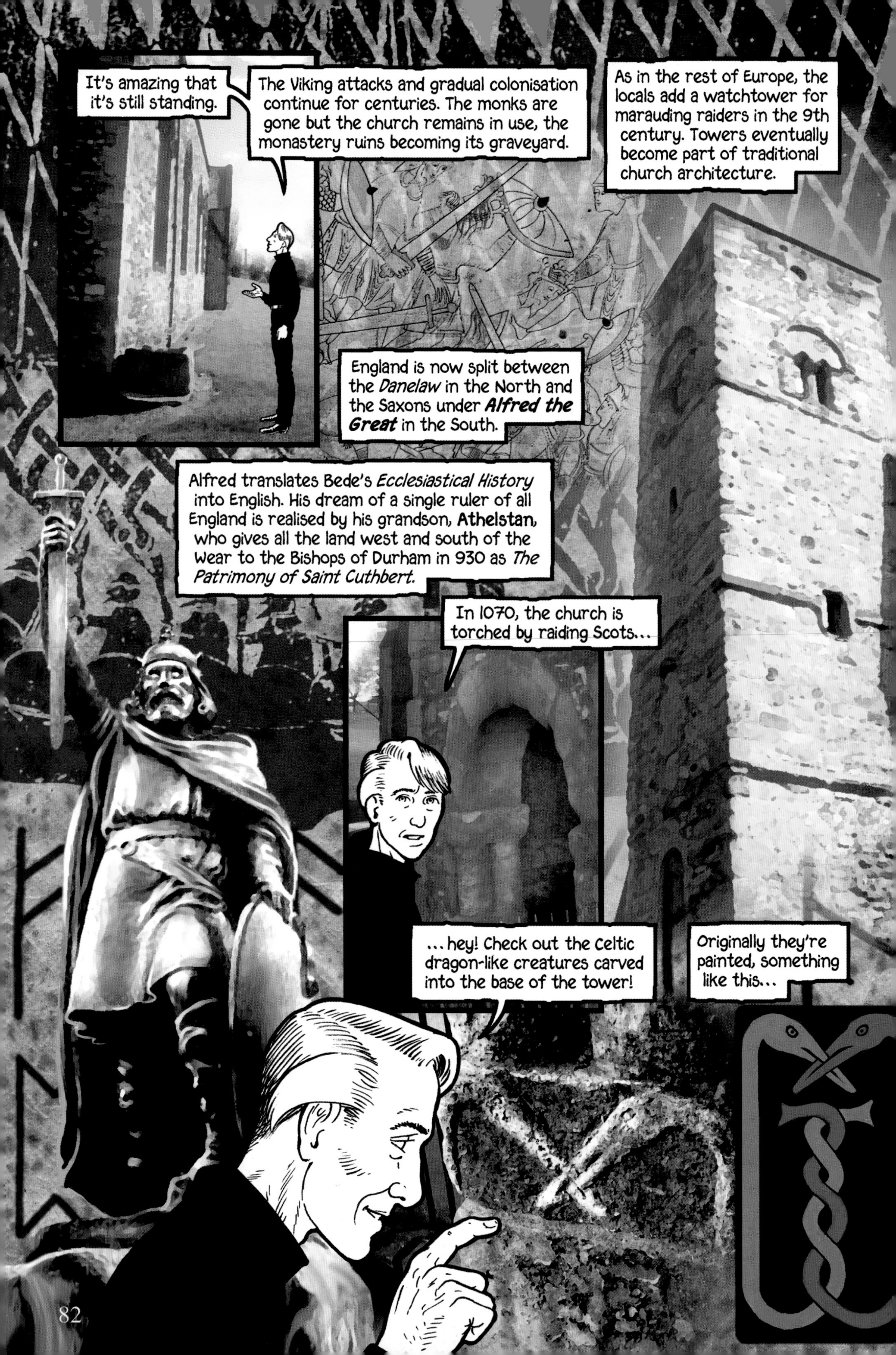

It's amazing that it's still standing.
The Viking attacks and gradual colonisation continue for centuries. The monks are gone but the church remains in use, the monastery ruins becoming its graveyard.
As in the rest of Europe, the locals add a watchtower for marauding raiders in the 9th century. Towers eventually become part of traditional church architecture.
England is now split between the *Danelaw* in the North and the Saxons under ***Alfred the Great*** in the South.
Alfred translates Bede's *Ecclesiastical History* into English. His dream of a single ruler of all England is realised by his grandson, **Athelstan**, who gives all the land west and south of the Wear to the Bishops of Durham in 930 as *The Patrimony of Saint Cuthbert.*
In 1070, the church is torched by raiding Scots...
...hey! Check out the Celtic dragon-like creatures carved into the base of the tower!
Originally they're painted, something like this...

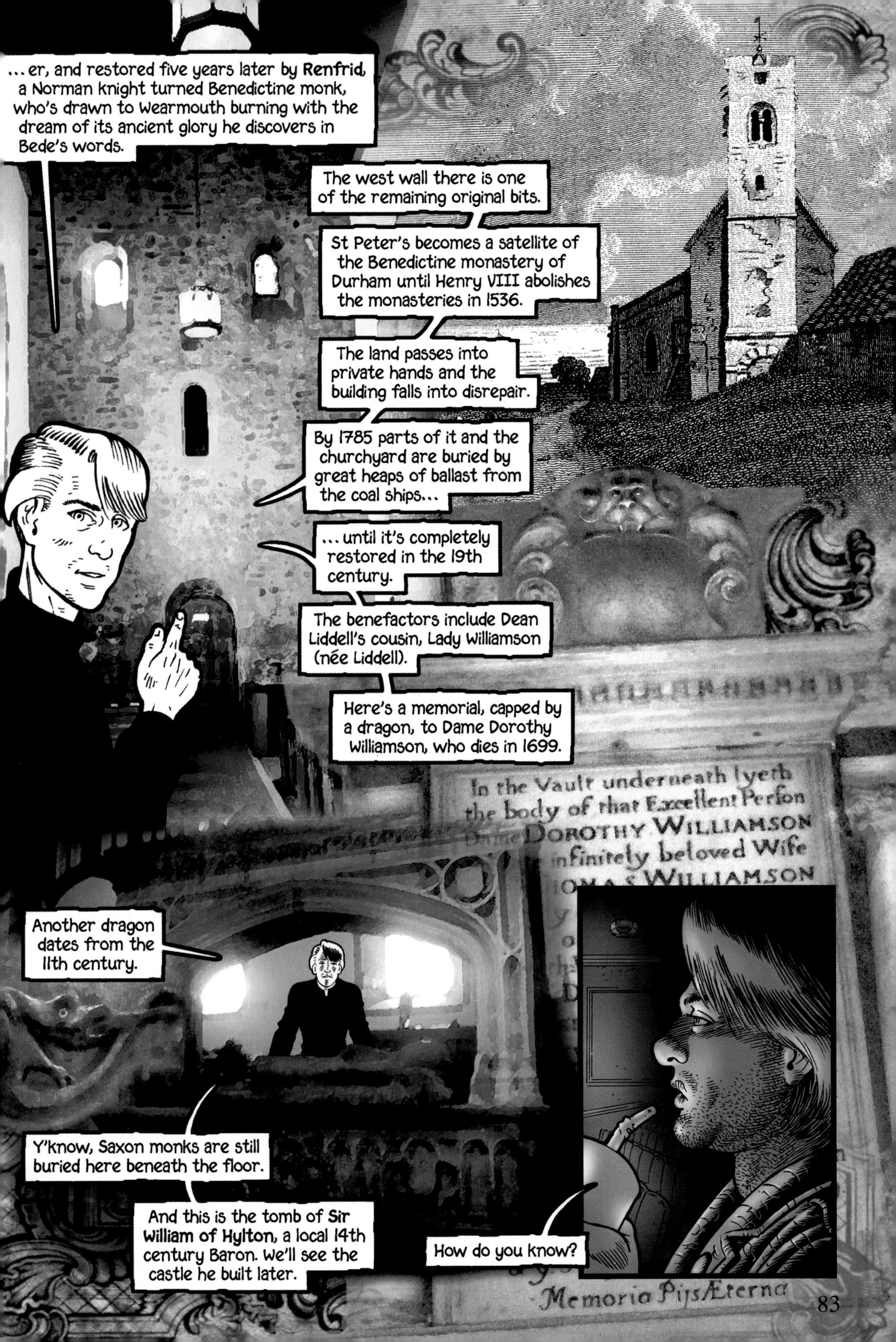

...er, and restored five years later by **Renfrid**, a Norman knight turned Benedictine monk, who's drawn to Wearmouth burning with the dream of its ancient glory he discovers in Bede's words.
The west wall there is one of the remaining original bits.
St Peter's becomes a satellite of the Benedictine monastery of Durham until Henry VIII abolishes the monasteries in 1536.
The land passes into private hands and the building falls into disrepair.
By 1785 parts of it and the churchyard are buried by great heaps of ballast from the coal ships...
...until it's completely restored in the 19th century.
The benefactors include Dean Liddell's cousin, Lady Williamson (née Liddell).
Here's a memorial, capped by a dragon, to Dame Dorothy Williamson, who dies in 1699.
In the Vault underneath lyeth
the body of that Excellent Perſon
DOROTHY WILLIAMSON
infinitely beloved Wife
Another dragon dates from the 11th century.
Y'know, Saxon monks are still buried here beneath the floor.
And this is the tomb of **Sir William of Hylton**, a local 14th century Baron. We'll see the castle he built later.
How do you know?
Memoria Pijs Æterna

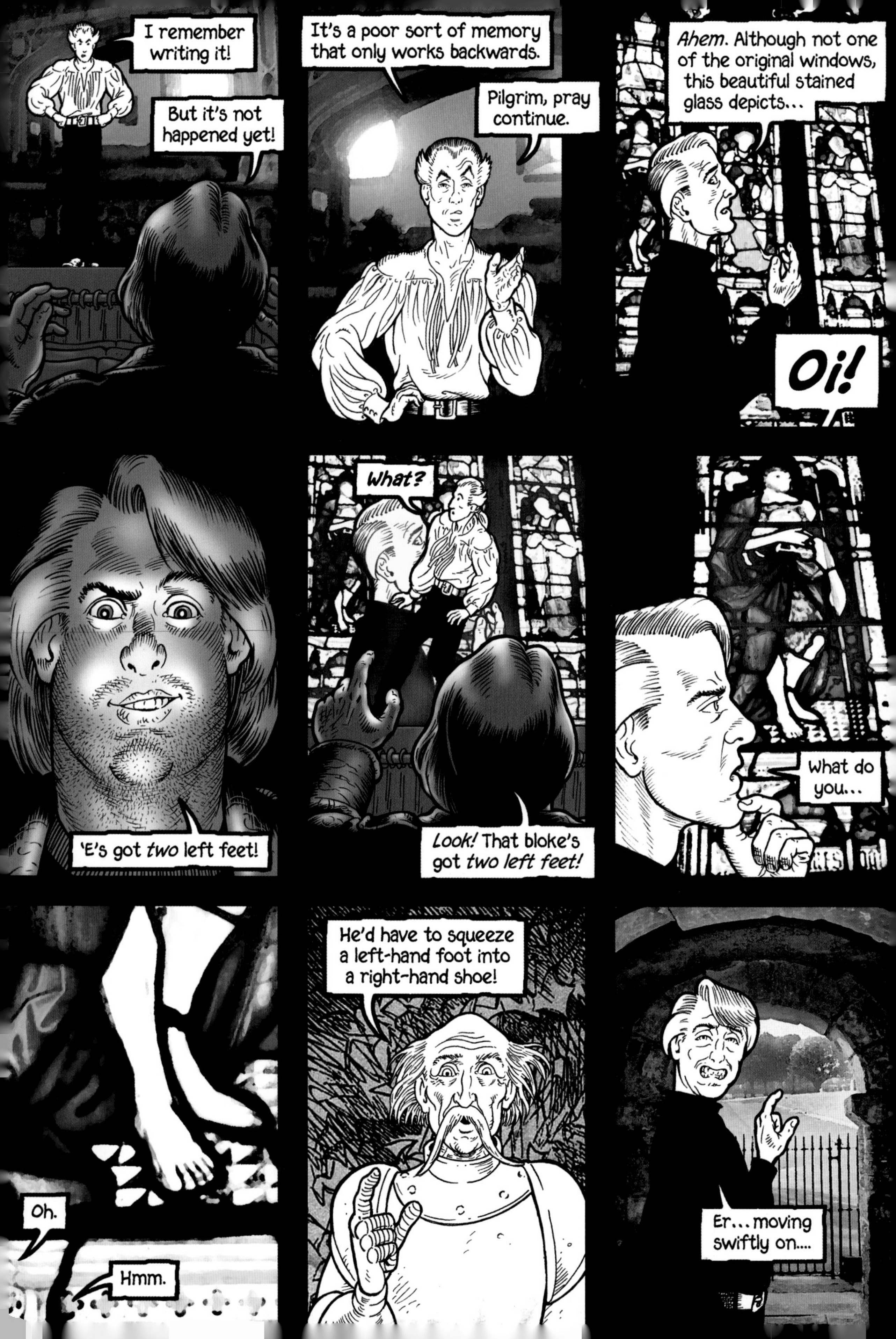
I remember writing it!
But it's not happened yet!
It's a poor sort of memory that only works backwards.
Pilgrim, pray continue.
Ahem. Although not one of the original windows, this beautiful stained glass depicts...
Oi!
'E's got *two* left feet!
What?
Look! That bloke's got *two left feet!*
What do you...
Oh.
Hmm.
He'd have to squeeze a left-hand foot into a right-hand shoe!
Er... moving swiftly on....

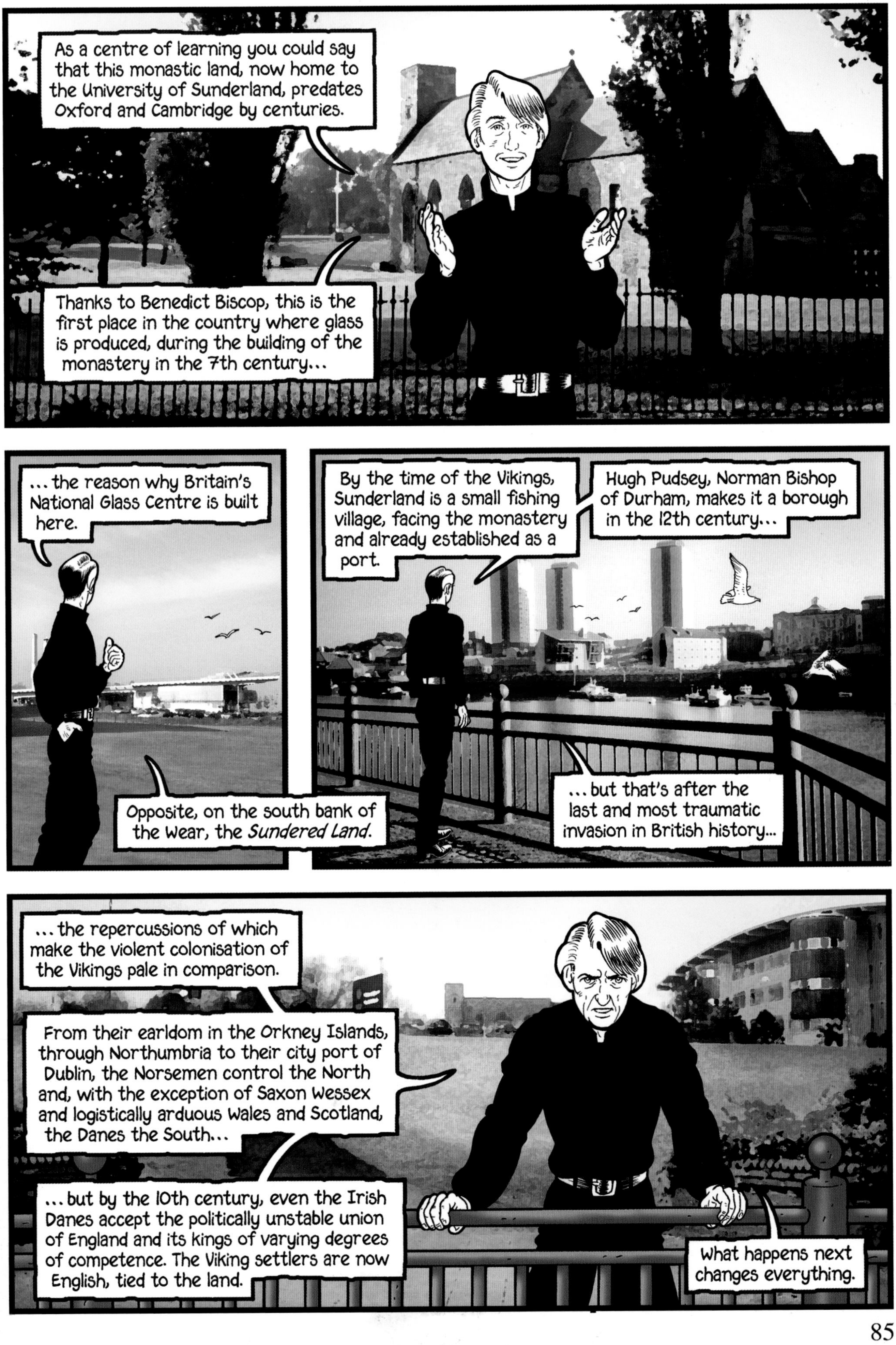
As a centre of learning you could say that this monastic land, now home to the University of Sunderland, predates Oxford and Cambridge by centuries.
Thanks to Benedict Biscop, this is the first place in the country where glass is produced, during the building of the monastery in the 7th century...
...the reason why Britain's National Glass Centre is built here.
Opposite, on the south bank of the Wear, the *Sundered Land.*
By the time of the Vikings, Sunderland is a small fishing village, facing the monastery and already established as a port.
Hugh Pudsey, Norman Bishop of Durham, makes it a borough in the 12th century...
...but that's after the last and most traumatic invasion in British history...
...the repercussions of which make the violent colonisation of the Vikings pale in comparison.
From their earldom in the Orkney Islands, through Northumbria to their city port of Dublin, the Norsemen control the North and, with the exception of Saxon Wessex and logistically arduous Wales and Scotland, the Danes the South...
...but by the 10th century, even the Irish Danes accept the politically unstable union of England and its kings of varying degrees of competence. The Viking settlers are now English, tied to the land.
What happens next changes everything.

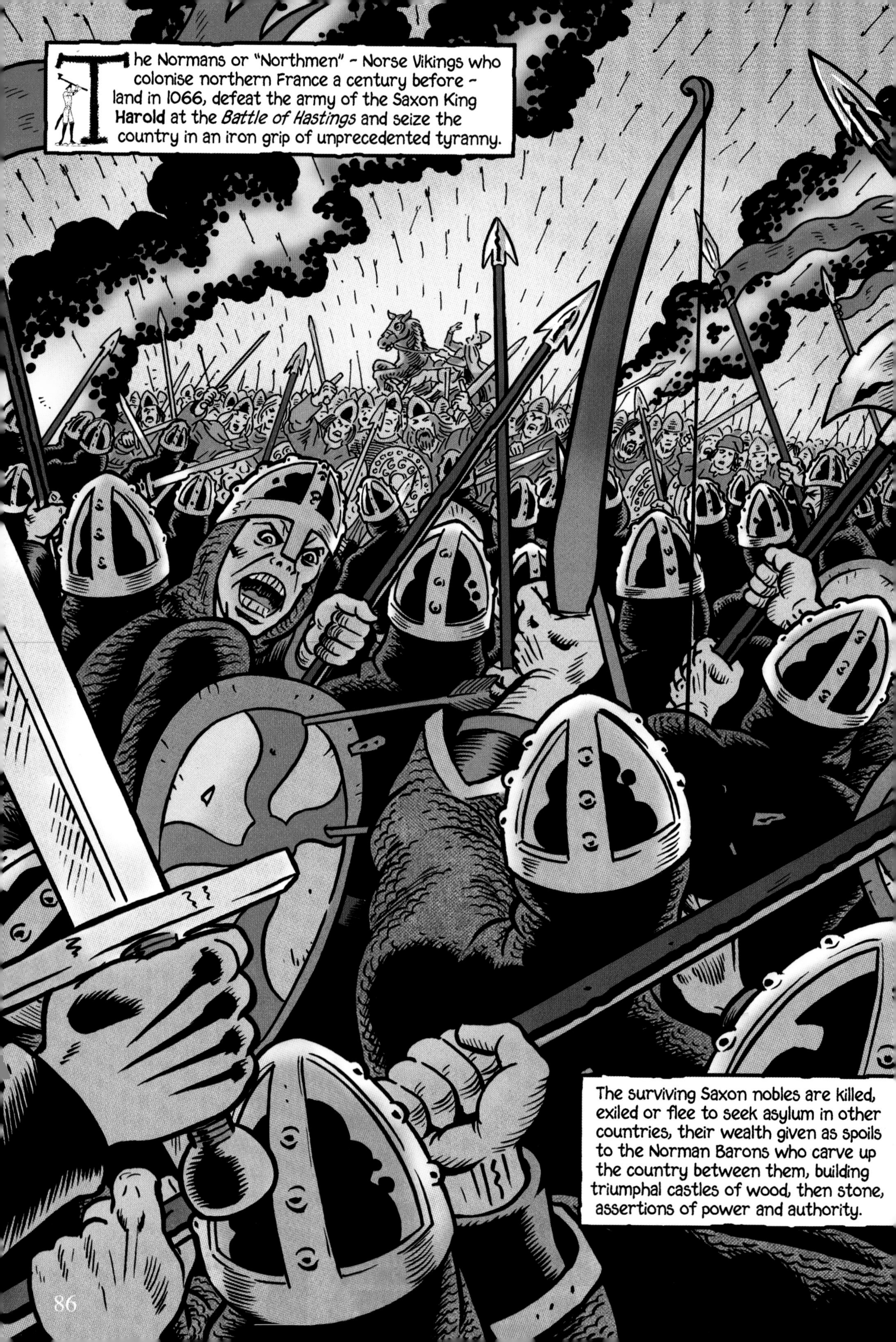
The Normans or "Northmen" - Norse Vikings who colonise northern France a century before - land in 1066, defeat the army of the Saxon King **Harold** at the *Battle of Hastings* and seize the country in an iron grip of unprecedented tyranny.
The surviving Saxon nobles are killed, exiled or flee to seek asylum in other countries, their wealth given as spoils to the Norman Barons who carve up the country between them, building triumphal castles of wood, then stone, assertions of power and authority.

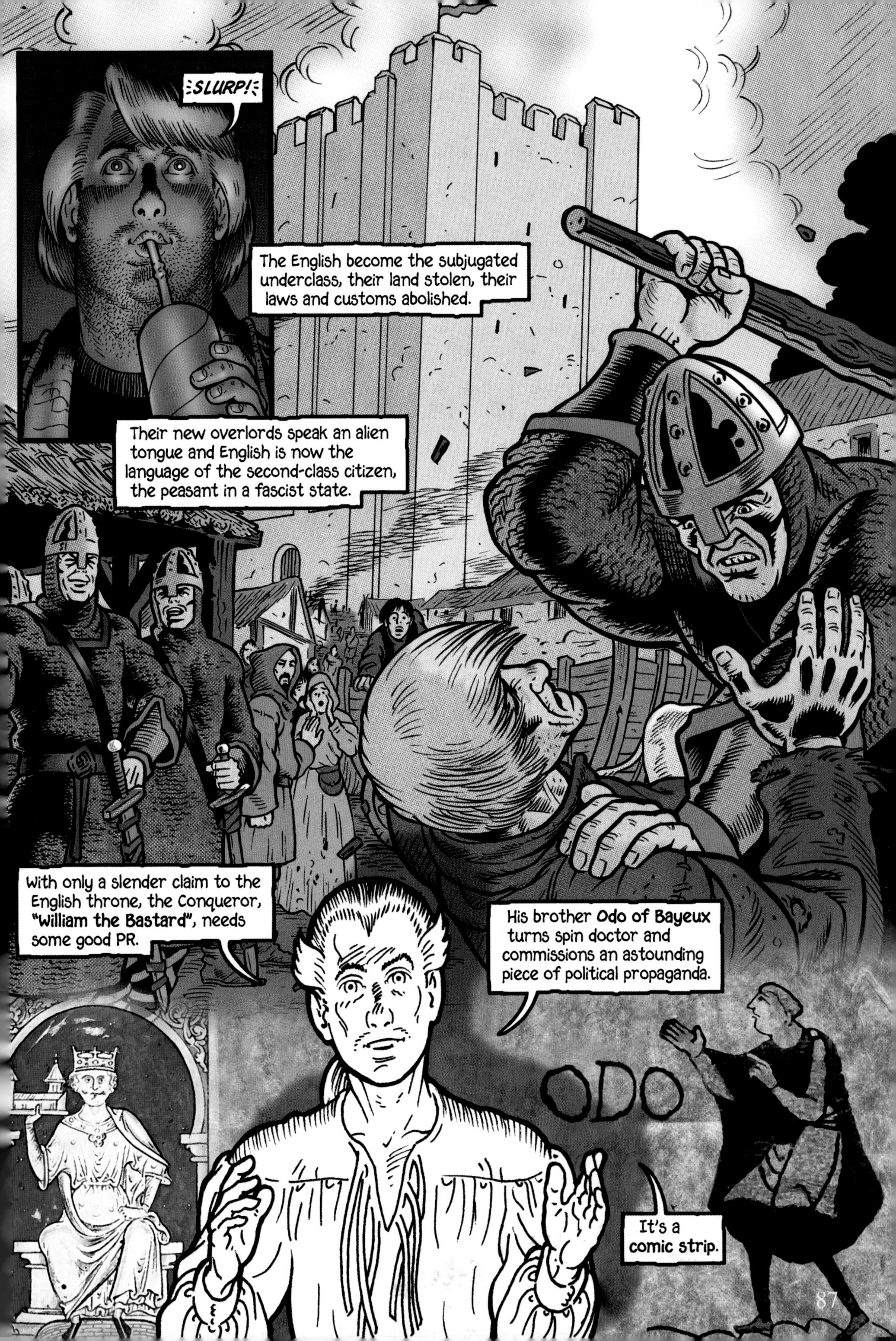
SLURP!
The English become the subjugated underclass, their land stolen, their laws and customs abolished.
Their new overlords speak an alien tongue and English is now the language of the second-class citizen, the peasant in a fascist state.
With only a slender claim to the English throne, the Conqueror, "William the Bastard", needs some good PR.
His brother Odo of Bayeux turns spin doctor and commissions an astounding piece of political propaganda.
ODO
It's a comic strip.

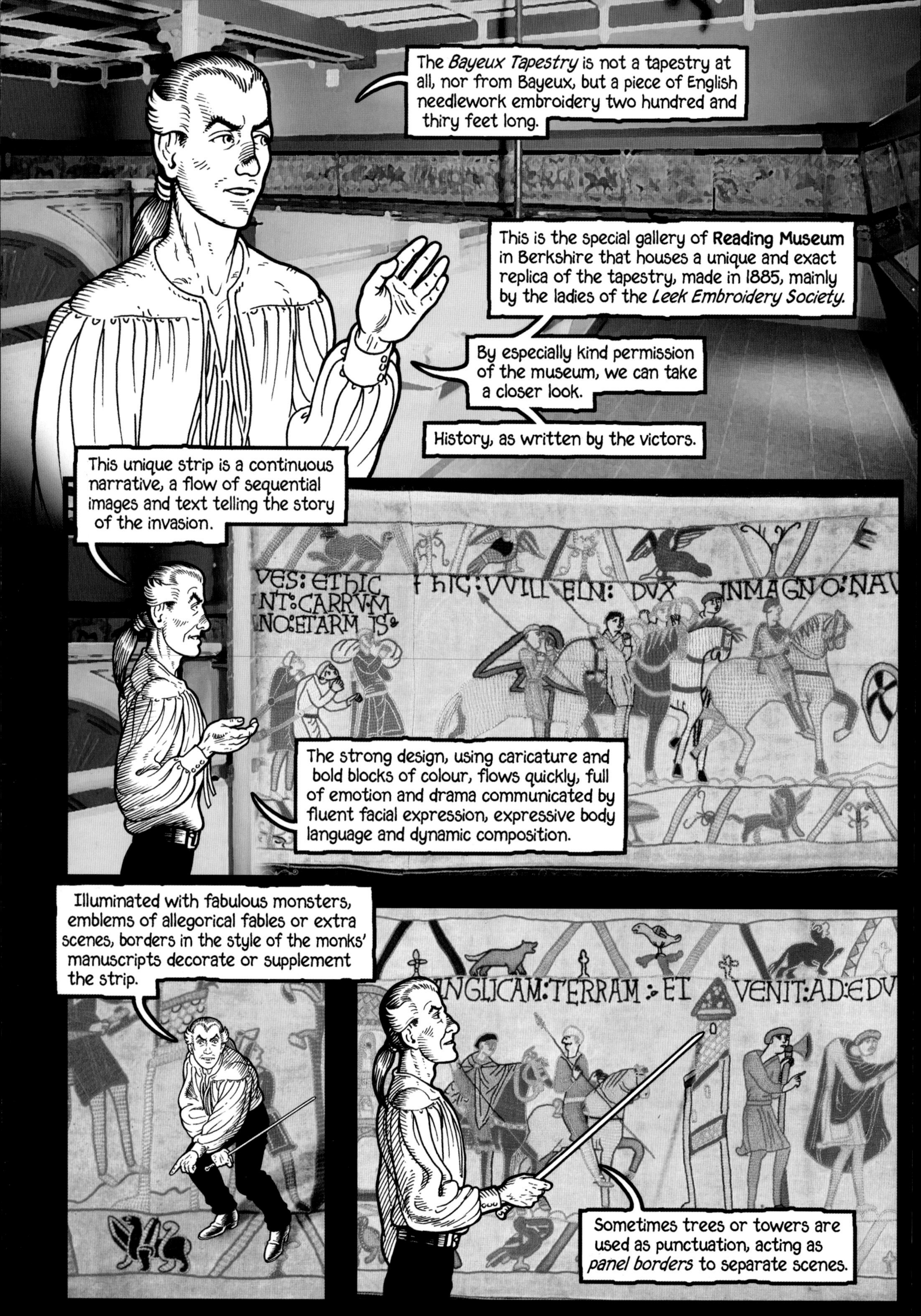
The *Bayeux Tapestry* is not a tapestry at all, nor from Bayeux, but a piece of English needlework embroidery two hundred and thiry feet long.
This is the special gallery of **Reading Museum** in Berkshire that houses a unique and exact replica of the tapestry, made in 1885, mainly by the ladies of the *Leek Embroidery Society*.
By especially kind permission of the museum, we can take a closer look.
History, as written by the victors.
This unique strip is a continuous narrative, a flow of sequential images and text telling the story of the invasion.
The strong design, using caricature and bold blocks of colour, flows quickly, full of emotion and drama communicated by fluent facial expression, expressive body language and dynamic composition.
Illuminated with fabulous monsters, emblems of allegorical fables or extra scenes, borders in the style of the monks' manuscripts decorate or supplement the strip.
Sometimes trees or towers are used as punctuation, acting as *panel borders* to separate scenes.

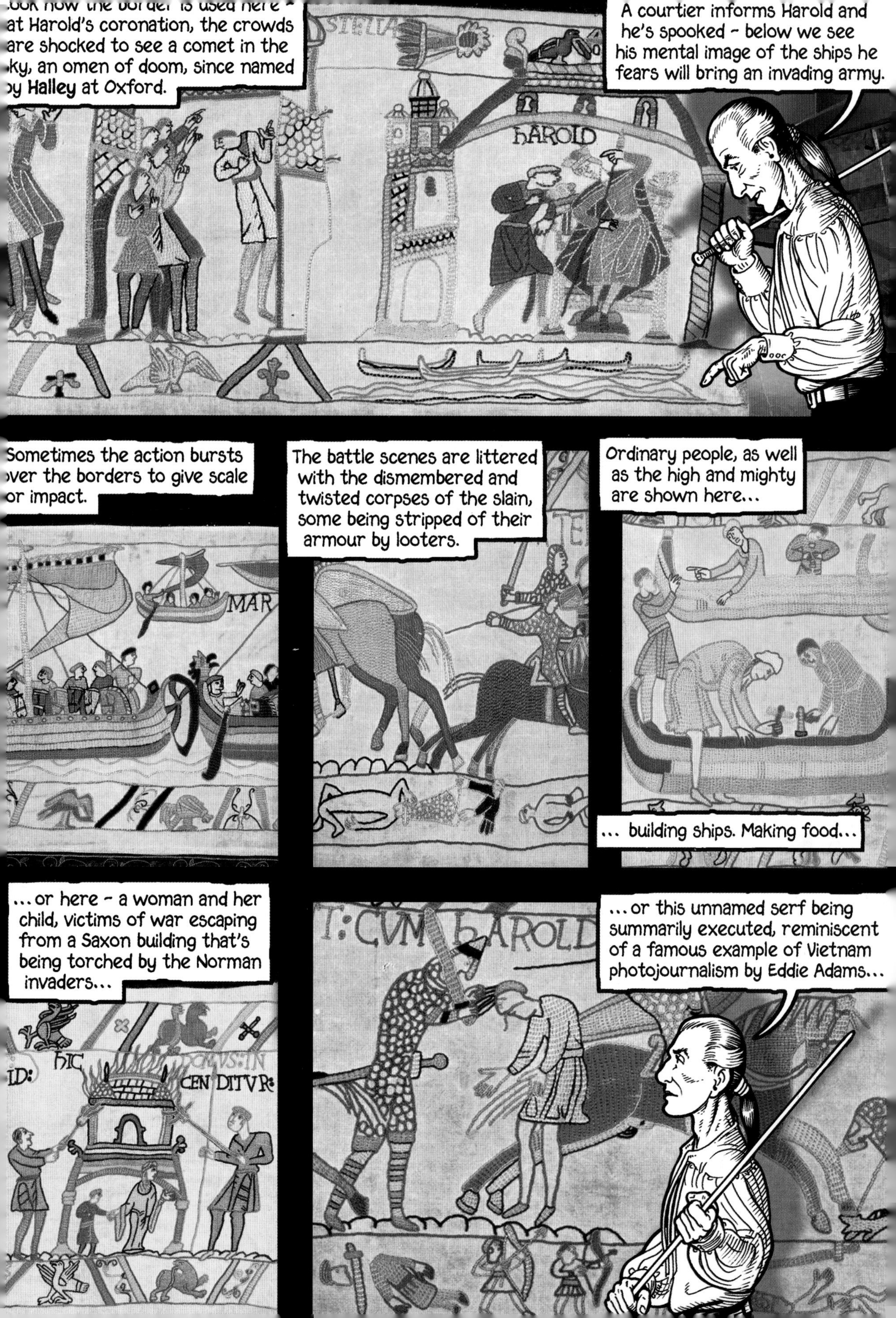ook how the border is used here – at Harold's coronation, the crowds are shocked to see a comet in the ky, an omen of doom, since named y **Halley** at Oxford.
STELLA
A courtier informs Harold and he's spooked – below we see his mental image of the ships he fears will bring an invading army.
HAROLD
Sometimes the action bursts ver the borders to give scale or impact.
MAR
The battle scenes are littered with the dismembered and twisted corpses of the slain, some being stripped of their armour by looters.
Ordinary people, as well as the high and mighty are shown here...
... building ships. Making food...
... or here – a woman and her child, victims of war escaping from a Saxon building that's being torched by the Norman invaders...
HIC
CEN DITVR:
T:CVM HAROLD
... or this unnamed serf being summarily executed, reminiscent of a famous example of Vietnam photojournalism by Eddie Adams...

...a connection I make in my graphic novel *The Adventures of Luther Arkwright*, by the way.

On sale in the foyer.

The Adventures of Luther Arkwright by Bryan Talbot

with an introduction by Michael Moorcock

Produced in England by a team of embroiderers, the pacing, the uniformity of art style and the consistency of structure show it to be the reproduction of an original draft drawing designed by a *single* artist...

...the anonymous first British comic artist... the beginning of *British Comic Strip history!*

⌐BUUURP!⌐

Eh, heh... sorry, squire!

Er, go on! What about these *Normans* then?

Cool!

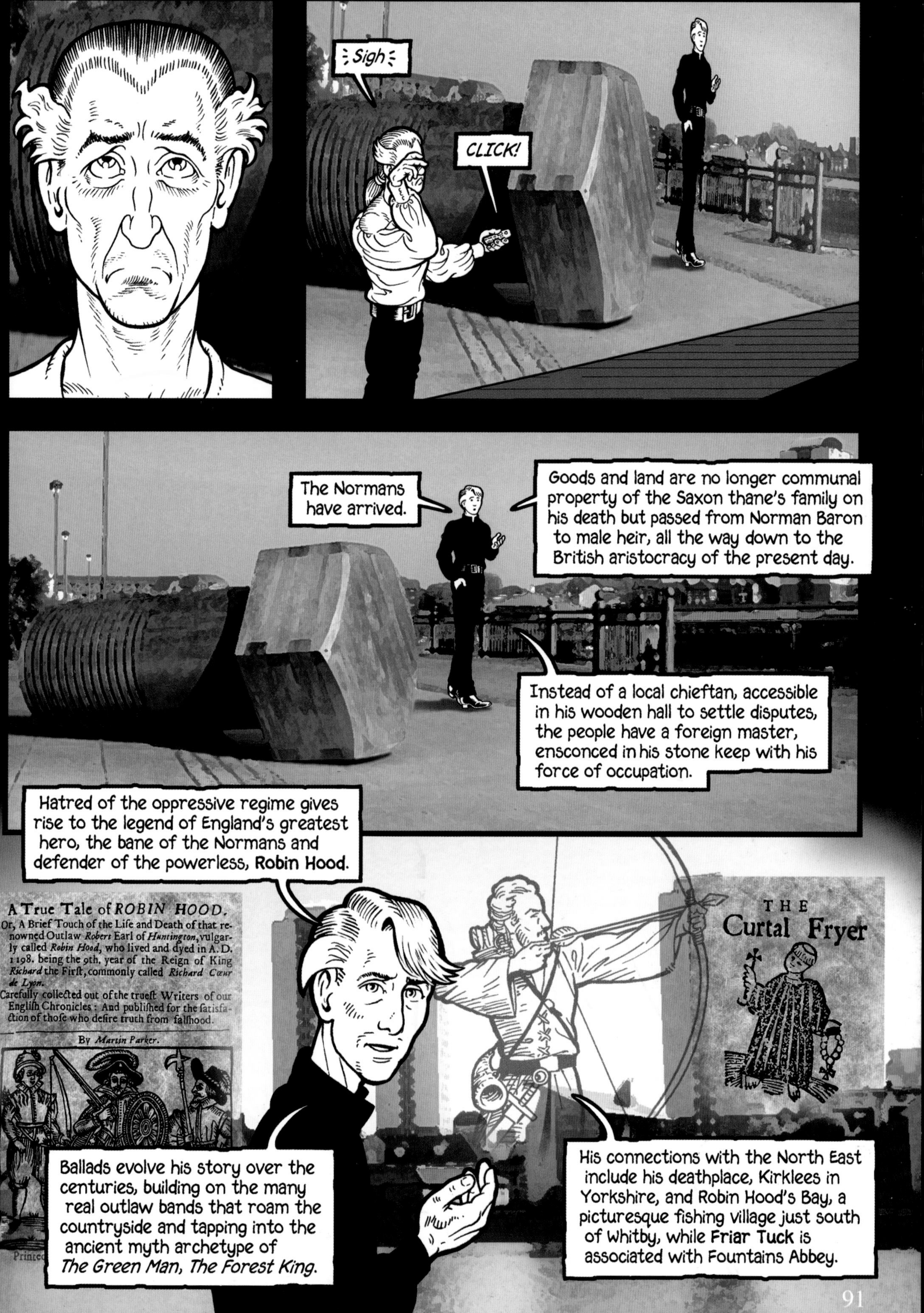

Sigh
CLICK!
The Normans have arrived.
Goods and land are no longer communal property of the Saxon thane's family on his death but passed from Norman Baron to male heir, all the way down to the British aristocracy of the present day.
Instead of a local chieftan, accessible in his wooden hall to settle disputes, the people have a foreign master, ensconced in his stone keep with his force of occupation.
Hatred of the oppressive regime gives rise to the legend of England's greatest hero, the bane of the Normans and defender of the powerless, **Robin Hood**.
A True Tale of ROBIN HOOD.
Or, A Brief Touch of the Life and Death of that renowned Outlaw Robert Earl of Huntington, vulgarly called Robin Hood, who lived and dyed in A. D. 1198. being the 9th. year of the Reign of King Richard the First, commonly called Richard Cœur de Lyon.
Carefully collected out of the truest Writers of our English Chronicles: And published for the satisfaction of those who desire truth from falshood.
By Martin Parker.
THE Curtal Fryer
Ballads evolve his story over the centuries, building on the many real outlaw bands that roam the countryside and tapping into the ancient myth archetype of *The Green Man, The Forest King*.
His connections with the North East include his deathplace, Kirklees in Yorkshire, and Robin Hood's Bay, a picturesque fishing village just south of Whitby, while **Friar Tuck** is associated with Fountains Abbey.

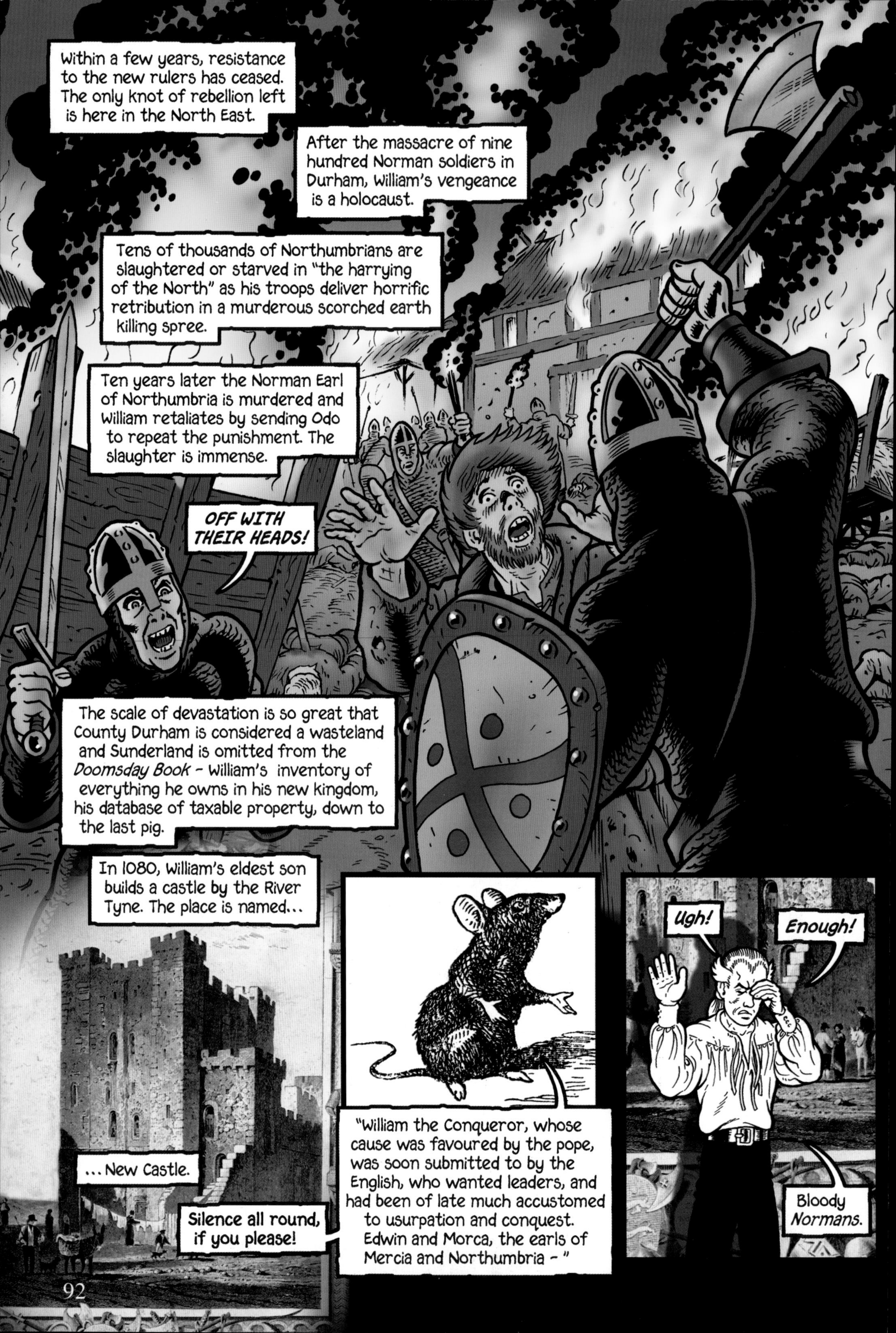
Within a few years, resistance to the new rulers has ceased. The only knot of rebellion left is here in the North East.
After the massacre of nine hundred Norman soldiers in Durham, William's vengeance is a holocaust.
Tens of thousands of Northumbrians are slaughtered or starved in "the harrying of the North" as his troops deliver horrific retribution in a murderous scorched earth killing spree.
Ten years later the Norman Earl of Northumbria is murdered and William retaliates by sending Odo to repeat the punishment. The slaughter is immense.
OFF WITH THEIR HEADS!
The scale of devastation is so great that County Durham is considered a wasteland and Sunderland is omitted from the *Doomsday Book* - William's inventory of everything he owns in his new kingdom, his database of taxable property, down to the last pig.
In 1080, William's eldest son builds a castle by the River Tyne. The place is named...
...New Castle.
Silence all round, if you please!
"William the Conqueror, whose cause was favoured by the pope, was soon submitted to by the English, who wanted leaders, and had been of late much accustomed to usurpation and conquest. Edwin and Morca, the earls of Mercia and Northumbria - "
Ugh!
Enough!
Bloody *Normans*.

I've no need to talk.

The Talbots are Norman. **Richard Talbot** is one of William's commanders. We're a pedigree breed.

A Talbot is mentioned in Chaucer's *Nun's Priest's Tale* and in the *St Crispin Day* speech in *Henry V* as a noble lineage.

The Earls of Shrewsbury are Talbots.

I still have the aristocratic conk.

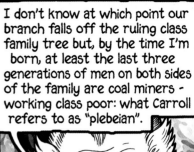

I don't know at which point our branch falls off the ruling class family tree but, by the time I'm born, at least the last three generations of men on both sides of the family are coal miners - working class poor: what Carroll refers to as "plebeian".

My Grandad is even a communist in the 30s. This is his party badge.

Hm. I should probably also point out that I'm not from Sunderland either. I've only lived here a few years...

Yeah, we know that, you great berk! You're from Wigan, you told us before.

Hey, pal, I met George Formby, y'know...

Look, can you shut up?

And stop pretending you're a cockney! It's a myth!

Me, fake?

It's an act! You're from South Africa! Now go away!

Okay, mush. Keep yer 'air on.

Blimey!

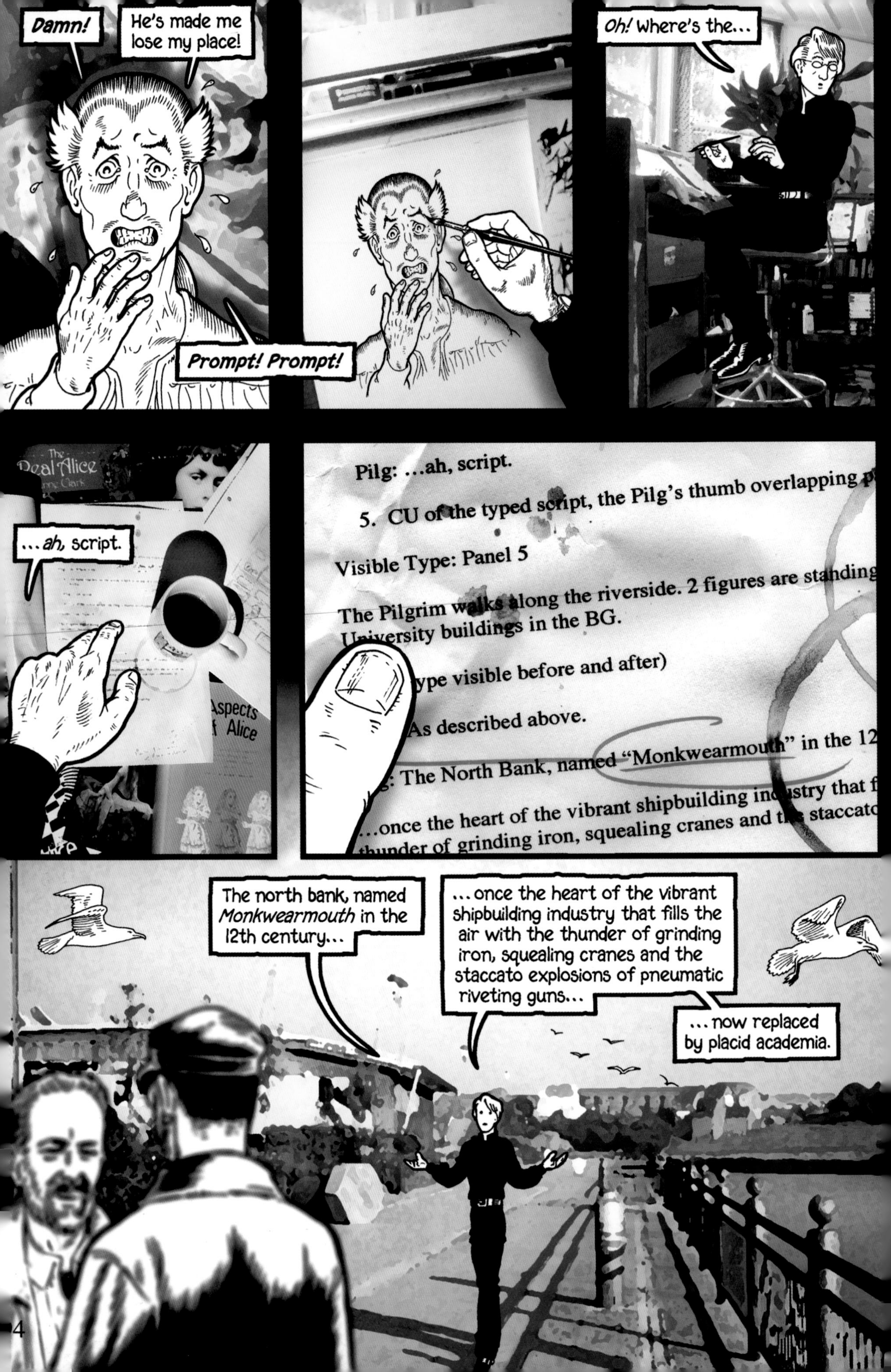

Damn!
He's made me lose my place!
Prompt! Prompt!
Oh! Where's the...
...ah, script.
Pilg: ...ah, script.
5. CU of the typed script, the Pilg's thumb overlapping
Visible Type: Panel 5
The Pilgrim walks along the riverside. 2 figures are standing
University buildings in the BG.
As described above.
The North Bank, named "Monkwearmouth" in the 12
...once the heart of the vibrant shipbuilding industry that f
thunder of grinding iron, squealing cranes and the staccato
The north bank, named *Monkwearmouth* in the 12th century...
...once the heart of the vibrant shipbuilding industry that fills the air with the thunder of grinding iron, squealing cranes and the staccato explosions of pneumatic riveting guns...
...now replaced by placid academia.

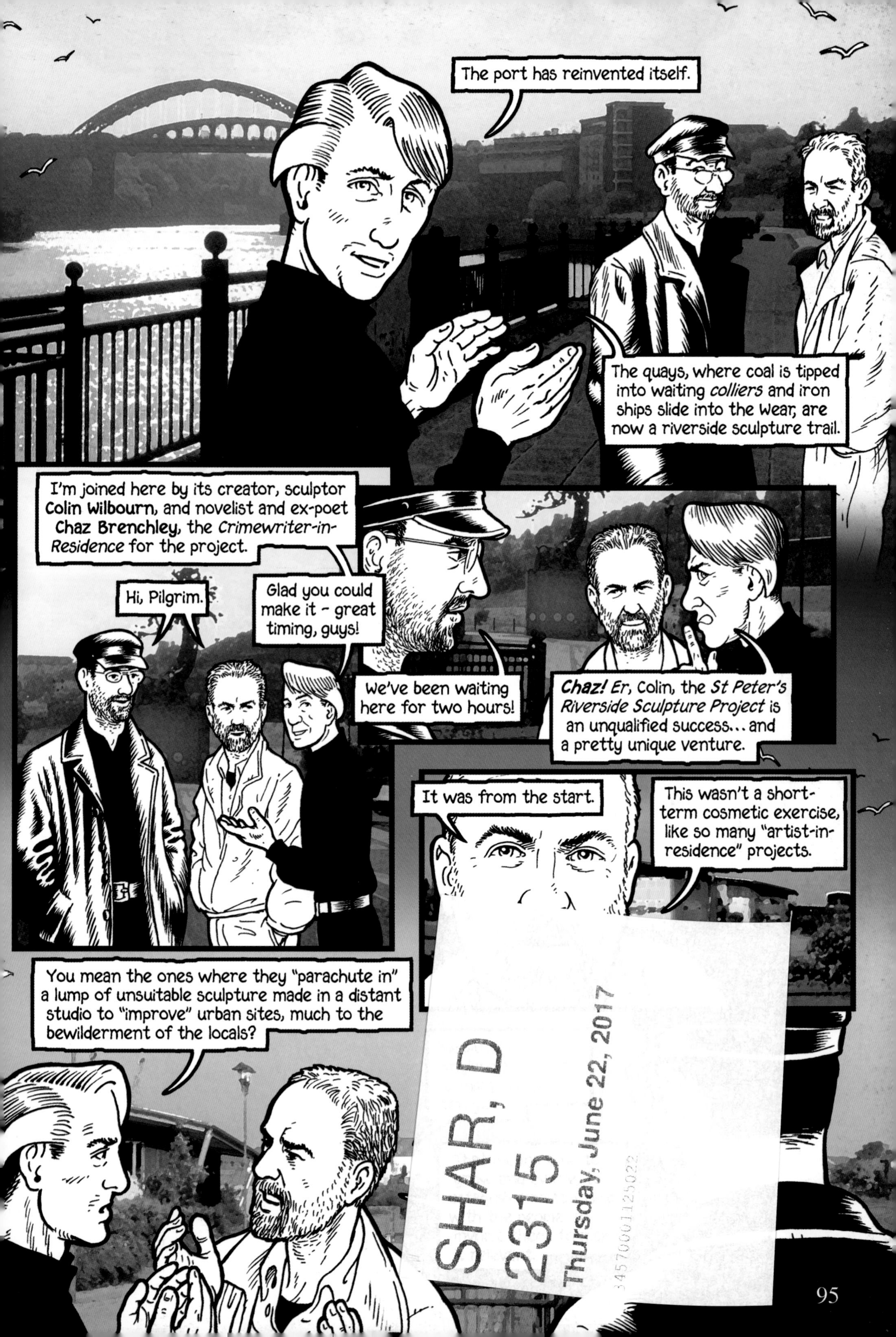
The port has reinvented itself.
The quays, where coal is tipped into waiting *colliers* and iron ships slide into the Wear, are now a riverside sculpture trail.
I'm joined here by its creator, sculptor **Colin Wilbourn**, and novelist and ex-poet **Chaz Brenchley**, the *Crimewriter-in-Residence* for the project.
Hi, Pilgrim.
Glad you could make it - great timing, guys!
We've been waiting here for two hours!
Chaz! *Er,* Colin, the *St Peter's Riverside Sculpture Project* is an unqualified success... and a pretty unique venture.
It was from the start.
This wasn't a short-term cosmetic exercise, like so many "artist-in-residence" projects.
You mean the ones where they "parachute in" a lump of unsuitable sculpture made in a distant studio to "improve" urban sites, much to the bewilderment of the locals?

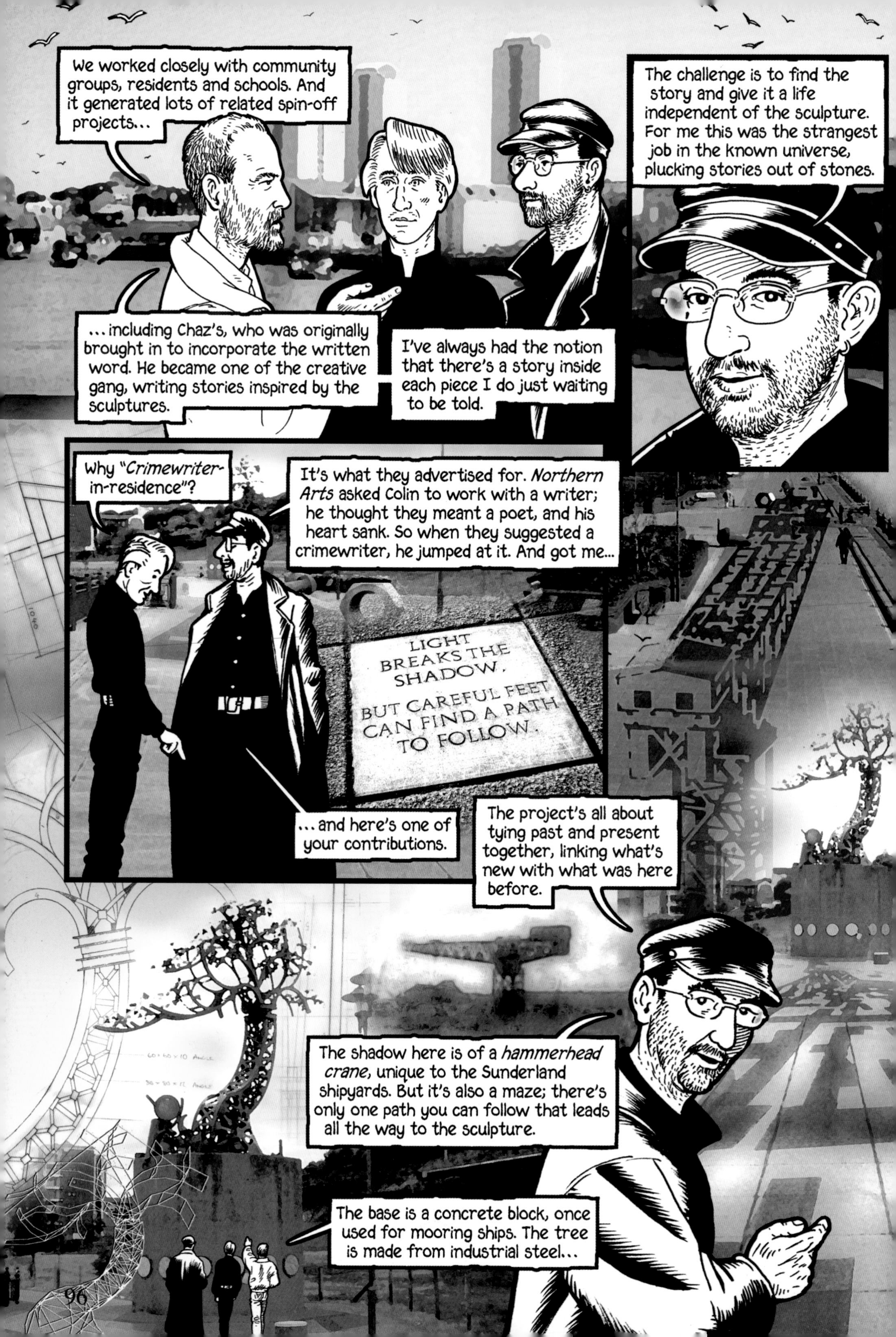

We worked closely with community groups, residents and schools. And it generated lots of related spin-off projects...
...including Chaz's, who was originally brought in to incorporate the written word. He became one of the creative gang, writing stories inspired by the sculptures.
I've always had the notion that there's a story inside each piece I do just waiting to be told.
The challenge is to find the story and give it a life independent of the sculpture. For me this was the strangest job in the known universe, plucking stories out of stones.
Why "Crimewriter-in-residence"?
It's what they advertised for. Northern Arts asked Colin to work with a writer; he thought they meant a poet, and his heart sank. So when they suggested a crimewriter, he jumped at it. And got me...
LIGHT BREAKS THE SHADOW, BUT CAREFUL FEET CAN FIND A PATH TO FOLLOW.
...and here's one of your contributions.
The project's all about tying past and present together, linking what's new with what was here before.
The shadow here is of a hammerhead crane, unique to the Sunderland shipyards. But it's also a maze; there's only one path you can follow that leads all the way to the sculpture.
The base is a concrete block, once used for mooring ships. The tree is made from industrial steel...

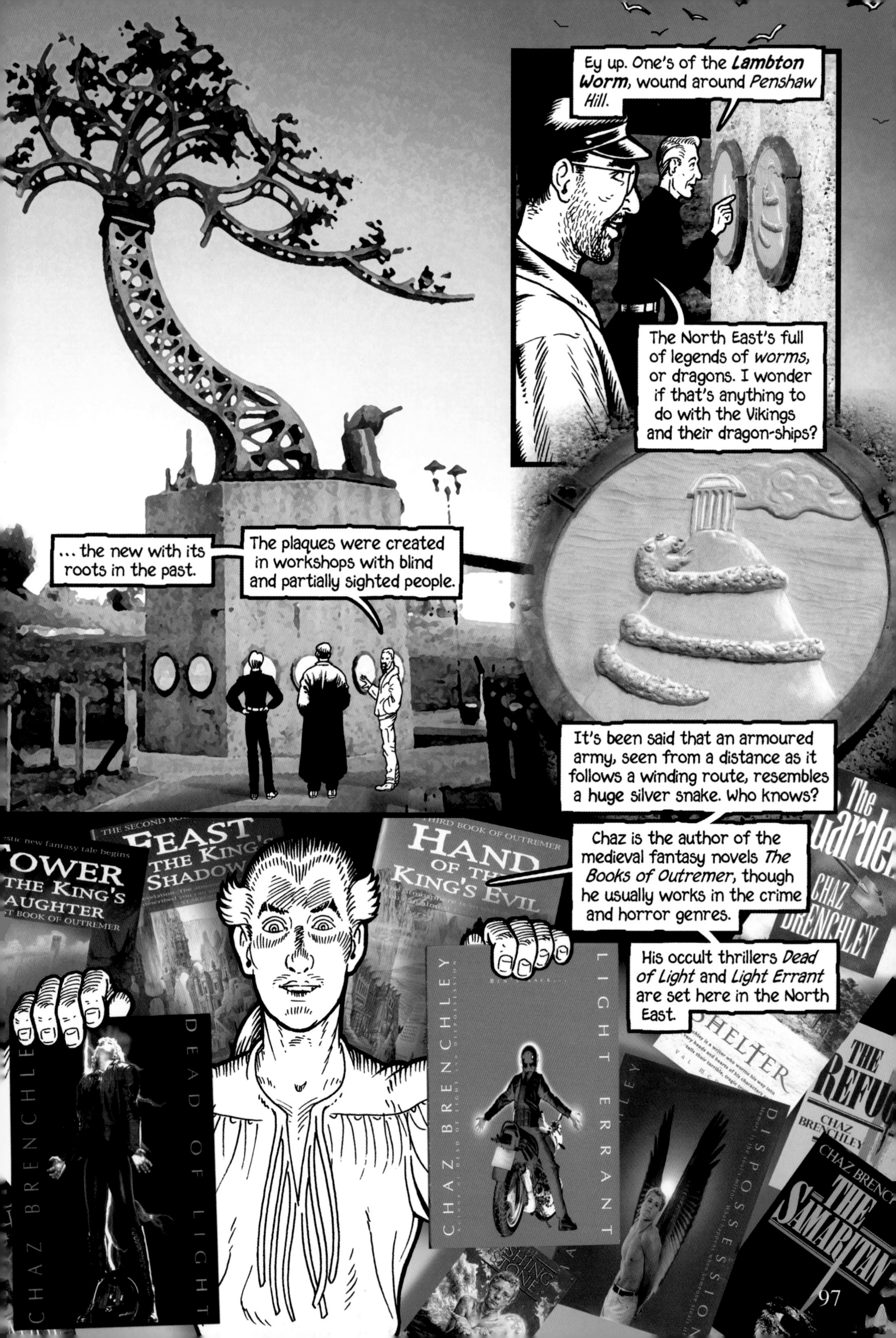
Ey up. One's of the **Lambton Worm**, wound around *Penshaw Hill*.
The North East's full of legends of *worms*, or dragons. I wonder if that's anything to do with the Vikings and their dragon-ships?
... the new with its roots in the past.
The plaques were created in workshops with blind and partially sighted people.
It's been said that an armoured army, seen from a distance as it follows a winding route, resembles a huge silver snake. Who knows?
Chaz is the author of the medieval fantasy novels *The Books of Outremer*, though he usually works in the crime and horror genres.
His occult thrillers *Dead of Light* and *Light Errant* are set here in the North East.
CHAZ BRENCHLEY
DEAD OF LIGHT
CHAZ BRENCHLEY
LIGHT ERRANT
DISPOSSESSION

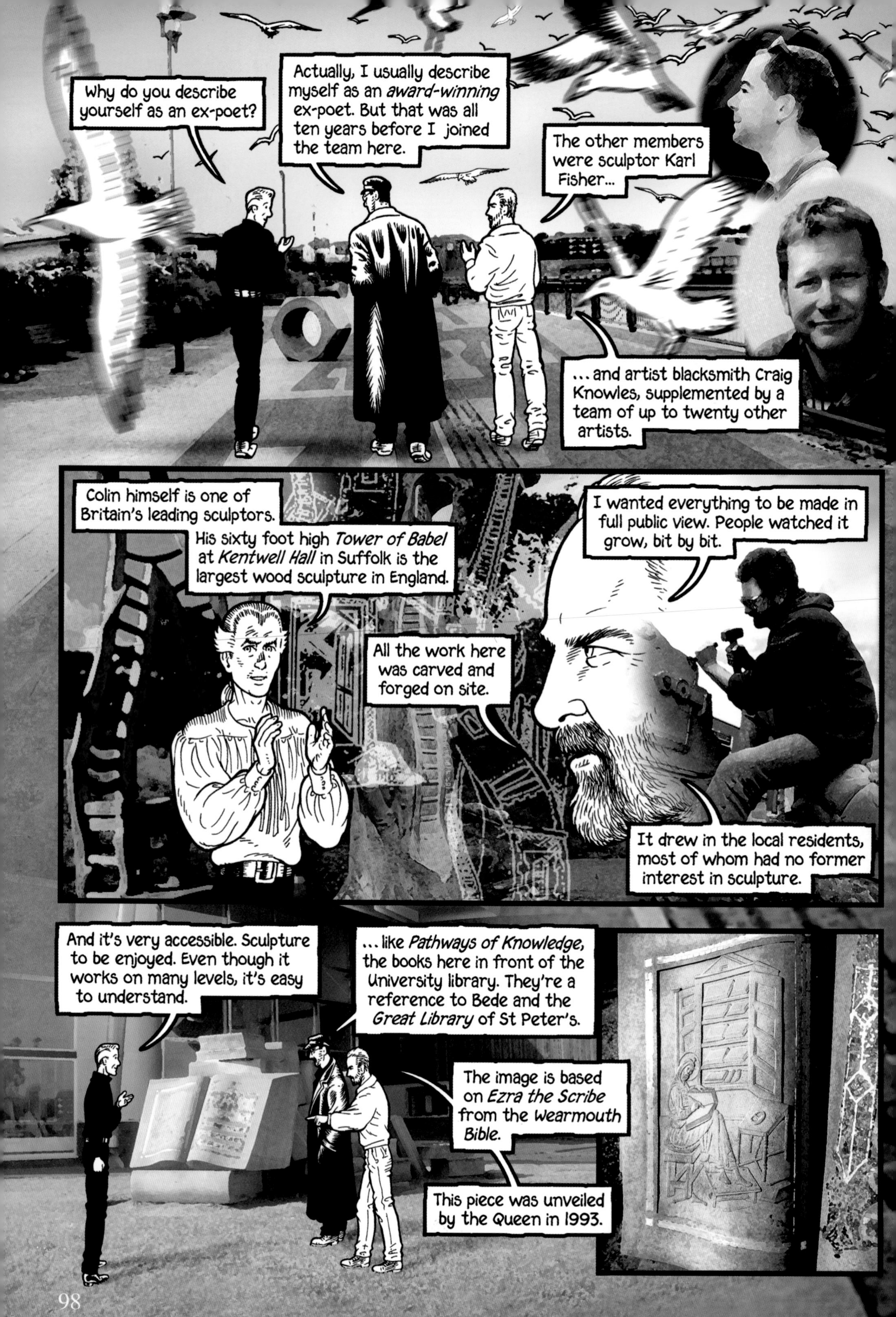
Why do you describe yourself as an ex-poet?
Actually, I usually describe myself as an *award-winning* ex-poet. But that was all ten years before I joined the team here.
The other members were sculptor Karl Fisher...
...and artist blacksmith Craig Knowles, supplemented by a team of up to twenty other artists.
Colin himself is one of Britain's leading sculptors.
His sixty foot high *Tower of Babel* at *Kentwell Hall* in Suffolk is the largest wood sculpture in England.
All the work here was carved and forged on site.
I wanted everything to be made in full public view. People watched it grow, bit by bit.
It drew in the local residents, most of whom had no former interest in sculpture.
And it's very accessible. Sculpture to be enjoyed. Even though it works on many levels, it's easy to understand.
...like *Pathways of Knowledge*, the books here in front of the University library. They're a reference to Bede and the *Great Library* of St Peter's.
The image is based on *Ezra the Scribe* from the Wearmouth Bible.
This piece was unveiled by the Queen in 1993.

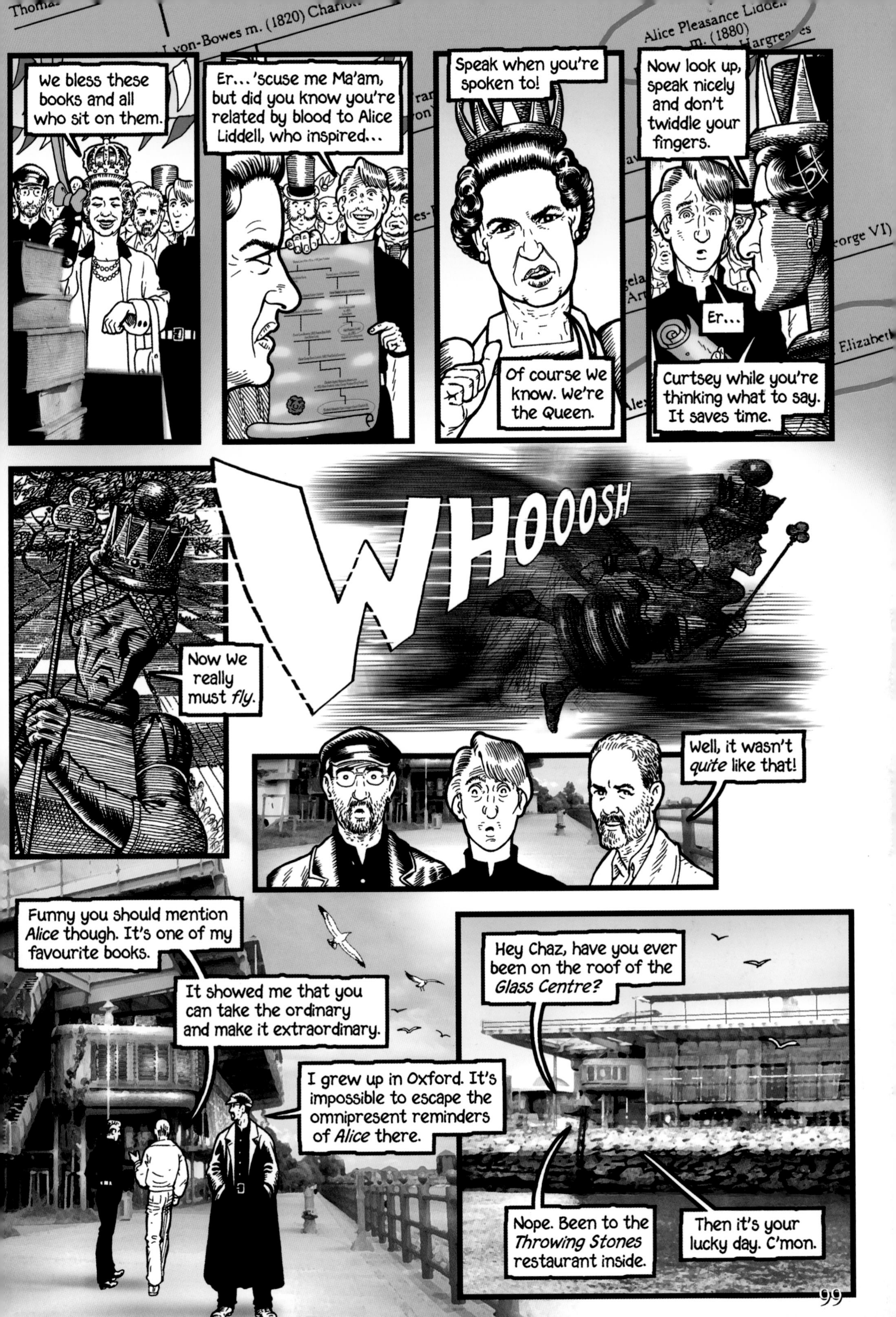

Thomas
Lyon-Bowes m. (1820) Charlotte
Alice Pleasance Liddell
m. (1880)
Hargreaves
We bless these books and all who sit on them.
Er...'scuse me Ma'am, but did you know you're related by blood to Alice Liddell, who inspired...
Speak when you're spoken to!
Of course We know. We're the Queen.
Now look up, speak nicely and don't twiddle your fingers.
Er...
Curtsey while you're thinking what to say. It saves time.
George VI)
Elizabeth
Now We really must *fly*.
WHOOOSH
Well, it wasn't *quite* like that!
Funny you should mention *Alice* though. It's one of my favourite books.
It showed me that you can take the ordinary and make it extraordinary.
I grew up in Oxford. It's impossible to escape the omnipresent reminders of *Alice* there.
Hey Chaz, have you ever been on the roof of the *Glass Centre?*
Nope. Been to the *Throwing Stones* restaurant inside.
Then it's your lucky day. C'mon.

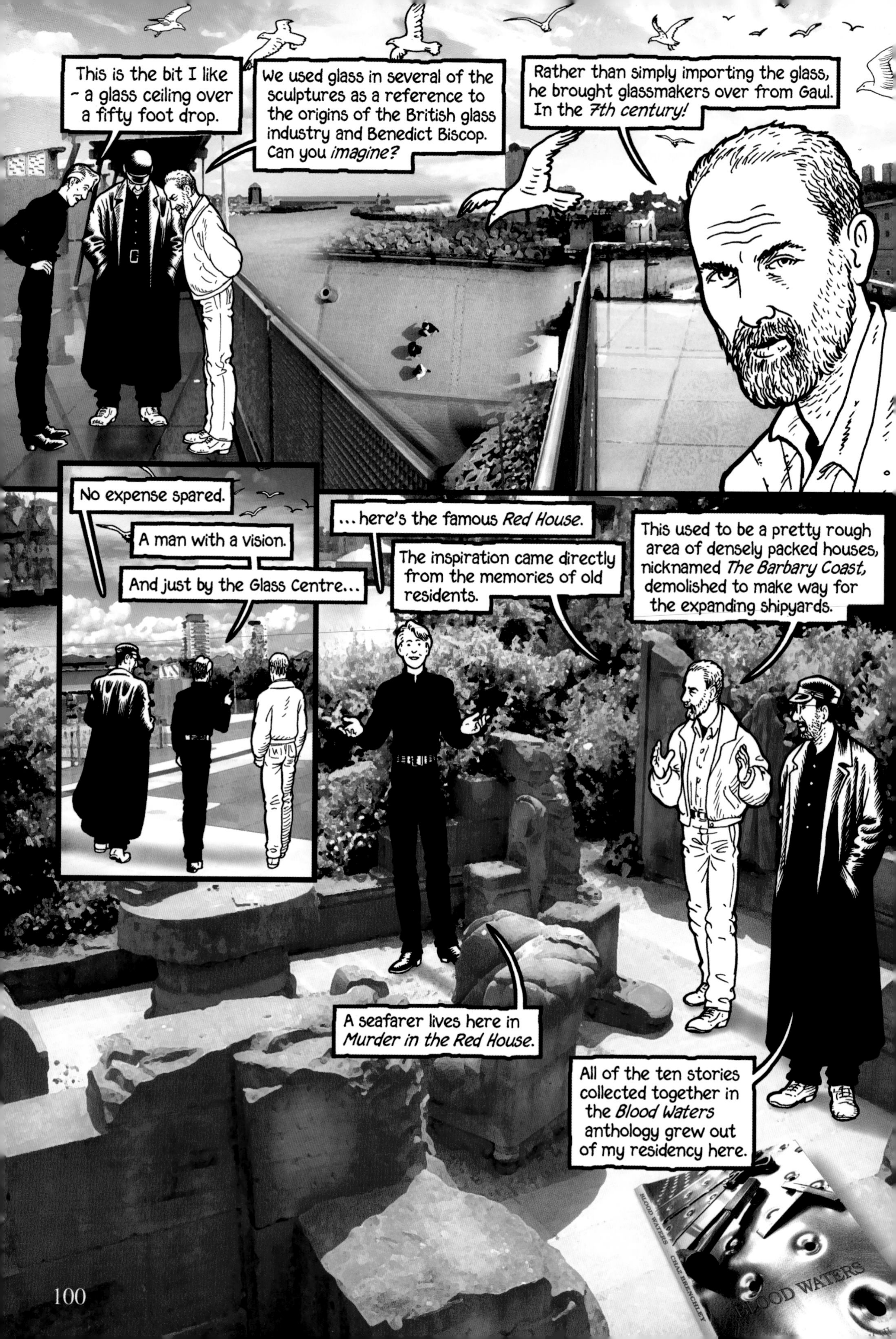
This is the bit I like – a glass ceiling over a fifty foot drop.
We used glass in several of the sculptures as a reference to the origins of the British glass industry and Benedict Biscop. Can you *imagine?*
Rather than simply importing the glass, he brought glassmakers over from Gaul. In the *7th century!*
No expense spared.
A man with a vision.
And just by the Glass Centre...
...here's the famous *Red House*.
The inspiration came directly from the memories of old residents.
This used to be a pretty rough area of densely packed houses, nicknamed *The Barbary Coast,* demolished to make way for the expanding shipyards.
A seafarer lives here in *Murder in the Red House*.
All of the ten stories collected together in the *Blood Waters* anthology grew out of my residency here.
BLOOD WATERS
CHAZ BRENCHLEY

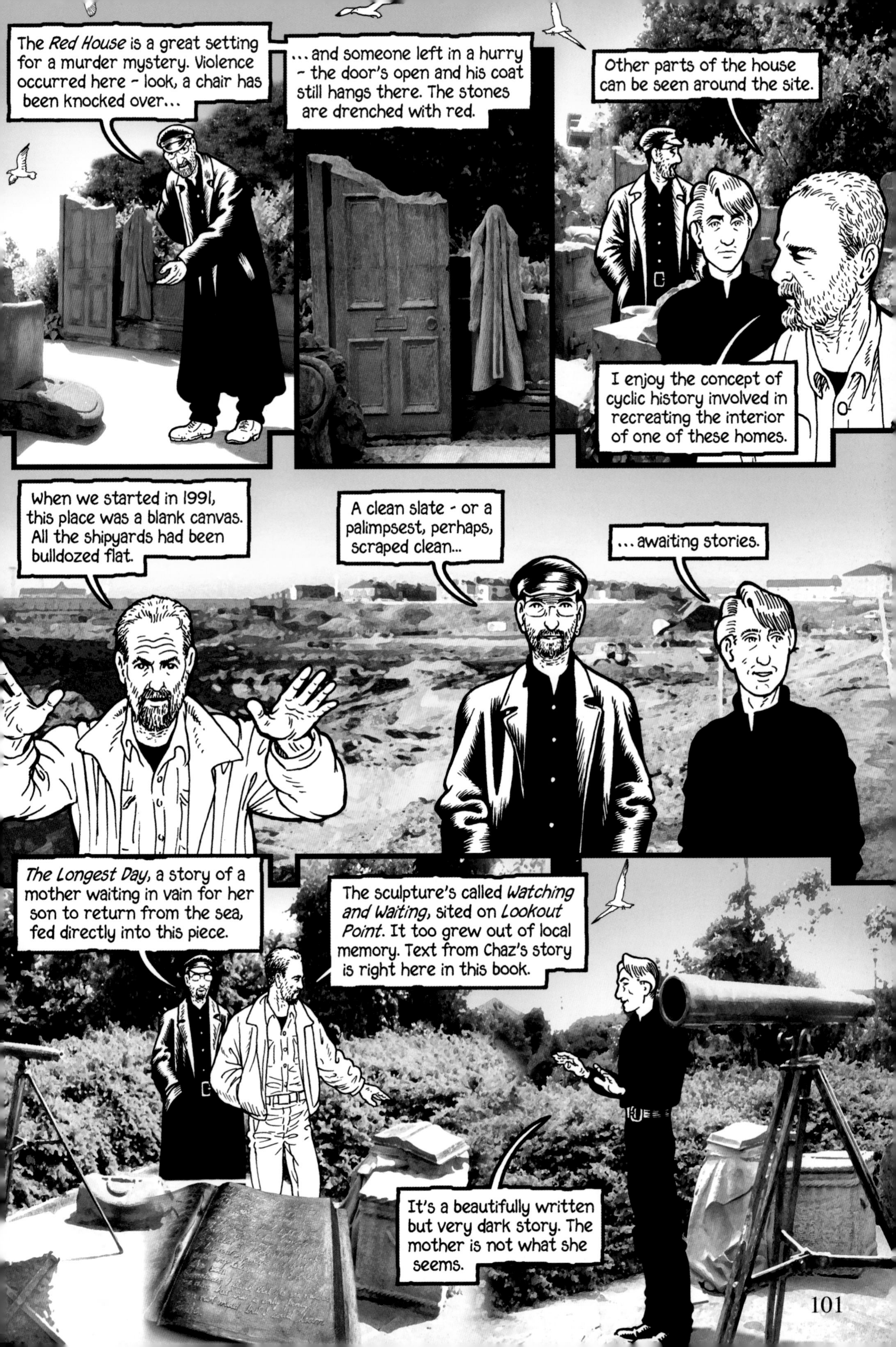
The *Red House* is a great setting for a murder mystery. Violence occurred here - look, a chair has been knocked over...
...and someone left in a hurry - the door's open and his coat still hangs there. The stones are drenched with red.
Other parts of the house can be seen around the site.
I enjoy the concept of cyclic history involved in recreating the interior of one of these homes.
When we started in 1991, this place was a blank canvas. All the shipyards had been bulldozed flat.
A clean slate - or a palimpsest, perhaps, scraped clean...
...awaiting stories.
The Longest Day, a story of a mother waiting in vain for her son to return from the sea, fed directly into this piece.
The sculpture's called *Watching and Waiting*, sited on *Lookout Point*. It too grew out of local memory. Text from Chaz's story is right here in this book.
It's a beautifully written but very dark story. The mother is not what she seems.

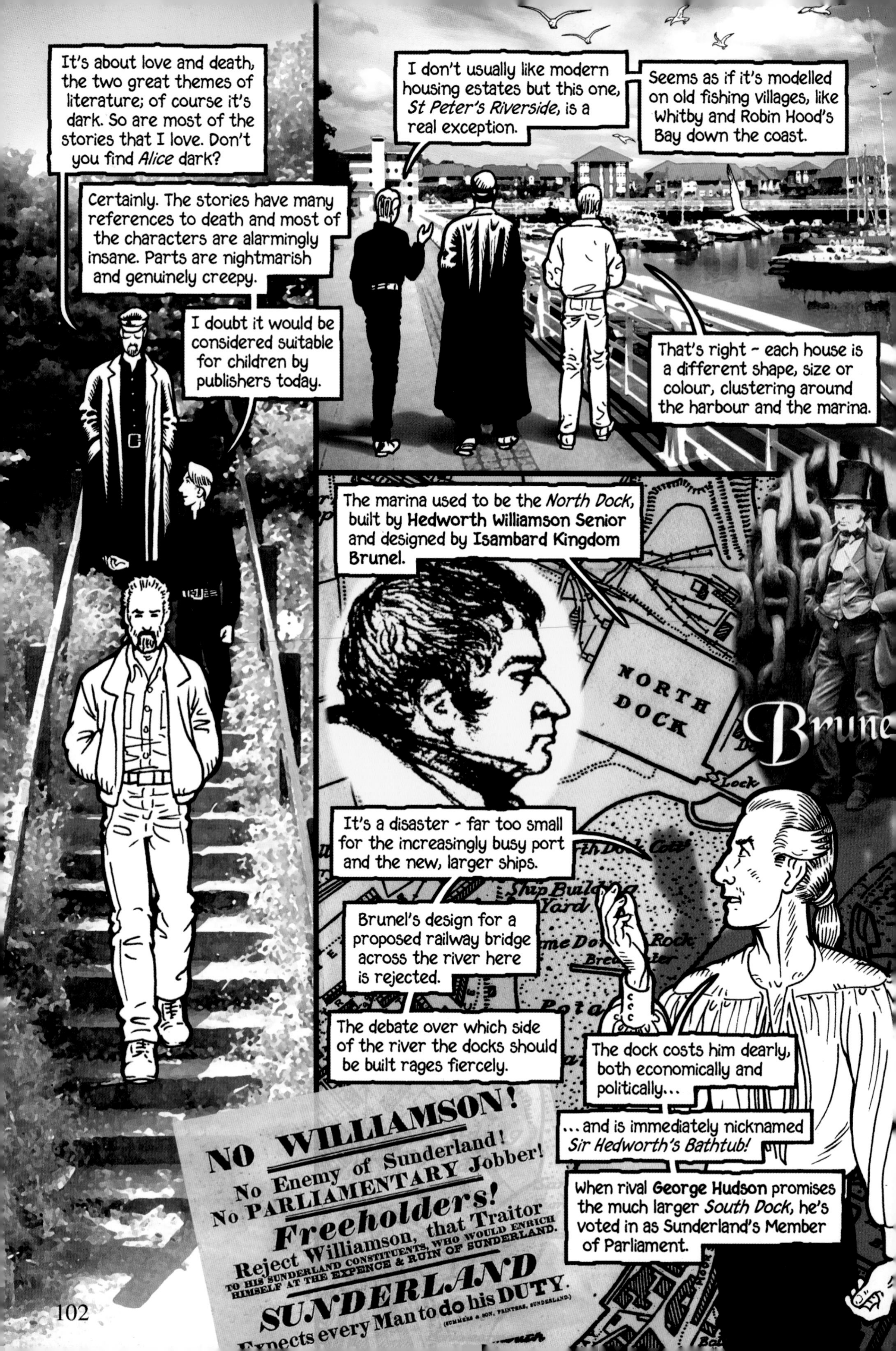
It's about love and death, the two great themes of literature; of course it's dark. So are most of the stories that I love. Don't you find *Alice* dark?
Certainly. The stories have many references to death and most of the characters are alarmingly insane. Parts are nightmarish and genuinely creepy.
I doubt it would be considered suitable for children by publishers today.
I don't usually like modern housing estates but this one, *St Peter's Riverside*, is a real exception.
Seems as if it's modelled on old fishing villages, like Whitby and Robin Hood's Bay down the coast.
That's right – each house is a different shape, size or colour, clustering around the harbour and the marina.
The marina used to be the *North Dock*, built by **Hedworth Williamson Senior** and designed by **Isambard Kingdom Brunel.**
NORTH DOCK
Lock
It's a disaster – far too small for the increasingly busy port and the new, larger ships.
Brunel's design for a proposed railway bridge across the river here is rejected.
The debate over which side of the river the docks should be built rages fiercely.
The dock costs him dearly, both economically and politically…
…and is immediately nicknamed *Sir Hedworth's Bathtub!*
When rival **George Hudson** promises the much larger *South Dock*, he's voted in as Sunderland's Member of Parliament.
NO WILLIAMSON!
No Enemy of Sunderland!
No PARLIAMENTARY Jobber!
Freeholders!
Reject Williamson, that Traitor
TO HIS SUNDERLAND CONSTITUENTS, WHO WOULD ENRICH HIMSELF AT THE EXPENCE & RUIN OF SUNDERLAND.
SUNDERLAND
Expects every Man to do his DUTY.
(SUMMERS & SON, PRINTERS, SUNDERLAND.)

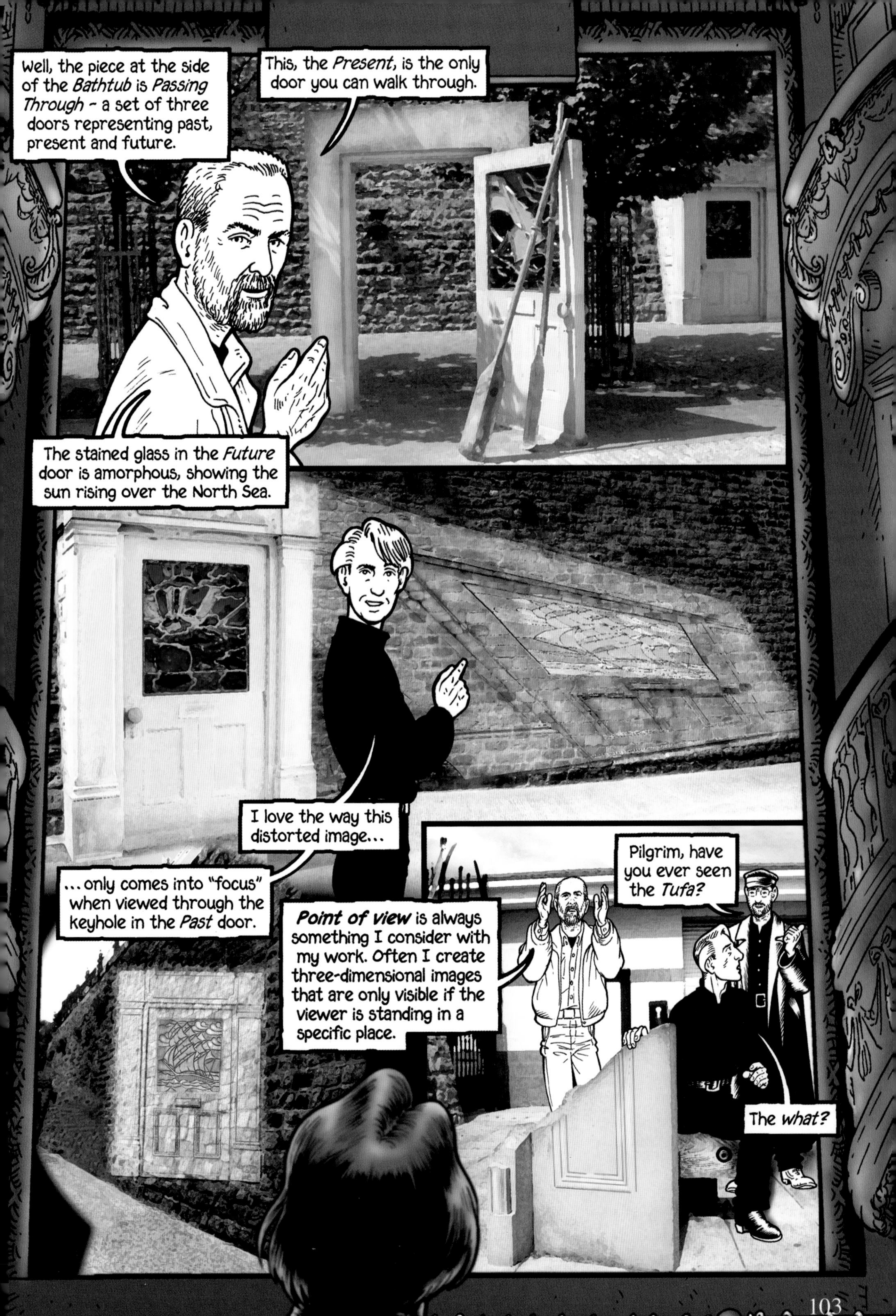
Well, the piece at the side of the *Bathtub* is *Passing Through* - a set of three doors representing past, present and future.
This, the *Present*, is the only door you can walk through.
The stained glass in the *Future* door is amorphous, showing the sun rising over the North Sea.
I love the way this distorted image...
...only comes into "focus" when viewed through the keyhole in the *Past* door.
Point of view is always something I consider with my work. Often I create three-dimensional images that are only visible if the viewer is standing in a specific place.
Pilgrim, have you ever seen the *Tufa?*
The *what?*

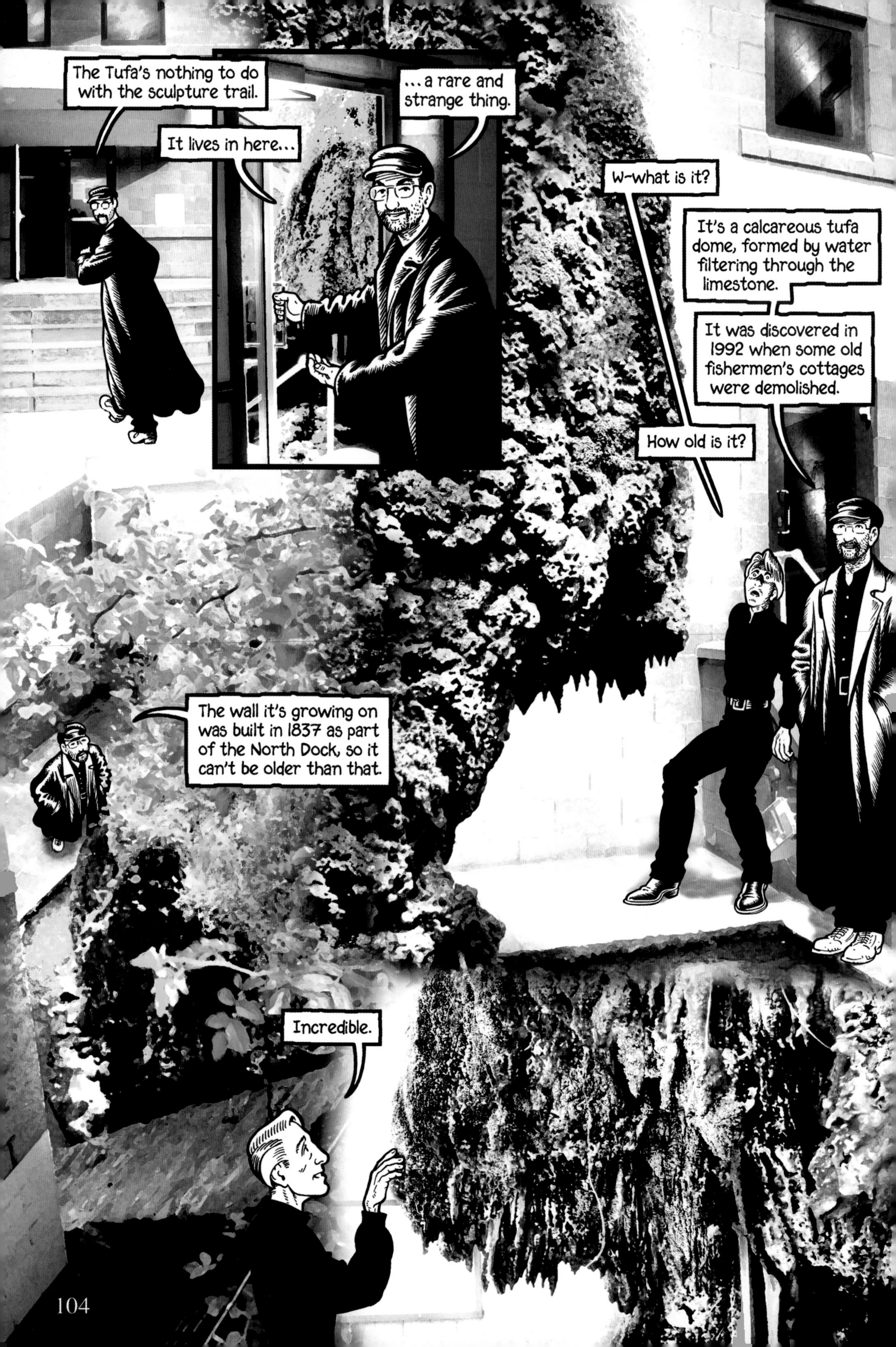
The Tufa's nothing to do with the sculpture trail.
It lives in here...
...a rare and strange thing.
W-what is it?
It's a calcareous tufa dome, formed by water filtering through the limestone.
It was discovered in 1992 when some old fishermen's cottages were demolished.
How old is it?
The wall it's growing on was built in 1837 as part of the North Dock, so it can't be older than that.
Incredible.

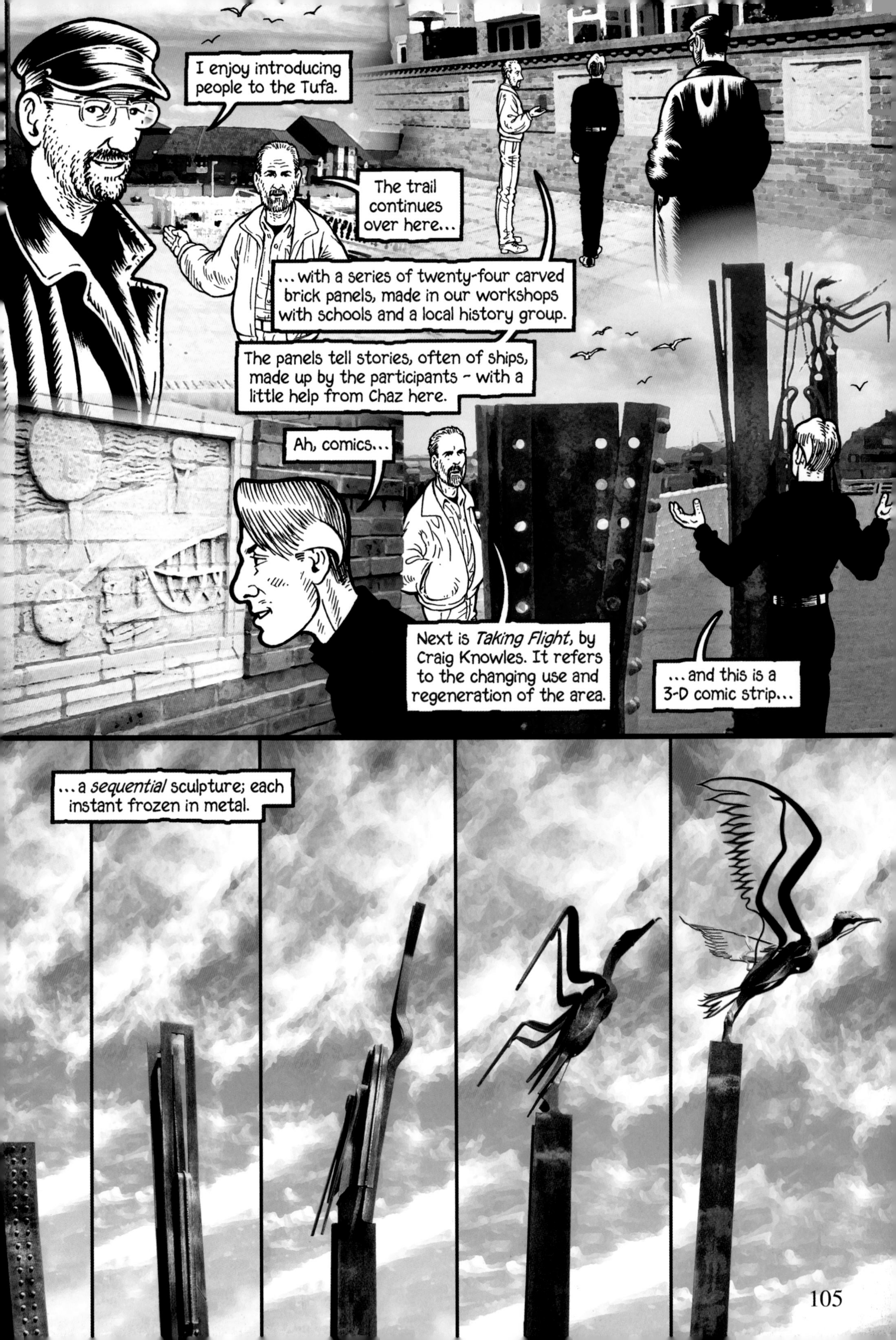

I enjoy introducing people to the Tufa.
The trail continues over here...
...with a series of twenty-four carved brick panels, made in our workshops with schools and a local history group.
The panels tell stories, often of ships, made up by the participants - with a little help from Chaz here.
Ah, comics...
Next is *Taking Flight*, by Craig Knowles. It refers to the changing use and regeneration of the area.
...and this is a 3-D comic strip...
...a *sequential* sculpture; each instant frozen in metal.

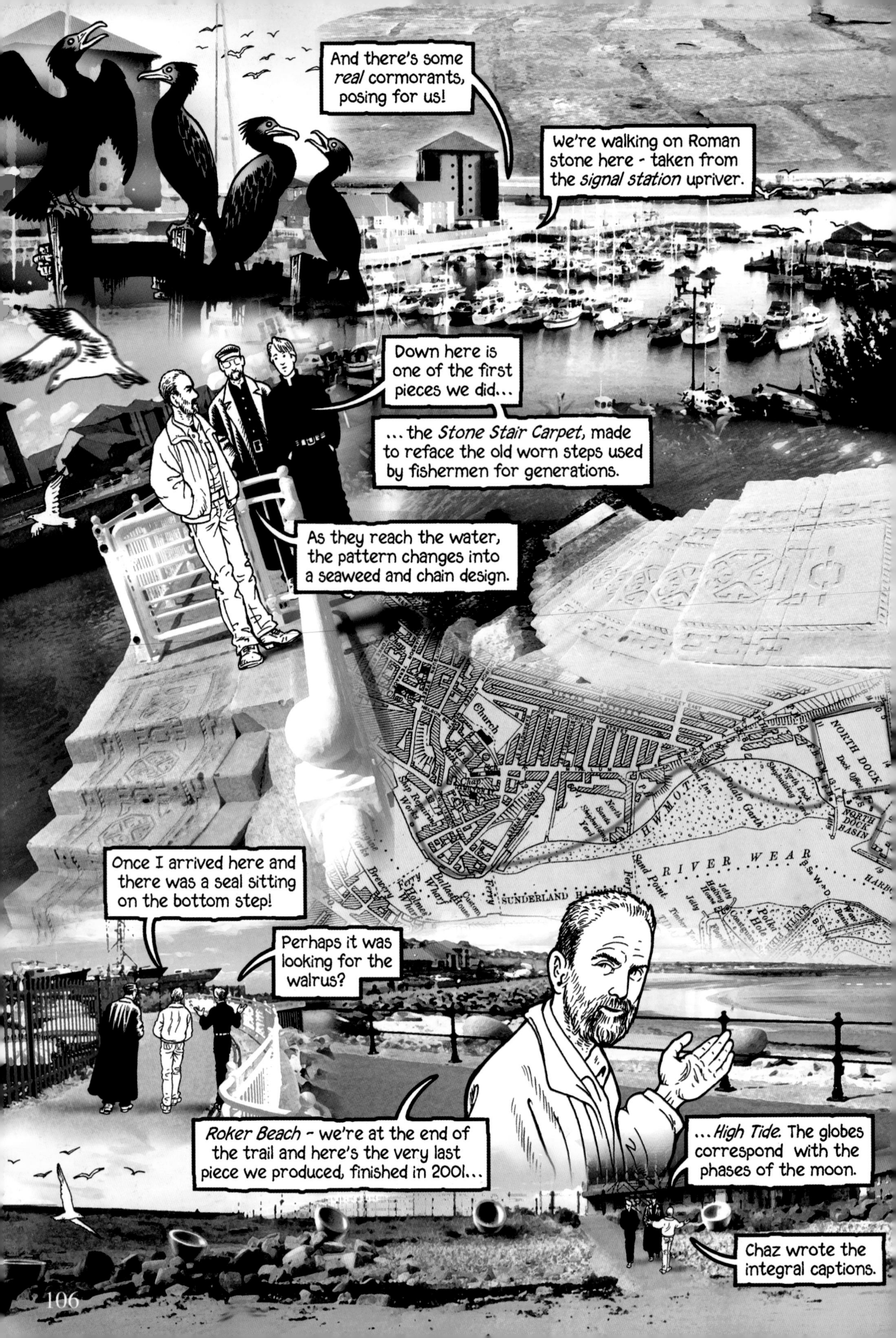
And there's some *real* cormorants, posing for us!
We're walking on Roman stone here - taken from the *signal station* upriver.
Down here is one of the first pieces we did...
...the *Stone Stair Carpet*, made to reface the old worn steps used by fishermen for generations.
As they reach the water, the pattern changes into a seaweed and chain design.
Church
NORTH DOCK
NORTH DOCK BASIN
RIVER WEAR
Once I arrived here and there was a seal sitting on the bottom step!
Perhaps it was looking for the walrus?
Roker Beach - we're at the end of the trail and here's the very last piece we produced, finished in 2001...
...*High Tide*. The globes correspond with the phases of the moon.
Chaz wrote the integral captions.

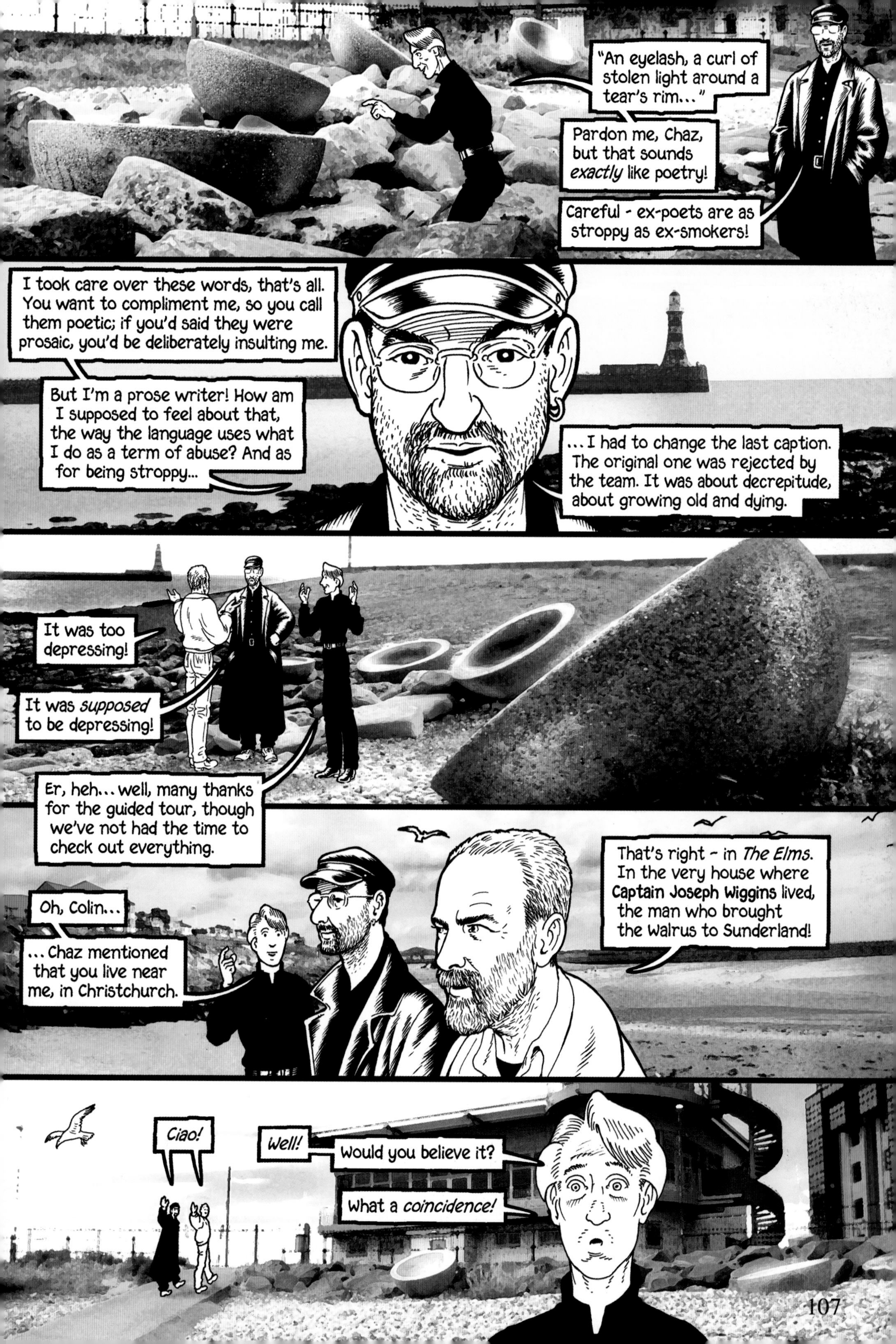
"An eyelash, a curl of stolen light around a tear's rim..."
Pardon me, Chaz, but that sounds *exactly* like poetry!
Careful - ex-poets are as stroppy as ex-smokers!
I took care over these words, that's all. You want to compliment me, so you call them poetic; if you'd said they were prosaic, you'd be deliberately insulting me.
But I'm a prose writer! How am I supposed to feel about that, the way the language uses what I do as a term of abuse? And as for being stroppy...
...I had to change the last caption. The original one was rejected by the team. It was about decrepitude, about growing old and dying.
It was too depressing!
It was *supposed* to be depressing!
Er, heh... well, many thanks for the guided tour, though we've not had the time to check out everything.
Oh, Colin...
...Chaz mentioned that you live near me, in Christchurch.
That's right - in *The Elms*. In the very house where **Captain Joseph Wiggins** lived, the man who brought the Walrus to Sunderland!
Ciao!
Well!
Would you believe it?
What a *coincidence!*

SIR HENRY IRVING'S MANAGER TALKS
OF PLAYS, BOOKS, PICTURES AN

Bram Stoker Visible But Thirty Minutes ... Day, But
Accomplishes Wonders.

HE ...CUSSES ...Y LOFTUS AND ELLEN TERRY

Oh, look – there's Henry Irving...

... the first actor to be knighted for his services to theatre.

He learns the lines for his very first stage appearance – at the *Lyceum*, here in Sunderland – walking on this beach in 1856.

Lewis Carroll, an avid lover of the theatre, is a great fan of his and sees him perform many times.

Irving returns here forty-eight years later on his farewell tour, accompanied by Bram Stoker who bases the look of *Dracula* on him.

Irving collapses and dies later in the tour.

Above the beach is a monument to Bede...

...and beyond is something unique, "the Cathedral of the *Arts and Crafts Movement*", *St Andrew's Church.*

It's incredible.

The story that its nave is meant to represent the inside of an overturned boat is a myth created by local tourist literature.

But just look at *this!*

AVENUE THEATR.
And Opera House, Sunderland.
TELEPHONE NO. 680.
Proprietors ... SUNDERLAND THEATRES LIMITED
Managing Director ... Mr. CHAS. E. MACK
Business Manager ... Mr. PERCIVAL GRA
WEDNESDAY, OCTOBER 26th. LAST PERFORMANCE
'MRS. DANE'S DEFENCE.'
THURSDAY, OCT. 27, 28 & 2
FOR 3 NIGHTS AND MATINEE SATURDAY.
FAREWELL
VISIT OF
HENRY
IRVING
AND HIS COMPANY. (Previous to his Retirement from the Stage).
THURSDAY NIGHT, OCT. 27th.
AND SATURDAY MATINEE, OCT. 29th.
THE MERCHANT OF VENICE
Shylock ... HENRY IRV
FRIDAY NIGHT, OCT. 28th.
BECKET
By ALFRED LORD TENNYSON. Adapted for the stage by HENRY IRVI
Becket (Chancellor and Archbishop) ... HENRY IR
SATURDAY NIGHT, OCT. 29th.
WATERLOO
Corporal Brewster ... HENRY IRVING
(FAREWELL PERFORMANCE)
THE BELL

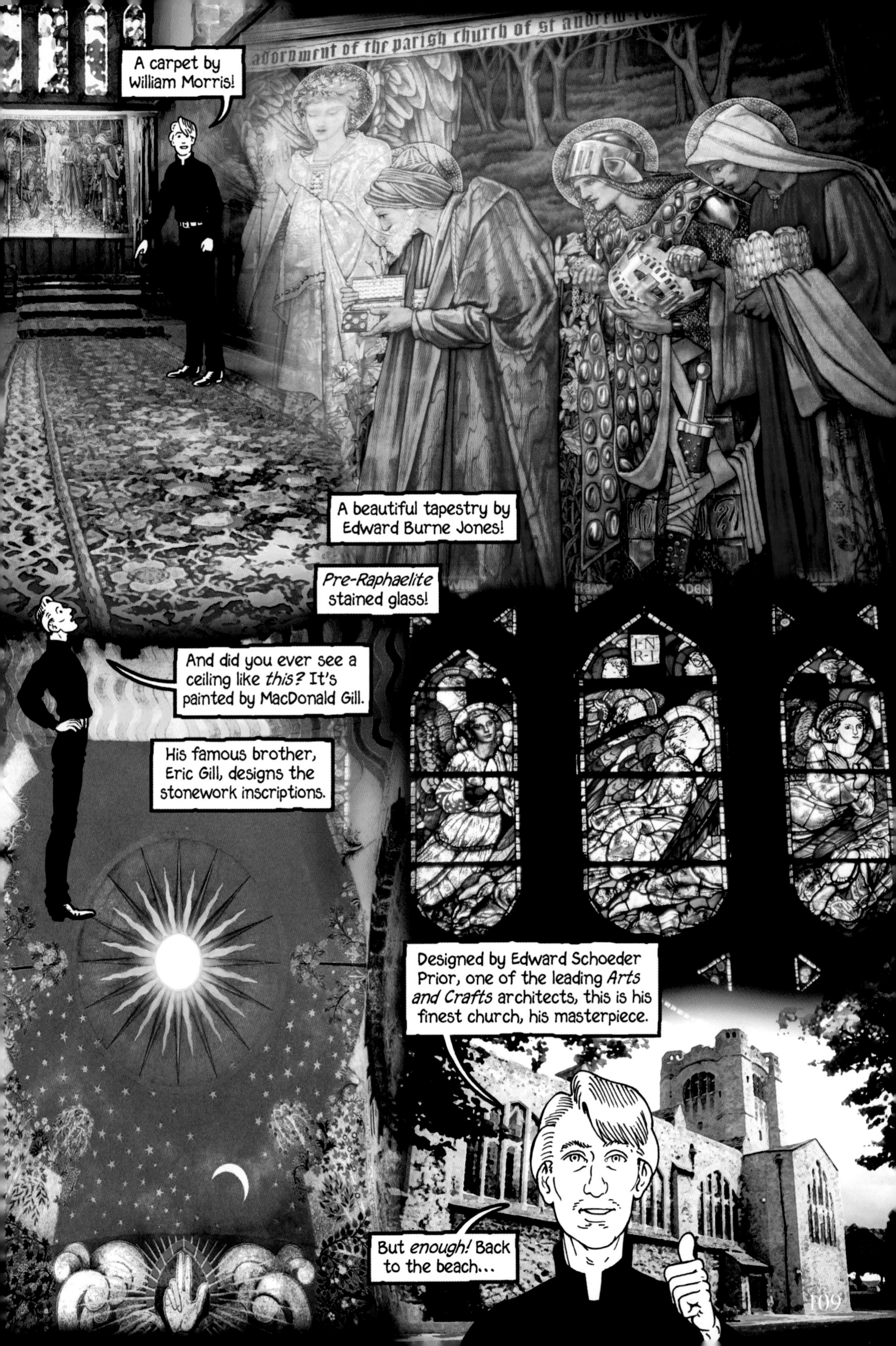
adornment of the parish church of st
A carpet by William Morris!
A beautiful tapestry by Edward Burne Jones!
Pre-Raphaelite stained glass!
And did you ever see a ceiling like *this?* It's painted by MacDonald Gill.
His famous brother, Eric Gill, designs the stonework inscriptions.
I·N R·I
Designed by Edward Schoeder Prior, one of the leading *Arts and Crafts* architects, this is his finest church, his masterpiece.
But *enough!* Back to the beach...

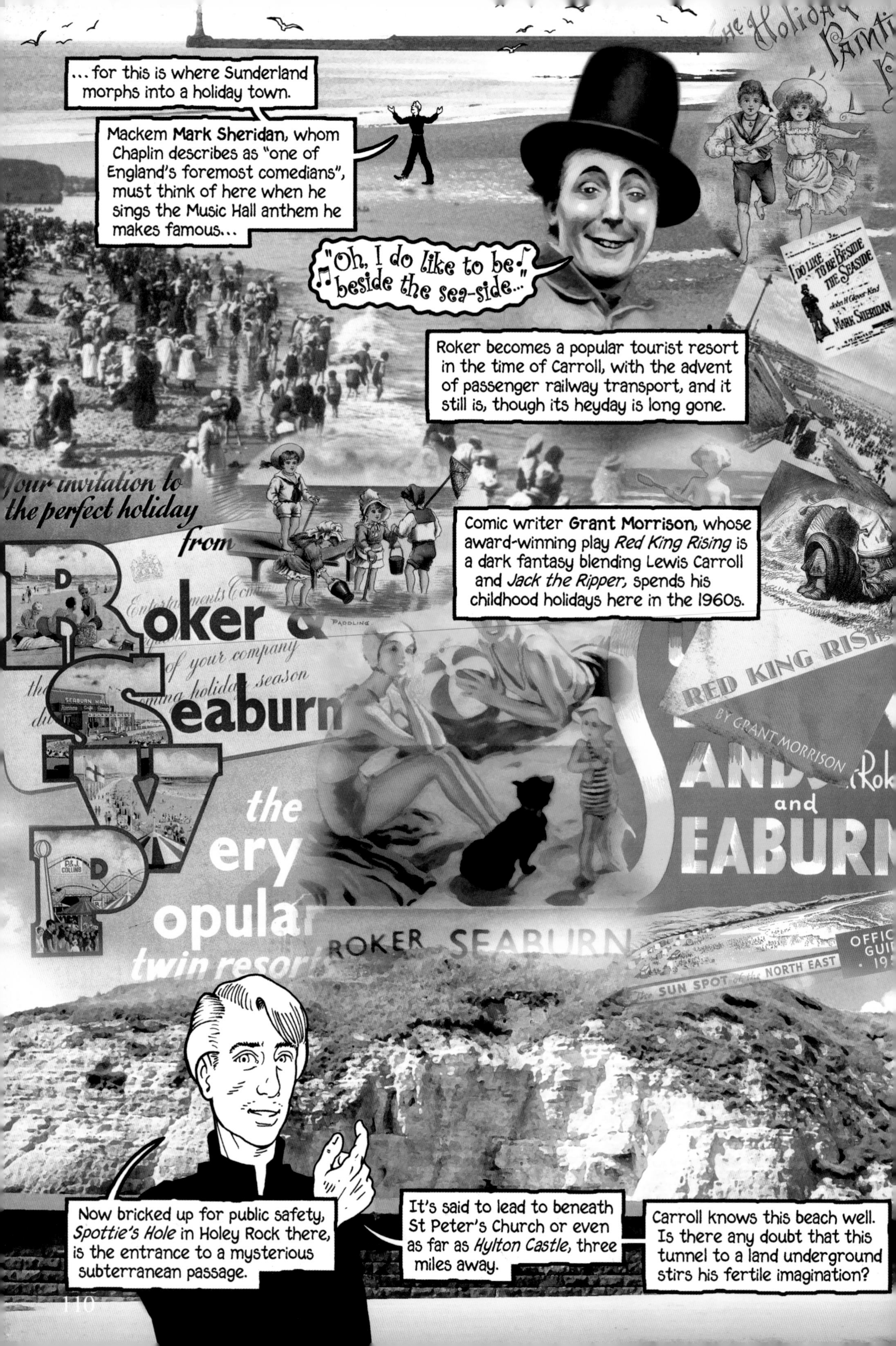

... for this is where Sunderland morphs into a holiday town.
Mackem **Mark Sheridan**, whom Chaplin describes as "one of England's foremost comedians", must think of here when he sings the Music Hall anthem he makes famous...
"Oh, I do like to be beside the sea-side..."
I DO LIKE TO BE BESIDE THE SEASIDE
MARK SHERIDAN
Roker becomes a popular tourist resort in the time of Carroll, with the advent of passenger railway transport, and it still is, though its heyday is long gone.
Your invitation to the perfect holiday from Roker & Seaburn
PADDLING
Comic writer **Grant Morrison**, whose award-winning play *Red King Rising* is a dark fantasy blending Lewis Carroll and *Jack the Ripper*, spends his childhood holidays here in the 1960s.
RED KING RIS
BY GRANT MORRISON
and
SEABURN HALL
the Very Popular twin resorts
ROKER SEABURN
The SUN SPOT of the NORTH EAST
Now bricked up for public safety, *Spottie's Hole* in Holey Rock there, is the entrance to a mysterious subterranean passage.
It's said to lead to beneath St Peter's Church or even as far as *Hylton Castle*, three miles away.
Carroll knows this beach well. Is there any doubt that this tunnel to a land underground stirs his fertile imagination?

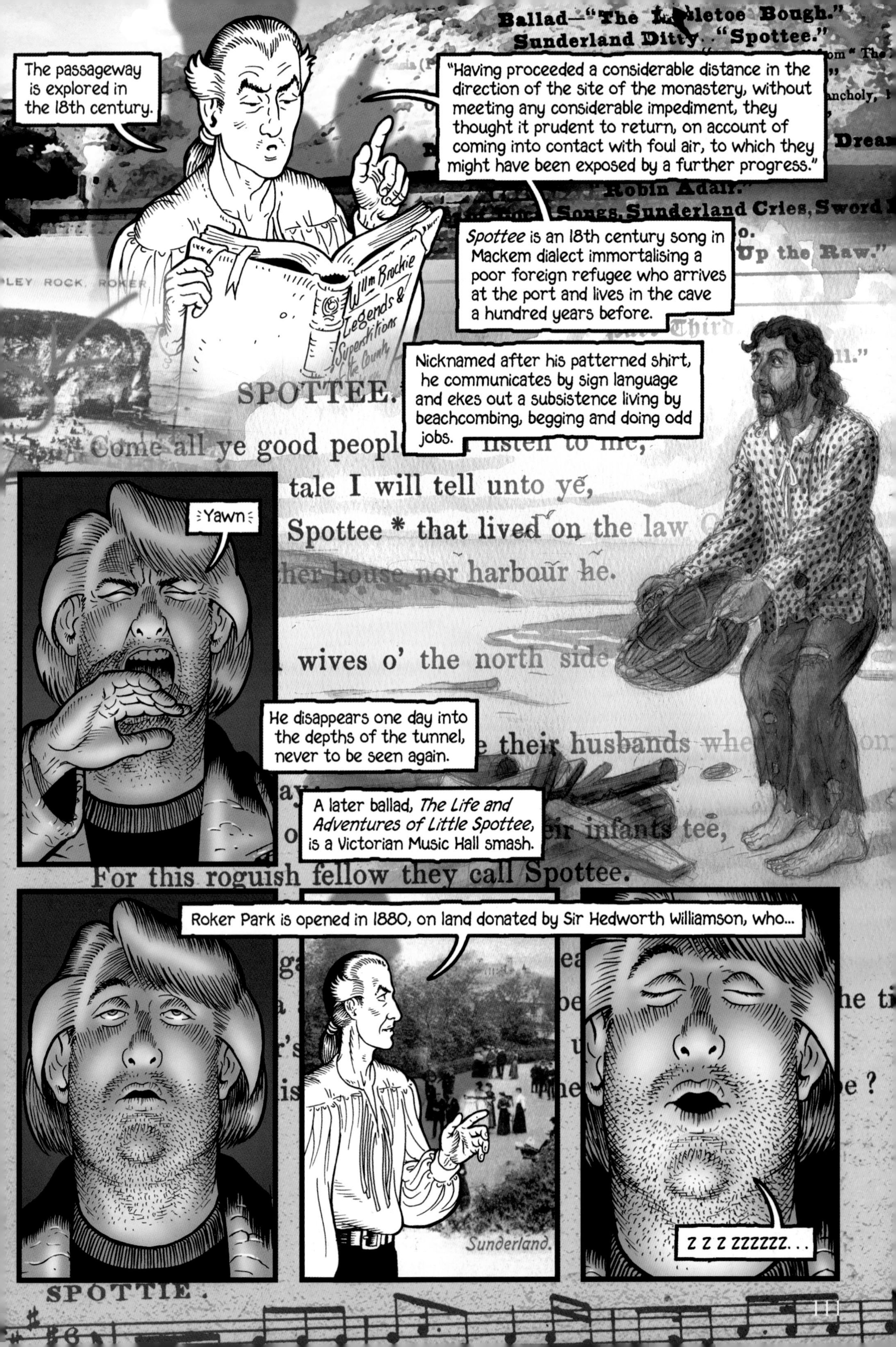
The passageway is explored in the 18th century.
"Having proceeded a considerable distance in the direction of the site of the monastery, without meeting any considerable impediment, they thought it prudent to return, on account of coming into contact with foul air, to which they might have been exposed by a further progress."
Spottee is an 18th century song in Mackem dialect immortalising a poor foreign refugee who arrives at the port and lives in the cave a hundred years before.
Nicknamed after his patterned shirt, he communicates by sign language and ekes out a subsistence living by beachcombing, begging and doing odd jobs.
Yawn
He disappears one day into the depths of the tunnel, never to be seen again.
A later ballad, The Life and Adventures of Little Spottee, is a Victorian Music Hall smash.
Roker Park is opened in 1880, on land donated by Sir Hedworth Williamson, who...
Sunderland.
Z Z Z ZZZZZZ. . .
SPOTTEE.
Come all ye good people
tale I will tell unto ye,
Spottee * that lived on the law
her house nor harbour he.
wives o' the north side
their husbands whe
their infants tee,
For this roguish fellow they call Spottee.
Ballad—"The Mistletoe Bough."
Sunderland Ditty . "Spottee."
Robin Adair."
Songs, Sunderland Cries, Sword
"Up the Raw."
SPOTTIE.

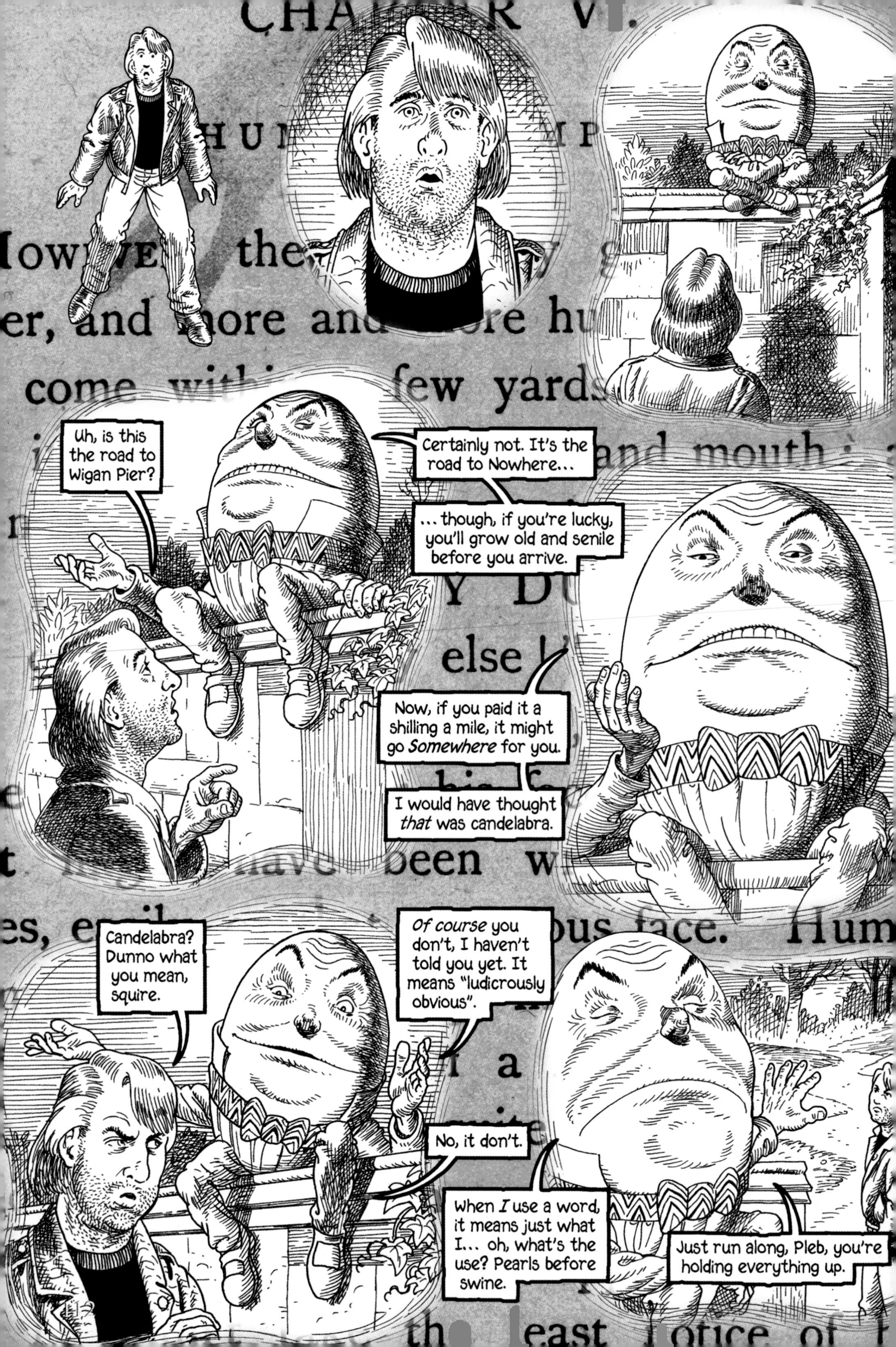
Uh, is this the road to Wigan Pier?
Certainly not. It's the road to Nowhere...
... though, if you're lucky, you'll grow old and senile before you arrive.
Now, if you paid it a shilling a mile, it might go *Somewhere* for you.
I would have thought *that* was candelabra.
Candelabra? Dunno what you mean, squire.
Of course you don't, I haven't told you yet. It means "ludicrously obvious".
No, it don't.
When *I* use a word, it means just what I... oh, what's the use? Pearls before swine.
Just run along, Pleb, you're holding everything up.

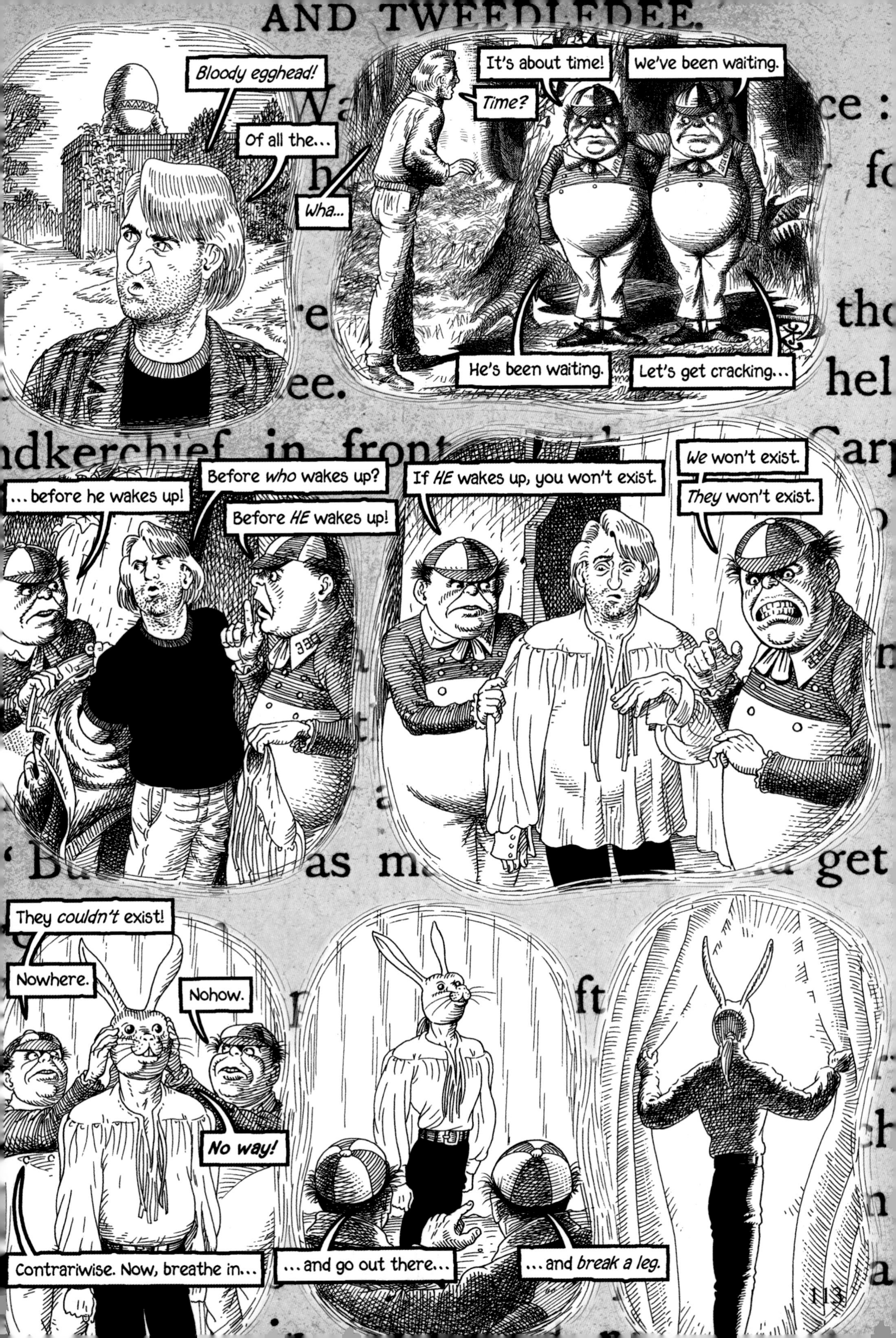
AND TWEEDLEDEE.
Bloody egghead!
Of all the...
Wha...
Time?
It's about time!
We've been waiting.
He's been waiting.
Let's get cracking...
...before he wakes up!
Before who wakes up?
Before HE wakes up!
If HE wakes up, you won't exist.
We won't exist.
They won't exist.
They couldn't exist!
Nowhere.
Nohow.
No way!
Contrariwise. Now, breathe in...
...and go out there...
...and break a leg.

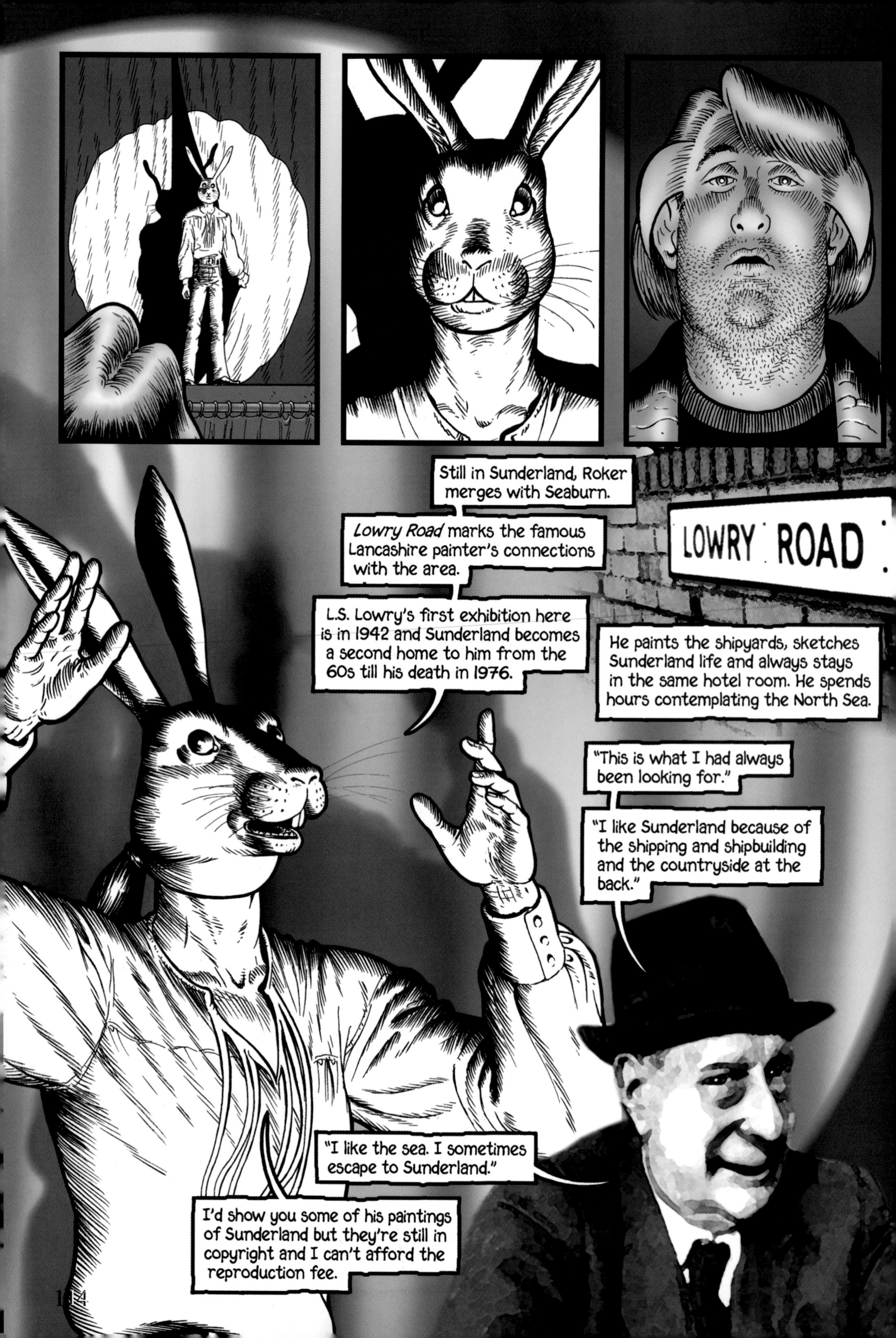
Still in Sunderland, Roker merges with Seaburn.
Lowry Road marks the famous Lancashire painter's connections with the area.
LOWRY ROAD
L.S. Lowry's first exhibition here is in 1942 and Sunderland becomes a second home to him from the 60s till his death in 1976.
He paints the shipyards, sketches Sunderland life and always stays in the same hotel room. He spends hours contemplating the North Sea.
"This is what I had always been looking for."
"I like Sunderland because of the shipping and shipbuilding and the countryside at the back."
"I like the sea. I sometimes escape to Sunderland."
I'd show you some of his paintings of Sunderland but they're still in copyright and I can't afford the reproduction fee.

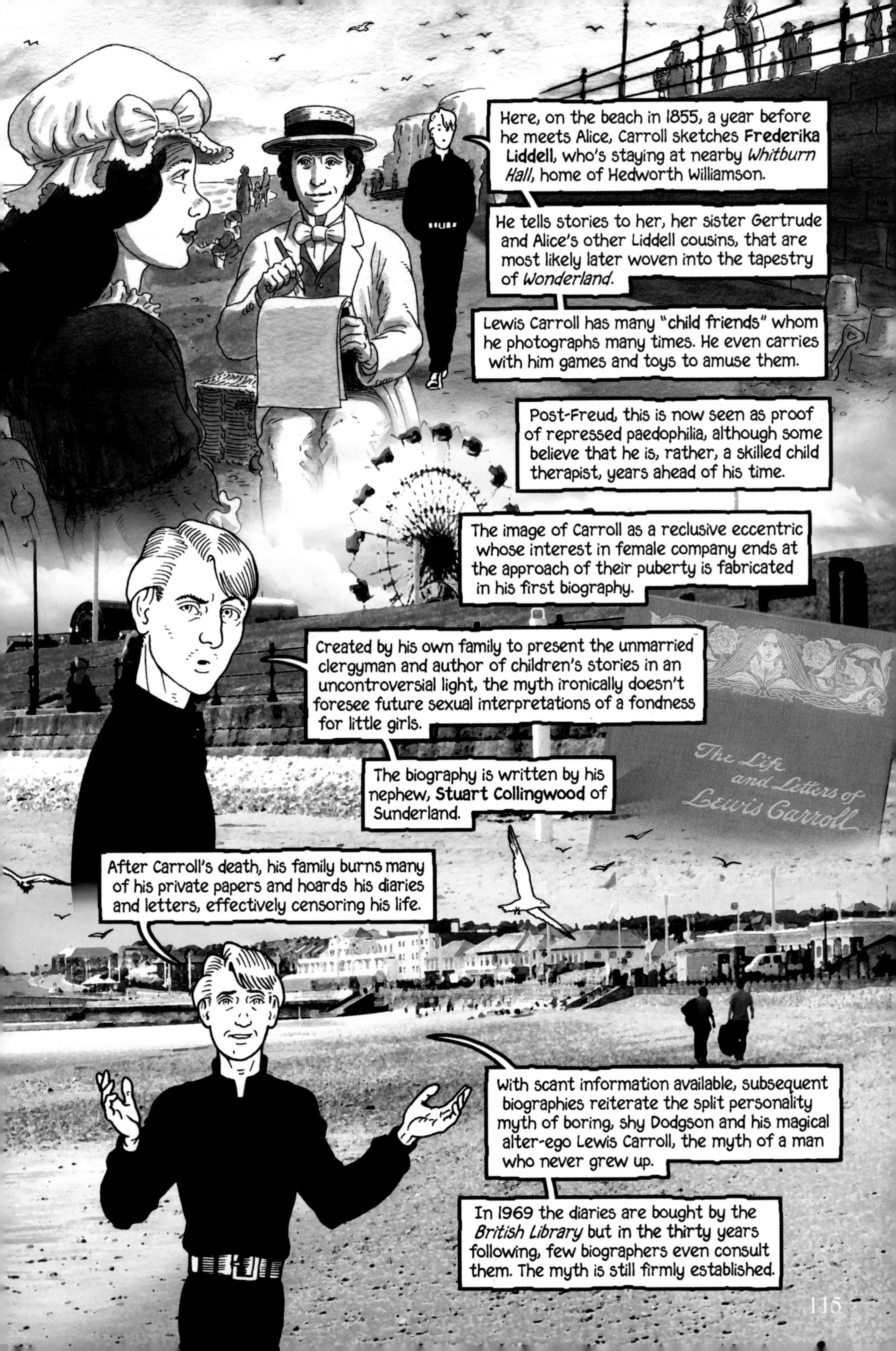

Here, on the beach in 1855, a year before he meets Alice, Carroll sketches **Frederika Liddell**, who's staying at nearby *Whitburn Hall*, home of Hedworth Williamson.
He tells stories to her, her sister Gertrude and Alice's other Liddell cousins, that are most likely later woven into the tapestry of *Wonderland*.
Lewis Carroll has many "**child friends**" whom he photographs many times. He even carries with him games and toys to amuse them.
Post-Freud, this is now seen as proof of repressed paedophilia, although some believe that he is, rather, a skilled child therapist, years ahead of his time.
The image of Carroll as a reclusive eccentric whose interest in female company ends at the approach of their puberty is fabricated in his first biography.
Created by his own family to present the unmarried clergyman and author of children's stories in an uncontroversial light, the myth ironically doesn't foresee future sexual interpretations of a fondness for little girls.
The biography is written by his nephew, **Stuart Collingwood** of Sunderland.
The Life and Letters of Lewis Carroll
After Carroll's death, his family burns many of his private papers and hoards his diaries and letters, effectively censoring his life.
With scant information available, subsequent biographies reiterate the split personality myth of boring, shy Dodgson and his magical alter-ego Lewis Carroll, the myth of a man who never grew up.
In 1969 the diaries are bought by the *British Library* but in the thirty years following, few biographers even consult them. The myth is still firmly established.

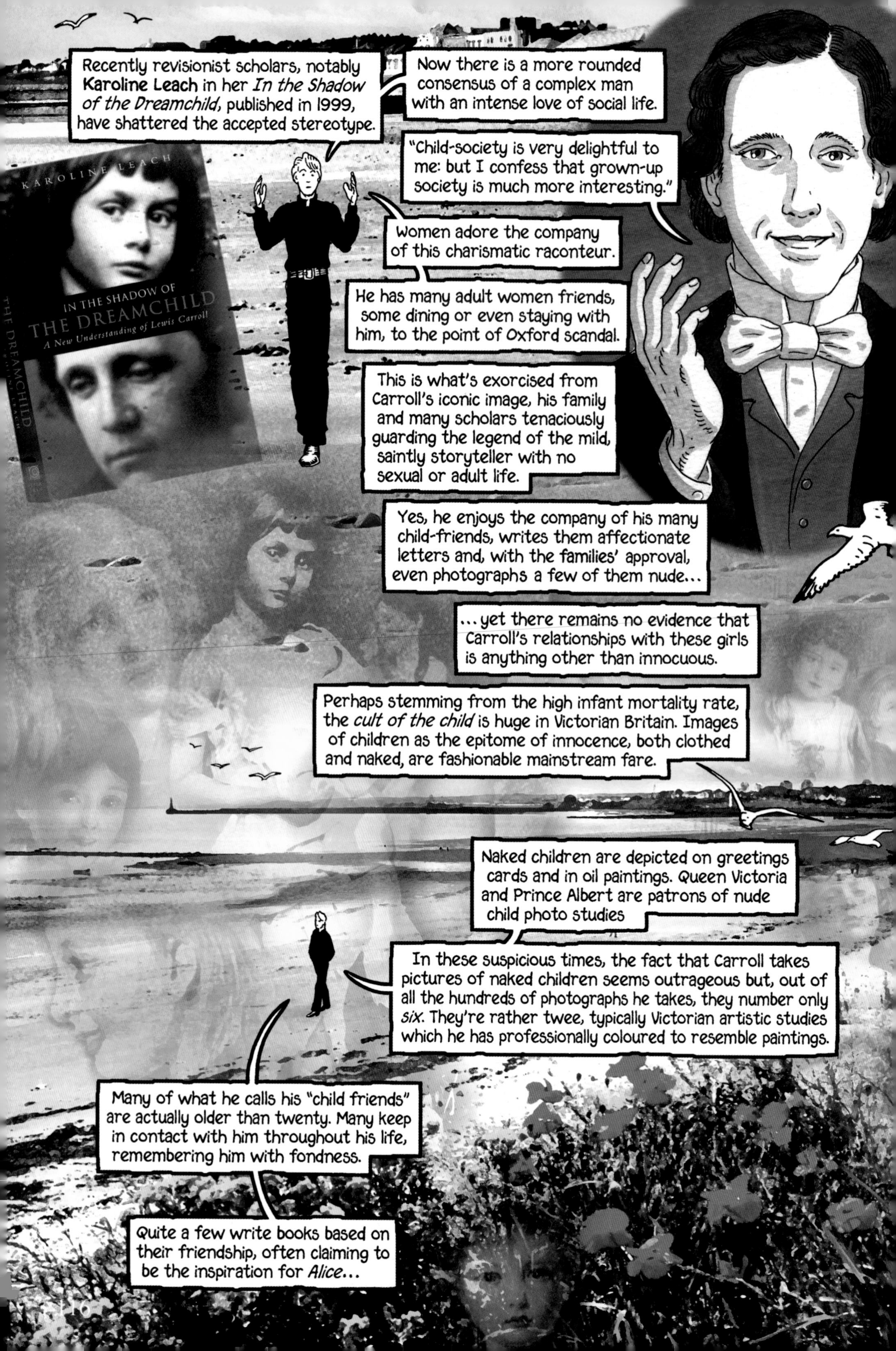
Recently revisionist scholars, notably Karoline Leach in her In the Shadow of the Dreamchild, published in 1999, have shattered the accepted stereotype.
Now there is a more rounded consensus of a complex man with an intense love of social life.
"Child-society is very delightful to me: but I confess that grown-up society is much more interesting."
KAROLINE LEACH
IN THE SHADOW OF THE DREAMCHILD
A New Understanding of Lewis Carroll
Women adore the company of this charismatic raconteur.
He has many adult women friends, some dining or even staying with him, to the point of Oxford scandal.
This is what's exorcised from Carroll's iconic image, his family and many scholars tenaciously guarding the legend of the mild, saintly storyteller with no sexual or adult life.
Yes, he enjoys the company of his many child-friends, writes them affectionate letters and, with the families' approval, even photographs a few of them nude...
...yet there remains no evidence that Carroll's relationships with these girls is anything other than innocuous.
Perhaps stemming from the high infant mortality rate, the cult of the child is huge in Victorian Britain. Images of children as the epitome of innocence, both clothed and naked, are fashionable mainstream fare.
Naked children are depicted on greetings cards and in oil paintings. Queen Victoria and Prince Albert are patrons of nude child photo studies
In these suspicious times, the fact that Carroll takes pictures of naked children seems outrageous but, out of all the hundreds of photographs he takes, they number only six. They're rather twee, typically Victorian artistic studies which he has professionally coloured to resemble paintings.
Many of what he calls his "child friends" are actually older than twenty. Many keep in contact with him throughout his life, remembering him with fondness.
Quite a few write books based on their friendship, often claiming to be the inspiration for Alice...

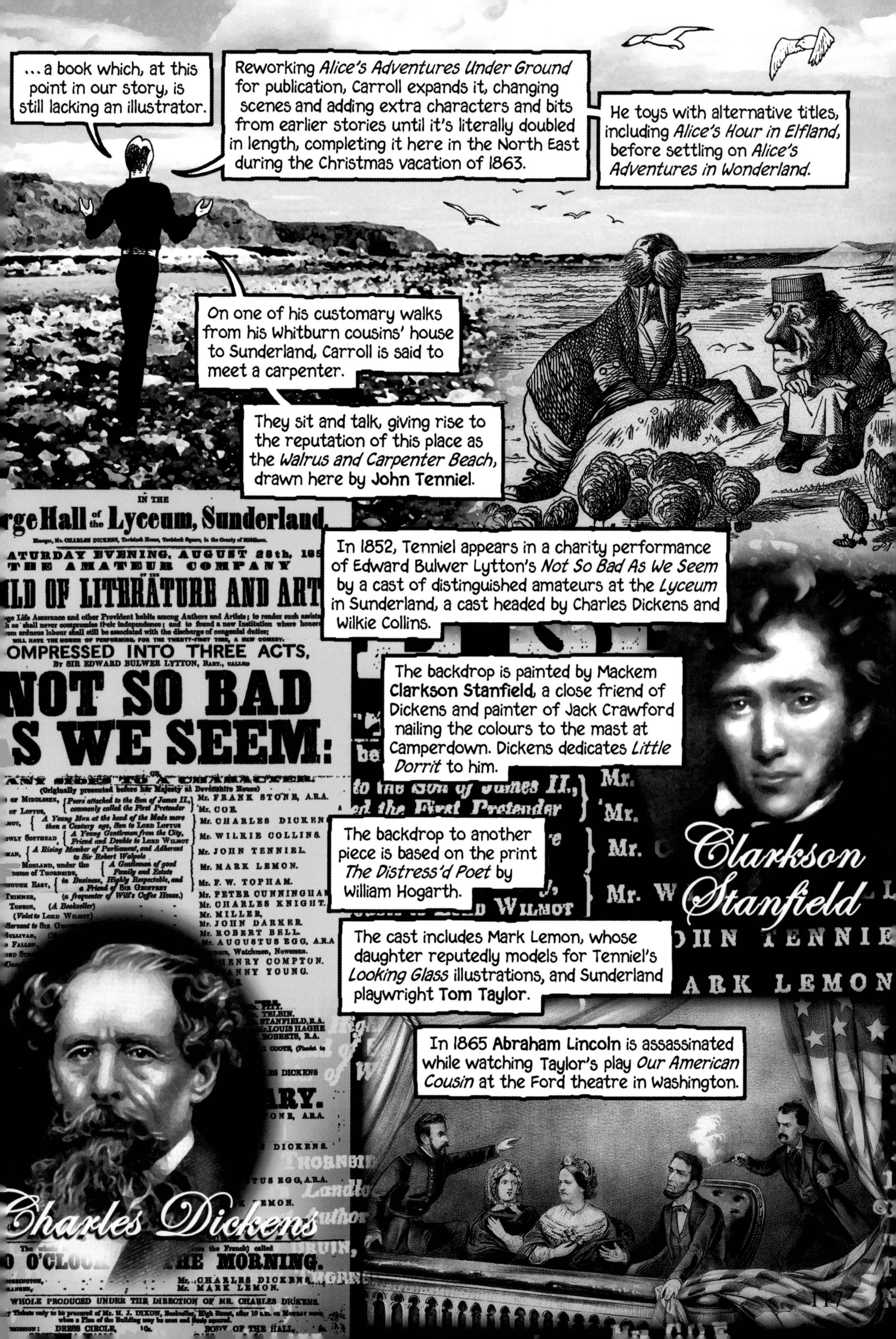
...a book which, at this point in our story, is still lacking an illustrator.
Reworking Alice's Adventures Under Ground for publication, Carroll expands it, changing scenes and adding extra characters and bits from earlier stories until it's literally doubled in length, completing it here in the North East during the Christmas vacation of 1863.
He toys with alternative titles, including Alice's Hour in Elfland, before settling on Alice's Adventures in Wonderland.
On one of his customary walks from his Whitburn cousins' house to Sunderland, Carroll is said to meet a carpenter.
They sit and talk, giving rise to the reputation of this place as the Walrus and Carpenter Beach, drawn here by John Tenniel.
rge Hall of the Lyceum, Sunderland
ATURDAY EVENING, AUGUST 28th, 185
THE AMATEUR COMPANY
ILD OF LITERATURE AND ART
OMPRESSED INTO THREE ACTS,
NOT SO BAD
S WE SEEM:
In 1852, Tenniel appears in a charity performance of Edward Bulwer Lytton's Not So Bad As We Seem by a cast of distinguished amateurs at the Lyceum in Sunderland, a cast headed by Charles Dickens and Wilkie Collins.
The backdrop is painted by Mackem Clarkson Stanfield, a close friend of Dickens and painter of Jack Crawford nailing the colours to the mast at Camperdown. Dickens dedicates Little Dorrit to him.
The backdrop to another piece is based on the print The Distress'd Poet by William Hogarth.
Clarkson Stanfield
The cast includes Mark Lemon, whose daughter reputedly models for Tenniel's Looking Glass illustrations, and Sunderland playwright Tom Taylor.
In 1865 Abraham Lincoln is assassinated while watching Taylor's play Our American Cousin at the Ford theatre in Washington.
Charles Dickens
O'CLOC HE MORNING.
WHOLE PRODUCED UNDER THE DIRECTION OF MR. CHARLES DICKENS.

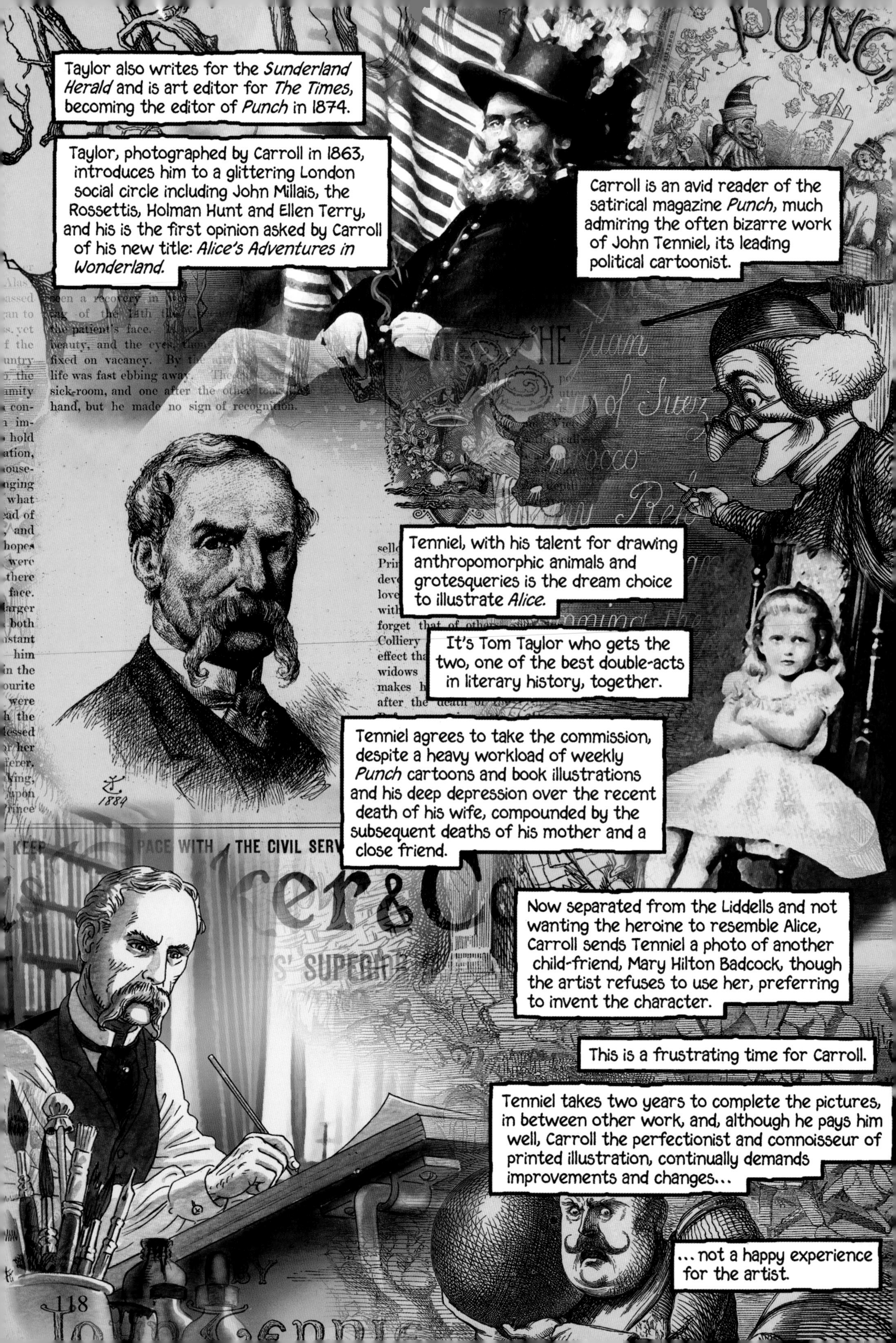
Taylor also writes for the *Sunderland Herald* and is art editor for *The Times*, becoming the editor of *Punch* in 1874.
Taylor, photographed by Carroll in 1863, introduces him to a glittering London social circle including John Millais, the Rossettis, Holman Hunt and Ellen Terry, and his is the first opinion asked by Carroll of his new title: *Alice's Adventures in Wonderland.*
Carroll is an avid reader of the satirical magazine *Punch*, much admiring the often bizarre work of John Tenniel, its leading political cartoonist.
Tenniel, with his talent for drawing anthropomorphic animals and grotesqueries is the dream choice to illustrate *Alice.*
It's Tom Taylor who gets the two, one of the best double-acts in literary history, together.
Tenniel agrees to take the commission, despite a heavy workload of weekly *Punch* cartoons and book illustrations and his deep depression over the recent death of his wife, compounded by the subsequent deaths of his mother and a close friend.
Now separated from the Liddells and not wanting the heroine to resemble Alice, Carroll sends Tenniel a photo of another child-friend, Mary Hilton Badcock, though the artist refuses to use her, preferring to invent the character.
This is a frustrating time for Carroll.
Tenniel takes two years to complete the pictures, in between other work, and, although he pays him well, Carroll the perfectionist and connoisseur of printed illustration, continually demands improvements and changes...
...not a happy experience for the artist.

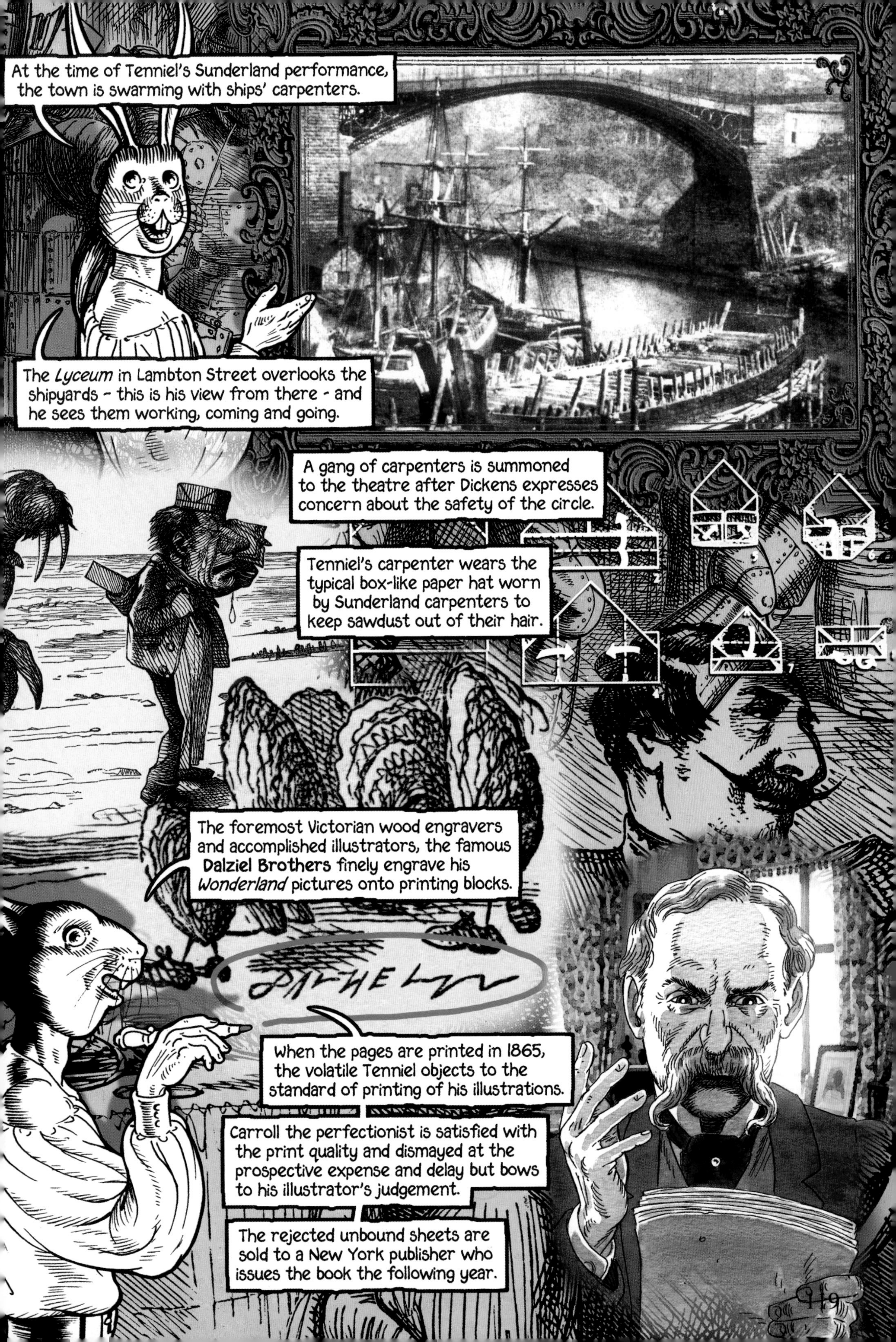

At the time of Tenniel's Sunderland performance, the town is swarming with ships' carpenters.
The *Lyceum* in Lambton Street overlooks the shipyards - this is his view from there - and he sees them working, coming and going.
A gang of carpenters is summoned to the theatre after Dickens expresses concern about the safety of the circle.
Tenniel's carpenter wears the typical box-like paper hat worn by Sunderland carpenters to keep sawdust out of their hair.
The foremost Victorian wood engravers and accomplished illustrators, the famous **Dalziel Brothers** finely engrave his *Wonderland* pictures onto printing blocks.
When the pages are printed in 1865, the volatile Tenniel objects to the standard of printing of his illustrations.
Carroll the perfectionist is satisfied with the print quality and dismayed at the prospective expense and delay but bows to his illustrator's judgement.
The rejected unbound sheets are sold to a New York publisher who issues the book the following year.

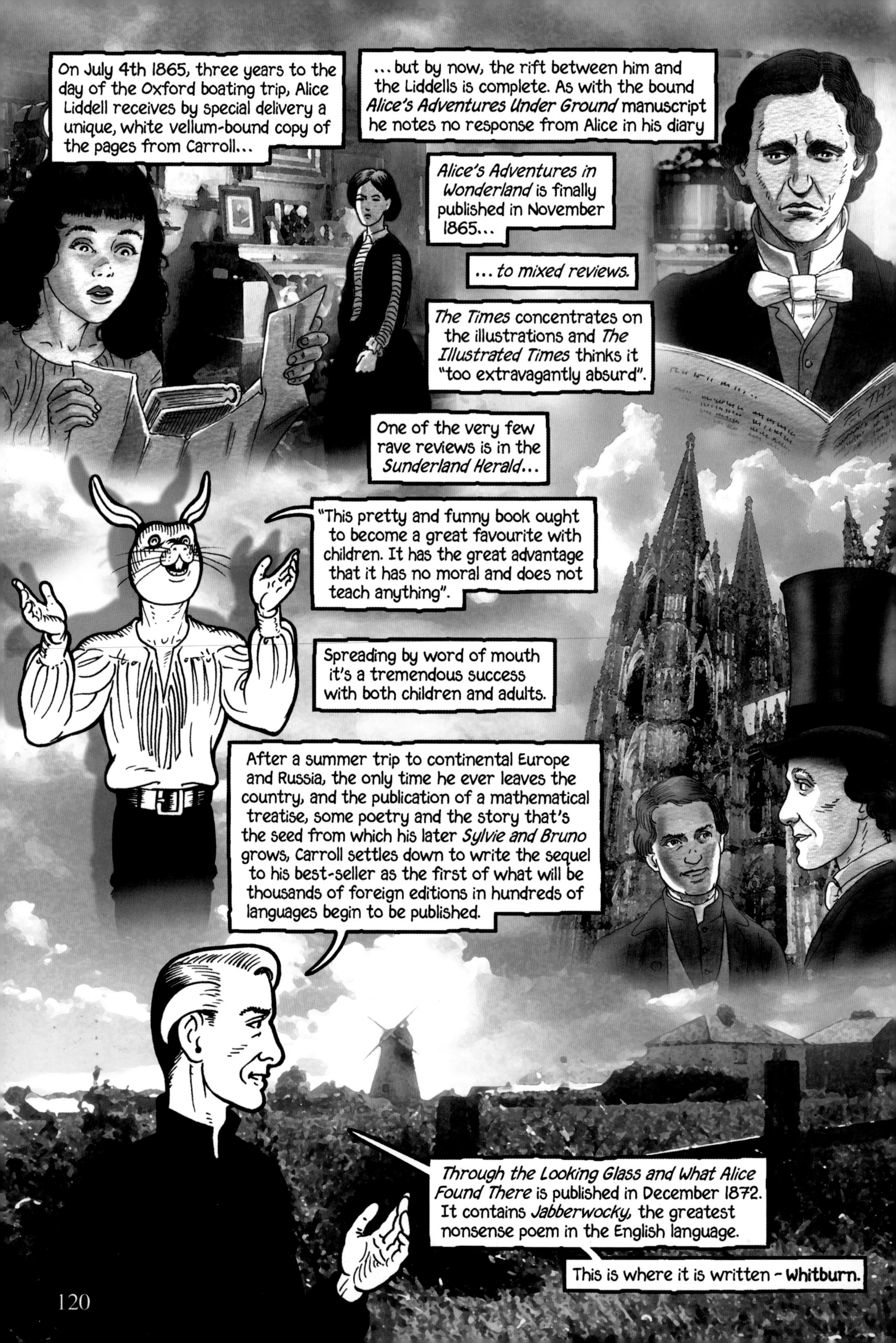

On July 4th 1865, three years to the day of the Oxford boating trip, Alice Liddell receives by special delivery a unique, white vellum-bound copy of the pages from Carroll...
...but by now, the rift between him and the Liddells is complete. As with the bound *Alice's Adventures Under Ground* manuscript he notes no response from Alice in his diary
Alice's Adventures in Wonderland is finally published in November 1865...
...to mixed reviews.
The Times concentrates on the illustrations and *The Illustrated Times* thinks it "too extravagantly absurd".
One of the very few rave reviews is in the *Sunderland Herald*...
"This pretty and funny book ought to become a great favourite with children. It has the great advantage that it has no moral and does not teach anything".
Spreading by word of mouth it's a tremendous success with both children and adults.
After a summer trip to continental Europe and Russia, the only time he ever leaves the country, and the publication of a mathematical treatise, some poetry and the story that's the seed from which his later *Sylvie and Bruno* grows, Carroll settles down to write the sequel to his best-seller as the first of what will be thousands of foreign editions in hundreds of languages begin to be published.
Through the Looking Glass and What Alice Found There is published in December 1872. It contains *Jabberwocky,* the greatest nonsense poem in the English language.
This is where it is written – **Whitburn.**

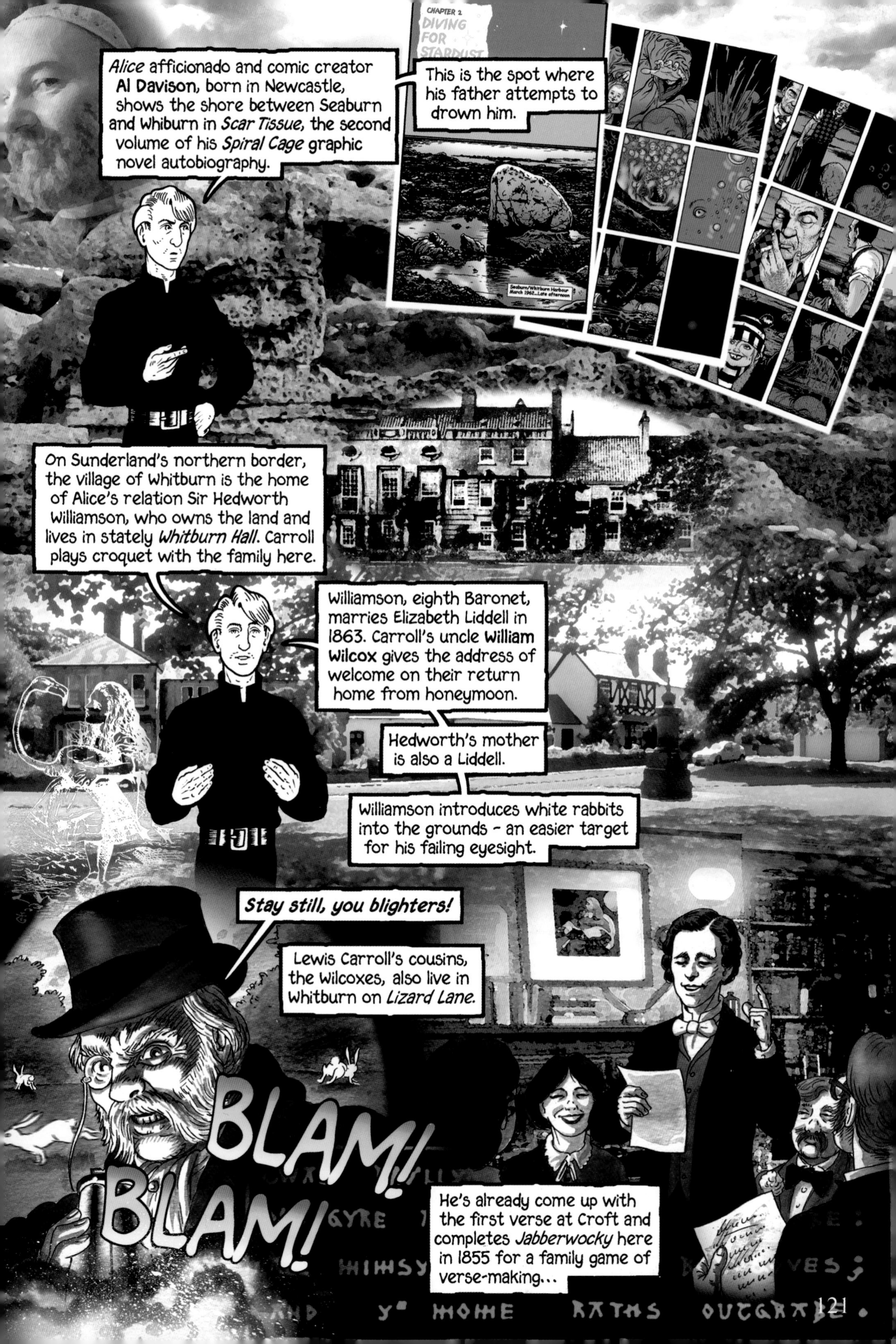

Alice afficionado and comic creator Al Davison, born in Newcastle, shows the shore between Seaburn and Whiburn in Scar Tissue, the second volume of his Spiral Cage graphic novel autobiography.
CHAPTER 2
DIVING FOR STARDUST
This is the spot where his father attempts to drown him.
On Sunderland's northern border, the village of Whitburn is the home of Alice's relation Sir Hedworth Williamson, who owns the land and lives in stately Whitburn Hall. Carroll plays croquet with the family here.
Williamson, eighth Baronet, marries Elizabeth Liddell in 1863. Carroll's uncle William Wilcox gives the address of welcome on their return home from honeymoon.
Hedworth's mother is also a Liddell.
Williamson introduces white rabbits into the grounds - an easier target for his failing eyesight.
Stay still, you blighters!
Lewis Carroll's cousins, the Wilcoxes, also live in Whitburn on Lizard Lane.
BLAM! BLAM!
He's already come up with the first verse at Croft and completes Jabberwocky here in 1855 for a family game of verse-making...

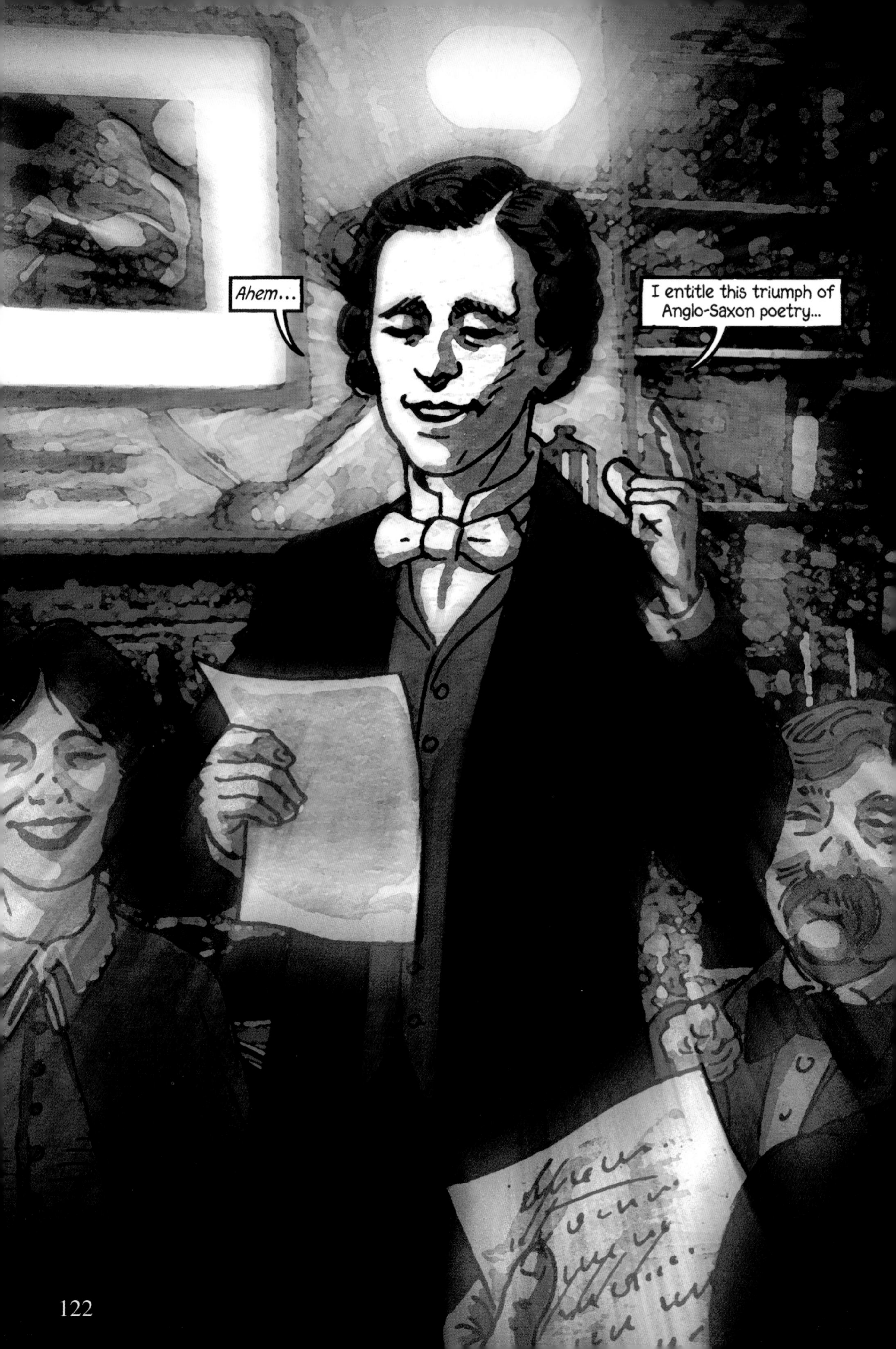
Ahem...
I entitle this triumph of Anglo-Saxon poetry...

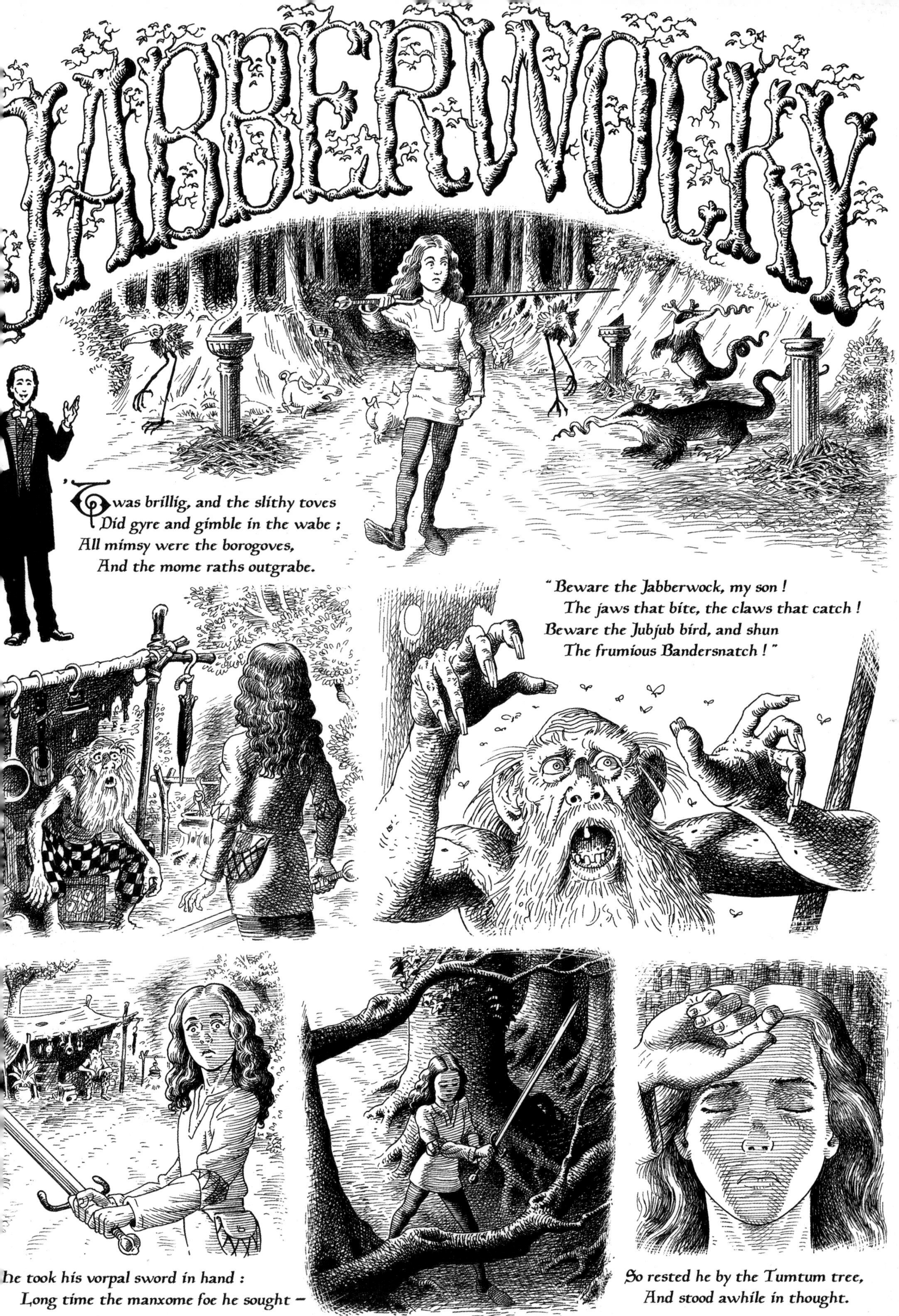
JABBERWOCKY
'Twas brillig, and the slithy toves
Did gyre and gimble in the wabe ;
All mimsy were the borogoves,
And the mome raths outgrabe.
"Beware the Jabberwock, my son !
The jaws that bite, the claws that catch !
Beware the Jubjub bird, and shun
The frumious Bandersnatch !"
He took his vorpal sword in hand :
Long time the manxome foe he sought –
So rested he by the Tumtum tree,
And stood awhile in thought.

And as in uffish thought he stood,
The Jabberwock, with eyes of flame,
Came whiffling through the tulgey wood,
And burbled as it came!

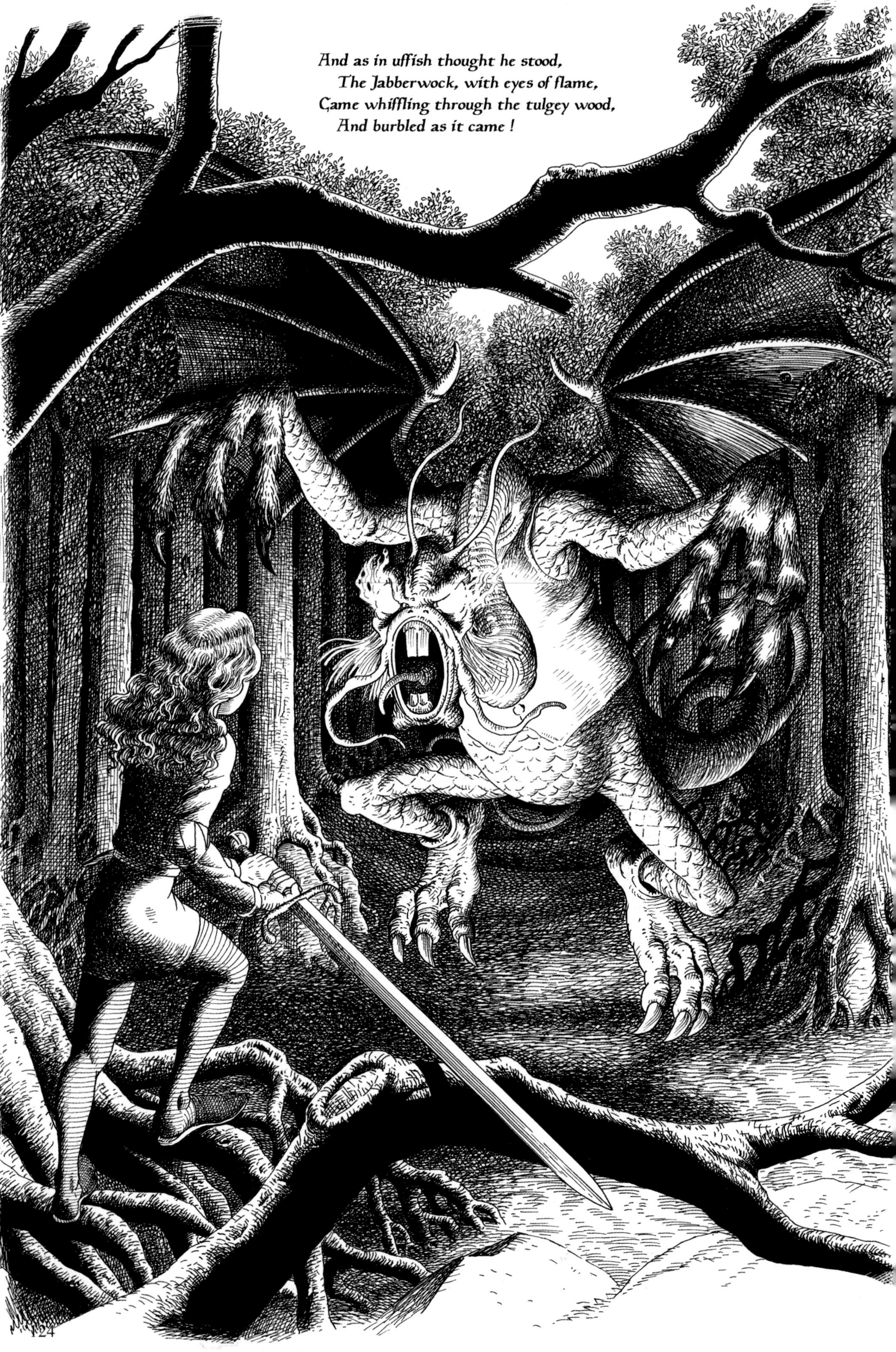

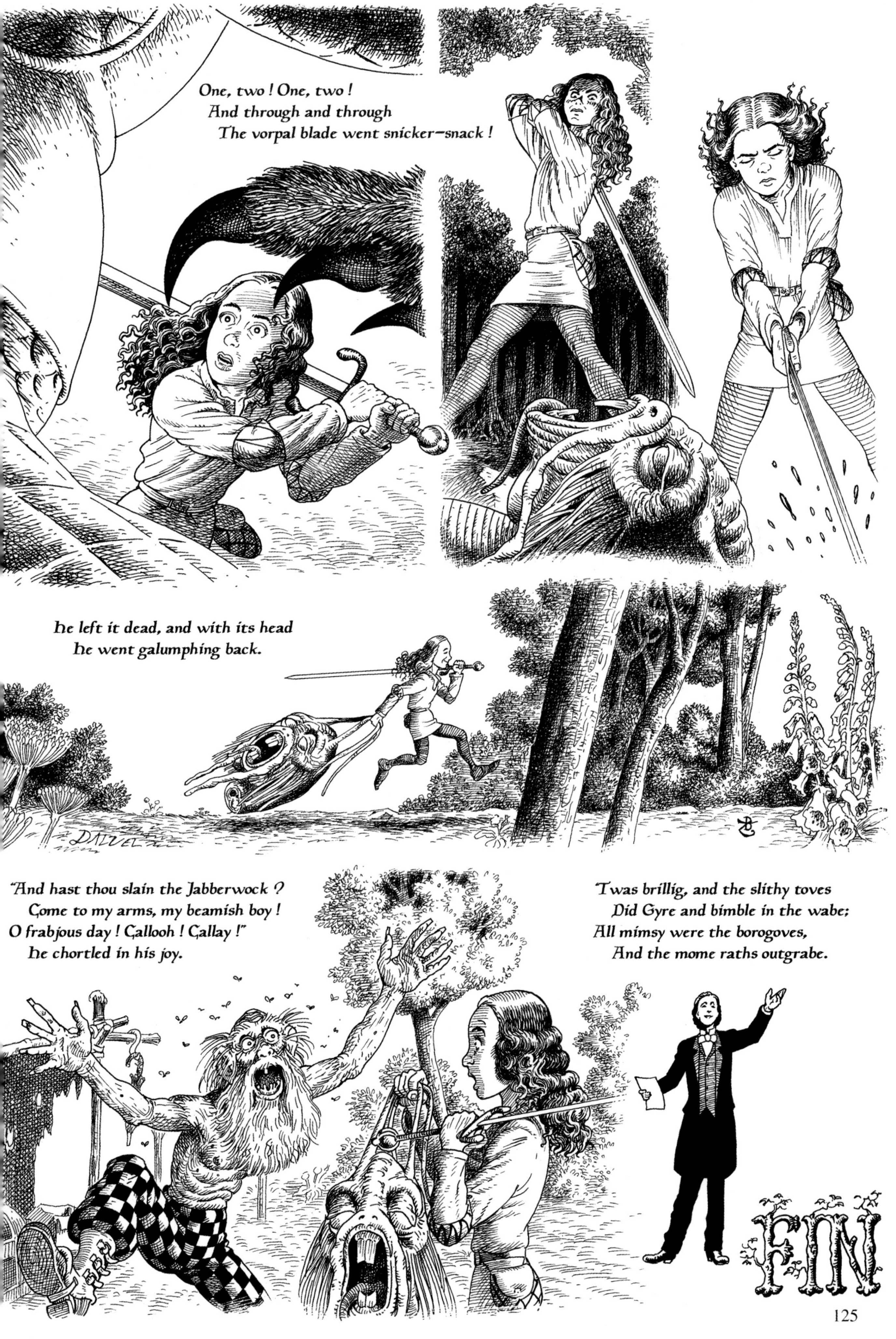
One, two! One, two!
And through and through
The vorpal blade went snicker–snack!
He left it dead, and with its head
He went galumphing back.
"And hast thou slain the Jabberwock?
Come to my arms, my beamish boy!
O frabjous day! Callooh! Callay!"
He chortled in his joy.
'Twas brillig, and the slithy toves
Did Gyre and bimble in the wabe;
All mimsy were the borogoves,
And the mome raths outgrabe.
FIN

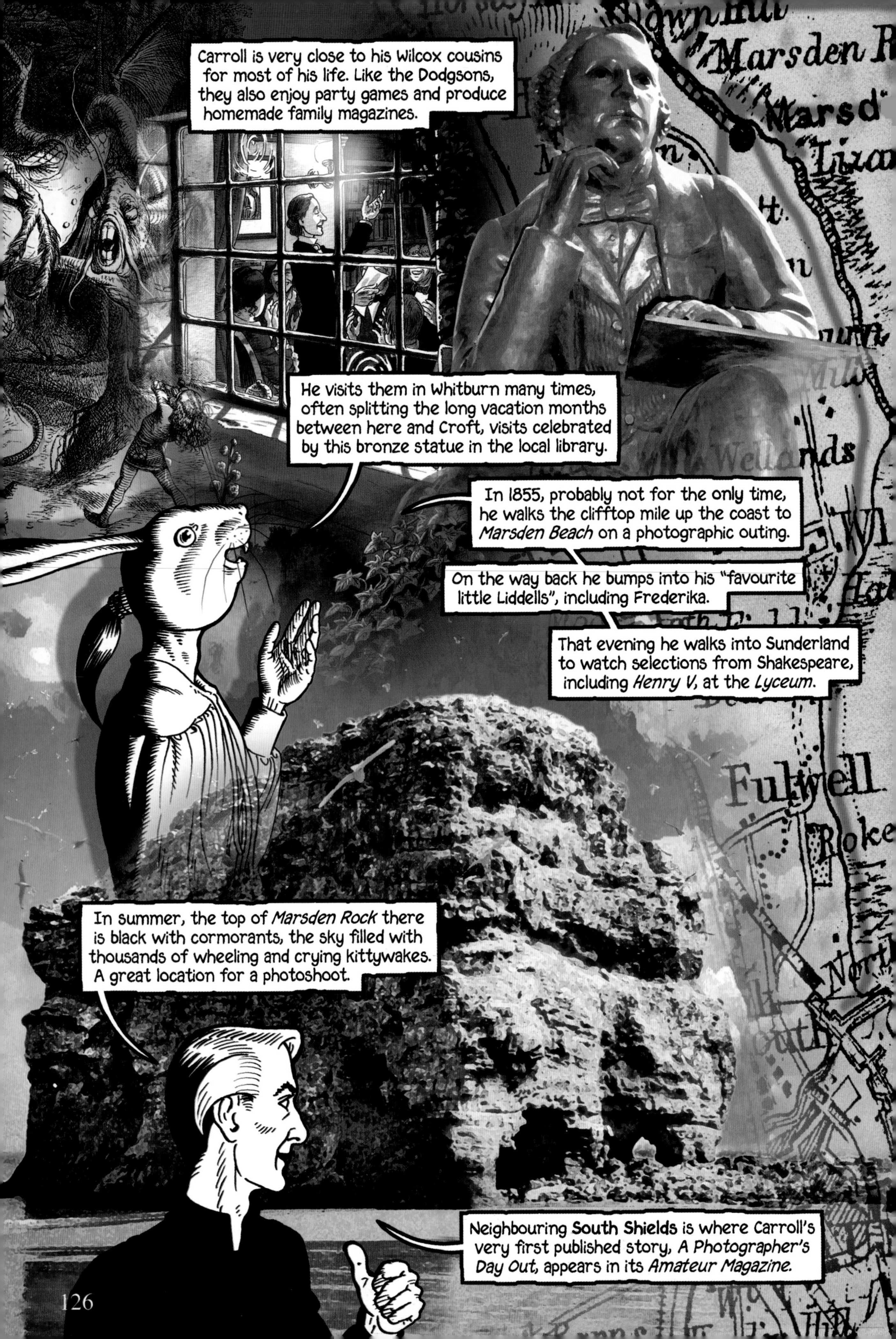
Carroll is very close to his Wilcox cousins for most of his life. Like the Dodgsons, they also enjoy party games and produce homemade family magazines.
He visits them in Whitburn many times, often splitting the long vacation months between here and Croft, visits celebrated by this bronze statue in the local library.
In 1855, probably not for the only time, he walks the clifftop mile up the coast to *Marsden Beach* on a photographic outing.
On the way back he bumps into his "favourite little Liddells", including Frederika.
That evening he walks into Sunderland to watch selections from Shakespeare, including *Henry V*, at the *Lyceum*.
Fulwell
In summer, the top of *Marsden Rock* there is black with cormorants, the sky filled with thousands of wheeling and crying kittywakes. A great location for a photoshoot.
Neighbouring **South Shields** is where Carroll's very first published story, *A Photographer's Day Out*, appears in its *Amateur Magazine*.

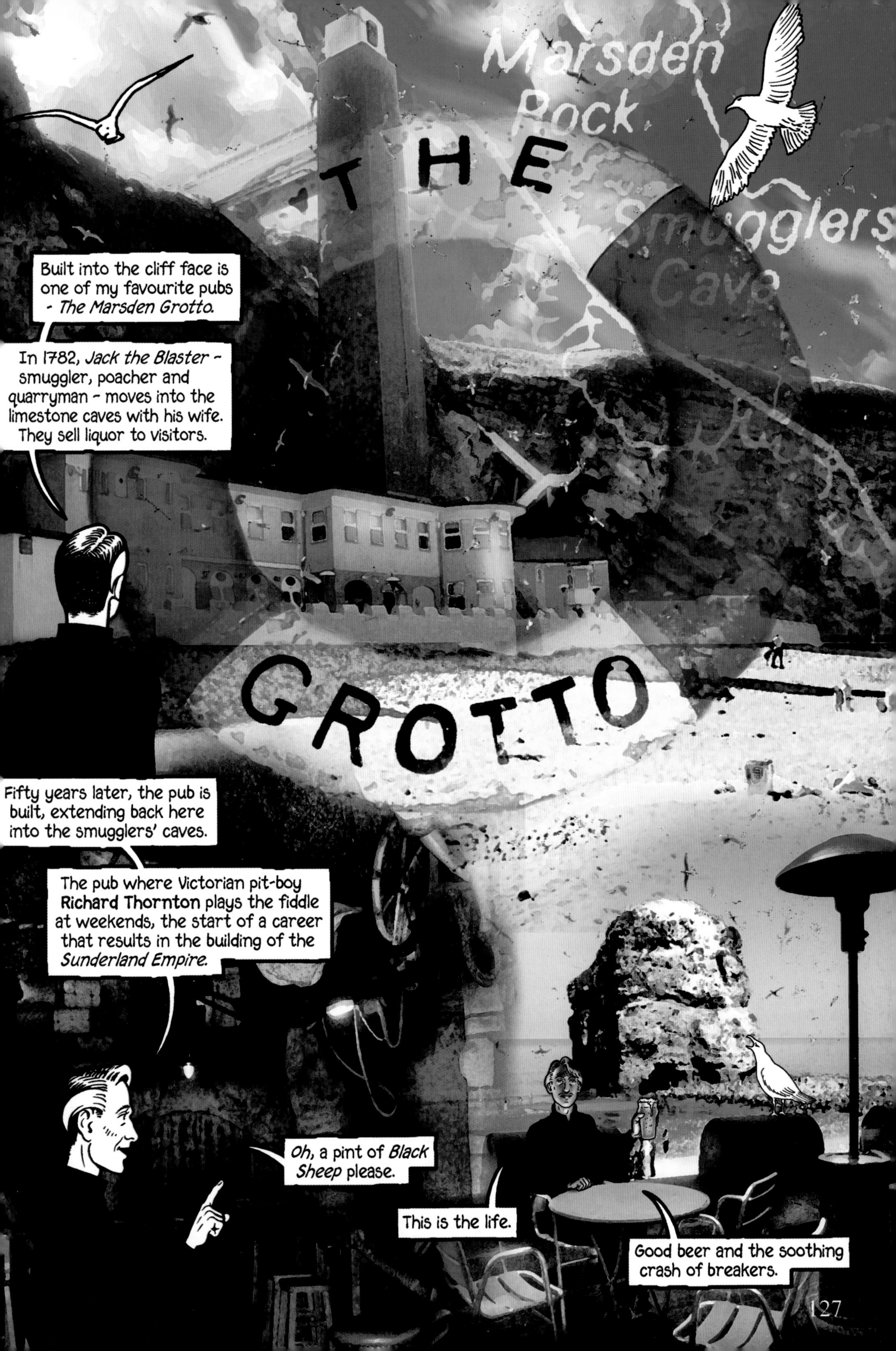
Marsden Rock
THE
Smugglers Cave
Built into the cliff face is one of my favourite pubs - *The Marsden Grotto.*
In 1782, *Jack the Blaster* - smuggler, poacher and quarryman - moves into the limestone caves with his wife. They sell liquor to visitors.
GROTTO
Fifty years later, the pub is built, extending back here into the smugglers' caves.
The pub where Victorian pit-boy **Richard Thornton** plays the fiddle at weekends, the start of a career that results in the building of the *Sunderland Empire.*
Oh, a pint of *Black Sheep* please.
This is the life.
Good beer and the soothing crash of breakers.

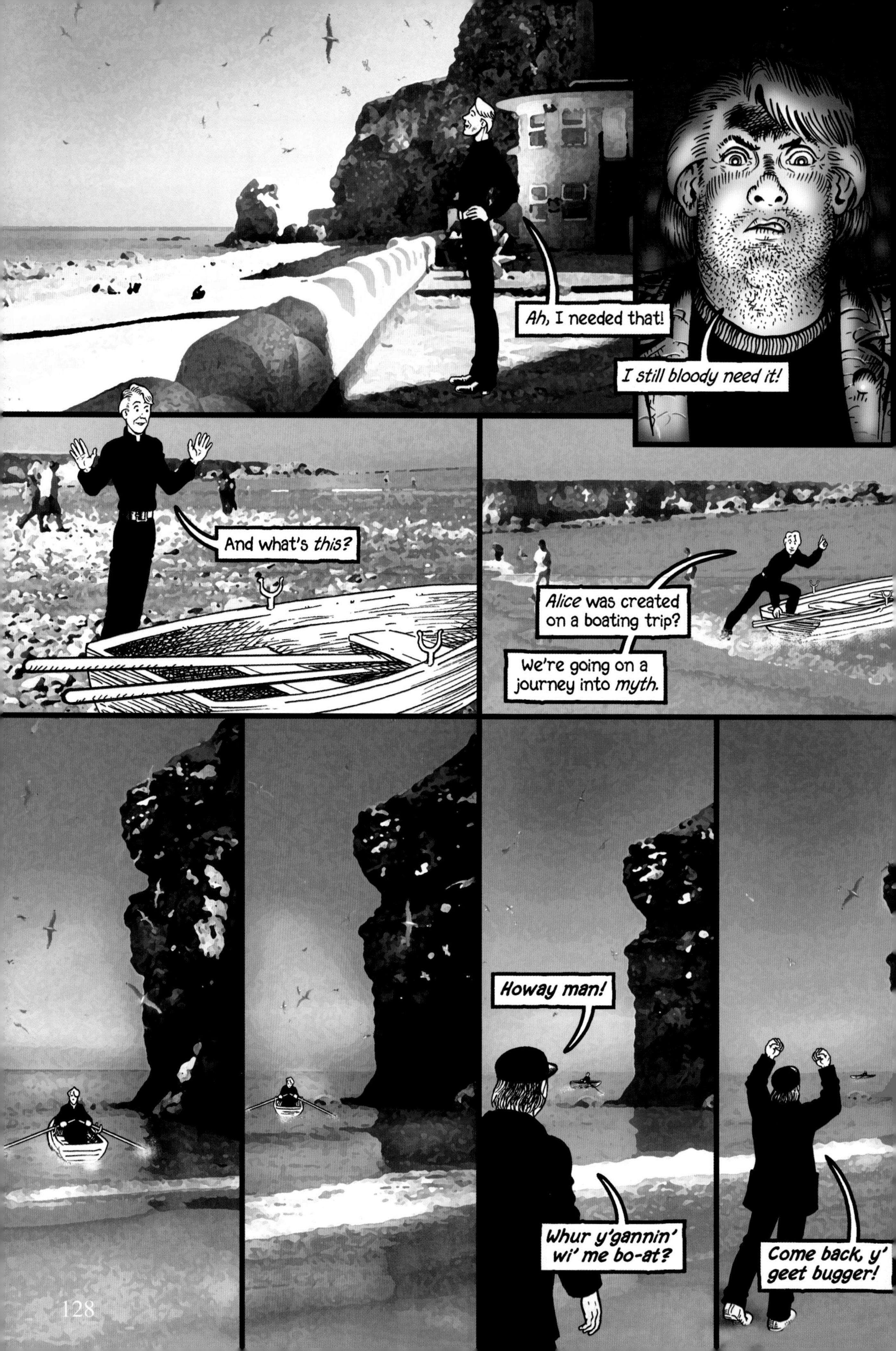
Ah, I needed that!
I still bloody need it!
And what's this?
Alice was created on a boating trip?
We're going on a journey into myth.
Howay man!
Whur y'gannin' wi' me bo-at?
Come back, y' geet bugger!

INTERMISSION

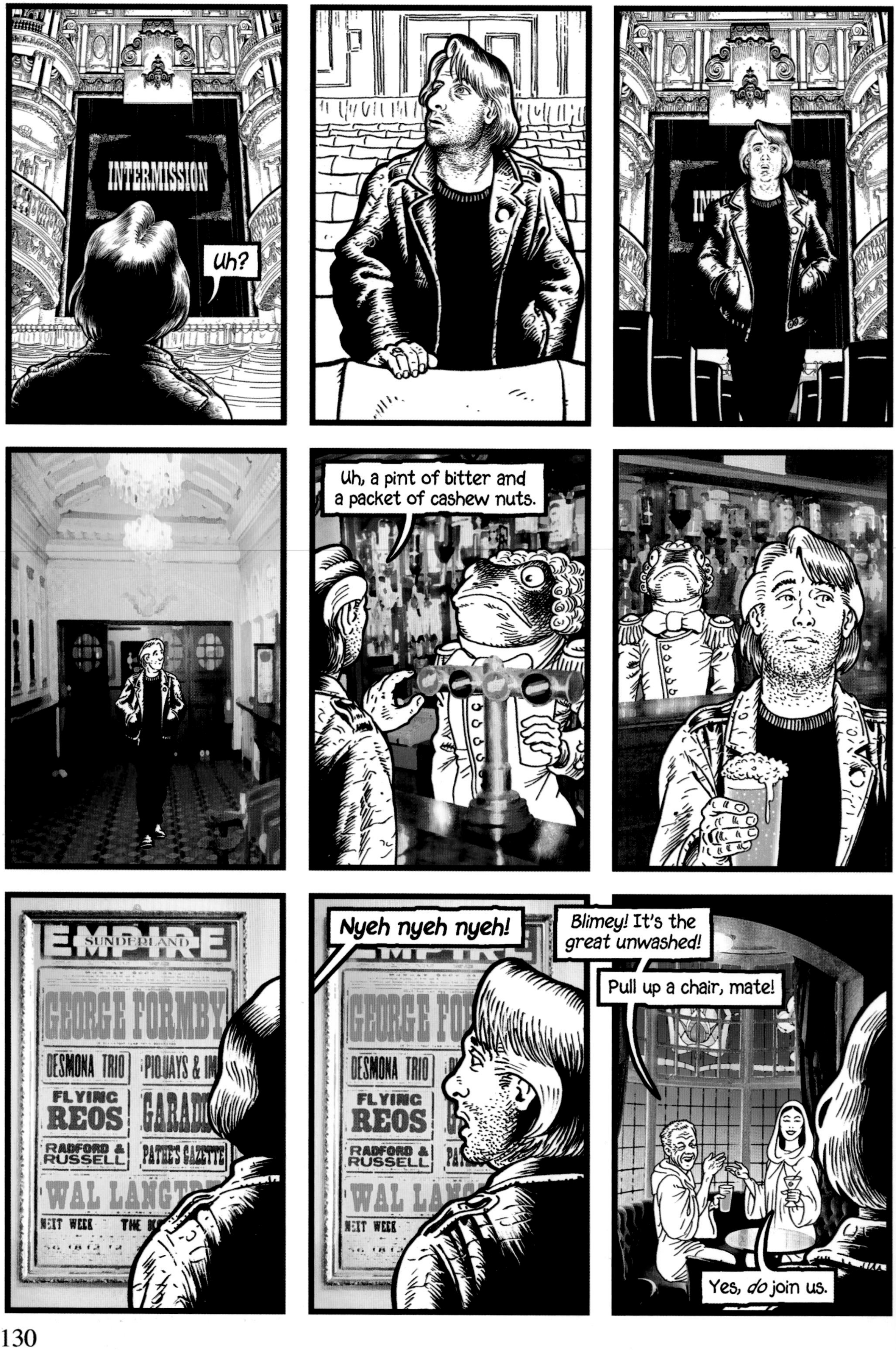
INTERMISSION
Uh?
Uh, a pint of bitter and a packet of cashew nuts.
EMPIRE
SUNDERLAND
GEORGE FORMBY
DESMONA TRIO
FLYING REOS
RADFORD & RUSSELL
PATHE'S GAZETTE
NEXT WEEK
Nyeh nyeh nyeh!
Blimey! It's the great unwashed!
Pull up a chair, mate!
Yes, *do* join us.

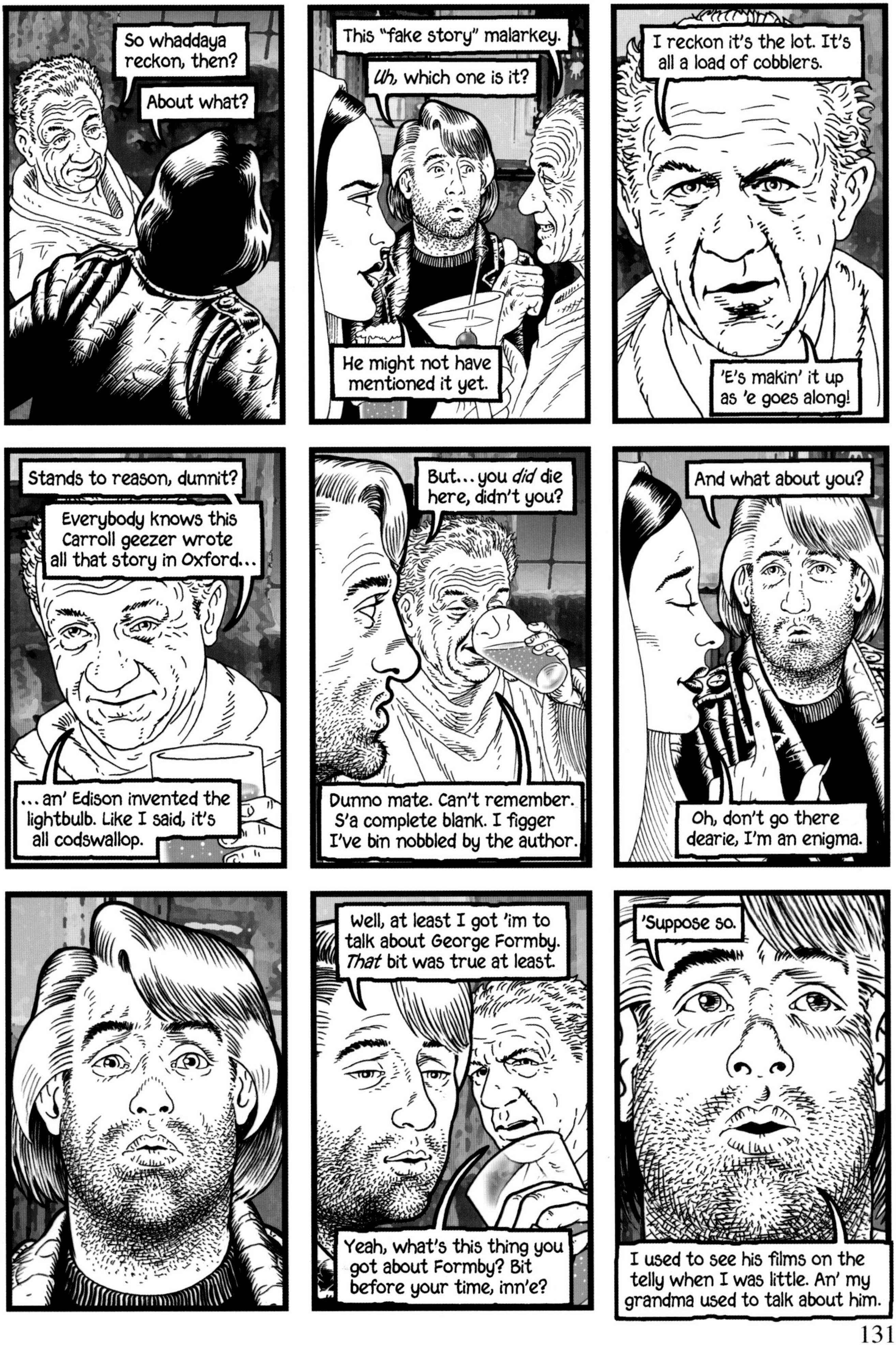
So whaddaya reckon, then?
About what?
This "fake story" malarkey.
Uh, which one is it?
He might not have mentioned it yet.
I reckon it's the lot. It's all a load of cobblers.
'E's makin' it up as 'e goes along!
Stands to reason, dunnit?
Everybody knows this Carroll geezer wrote all that story in Oxford...
...an' Edison invented the lightbulb. Like I said, it's all codswallop.
But... you *did* die here, didn't you?
Dunno mate. Can't remember. S'a complete blank. I figger I've bin nobbled by the author.
And what about you?
Oh, don't go there dearie, I'm an enigma.
Well, at least I got 'im to talk about George Formby. *That* bit was true at least.
Yeah, what's this thing you got about Formby? Bit before your time, inn'e?
'Suppose so.
I used to see his films on the telly when I was little. An' my grandma used to talk about him.

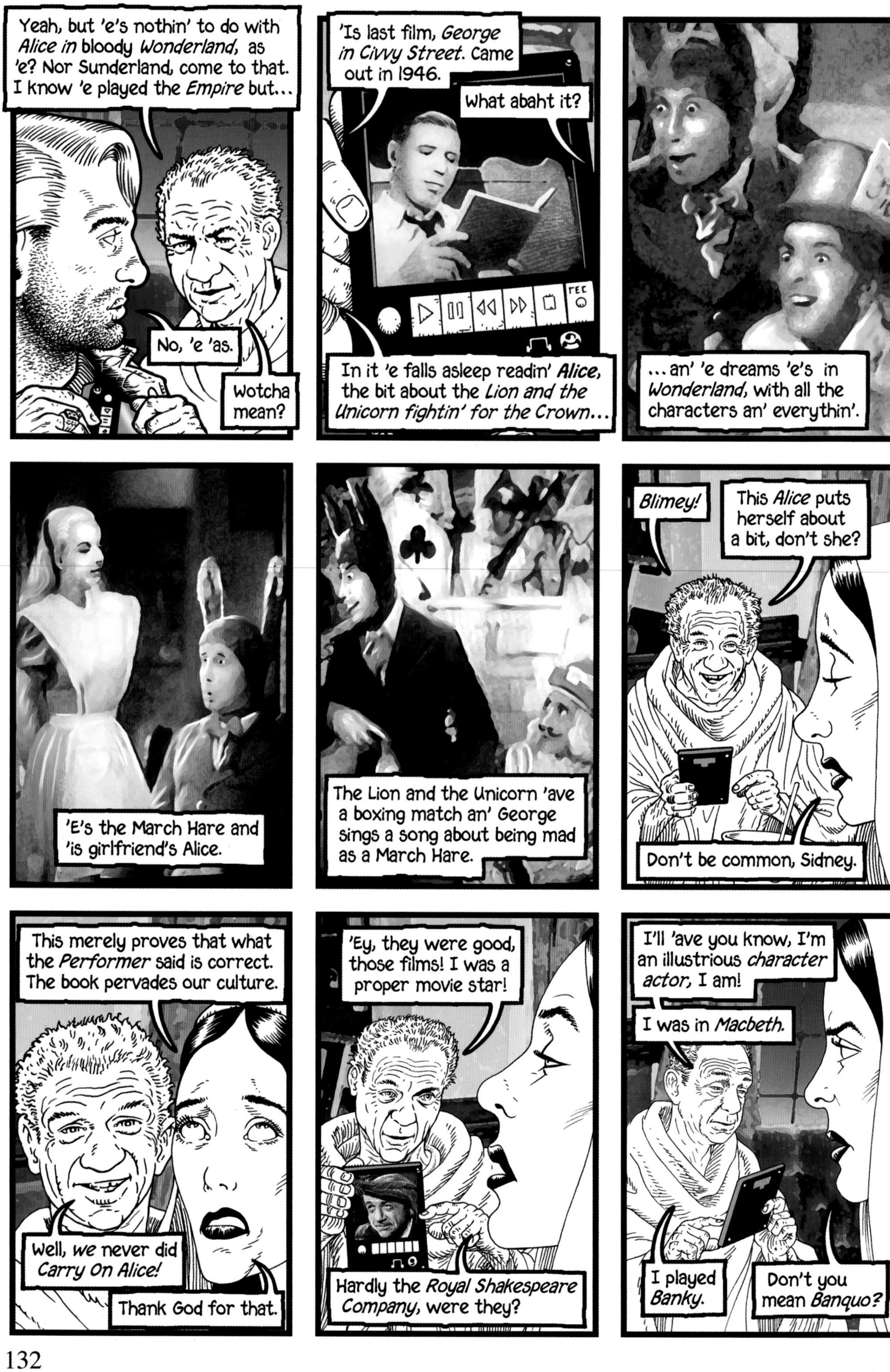

Yeah, but 'e's nothin' to do with Alice in bloody Wonderland, as 'e? Nor Sunderland, come to that. I know 'e played the Empire but...
No, 'e 'as.
Wotcha mean?
'Is last film, George in Civvy Street. Came out in 1946.
What abaht it?
In it 'e falls asleep readin' Alice, the bit about the Lion and the Unicorn fightin' for the Crown...
...an' 'e dreams 'e's in Wonderland, with all the characters an' everythin'.
'E's the March Hare and 'is girlfriend's Alice.
The Lion and the Unicorn 'ave a boxing match an' George sings a song about being mad as a March Hare.
Blimey!
This Alice puts herself about a bit, don't she?
Don't be common, Sidney.
This merely proves that what the Performer said is correct. The book pervades our culture.
Well, we never did Carry On Alice!
Thank God for that.
'Ey, they were good, those films! I was a proper movie star!
Hardly the Royal Shakespeare Company, were they?
I'll 'ave you know, I'm an illustrious character actor, I am!
I was in Macbeth.
I played Banky.
Don't you mean Banquo?

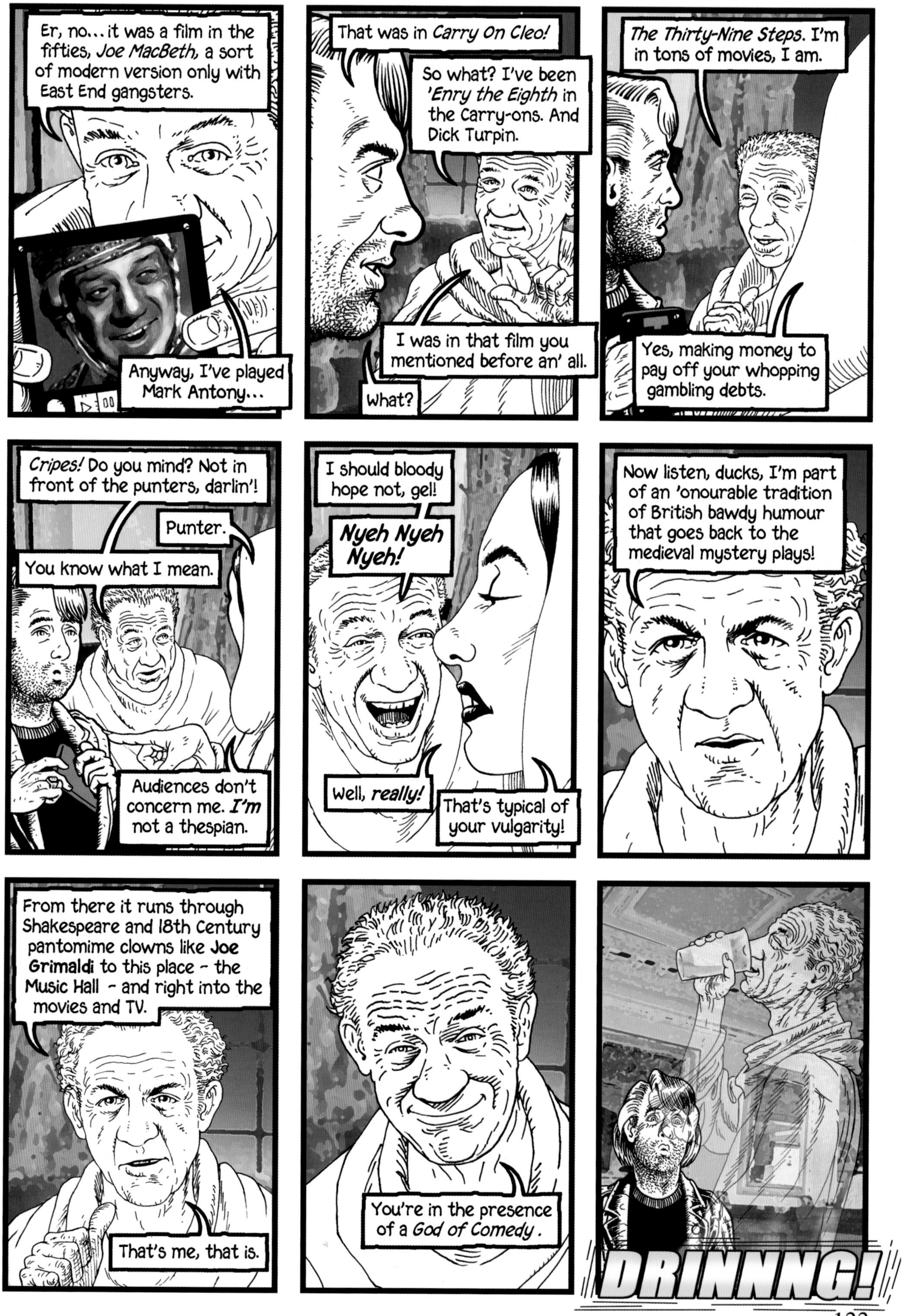
Er, no... it was a film in the fifties, *Joe MacBeth*, a sort of modern version only with East End gangsters.
Anyway, I've played Mark Antony...
That was in *Carry On Cleo!*
So what? I've been *'Enry the Eighth* in the Carry-ons. And Dick Turpin.
I was in that film you mentioned before an' all.
What?
The Thirty-Nine Steps. I'm in tons of movies, I am.
Yes, making money to pay off your whopping gambling debts.
Cripes! Do you mind? Not in front of the punters, darlin'!
Punter.
You know what I mean.
Audiences don't concern me. *I'm* not a thespian.
I should bloody hope not, gel!
Nyeh Nyeh Nyeh!
Well, *really!*
That's typical of your vulgarity!
Now listen, ducks, I'm part of an 'onourable tradition of British bawdy humour that goes back to the medieval mystery plays!
From there it runs through Shakespeare and 18th Century pantomime clowns like **Joe Grimaldi** to this place - the Music Hall - and right into the movies and TV.
That's me, that is.
You're in the presence of a *God of Comedy*.
DRINNNG!

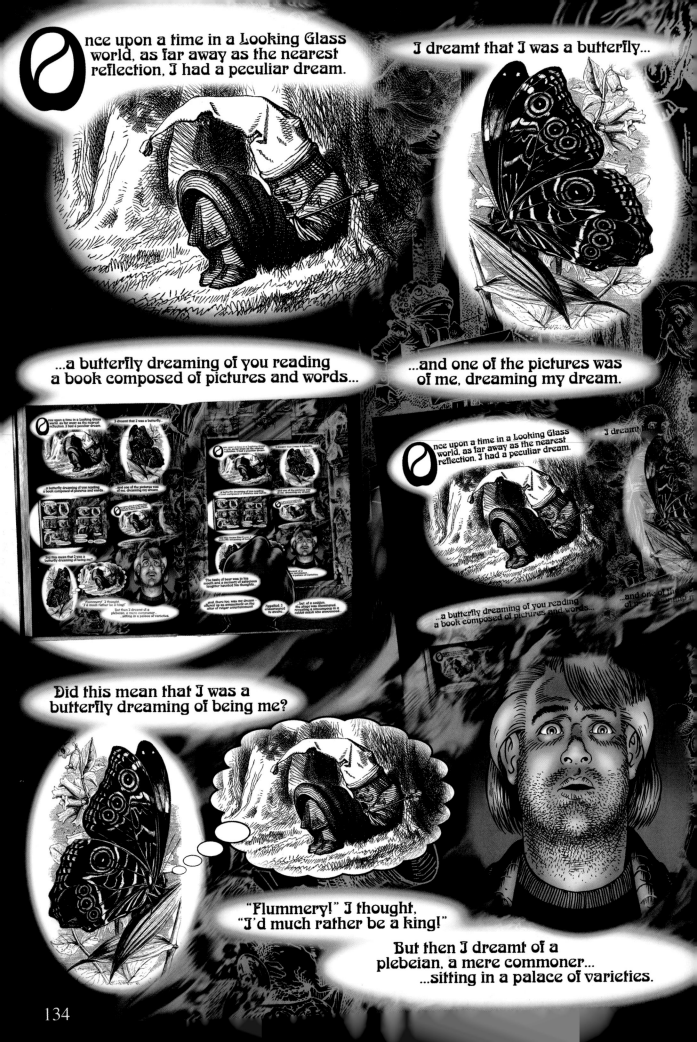

Once upon a time in a Looking Glass world, as far away as the nearest reflection, I had a peculiar dream.

I dreamt that I was a butterfly...

...a butterfly dreaming of you reading a book composed of pictures and words...

...and one of the pictures was of me, dreaming my dream.

Once upon a time in a Looking Glass world, as far away as the nearest reflection, I had a peculiar dream.

I dreamt

...a butterfly dreaming of you reading a book composed of pictures and words...

...and one of

Did this mean that I was a butterfly dreaming of being me?

"Flummery!" I thought, "I'd much rather be a king!"

But then I dreamt of a plebeian, a mere commoner... ...sitting in a palace of varieties.

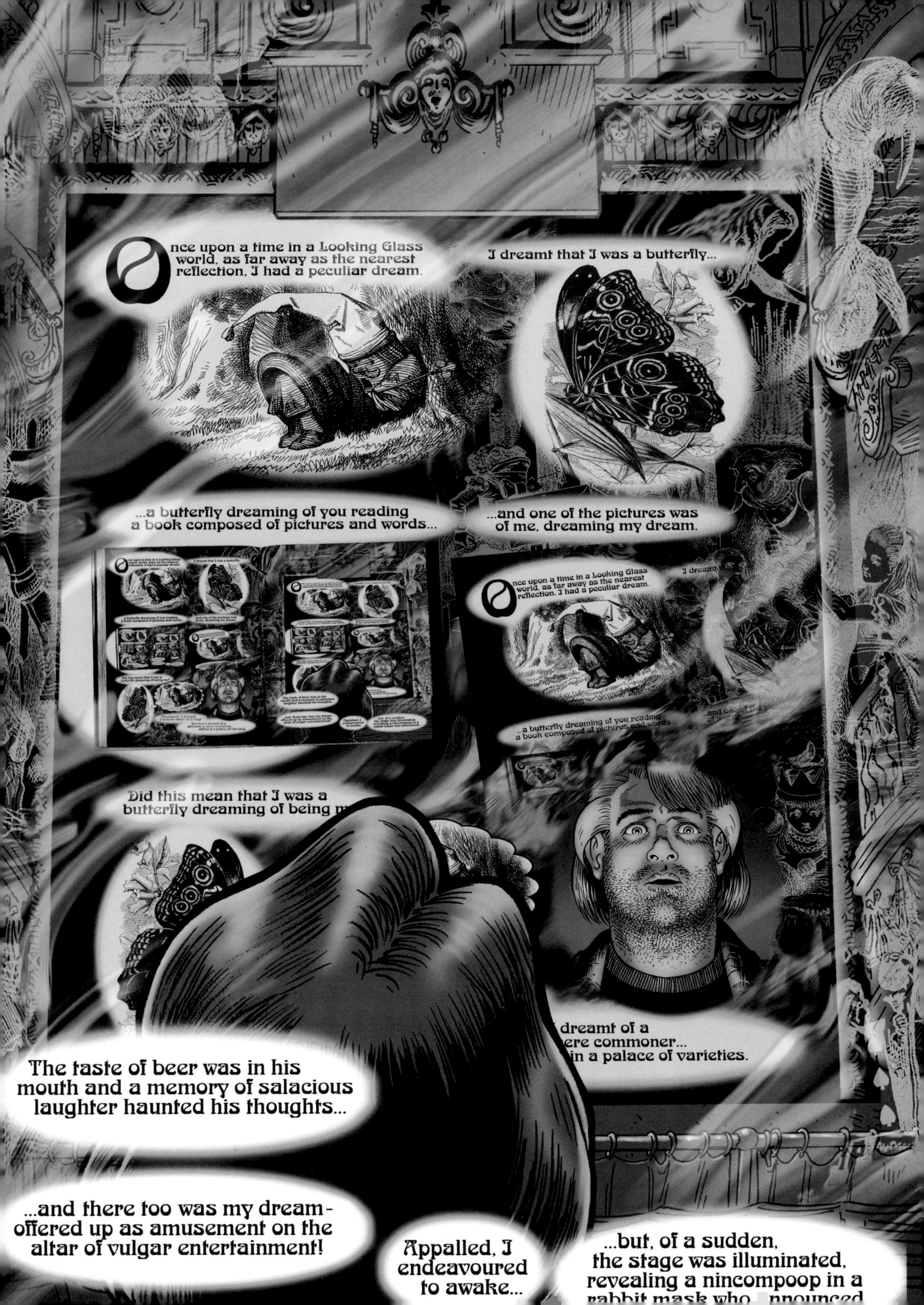

Once upon a time in a Looking Glass world, as far away as the nearest reflection, I had a peculiar dream.
I dreamt that I was a butterfly...
...a butterfly dreaming of you reading a book composed of pictures and words...
...and one of the pictures was of me, dreaming my dream.
Once upon a time in a Looking Glass world, as far away as the nearest reflection, I had a peculiar dream.
...a butterfly dreaming of you reading a book composed of pictures and words...
Did this mean that I was a butterfly dreaming of being m
dreamt of a ere commoner... in a palace of varieties.
The taste of beer was in his mouth and a memory of salacious laughter haunted his thoughts...
...and there too was my dream - offered up as amusement on the altar of vulgar entertainment!
Appalled, I endeavoured to awake...
...but, of a sudden, the stage was illuminated, revealing a nincompoop in a rabbit mask who

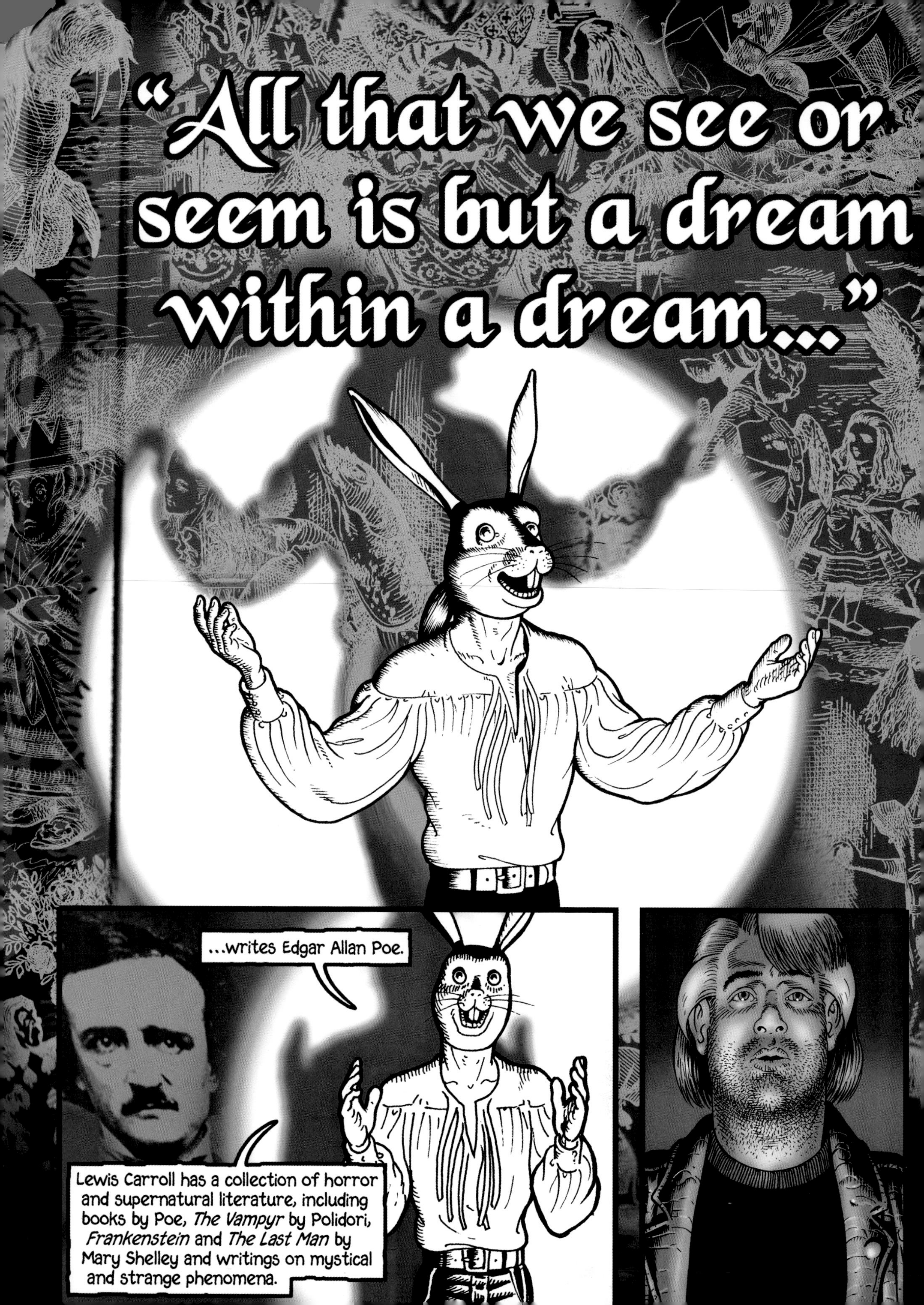
"All that we see or seem is but a dream within a dream..."
...writes Edgar Allan Poe.
Lewis Carroll has a collection of horror and supernatural literature, including books by Poe, The Vampyr by Polidori, Frankenstein and The Last Man by Mary Shelley and writings on mystical and strange phenomena.

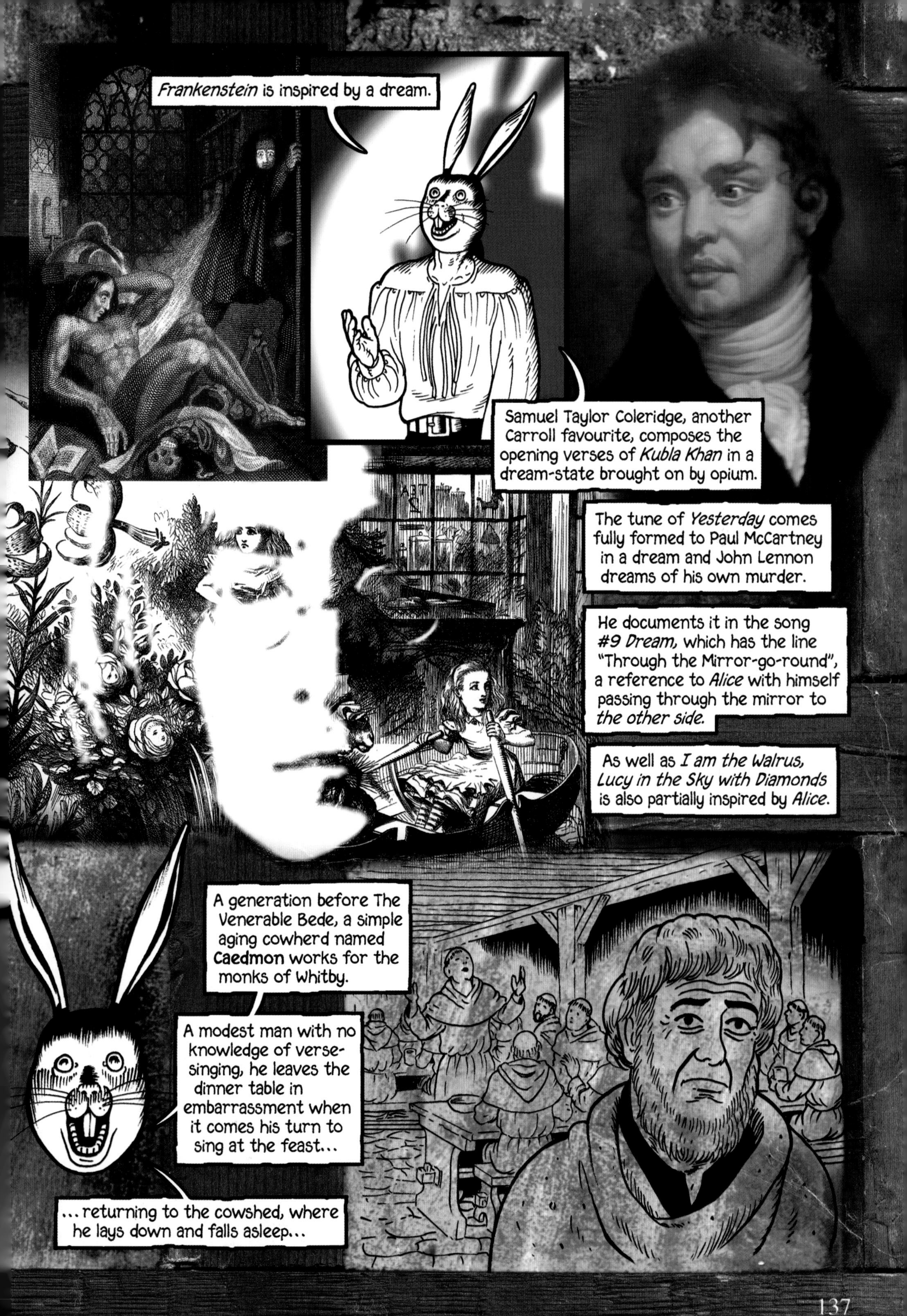
Frankenstein is inspired by a dream.
Samuel Taylor Coleridge, another Carroll favourite, composes the opening verses of Kubla Khan in a dream-state brought on by opium.
The tune of Yesterday comes fully formed to Paul McCartney in a dream and John Lennon dreams of his own murder.
He documents it in the song #9 Dream, which has the line "Through the Mirror-go-round", a reference to Alice with himself passing through the mirror to the other side.
As well as I am the Walrus, Lucy in the Sky with Diamonds is also partially inspired by Alice.
A generation before The Venerable Bede, a simple aging cowherd named Caedmon works for the monks of Whitby.
A modest man with no knowledge of verse-singing, he leaves the dinner table in embarrassment when it comes his turn to sing at the feast...
...returning to the cowshed, where he lays down and falls asleep...

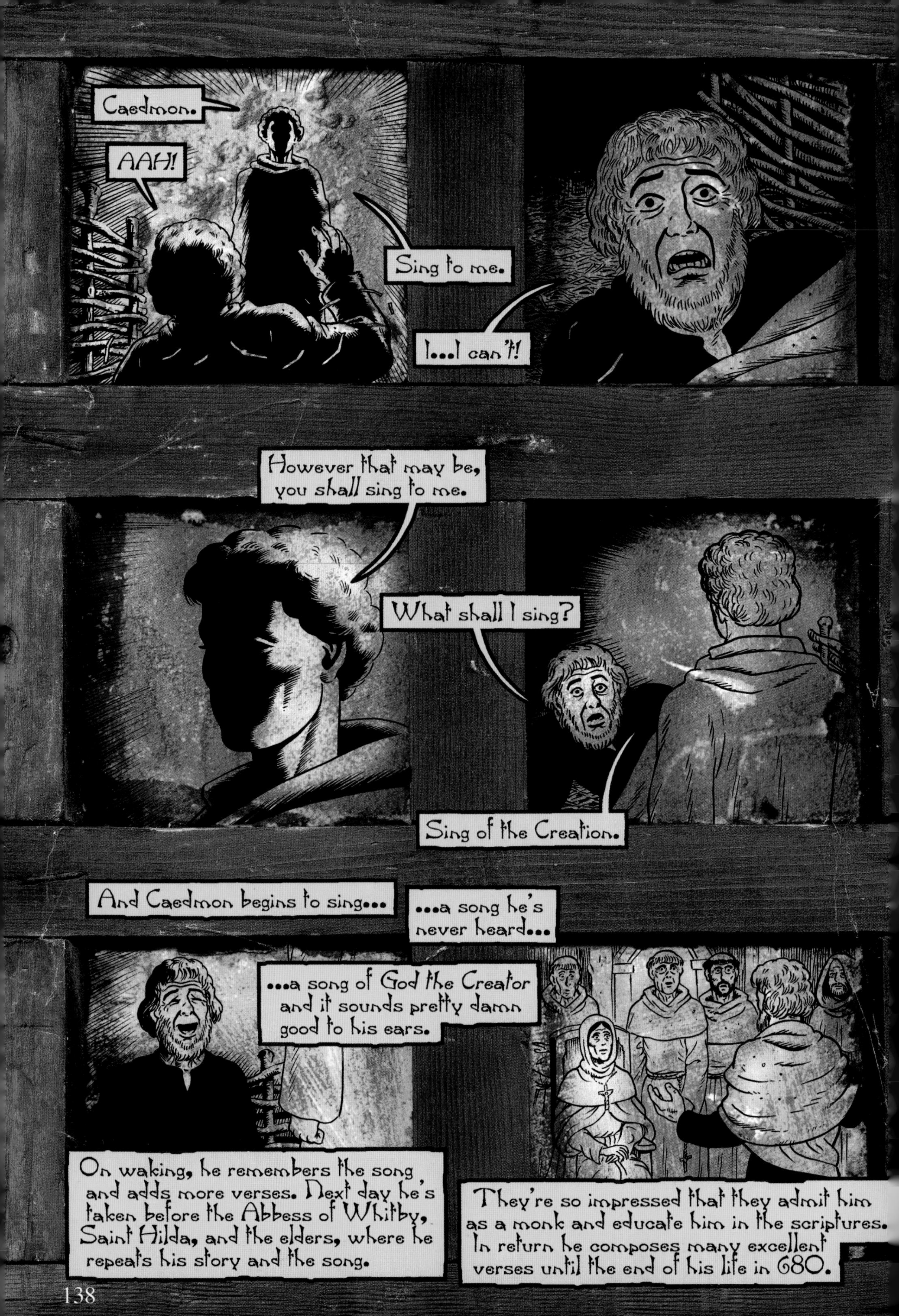
Caedmon.
AAH!
Sing to me.
I...I can't!
However that may be, you shall sing to me.
What shall I sing?
Sing of the Creation.
And Caedmon begins to sing...
...a song he's never heard...
...a song of God the Creator and it sounds pretty damn good to his ears.
On waking, he remembers the song and adds more verses. Next day he's taken before the Abbess of Whitby, Saint Hilda, and the elders, where he repeats his story and the song.
They're so impressed that they admit him as a monk and educate him in the scriptures. In return he composes many excellent verses until the end of his life in 680.

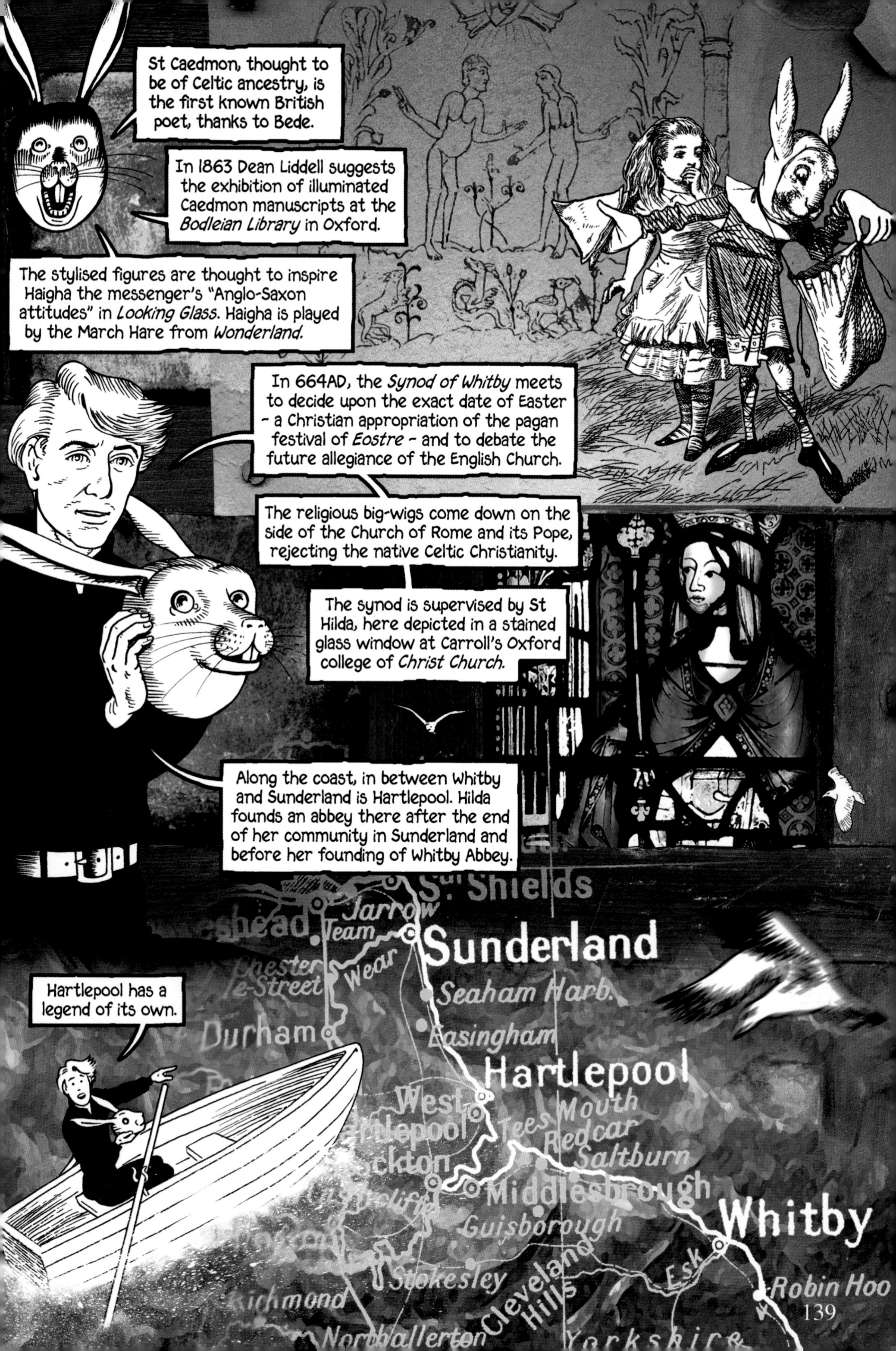
St Caedmon, thought to be of Celtic ancestry, is the first known British poet, thanks to Bede.
In 1863 Dean Liddell suggests the exhibition of illuminated Caedmon manuscripts at the *Bodleian Library* in Oxford.
The stylised figures are thought to inspire Haigha the messenger's "Anglo-Saxon attitudes" in *Looking Glass*. Haigha is played by the March Hare from *Wonderland*.
In 664AD, the *Synod of Whitby* meets to decide upon the exact date of Easter – a Christian appropriation of the pagan festival of *Eostre* – and to debate the future allegiance of the English Church.
The religious big-wigs come down on the side of the Church of Rome and its Pope, rejecting the native Celtic Christianity.
The synod is supervised by St Hilda, here depicted in a stained glass window at Carroll's Oxford college of *Christ Church*.
Along the coast, in between Whitby and Sunderland is Hartlepool. Hilda founds an abbey there after the end of her community in Sunderland and before her founding of Whitby Abbey.
Hartlepool has a legend of its own.
S. Shields
Jarrow
Team
Sunderland
Wear
Chester le-Street
Seaham Harb.
Durham
Easingham
Hartlepool
West Hartlepool
Tees Mouth
Redcar
Saltburn
Middlesbrough
Whitby
Guisborough
Stokesley
Cleveland Hills
Esk
Robin Hoo
Richmond
Northallerton
Yorkshire

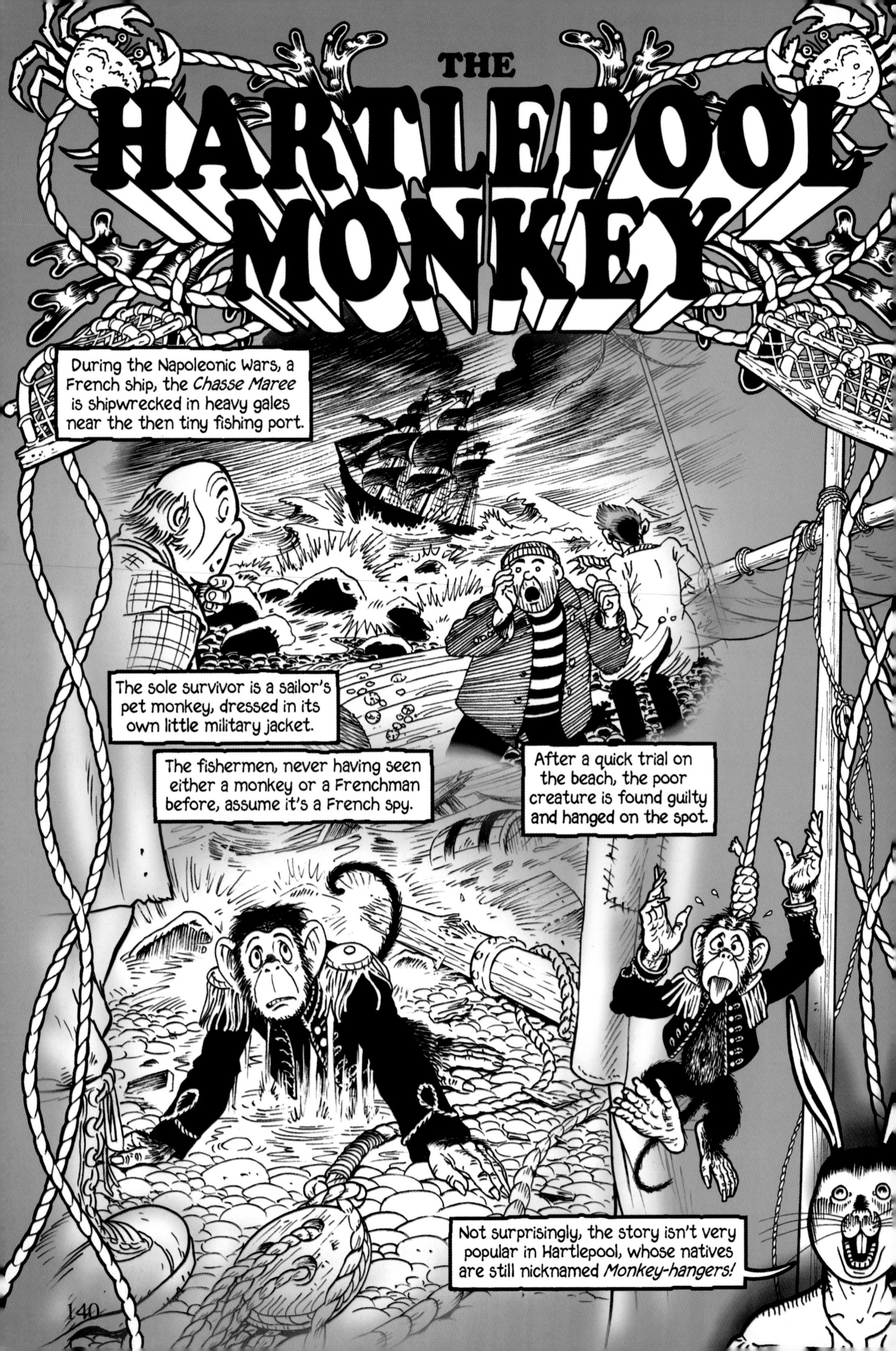
THE HARTLEPOOL MONKEY
During the Napoleonic Wars, a French ship, the *Chasse Maree* is shipwrecked in heavy gales near the then tiny fishing port.
The sole survivor is a sailor's pet monkey, dressed in its own little military jacket.
The fishermen, never having seen either a monkey or a Frenchman before, assume it's a French spy.
After a quick trial on the beach, the poor creature is found guilty and hanged on the spot.
Not surprisingly, the story isn't very popular in Hartlepool, whose natives are still nicknamed *Monkey-hangers!*

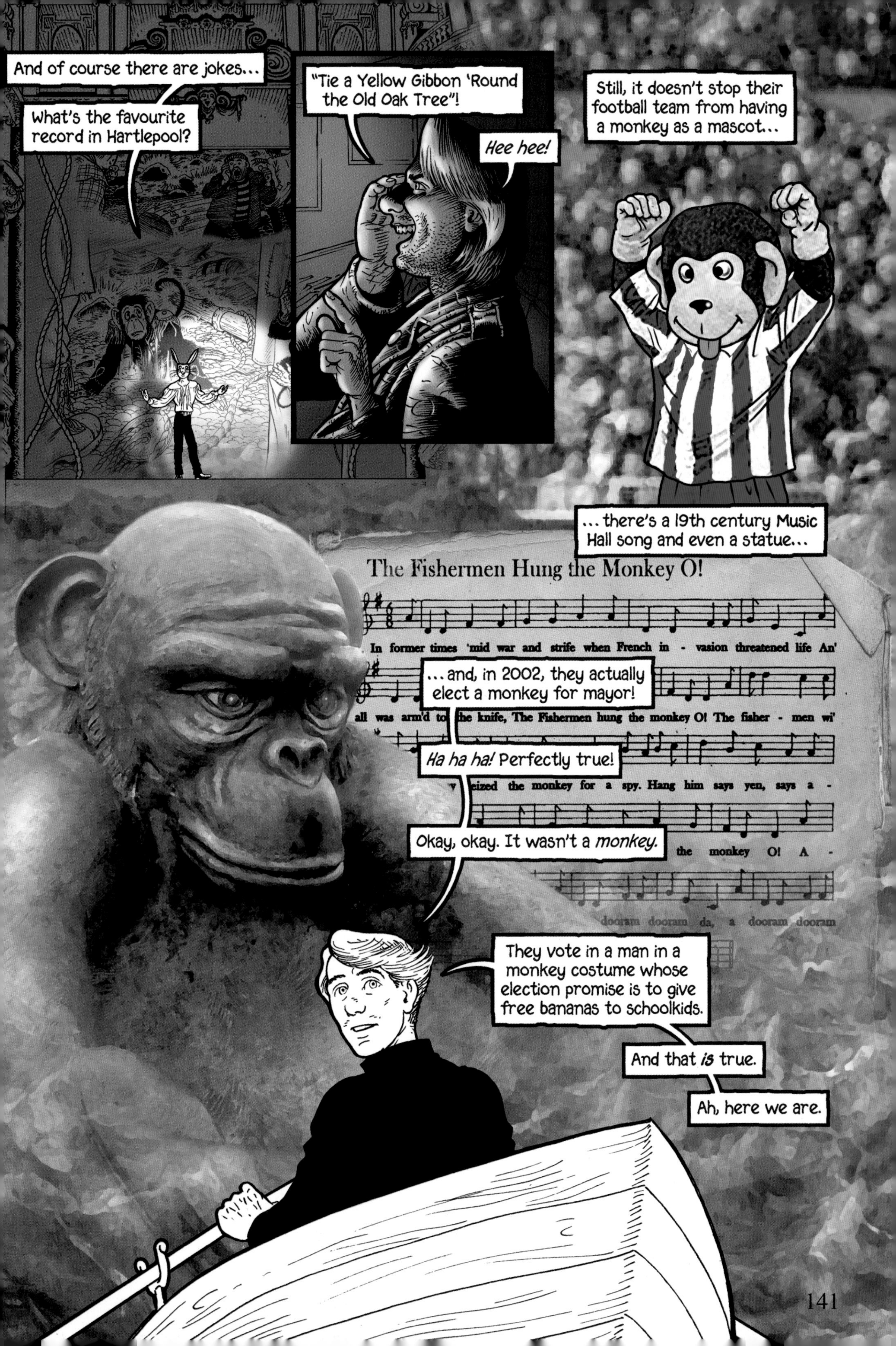
And of course there are jokes...
What's the favourite record in Hartlepool?
"Tie a Yellow Gibbon 'Round the Old Oak Tree"!
Hee hee!
Still, it doesn't stop their football team from having a monkey as a mascot...
... there's a 19th century Music Hall song and even a statue...
The Fishermen Hung the Monkey O!
In former times 'mid war and strife when French in - vasion threatened life An'
all was arm'd to the knife, The Fishermen hung the monkey O! The fisher - men wi'
eized the monkey for a spy. Hang him says yen, says a -
the monkey O! A -
dooram dooram da, a dooram dooram
... and, in 2002, they actually elect a monkey for mayor!
Ha ha ha! Perfectly true!
Okay, okay. It wasn't a monkey.
They vote in a man in a monkey costume whose election promise is to give free bananas to schoolkids.
And that is true.
Ah, here we are.

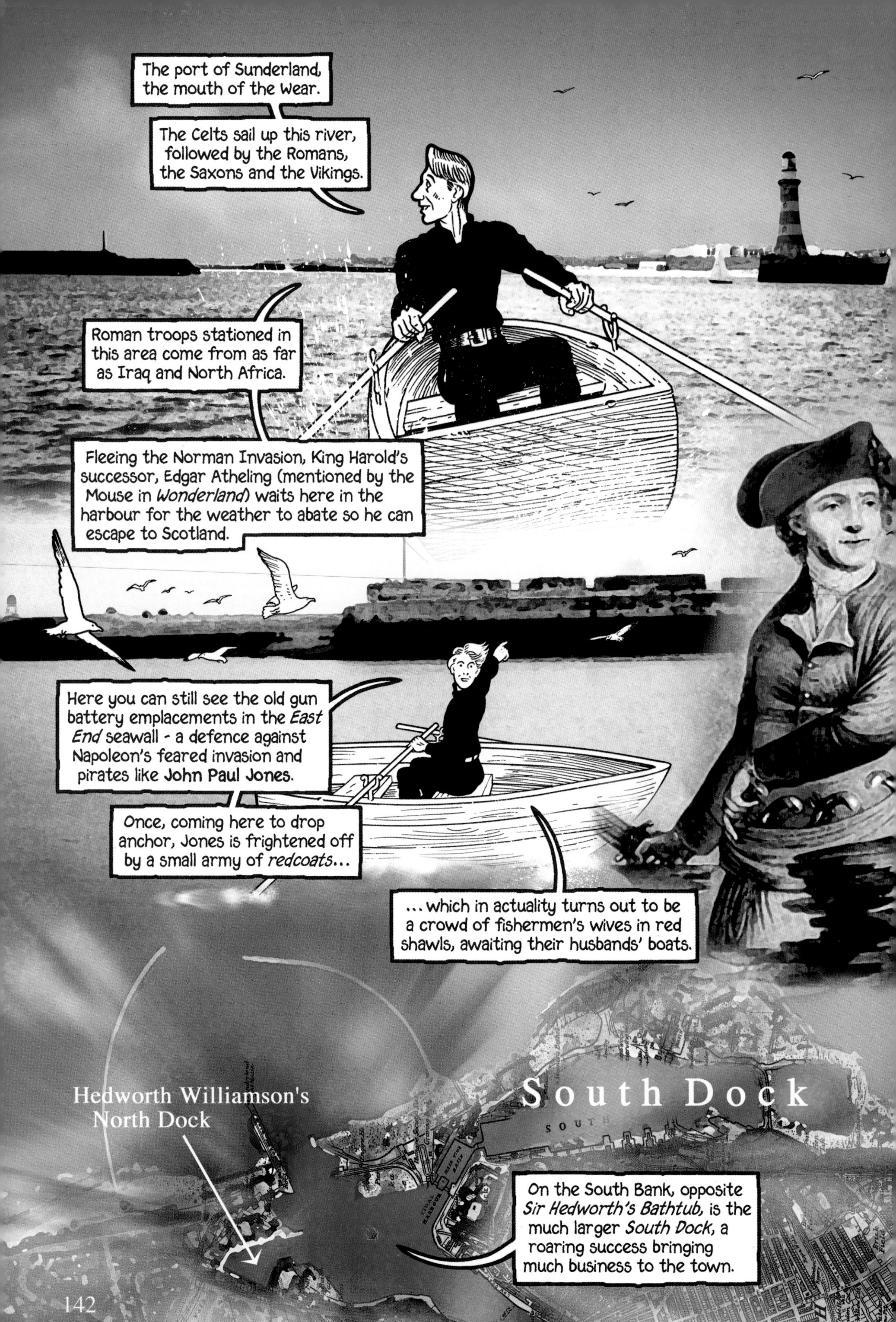

The port of Sunderland, the mouth of the Wear.
The Celts sail up this river, followed by the Romans, the Saxons and the Vikings.
Roman troops stationed in this area come from as far as Iraq and North Africa.
Fleeing the Norman Invasion, King Harold's successor, Edgar Atheling (mentioned by the Mouse in *Wonderland*) waits here in the harbour for the weather to abate so he can escape to Scotland.
Here you can still see the old gun battery emplacements in the *East End* seawall - a defence against Napoleon's feared invasion and pirates like **John Paul Jones**.
Once, coming here to drop anchor, Jones is frightened off by a small army of *redcoats*...
...which in actuality turns out to be a crowd of fishermen's wives in red shawls, awaiting their husbands' boats.
Hedworth Williamson's North Dock
South Dock
On the South Bank, opposite *Sir Hedworth's Bathtub*, is the much larger *South Dock*, a roaring success bringing much business to the town.

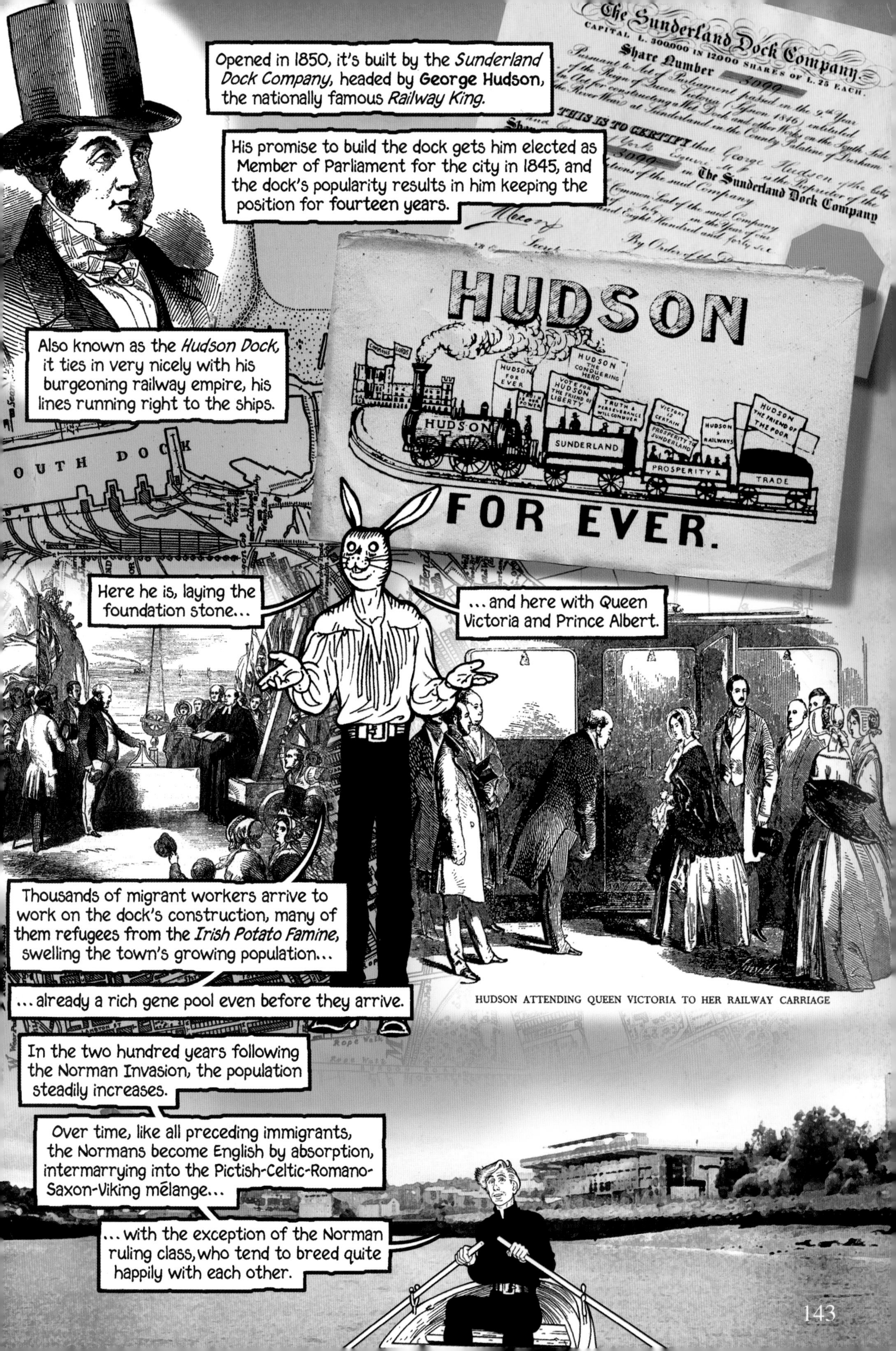
Opened in 1850, it's built by the *Sunderland Dock Company*, headed by **George Hudson**, the nationally famous *Railway King*.
The Sunderland Dock Company
Share Number
His promise to build the dock gets him elected as Member of Parliament for the city in 1845, and the dock's popularity results in him keeping the position for fourteen years.
THIS IS TO CERTIFY that George Hudson
The Sunderland Dock Company
HUDSON
Also known as the *Hudson Dock*, it ties in very nicely with his burgeoning railway empire, his lines running right to the ships.
HUDSON THE CONQUERING HERO
HUDSON FOR EVER
VOTE FOR HUDSON THE FRIEND OF LIBERTY
TRUTH & PERSEVERANCE WILL CONQUER
VICTORY IS CERTAIN
PROSPERITY TO SUNDERLAND
HUDSON & RAILWAYS
HUDSON THE FRIEND OF THE POOR
HUDSON
SUNDERLAND
PROSPERITY &
TRADE
FOR EVER.
SOUTH DOCK
Here he is, laying the foundation stone...
... and here with Queen Victoria and Prince Albert.
Thousands of migrant workers arrive to work on the dock's construction, many of them refugees from the *Irish Potato Famine*, swelling the town's growing population...
... already a rich gene pool even before they arrive.
HUDSON ATTENDING QUEEN VICTORIA TO HER RAILWAY CARRIAGE
In the two hundred years following the Norman Invasion, the population steadily increases.
Over time, like all preceding immigrants, the Normans become English by absorption, intermarrying into the Pictish-Celtic-Romano-Saxon-Viking mélange...
... with the exception of the Norman ruling class, who tend to breed quite happily with each other.

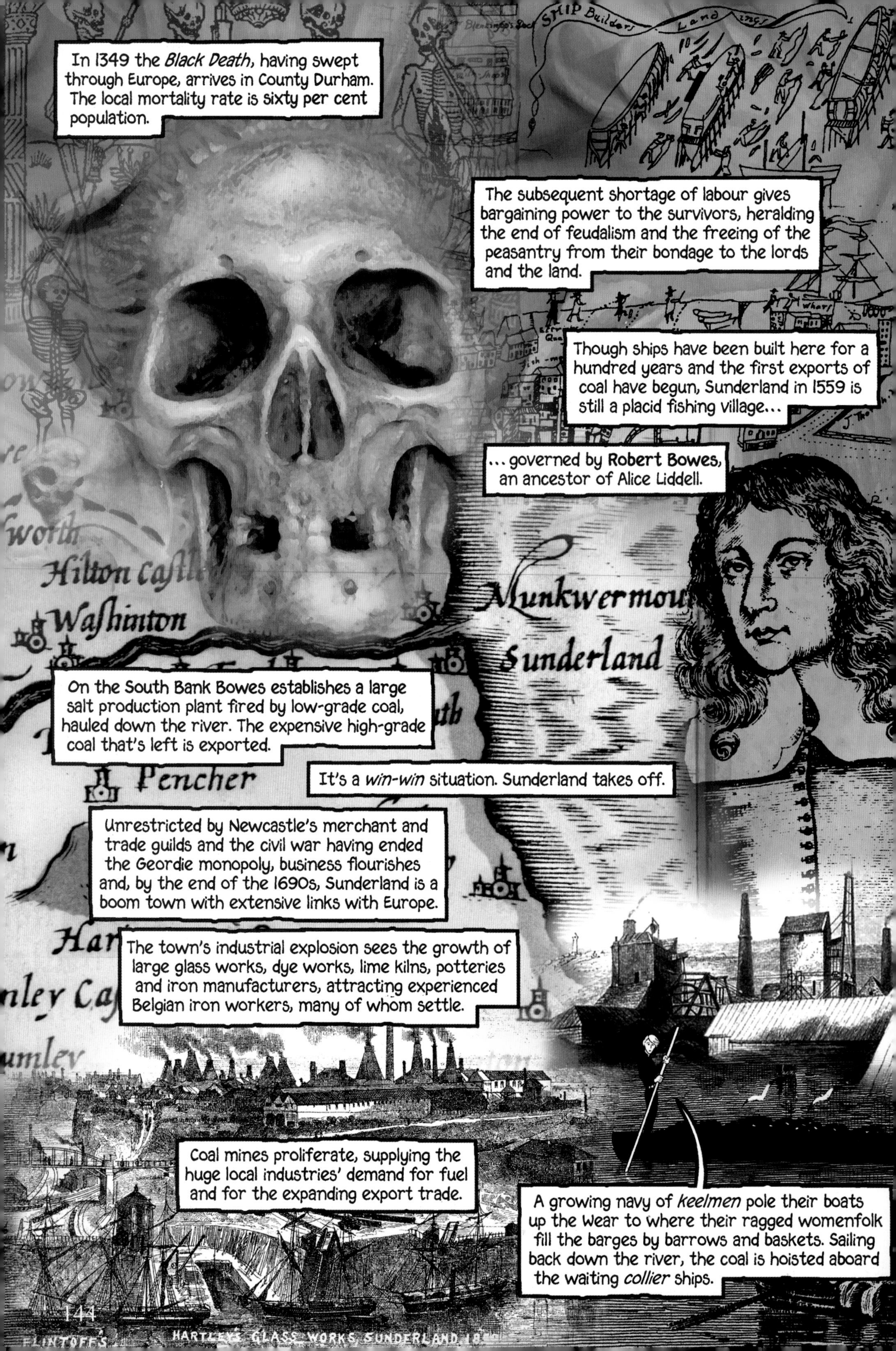
In 1349 the *Black Death*, having swept through Europe, arrives in County Durham. The local mortality rate is sixty per cent population.
The subsequent shortage of labour gives bargaining power to the survivors, heralding the end of feudalism and the freeing of the peasantry from their bondage to the lords and the land.
Though ships have been built here for a hundred years and the first exports of coal have begun, Sunderland in 1559 is still a placid fishing village...
... governed by **Robert Bowes**, an ancestor of Alice Liddell.
Washinton
Sunderland
On the South Bank Bowes establishes a large salt production plant fired by low-grade coal, hauled down the river. The expensive high-grade coal that's left is exported.
Pencher
It's a *win-win* situation. Sunderland takes off.
Unrestricted by Newcastle's merchant and trade guilds and the civil war having ended the Geordie monopoly, business flourishes and, by the end of the 1690s, Sunderland is a boom town with extensive links with Europe.
The town's industrial explosion sees the growth of large glass works, dye works, lime kilns, potteries and iron manufacturers, attracting experienced Belgian iron workers, many of whom settle.
Coal mines proliferate, supplying the huge local industries' demand for fuel and for the expanding export trade.
A growing navy of *keelmen* pole their boats up the Wear to where their ragged womenfolk fill the barges by barrows and baskets. Sailing back down the river, the coal is hoisted aboard the waiting *collier* ships.
HARTLEYS GLASS WORKS, SUNDERLAND

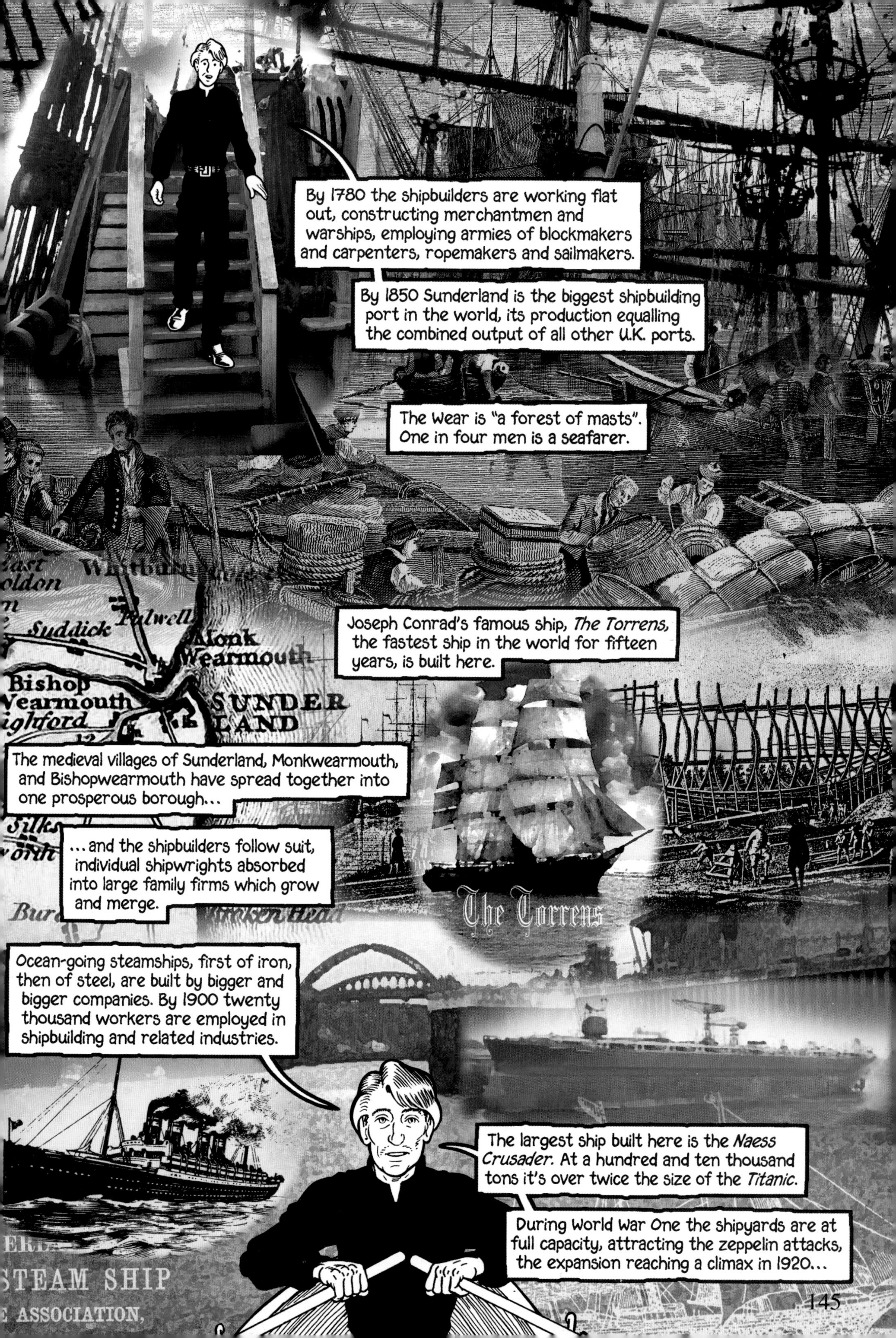
By 1780 the shipbuilders are working flat out, constructing merchantmen and warships, employing armies of blockmakers and carpenters, ropemakers and sailmakers.
By 1850 Sunderland is the biggest shipbuilding port in the world, its production equalling the combined output of all other U.K. ports.
The Wear is "a forest of masts". One in four men is a seafarer.
Joseph Conrad's famous ship, *The Torrens*, the fastest ship in the world for fifteen years, is built here.
The medieval villages of Sunderland, Monkwearmouth, and Bishopwearmouth have spread together into one prosperous borough...
...and the shipbuilders follow suit, individual shipwrights absorbed into large family firms which grow and merge.
The Torrens
Ocean-going steamships, first of iron, then of steel, are built by bigger and bigger companies. By 1900 twenty thousand workers are employed in shipbuilding and related industries.
The largest ship built here is the *Naess Crusader*. At a hundred and ten thousand tons it's over twice the size of the *Titanic*.
During World War One the shipyards are at full capacity, attracting the zeppelin attacks, the expansion reaching a climax in 1920...
STEAM SHIP
ASSOCIATION,

... followed by the *Depression*, hitting the town hard. The unemployment rate is seventy-five per cent. Coal and iron exports dwindle.

North Mail
Newcastle Daily Chronicle
CITY EDITION.
No. 16,934. TUESDAY, MAY 4, 1926. PRICE ONE PENNY.

BIGGEST STRIKE IN BRITAIN'S HISTORY BEGUN.

N.U.R.'S FINAL INSTRUCTION. | SOLDIERS' LEAVE STOPPED.

NEARLY 5,000,000 WORKERS INVOLVED IN STOPPAGE.

MR. J. H. THOMAS MAKES FINAL BUT FUTILE MEDIATION EFFORT.

PREMIER'S REPLY TO CHALLENGE

EMERGENCY PLANS OF GOVERNMENT. | WIDE POWERS THE STATE.

The *General Strike* of 1926 sees none of the violence that takes place elsewhere, but by 1930 shipbuilding comes to a virtual standstill.

The breweries are forced to close but, strangely enough, there seems to be no shortage of beer!

The shipyards burst into life again during World War Two, and Sunderland is a major contributor to the *War Effort*, paying the price by once more becoming a target for enemy bombers.

The *Empire Liberty* is made here; its clever design using prefabricated parts is adopted by the U.S.A., which produces a fleet of over twenty-seven hundred *Liberty Ships* to ferry soldiers and material to war zones, a key factor in the Allies' victory.

The new boom continues into the 1960s until ferocious global competition sinks the market.

There's a world-wide slump. The shipyards amalgamate or close.

The last yards here close after a deal, brokered by the government of Margaret Thatcher, grants Scottish shipbuilders a large European subsidy.

A condition of the subsidy is that Britain loses a major shipbuilder.

Sunderland is sacrificed. The last ship is launched here in 1990.

It's the end of an era.

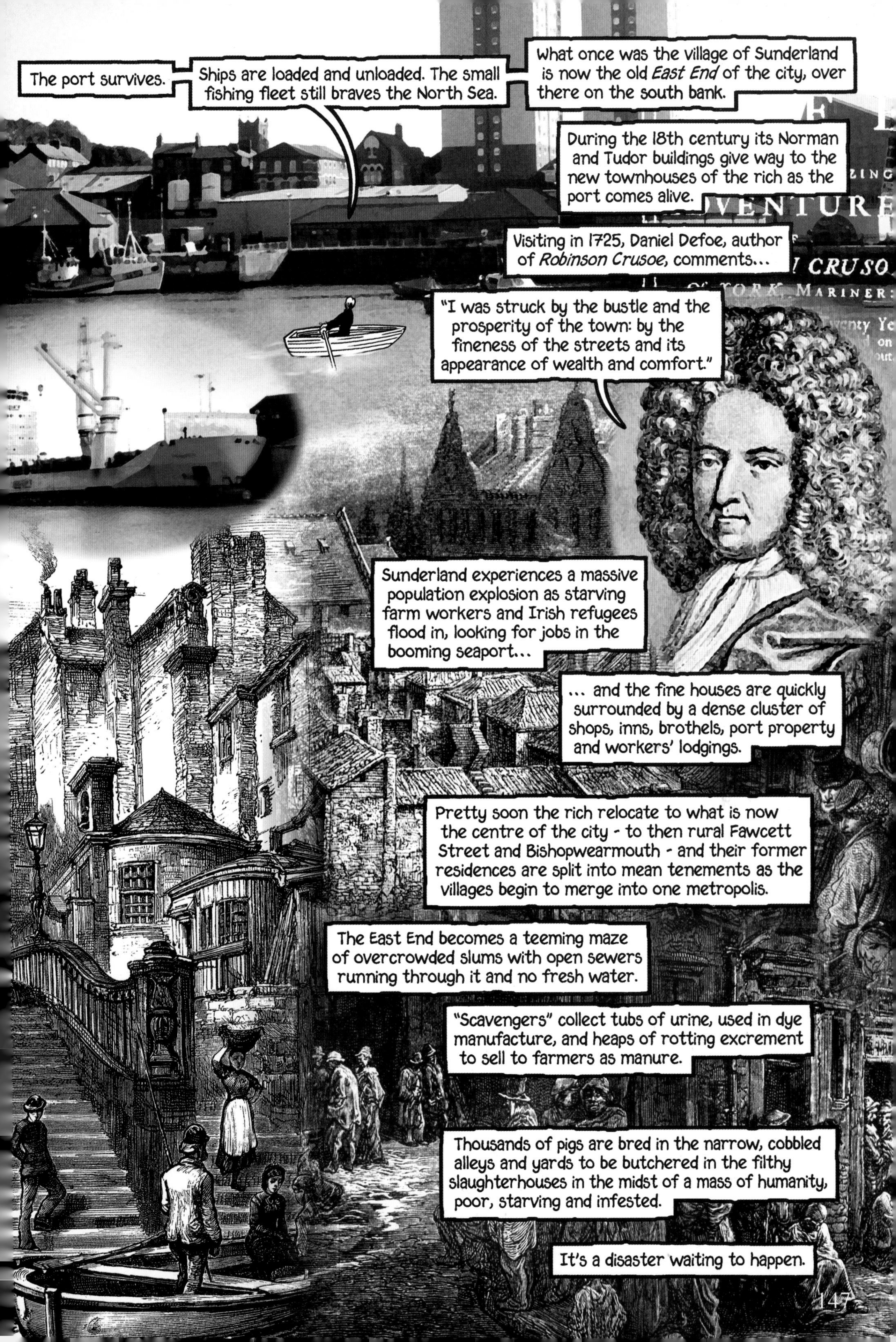
The port survives.
Ships are loaded and unloaded. The small fishing fleet still braves the North Sea.
What once was the village of Sunderland is now the old *East End* of the city, over there on the south bank.
During the 18th century its Norman and Tudor buildings give way to the new townhouses of the rich as the port comes alive.
Visiting in 1725, Daniel Defoe, author of *Robinson Crusoe*, comments...
"I was struck by the bustle and the prosperity of the town: by the fineness of the streets and its appearance of wealth and comfort."
Sunderland experiences a massive population explosion as starving farm workers and Irish refugees flood in, looking for jobs in the booming seaport...
... and the fine houses are quickly surrounded by a dense cluster of shops, inns, brothels, port property and workers' lodgings.
Pretty soon the rich relocate to what is now the centre of the city - to then rural Fawcett Street and Bishopwearmouth - and their former residences are split into mean tenements as the villages begin to merge into one metropolis.
The East End becomes a teeming maze of overcrowded slums with open sewers running through it and no fresh water.
"Scavengers" collect tubs of urine, used in dye manufacture, and heaps of rotting excrement to sell to farmers as manure.
Thousands of pigs are bred in the narrow, cobbled alleys and yards to be butchered in the filthy slaughterhouses in the midst of a mass of humanity, poor, starving and infested.
It's a disaster waiting to happen.

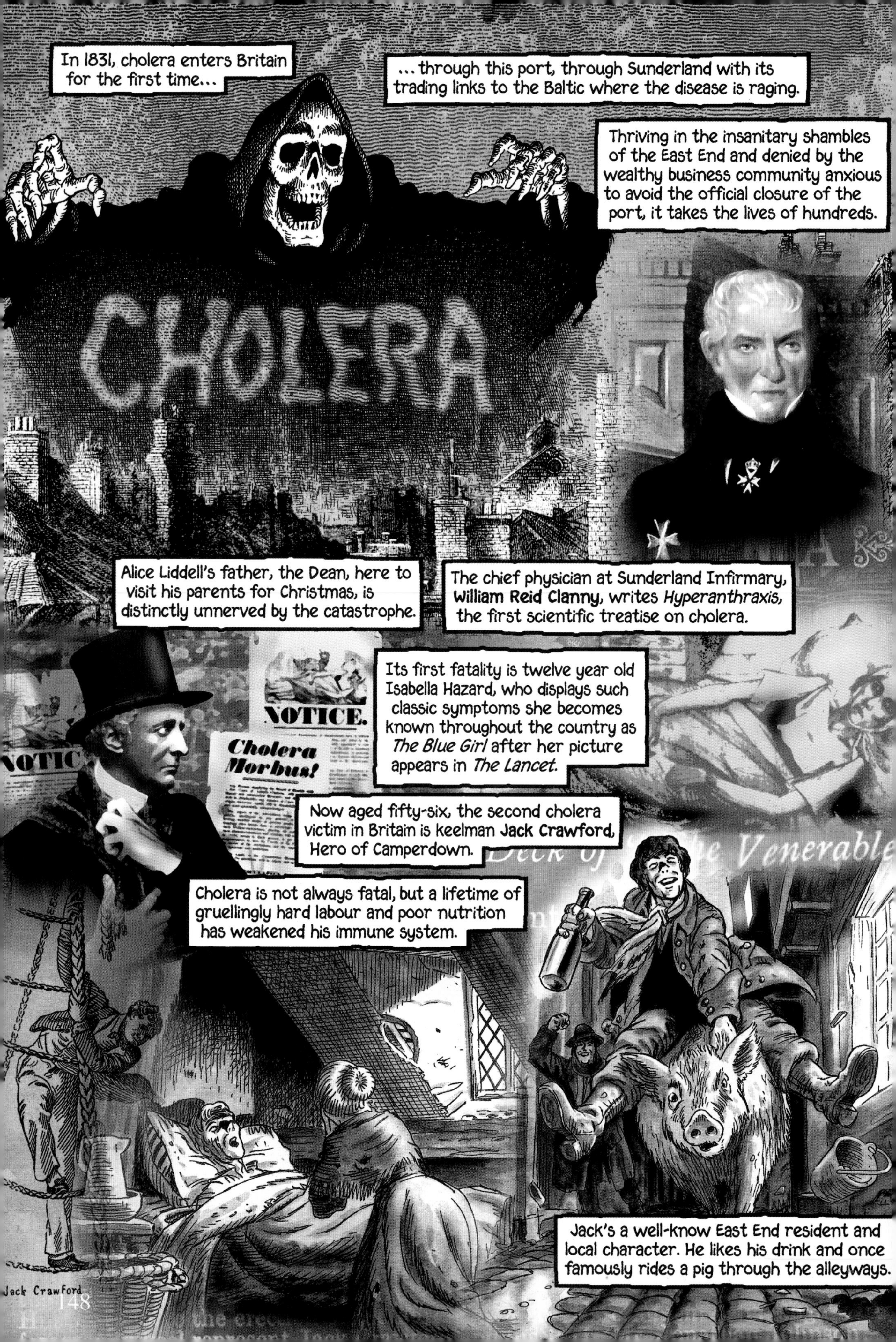

In 1831, cholera enters Britain for the first time...
... through this port, through Sunderland with its trading links to the Baltic where the disease is raging.
Thriving in the insanitary shambles of the East End and denied by the wealthy business community anxious to avoid the official closure of the port, it takes the lives of hundreds.
CHOLERA
Alice Liddell's father, the Dean, here to visit his parents for Christmas, is distinctly unnerved by the catastrophe.
The chief physician at Sunderland Infirmary, **William Reid Clanny**, writes *Hyperanthraxis*, the first scientific treatise on cholera.
NOTICE.
Cholera Morbus!
Its first fatality is twelve year old Isabella Hazard, who displays such classic symptoms she becomes known throughout the country as *The Blue Girl* after her picture appears in *The Lancet*.
Now aged fifty-six, the second cholera victim in Britain is keelman **Jack Crawford**, Hero of Camperdown.
Cholera is not always fatal, but a lifetime of gruellingly hard labour and poor nutrition has weakened his immune system.
Jack's a well-know East End resident and local character. He likes his drink and once famously rides a pig through the alleyways.
Jack Crawford

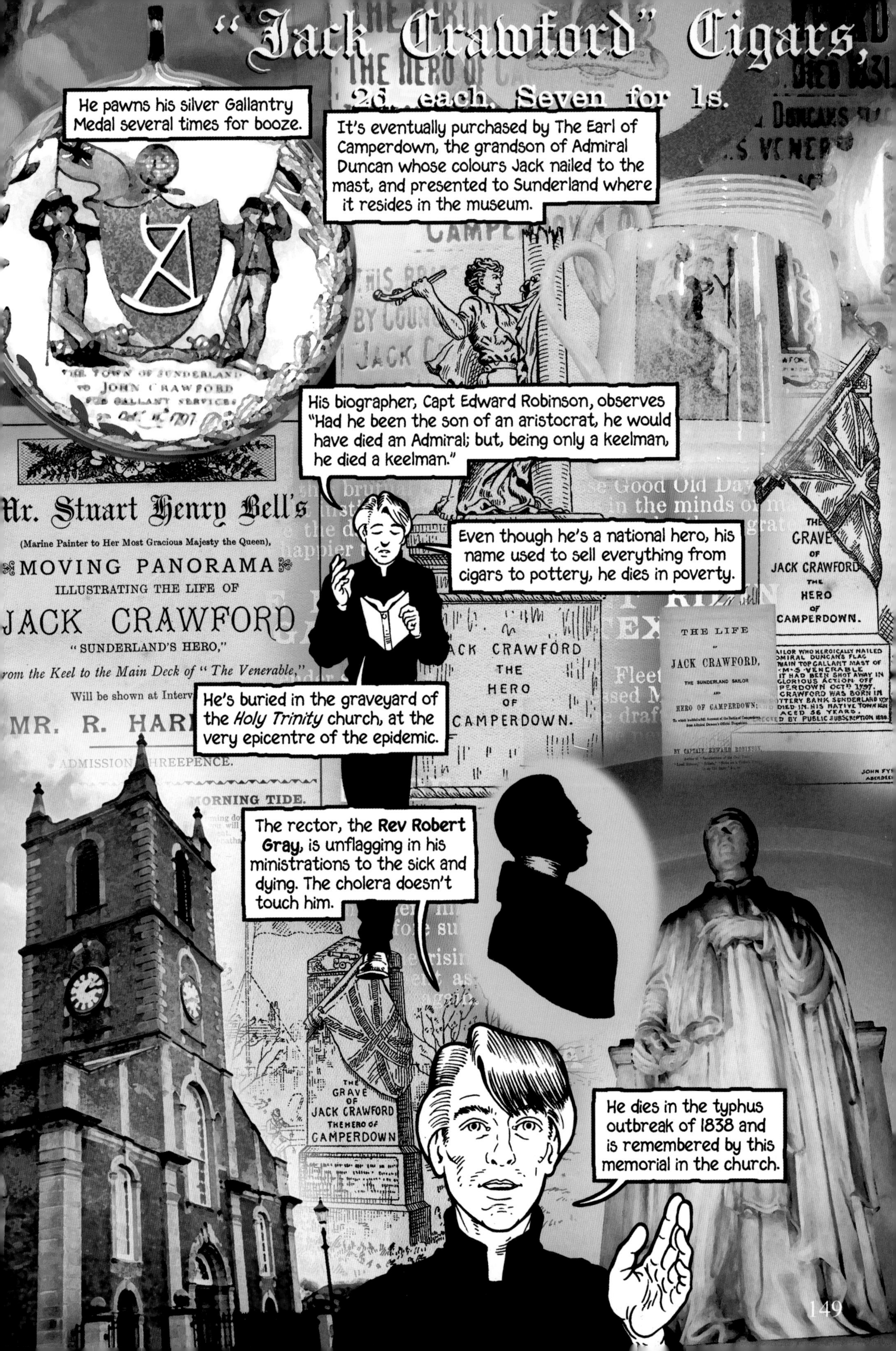

"Jack Crawford" Cigars,
2d. each. Seven for 1s.
He pawns his silver Gallantry Medal several times for booze.
It's eventually purchased by The Earl of Camperdown, the grandson of Admiral Duncan whose colours Jack nailed to the mast, and presented to Sunderland where it resides in the museum.
His biographer, Capt Edward Robinson, observes "Had he been the son of an aristocrat, he would have died an Admiral; but, being only a keelman, he died a keelman."
Even though he's a national hero, his name used to sell everything from cigars to pottery, he dies in poverty.
He's buried in the graveyard of the *Holy Trinity* church, at the very epicentre of the epidemic.
The rector, the **Rev Robert Gray**, is unflagging in his ministrations to the sick and dying. The cholera doesn't touch him.
He dies in the typhus outbreak of 1838 and is remembered by this memorial in the church.
Mr. Stuart Henry Bell's
(Marine Painter to Her Most Gracious Majesty the Queen),
MOVING PANORAMA
ILLUSTRATING THE LIFE OF
JACK CRAWFORD
"SUNDERLAND'S HERO,"
THE LIFE OF JACK CRAWFORD, THE SUNDERLAND SAILOR AND HERO OF CAMPERDOWN
THE GRAVE OF JACK CRAWFORD THE HERO OF CAMPERDOWN.

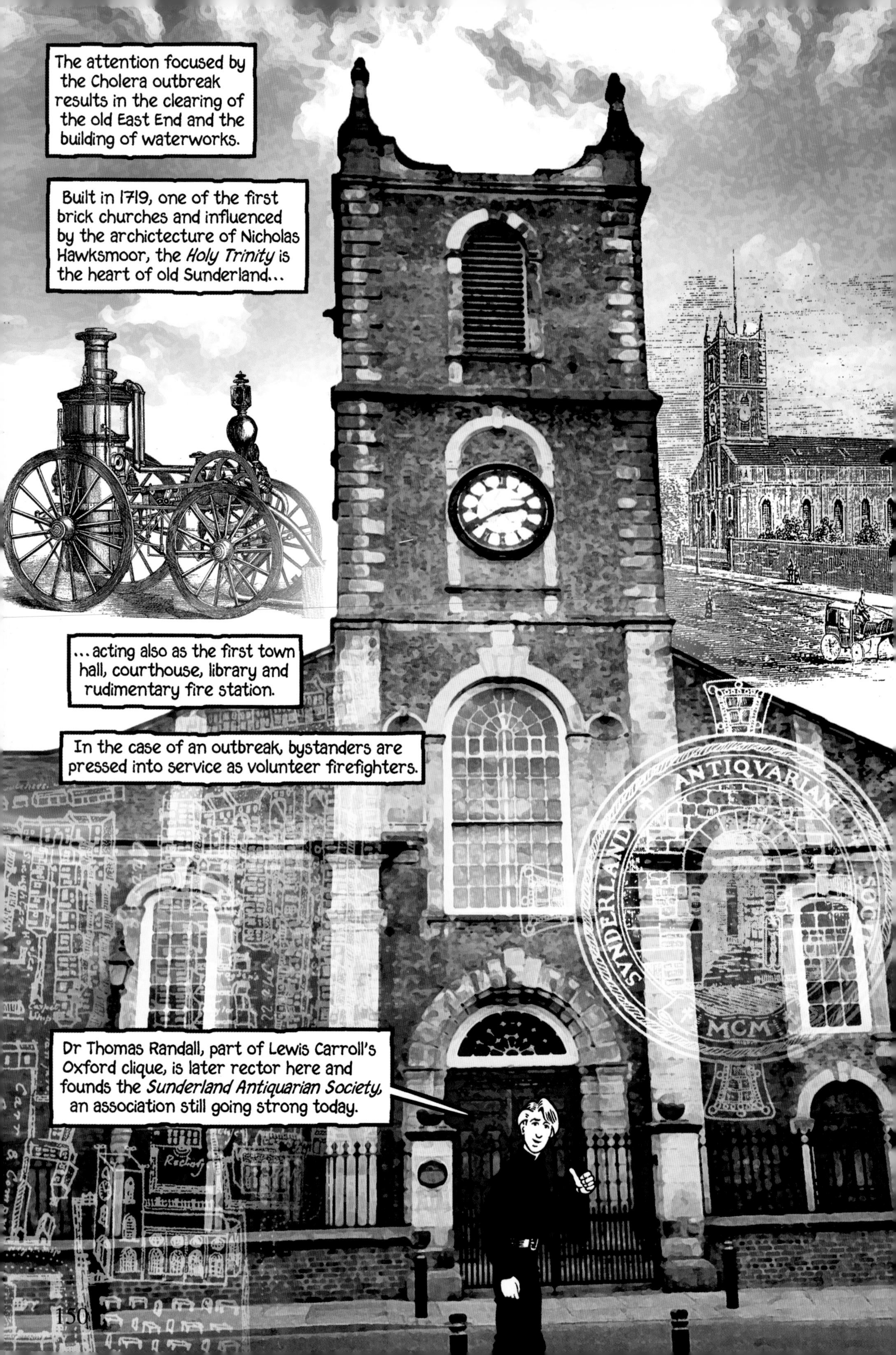

The attention focused by the Cholera outbreak results in the clearing of the old East End and the building of waterworks.
Built in 1719, one of the first brick churches and influenced by the architecture of Nicholas Hawksmoor, the *Holy Trinity* is the heart of old Sunderland...
...acting also as the first town hall, courthouse, library and rudimentary fire station.
In the case of an outbreak, bystanders are pressed into service as volunteer firefighters.
SUNDERLAND ANTIQUARIAN
MCM
Dr Thomas Randall, part of Lewis Carroll's Oxford clique, is later rector here and founds the *Sunderland Antiquarian Society*, an association still going strong today.

In the 1820s, *bodysnatchers* raid the Holy Trinity graveyard, then the largest burial ground in North England, for corpses to meet the high demand of Edinburgh's medical schools.

Irish immigrants **Burke and Hare** ply their gruesome trade here. The filthy, overcrowded East End tenements with their high mortality rate provide a constant supply of fresh cadavers.

Selling mutton pies and Chelsea buns as a front, they use the food wagon to transport their exhumations to Edinburgh.

No comments about the quality of their pies are documented.

Burke, often seen strolling down High Street at night, is described as "a very obliging man, with many a kind word".

They escape detection in Sunderland but aren't as lucky back in Edinburgh, where Hare turns King's evidence and Burke's hanged for murder in 1828.

Resurrectionists snatch so many bodies that watchmen and vigilante groups patrol by torchlight, keeping a watch over their family graves...

...and, in 1824, a Scots surgeon and a medical student are imprisoned in Durham Gaol after being caught here red-handed and in possession of a recently buried child's body, all packed up and ready to be posted to Edinburgh.

If any of this sounds familiar – the bodysnatchers, the cholera epidemic, the slums and the death of Jack Crawford - it may be because you've read the best-selling novel *The Dress Lodger* by **Sheri Holman**.

This dark historical thriller paints a vivid and realistic picture of the squalor of the old East End.

Holman comes to Sunderland in the 1990s to research the history of her story's location.

TIONAL BESTSELLER

...man seduces you. Her prose, tart, racy, and somber, will sing in your soul a long while.
—FRANK McCOURT, author of *Angela's Ashes*

The Dress Lodger

SHERI HOL

151

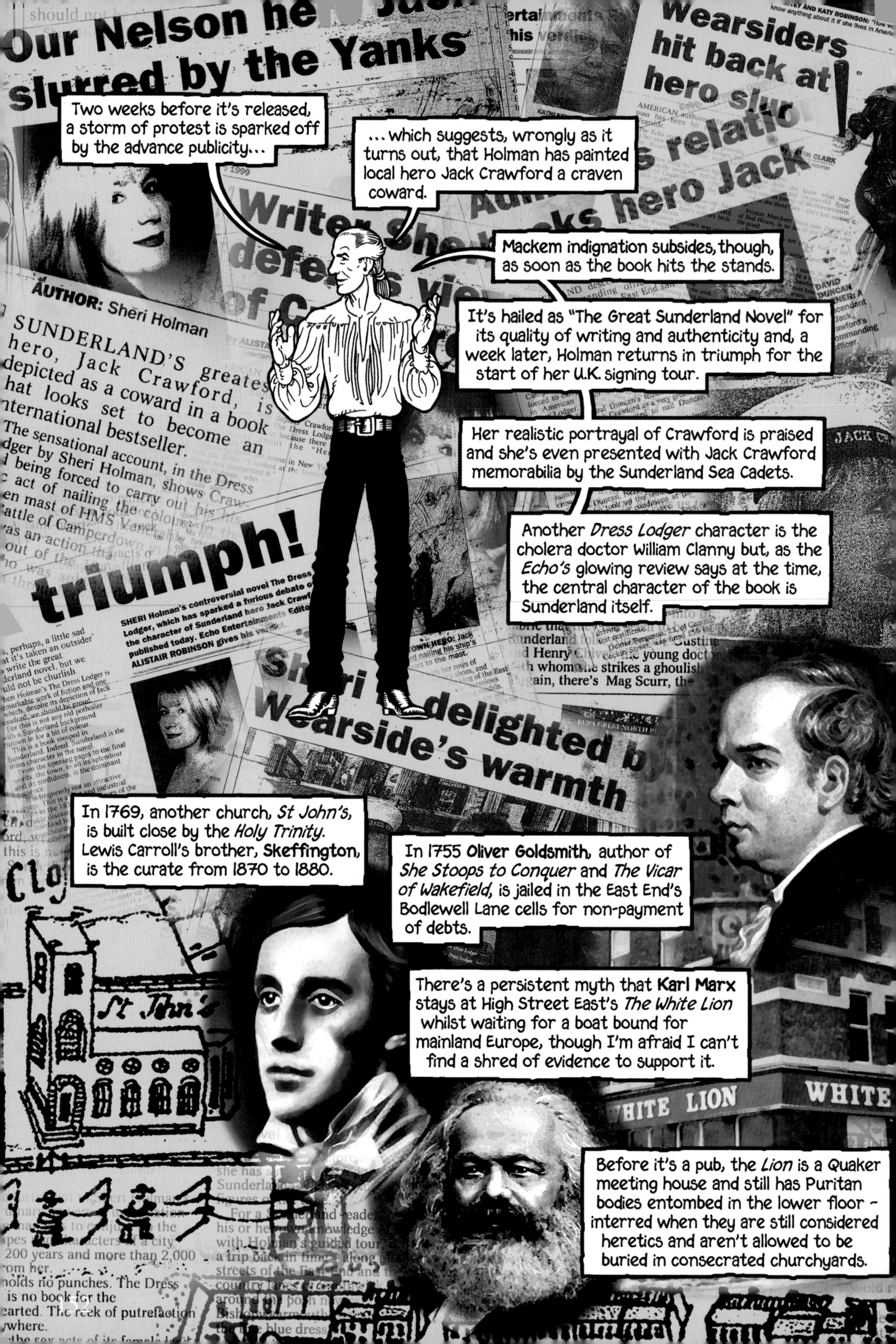

Two weeks before it's released, a storm of protest is sparked off by the advance publicity...
...which suggests, wrongly as it turns out, that Holman has painted local hero Jack Crawford a craven coward.
Mackem indignation subsides, though, as soon as the book hits the stands.
It's hailed as "The Great Sunderland Novel" for its quality of writing and authenticity and, a week later, Holman returns in triumph for the start of her U.K. signing tour.
Her realistic portrayal of Crawford is praised and she's even presented with Jack Crawford memorabilia by the Sunderland Sea Cadets.
Another *Dress Lodger* character is the cholera doctor William Clanny but, as the *Echo's* glowing review says at the time, the central character of the book is Sunderland itself.
In 1769, another church, *St John's*, is built close by the *Holy Trinity*. Lewis Carroll's brother, **Skeffington**, is the curate from 1870 to 1880.
In 1755 **Oliver Goldsmith**, author of *She Stoops to Conquer* and *The Vicar of Wakefield*, is jailed in the East End's Bodlewell Lane cells for non-payment of debts.
There's a persistent myth that **Karl Marx** stays at High Street East's *The White Lion* whilst waiting for a boat bound for mainland Europe, though I'm afraid I can't find a shred of evidence to support it.
Before it's a pub, the *Lion* is a Quaker meeting house and still has Puritan bodies entombed in the lower floor - interred when they are still considered heretics and aren't allowed to be buried in consecrated churchyards.
Our Nelson hero slurred by the Yanks
Wearsiders hit back at hero slur
triumph!
Sheri delighted by Wearside's warmth
AUTHOR: Sheri Holman
St John's
WHITE LION

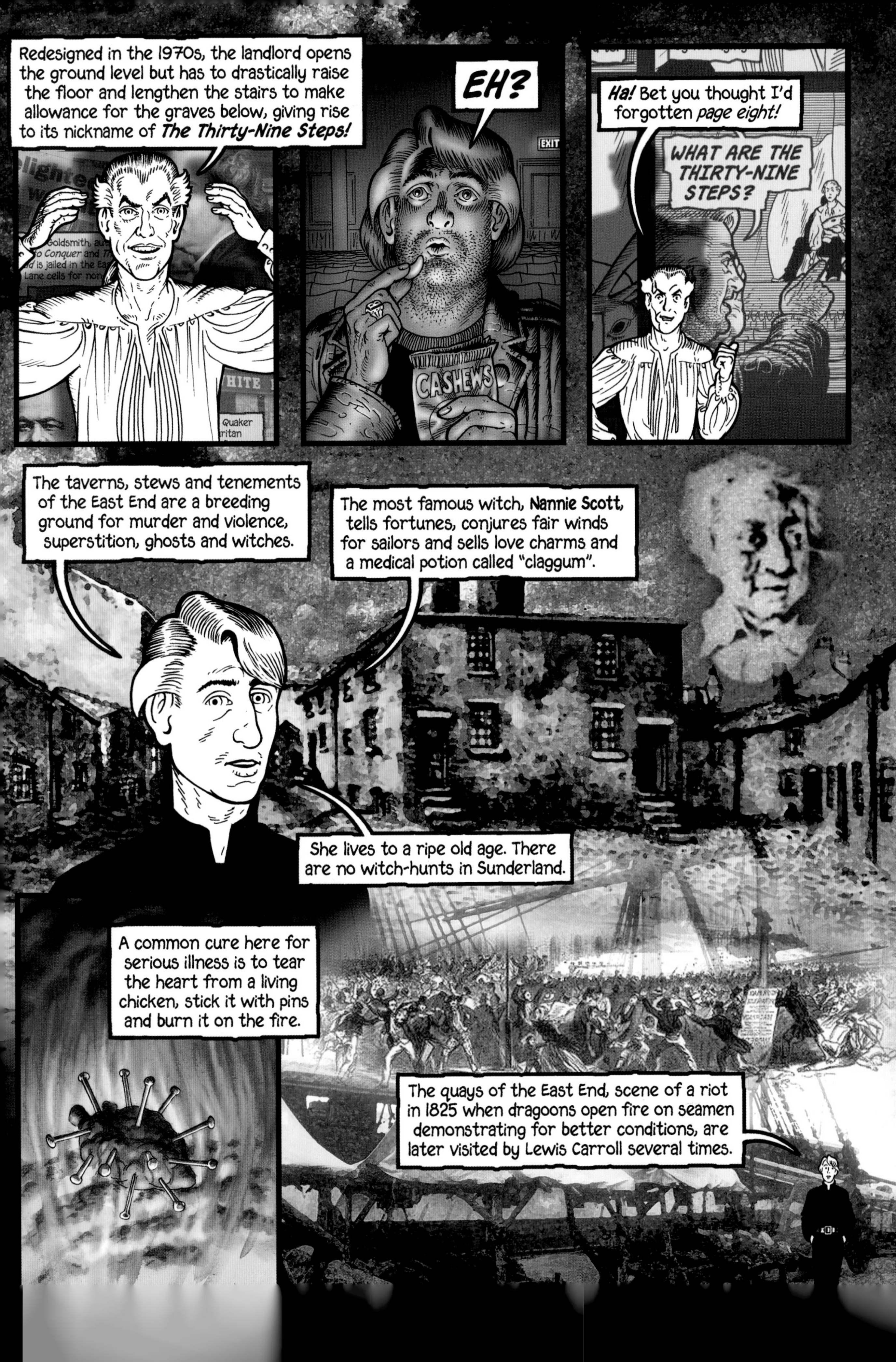
Redesigned in the 1970s, the landlord opens the ground level but has to drastically raise the floor and lengthen the stairs to make allowance for the graves below, giving rise to its nickname of ***The Thirty-Nine Steps!***
EH?
EXIT
CASHEWS
Ha! Bet you thought I'd forgotten *page eight!*
WHAT ARE THE THIRTY-NINE STEPS?
The taverns, stews and tenements of the East End are a breeding ground for murder and violence, superstition, ghosts and witches.
The most famous witch, **Nannie Scott**, tells fortunes, conjures fair winds for sailors and sells love charms and a medical potion called "claggum".
She lives to a ripe old age. There are no witch-hunts in Sunderland.
A common cure here for serious illness is to tear the heart from a living chicken, stick it with pins and burn it on the fire.
The quays of the East End, scene of a riot in 1825 when dragoons open fire on seamen demonstrating for better conditions, are later visited by Lewis Carroll several times.

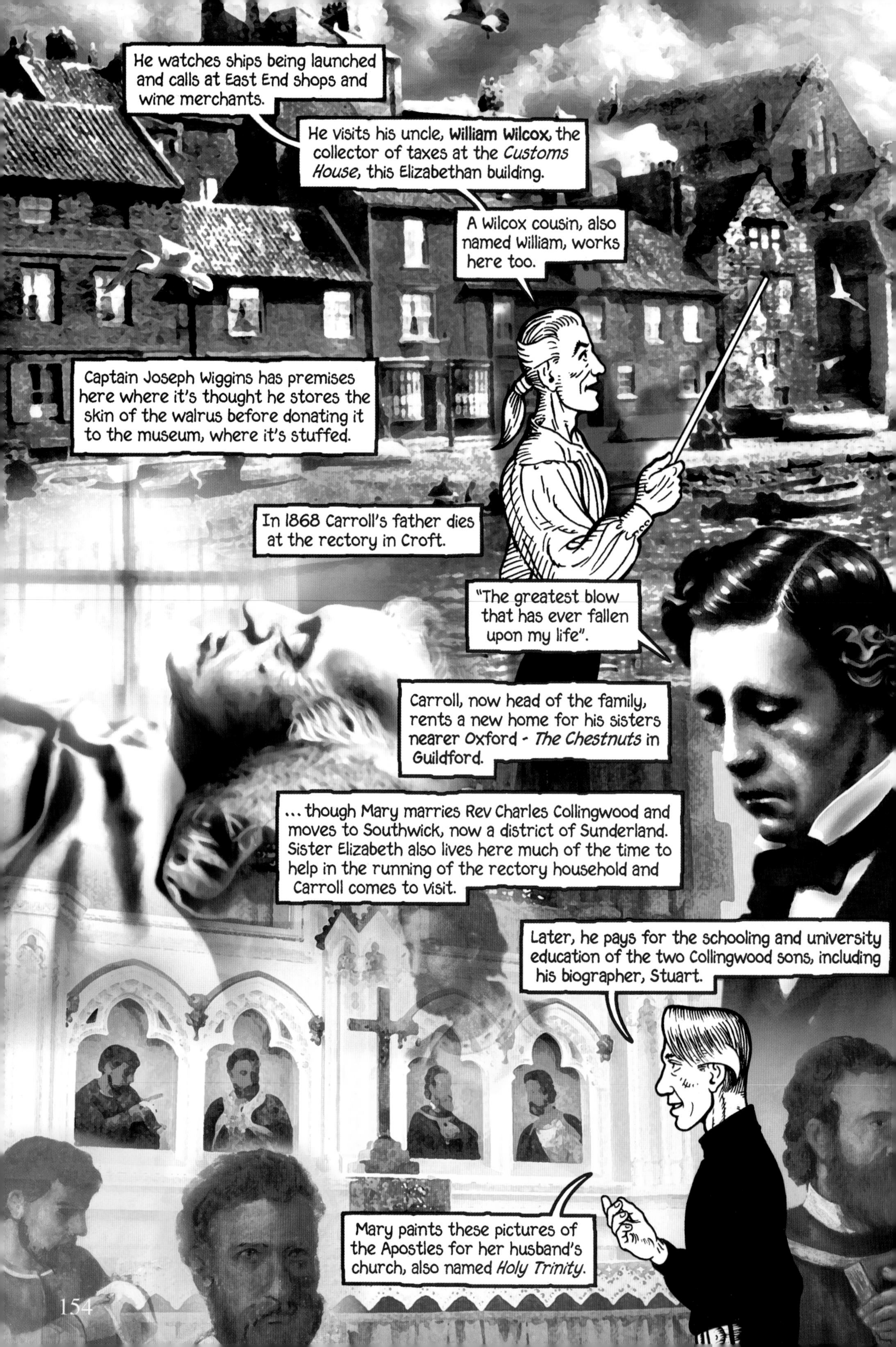
He watches ships being launched and calls at East End shops and wine merchants.
He visits his uncle, **William Wilcox**, the collector of taxes at the *Customs House*, this Elizabethan building.
A Wilcox cousin, also named William, works here too.
Captain Joseph Wiggins has premises here where it's thought he stores the skin of the walrus before donating it to the museum, where it's stuffed.
In 1868 Carroll's father dies at the rectory in Croft.
"The greatest blow that has ever fallen upon my life".
Carroll, now head of the family, rents a new home for his sisters nearer Oxford - *The Chestnuts* in Guildford.
... though Mary marries Rev Charles Collingwood and moves to Southwick, now a district of Sunderland. Sister Elizabeth also lives here much of the time to help in the running of the rectory household and Carroll comes to visit.
Later, he pays for the schooling and university education of the two Collingwood sons, including his biographer, Stuart.
Mary paints these pictures of the Apostles for her husband's church, also named *Holy Trinity*.

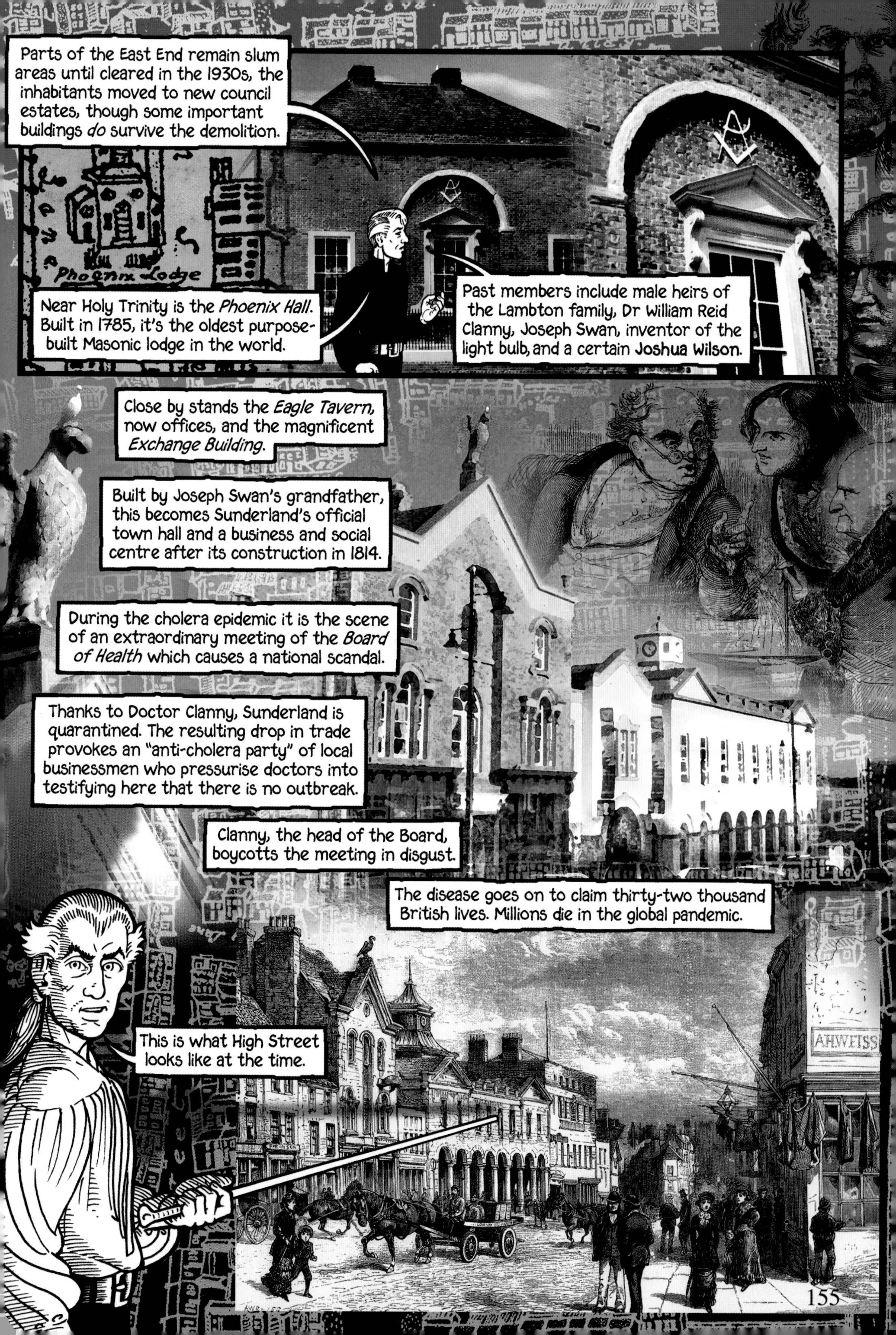

Parts of the East End remain slum areas until cleared in the 1930s, the inhabitants moved to new council estates, though some important buildings *do* survive the demolition.
Phoenix Lodge
Near Holy Trinity is the *Phoenix Hall*. Built in 1785, it's the oldest purpose-built Masonic lodge in the world.
Past members include male heirs of the Lambton family, Dr William Reid Clanny, Joseph Swan, inventor of the light bulb, and a certain **Joshua Wilson**.
Close by stands the *Eagle Tavern*, now offices, and the magnificent *Exchange Building*.
Built by Joseph Swan's grandfather, this becomes Sunderland's official town hall and a business and social centre after its construction in 1814.
During the cholera epidemic it is the scene of an extraordinary meeting of the *Board of Health* which causes a national scandal.
Thanks to Doctor Clanny, Sunderland is quarantined. The resulting drop in trade provokes an "anti-cholera party" of local businessmen who pressurise doctors into testifying here that there is no outbreak.
Clanny, the head of the Board, boycotts the meeting in disgust.
The disease goes on to claim thirty-two thousand British lives. Millions die in the global pandemic.
This is what High Street looks like at the time.
A.H.WEISS

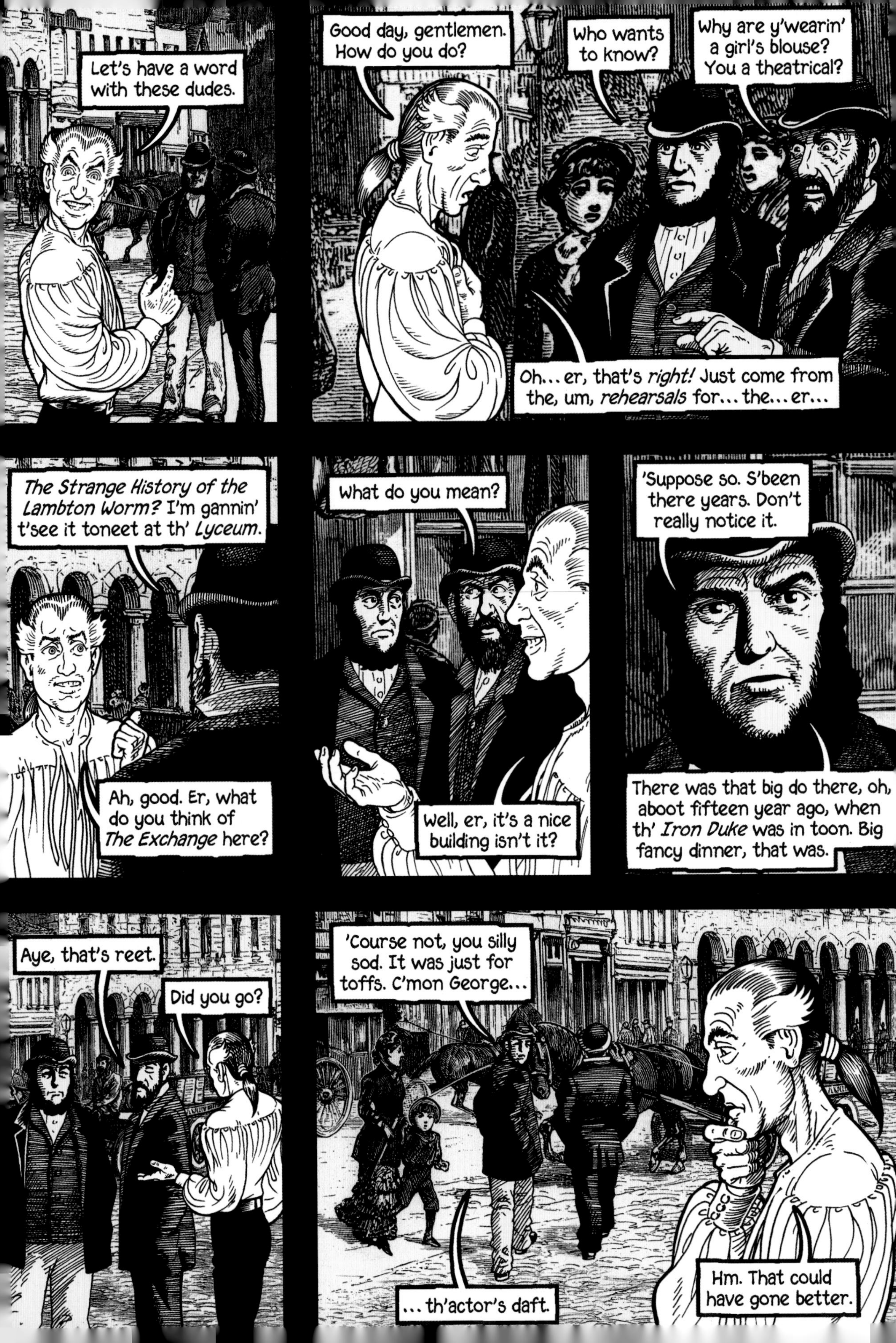
Let's have a word with these dudes.
Good day, gentlemen. How do you do?
Who wants to know?
Why are y'wearin' a girl's blouse? You a theatrical?
Oh... er, that's *right!* Just come from the, um, *rehearsals* for... the... er...
The Strange History of the Lambton Worm? I'm gannin' t'see it toneet at th' *Lyceum*.
Ah, good. Er, what do you think of *The Exchange* here?
What do you mean?
Well, er, it's a nice building isn't it?
'Suppose so. S'been there years. Don't really notice it.
There was that big do there, oh, aboot fifteen year ago, when th' *Iron Duke* was in toon. Big fancy dinner, that was.
Aye, that's reet.
Did you go?
'Course not, you silly sod. It was just for toffs. C'mon George...
... th'actor's daft.
Hm. That could have gone better.

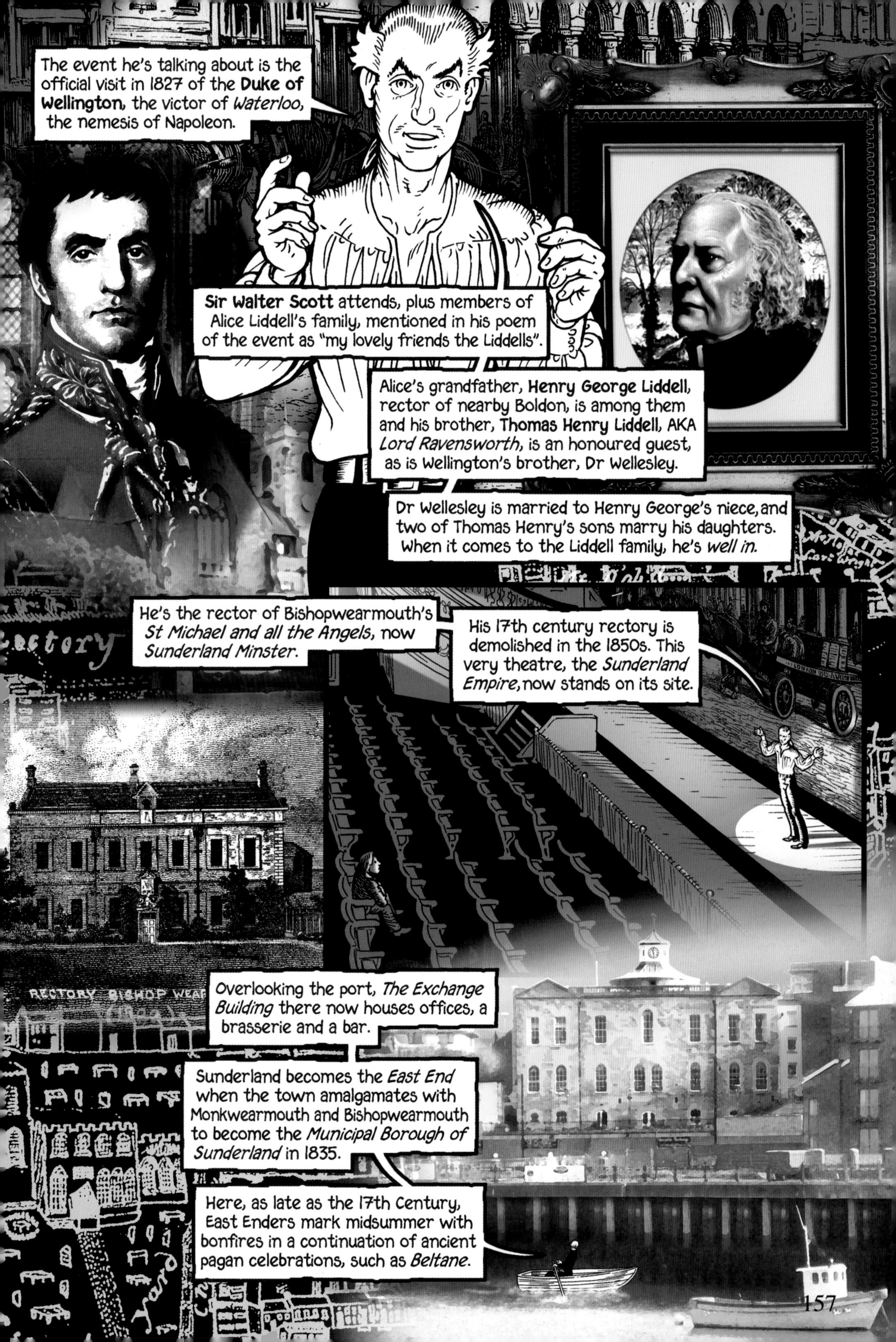
The event he's talking about is the official visit in 1827 of the **Duke of Wellington**, the victor of *Waterloo*, the nemesis of Napoleon.
Sir Walter Scott attends, plus members of Alice Liddell's family, mentioned in his poem of the event as "my lovely friends the Liddells".
Alice's grandfather, **Henry George Liddell**, rector of nearby Boldon, is among them and his brother, **Thomas Henry Liddell**, AKA *Lord Ravensworth*, is an honoured guest, as is Wellington's brother, Dr Wellesley.
Dr Wellesley is married to Henry George's niece, and two of Thomas Henry's sons marry his daughters. When it comes to the Liddell family, he's *well in*.
He's the rector of Bishopwearmouth's *St Michael and all the Angels*, now *Sunderland Minster*.
His 17th century rectory is demolished in the 1850s. This very theatre, the *Sunderland Empire*, now stands on its site.
RECTORY BISHOP WEAR
Overlooking the port, *The Exchange Building* there now houses offices, a brasserie and a bar.
Sunderland becomes the *East End* when the town amalgamates with Monkwearmouth and Bishopwearmouth to become the *Municipal Borough of Sunderland* in 1835.
Here, as late as the 17th Century, East Enders mark midsummer with bonfires in a continuation of ancient pagan celebrations, such as *Beltane*.

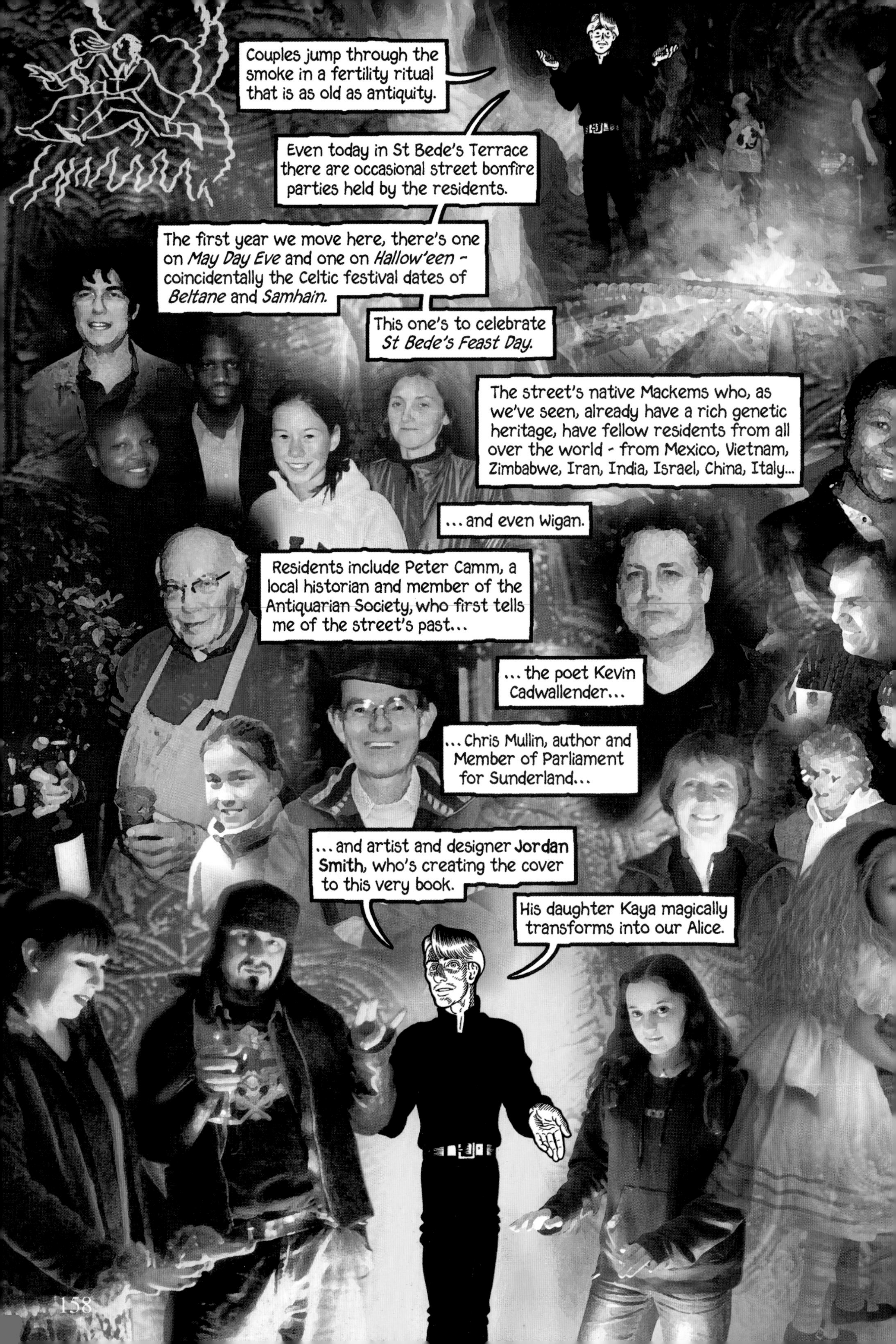
Couples jump through the smoke in a fertility ritual that is as old as antiquity.
Even today in St Bede's Terrace there are occasional street bonfire parties held by the residents.
The first year we move here, there's one on May Day Eve and one on Hallow'een - coincidentally the Celtic festival dates of Beltane and Samhain.
This one's to celebrate St Bede's Feast Day.
The street's native Mackems who, as we've seen, already have a rich genetic heritage, have fellow residents from all over the world - from Mexico, Vietnam, Zimbabwe, Iran, India, Israel, China, Italy...
... and even Wigan.
Residents include Peter Camm, a local historian and member of the Antiquarian Society, who first tells me of the street's past...
... the poet Kevin Cadwallender...
... Chris Mullin, author and Member of Parliament for Sunderland...
... and artist and designer Jordan Smith, who's creating the cover to this very book.
His daughter Kaya magically transforms into our Alice.

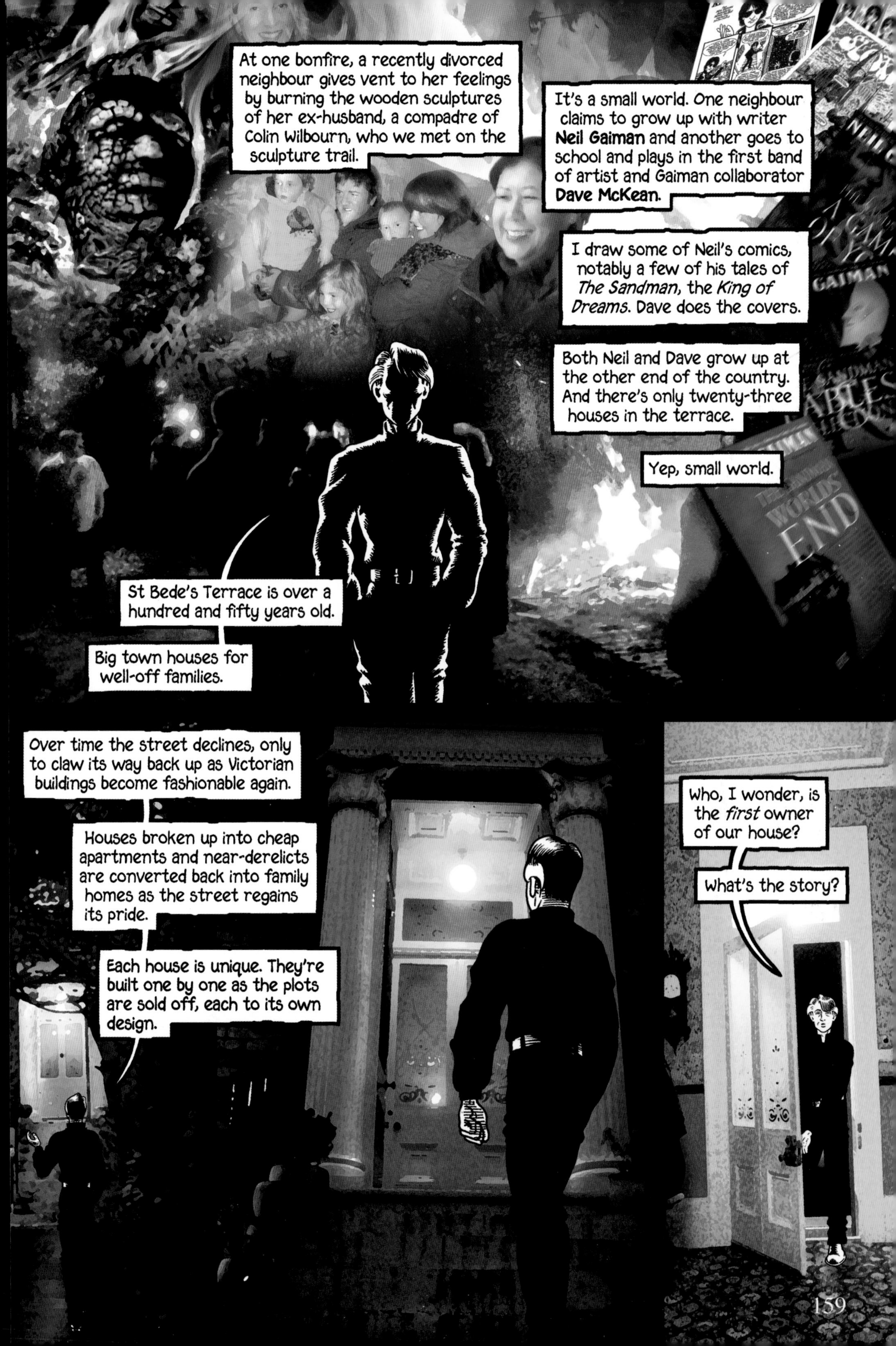
At one bonfire, a recently divorced neighbour gives vent to her feelings by burning the wooden sculptures of her ex-husband, a compadre of Colin Wilbourn, who we met on the sculpture trail.
It's a small world. One neighbour claims to grow up with writer **Neil Gaiman** and another goes to school and plays in the first band of artist and Gaiman collaborator **Dave McKean**.
I draw some of Neil's comics, notably a few of his tales of *The Sandman*, the *King of Dreams*. Dave does the covers.
Both Neil and Dave grow up at the other end of the country. And there's only twenty-three houses in the terrace.
Yep, small world.
St Bede's Terrace is over a hundred and fifty years old.
Big town houses for well-off families.
Over time the street declines, only to claw its way back up as Victorian buildings become fashionable again.
Houses broken up into cheap apartments and near-derelicts are converted back into family homes as the street regains its pride.
Each house is unique. They're built one by one as the plots are sold off, each to its own design.
Who, I wonder, is the *first* owner of our house?
What's the story?

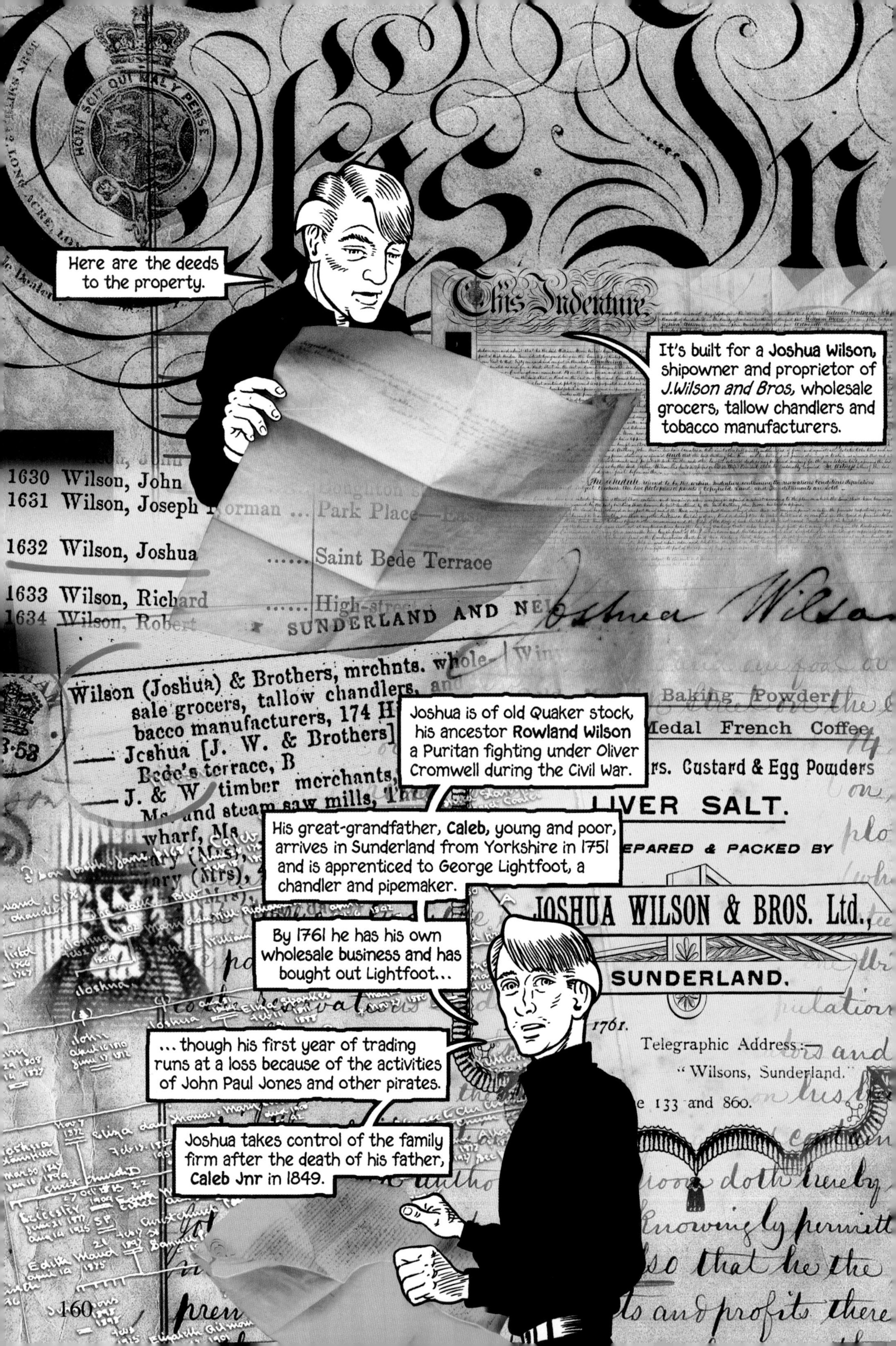
HONI SOIT QUI MAL Y PENSE
This Indenture
Here are the deeds to the property.
It's built for a **Joshua Wilson**, shipowner and proprietor of *J.Wilson and Bros*, wholesale grocers, tallow chandlers and tobacco manufacturers.
1630 Wilson, John
1631 Wilson, Joseph
1632 Wilson, Joshua ...... Saint Bede Terrace
1633 Wilson, Richard
SUNDERLAND AND NE
Joshua Wilson
Wilson (Joshua) & Brothers, mrchnts. whole-sale grocers, tallow chandlers, and bacco manufacturers, 174 H
— Joshua [J. W. & Brothers]
Bede's terrace, B
— J. & W timber merchants,
Baking Powder
Medal French Coffee
rs. Custard & Egg Powders
LIVER SALT.
EPARED & PACKED BY
JOSHUA WILSON & BROS. Ltd.,
SUNDERLAND.
1761.
Telegraphic Address:—
"Wilsons, Sunderland."
e 133 and 860.
Joshua is of old Quaker stock, his ancestor **Rowland Wilson** a Puritan fighting under Oliver Cromwell during the Civil War.
His great-grandfather, **Caleb**, young and poor, arrives in Sunderland from Yorkshire in 1751 and is apprenticed to George Lightfoot, a chandler and pipemaker.
By 1761 he has his own wholesale business and has bought out Lightfoot...
... though his first year of trading runs at a loss because of the activities of John Paul Jones and other pirates.
Joshua takes control of the family firm after the death of his father, **Caleb Jnr** in 1849.

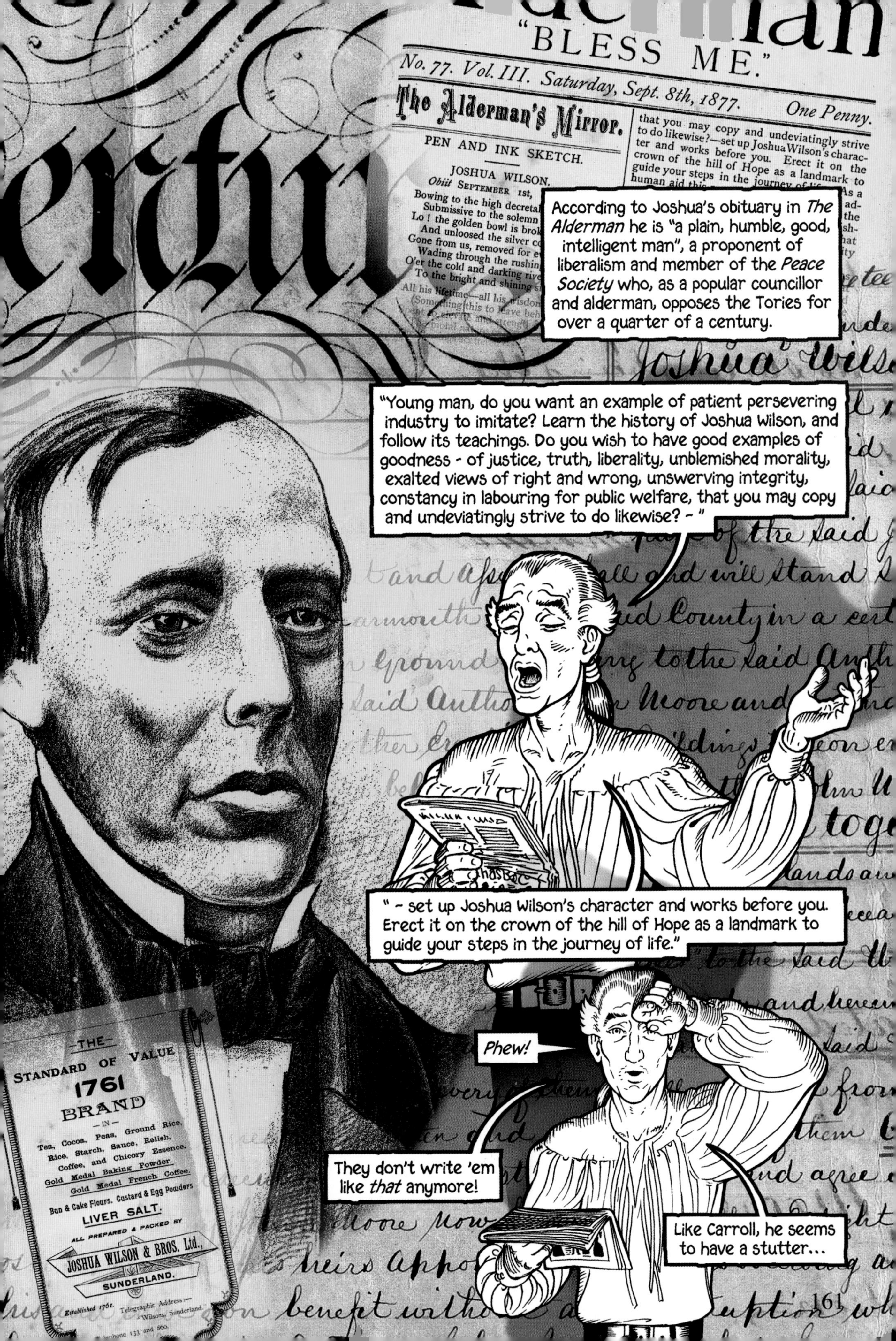
"BLESS ME."
No. 77. Vol. III. Saturday, Sept. 8th, 1877. One Penny.
The Alderman's Mirror.
PEN AND INK SKETCH.
JOSHUA WILSON.
According to Joshua's obituary in *The Alderman* he is "a plain, humble, good, intelligent man", a proponent of liberalism and member of the *Peace Society* who, as a popular councillor and alderman, opposes the Tories for over a quarter of a century.
"Young man, do you want an example of patient persevering industry to imitate? Learn the history of Joshua Wilson, and follow its teachings. Do you wish to have good examples of goodness - of justice, truth, liberality, unblemished morality, exalted views of right and wrong, unswerving integrity, constancy in labouring for public welfare, that you may copy and undeviatingly strive to do likewise? - "
" - set up Joshua Wilson's character and works before you. Erect it on the crown of the hill of Hope as a landmark to guide your steps in the journey of life."
Phew!
They don't write 'em like *that* anymore!
Like Carroll, he seems to have a stutter...
THE STANDARD OF VALUE 1761 BRAND
JOSHUA WILSON & BROS. Ltd., SUNDERLAND.

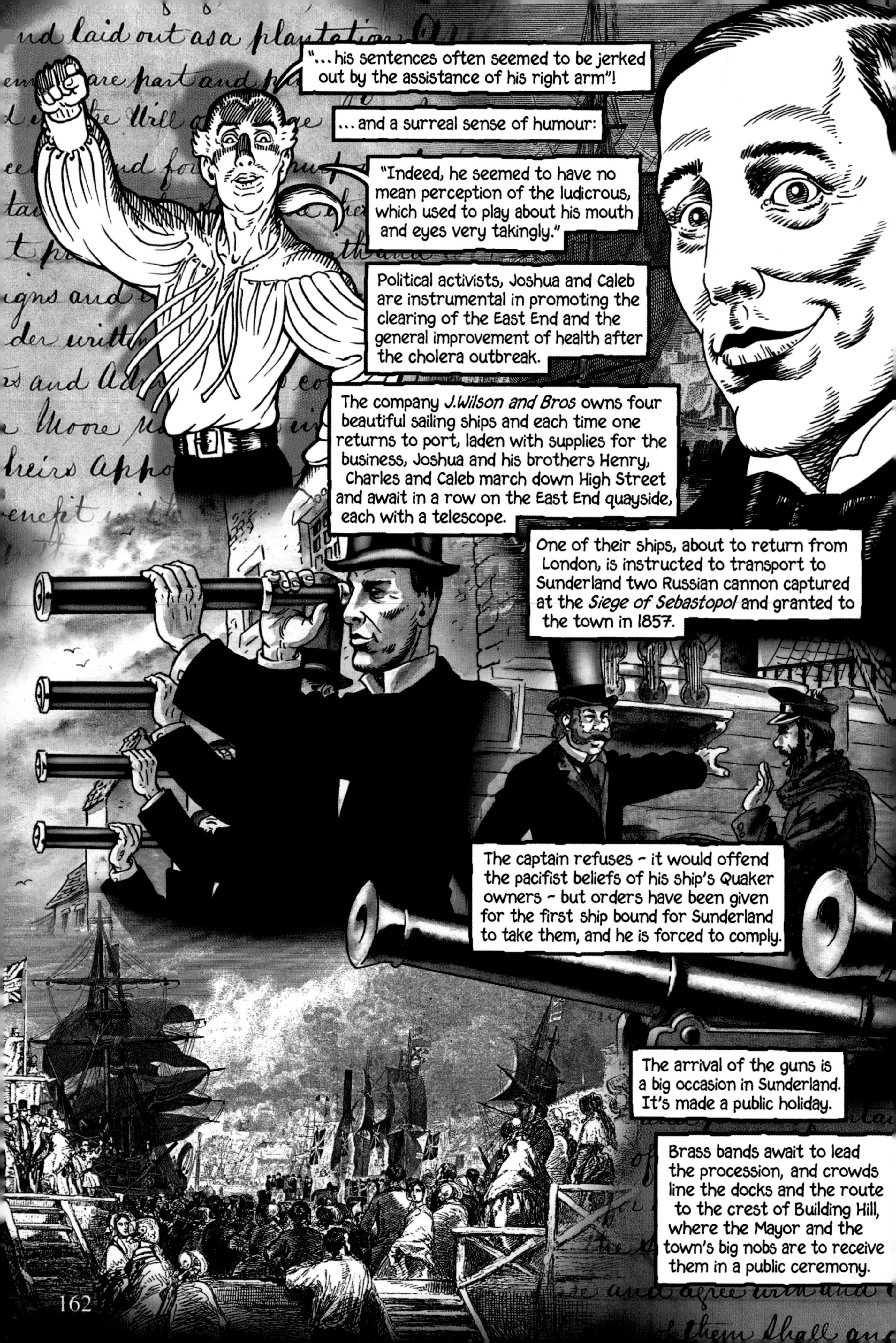

"...his sentences often seemed to be jerked out by the assistance of his right arm"!
...and a surreal sense of humour:
"Indeed, he seemed to have no mean perception of the ludicrous, which used to play about his mouth and eyes very takingly."
Political activists, Joshua and Caleb are instrumental in promoting the clearing of the East End and the general improvement of health after the cholera outbreak.
The company *J.Wilson and Bros* owns four beautiful sailing ships and each time one returns to port, laden with supplies for the business, Joshua and his brothers Henry, Charles and Caleb march down High Street and await in a row on the East End quayside, each with a telescope.
One of their ships, about to return from London, is instructed to transport to Sunderland two Russian cannon captured at the *Siege of Sebastopol* and granted to the town in 1857.
The captain refuses - it would offend the pacifist beliefs of his ship's Quaker owners - but orders have been given for the first ship bound for Sunderland to take them, and he is forced to comply.
The arrival of the guns is a big occasion in Sunderland. It's made a public holiday.
Brass bands await to lead the procession, and crowds line the docks and the route to the crest of Building Hill, where the Mayor and the town's big nobs are to receive them in a public ceremony.

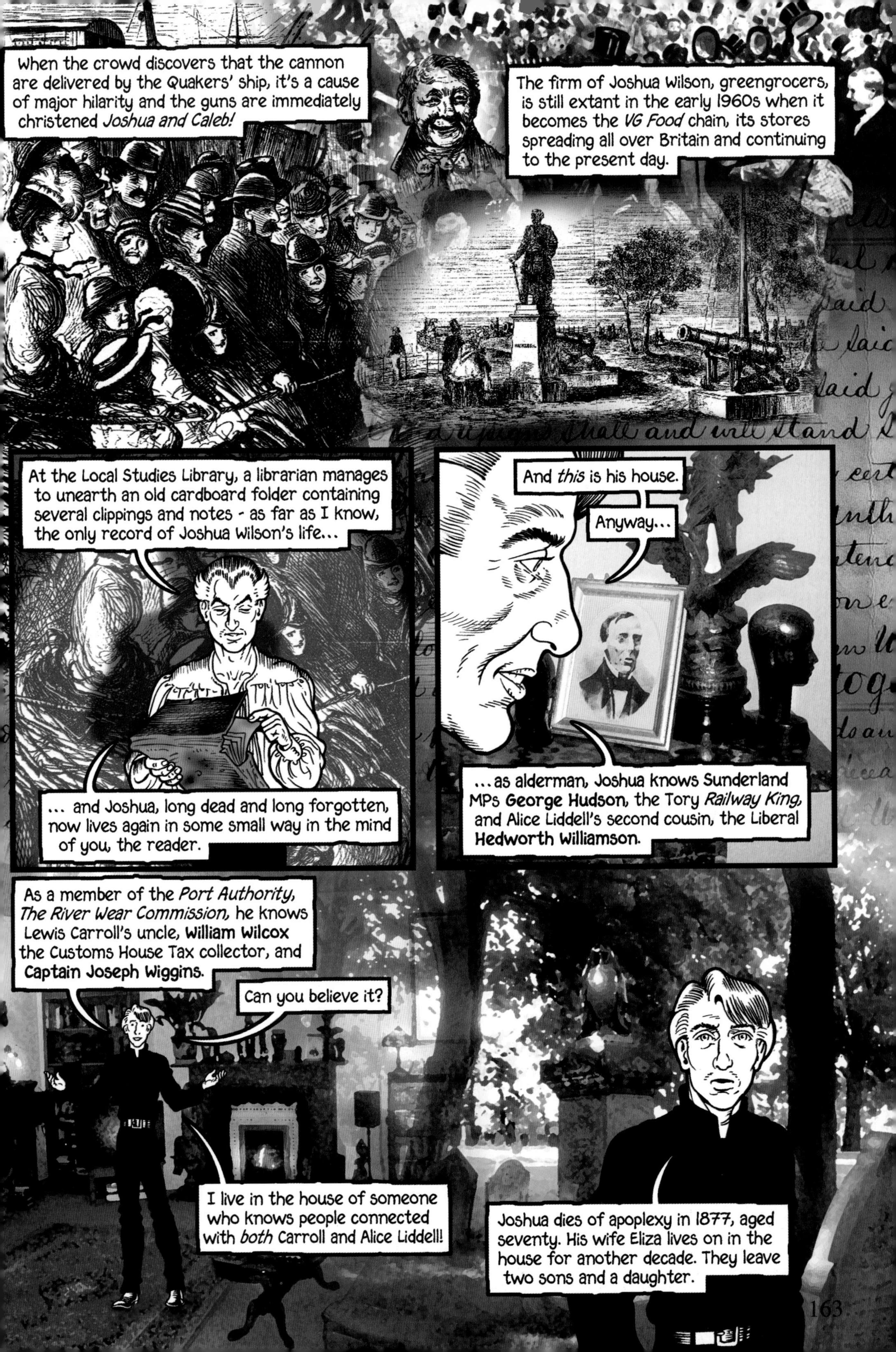

When the crowd discovers that the cannon are delivered by the Quakers' ship, it's a cause of major hilarity and the guns are immediately christened *Joshua and Caleb!*
The firm of Joshua Wilson, greengrocers, is still extant in the early 1960s when it becomes the *VG Food* chain, its stores spreading all over Britain and continuing to the present day.
At the Local Studies Library, a librarian manages to unearth an old cardboard folder containing several clippings and notes - as far as I know, the only record of Joshua Wilson's life...
... and Joshua, long dead and long forgotten, now lives again in some small way in the mind of you, the reader.
And *this* is his house.
Anyway...
...as alderman, Joshua knows Sunderland MPs **George Hudson**, the Tory *Railway King*, and Alice Liddell's second cousin, the Liberal **Hedworth Williamson**.
As a member of the *Port Authority, The River Wear Commission,* he knows Lewis Carroll's uncle, **William Wilcox** the Customs House Tax collector, and **Captain Joseph Wiggins**.
Can you believe it?
I live in the house of someone who knows people connected with *both* Carroll and Alice Liddell!
Joshua dies of apoplexy in 1877, aged seventy. His wife Eliza lives on in the house for another decade. They leave two sons and a daughter.

FUNERAL OF THE LATE MR. JOSHUA WILSON.
Yesterday afternoon the remains of the late Mr. Joshua Wilson were interred in the family burying ground in Bishopwearmouth Cemetery.

Joshua's funeral is a big affair, attended by a huge crowd and many local dignitaries...

...and he's interred here, in the *Quaker Field* of Bishopwearmouth Cemetery.

A small, unostentatious gravestone marks the spot.

Eliza is buried next door.

JOSHUA WILSON.

ELIZA WILSON

Strange to think that I'm only six feet away from him now...

...as he lies in *cold storage.*

God, how *depressing!*

I only introduce him four pages ago and he's already dead and buried!

Such is life.

Here, *Autumn Leaves* by the *Pre-Raphaelite* John Millais - mate of Lewis Carroll. Different medium. Same message.

The brevity of existence.

Carry on Pilgrim.

I'm going for a drink!

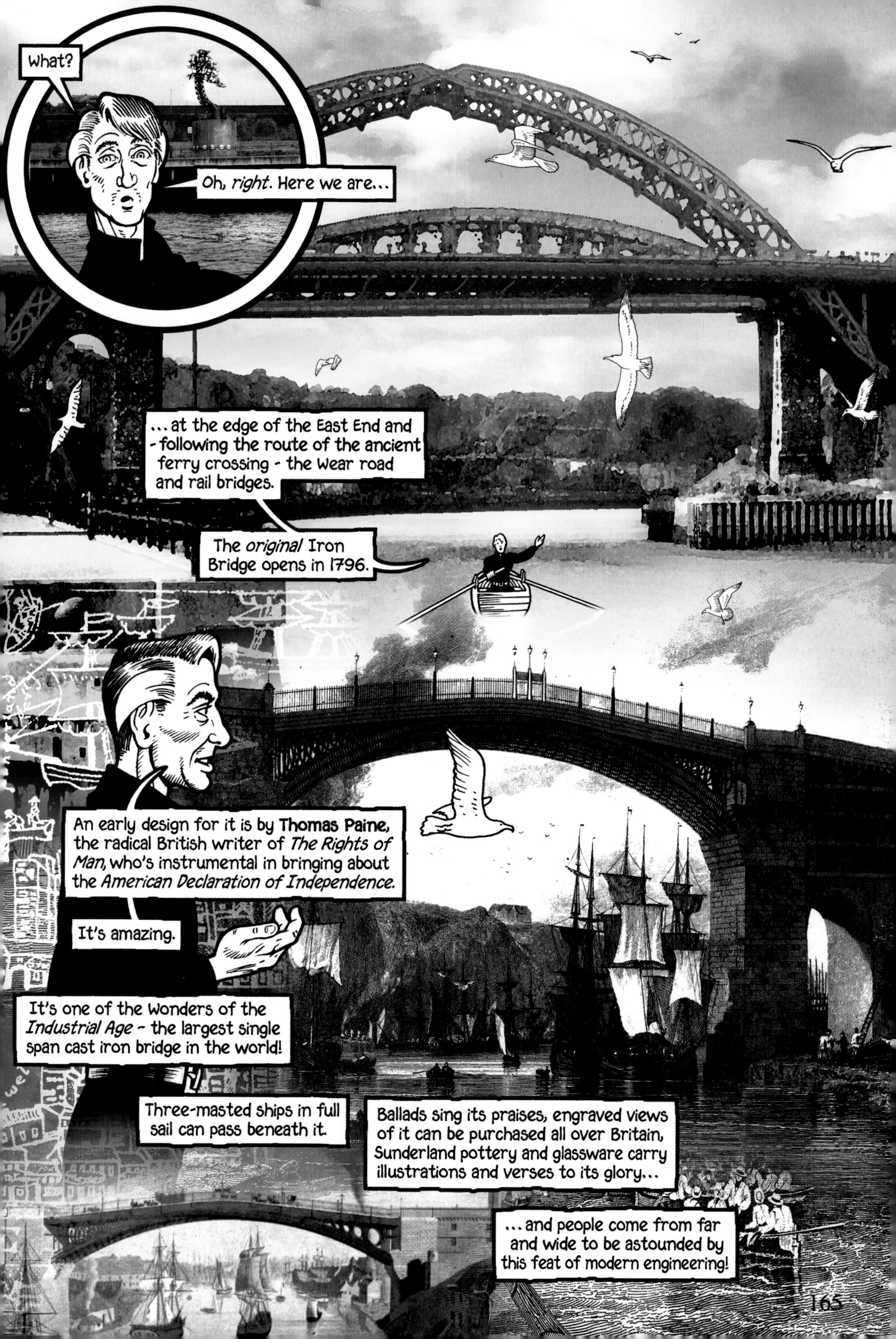

What?
Oh, *right*. Here we are...
...at the edge of the East End and - following the route of the ancient ferry crossing - the Wear road and rail bridges.
The *original* Iron Bridge opens in 1796.
An early design for it is by **Thomas Paine**, the radical British writer of *The Rights of Man,* who's instrumental in bringing about the *American Declaration of Independence.*
It's amazing.
It's one of the Wonders of the *Industrial Age* - the largest single span cast iron bridge in the world!
Three-masted ships in full sail can pass beneath it.
Ballads sing its praises, engraved views of it can be purchased all over Britain, Sunderland pottery and glassware carry illustrations and verses to its glory...
...and people come from far and wide to be astounded by this feat of modern engineering!

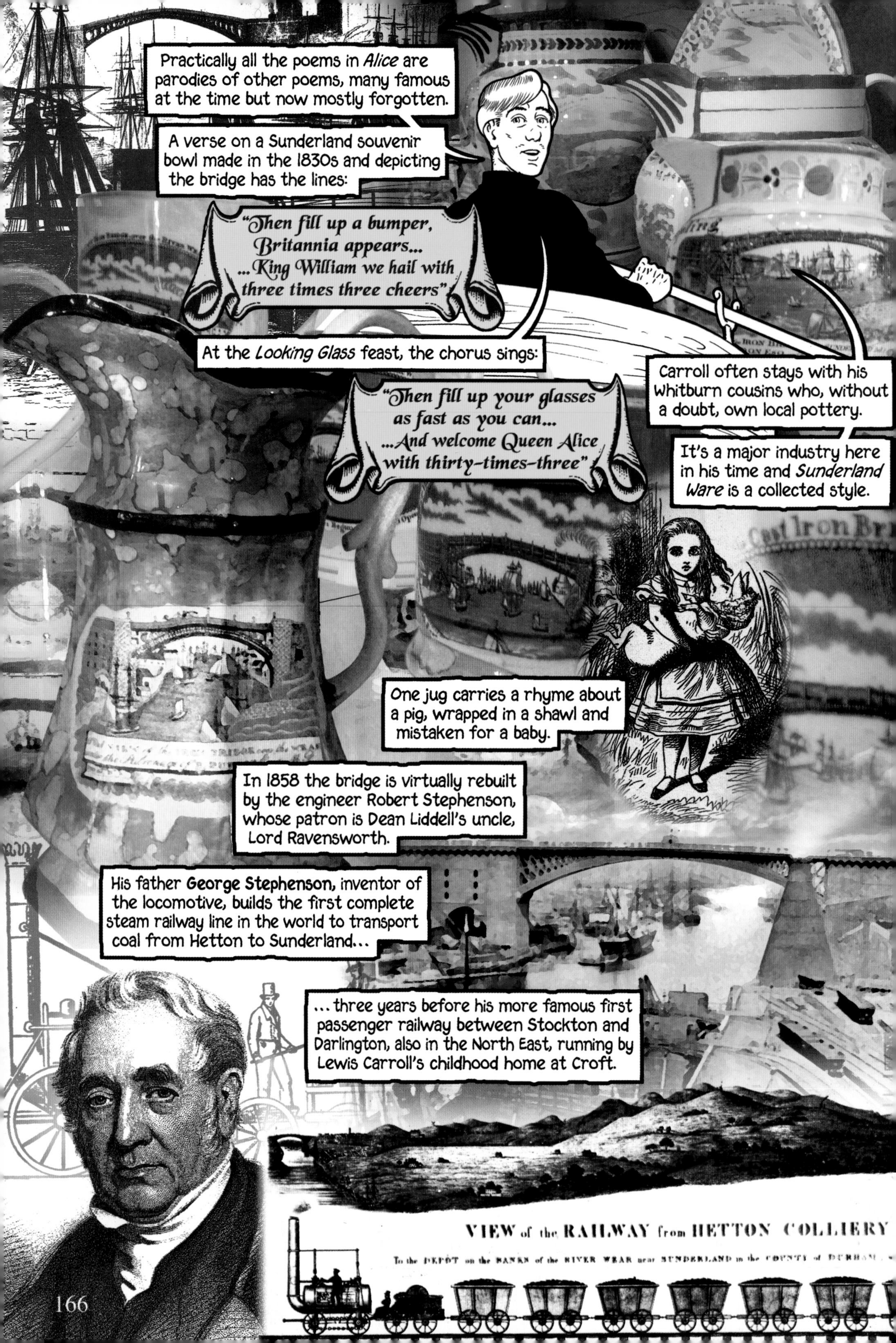

Practically all the poems in *Alice* are parodies of other poems, many famous at the time but now mostly forgotten.
A verse on a Sunderland souvenir bowl made in the 1830s and depicting the bridge has the lines:
"Then fill up a bumper, Britannia appears... ...King William we hail with three times three cheers"
At the *Looking Glass* feast, the chorus sings:
"Then fill up your glasses as fast as you can... ...And welcome Queen Alice with thirty-times-three"
Carroll often stays with his Whitburn cousins who, without a doubt, own local pottery.
It's a major industry here in his time and *Sunderland Ware* is a collected style.
One jug carries a rhyme about a pig, wrapped in a shawl and mistaken for a baby.
In 1858 the bridge is virtually rebuilt by the engineer Robert Stephenson, whose patron is Dean Liddell's uncle, Lord Ravensworth.
His father **George Stephenson**, inventor of the locomotive, builds the first complete steam railway line in the world to transport coal from Hetton to Sunderland...
... three years before his more famous first passenger railway between Stockton and Darlington, also in the North East, running by Lewis Carroll's childhood home at Croft.
VIEW of the RAILWAY from HETTON COLLIERY
To the DEPOT on the BANKS of the RIVER WEAR near SUNDERLAND in the COUNTY of DURHAM

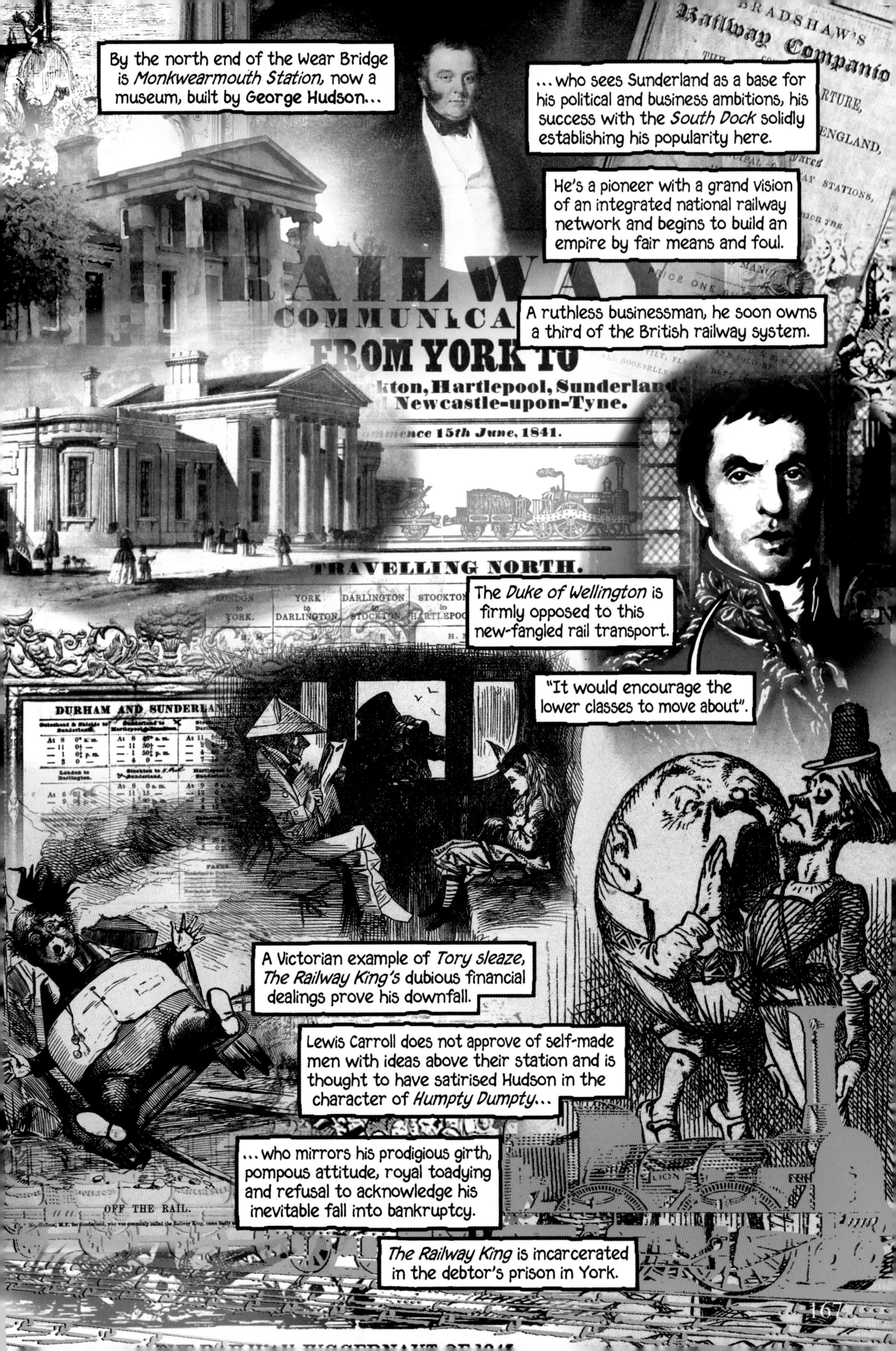

By the north end of the Wear Bridge is *Monkwearmouth Station,* now a museum, built by **George Hudson**...
...who sees Sunderland as a base for his political and business ambitions, his success with the *South Dock* solidly establishing his popularity here.
He's a pioneer with a grand vision of an integrated national railway network and begins to build an empire by fair means and foul.
A ruthless businessman, he soon owns a third of the British railway system.
FROM YORK TO
Newcastle-upon-Tyne.
TRAVELLING NORTH.
The *Duke of Wellington* is firmly opposed to this new-fangled rail transport.
"It would encourage the lower classes to move about".
A Victorian example of *Tory sleaze, The Railway King's* dubious financial dealings prove his downfall.
Lewis Carroll does not approve of self-made men with ideas above their station and is thought to have satirised Hudson in the character of *Humpty Dumpty*...
...who mirrors his prodigious girth, pompous attitude, royal toadying and refusal to acknowledge his inevitable fall into bankruptcy.
OFF THE RAIL.
The Railway King is incarcerated in the debtor's prison in York.

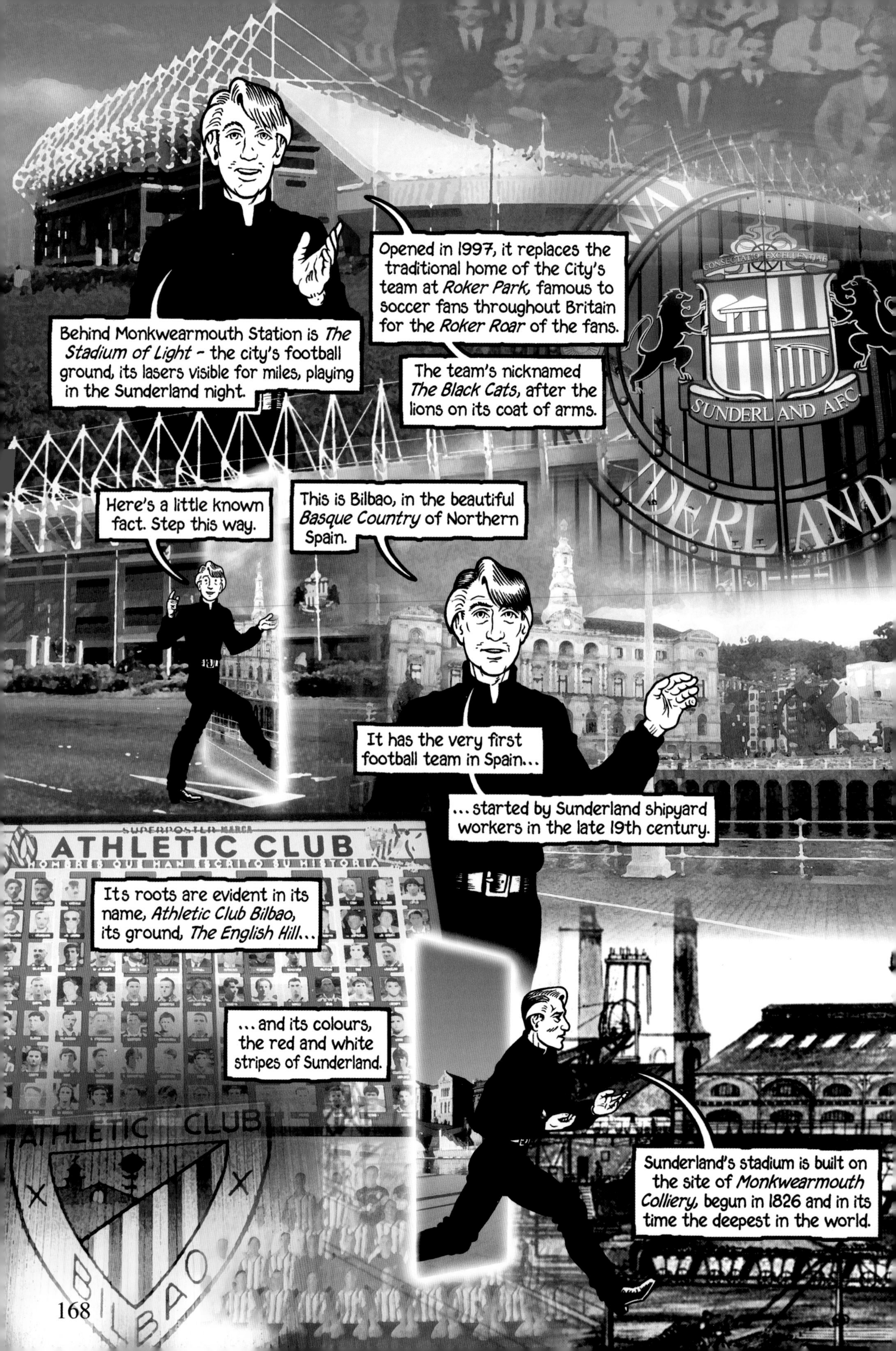
Behind Monkwearmouth Station is *The Stadium of Light* – the city's football ground, its lasers visible for miles, playing in the Sunderland night.
Opened in 1997, it replaces the traditional home of the City's team at *Roker Park*, famous to soccer fans throughout Britain for the *Roker Roar* of the fans.
The team's nicknamed *The Black Cats*, after the lions on its coat of arms.
SUNDERLAND A.F.C.
Here's a little known fact. Step this way.
This is Bilbao, in the beautiful *Basque Country* of Northern Spain.
It has the very first football team in Spain...
...started by Sunderland shipyard workers in the late 19th century.
ATHLETIC CLUB
Its roots are evident in its name, *Athletic Club Bilbao*, its ground, *The English Hill*...
...and its colours, the red and white stripes of Sunderland.
ATHLETIC CLUB
BILBAO
Sunderland's stadium is built on the site of *Monkwearmouth Colliery*, begun in 1826 and in its time the deepest in the world.

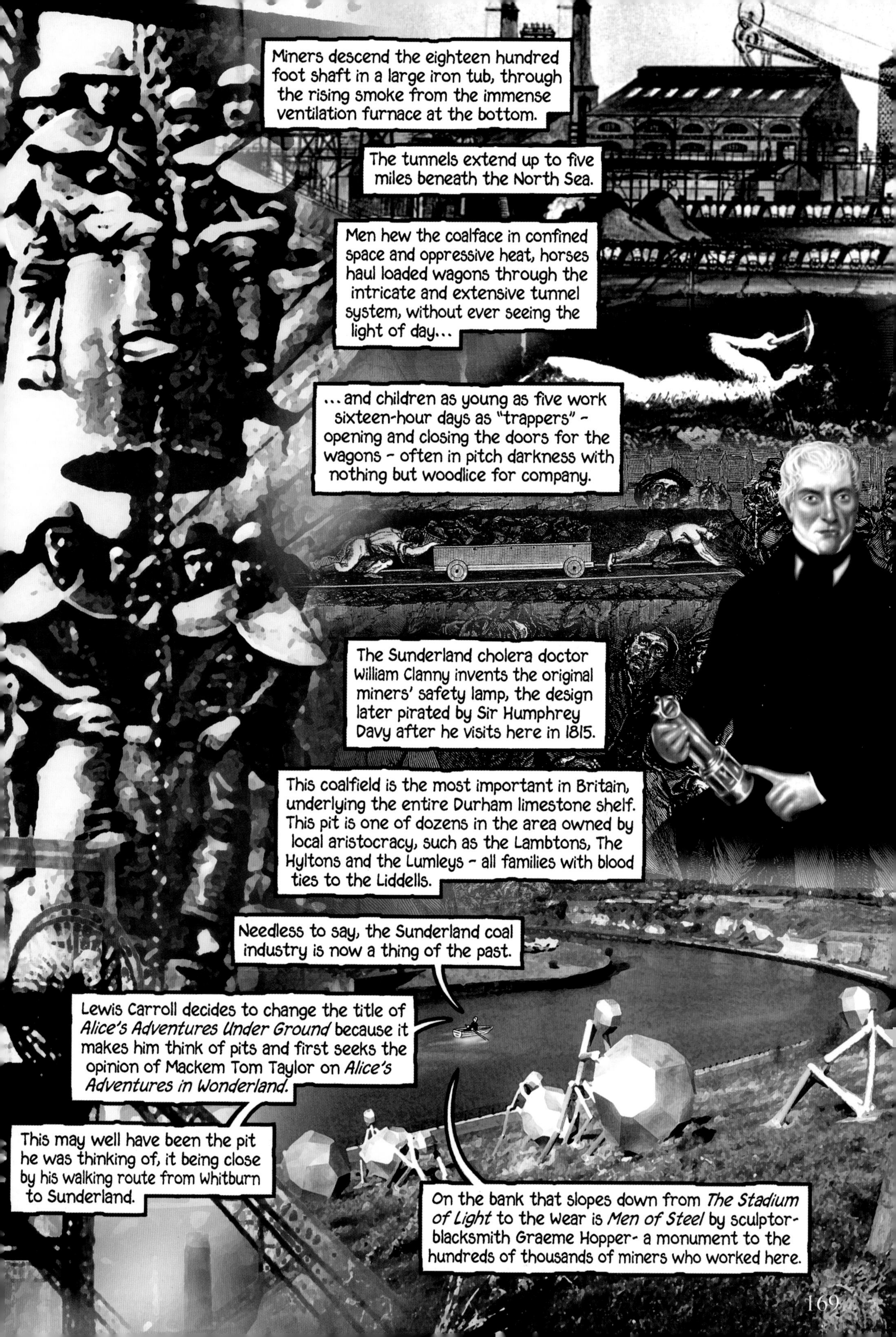

Miners descend the eighteen hundred foot shaft in a large iron tub, through the rising smoke from the immense ventilation furnace at the bottom.
The tunnels extend up to five miles beneath the North Sea.
Men hew the coalface in confined space and oppressive heat, horses haul loaded wagons through the intricate and extensive tunnel system, without ever seeing the light of day...
...and children as young as five work sixteen-hour days as "trappers" - opening and closing the doors for the wagons - often in pitch darkness with nothing but woodlice for company.
The Sunderland cholera doctor William Clanny invents the original miners' safety lamp, the design later pirated by Sir Humphrey Davy after he visits here in 1815.
This coalfield is the most important in Britain, underlying the entire Durham limestone shelf. This pit is one of dozens in the area owned by local aristocracy, such as the Lambtons, The Hyltons and the Lumleys - all families with blood ties to the Liddells.
Needless to say, the Sunderland coal industry is now a thing of the past.
Lewis Carroll decides to change the title of *Alice's Adventures Under Ground* because it makes him think of pits and first seeks the opinion of Mackem Tom Taylor on *Alice's Adventures in Wonderland.*
This may well have been the pit he was thinking of, it being close by his walking route from Whitburn to Sunderland.
On the bank that slopes down from *The Stadium of Light* to the Wear is *Men of Steel* by sculptor-blacksmith Graeme Hopper- a monument to the hundreds of thousands of miners who worked here.

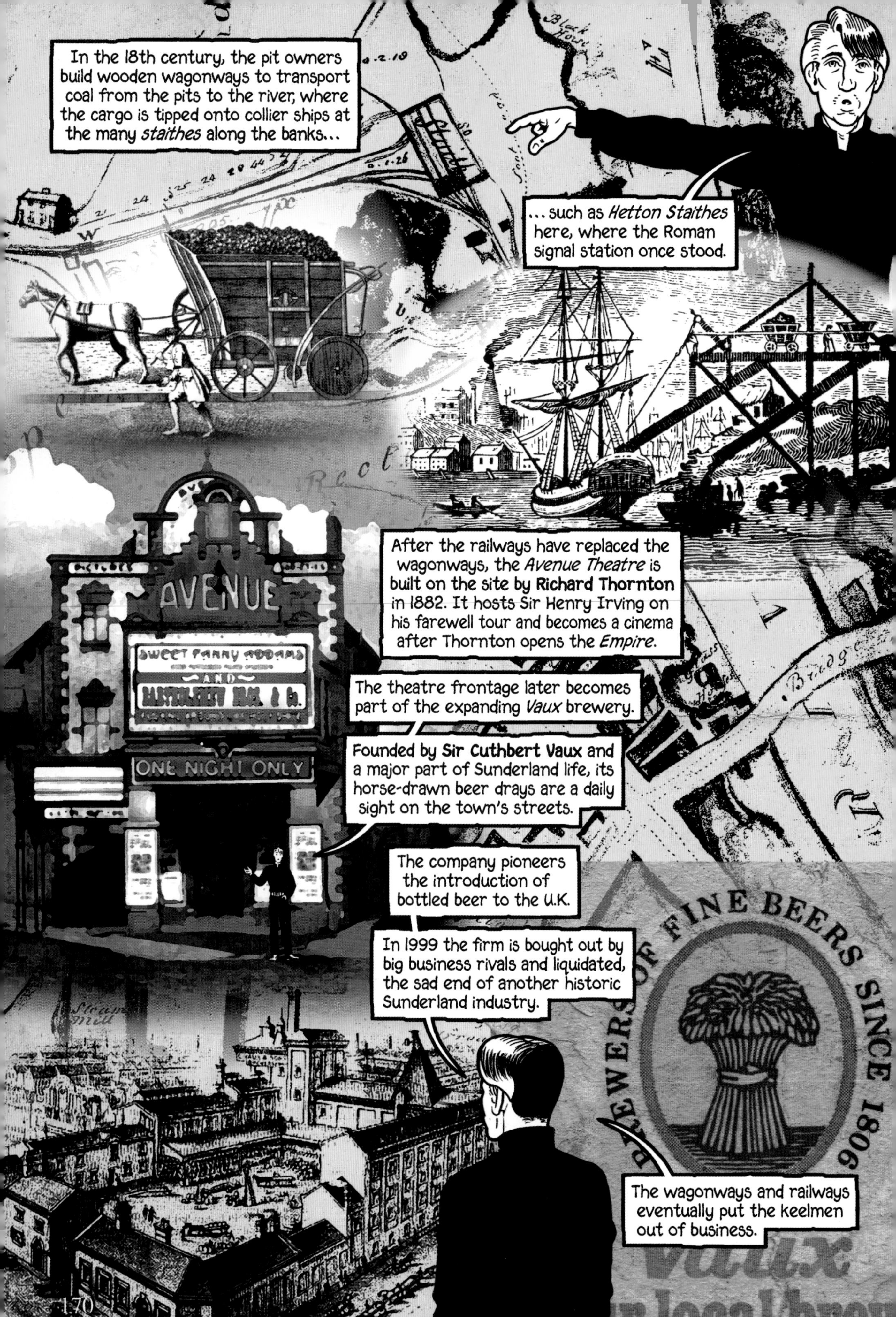

In the 18th century, the pit owners build wooden wagonways to transport coal from the pits to the river, where the cargo is tipped onto collier ships at the many *staithes* along the banks...
...such as *Hetton Staithes* here, where the Roman signal station once stood.
After the railways have replaced the wagonways, the *Avenue Theatre* is **built on the site by Richard Thornton** in 1882. It hosts Sir Henry Irving on his farewell tour and becomes a cinema after Thornton opens the *Empire*.
AVENUE
SWEET FANNY ADAMS
AND
ONE NIGHT ONLY
The theatre frontage later becomes part of the expanding *Vaux* brewery.
Founded by Sir Cuthbert Vaux and a major part of Sunderland life, its horse-drawn beer drays are a daily sight on the town's streets.
The company pioneers the introduction of bottled beer to the U.K.
In 1999 the firm is bought out by big business rivals and liquidated, the sad end of another historic Sunderland industry.
BREWERS OF FINE BEERS SINCE 1806
Vaux
The wagonways and railways eventually put the keelmen out of business.

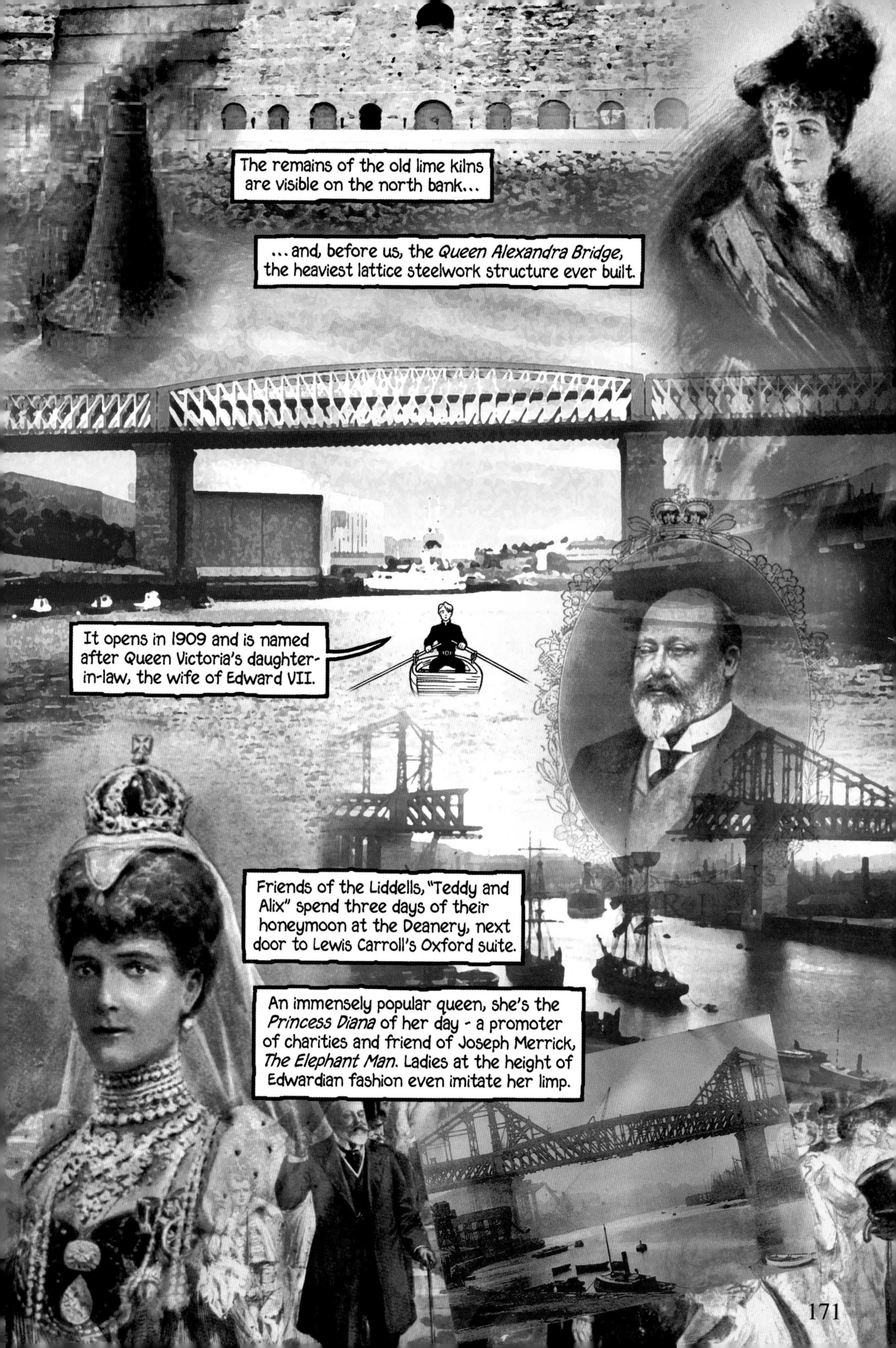
The remains of the old lime kilns are visible on the north bank...
...and, before us, the *Queen Alexandra Bridge*, the heaviest lattice steelwork structure ever built.
It opens in 1909 and is named after Queen Victoria's daughter-in-law, the wife of Edward VII.
Friends of the Liddells, "Teddy and Alix" spend three days of their honeymoon at the Deanery, next door to Lewis Carroll's Oxford suite.
An immensely popular queen, she's the *Princess Diana* of her day - a promoter of charities and friend of Joseph Merrick, *The Elephant Man*. Ladies at the height of Edwardian fashion even imitate her limp.

Incidentally, John Lawrence, grandfather of **Thomas Edward Lawrence** - *Lawrence of Arabia* - is a ship's carpenter in Sunderland.

T E himself is the result of an affair between a married baronet, Thomas Chapman, and the illegitimate Mackem nanny of his children, **Sarah Junner**, who reclaims the name Lawrence when they elope.

T E hates the name, believing it to be chosen at random as a cover for their affair.

Incredibly, the father of Peter O'Toole, who plays T E Lawrence in the movie, is also a Sunderland shipwright, later becoming a bookmaker here before moving to Leeds.

On the south bank by the Alexandra Bridge is *Webster's Ropery*. Built in 1794 at the dawn of the *Industrial Revolution*, it's the first mechanised rope factory in the world.

Before this, rope is made by hand, the strands interwoven down long *ropewalks*.

In 1892 websters produce a giant steel rope six miles long that weighs twenty-five tons. Thirty horses are needed to cart it to the Railway station.

The building is now offices and a rather nice pub.

Borough of Sunderland
WEBSTER'S ROPERY
(originally built in 1793)
After a long and eventful history, this, the World's first patent ropeworks became derelict and remained so for many years. Restored between 1985 and 1987, the Ropery now provides commercial and leisure facilities.
Urban Programme

To the north of the bridge is the district of *Southwick*...

...pronounced "Suddick"...

...hang on a second...

Sarah Lawrence

Rope Walk

172

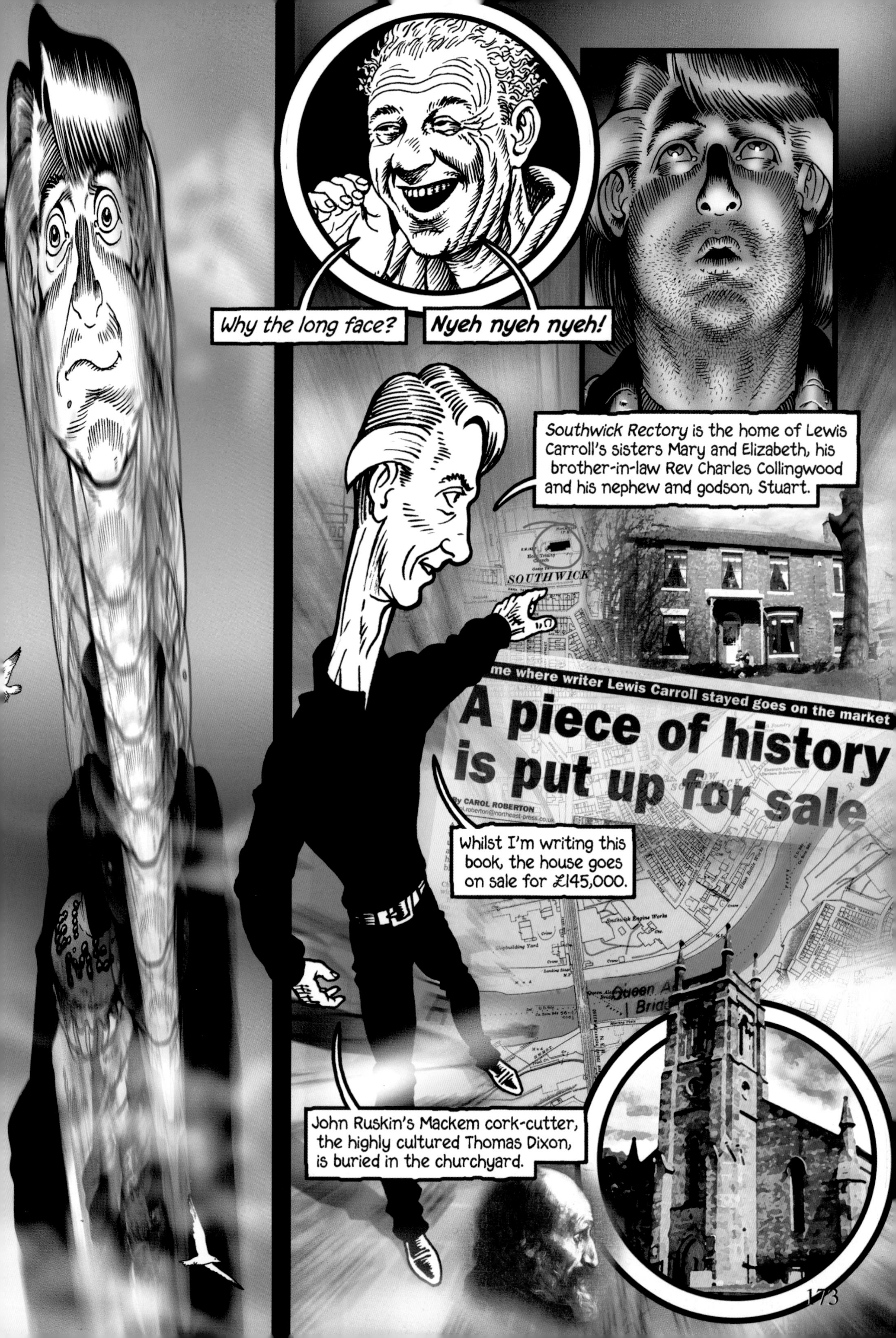

Why the long face?
Nyeh nyeh nyeh!
Southwick Rectory is the home of Lewis Carroll's sisters Mary and Elizabeth, his brother-in-law Rev Charles Collingwood and his nephew and godson, Stuart.
SOUTHWICK
me where writer Lewis Carroll stayed goes on the market
A piece of history is put up for sale
By CAROL ROBERTON
Whilst I'm writing this book, the house goes on sale for £145,000.
John Ruskin's Mackem cork-cutter, the highly cultured Thomas Dixon, is buried in the churchyard.

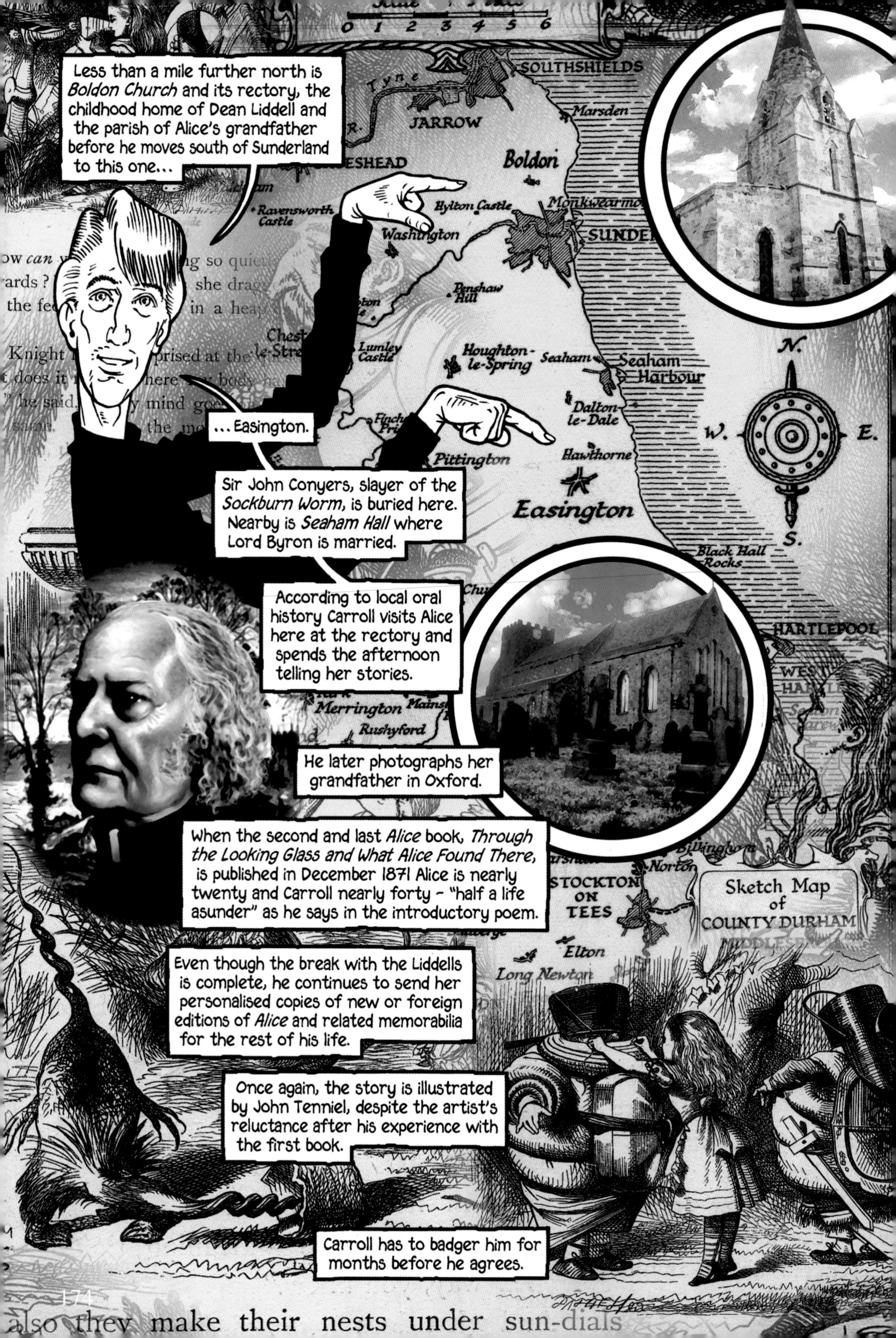

Less than a mile further north is *Boldon Church* and its rectory, the childhood home of Dean Liddell and the parish of Alice's grandfather before he moves south of Sunderland to this one...
...Easington.
Sir John Conyers, slayer of the *Sockburn Worm*, is buried here. Nearby is *Seaham Hall* where Lord Byron is married.
According to local oral history Carroll visits Alice here at the rectory and spends the afternoon telling her stories.
He later photographs her grandfather in Oxford.
When the second and last *Alice* book, *Through the Looking Glass and What Alice Found There*, is published in December 1871 Alice is nearly twenty and Carroll nearly forty – "half a life asunder" as he says in the introductory poem.
Even though the break with the Liddells is complete, he continues to send her personalised copies of new or foreign editions of *Alice* and related memorabilia for the rest of his life.
Once again, the story is illustrated by John Tenniel, despite the artist's reluctance after his experience with the first book.
Carroll has to badger him for months before he agrees.
Sketch Map of COUNTY DURHAM
SOUTHSHIELDS
JARROW
Boldon
Easington
Seaham Harbour
HARTLEPOOL
STOCKTON ON TEES
also they make their nests under sun-dials

This time it takes him three years and his patience with the exacting Carroll wears extremely thin.

"He is *impossible!*"

Perhaps by way of revenge, he argues Carroll into editing out a whole sequence, *Wasp in a Wig*, claiming that a drawing of the character is inconceivable and that the writing is below standard.

Lost for over a hundred years, the missing chapter turns up in an auction at *Sotheby's* and is published for the first time in 1977, here illustrated by Ralph Steadman, though there remains the possibility that it's a forgery and the original is lost forever.

Tenniel never illustrates another book...

LEWIS CARROLL
THE WASP
IN A WIG

A WASP IN A WIG
Exclusive: the missing chapter
Number 51 September 4 1977

THROUGH THE LOOKING-GLASS
AND WHAT ALICE FOUND THERE

... despite the immediate success of *Looking Glass* and the popularity of his drawings, which are of pure genius.

LEWIS CARROLL

Alice works in some ways that are very similar to the comic strip. Carroll's descriptions are minimal and sometimes nonexistent. The words and pictures come together to form a whole.

JOHN TENNIEL

For example, the only description of the *Mad Hatter* is his name. Our image of him and the surrounding dreamworld comes straight from Tenniel.

Ah, *there* you are.

Well, did you succeed? Did you kill *Time*?

I'm afraid not, Spottie, old fruit.

I burst into his house but...

... *Time* ran out.

Next time I'll use a *Time* bomb.

Now, *that* really is *Time*-consuming!

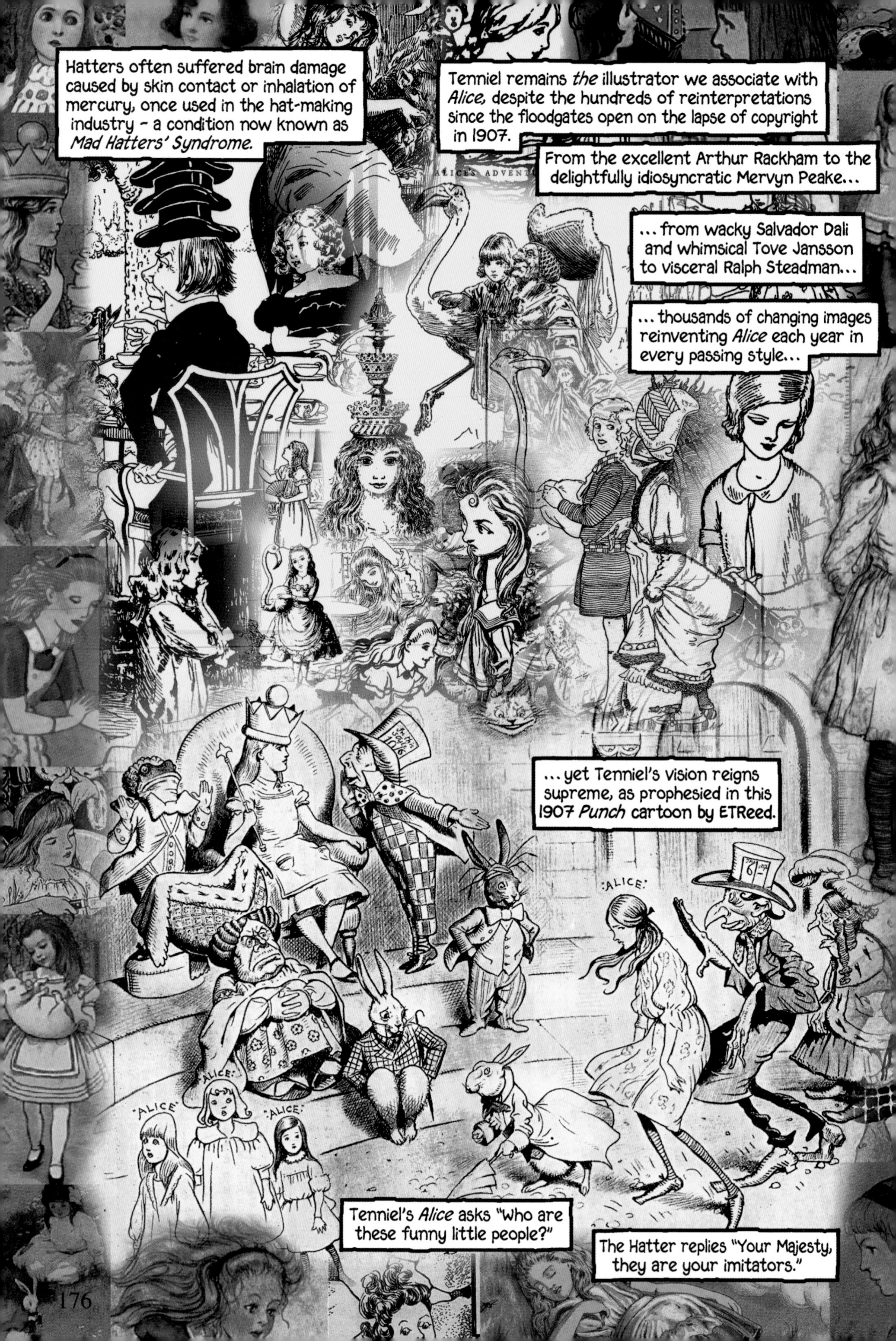
Hatters often suffered brain damage caused by skin contact or inhalation of mercury, once used in the hat-making industry – a condition now known as *Mad Hatters' Syndrome.*
Tenniel remains *the* illustrator we associate with *Alice,* despite the hundreds of reinterpretations since the floodgates open on the lapse of copyright in 1907.
From the excellent Arthur Rackham to the delightfully idiosyncratic Mervyn Peake…
… from wacky Salvador Dali and whimsical Tove Jansson to visceral Ralph Steadman…
… thousands of changing images reinventing *Alice* each year in every passing style…
… yet Tenniel's vision reigns supreme, as prophesied in this 1907 *Punch* cartoon by ETReed.
"ALICE"
"ALICE"
"ALICE"
"ALICE"
Tenniel's *Alice* asks "Who are these funny little people?"
The Hatter replies "Your Majesty, they are your imitators."

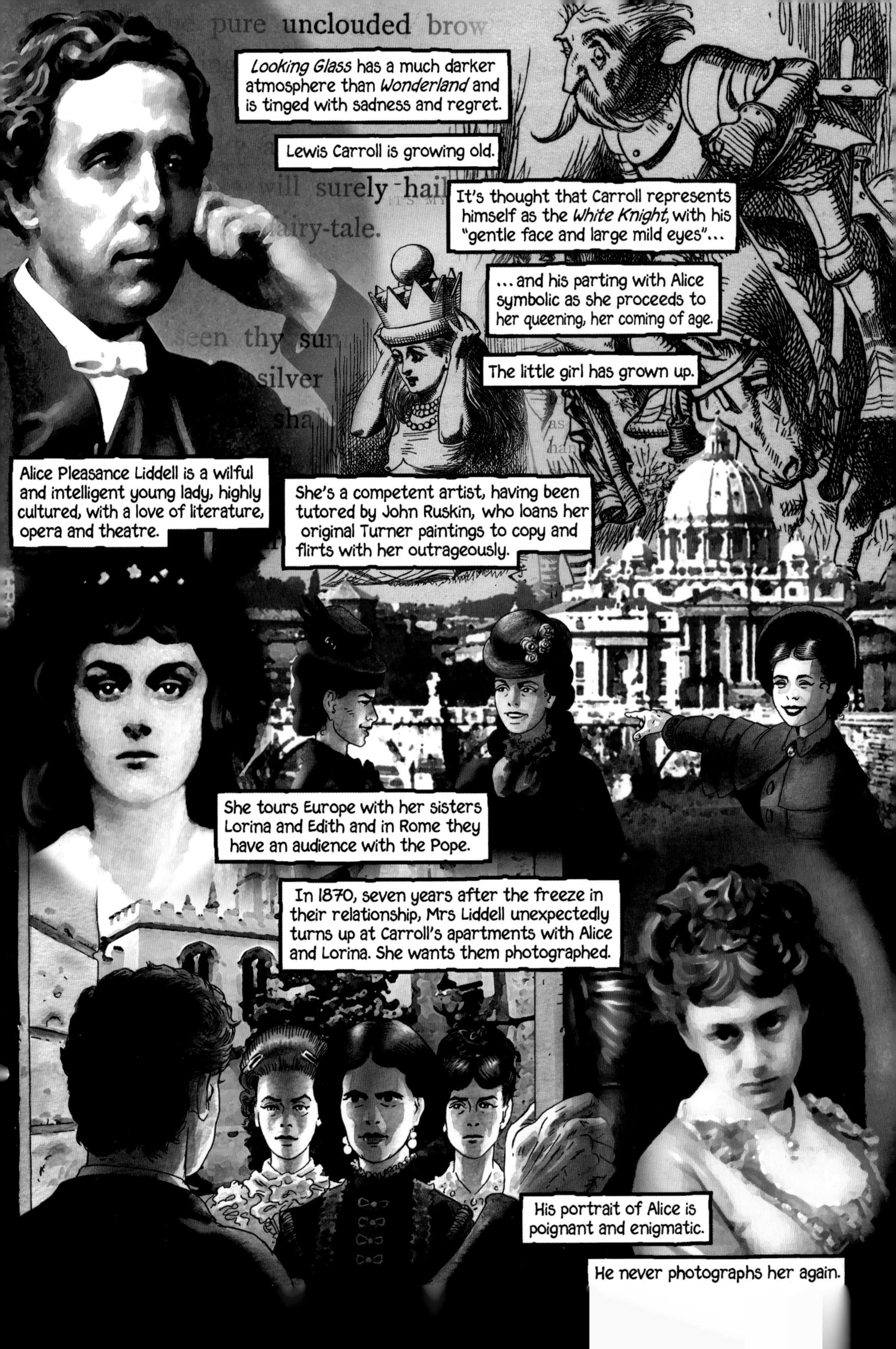
pure unclouded brow
Looking Glass has a much darker atmosphere than *Wonderland* and is tinged with sadness and regret.
Lewis Carroll is growing old.
will surely hail
It's thought that Carroll represents himself as the *White Knight*, with his "gentle face and large mild eyes"...
...and his parting with Alice symbolic as she proceeds to her queening, her coming of age.
The little girl has grown up.
Alice Pleasance Liddell is a wilful and intelligent young lady, highly cultured, with a love of literature, opera and theatre.
She's a competent artist, having been tutored by John Ruskin, who loans her original Turner paintings to copy and flirts with her outrageously.
She tours Europe with her sisters Lorina and Edith and in Rome they have an audience with the Pope.
In 1870, seven years after the freeze in their relationship, Mrs Liddell unexpectedly turns up at Carroll's apartments with Alice and Lorina. She wants them photographed.
His portrait of Alice is poignant and enigmatic.
He never photographs her again.

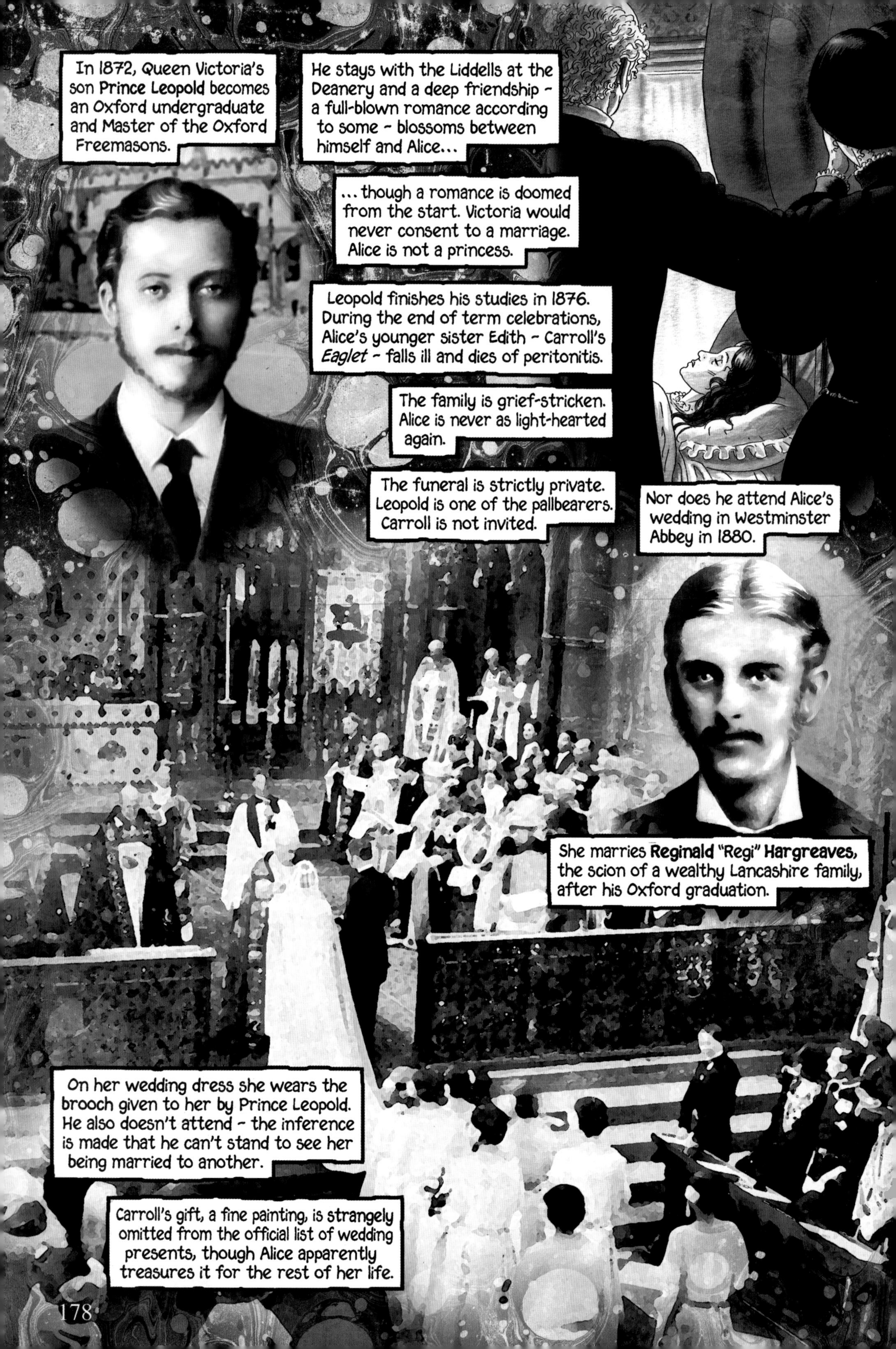
In 1872, Queen Victoria's son **Prince Leopold** becomes an Oxford undergraduate and Master of the Oxford Freemasons.
He stays with the Liddells at the Deanery and a deep friendship - a full-blown romance according to some - blossoms between himself and Alice...
...though a romance is doomed from the start. Victoria would never consent to a marriage. Alice is not a princess.
Leopold finishes his studies in 1876. During the end of term celebrations, Alice's younger sister Edith - Carroll's *Eaglet* - falls ill and dies of peritonitis.
The family is grief-stricken. Alice is never as light-hearted again.
The funeral is strictly private. Leopold is one of the pallbearers. Carroll is not invited.
Nor does he attend Alice's wedding in Westminster Abbey in 1880.
She marries **Reginald "Regi" Hargreaves,** the scion of a wealthy Lancashire family, after his Oxford graduation.
On her wedding dress she wears the brooch given to her by Prince Leopold. He also doesn't attend - the inference is made that he can't stand to see her being married to another.
Carroll's gift, a fine painting, is strangely omitted from the official list of wedding presents, though Alice apparently treasures it for the rest of her life.

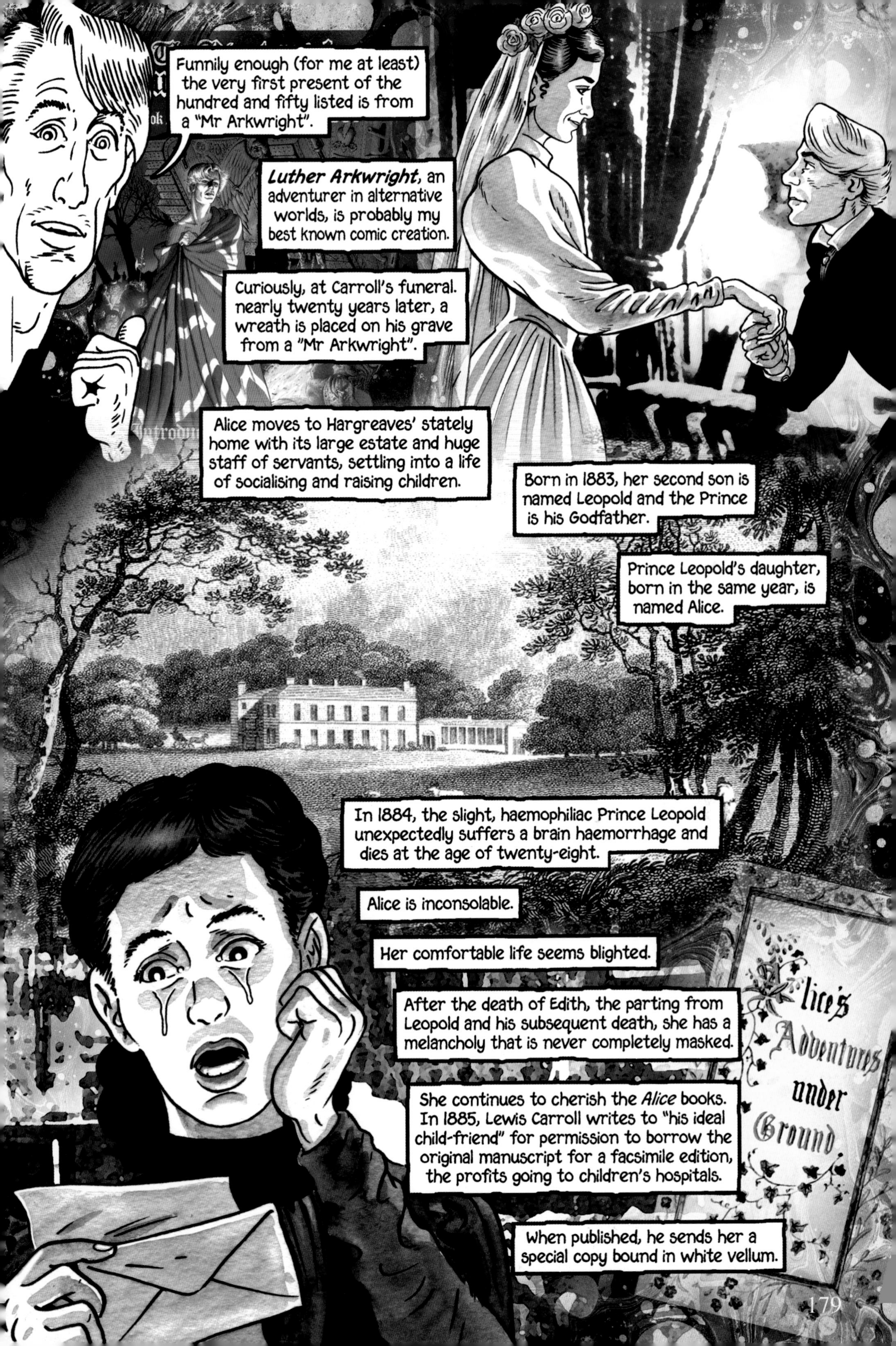

Funnily enough (for me at least) the very first present of the hundred and fifty listed is from a "Mr Arkwright".
Luther Arkwright, an adventurer in alternative worlds, is probably my best known comic creation.
Curiously, at Carroll's funeral. nearly twenty years later, a wreath is placed on his grave from a "Mr Arkwright".
Alice moves to Hargreaves' stately home with its large estate and huge staff of servants, settling into a life of socialising and raising children.
Born in 1883, her second son is named Leopold and the Prince is his Godfather.
Prince Leopold's daughter, born in the same year, is named Alice.
In 1884, the slight, haemophiliac Prince Leopold unexpectedly suffers a brain haemorrhage and dies at the age of twenty-eight.
Alice is inconsolable.
Her comfortable life seems blighted.
After the death of Edith, the parting from Leopold and his subsequent death, she has a melancholy that is never completely masked.
She continues to cherish the *Alice* books. In 1885, Lewis Carroll writes to "his ideal child-friend" for permission to borrow the original manuscript for a facsimile edition, the profits going to children's hospitals.
When published, he sends her a special copy bound in white vellum.
Alice's Adventures under Ground

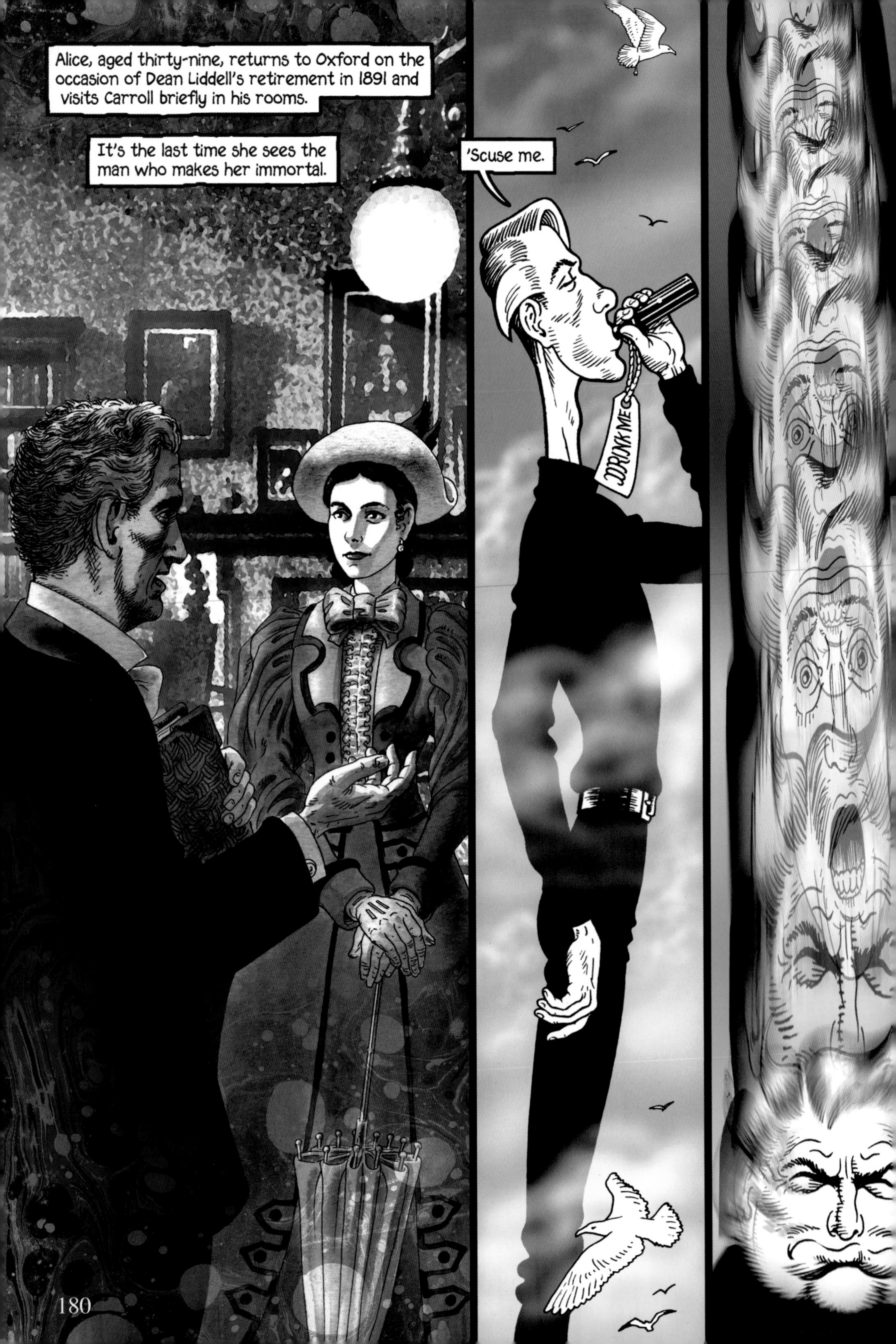

Alice, aged thirty-nine, returns to Oxford on the occasion of Dean Liddell's retirement in 1891 and visits Carroll briefly in his rooms.
It's the last time she sees the man who makes her immortal.
'Scuse me.
DRINK ME

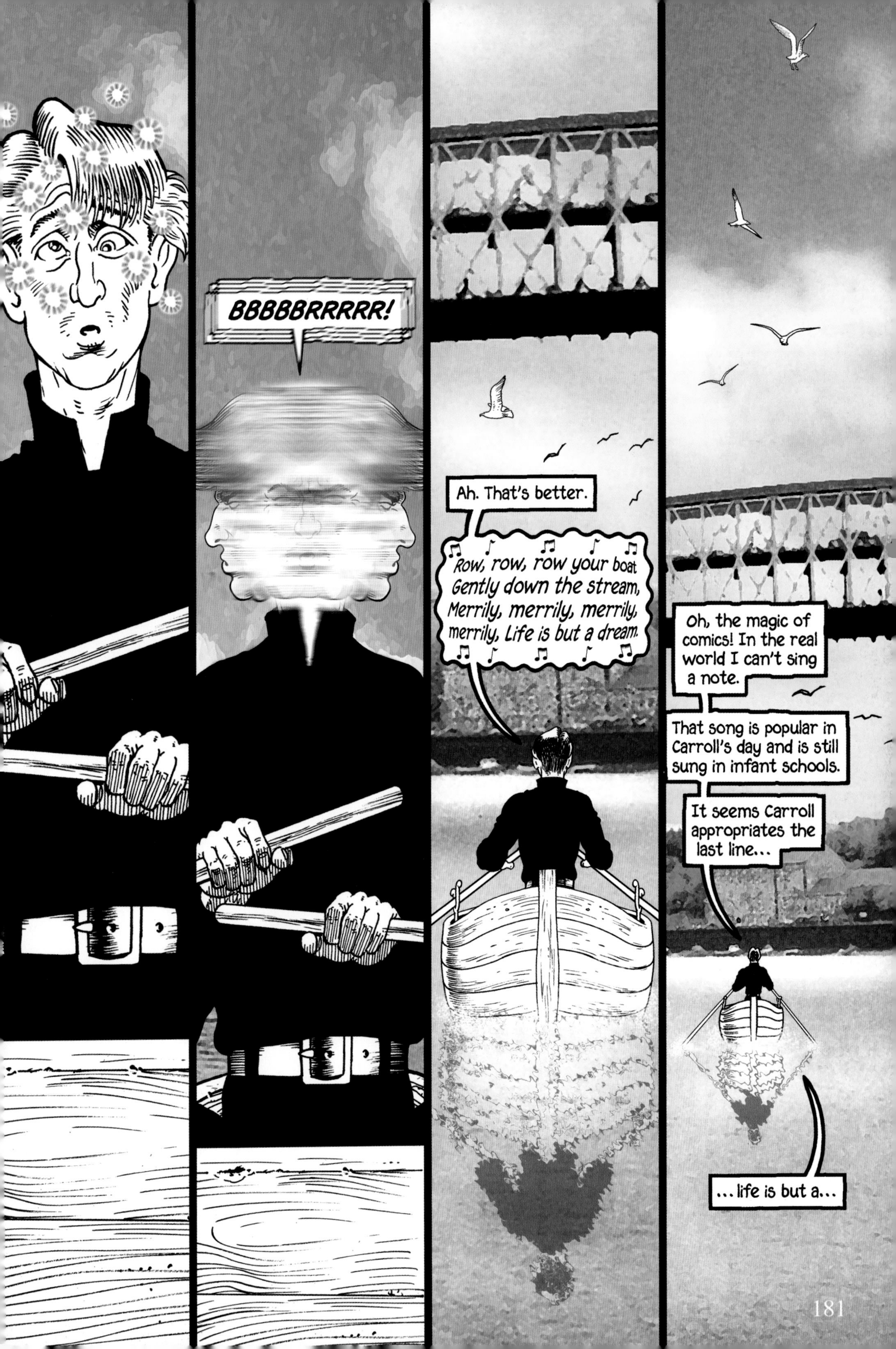

BBBBBRRRRR!
Ah. That's better.
Row, row, row your boat
Gently down the stream,
Merrily, merrily, merrily,
merrily, Life is but a dream.
Oh, the magic of comics! In the real world I can't sing a note.
That song is popular in Carroll's day and is still sung in infant schools.
It seems Carroll appropriates the last line...
...life is but a...

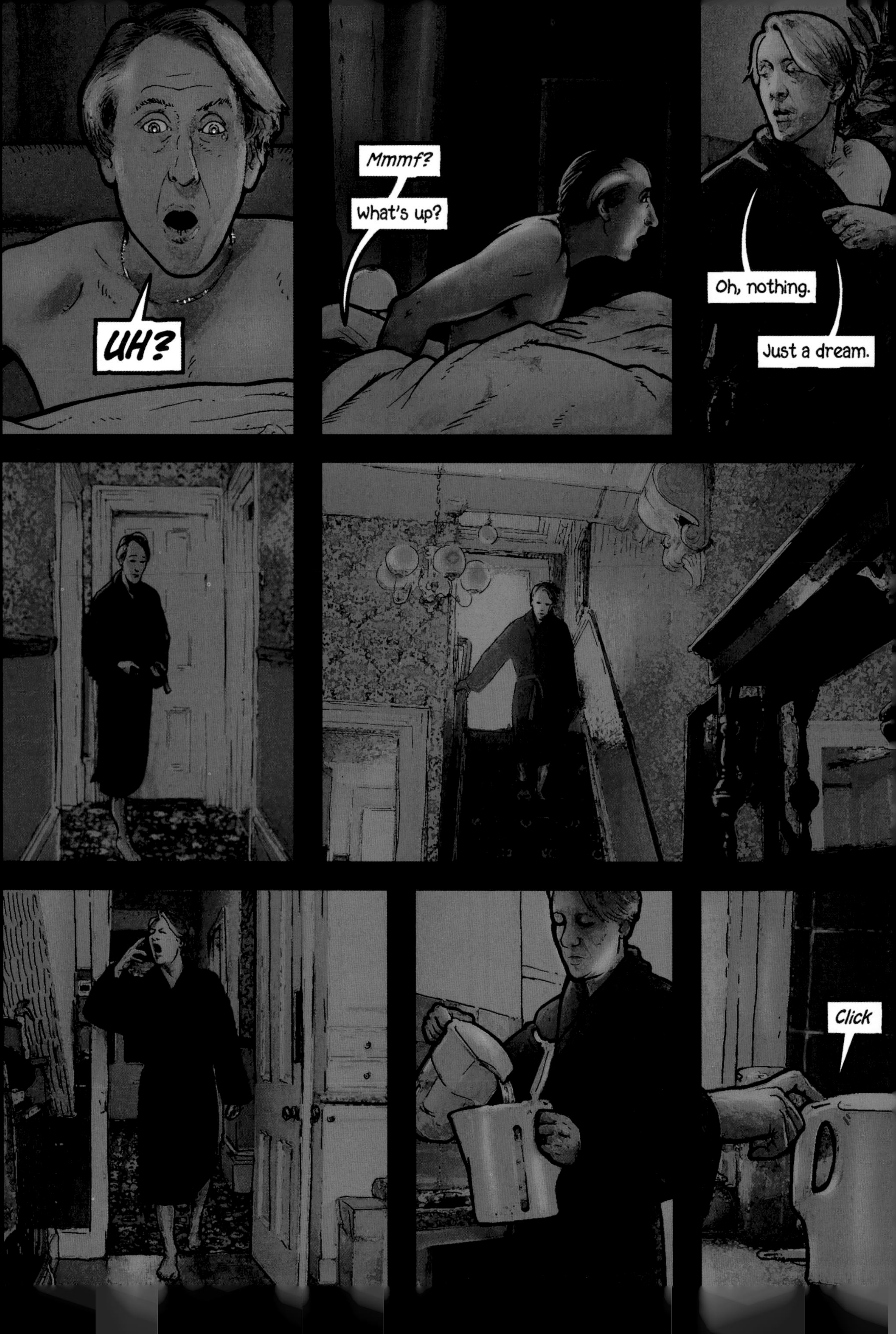
UH?
Mmmf?
What's up?
Oh, nothing.
Just a dream.
Click

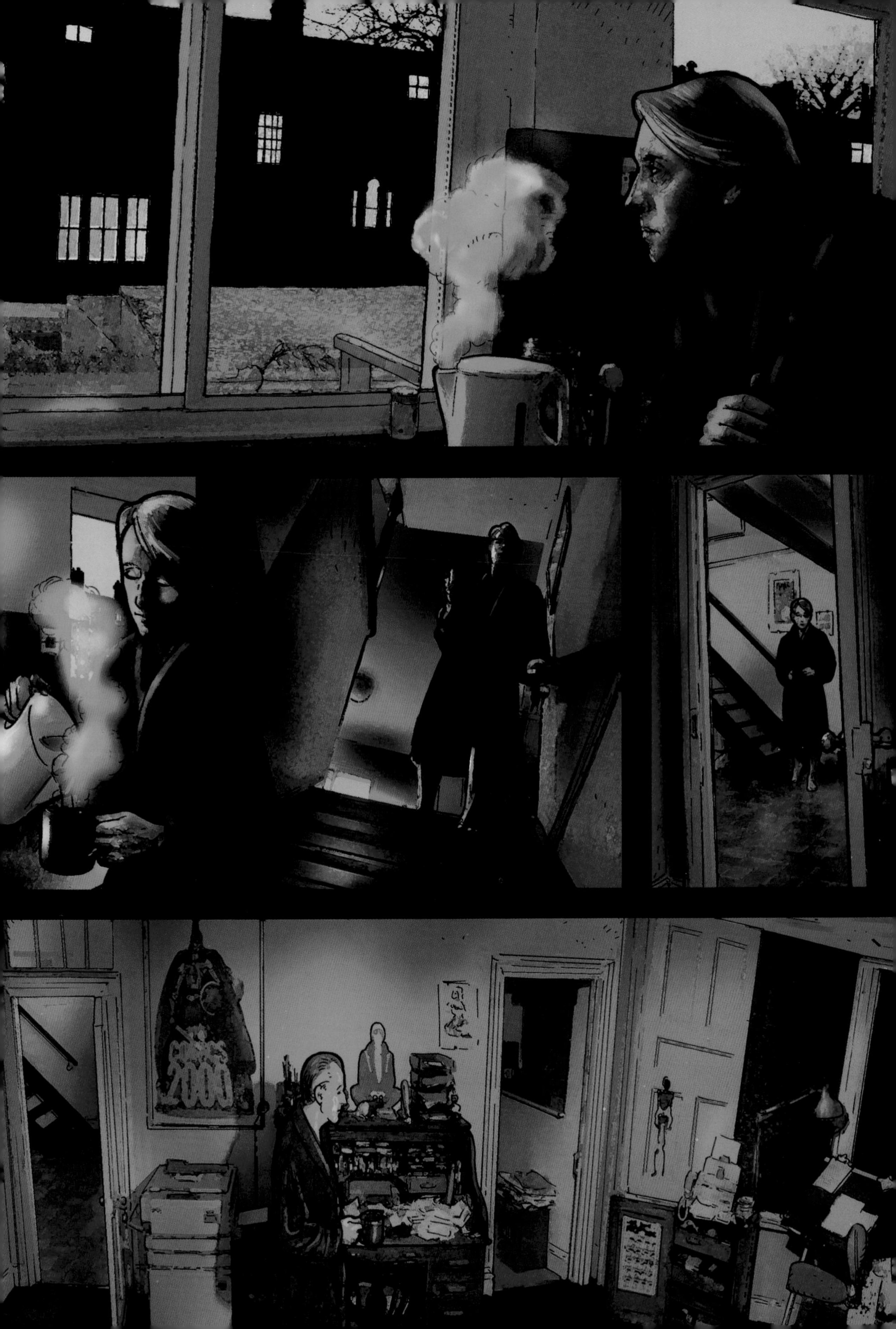

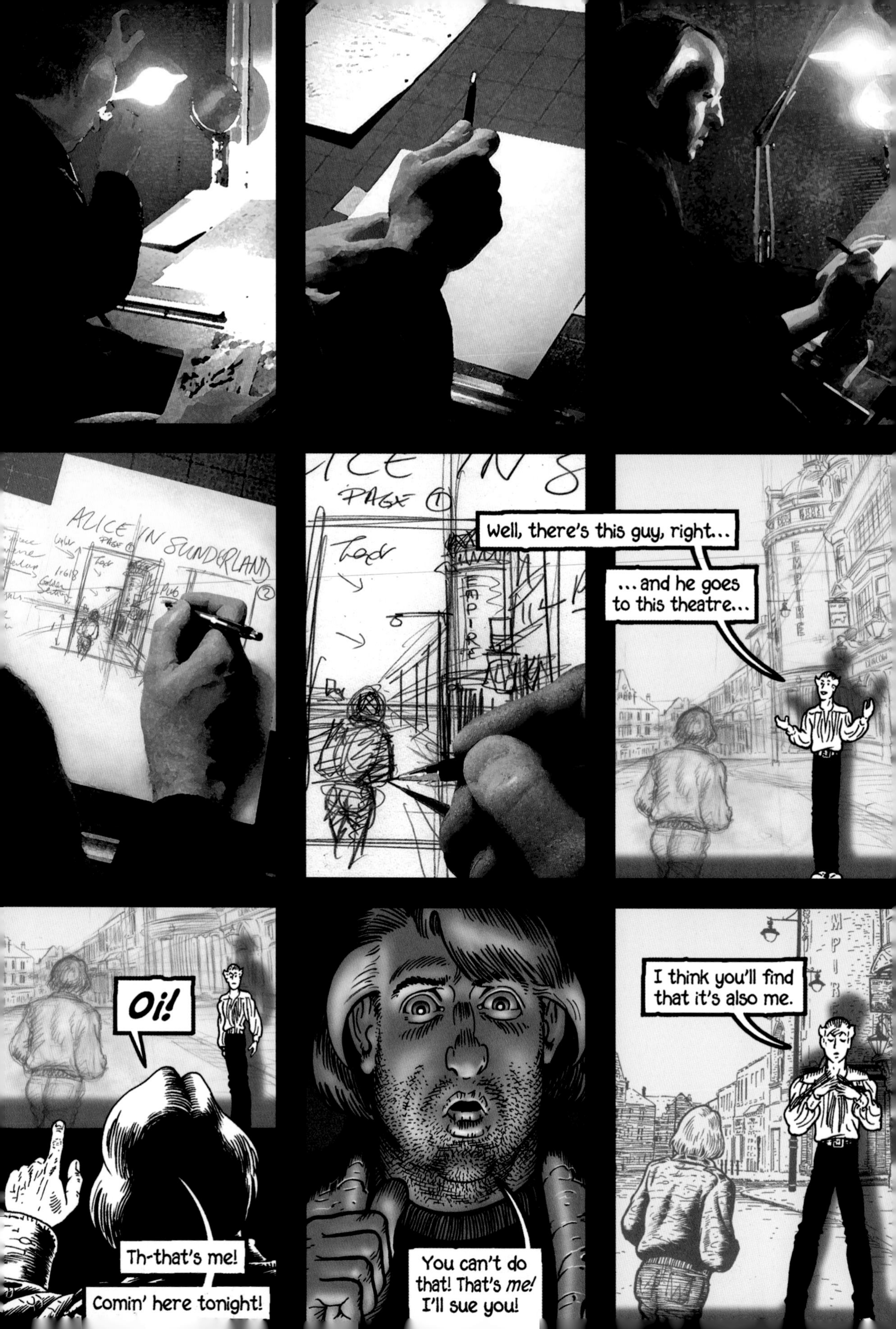
ALICE IN SUNDERLAND
PAGE 1
EMPIRE
Well, there's this guy, right...
...and he goes to this theatre...
EMPIRE
Oi!
Th-that's me!
Comin' here tonight!
You can't do that! That's *me!* I'll sue you!
I think you'll find that it's also me.

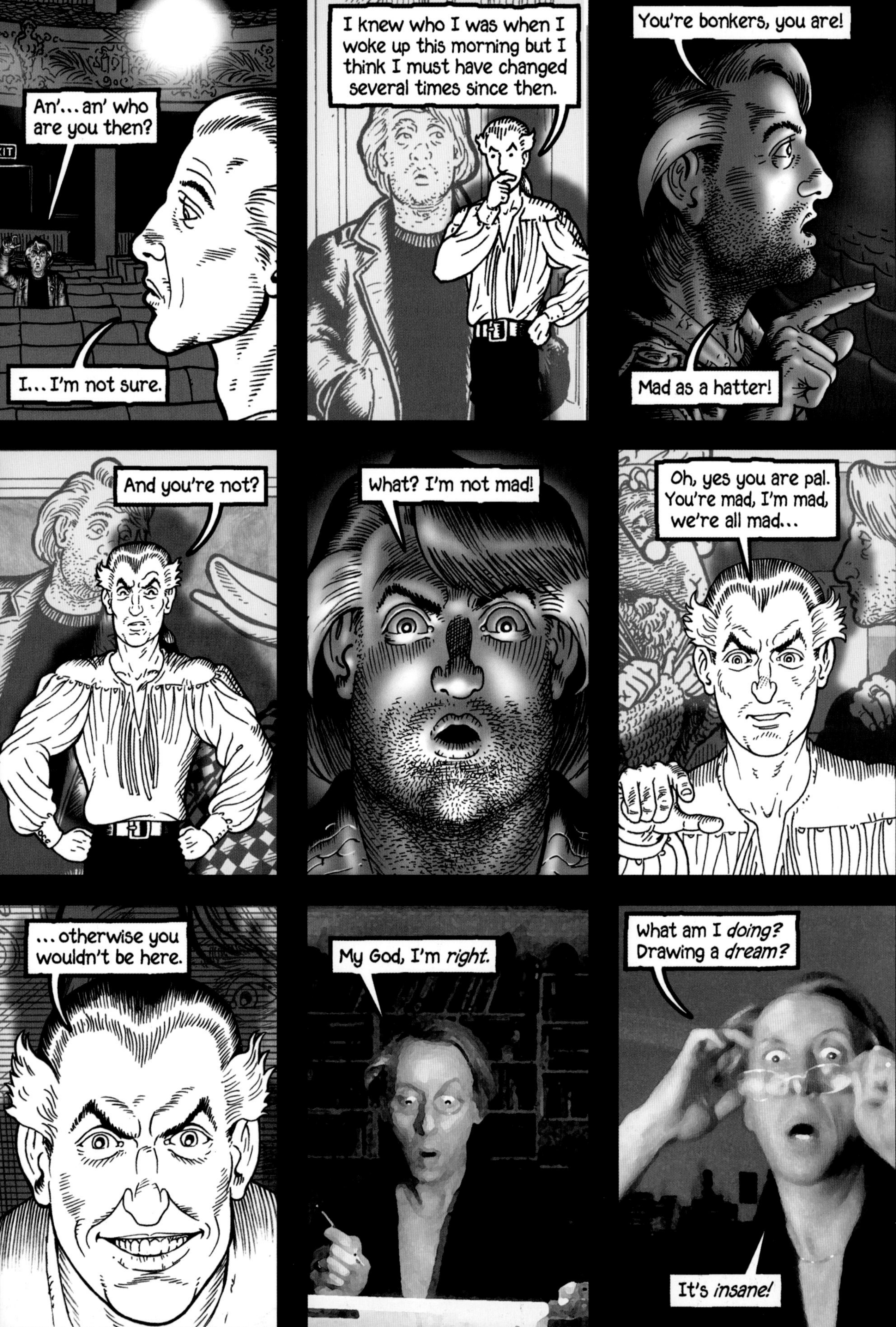

An'...an' who are you then?
I... I'm not sure.
I knew who I was when I woke up this morning but I think I must have changed several times since then.
You're bonkers, you are!
Mad as a hatter!
And you're not?
What? I'm not mad!
Oh, yes you are pal. You're mad, I'm mad, we're all mad...
...otherwise you wouldn't be here.
My God, I'm *right.*
What am I *doing?* Drawing a *dream?*
It's *insane!*

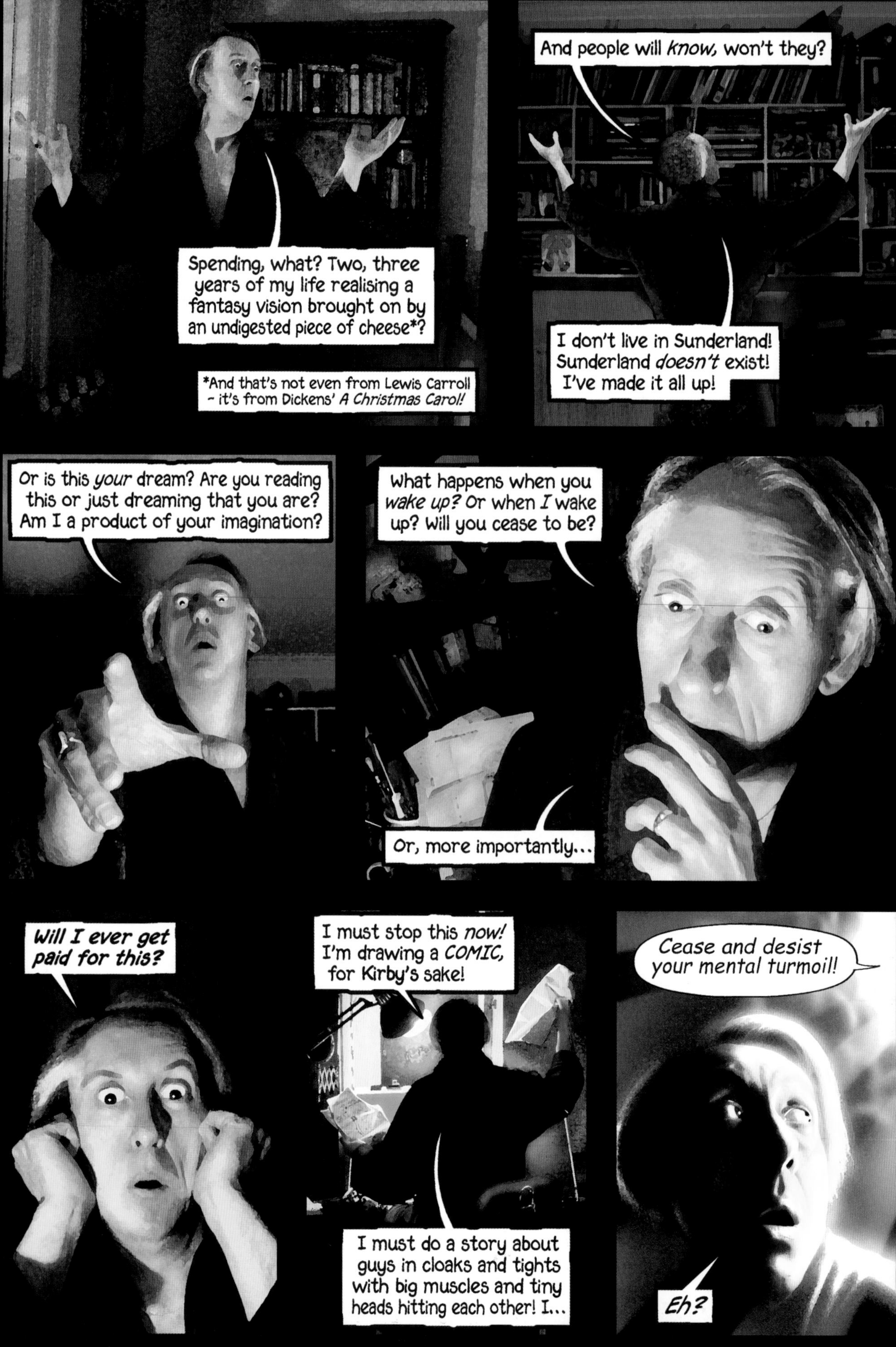
Spending, what? Two, three years of my life realising a fantasy vision brought on by an undigested piece of cheese*?
*And that's not even from Lewis Carroll – it's from Dickens' *A Christmas Carol!*
And people will *know*, won't they?
I don't live in Sunderland! Sunderland *doesn't* exist! I've made it all up!
Or is this *your* dream? Are you reading this or just dreaming that you are? Am I a product of your imagination?
What happens when you *wake up?* Or when *I* wake up? Will you cease to be?
Or, more importantly...
Will I ever get paid for this?
I must stop this *now!* I'm drawing a *COMIC,* for Kirby's sake!
I must do a story about guys in cloaks and tights with big muscles and tiny heads hitting each other! I...
Cease and desist your mental turmoil!
Eh?

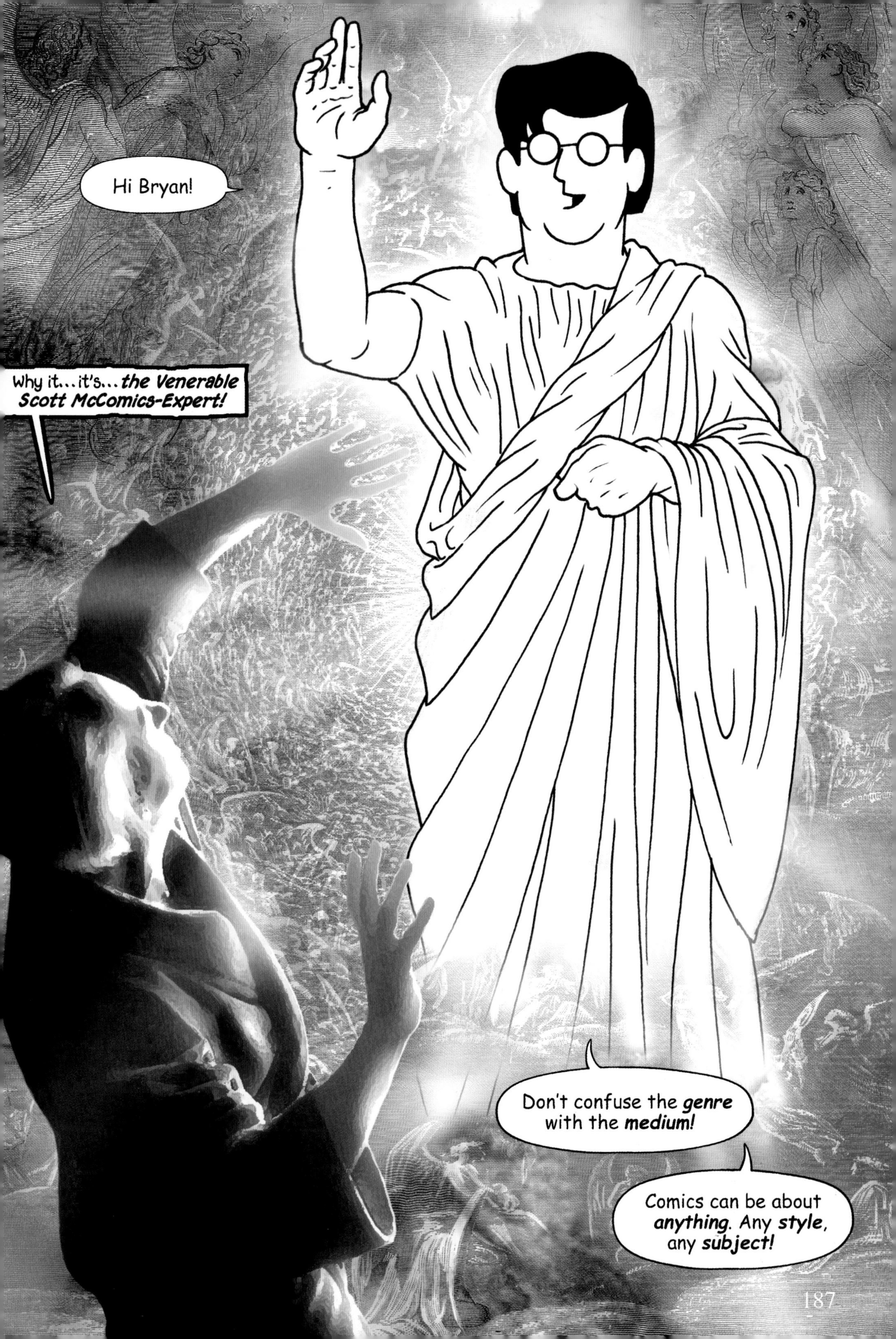
Hi Bryan!
Why it...it's...the Venerable Scott McComics-Expert!
Don't confuse the genre with the medium!
Comics can be about anything. Any style, any subject!

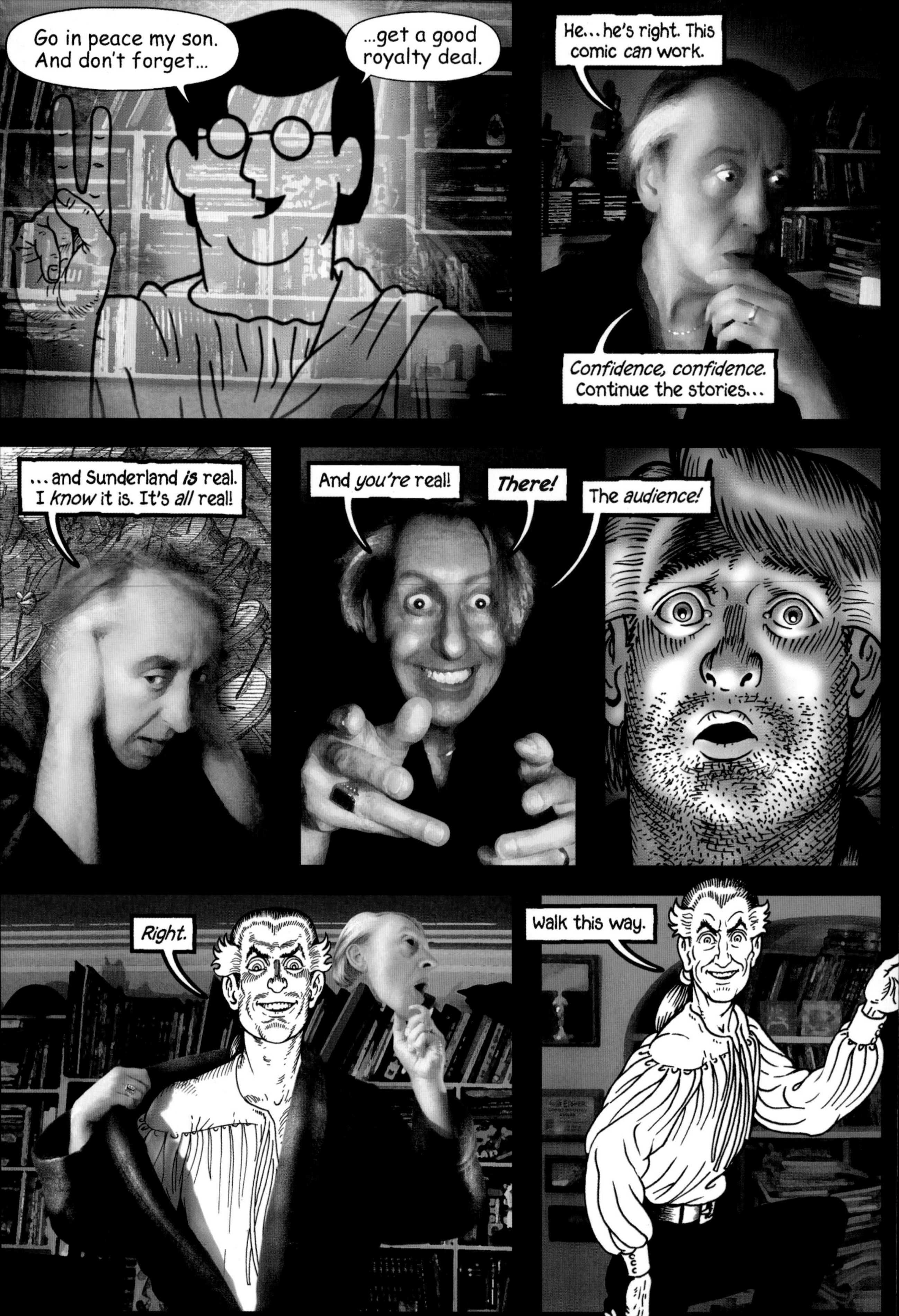
Go in peace my son. And don't forget...
...get a good royalty deal.
He...he's right. This comic *can* work.
Confidence, confidence. Continue the stories...
...and Sunderland *is* real. I *know* it is. It's *all* real!
And *you're* real!
There!
The *audience!*
Right.
Walk this way.

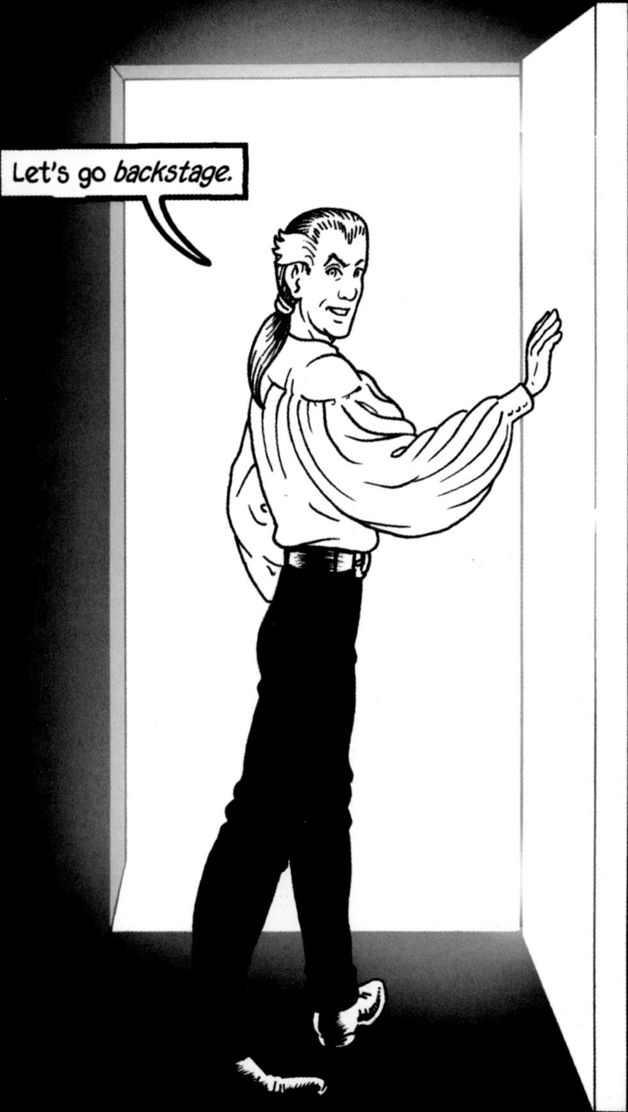
Let's go *backstage.*

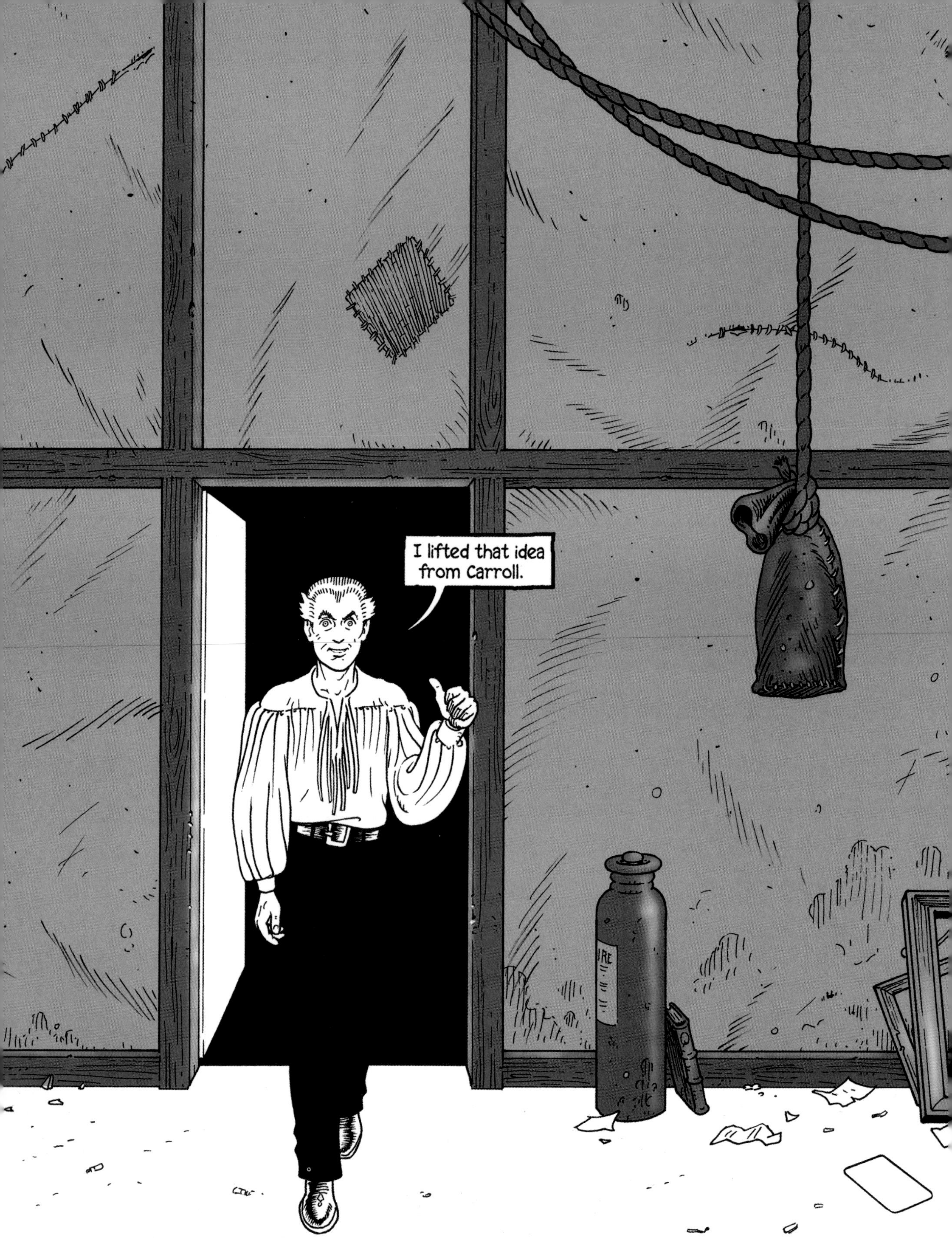
I lifted that idea from Carroll.

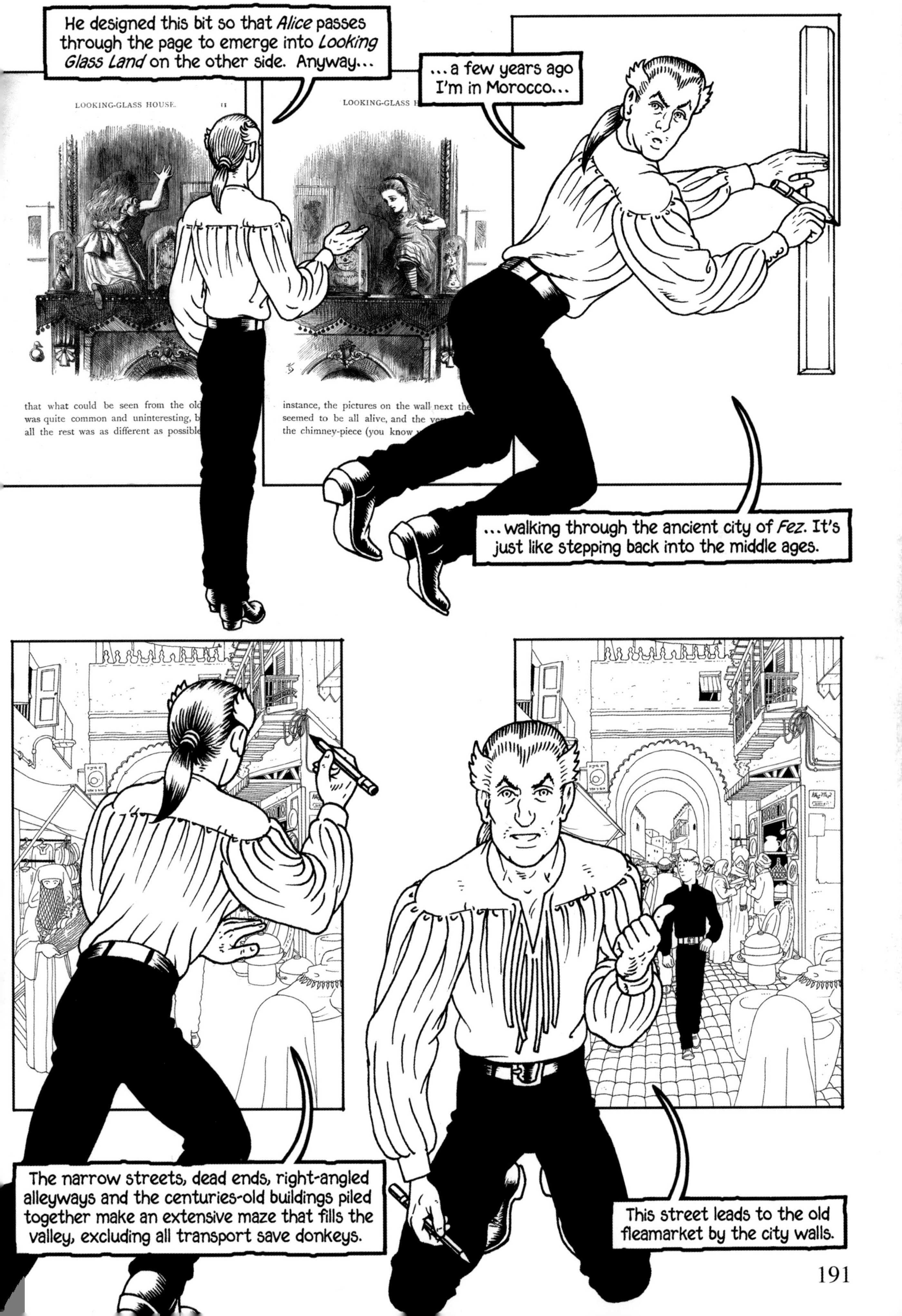
He designed this bit so that *Alice* passes through the page to emerge into *Looking Glass Land* on the other side. Anyway...
LOOKING-GLASS HOUSE. 11
LOOKING-GLASS H
that what could be seen from the old
was quite common and uninteresting, b
all the rest was as different as possible
instance, the pictures on the wall next the
seemed to be all alive, and the ve
the chimney-piece (you know
...a few years ago I'm in Morocco...
...walking through the ancient city of *Fez*. It's just like stepping back into the middle ages.
The narrow streets, dead ends, right-angled alleyways and the centuries-old buildings piled together make an extensive maze that fills the valley, excluding all transport save donkeys.
This street leads to the old fleamarket by the city walls.

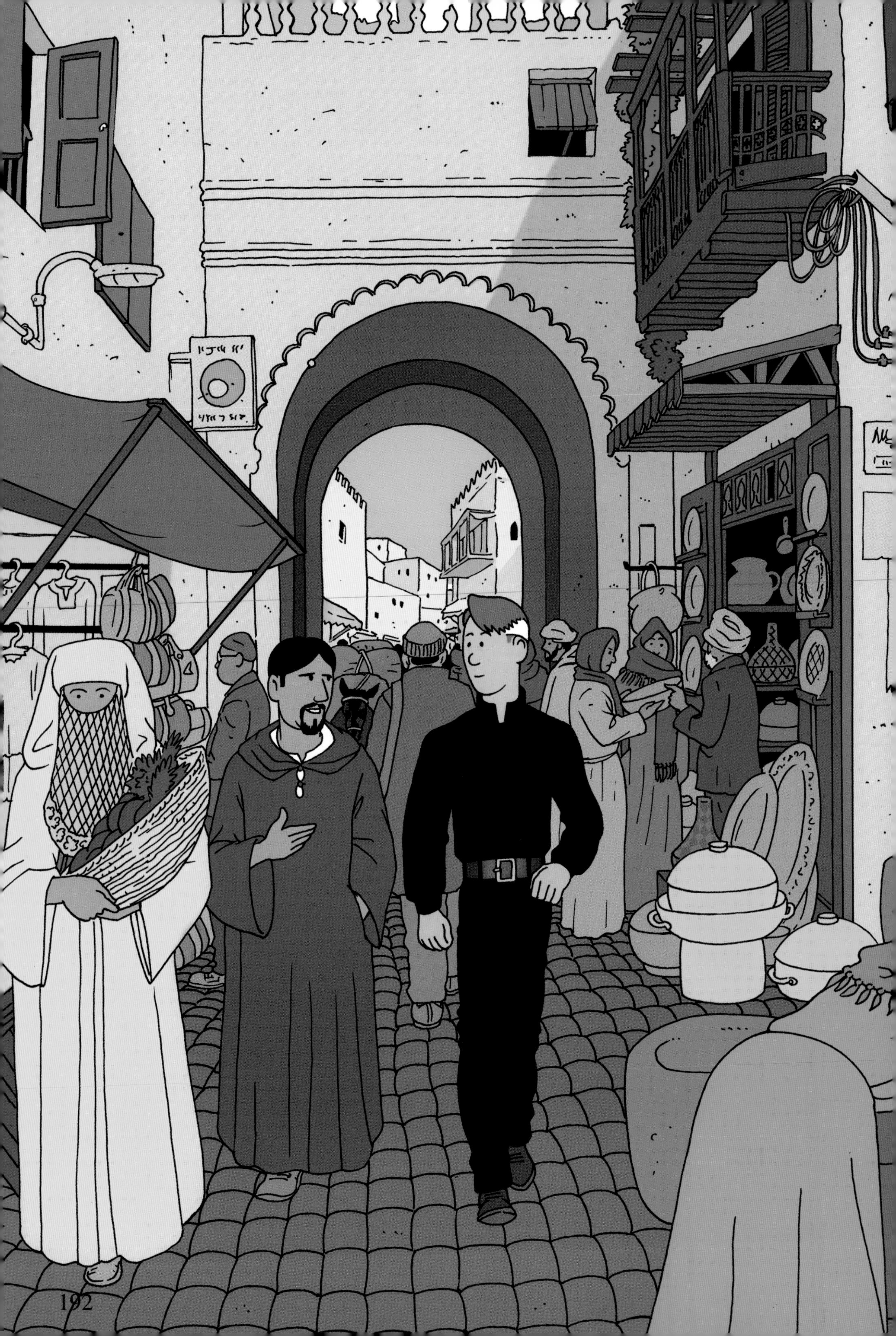

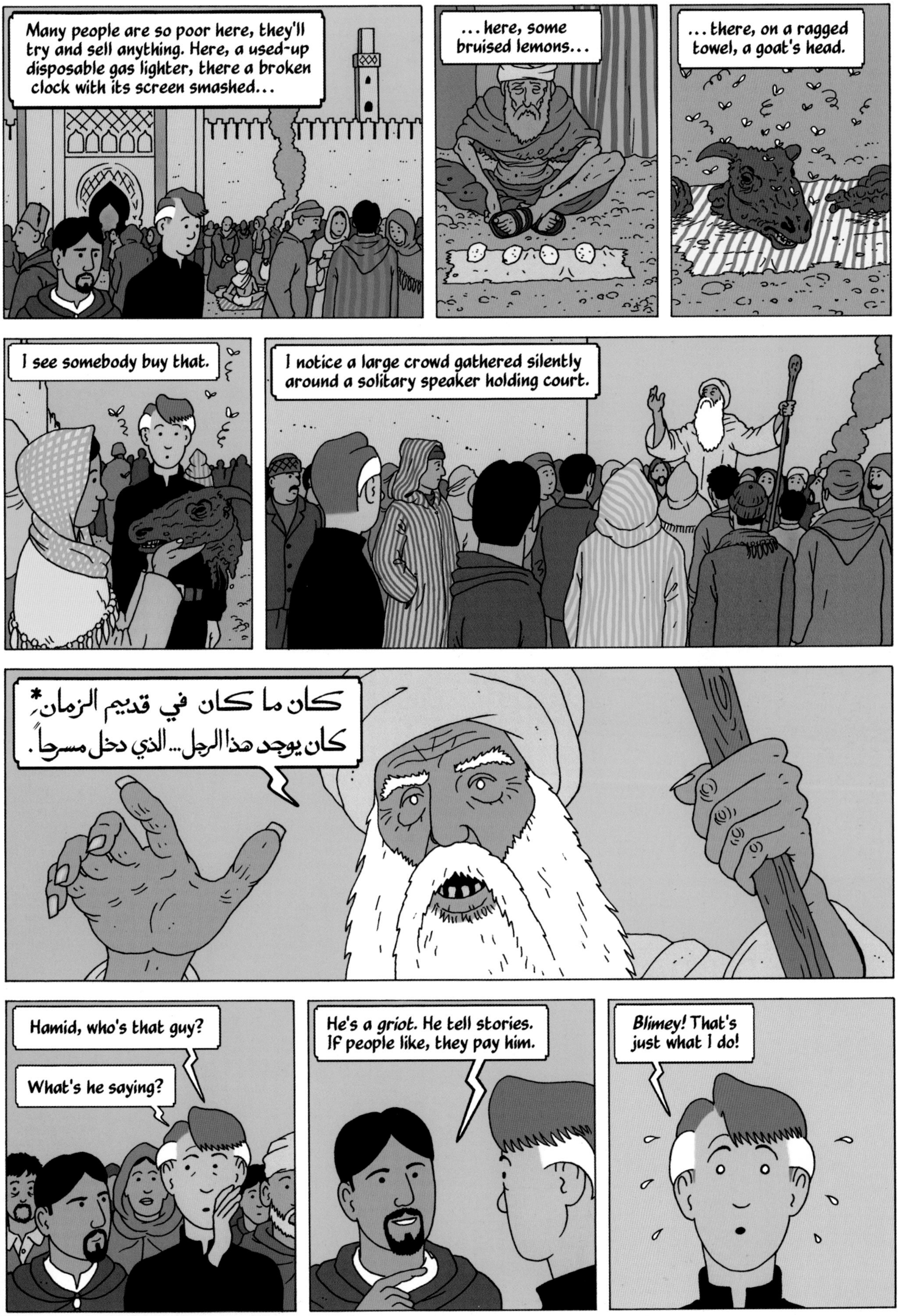
Many people are so poor here, they'll try and sell anything. Here, a used-up disposable gas lighter, there a broken clock with its screen smashed...
...here, some bruised lemons...
...there, on a ragged towel, a goat's head.
I see somebody buy that.
I notice a large crowd gathered silently around a solitary speaker holding court.
كان ما كان في قديم الزمان،* كان يوجد هذا الرجل... الذي دخل مسرحاً.
Hamid, who's that guy?
What's he saying?
He's a *griot*. He tell stories. If people like, they pay him.
Blimey! That's just what I do!

* Moroccan Arabic: "Once upon a time, there was this man...and he entered a theatre..."

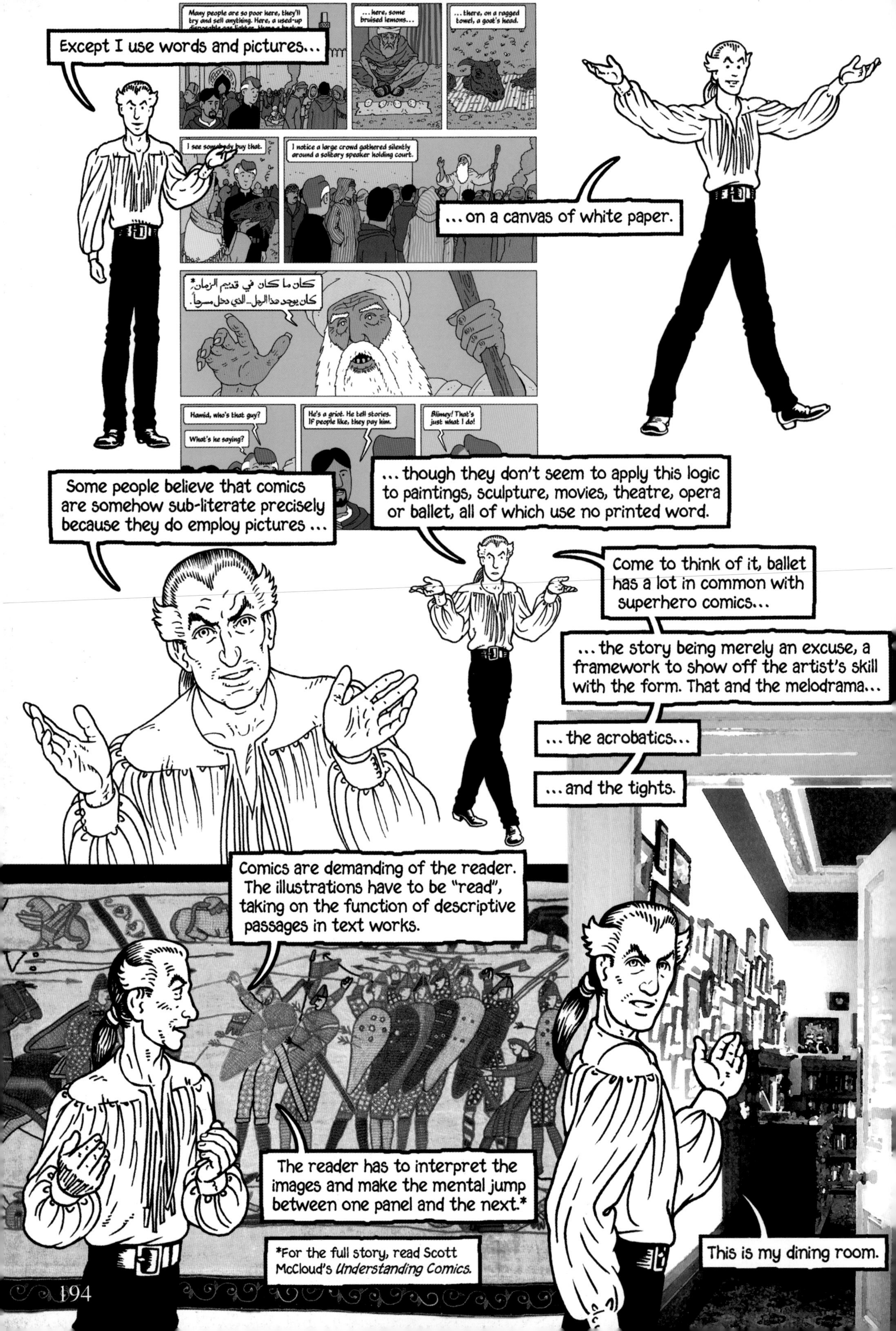
Many people are so poor here, they'll try and sell anything. Here, a used-up
Except I use words and pictures...
...here, some bruised lemons...
...there, on a ragged towel, a goat's head.
I see somebody buy that.
I notice a large crowd gathered silently around a solitary speaker holding court.
...on a canvas of white paper.
كان ما كان في قديم الزمان،*
كان يوجد هذا الرجل... الذي دخل مسرحاً.
Hamid, who's that guy?
What's he saying?
He's a griot. He tell stories. If people like, they pay him.
Blimey! That's just what I do!
Some people believe that comics are somehow sub-literate precisely because they do employ pictures ...
... though they don't seem to apply this logic to paintings, sculpture, movies, theatre, opera or ballet, all of which use no printed word.
Come to think of it, ballet has a lot in common with superhero comics...
... the story being merely an excuse, a framework to show off the artist's skill with the form. That and the melodrama...
... the acrobatics...
... and the tights.
Comics are demanding of the reader. The illustrations have to be "read", taking on the function of descriptive passages in text works.
The reader has to interpret the images and make the mental jump between one panel and the next.*
*For the full story, read Scott McCloud's *Understanding Comics*.
This is my dining room.

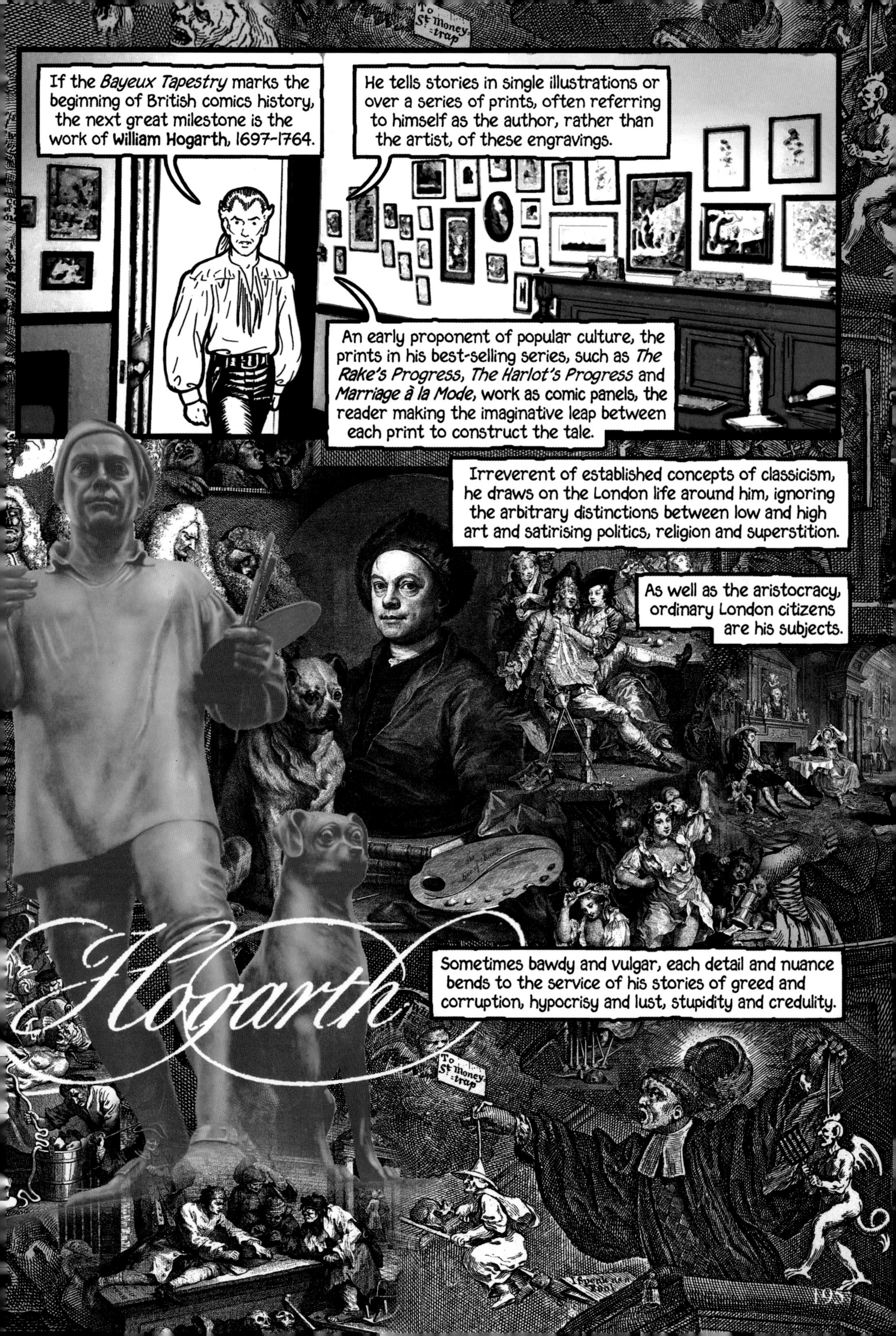

To St Money-trap
If the *Bayeux Tapestry* marks the beginning of British comics history, the next great milestone is the work of **William Hogarth**, 1697–1764.
He tells stories in single illustrations or over a series of prints, often referring to himself as the author, rather than the artist, of these engravings.
An early proponent of popular culture, the prints in his best-selling series, such as *The Rake's Progress*, *The Harlot's Progress* and *Marriage à la Mode*, work as comic panels, the reader making the imaginative leap between each print to construct the tale.
Irreverent of established concepts of classicism, he draws on the London life around him, ignoring the arbitrary distinctions between low and high art and satirising politics, religion and superstition.
As well as the aristocracy, ordinary London citizens are his subjects.
Hogarth
Sometimes bawdy and vulgar, each detail and nuance bends to the service of his stories of greed and corruption, hypocrisy and lust, stupidity and credulity.
To St Money-trap

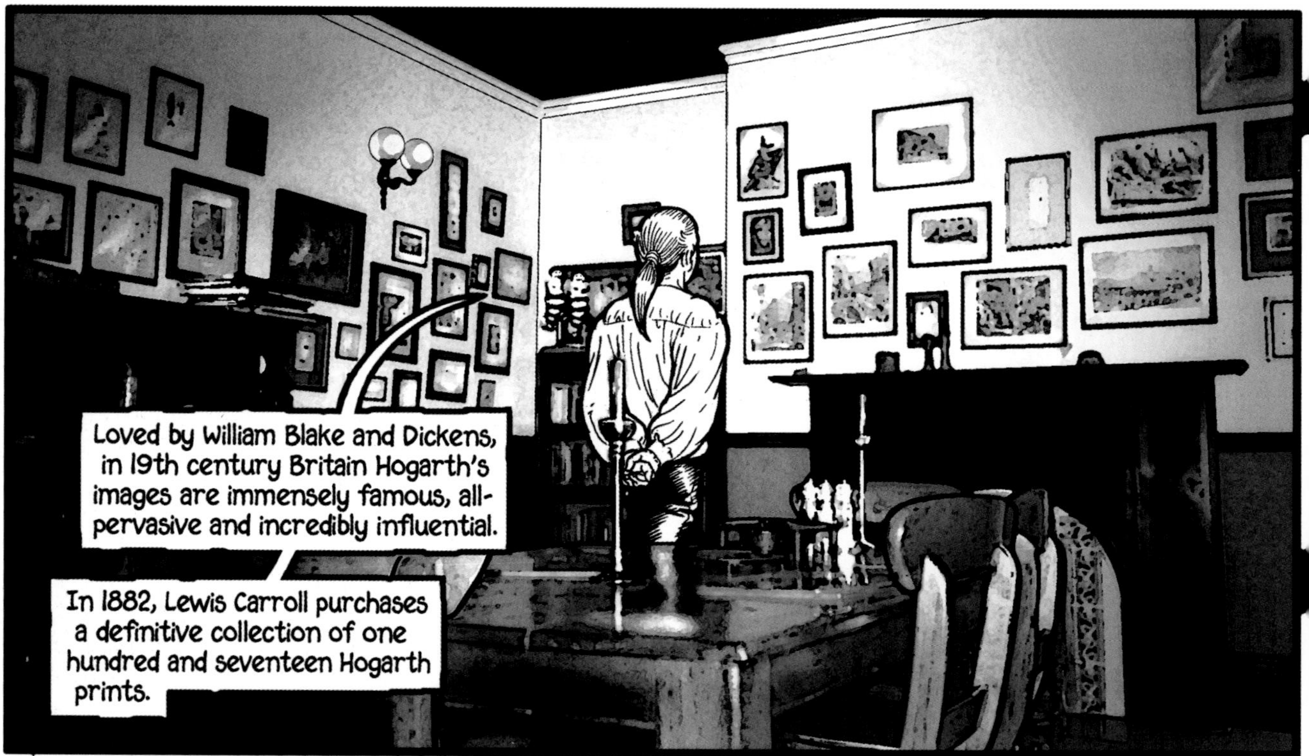
Loved by William Blake and Dickens, in 19th century Britain Hogarth's images are immensely famous, all-pervasive and incredibly influential.
In 1882, Lewis Carroll purchases a definitive collection of one hundred and seventeen Hogarth prints.

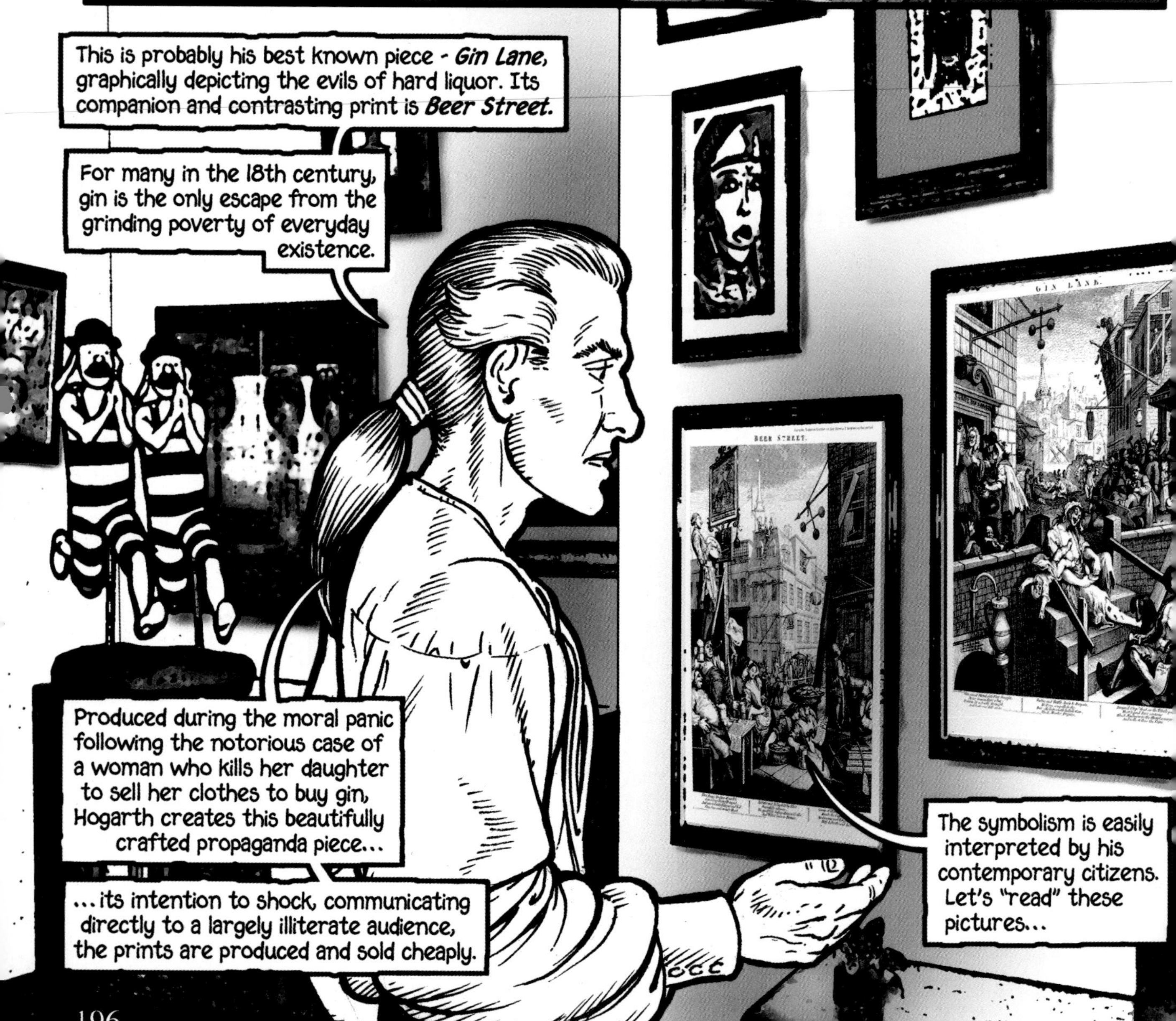
This is probably his best known piece - *Gin Lane*, graphically depicting the evils of hard liquor. Its companion and contrasting print is *Beer Street*.
For many in the 18th century, gin is the only escape from the grinding poverty of everyday existence.
GIN LANE.
BEER STREET.
Produced during the moral panic following the notorious case of a woman who kills her daughter to sell her clothes to buy gin, Hogarth creates this beautifully crafted propaganda piece...
...its intention to shock, communicating directly to a largely illiterate audience, the prints are produced and sold cheaply.
The symbolism is easily interpreted by his contemporary citizens. Let's "read" these pictures...

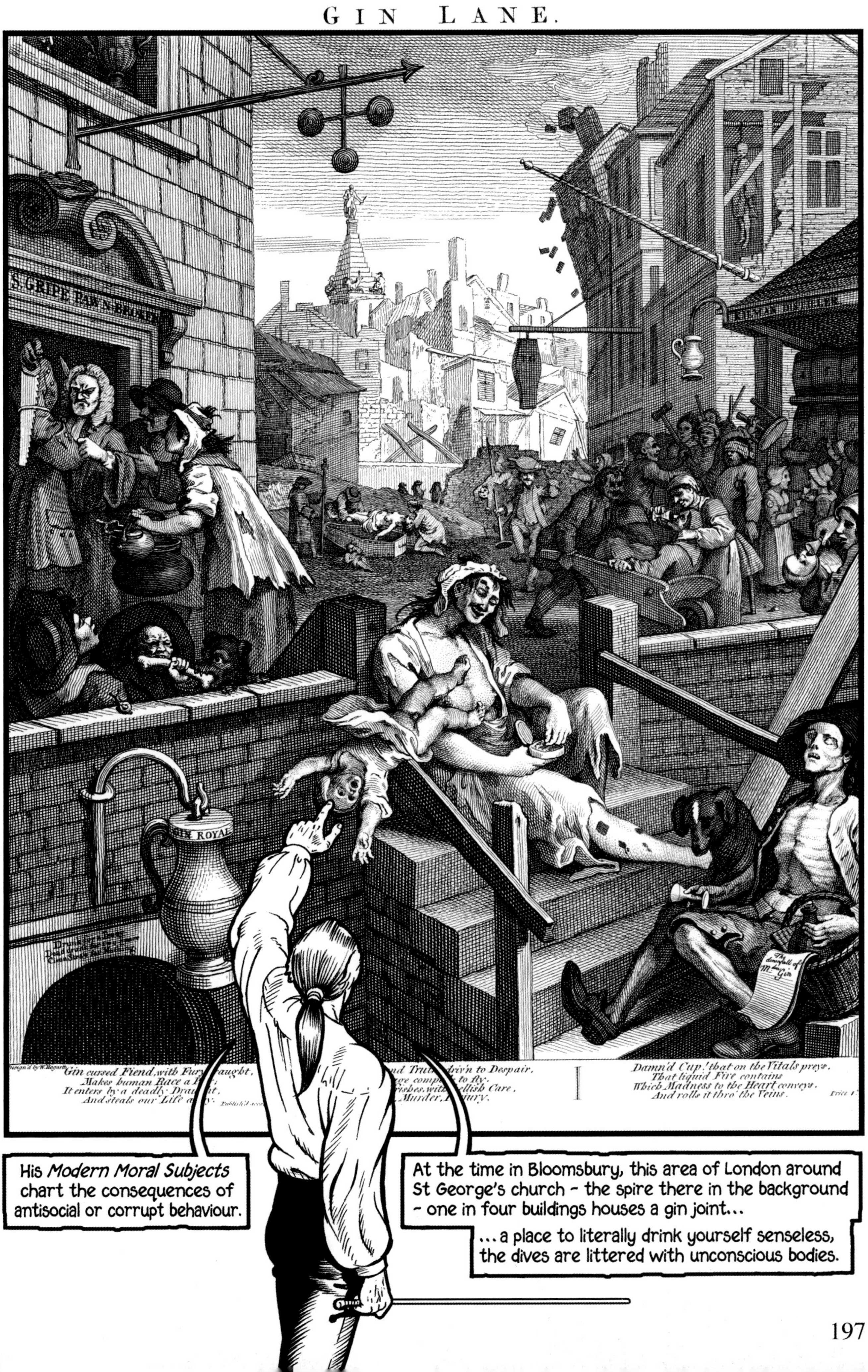
GIN LANE.
Damn'd Cup! that on the Vitals preys,
That liquid Fire contains
Which Madness to the Heart conveys,
And rolls it thro' the Veins.
His *Modern Moral Subjects* chart the consequences of antisocial or corrupt behaviour.
At the time in Bloomsbury, this area of London around St George's church – the spire there in the background – one in four buildings houses a gin joint...
...a place to literally drink yourself senseless, the dives are littered with unconscious bodies.

Cheap, too. See the sign above the door, behind the gin flask...

The child tumbles from the arms of its ragged, inebriated mother as she helps herself to another pinch of snuff.

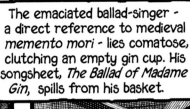

The emaciated ballad-singer - a direct reference to medieval *memento mori* - lies comatose, clutching an empty gin cup. His songsheet, *The Ballad of Madame Gin*, spills from his basket.

... "Drunk for a penny. Dead drunk for twopence. Clean straw for nothing."

This guy's so plastered a snail has time to crawl onto his shoulder.

His companion is also an addict who's lost all sense of dignity!

Behind them a carpenter and a cook sell the means of their livelihood to a pawnbroker for gin money.

In the background a woman doses her baby, and two girls from the charity school of *St Giles* drink at the gin-stall.

A barber, we tell from his pole, his business gone and himself bankrupted, hangs himself.

The gin-sodden spend no cash on haircuts.

Everywhere, there are signs of death...

...and madness...

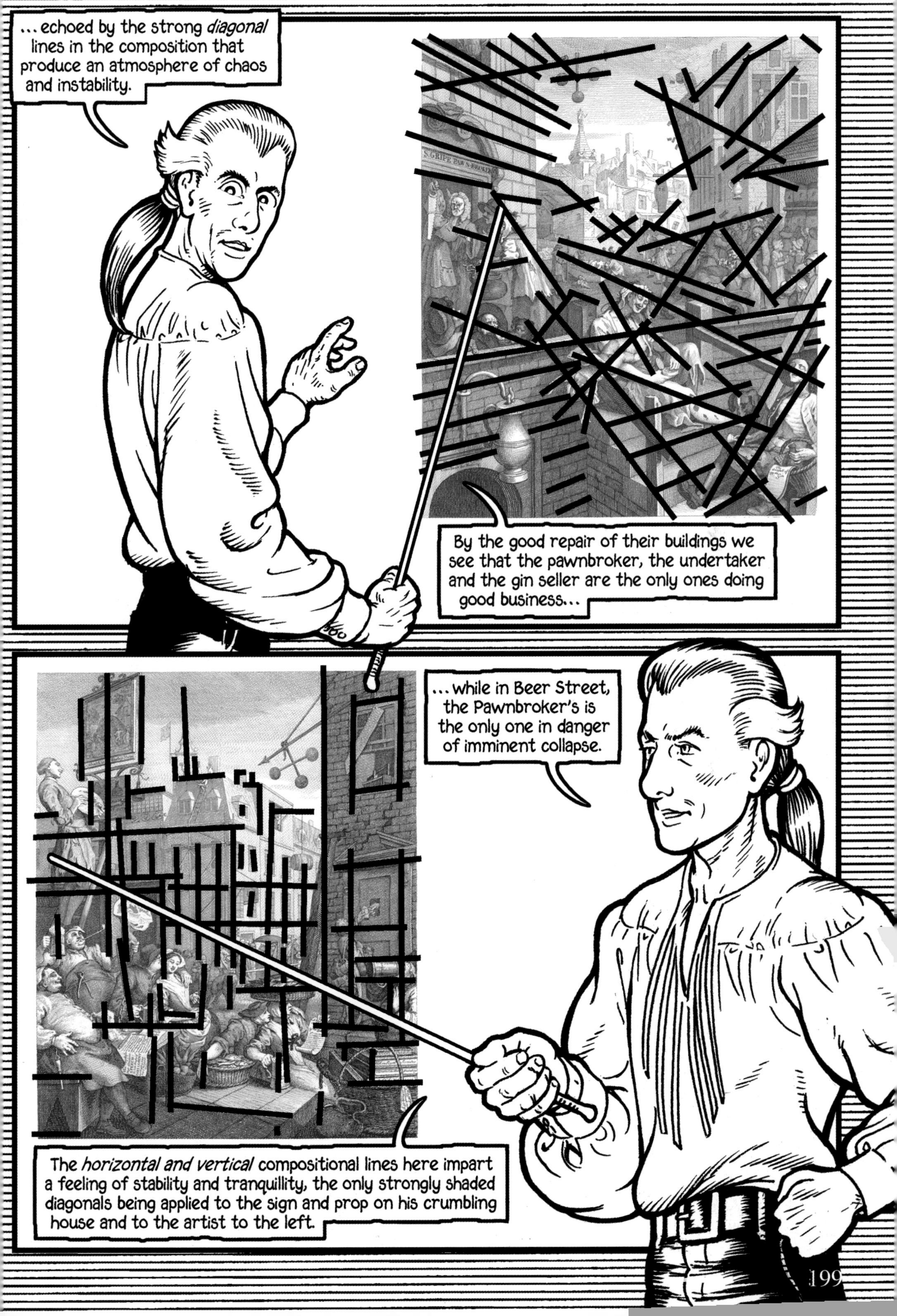

...echoed by the strong *diagonal* lines in the composition that produce an atmosphere of chaos and instability.
S. GRIPE PAWN BROKER
By the good repair of their buildings we see that the pawnbroker, the undertaker and the gin seller are the only ones doing good business...
...while in Beer Street, the Pawnbroker's is the only one in danger of imminent collapse.
The *horizontal and vertical* compositional lines here impart a feeling of stability and tranquillity, the only strongly shaded diagonals being applied to the sign and prop on his crumbling house and to the artist to the left.

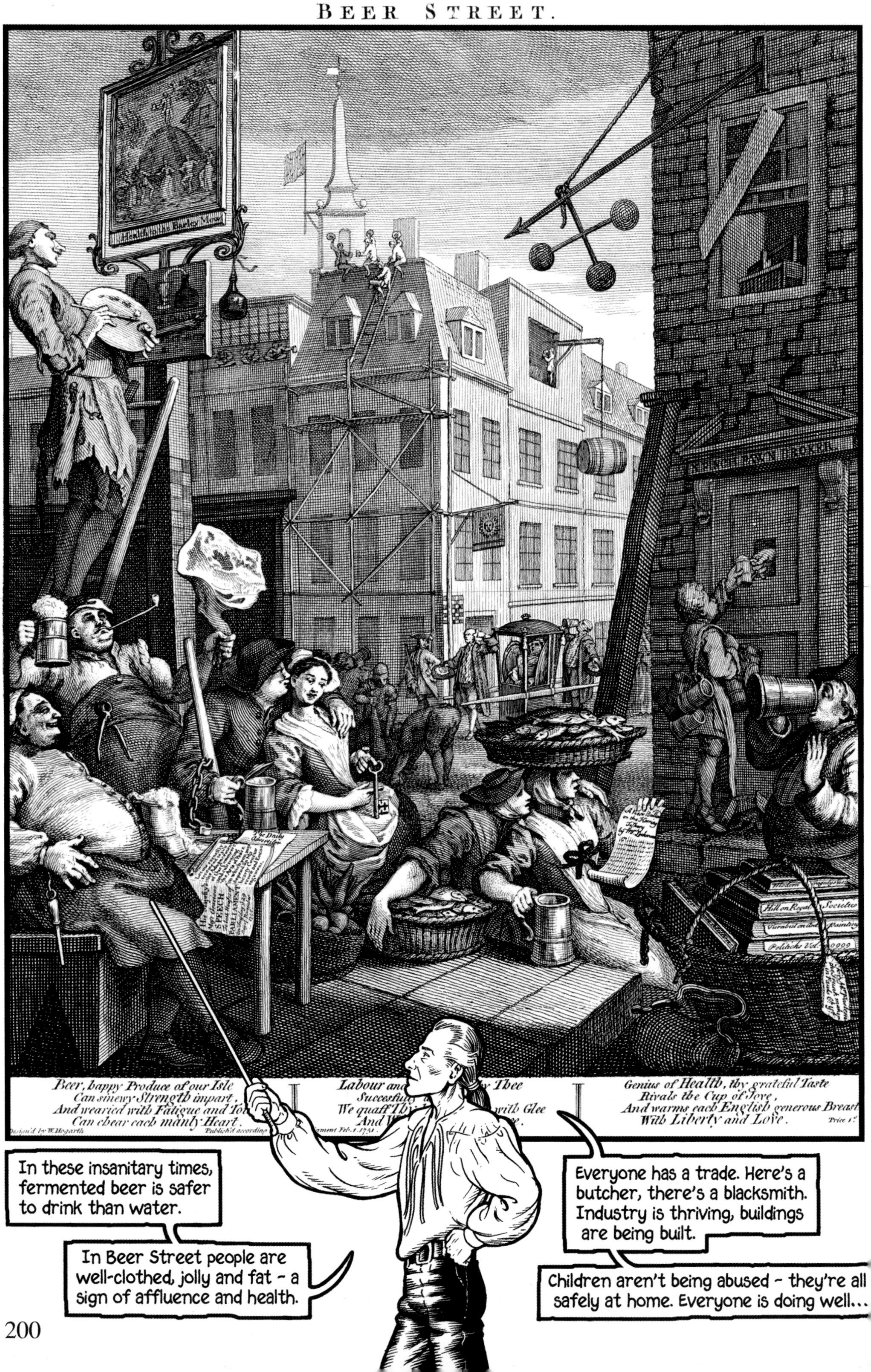
BEER STREET.
Beer, happy Produce of our Isle
Can sinewy Strength impart,
And wearied with Fatigue and Toil
Can chear each manly Heart.
Genius of Health, thy grateful Taste
Rivals the Cup of Jove,
And warms each English generous Breast
With Liberty and Love.
In these insanitary times, fermented beer is safer to drink than water.
In Beer Street people are well-clothed, jolly and fat – a sign of affluence and health.
Everyone has a trade. Here's a butcher, there's a blacksmith. Industry is thriving, buildings are being built.
Children aren't being abused – they're all safely at home. Everyone is doing well...

...with the exception of the pawnbroker and the artist, who's poor and ragged, reduced to using his skills to paint pub signs...

...because he's still a gin addict. *See* — he paints a gin flask, not a beer bottle on the sign.

On Beer Street, literacy abounds...

...and love is in the air.

All is harmonious and stable...

...partly due to Hogarth's placement of our eye level.

We gaze at the scene with our feet firmly planted on the pavement.

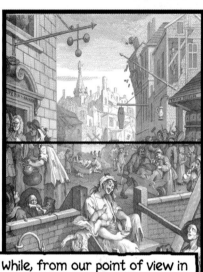

While, from our point of view in Gin Lane, we float unnervingly in space, nothing beneath our feet...

...as we hover, almost literally, over **the abyss.**

The prints help to bring about the 1751 *Gin Act* and gin is reinvented as a drink for toffs.

Ah, a nice *G & T.* In Quaker and teetotaller Joshua Wilson's house too.

There's even a brand now called *Hogarth Gin*, with his portrait on the front!

They both must be spinning in their graves.

Bottoms up!

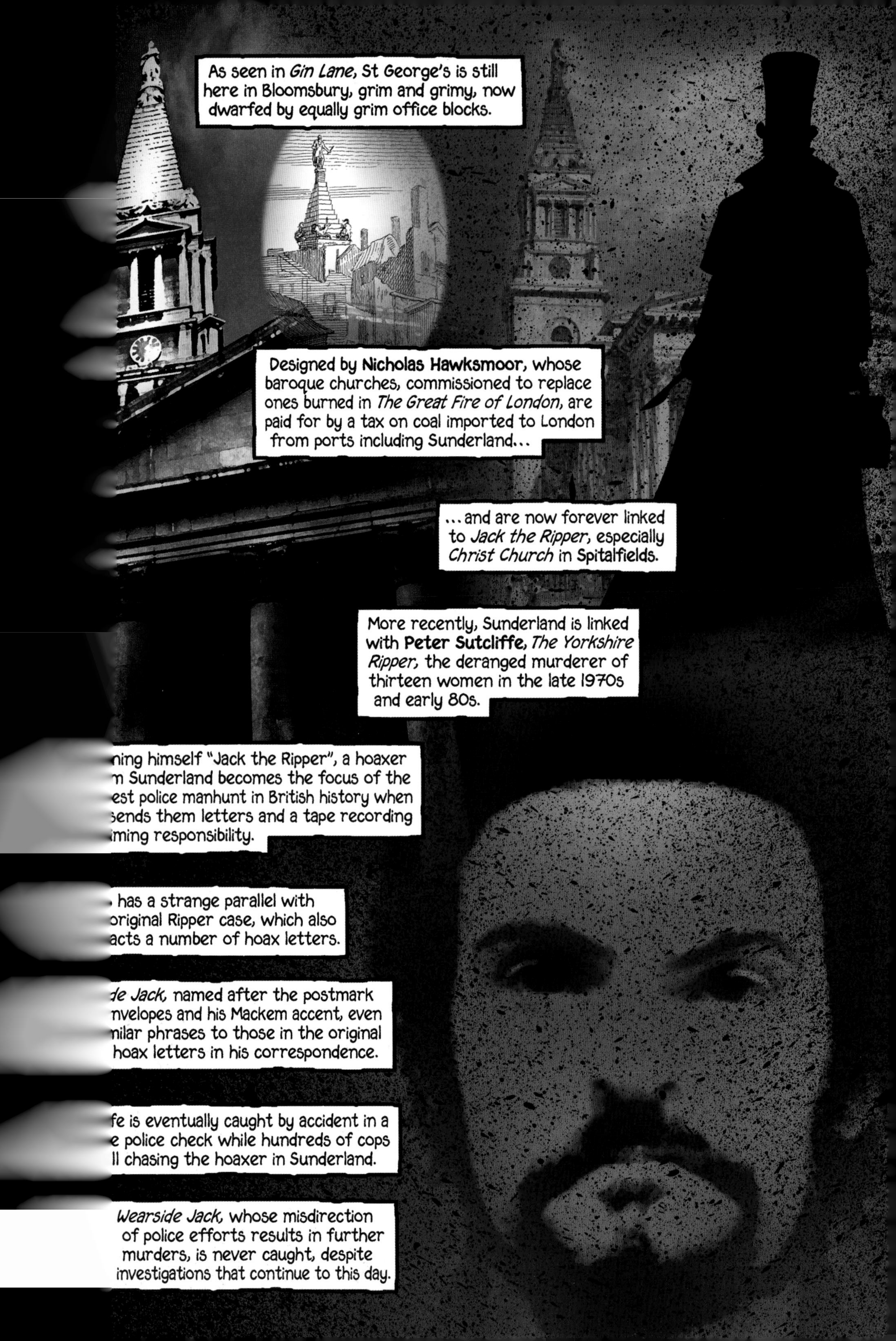

As seen in *Gin Lane*, St George's is still here in Bloomsbury, grim and grimy, now dwarfed by equally grim office blocks.
Designed by **Nicholas Hawksmoor**, whose baroque churches, commissioned to replace ones burned in *The Great Fire of London*, are paid for by a tax on coal imported to London from ports including Sunderland...
...and are now forever linked to *Jack the Ripper*, especially *Christ Church* in **Spitalfields**.
More recently, Sunderland is linked with **Peter Sutcliffe**, *The Yorkshire Ripper*, the deranged murderer of thirteen women in the late 1970s and early 80s.
ning himself "Jack the Ripper", a hoaxer m Sunderland becomes the focus of the est police manhunt in British history when sends them letters and a tape recording iming responsibility.
has a strange parallel with original Ripper case, which also acts a number of hoax letters.
de Jack, named after the postmark nvelopes and his Mackem accent, even nilar phrases to those in the original hoax letters in his correspondence.
fe is eventually caught by accident in a e police check while hundreds of cops ll chasing the hoaxer in Sunderland.
Wearside Jack, whose misdirection of police efforts results in further murders, is never caught, despite investigations that continue to this day.

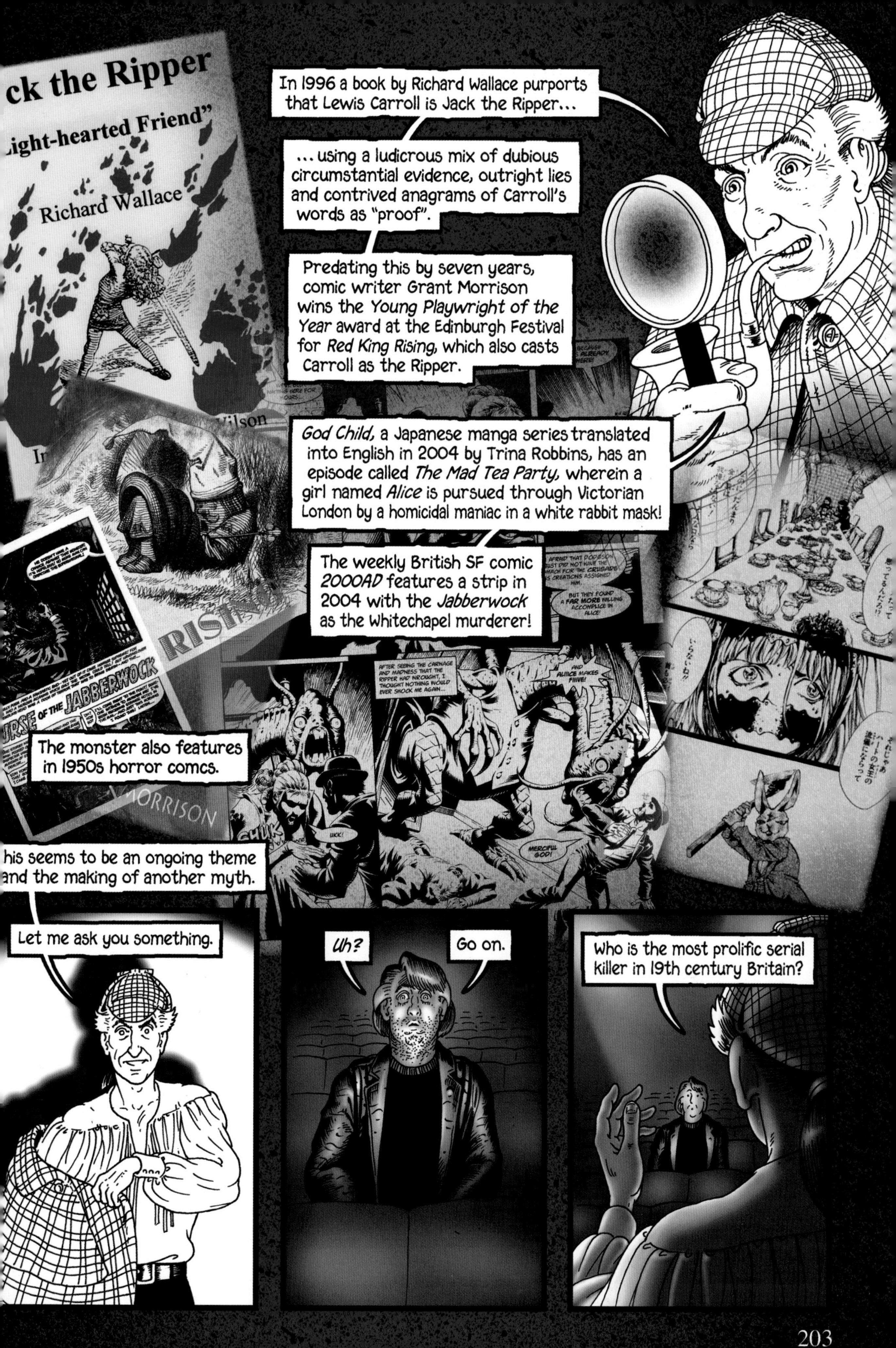
ck the Ripper
Light-hearted Friend"
Richard Wallace
In 1996 a book by Richard Wallace purports that Lewis Carroll is Jack the Ripper...
... using a ludicrous mix of dubious circumstantial evidence, outright lies and contrived anagrams of Carroll's words as "proof".
Predating this by seven years, comic writer Grant Morrison wins the *Young Playwright of the Year* award at the Edinburgh Festival for *Red King Rising*, which also casts Carroll as the Ripper.
God Child, a Japanese manga series translated into English in 2004 by Trina Robbins, has an episode called *The Mad Tea Party*, wherein a girl named *Alice* is pursued through Victorian London by a homicidal maniac in a white rabbit mask!
The weekly British SF comic *2000AD* features a strip in 2004 with the *Jabberwock* as the Whitechapel murderer!
BUT THEY FOUND A FAR MORE WILLING ACCOMPLICE IN ALICE!
JABBERWOCK
RISING
The monster also features in 1950s horror comcs.
MORRISON
UKK!
MERCIFUL GOD!
his seems to be an ongoing theme and the making of another myth.
Let me ask you something.
Uh?
Go on.
Who is the most prolific serial killer in 19th century Britain?

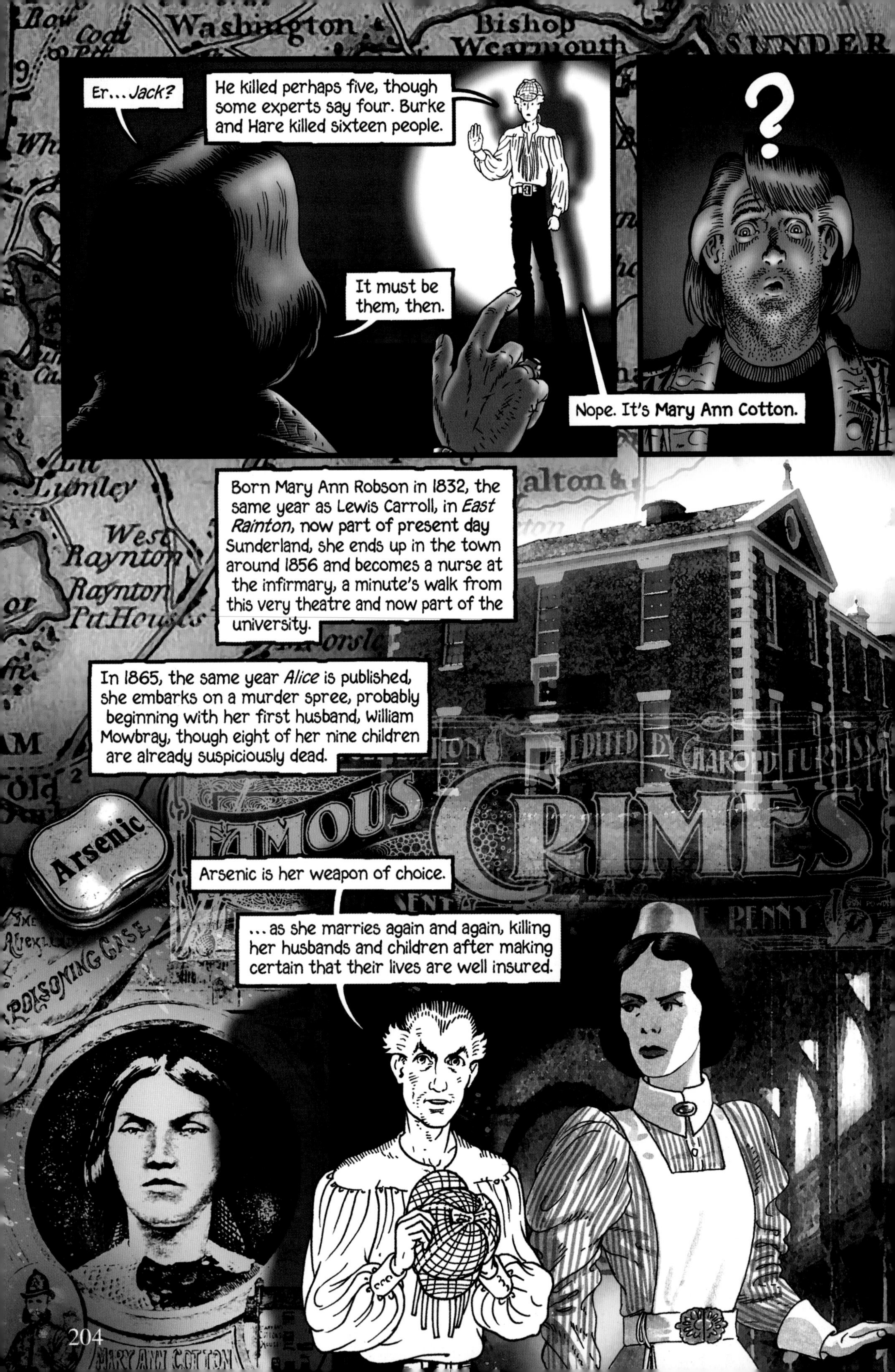

Er... *Jack?*
He killed perhaps five, though some experts say four. Burke and Hare killed sixteen people.
It must be them, then.
?
Nope. It's Mary Ann Cotton.
Born Mary Ann Robson in 1832, the same year as Lewis Carroll, in *East Rainton*, now part of present day Sunderland, she ends up in the town around 1856 and becomes a nurse at the infirmary, a minute's walk from this very theatre and now part of the university.
In 1865, the same year *Alice* is published, she embarks on a murder spree, probably beginning with her first husband, William Mowbray, though eight of her nine children are already suspiciously dead.
Arsenic
FAMOUS CRIMES
Arsenic is her weapon of choice.
...as she marries again and again, killing her husbands and children after making certain that their lives are well insured.
POISONING CASE
MARY ANN COTTON

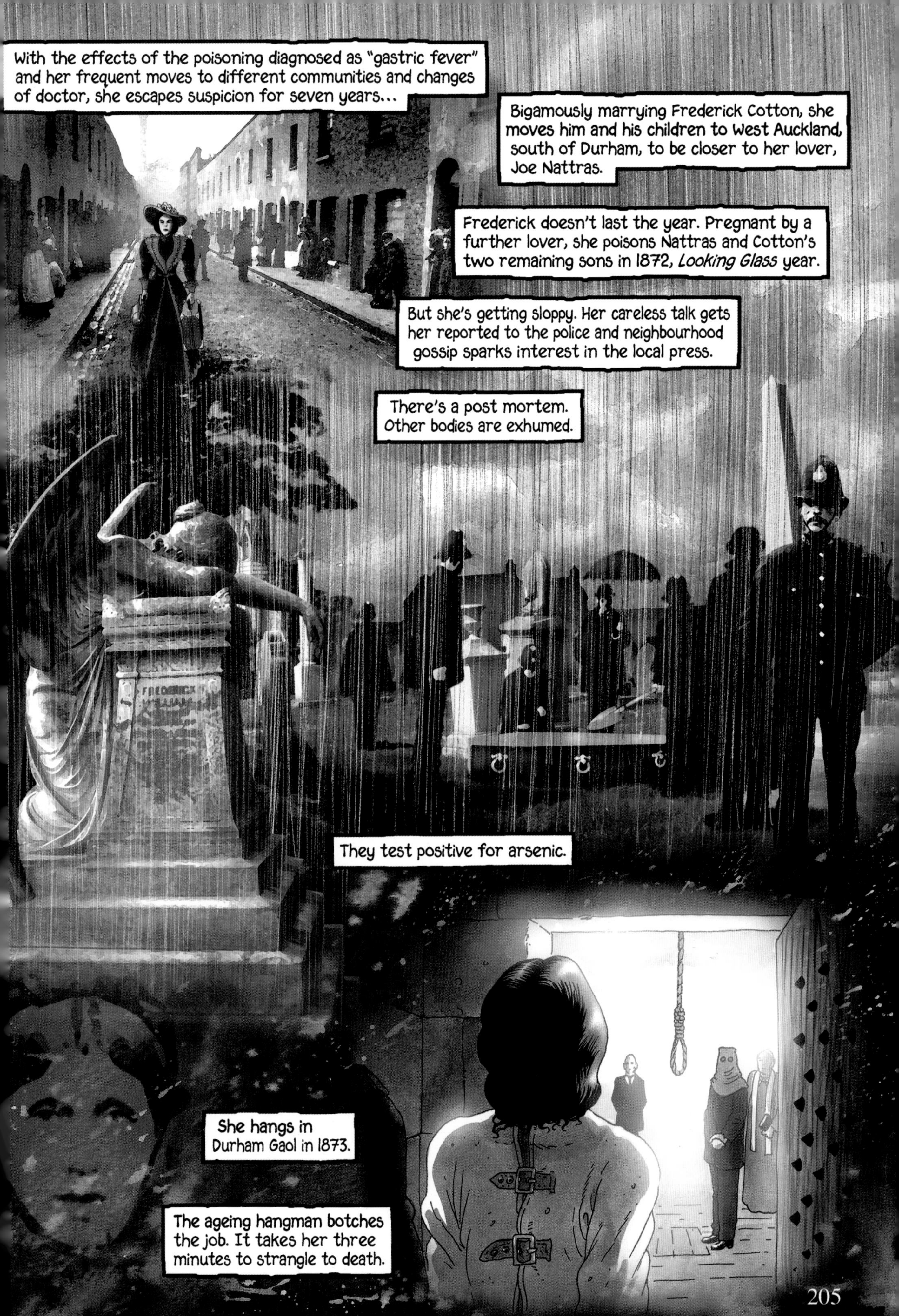
With the effects of the poisoning diagnosed as "gastric fever" and her frequent moves to different communities and changes of doctor, she escapes suspicion for seven years...
Bigamously marrying Frederick Cotton, she moves him and his children to West Auckland, south of Durham, to be closer to her lover, Joe Nattras.
Frederick doesn't last the year. Pregnant by a further lover, she poisons Nattras and Cotton's two remaining sons in 1872, *Looking Glass* year.
But she's getting sloppy. Her careless talk gets her reported to the police and neighbourhood gossip sparks interest in the local press.
There's a post mortem. Other bodies are exhumed.
FREDERICK
They test positive for arsenic.
She hangs in Durham Gaol in 1873.
The ageing hangman botches the job. It takes her three minutes to strangle to death.

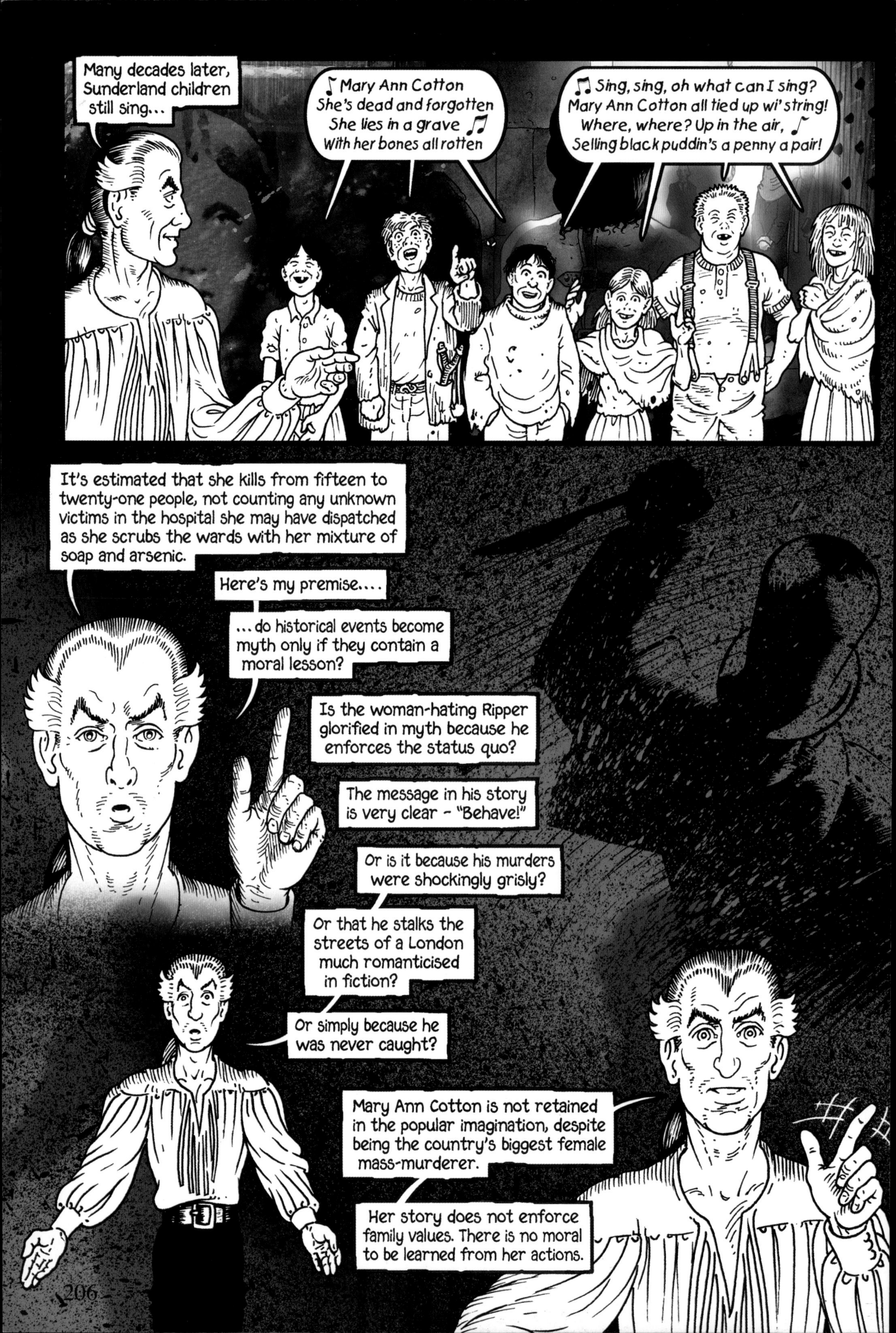

Many decades later, Sunderland children still sing...
Mary Ann Cotton She's dead and forgotten She lies in a grave With her bones all rotten
Sing, sing, oh what can I sing? Mary Ann Cotton all tied up wi' string! Where, where? Up in the air, Selling black puddin's a penny a pair!
It's estimated that she kills from fifteen to twenty-one people, not counting any unknown victims in the hospital she may have dispatched as she scrubs the wards with her mixture of soap and arsenic.
Here's my premise....
...do historical events become myth only if they contain a moral lesson?
Is the woman-hating Ripper glorified in myth because he enforces the status quo?
The message in his story is very clear - "Behave!"
Or is it because his murders were shockingly grisly?
Or that he stalks the streets of a London much romanticised in fiction?
Or simply because he was never caught?
Mary Ann Cotton is not retained in the popular imagination, despite being the country's biggest female mass-murderer.
Her story does not enforce family values. There is no moral to be learned from her actions.

There's *always* a moral if you look for one!

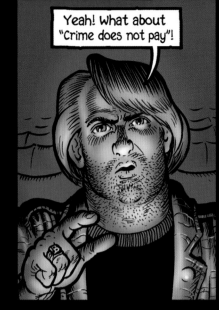

Yeah! What about "Crime does not pay"!

What?

'E's right! She was caught! "The seeds of crime bear bitter fruit"!

That's your theory right up the spout, mate! *Nyeh nyeh nyeh!*

Hee hee hee!

Ha ha ha!

Nyeh nyeh nyeh nyeh!

Hee hee hee hee!

Snort!

Hee hee hee!

Ha ha ha!

Nyeh nyeh nyeh!

Hee hee hee!

CUT!

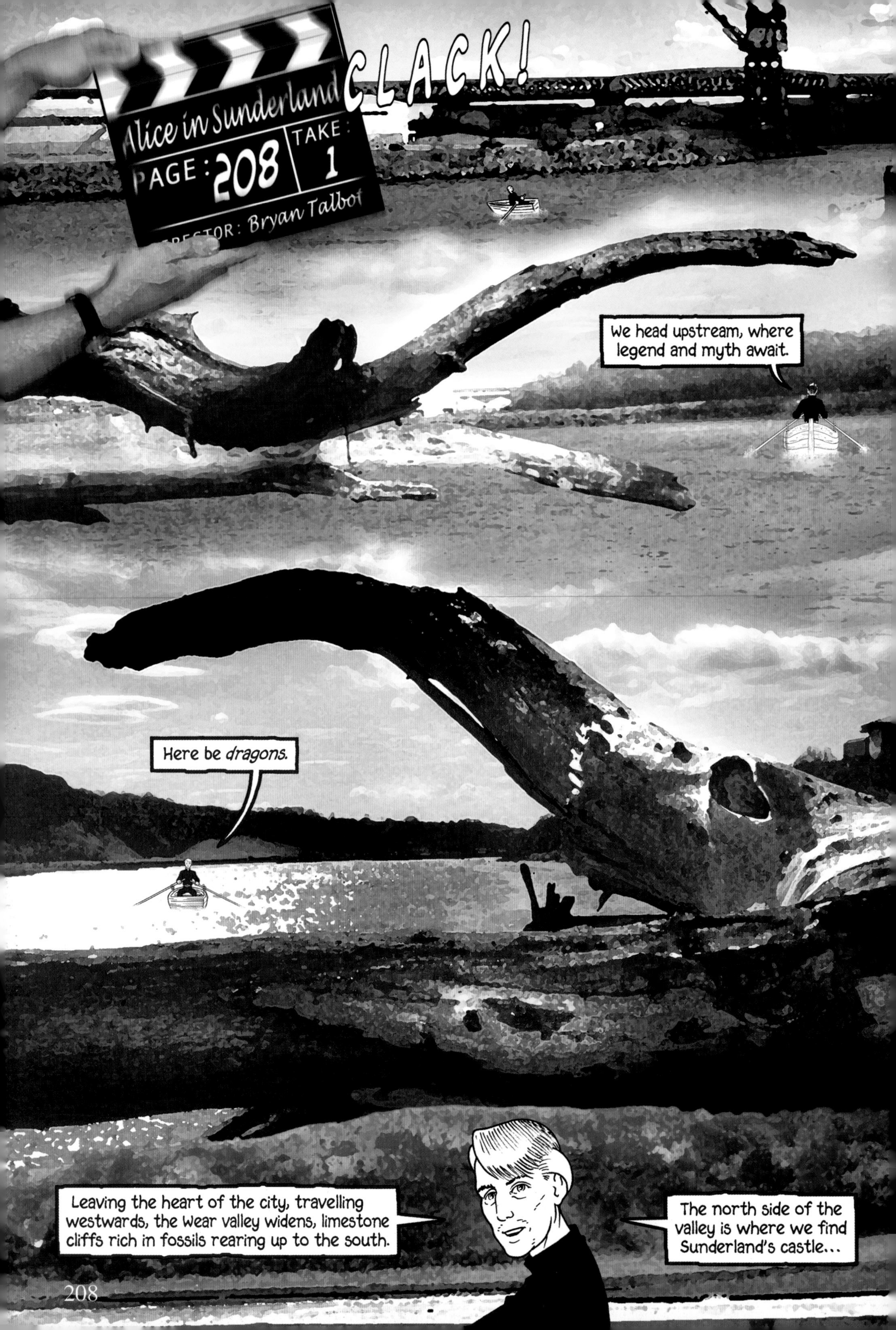

Alice in Sunderland
PAGE : 208
TAKE : 1
Bryan Talbot
CLACK!
We head upstream, where legend and myth await.
Here be *dragons*.
Leaving the heart of the city, travelling westwards, the Wear valley widens, limestone cliffs rich in fossils rearing up to the south.
The north side of the valley is where we find Sunderland's castle...

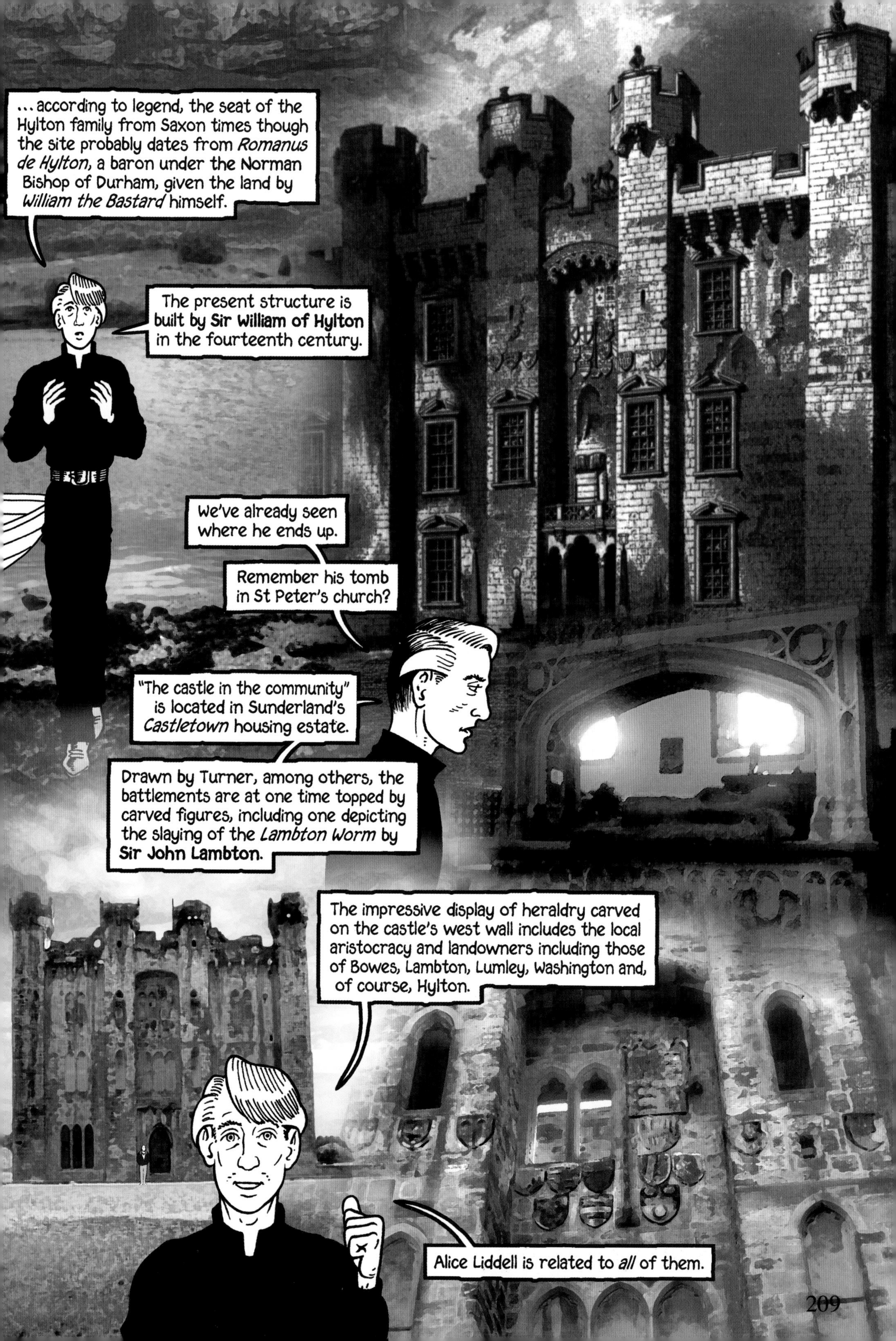

...according to legend, the seat of the Hylton family from Saxon times though the site probably dates from *Romanus de Hylton*, a baron under the Norman Bishop of Durham, given the land by *William the Bastard* himself.
The present structure is built by **Sir William of Hylton** in the fourteenth century.
We've already seen where he ends up.
Remember his tomb in St Peter's church?
"The castle in the community" is located in Sunderland's *Castletown* housing estate.
Drawn by Turner, among others, the battlements are at one time topped by carved figures, including one depicting the slaying of the *Lambton Worm* by **Sir John Lambton**.
The impressive display of heraldry carved on the castle's west wall includes the local aristocracy and landowners including those of Bowes, Lambton, Lumley, Washington and, of course, Hylton.
Alice Liddell is related to *all* of them.

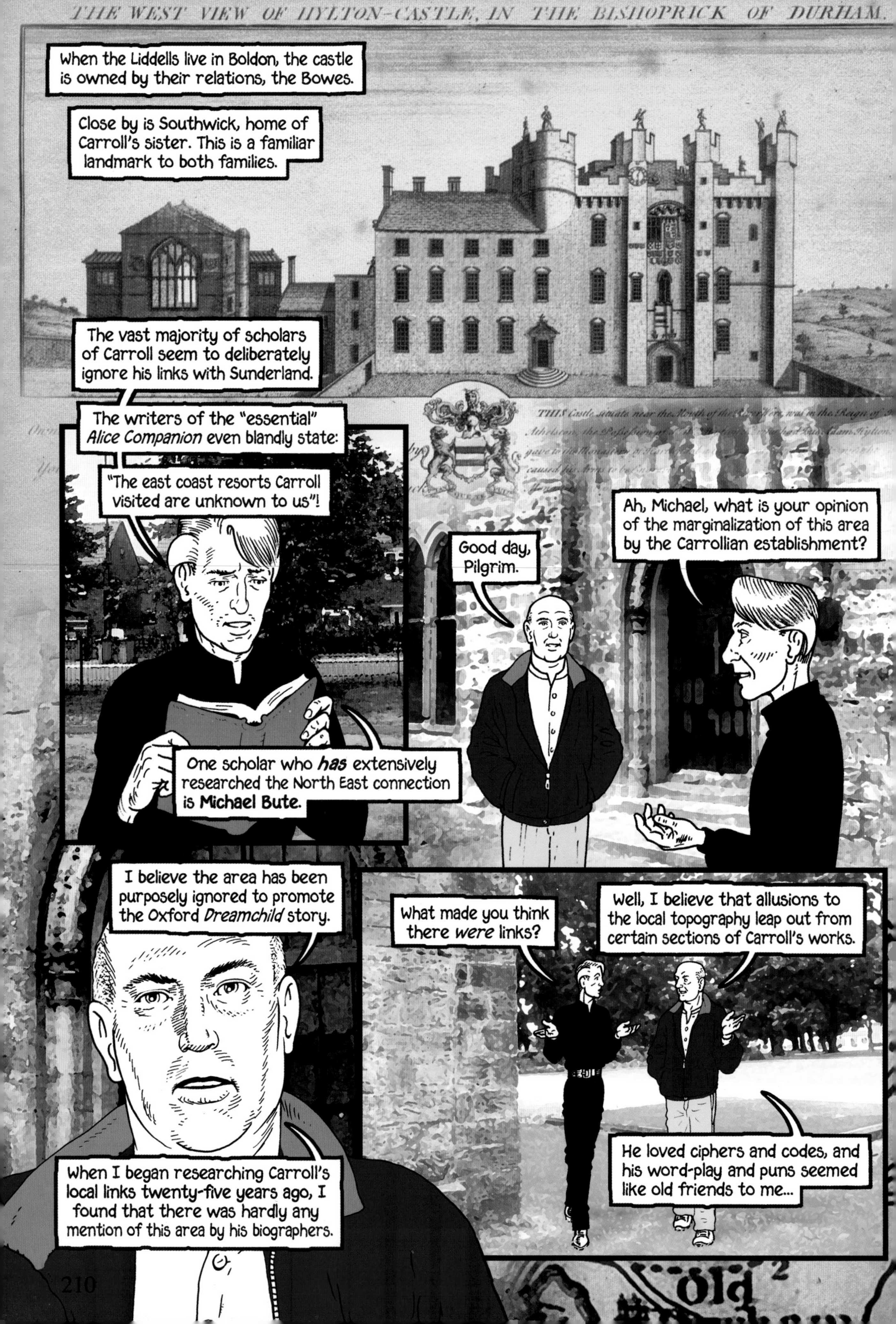
THE WEST VIEW OF HYLTON-CASTLE, IN THE BISHOPRICK OF DURHAM.
When the Liddells live in Boldon, the castle is owned by their relations, the Bowes.
Close by is Southwick, home of Carroll's sister. This is a familiar landmark to both families.
The vast majority of scholars of Carroll seem to deliberately ignore his links with Sunderland.
The writers of the "essential" *Alice Companion* even blandly state:
"The east coast resorts Carroll visited are unknown to us"!
One scholar who ***has*** extensively researched the North East connection is **Michael Bute**.
Good day, Pilgrim.
Ah, Michael, what is your opinion of the marginalization of this area by the Carrollian establishment?
I believe the area has been purposely ignored to promote the Oxford *Dreamchild* story.
When I began researching Carroll's local links twenty-five years ago, I found that there was hardly any mention of this area by his biographers.
What made you think there *were* links?
Well, I believe that allusions to the local topography leap out from certain sections of Carroll's works.
He loved ciphers and codes, and his word-play and puns seemed like old friends to me...
Old

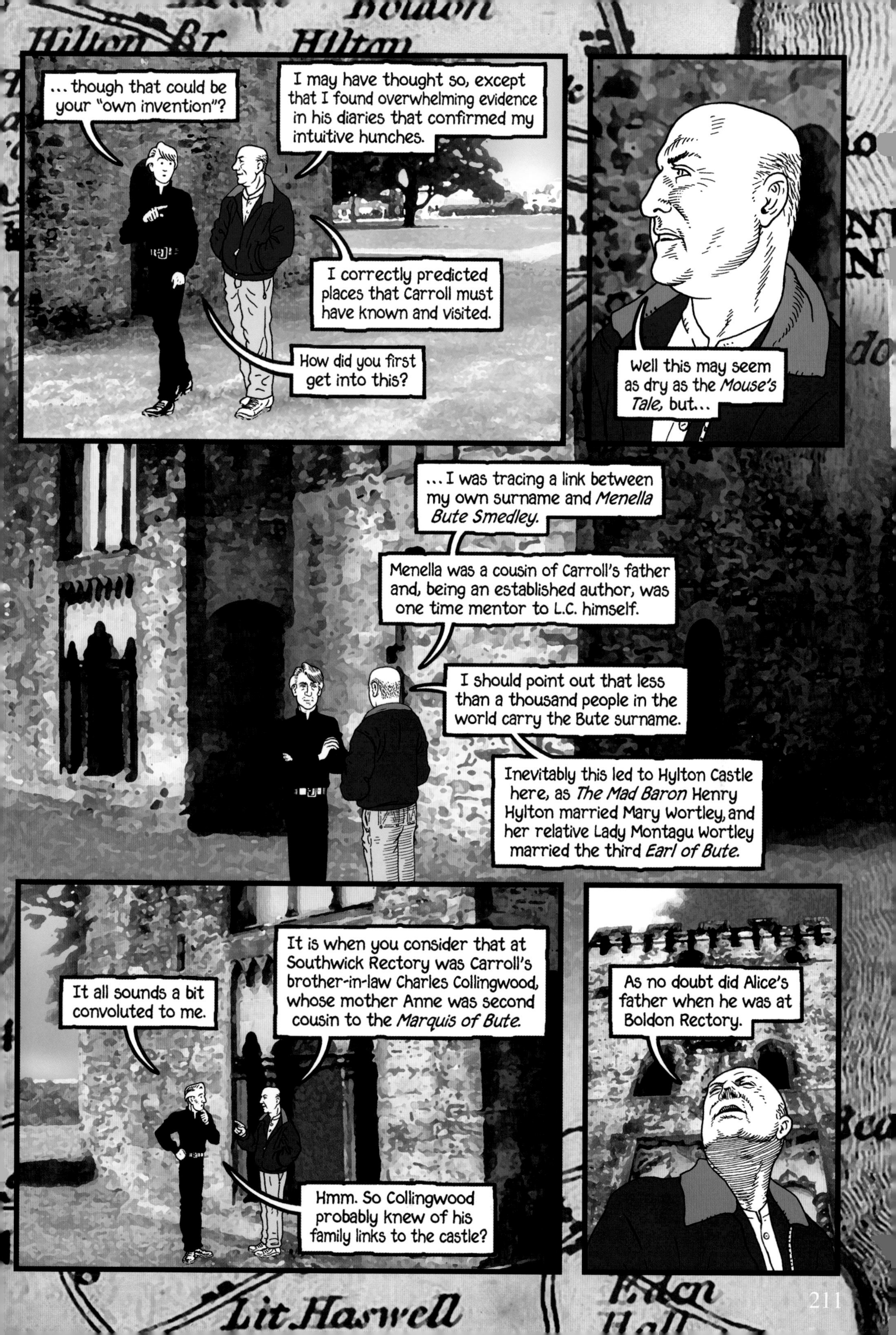
... though that could be your "own invention"?
I may have thought so, except that I found overwhelming evidence in his diaries that confirmed my intuitive hunches.
I correctly predicted places that Carroll must have known and visited.
How did you first get into this?
Well this may seem as dry as the *Mouse's Tale,* but...
... I was tracing a link between my own surname and *Menella Bute Smedley.*
Menella was a cousin of Carroll's father and, being an established author, was one time mentor to L.C. himself.
I should point out that less than a thousand people in the world carry the Bute surname.
Inevitably this led to Hylton Castle here, as *The Mad Baron* Henry Hylton married Mary Wortley, and her relative Lady Montagu Wortley married the third *Earl of Bute.*
It all sounds a bit convoluted to me.
It is when you consider that at Southwick Rectory was Carroll's brother-in-law Charles Collingwood, whose mother Anne was second cousin to the *Marquis of Bute.*
Hmm. So Collingwood probably knew of his family links to the castle?
As no doubt did Alice's father when he was at Boldon Rectory.
Hilton
Lit Haswell

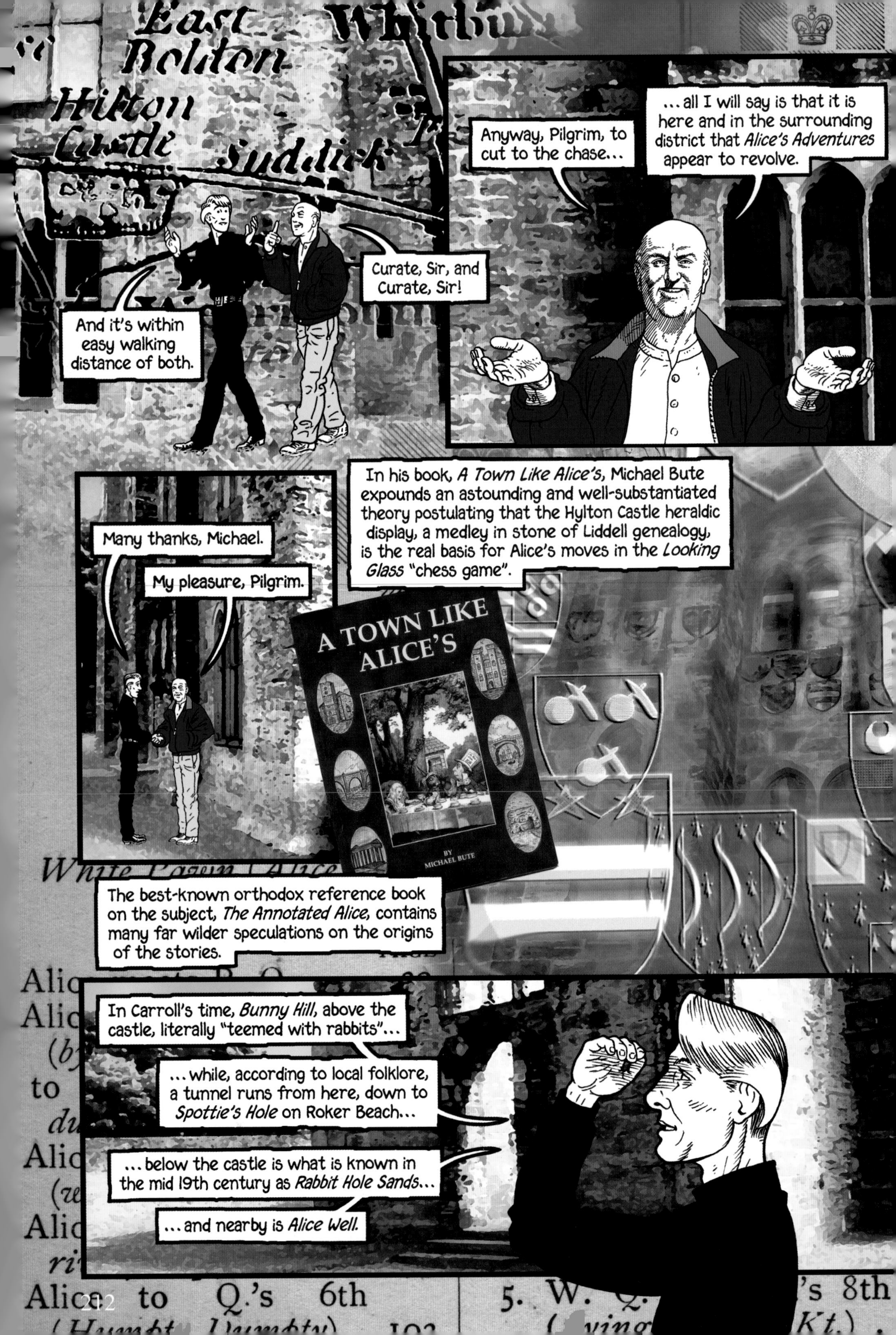
Curate, Sir, and Curate, Sir!
And it's within easy walking distance of both.
Anyway, Pilgrim, to cut to the chase...
...all I will say is that it is here and in the surrounding district that Alice's Adventures appear to revolve.
In his book, A Town Like Alice's, Michael Bute expounds an astounding and well-substantiated theory postulating that the Hylton Castle heraldic display, a medley in stone of Liddell genealogy, is the real basis for Alice's moves in the Looking Glass "chess game".
Many thanks, Michael.
My pleasure, Pilgrim.
A TOWN LIKE ALICE'S
BY MICHAEL BUTE
The best-known orthodox reference book on the subject, The Annotated Alice, contains many far wilder speculations on the origins of the stories.
In Carroll's time, Bunny Hill, above the castle, literally "teemed with rabbits"...
...while, according to local folklore, a tunnel runs from here, down to Spottie's Hole on Roker Beach...
...below the castle is what is known in the mid 19th century as Rabbit Hole Sands...
...and nearby is Alice Well.

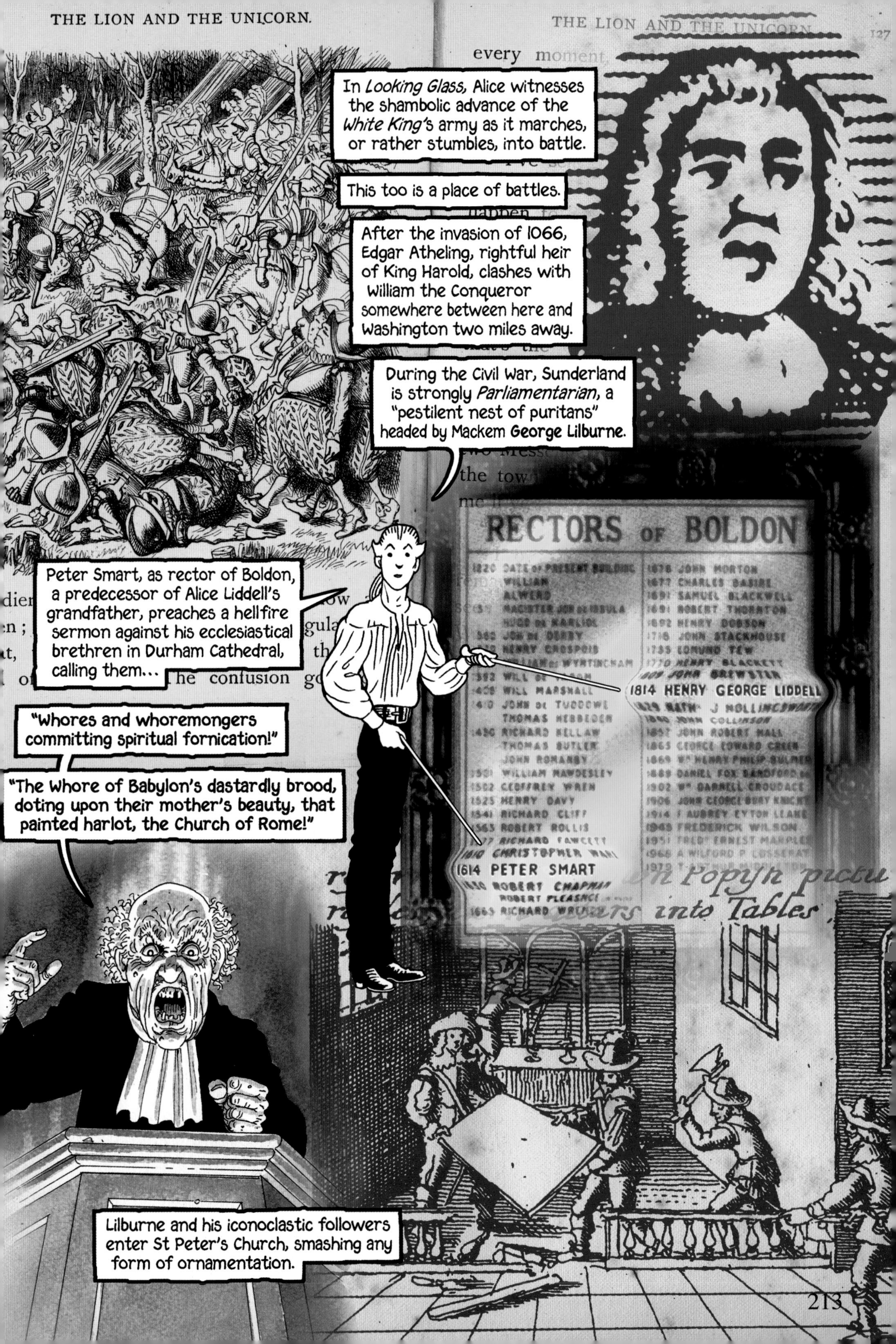
THE LION AND THE UNICORN.
THE LION AND THE UNICORN
In *Looking Glass*, Alice witnesses the shambolic advance of the *White King's* army as it marches, or rather stumbles, into battle.
This too is a place of battles.
After the invasion of 1066, Edgar Atheling, rightful heir of King Harold, clashes with William the Conqueror somewhere between here and Washington two miles away.
During the Civil War, Sunderland is strongly *Parliamentarian*, a "pestilent nest of puritans" headed by Mackem **George Lilburne**.
RECTORS OF BOLDON
1814 HENRY GEORGE LIDDELL
1614 PETER SMART
Peter Smart, as rector of Boldon, a predecessor of Alice Liddell's grandfather, preaches a hellfire sermon against his ecclesiastical brethren in Durham Cathedral, calling them…
"Whores and whoremongers committing spiritual fornication!"
"The Whore of Babylon's dastardly brood, doting upon their mother's beauty, that painted harlot, the Church of Rome!"
into Tables
Lilburne and his iconoclastic followers enter St Peter's Church, smashing any form of ornamentation.

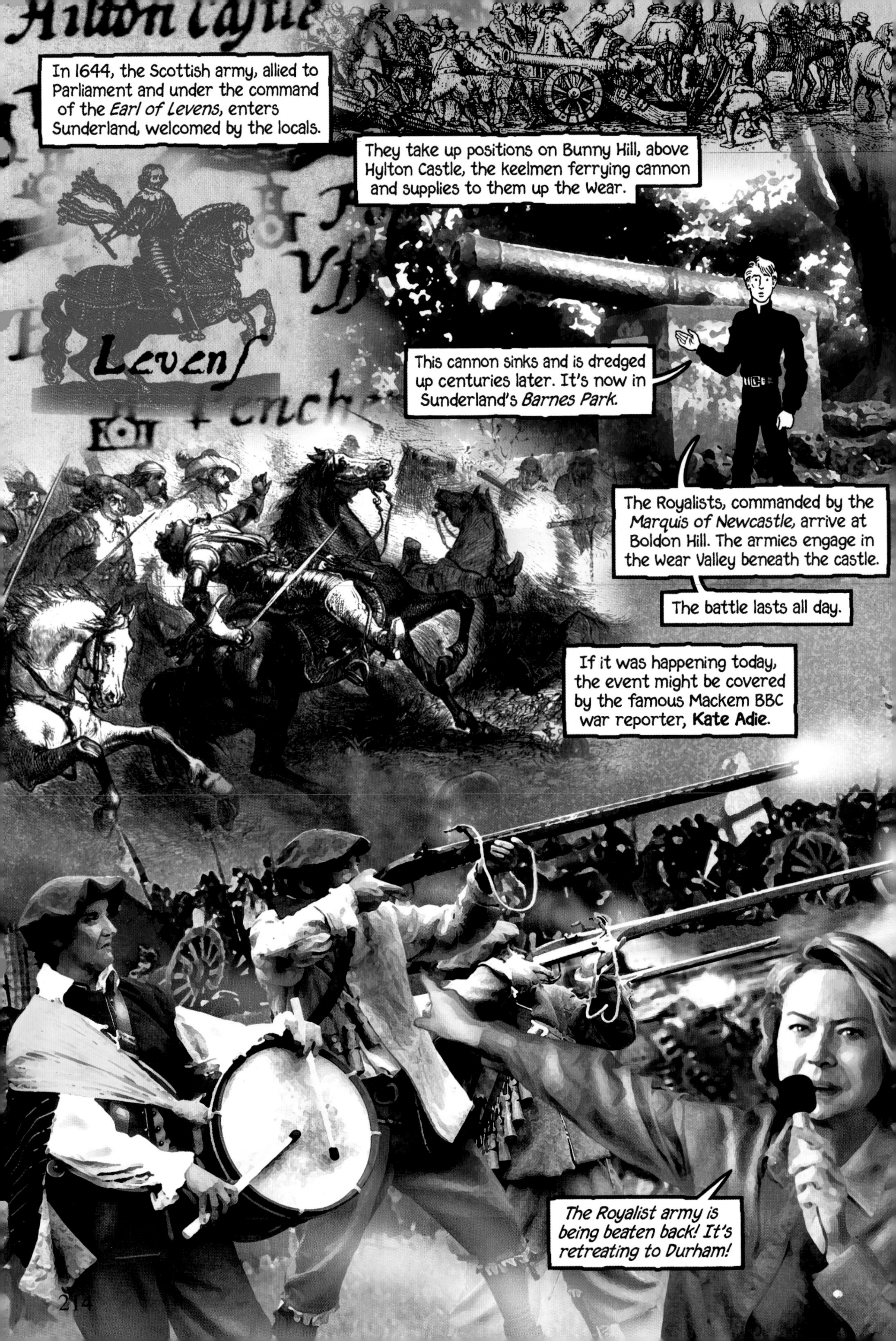
Hilton Castle
In 1644, the Scottish army, allied to Parliament and under the command of the *Earl of Levens*, enters Sunderland, welcomed by the locals.
They take up positions on Bunny Hill, above Hylton Castle, the keelmen ferrying cannon and supplies to them up the Wear.
Levens
This cannon sinks and is dredged up centuries later. It's now in Sunderland's *Barnes Park*.
The Royalists, commanded by the *Marquis of Newcastle*, arrive at Boldon Hill. The armies engage in the Wear Valley beneath the castle.
The battle lasts all day.
If it was happening today, the event might be covered by the famous Mackem BBC war reporter, **Kate Adie**.
The Royalist army is being beaten back! It's retreating to Durham!

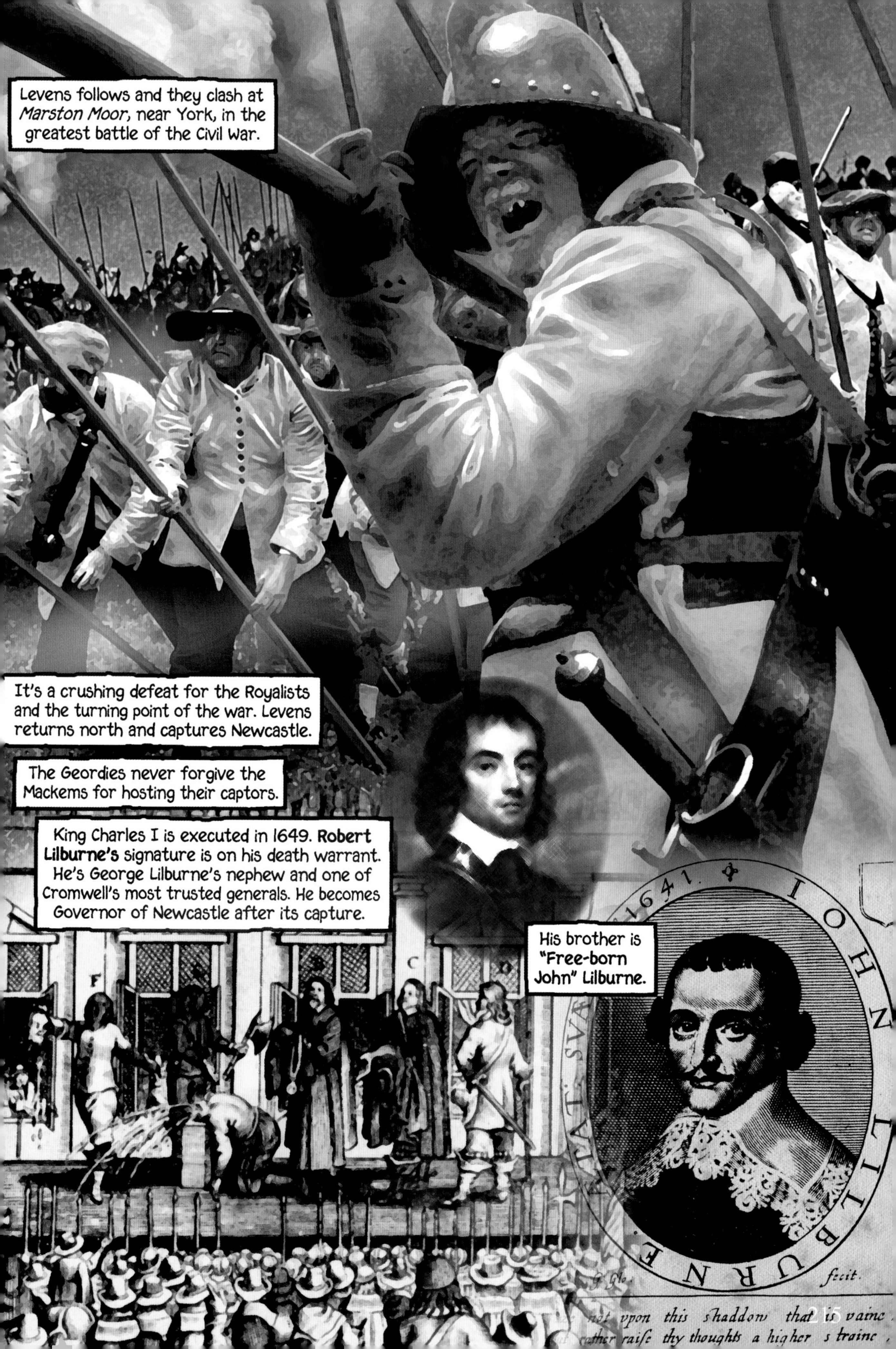
Levens follows and they clash at *Marston Moor*, near York, in the greatest battle of the Civil War.
It's a crushing defeat for the Royalists and the turning point of the war. Levens returns north and captures Newcastle.
The Geordies never forgive the Mackems for hosting their captors.
King Charles I is executed in 1649. **Robert Lilburne's** signature is on his death warrant. He's George Lilburne's nephew and one of Cromwell's most trusted generals. He becomes Governor of Newcastle after its capture.
His brother is **"Free-born John" Lilburne.**
IOHN LILBURNE
1641
fecit.
not vpon this shaddow that is vaine
rather raise thy thoughts a higher straine

Born in Sunderland in 1615, John, a Quaker and political activist, is the founder of the original communists, *The Levellers*. He spends much of his life in prison for being a thorn in the side of both the King before the *English Revolution* and Parliament afterwards.

It's believed that John Lilburne's writings of 1649 are the basis for the rights contained in the *Constitution of the United States*.

A fighter against hypocrisy and corruption, he's once whipped through the streets of London, while the crowds cheer him as a hero.

An officer in the Parliamentarian army, he fights with distinction at Marston Moor.

One hundred years later in 1745, Alice's great-grandfather, **Sir Thomas Liddell**, defends Newcastle against the Scots and is rewarded with the title and position of *Lord Ravensworth*.

Incidentally, Joseph Swan, inventor of the light bulb, is educated here when the castle is a school in the mid 19th century. By the time he...

Stone the bleedin' crows! 'E don't 'arf *rabbit* on!

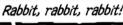

Rabbit, rabbit, rabbit!

And he's not even *mentioned* the ghost!

What you on abaht?

Why, the castle is haunted...

...by...

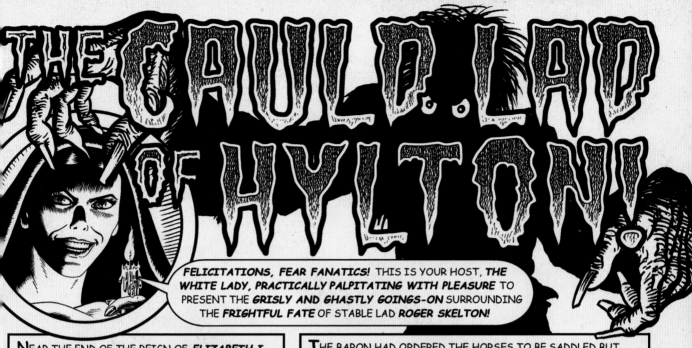

THE CAULD LAD OF HYLTON!

FELICITATIONS, FEAR FANATICS! THIS IS YOUR HOST, *THE WHITE LADY*, PRACTICALLY *PALPITATING WITH PLEASURE* TO PRESENT THE *GRISLY AND GHASTLY GOINGS-ON* SURROUNDING THE *FRIGHTFUL FATE* OF STABLE LAD *ROGER SKELTON!*

NEAR THE END OF THE REIGN OF *ELIZABETH I*, THE LORD OF *HYLTON CASTLE* WAS DISSOLUTE *BARON ROBERT*. EARLY ONE MORNING...

HA HA HA! ≈BUURP!≈

TO *THE HUNT!*

THE BARON HAD ORDERED THE HORSES TO BE SADDLED BUT...

IN GOD'S NAME! WHERE'S THE *HORSES*? WHERE'S THE *GROOM*?

DAMN THAT BOY STRAIGHT TO *HELL!*

HE STAGGERED DRUNKENLY TO THE *STABLES*, WHERE...

SKELTON! WHERE THE *DEVIL* ARE...

YOU *LAZY SWINE!*

S-S-SORRY, MILORD! I-I JUST...

YOU *JUST!* I'LL *TEACH YOU*...

THOK!

UHN!

217

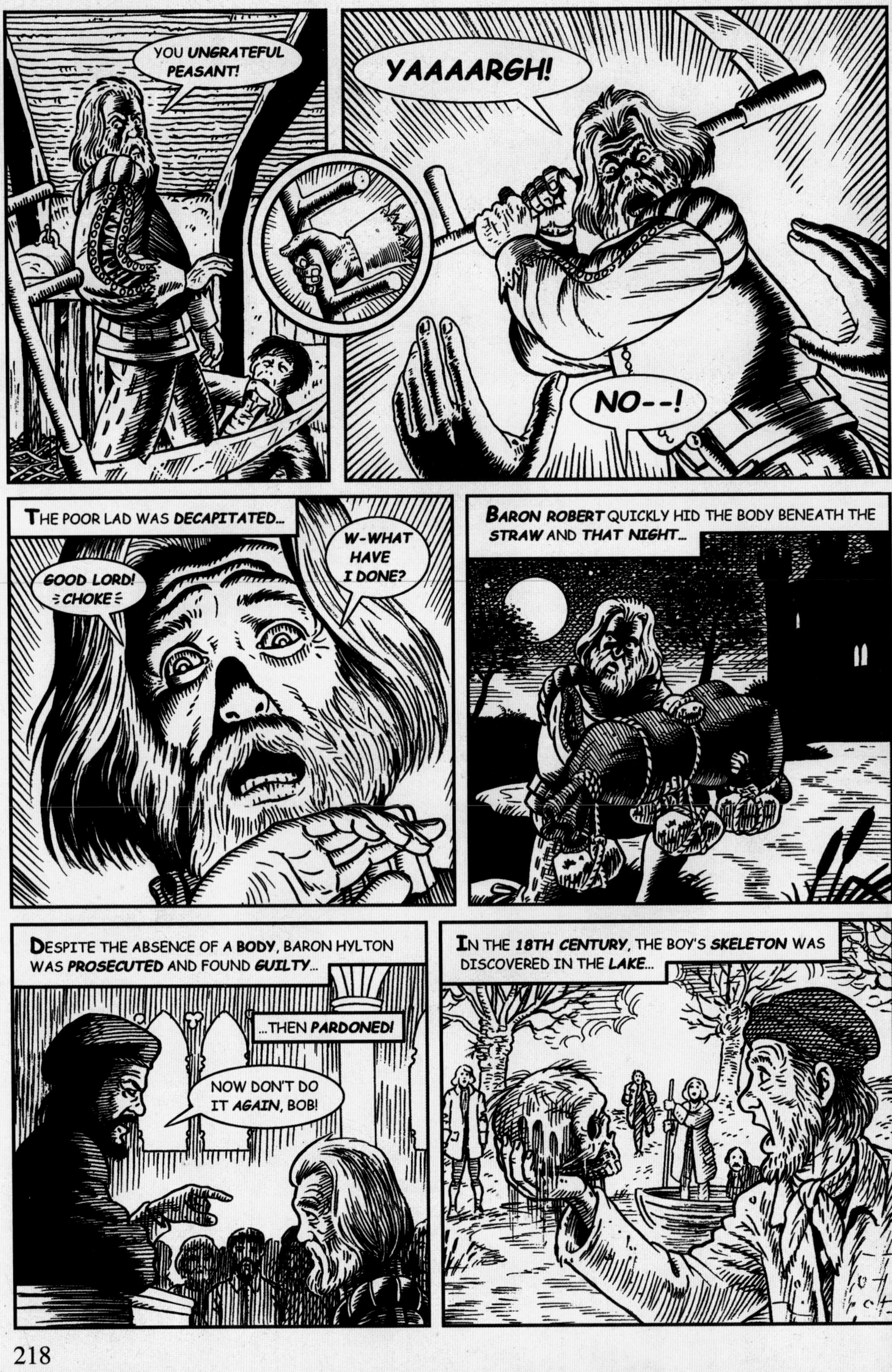
YOU UNGRATEFUL PEASANT!
YAAAARGH!
NO--!
THE POOR LAD WAS DECAPITATED...
GOOD LORD! CHOKE
W-WHAT HAVE I DONE?
BARON ROBERT QUICKLY HID THE BODY BENEATH THE STRAW AND THAT NIGHT...
DESPITE THE ABSENCE OF A BODY, BARON HYLTON WAS PROSECUTED AND FOUND GUILTY...
...THEN PARDONED!
NOW DON'T DO IT AGAIN, BOB!
IN THE 18TH CENTURY, THE BOY'S SKELETON WAS DISCOVERED IN THE LAKE...

AFTER THAT, THE CASTLE WAS PLAGUED BY MISCHIEVOUS **POLTERGEIST** ACTIVITY. **UNEARTHLY WAILING** AND **WEEPING** ECHOED THROUGH THE CORRIDORS AT NIGHT AS THE **TERRIFIED** SERVANTS **COWERED** IN THEIR BEDS...

UNPREDICTABLY, THE **BROWNIE** WOULD SOMETIMES **TIDY UP** THE **KITCHEN** OVERNIGHT...BUT THE COOKS WERE MORE LIKELY TO FIND **CATS** STUFFED INTO **HONEY JARS** OR **HUNG** ON **NAILS**...

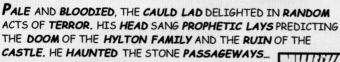

PALE AND **BLOODIED**, THE **CAULD LAD** DELIGHTED IN **RANDOM** ACTS OF **TERROR**. HIS **HEAD** SANG **PROPHETIC LAYS** PREDICTING THE **DOOM** OF THE **HYLTON FAMILY** AND THE **RUIN** OF THE **CASTLE**. HE **HAUNTED** THE STONE **PASSAGEWAYS**...

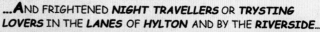

...AND FRIGHTENED **NIGHT TRAVELLERS** OR **TRYSTING LOVERS** IN THE **LANES** OF **HYLTON** AND BY THE **RIVERSIDE**...

AIEEEEEEEE!

HE WAS OFTEN SEEN **DRINKING ALE** IN THE **CELLAR**... BUT WHATEVER **CASK** HE DRANK FROM, EVEN IF THE CONTENTS WERE **OLD** AND **STALE**, THE **BEER** WAS ALWAYS **FRESH** IN THE **MORNING**...

IN AN ATTEMPT TO **EXORCISE** THE **CAULD LAD**, THE **SERVANTS** MADE A **GREEN CLOAK** AND LEFT IT FOR HIM - A TIME-HONOURED **BANISHING RITUAL**...

AND HE WAS **SATISFIED**. AT **COCKCROW**, HE SANG...

HERE'S A **CLOAK** AND HERE'S A **HOOD**, THE **CAULD LAD OF HYLTON** WILL DO **NO MORE GOOD!**

...AND PROMPTLY **VANISHED** FROM THE **CASTLE!**

THE SUBJECT OF SEVERAL **SONGS** AND **MUSIC HALL BALLADS** AND CELEBRATED IN THE 1856 **POEM** BY **T. ARTHUR**...

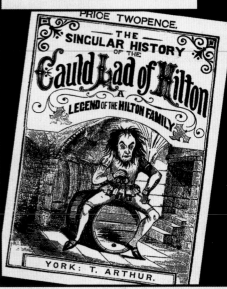

PRICE TWOPENCE.

THE **SINGULAR HISTORY** OF THE

Cauld Lad of Hilton

A

LEGEND OF THE HILTON FAMILY

YORK: T. ARTHUR.

...THE **CAULD LAD** STILL **HAUNTS** THE **BYWAYS** OF **HYLTON** AND THE **BANKS** OF THE **WEAR**, DOWN TO **THIS VERY DAY!**

DON'T FEEL SORRY FOR **ROGER** - HE SHOULDN'T HAVE **LOST HIS HEAD!** **HASTA LA VISTA** FROM YOUR **HORROR HOST, THE WHITE LADY!**

THE END

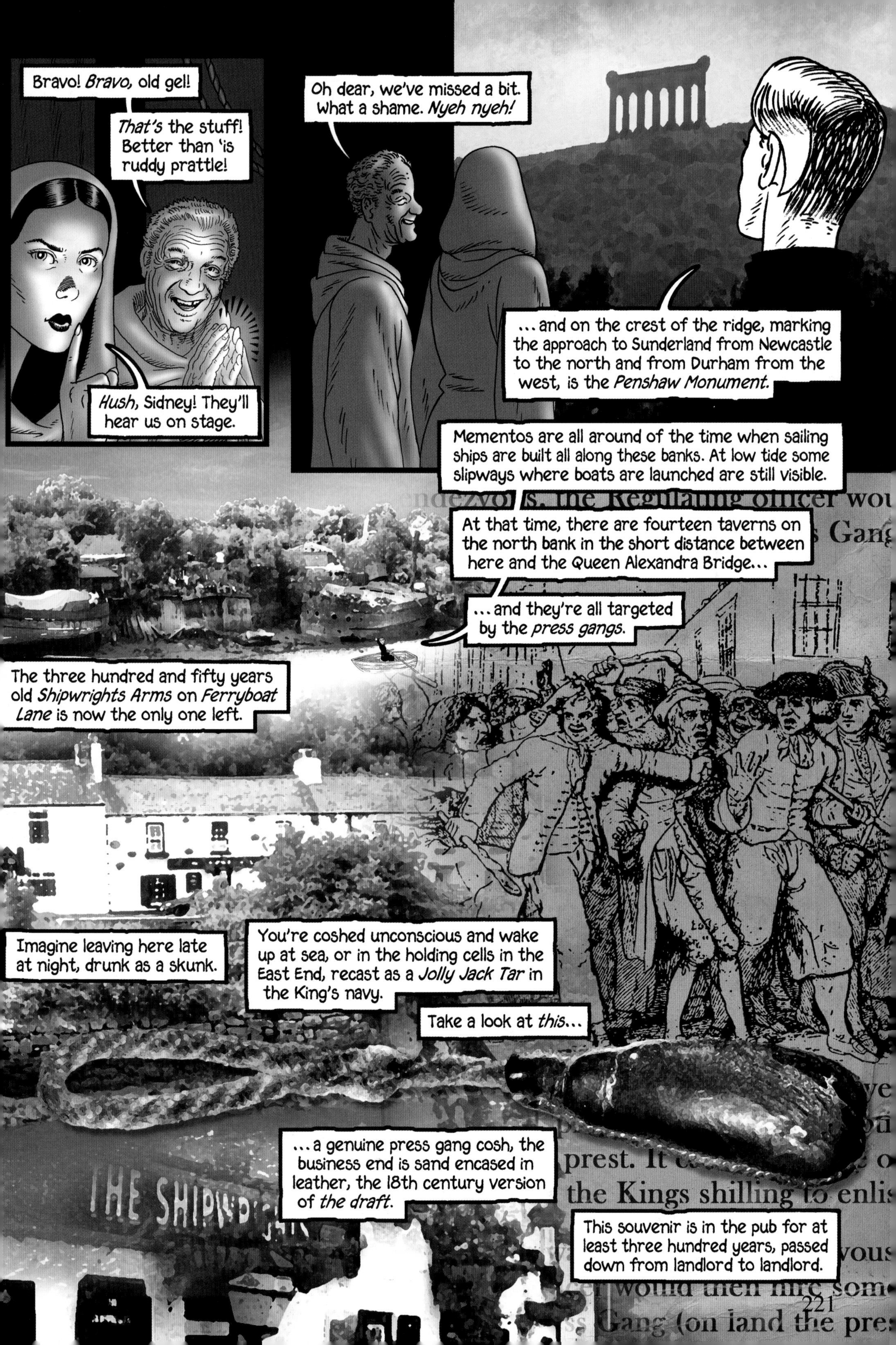
Bravo! *Bravo,* old gel!
That's the stuff! Better than 'is ruddy prattle!
Hush, Sidney! They'll hear us on stage.
Oh dear, we've missed a bit. What a shame. *Nyeh nyeh!*
...and on the crest of the ridge, marking the approach to Sunderland from Newcastle to the north and from Durham from the west, is the *Penshaw Monument.*
Mementos are all around of the time when sailing ships are built all along these banks. At low tide some slipways where boats are launched are still visible.
At that time, there are fourteen taverns on the north bank in the short distance between here and the Queen Alexandra Bridge...
...and they're all targeted by the *press gangs.*
The three hundred and fifty years old *Shipwrights Arms* on *Ferryboat Lane* is now the only one left.
Imagine leaving here late at night, drunk as a skunk.
You're coshed unconscious and wake up at sea, or in the holding cells in the East End, recast as a *Jolly Jack Tar* in the King's navy.
Take a look at *this*...
...a genuine press gang cosh, the business end is sand encased in leather, the 18th century version of *the draft.*
This souvenir is in the pub for at least three hundred years, passed down from landlord to landlord.

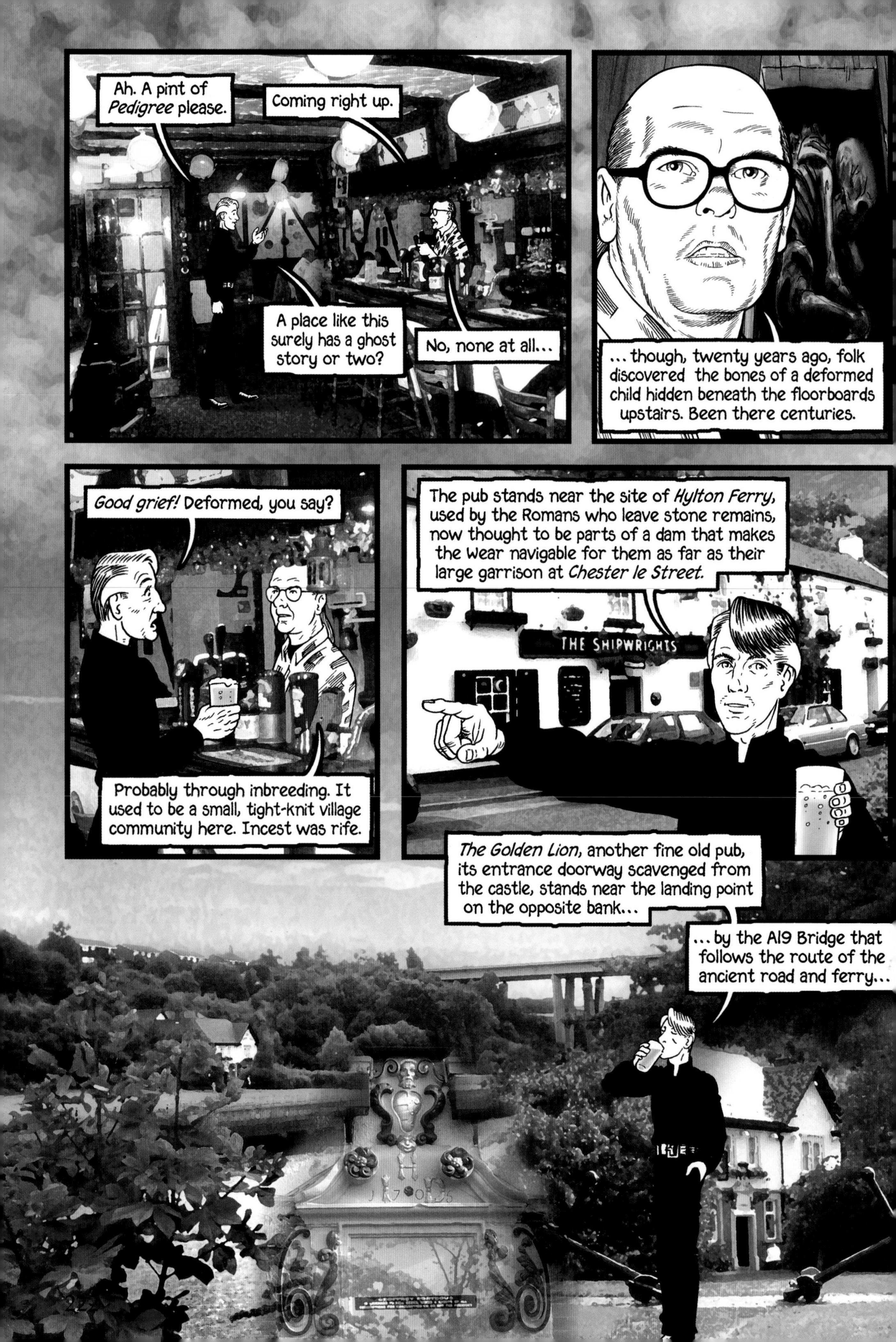

Ah. A pint of *Pedigree* please.
Coming right up.
A place like this surely has a ghost story or two?
No, none at all...
... though, twenty years ago, folk discovered the bones of a deformed child hidden beneath the floorboards upstairs. Been there centuries.
Good grief! Deformed, you say?
Probably through inbreeding. It used to be a small, tight-knit village community here. Incest was rife.
The pub stands near the site of *Hylton Ferry*, used by the Romans who leave stone remains, now thought to be parts of a dam that makes the Wear navigable for them as far as their large garrison at *Chester le Street*.
THE SHIPWRIGHTS
The Golden Lion, another fine old pub, its entrance doorway scavenged from the castle, stands near the landing point on the opposite bank...
... by the A19 Bridge that follows the route of the ancient road and ferry...

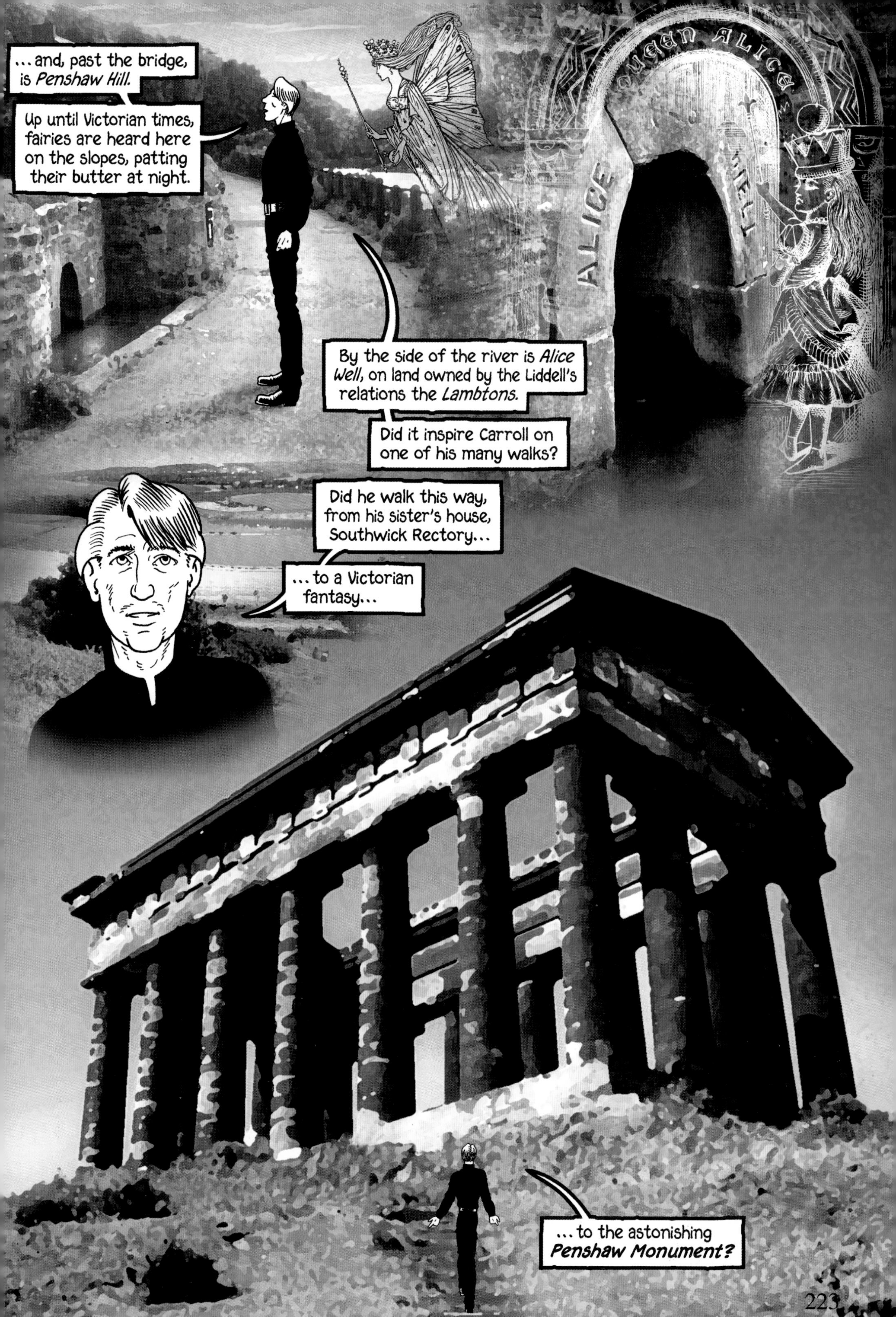

...and, past the bridge, is *Penshaw Hill.*
Up until Victorian times, fairies are heard here on the slopes, patting their butter at night.
QUEEN ALICE
ALICE
WELL
By the side of the river is *Alice Well,* on land owned by the Liddell's relations the *Lambtons.*
Did it inspire Carroll on one of his many walks?
Did he walk this way, from his sister's house, Southwick Rectory...
...to a Victorian fantasy...
...to the astonishing **Penshaw Monument?**

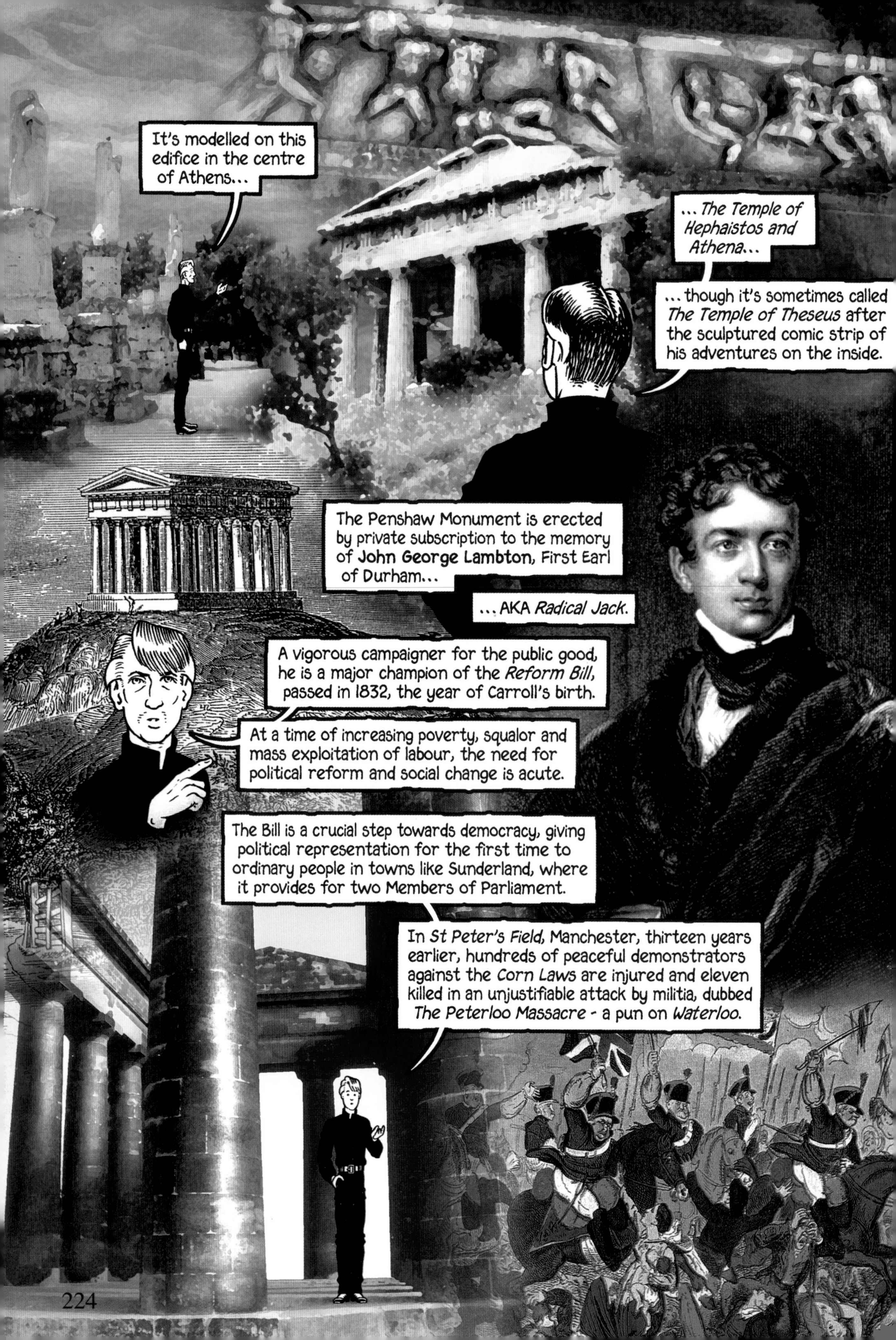

It's modelled on this edifice in the centre of Athens...
...The Temple of Hephaistos and Athena...
...though it's sometimes called The Temple of Theseus after the sculptured comic strip of his adventures on the inside.
The Penshaw Monument is erected by private subscription to the memory of John George Lambton, First Earl of Durham...
...AKA Radical Jack.
A vigorous campaigner for the public good, he is a major champion of the Reform Bill, passed in 1832, the year of Carroll's birth.
At a time of increasing poverty, squalor and mass exploitation of labour, the need for political reform and social change is acute.
The Bill is a crucial step towards democracy, giving political representation for the first time to ordinary people in towns like Sunderland, where it provides for two Members of Parliament.
In St Peter's Field, Manchester, thirteen years earlier, hundreds of peaceful demonstrators against the Corn Laws are injured and eleven killed in an unjustifiable attack by militia, dubbed The Peterloo Massacre - a pun on Waterloo.

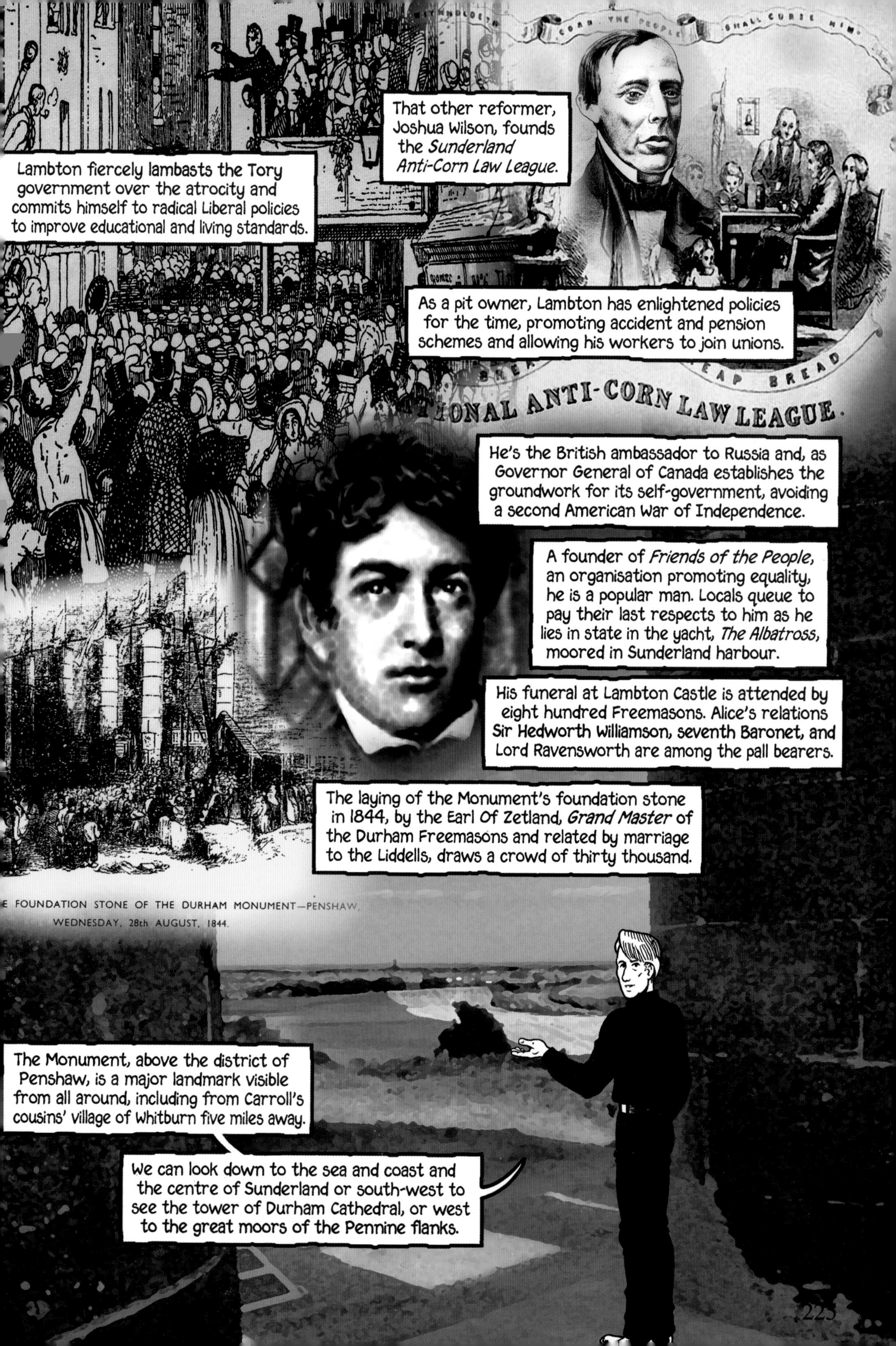
Lambton fiercely lambasts the Tory government over the atrocity and commits himself to radical Liberal policies to improve educational and living standards.
That other reformer, Joshua Wilson, founds the *Sunderland Anti-Corn Law League*.
As a pit owner, Lambton has enlightened policies for the time, promoting accident and pension schemes and allowing his workers to join unions.
ANTI-CORN LAW LEAGUE.
He's the British ambassador to Russia and, as Governor General of Canada establishes the groundwork for its self-government, avoiding a second American War of Independence.
A founder of *Friends of the People*, an organisation promoting equality, he is a popular man. Locals queue to pay their last respects to him as he lies in state in the yacht, *The Albatross*, moored in Sunderland harbour.
His funeral at Lambton Castle is attended by eight hundred Freemasons. Alice's relations Sir Hedworth Williamson, seventh Baronet, and Lord Ravensworth are among the pall bearers.
The laying of the Monument's foundation stone in 1844, by the Earl Of Zetland, *Grand Master* of the Durham Freemasons and related by marriage to the Liddells, draws a crowd of thirty thousand.
E FOUNDATION STONE OF THE DURHAM MONUMENT—PENSHAW.
WEDNESDAY, 28th AUGUST, 1844.
The Monument, above the district of Penshaw, is a major landmark visible from all around, including from Carroll's cousins' village of Whitburn five miles away.
We can look down to the sea and coast and the centre of Sunderland or south-west to see the tower of Durham Cathedral, or west to the great moors of the Pennine flanks.

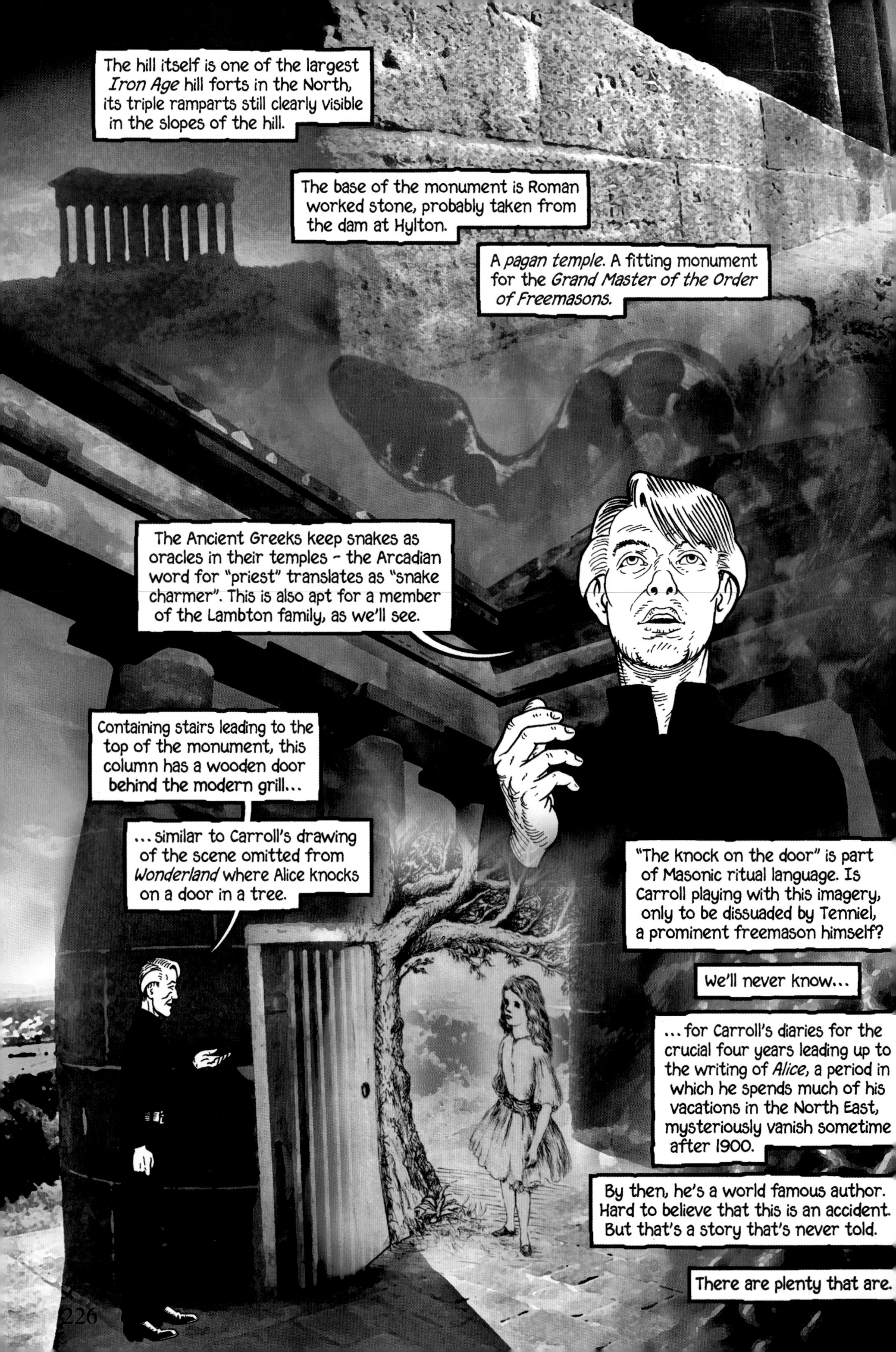
The hill itself is one of the largest *Iron Age* hill forts in the North, its triple ramparts still clearly visible in the slopes of the hill.
The base of the monument is Roman worked stone, probably taken from the dam at Hylton.
A *pagan temple*. A fitting monument for the *Grand Master of the Order of Freemasons.*
The Ancient Greeks keep snakes as oracles in their temples - the Arcadian word for "priest" translates as "snake charmer". This is also apt for a member of the Lambton family, as we'll see.
Containing stairs leading to the top of the monument, this column has a wooden door behind the modern grill...
...similar to Carroll's drawing of the scene omitted from *Wonderland* where Alice knocks on a door in a tree.
"The knock on the door" is part of Masonic ritual language. Is Carroll playing with this imagery, only to be dissuaded by Tenniel, a prominent freemason himself?
We'll never know...
...for Carroll's diaries for the crucial four years leading up to the writing of *Alice*, a period in which he spends much of his vacations in the North East, mysteriously vanish sometime after 1900.
By then, he's a world famous author. Hard to believe that this is an accident. But that's a story that's never told.
There are plenty that are.

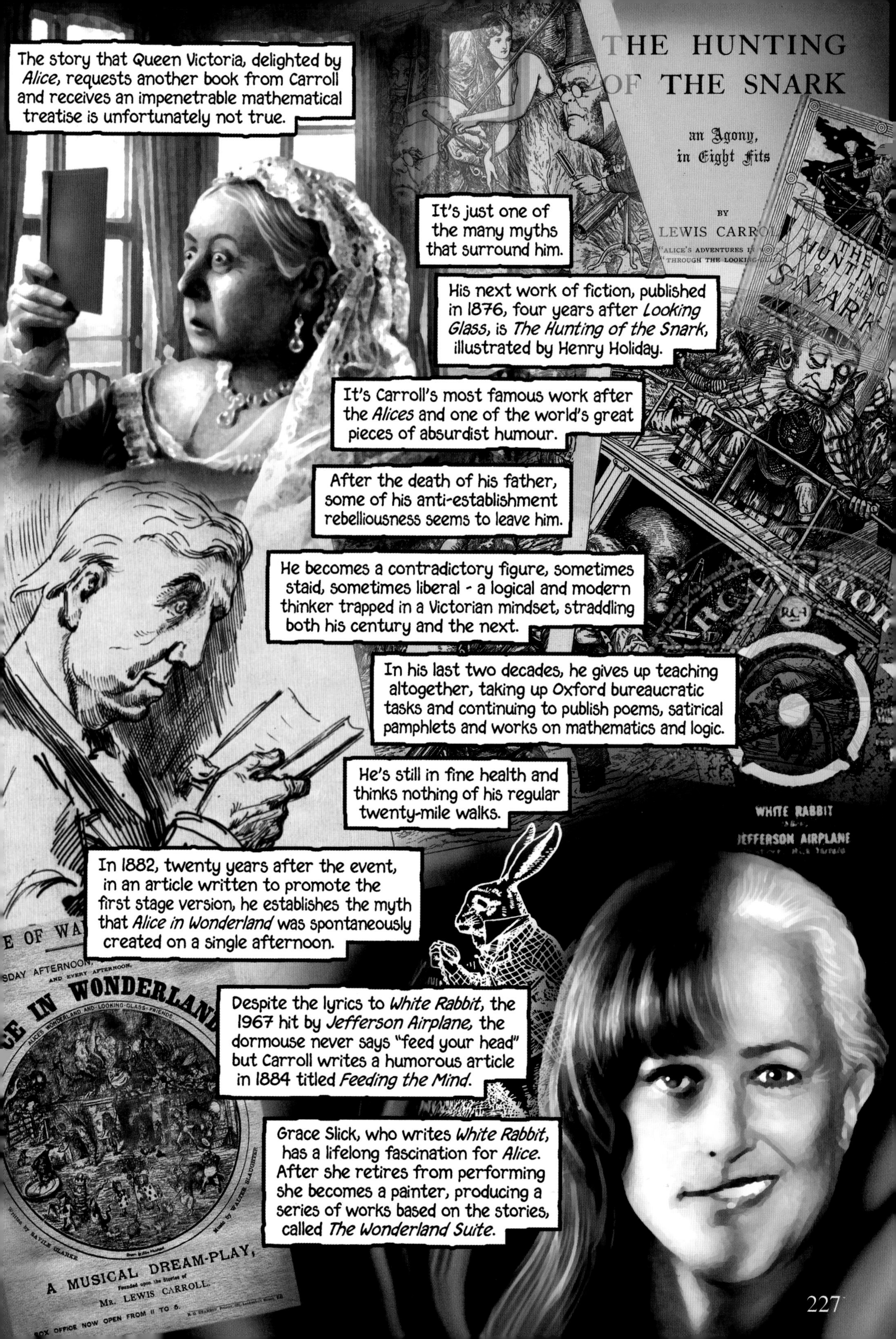

The story that Queen Victoria, delighted by *Alice*, requests another book from Carroll and receives an impenetrable mathematical treatise is unfortunately not true.
THE HUNTING OF THE SNARK
an Agony, in Eight Fits
BY
LEWIS CARRO
It's just one of the many myths that surround him.
His next work of fiction, published in 1876, four years after *Looking Glass*, is *The Hunting of the Snark*, illustrated by Henry Holiday.
It's Carroll's most famous work after the *Alices* and one of the world's great pieces of absurdist humour.
After the death of his father, some of his anti-establishment rebelliousness seems to leave him.
He becomes a contradictory figure, sometimes staid, sometimes liberal - a logical and modern thinker trapped in a Victorian mindset, straddling both his century and the next.
In his last two decades, he gives up teaching altogether, taking up Oxford bureaucratic tasks and continuing to publish poems, satirical pamphlets and works on mathematics and logic.
He's still in fine health and thinks nothing of his regular twenty-mile walks.
WHITE RABBIT
JEFFERSON AIRPLANE
In 1882, twenty years after the event, in an article written to promote the first stage version, he establishes the myth that *Alice in Wonderland* was spontaneously created on a single afternoon.
CE IN WONDERLAND
A MUSICAL DREAM-PLAY,
MR. LEWIS CARROLL.
BOX OFFICE NOW OPEN FROM 11 TO 5.
Despite the lyrics to *White Rabbit*, the 1967 hit by *Jefferson Airplane*, the dormouse never says "feed your head" but Carroll writes a humorous article in 1884 titled *Feeding the Mind*.
Grace Slick, who writes *White Rabbit*, has a lifelong fascination for *Alice*. After she retires from performing she becomes a painter, producing a series of works based on the stories, called *The Wonderland Suite*.

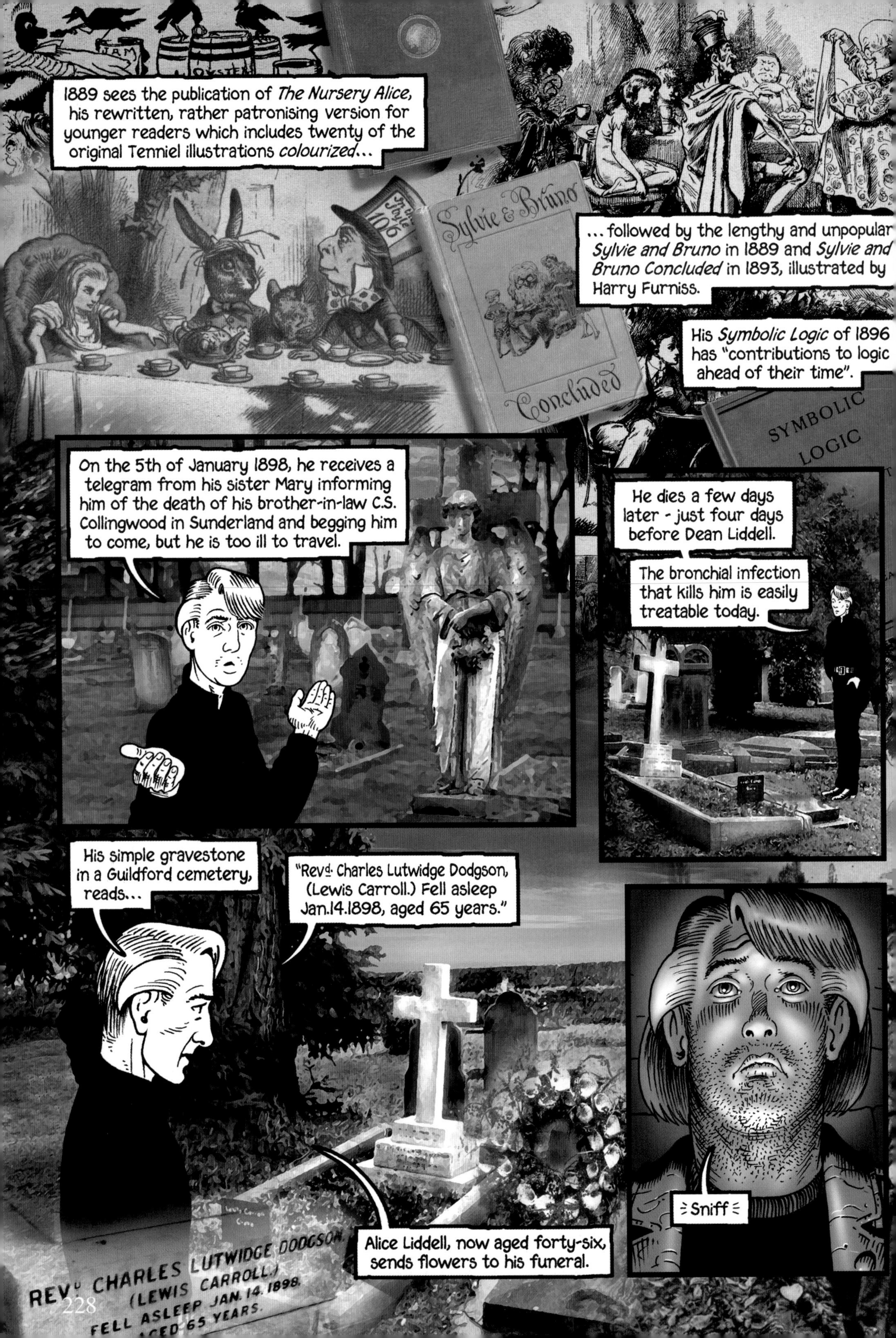

1889 sees the publication of *The Nursery Alice*, his rewritten, rather patronising version for younger readers which includes twenty of the original Tenniel illustrations *colourized*...
Sylvie & Bruno Concluded
... followed by the lengthy and unpopular *Sylvie and Bruno* in 1889 and *Sylvie and Bruno Concluded* in 1893, illustrated by Harry Furniss.
His *Symbolic Logic* of 1896 has "contributions to logic ahead of their time".
SYMBOLIC LOGIC
On the 5th of January 1898, he receives a telegram from his sister Mary informing him of the death of his brother-in-law C.S. Collingwood in Sunderland and begging him to come, but he is too ill to travel.
He dies a few days later - just four days before Dean Liddell.
The bronchial infection that kills him is easily treatable today.
His simple gravestone in a Guildford cemetery, reads...
"Revd. Charles Lutwidge Dodgson, (Lewis Carroll.) Fell asleep Jan.14.1898, aged 65 years."
Alice Liddell, now aged forty-six, sends flowers to his funeral.
Sniff
REVD CHARLES LUTWIDGE DODGSON
(LEWIS CARROLL.)
FELL ASLEEP JAN. 14. 1898.

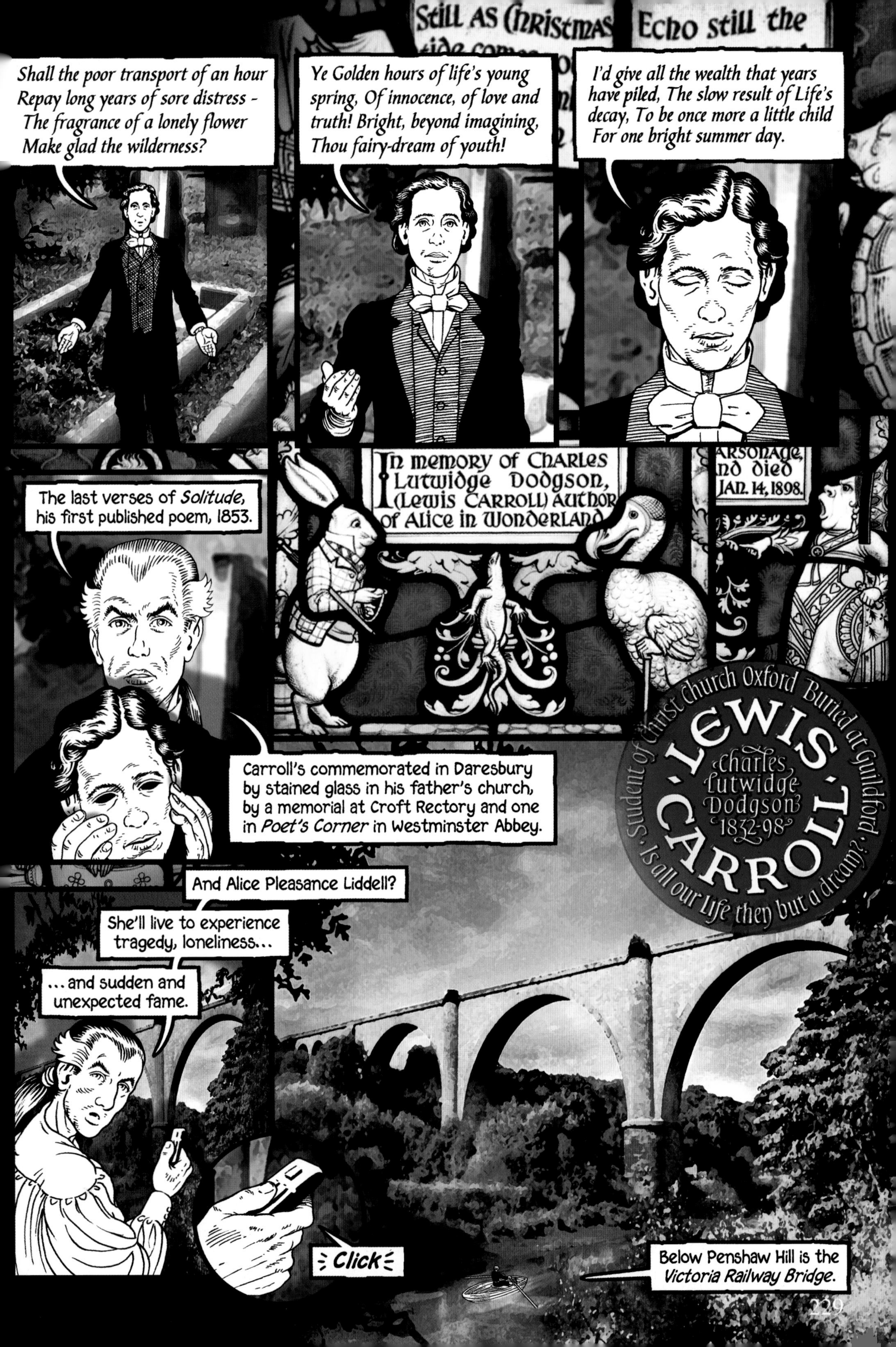

Still as Christmas
Echo still the
Shall the poor transport of an hour Repay long years of sore distress - The fragrance of a lonely flower Make glad the wilderness?
Ye Golden hours of life's young spring, Of innocence, of love and truth! Bright, beyond imagining, Thou fairy-dream of youth!
I'd give all the wealth that years have piled, The slow result of Life's decay, To be once more a little child For one bright summer day.
The last verses of *Solitude*, his first published poem, 1853.
In memory of Charles Lutwidge Dodgson, (Lewis Carroll) Author of Alice in Wonderland
arsonage, nd died Jan. 14, 1898.
Carroll's commemorated in Daresbury by stained glass in his father's church, by a memorial at Croft Rectory and one in *Poet's Corner* in Westminster Abbey.
Lewis Carroll
Charles Lutwidge Dodgson 1832-98
Student of Christ Church Oxford Buried at Guildford
Is all our Life then but a dream?
And Alice Pleasance Liddell?
She'll live to experience tragedy, loneliness...
...and sudden and unexpected fame.
Click
Below Penshaw Hill is the *Victoria Railway Bridge*.

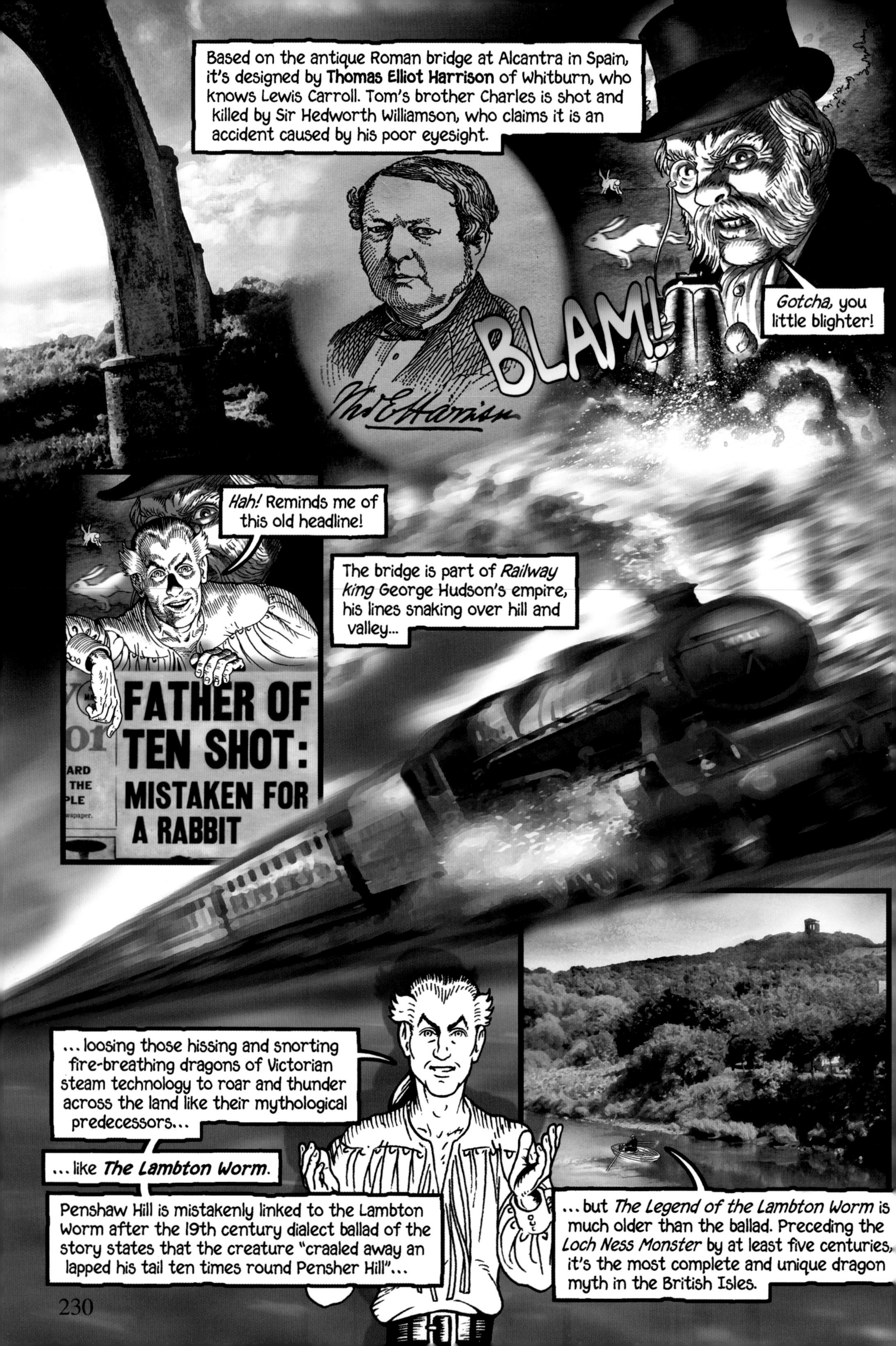
Based on the antique Roman bridge at Alcantra in Spain, it's designed by **Thomas Elliot Harrison** of Whitburn, who knows Lewis Carroll. Tom's brother Charles is shot and killed by Sir Hedworth Williamson, who claims it is an accident caused by his poor eyesight.
BLAM!!
Gotcha, you little blighter!
Hah! Reminds me of this old headline!
FATHER OF TEN SHOT: MISTAKEN FOR A RABBIT
The bridge is part of *Railway king* George Hudson's empire, his lines snaking over hill and valley...
... loosing those hissing and snorting fire-breathing dragons of Victorian steam technology to roar and thunder across the land like their mythological predecessors...
... like ***The Lambton Worm***.
Penshaw Hill is mistakenly linked to the Lambton Worm after the 19th century dialect ballad of the story states that the creature "craaled away an lapped his tail ten times round Pensher Hill"...
... but *The Legend of the Lambton Worm* is much older than the ballad. Preceding the *Loch Ness Monster* by at least five centuries, it's the most complete and unique dragon myth in the British Isles.

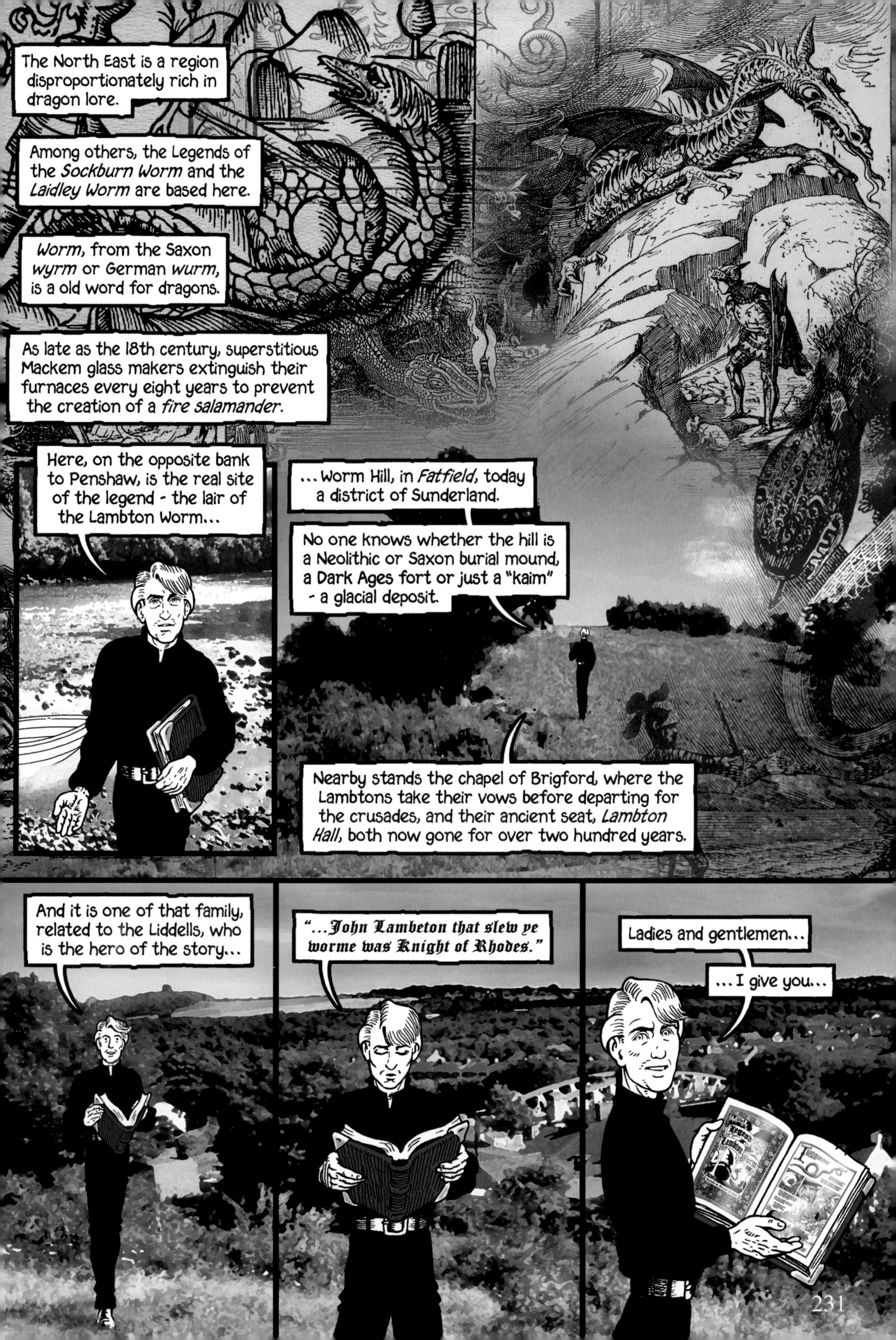
The North East is a region disproportionately rich in dragon lore.
Among others, the Legends of the *Sockburn Worm* and the *Laidley Worm* are based here.
Worm, from the Saxon *wyrm* or German *wurm*, is a old word for dragons.
As late as the 18th century, superstitious Mackem glass makers extinguish their furnaces every eight years to prevent the creation of a *fire salamander*.
Here, on the opposite bank to Penshaw, is the real site of the legend - the lair of the Lambton Worm...
...Worm Hill, in *Fatfield*, today a district of Sunderland.
No one knows whether the hill is a Neolithic or Saxon burial mound, a Dark Ages fort or just a "kaim" - a glacial deposit.
Nearby stands the chapel of Brigford, where the Lambtons take their vows before departing for the crusades, and their ancient seat, *Lambton Hall*, both now gone for over two hundred years.
And it is one of that family, related to the Liddells, who is the hero of the story...
"...John Lambeton that slew ye worme was Knight of Rhodes."
Ladies and gentlemen...
...I give you...

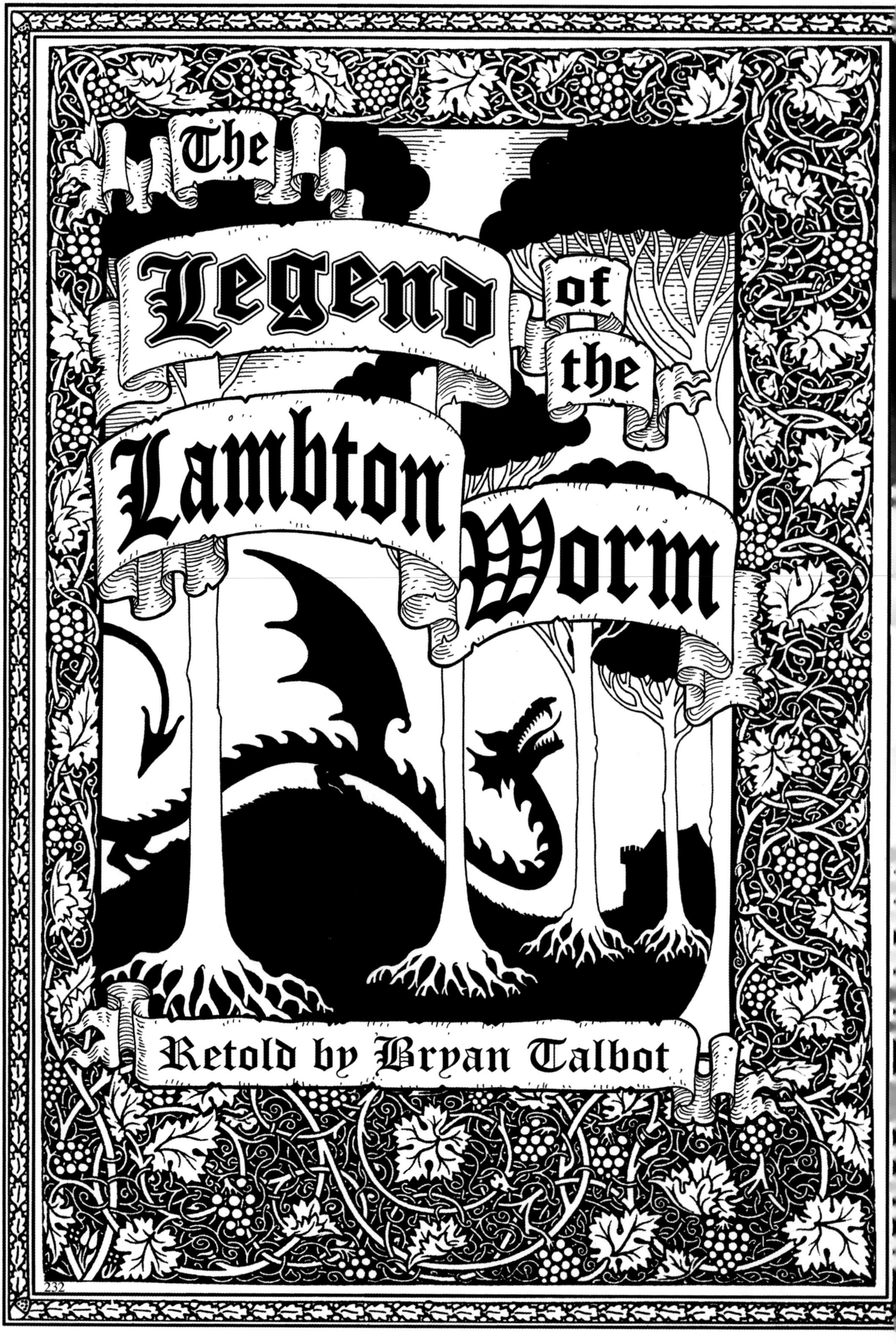
The Legend of the Lambton Worm
Retold by Bryan Talbot

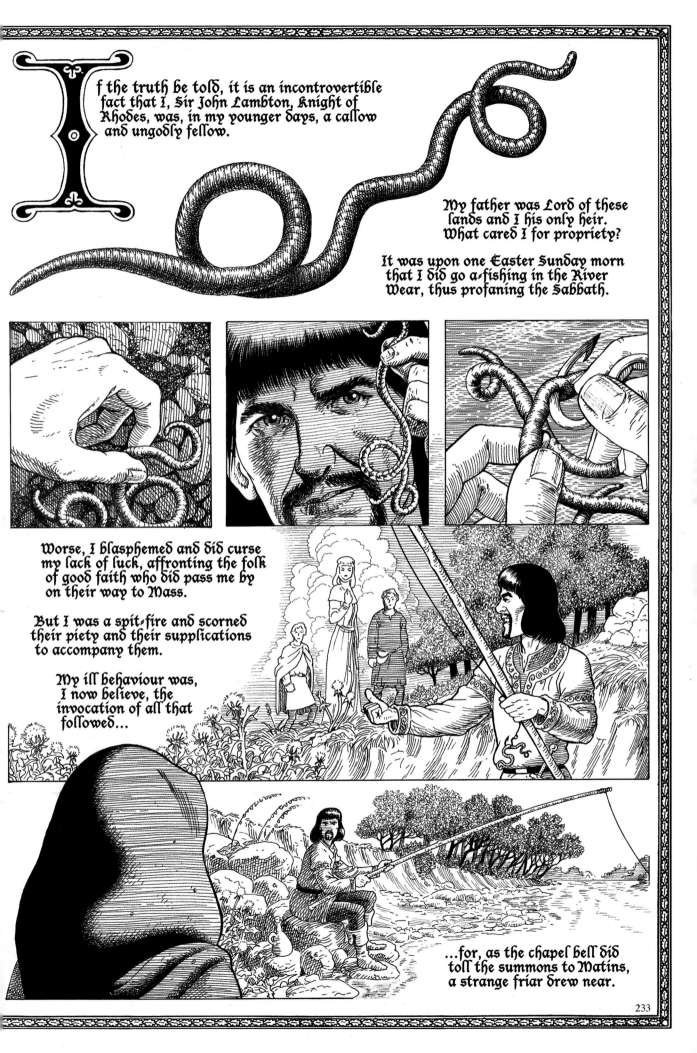

If the truth be told, it is an incontrovertible fact that I, Sir John Lambton, Knight of Rhodes, was, in my younger days, a callow and ungodly fellow.

My father was Lord of these lands and I his only heir. What cared I for propriety?

It was upon one Easter Sunday morn that I did go a-fishing in the River Wear, thus profaning the Sabbath.

Worse, I blasphemed and did curse my lack of luck, affronting the folk of good faith who did pass me by on their way to Mass.

But I was a spit-fire and scorned their piety and their supplications to accompany them.

My ill behaviour was, I now believe, the invocation of all that followed...

...for, as the chapel bell did toll the summons to Matins, a strange friar drew near.

233

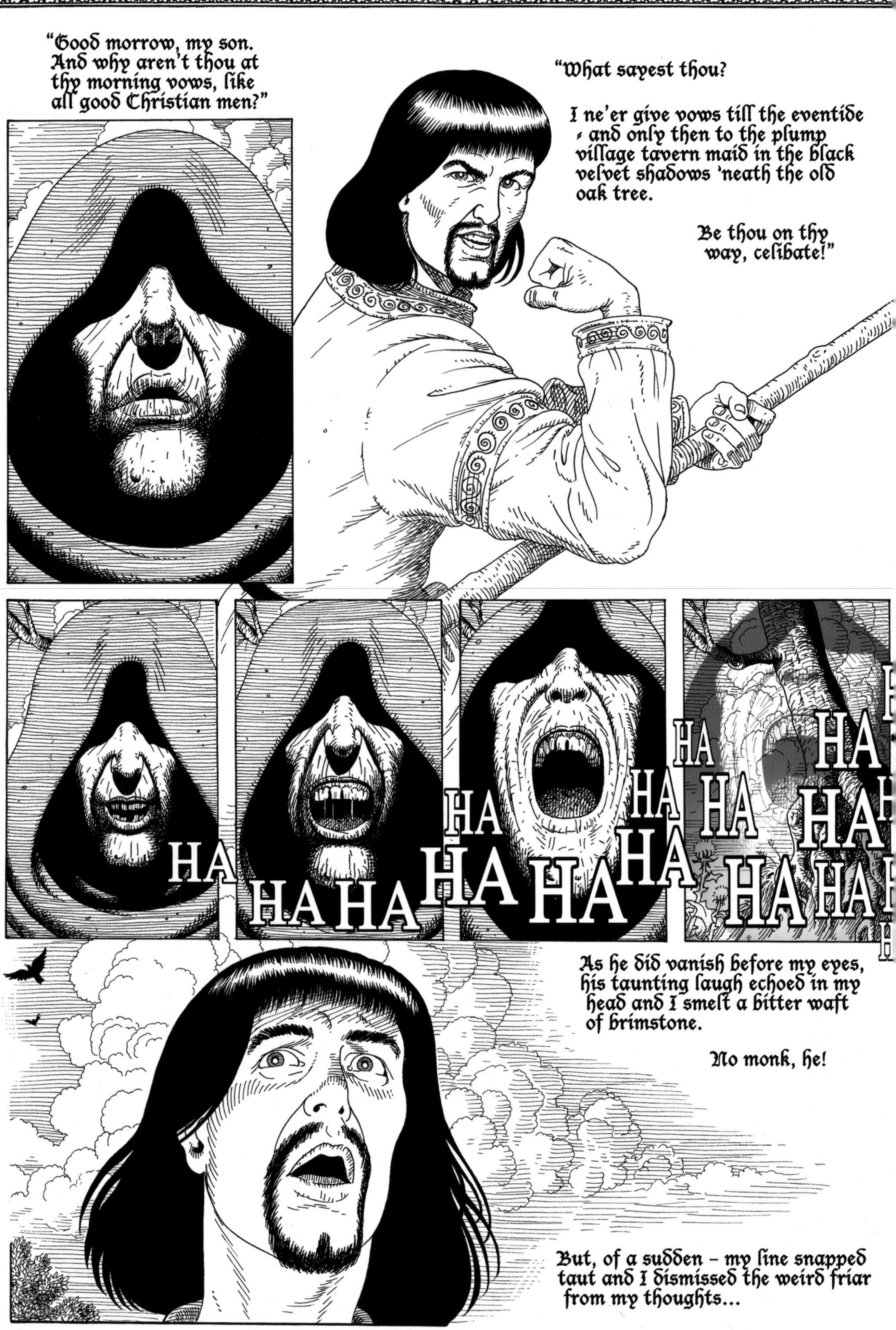
"Good morrow, my son. And why aren't thou at thy morning vows, like all good Christian men?"
"What sayest thou?
I ne'er give vows till the eventide - and only then to the plump village tavern maid in the black velvet shadows 'neath the old oak tree.
Be thou on thy way, celibate!"
HA HA HA HA HA HA HA HA HA HA HA HA HA HA HA
As he did vanish before my eyes, his taunting laugh echoed in my head and I smelt a bitter waft of brimstone.
No monk, he!
But, of a sudden - my line snapped taut and I dismissed the weird friar from my thoughts...

...for t'was certain that I'd hook'd a mighty catch!

For nigh on half an hour I struggled with all my might and cunning to land this indomitable fish, until...

"Good God Almighty, save us!"

I did stagger back under the weight and ferocity of this repulsive worm and, as soon as was able, tore the hook from its foul jaws and hoy'd it into the Fatfield well.

And, as I peer'd into that abyss...

HA HA HA HA HA HA HA HA HA HA HA HA HA HA HA HA HA HA HA HA HA HA HA HA HA HA HA HA HA HA HA HA HA HA HA HA HA HA HA HA HA HA HA HA HA HA HA HA HA HA HA HA HA HA HA HA HA HA HA HA HA HA HA HA HA HA HA HA HA HA HA

"Why, truly have I caught the Devil!"

235

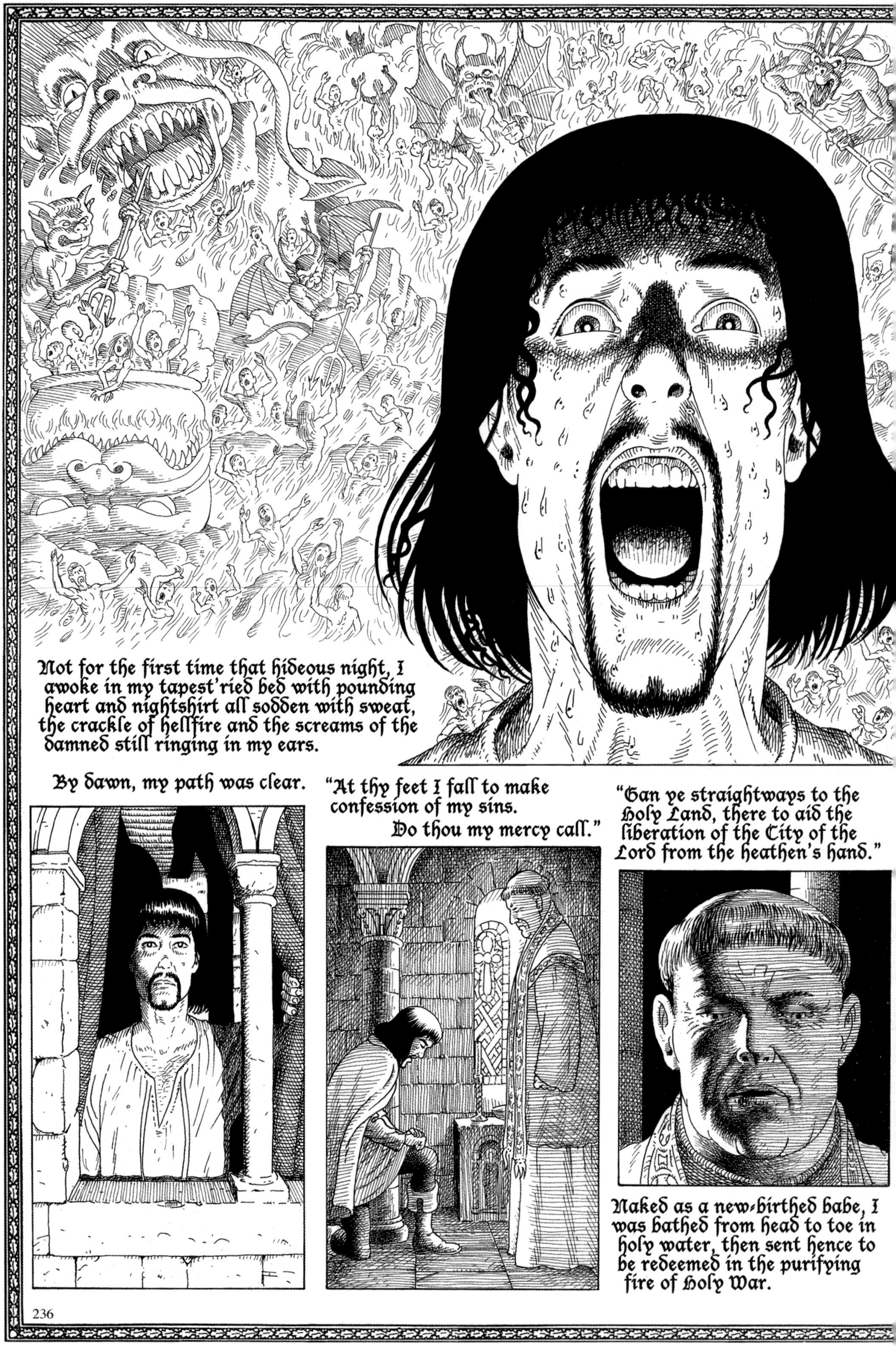

Not for the first time that hideous night, I awoke in my tapest'ried bed with pounding heart and nightshirt all sodden with sweat, the crackle of hellfire and the screams of the damned still ringing in my ears.
By dawn, my path was clear.
"At thy feet I fall to make confession of my sins. Do thou my mercy call."
"Gan ye straightways to the Holy Land, there to aid the liberation of the City of the Lord from the heathen's hand."
Naked as a new-birthed babe, I was bathed from head to toe in holy water, then sent hence to be redeemed in the purifying fire of Holy War.

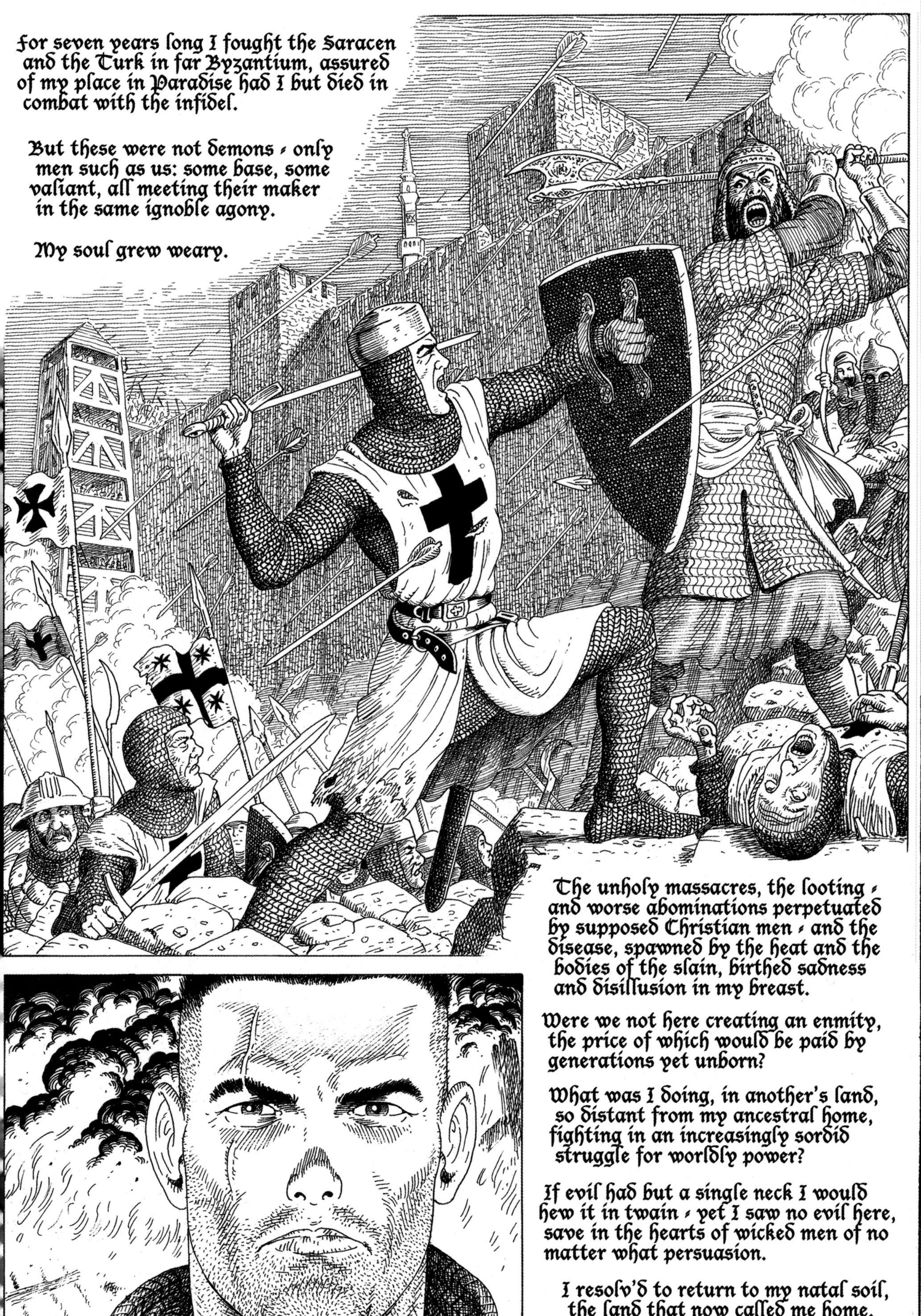
For seven years long I fought the Saracen and the Turk in far Byzantium, assured of my place in Paradise had I but died in combat with the infidel.
But these were not demons - only men such as us: some base, some valiant, all meeting their maker in the same ignoble agony.
My soul grew weary.
The unholy massacres, the looting - and worse abominations perpetuated by supposed Christian men - and the disease, spawned by the heat and the bodies of the slain, birthed sadness and disillusion in my breast.
Were we not here creating an enmity, the price of which would be paid by generations yet unborn?
What was I doing, in another's land, so distant from my ancestral home, fighting in an increasingly sordid struggle for worldly power?
If evil had but a single neck I would hew it in twain - yet I saw no evil here, save in the hearts of wicked men of no matter what persuasion.
I resolv'd to return to my natal soil, the land that now called me home.

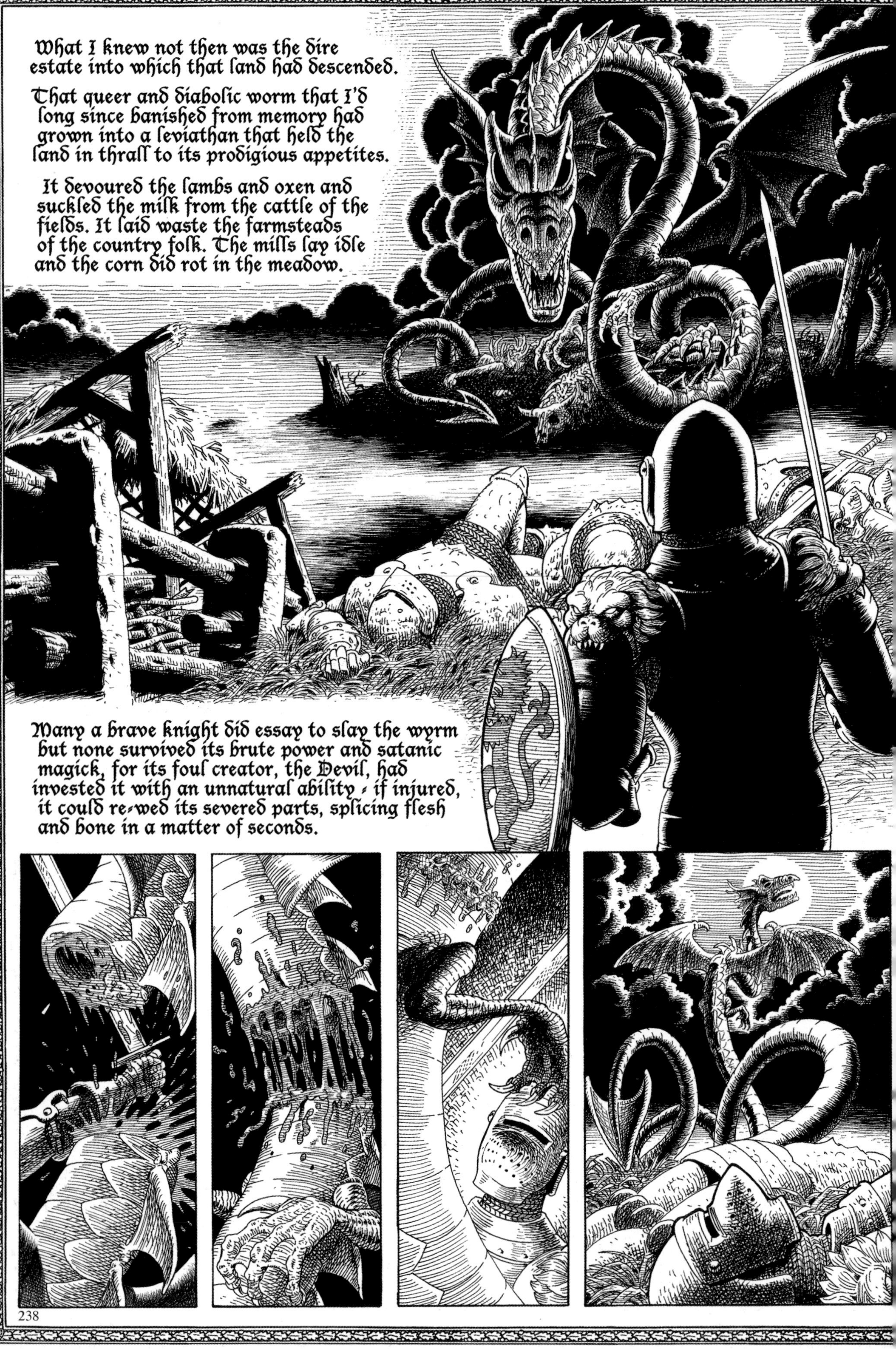
What I knew not then was the dire estate into which that land had descended.
That queer and diabolic worm that I'd long since banished from memory had grown into a leviathan that held the land in thrall to its prodigious appetites.
It devoured the lambs and oxen and suckled the milk from the cattle of the fields. It laid waste the farmsteads of the country folk. The mills lay idle and the corn did rot in the meadow.
Many a brave knight did essay to slay the wyrm but none survived its brute power and satanic magick, for its foul creator, the Devil, had invested it with an unnatural ability - if injured, it could re-wed its severed parts, splicing flesh and bone in a matter of seconds.

Lord Lambton, my dear father, a widower who long believed me slain in battle, had grown despondent.

He knew not how to assuage the plight of his people and his land, so took he counsel · and his ancient steward this plan did conceive...

"If we fill a trough with milk, it may appease the creature."

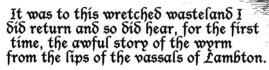

In faith, the ploy seemed to work. That day, the scourge of the Lambton lands did drink the milk from nine fat cows and, sated thus, retired to its hilltop lair, foregoing further mischief.

Each day did it return · but if by chance the milk filled not the trough, the dragon's wrath was fearsome to behold and much suffering would ensue.

It was to this wretched wasteland I did return and so did hear, for the first time, the awful story of the wyrm from the lips of the vassals of Lambton.

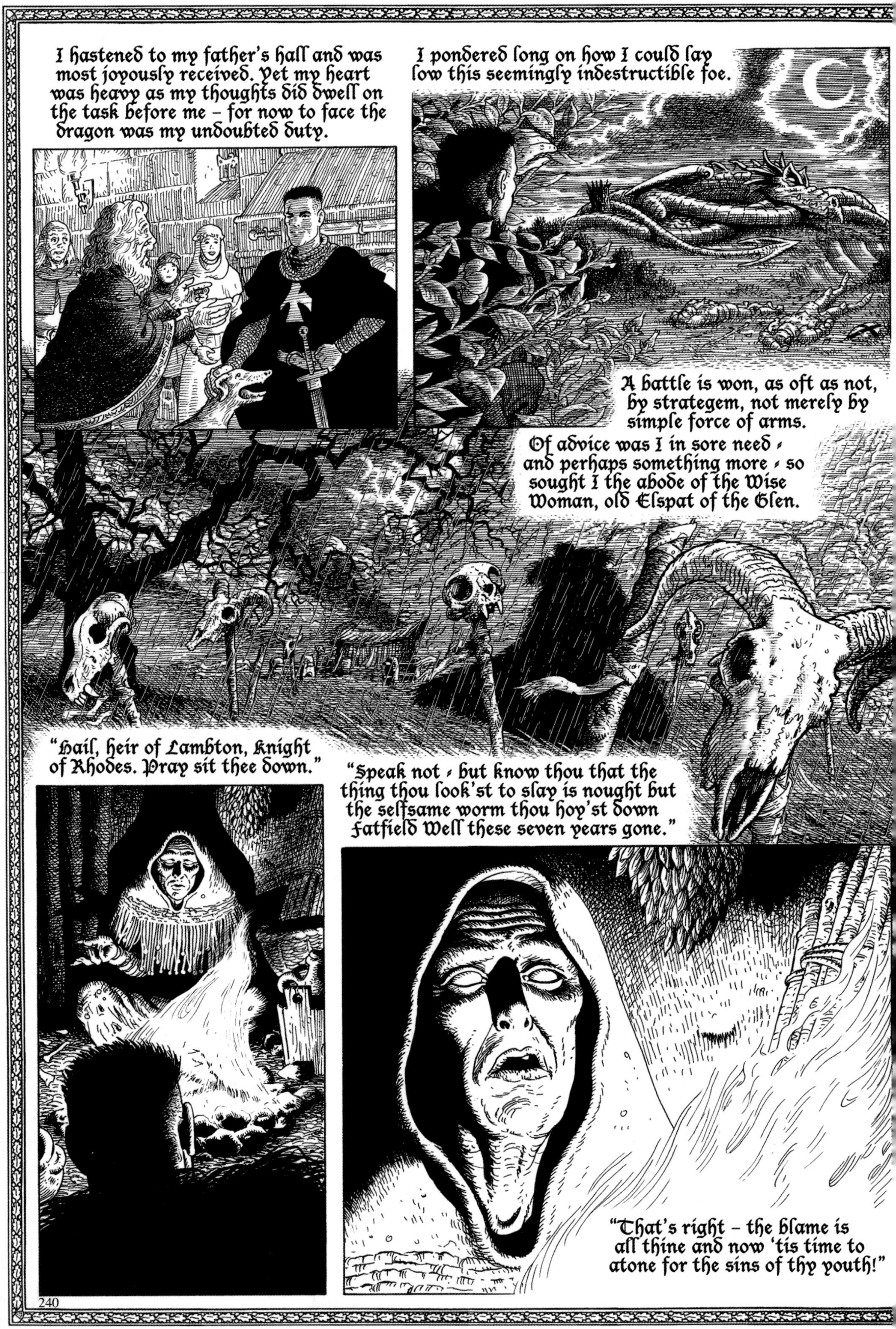
I hastened to my father's hall and was most joyously received. Yet my heart was heavy as my thoughts did dwell on the task before me – for now to face the dragon was my undoubted duty.
I pondered long on how I could slay this seemingly indestructible foe.
A battle is won, as oft as not, by strategem, not merely by simple force of arms.
Of advice was I in sore need – and perhaps something more – so sought I the abode of the Wise Woman, old Elspat of the Glen.
"Hail, heir of Lambton, knight of Rhodes. Pray sit thee down."
"Speak not – but know thou that the thing thou look'st to slay is nought but the selfsame worm thou hoy'st down Fatfield Well these seven years gone."
"That's right – the blame is all thine and now 'tis time to atone for the sins of thy youth!"

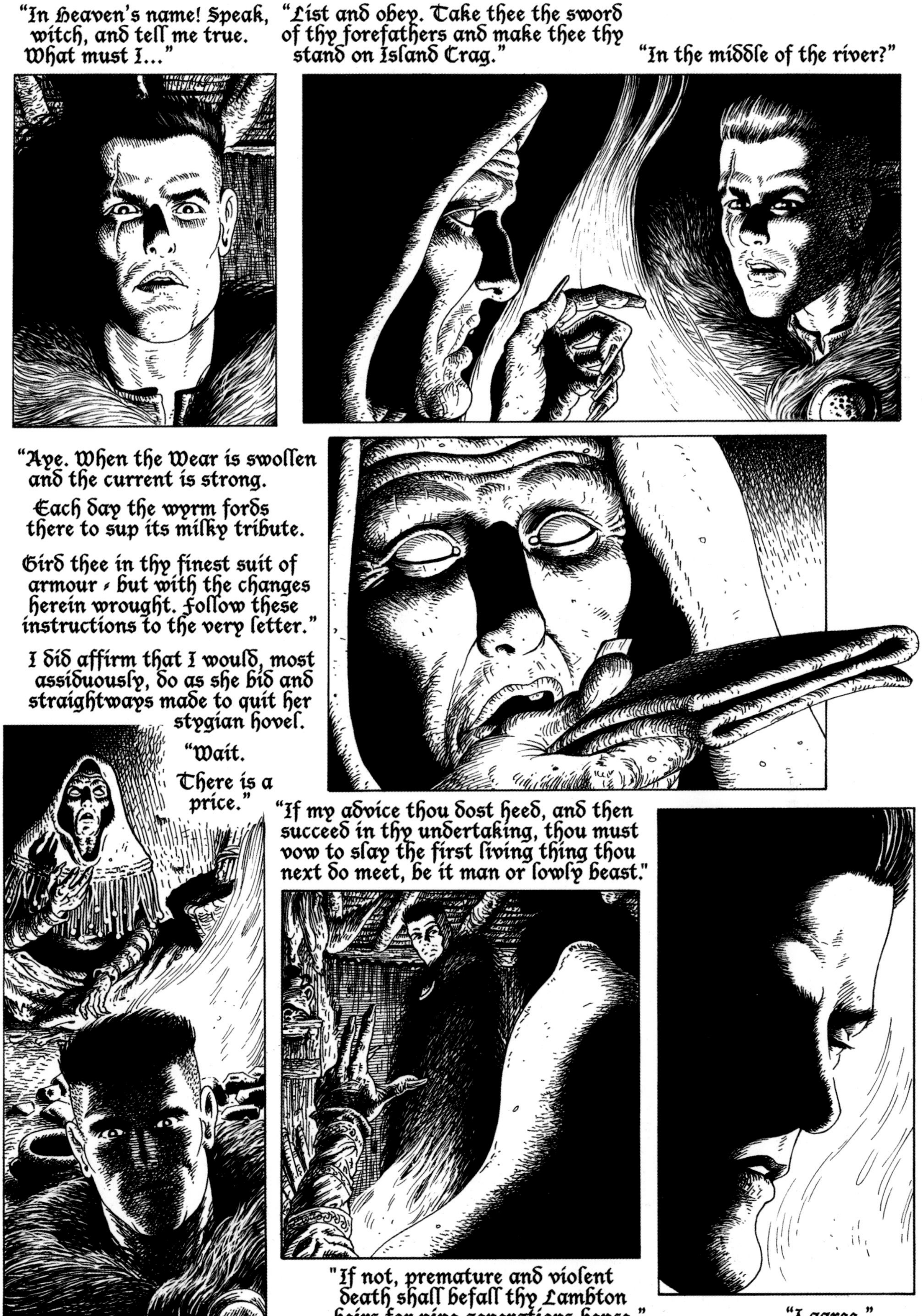
"In Heaven's name! Speak, witch, and tell me true. What must I..."
"List and obey. Take thee the sword of thy forefathers and make thee thy stand on Island Crag."
"In the middle of the river?"
"Aye. When the Wear is swollen and the current is strong.
Each day the wyrm fords there to sup its milky tribute.
Gird thee in thy finest suit of armour - but with the changes herein wrought. Follow these instructions to the very letter."
I did affirm that I would, most assiduously, do as she bid and straightways made to quit her stygian hovel.
"Wait. There is a price."
"If my advice thou dost heed, and then succeed in thy undertaking, thou must vow to slay the first living thing thou next do meet, be it man or lowly beast."
"If not, premature and violent death shall befall thy Lambton heirs for nine generations hence."
"I agree."

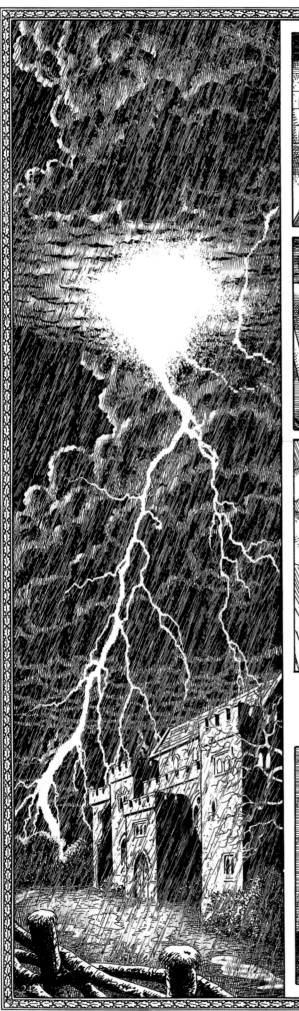

"Oh, my son, sore afraid am I for thy life! Beware those hellish claws, those monst'rous fangs…"

"Hush, father. I am ready and tomorrow the river shall be high."

"If I am victorious, I shall my horn sound three times. On that signal, release dear Ajax. The hound directly to me shall run. He shall be the witch's payment in blood."

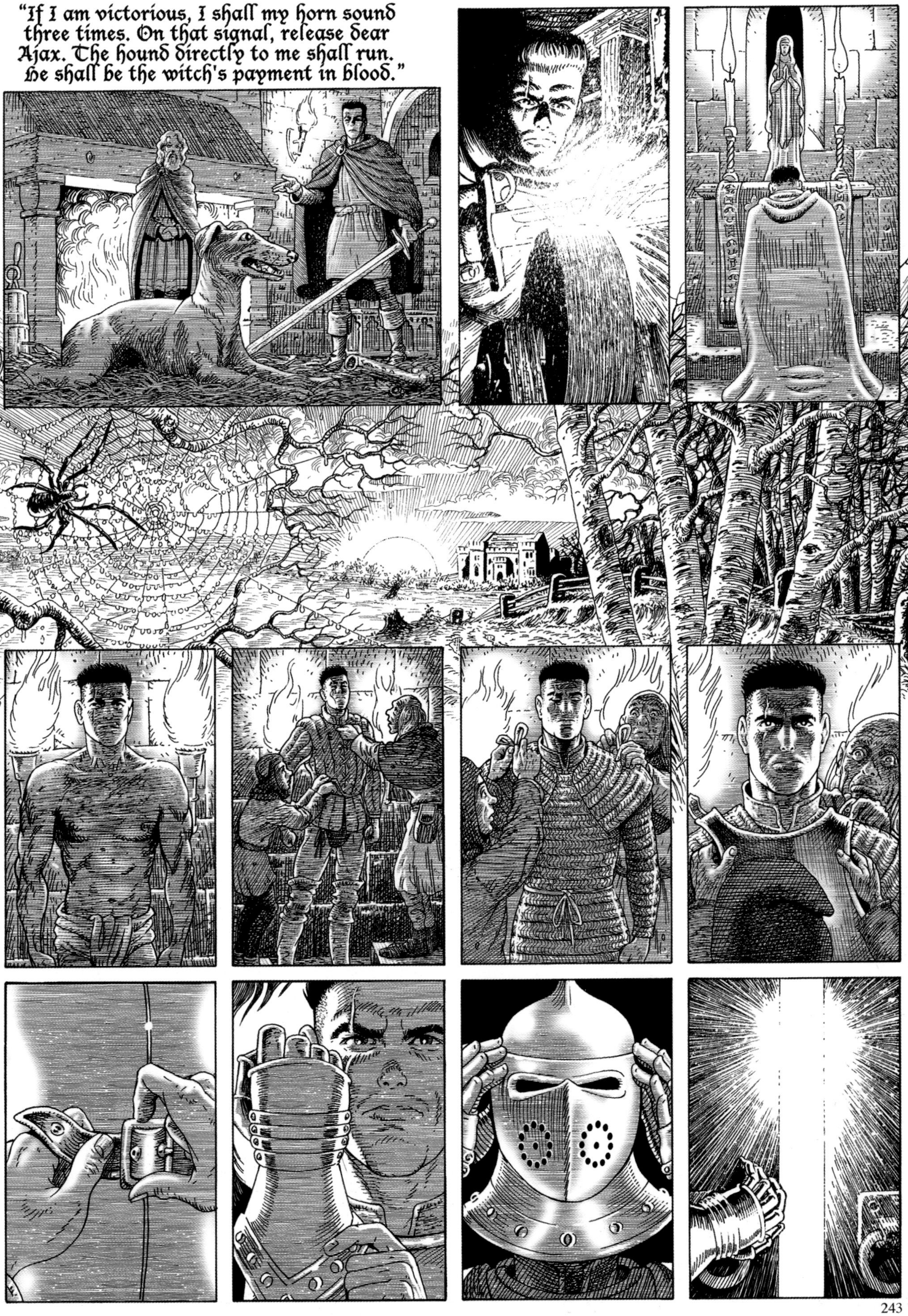

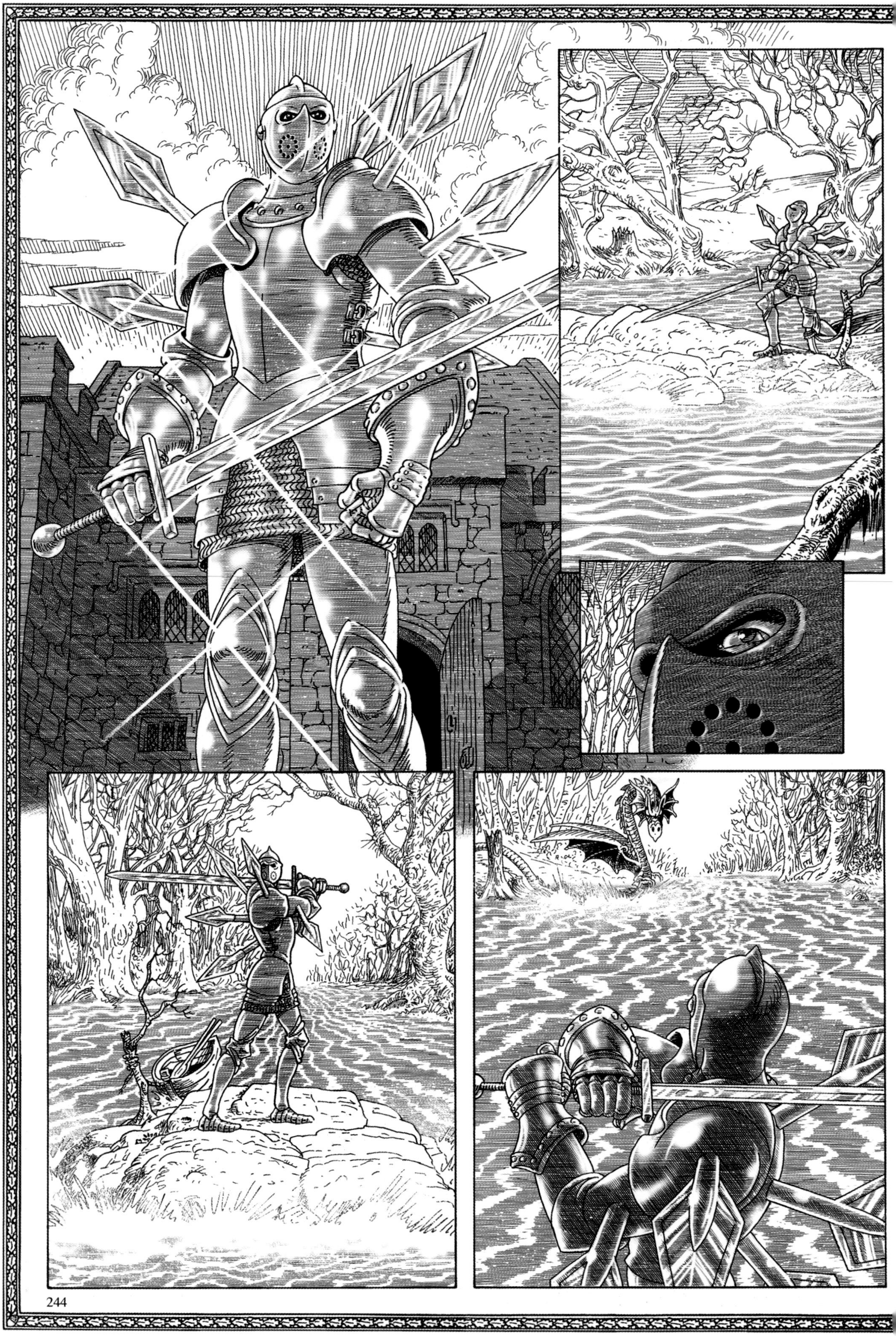

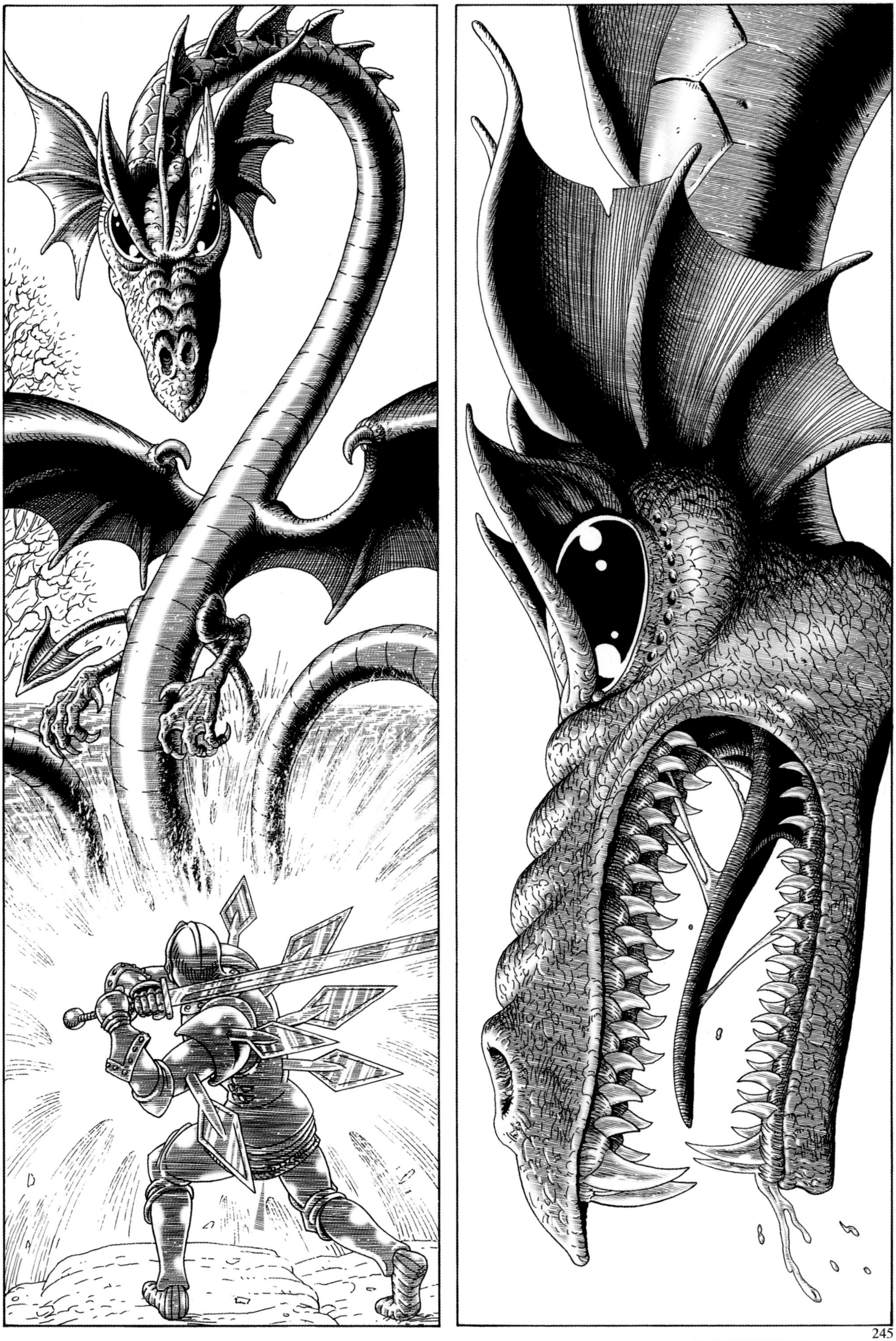

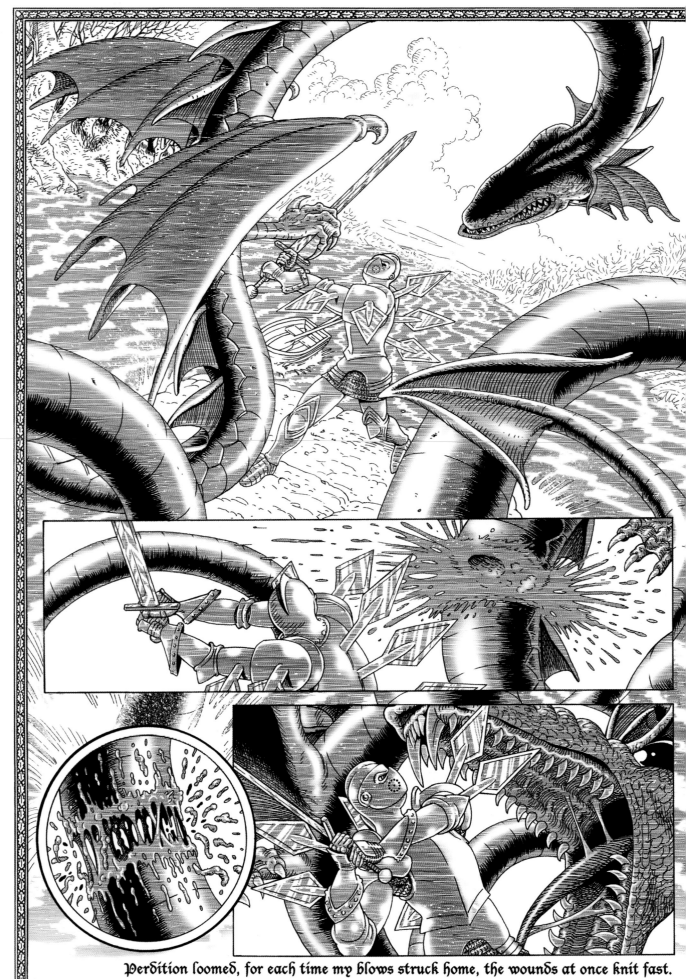

Perdition loomed, for each time my blows struck home, the wounds at once knit fast.

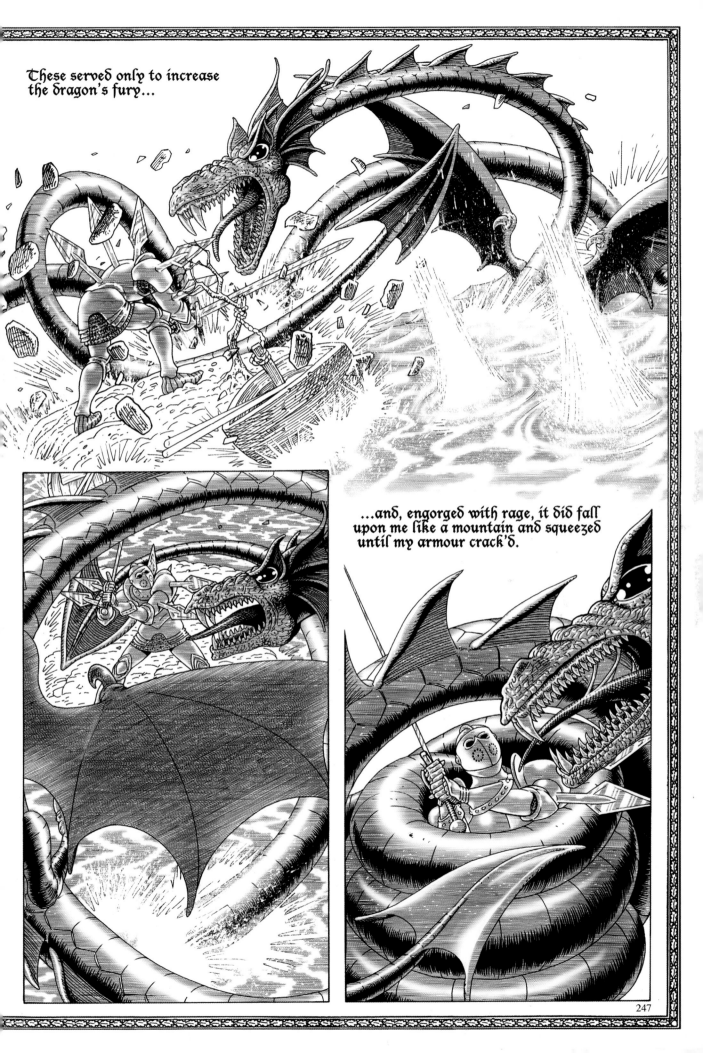

These served only to increase the dragon's fury...

...and, engorged with rage, it did fall upon me like a mountain and squeezed until my armour crack'd.

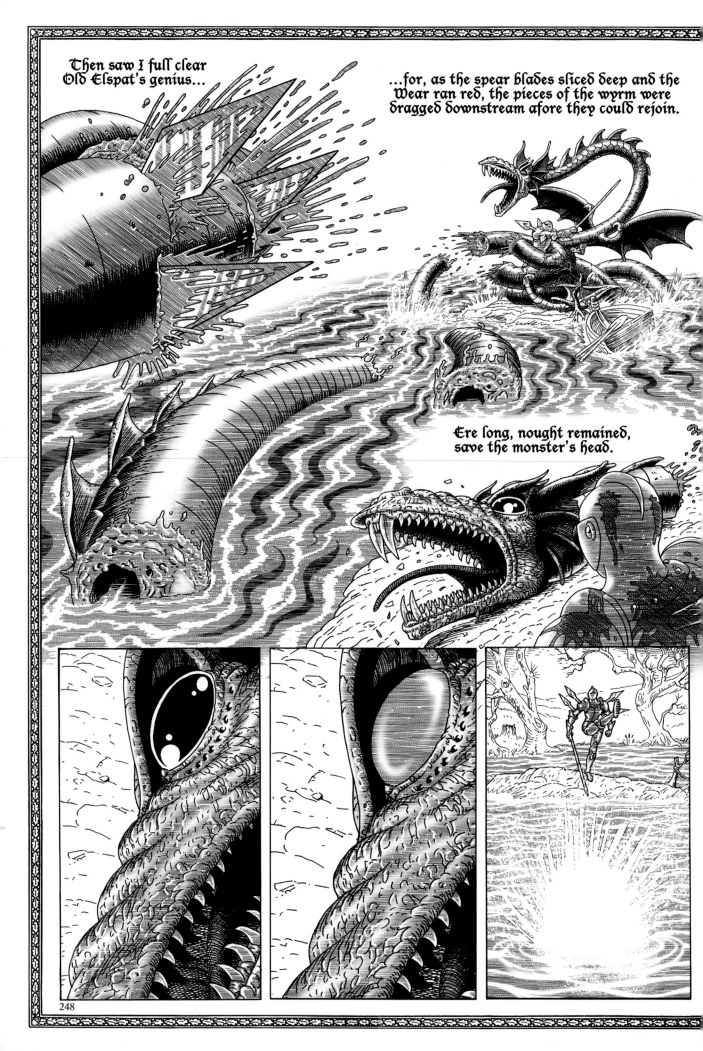

Then saw I full clear Old Elspat's genius...

...for, as the spear blades sliced deep and the Wear ran red, the pieces of the wyrm were dragged downstream afore they could rejoin.

Ere long, nought remained, save the monster's head.

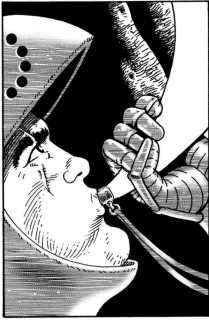

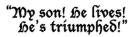

"My son! He lives! He's triumphed!"

"But my liege!"

"Father?"

"My boy! My dear boy! Come to my arms!"

Of course, my father I could not slay and so blew I the horn once more. And, when arrived the beloved hound...

"There is your sacrifice, witch."

...though I knew in my heart that I had reneged on our pact, thus damning my posterity to the curse of the Lambtons for the next nine generations.

The End

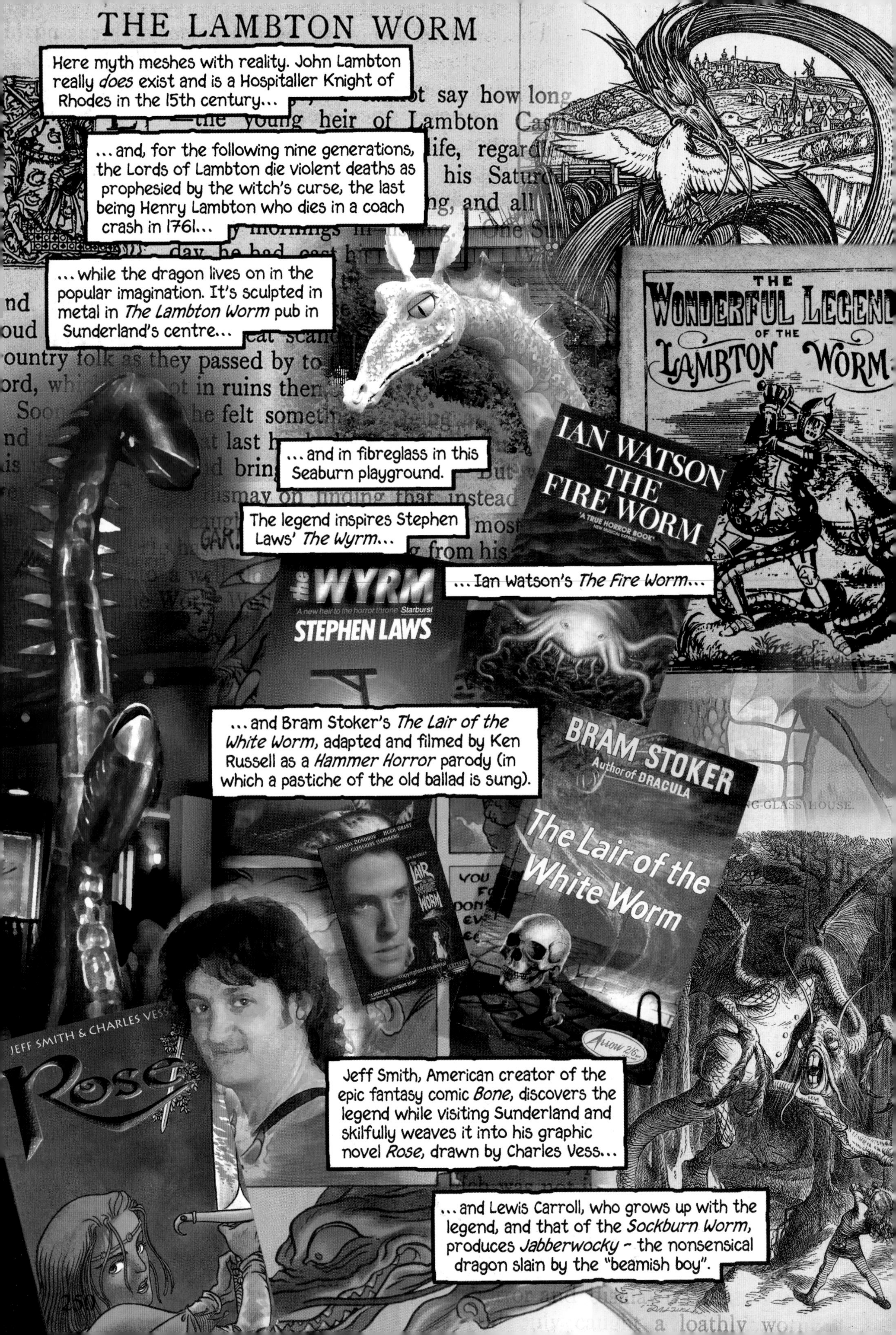

THE LAMBTON WORM
Here myth meshes with reality. John Lambton really *does* exist and is a Hospitaller Knight of Rhodes in the 15th century…
…and, for the following nine generations, the Lords of Lambton die violent deaths as prophesied by the witch's curse, the last being Henry Lambton who dies in a coach crash in 1761…
…while the dragon lives on in the popular imagination. It's sculpted in metal in *The Lambton Worm* pub in Sunderland's centre…
THE WONDERFUL LEGEND OF THE LAMBTON WORM
…and in fibreglass in this Seaburn playground.
IAN WATSON
THE FIRE WORM
The legend inspires Stephen Laws' *The Wyrm*…
the WYRM
'A new heir to the horror throne' Starburst
STEPHEN LAWS
…Ian Watson's *The Fire Worm*…
…and Bram Stoker's *The Lair of the White Worm*, adapted and filmed by Ken Russell as a *Hammer Horror* parody (in which a pastiche of the old ballad is sung).
BRAM STOKER
Author of DRACULA
The Lair of the White Worm
JEFF SMITH & CHARLES VESS
Rose
Jeff Smith, American creator of the epic fantasy comic *Bone*, discovers the legend while visiting Sunderland and skilfully weaves it into his graphic novel *Rose*, drawn by Charles Vess…
…and Lewis Carroll, who grows up with the legend, and that of the *Sockburn Worm*, produces *Jabberwocky* – the nonsensical dragon slain by the "beamish boy".

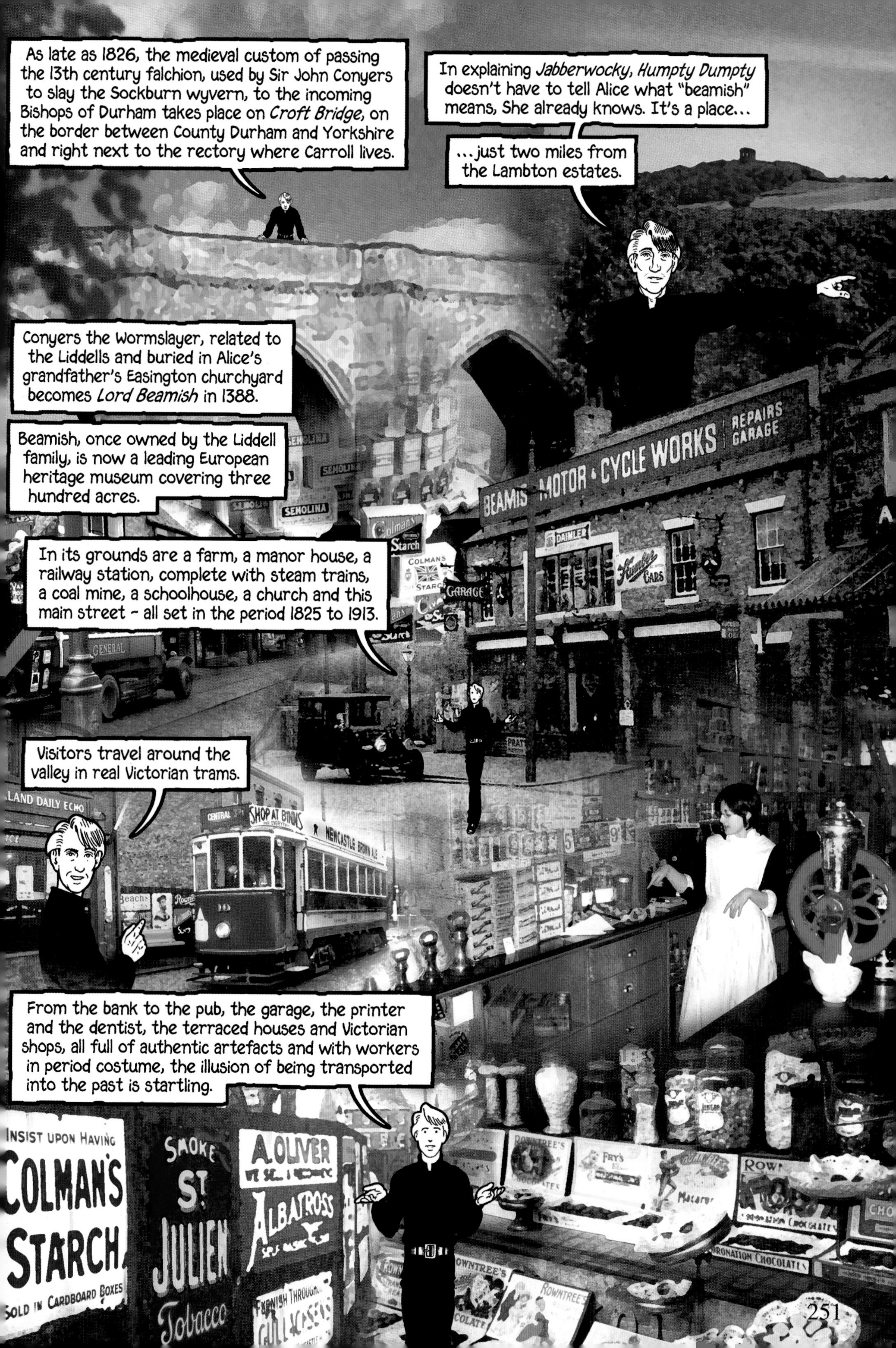
As late as 1826, the medieval custom of passing the 13th century falchion, used by Sir John Conyers to slay the Sockburn wyvern, to the incoming Bishops of Durham takes place on *Croft Bridge*, on the border between County Durham and Yorkshire and right next to the rectory where Carroll lives.
In explaining *Jabberwocky*, *Humpty Dumpty* doesn't have to tell Alice what "beamish" means, She already knows. It's a place...
...just two miles from the Lambton estates.
Conyers the Wormslayer, related to the Liddells and buried in Alice's grandfather's Easington churchyard becomes *Lord Beamish* in 1388.
Beamish, once owned by the Liddell family, is now a leading European heritage museum covering three hundred acres.
In its grounds are a farm, a manor house, a railway station, complete with steam trains, a coal mine, a schoolhouse, a church and this main street – all set in the period 1825 to 1913.
BEAMISH MOTOR & CYCLE WORKS
REPAIRS GARAGE
DAIMLER
GARAGE
SEMOLINA
Visitors travel around the valley in real Victorian trams.
SHOP AT BINNS
NEWCASTLE BROWN ALE
From the bank to the pub, the garage, the printer and the dentist, the terraced houses and Victorian shops, all full of authentic artefacts and with workers in period costume, the illusion of being transported into the past is startling.
INSIST UPON HAVING COLMAN'S STARCH SOLD IN CARDBOARD BOXES
SMOKE ST JULIEN Tobacco
A. OLIVER
ALBATROSS
ROWNTREE'S
CORONATION CHOCOLATES

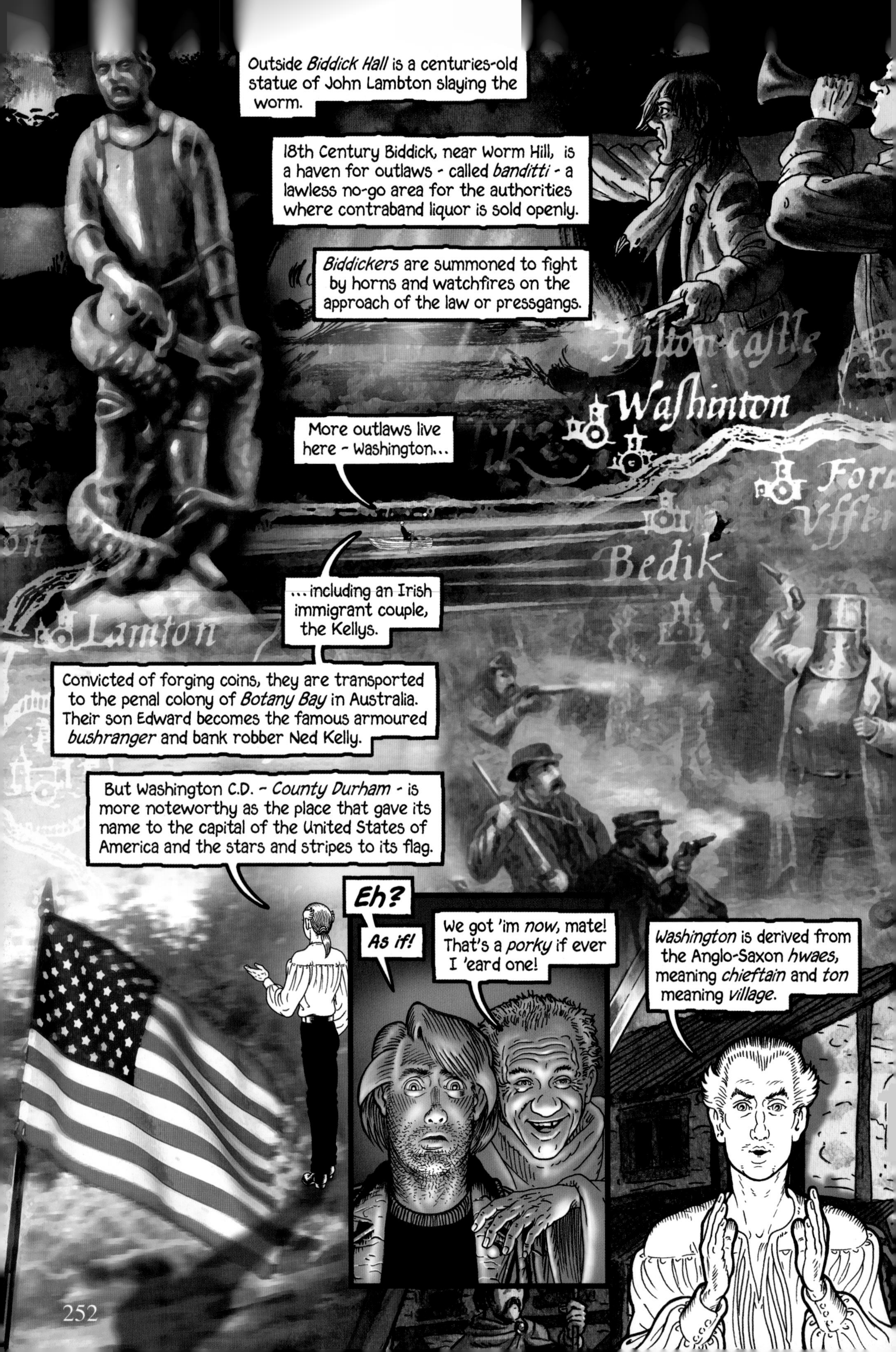

Outside *Biddick Hall* is a centuries-old statue of John Lambton slaying the worm.
18th Century Biddick, near Worm Hill, is a haven for outlaws - called *banditti* - a lawless no-go area for the authorities where contraband liquor is sold openly.
Biddickers are summoned to fight by horns and watchfires on the approach of the law or pressgangs.
Hilton castle
Washinton
Bedik
Lamton
More outlaws live here - Washington...
...including an Irish immigrant couple, the Kellys.
Convicted of forging coins, they are transported to the penal colony of *Botany Bay* in Australia. Their son Edward becomes the famous armoured *bushranger* and bank robber Ned Kelly.
But Washington C.D. - *County Durham* - is more noteworthy as the place that gave its name to the capital of the United States of America and the stars and stripes to its flag.
Eh?
As if!
We got 'im *now*, mate! That's a *porky* if ever I 'eard one!
Washington is derived from the Anglo-Saxon *hwaes*, meaning *chieftain* and *ton* meaning *village*.

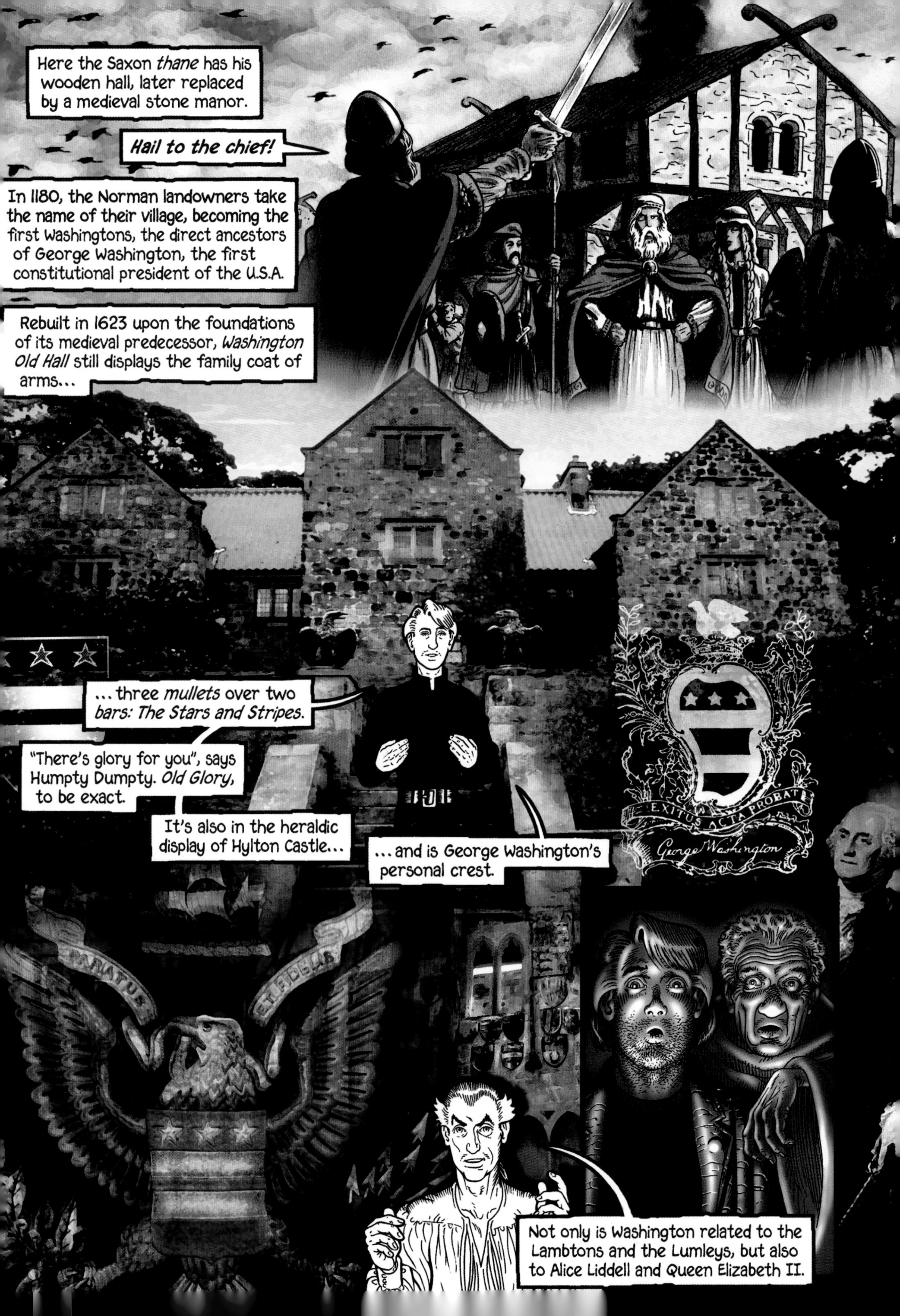
Here the Saxon *thane* has his wooden hall, later replaced by a medieval stone manor.
Hail to the chief!
In 1180, the Norman landowners take the name of their village, becoming the first Washingtons, the direct ancestors of George Washington, the first constitutional president of the U.S.A.
Rebuilt in 1623 upon the foundations of its medieval predecessor, *Washington Old Hall* still displays the family coat of arms…
… three *mullets* over two *bars: The Stars and Stripes.*
"There's glory for you", says Humpty Dumpty. *Old Glory,* to be exact.
It's also in the heraldic display of Hylton Castle…
… and is George Washington's personal crest.
EXITUS ACTA PROBAT
George Washington
PARATUS
ET FIDELIS
Not only is Washington related to the Lambtons and the Lumleys, but also to Alice Liddell and Queen Elizabeth II.

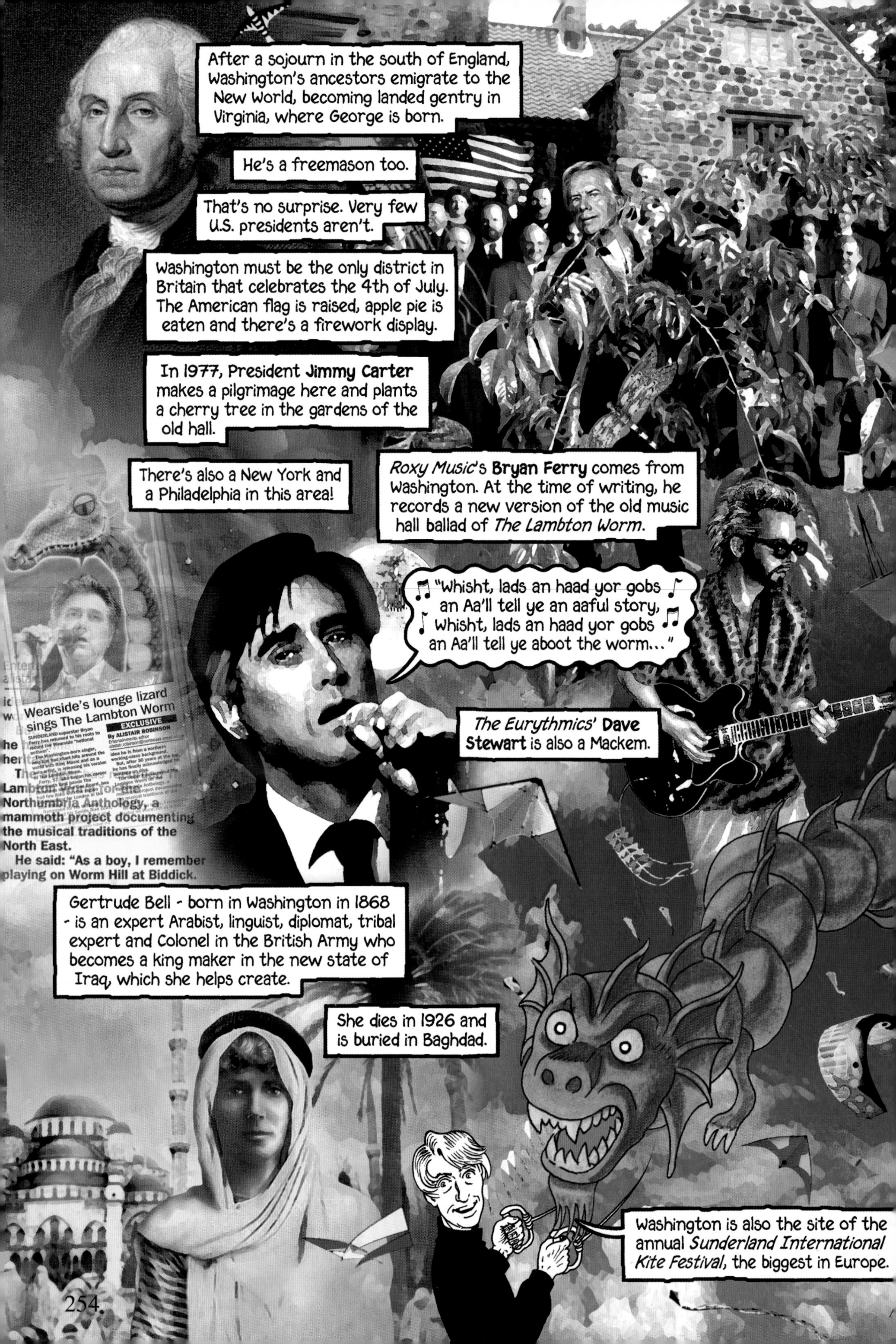
After a sojourn in the south of England, Washington's ancestors emigrate to the New World, becoming landed gentry in Virginia, where George is born.
He's a freemason too.
That's no surprise. Very few U.S. presidents aren't.
Washington must be the only district in Britain that celebrates the 4th of July. The American flag is raised, apple pie is eaten and there's a firework display.
In 1977, President **Jimmy Carter** makes a pilgrimage here and plants a cherry tree in the gardens of the old hall.
There's also a New York and a Philadelphia in this area!
Roxy Music's **Bryan Ferry** comes from Washington. At the time of writing, he records a new version of the old music hall ballad of *The Lambton Worm*.
"Whisht, lads an haad yor gobs an Aa'll tell ye an aaful story, Whisht, lads an haad yor gobs an Aa'll tell ye aboot the worm..."
Wearside's lounge lizard sings The Lambton Worm
EXCLUSIVE
By ALISTAIR ROBINSON
Northumbria Anthology, a mammoth project documenting the musical traditions of the North East.
He said: "As a boy, I remember playing on Worm Hill at Biddick.
The Eurythmics' **Dave Stewart** is also a Mackem.
Gertrude Bell - born in Washington in 1868 - is an expert Arabist, linguist, diplomat, tribal expert and Colonel in the British Army who becomes a king maker in the new state of Iraq, which she helps create.
She dies in 1926 and is buried in Baghdad.
Washington is also the site of the annual *Sunderland International Kite Festival*, the biggest in Europe.

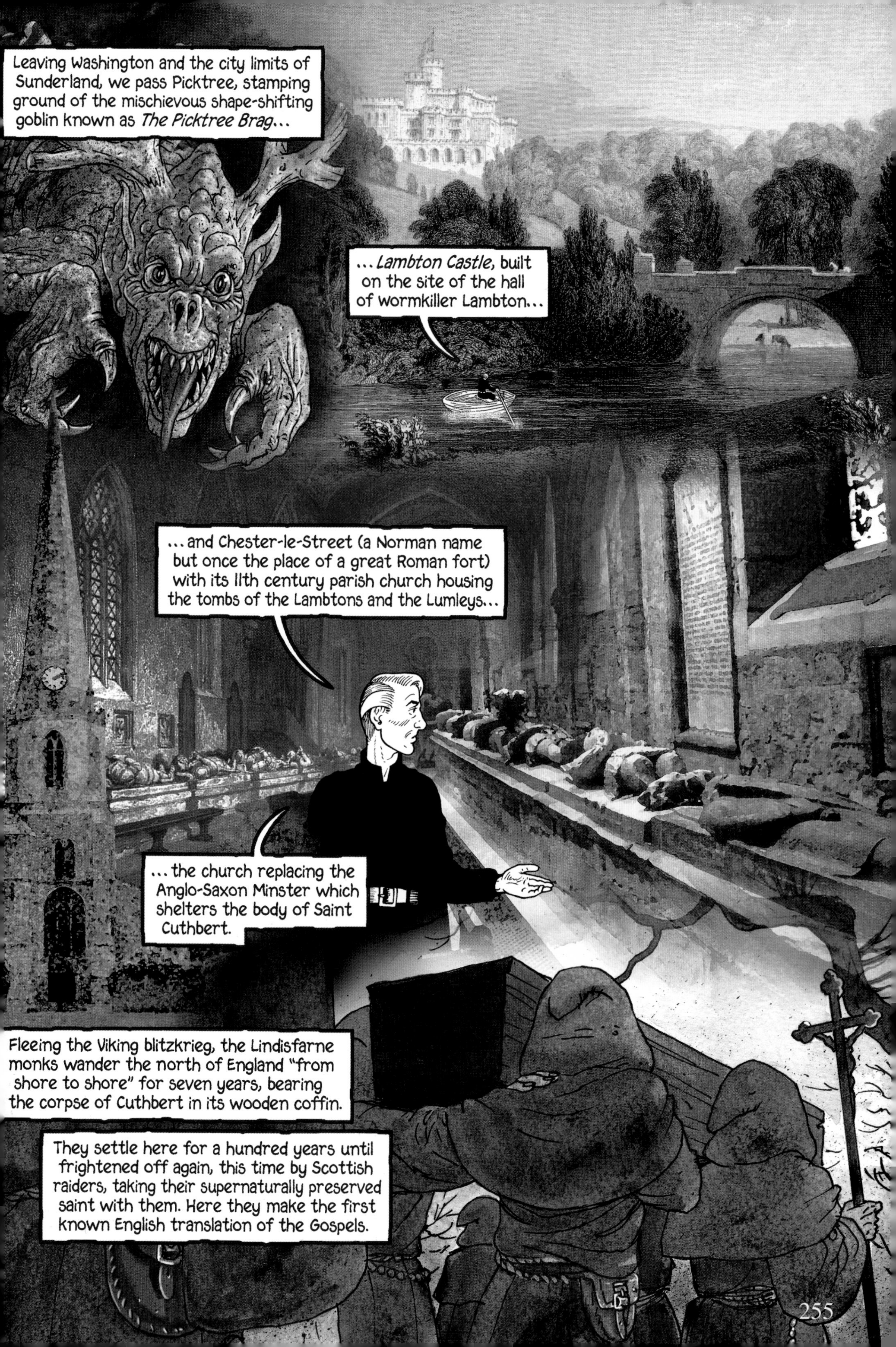
Leaving Washington and the city limits of Sunderland, we pass Picktree, stamping ground of the mischievous shape-shifting goblin known as *The Picktree Brag*...
...*Lambton Castle*, built on the site of the hall of Wormkiller Lambton...
...and Chester-le-Street (a Norman name but once the place of a great Roman fort) with its 11th century parish church housing the tombs of the Lambtons and the Lumleys...
...the church replacing the Anglo-Saxon Minster which shelters the body of Saint Cuthbert.
Fleeing the Viking blitzkrieg, the Lindisfarne monks wander the north of England "from shore to shore" for seven years, bearing the corpse of Cuthbert in its wooden coffin.
They settle here for a hundred years until frightened off again, this time by Scottish raiders, taking their supernaturally preserved saint with them. Here they make the first known English translation of the Gospels.

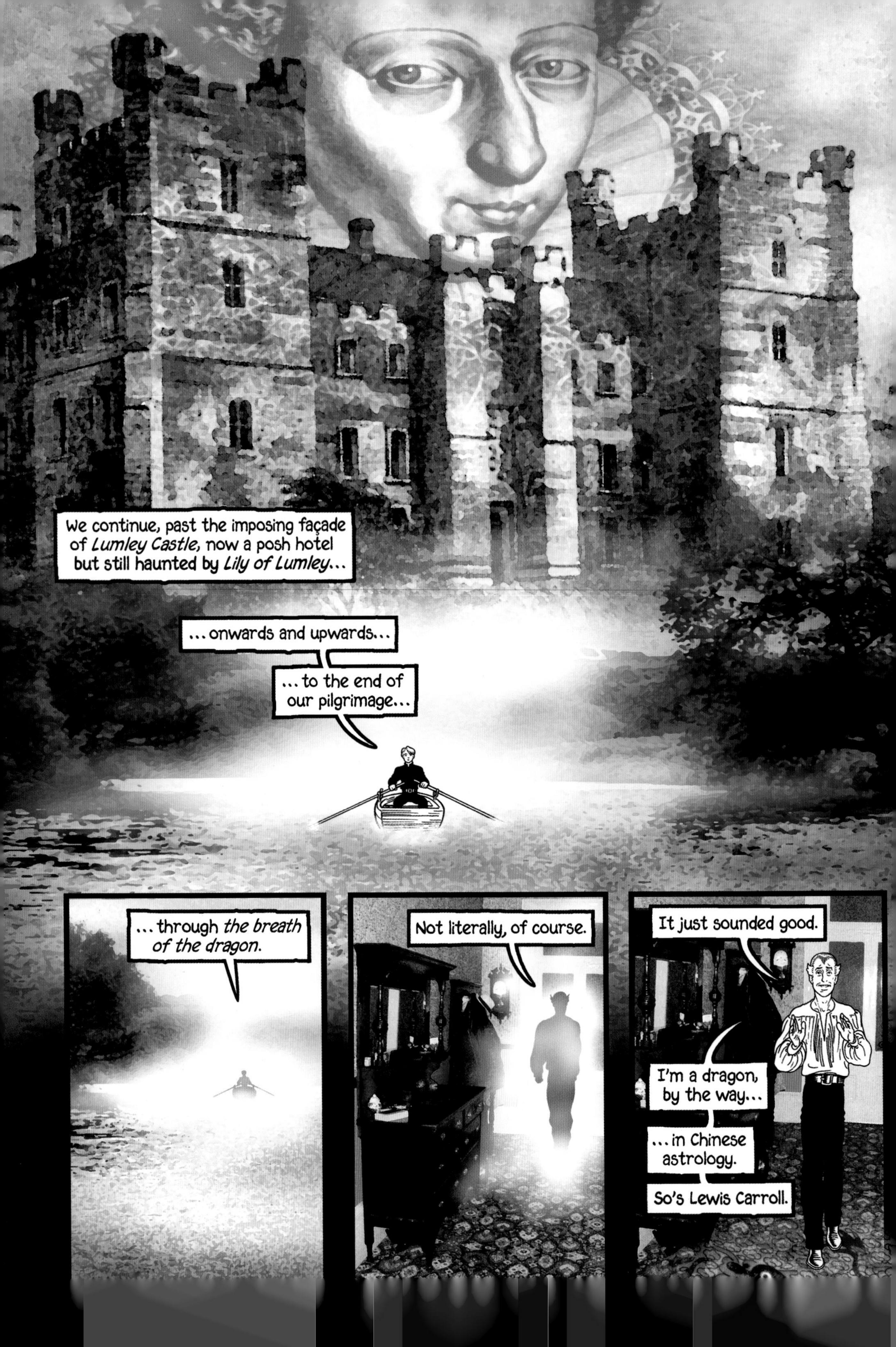

We continue, past the imposing façade of *Lumley Castle*, now a posh hotel but still haunted by *Lily of Lumley*...
...onwards and upwards...
...to the end of our pilgrimage...
...through *the breath of the dragon*.
Not literally, of course.
It just sounded good.
I'm a dragon, by the way...
...in Chinese astrology.
So's Lewis Carroll.

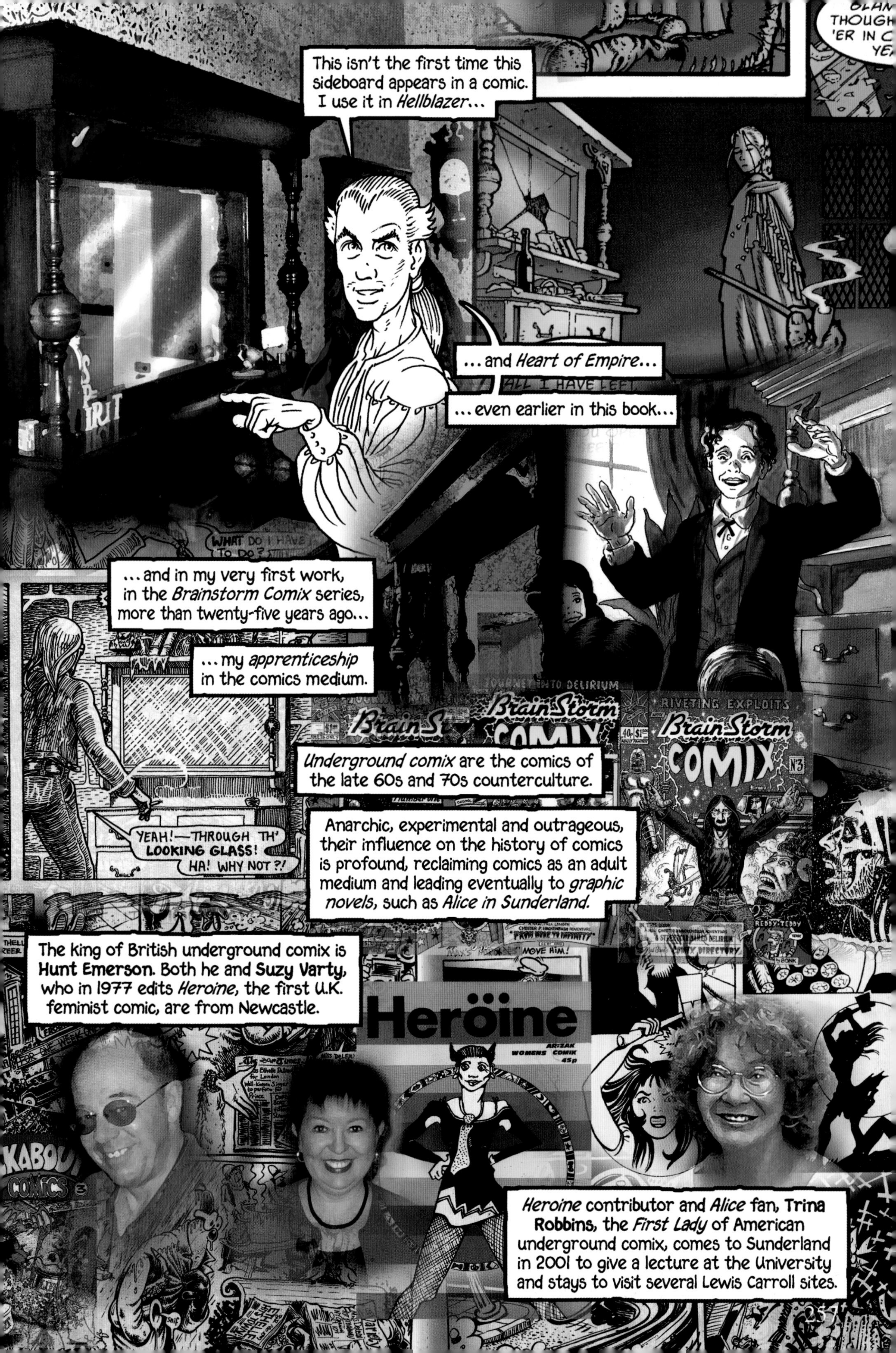

This isn't the first time this sideboard appears in a comic. I use it in *Hellblazer*...
...and *Heart of Empire*...
...even earlier in this book...
WHAT DO I HAVE TO DO?
...and in my very first work, in the *Brainstorm Comix* series, more than twenty-five years ago...
...my *apprenticeship* in the comics medium.
JOURNEY INTO DELIRIUM
Brain Storm COMIX
RIVETING EXPLOITS
Brain Storm COMIX Nº3
Underground comix are the comics of the late 60s and 70s counterculture.
YEAH!—THROUGH TH' LOOKING GLASS! HA! WHY NOT?!
Anarchic, experimental and outrageous, their influence on the history of comics is profound, reclaiming comics as an adult medium and leading eventually to *graphic novels*, such as *Alice in Sunderland*.
The king of British underground comix is **Hunt Emerson**. Both he and **Suzy Varty**, who in 1977 edits *Heroine*, the first U.K. feminist comic, are from Newcastle.
Heröine
AR:ZAK WOMENS COMIK 45p
Heroine contributor and *Alice* fan, **Trina Robbins**, the *First Lady* of American underground comix, comes to Sunderland in 2001 to give a lecture at the University and stays to visit several Lewis Carroll sites.

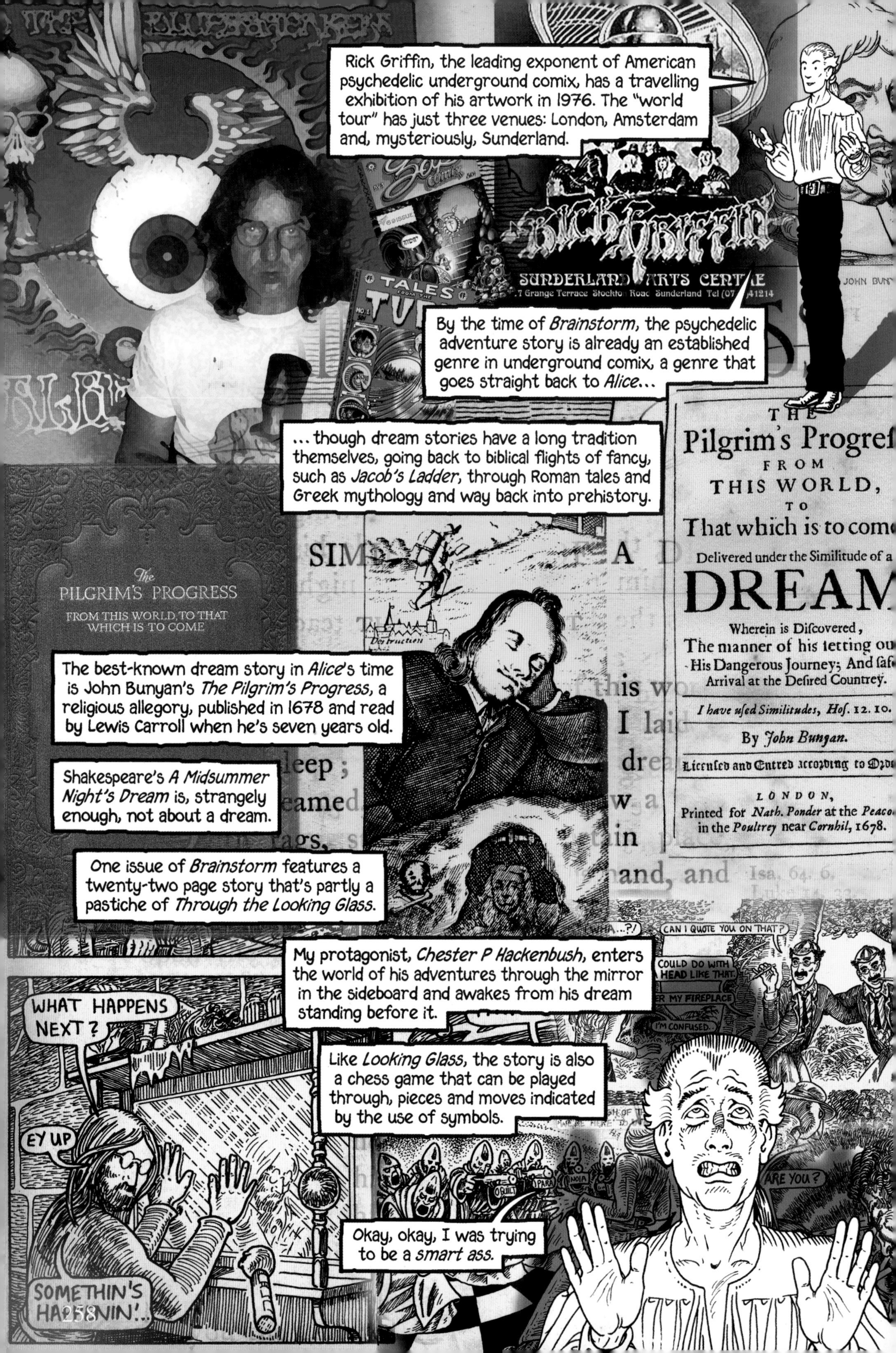
Rick Griffin, the leading exponent of American psychedelic underground comix, has a travelling exhibition of his artwork in 1976. The "world tour" has just three venues: London, Amsterdam and, mysteriously, Sunderland.
SUNDERLAND ARTS CENTRE
By the time of *Brainstorm*, the psychedelic adventure story is already an established genre in underground comix, a genre that goes straight back to *Alice*...
... though dream stories have a long tradition themselves, going back to biblical flights of fancy, such as *Jacob's Ladder*, through Roman tales and Greek mythology and way back into prehistory.
THE Pilgrim's Progress FROM THIS WORLD, TO That which is to come Delivered under the Similitude of a DREAM Wherein is Discovered, The manner of his setting out, His Dangerous Journey; And safe Arrival at the Desired Country.
I have used Similitudes, Hos. 12. 10.
By John Bunyan.
LONDON, Printed for Nath. Ponder at the Peacock in the Poultrey near Cornhil, 1678.
The PILGRIM'S PROGRESS FROM THIS WORLD, TO THAT WHICH IS TO COME
The best-known dream story in *Alice*'s time is John Bunyan's *The Pilgrim's Progress*, a religious allegory, published in 1678 and read by Lewis Carroll when he's seven years old.
Shakespeare's *A Midsummer Night's Dream* is, strangely enough, not about a dream.
One issue of *Brainstorm* features a twenty-two page story that's partly a pastiche of *Through the Looking Glass*.
My protagonist, *Chester P Hackenbush*, enters the world of his adventures through the mirror in the sideboard and awakes from his dream standing before it.
WHAT HAPPENS NEXT?
CAN I QUOTE YOU ON THAT?
COULD DO WITH HEAD LIKE THAT.
I'M CONFUSED.
Like *Looking Glass*, the story is also a chess game that can be played through, pieces and moves indicated by the use of symbols.
EY UP
ARE YOU?
Okay, okay, I was trying to be a *smart ass*.
SOMETHIN'S HAPPENIN'...

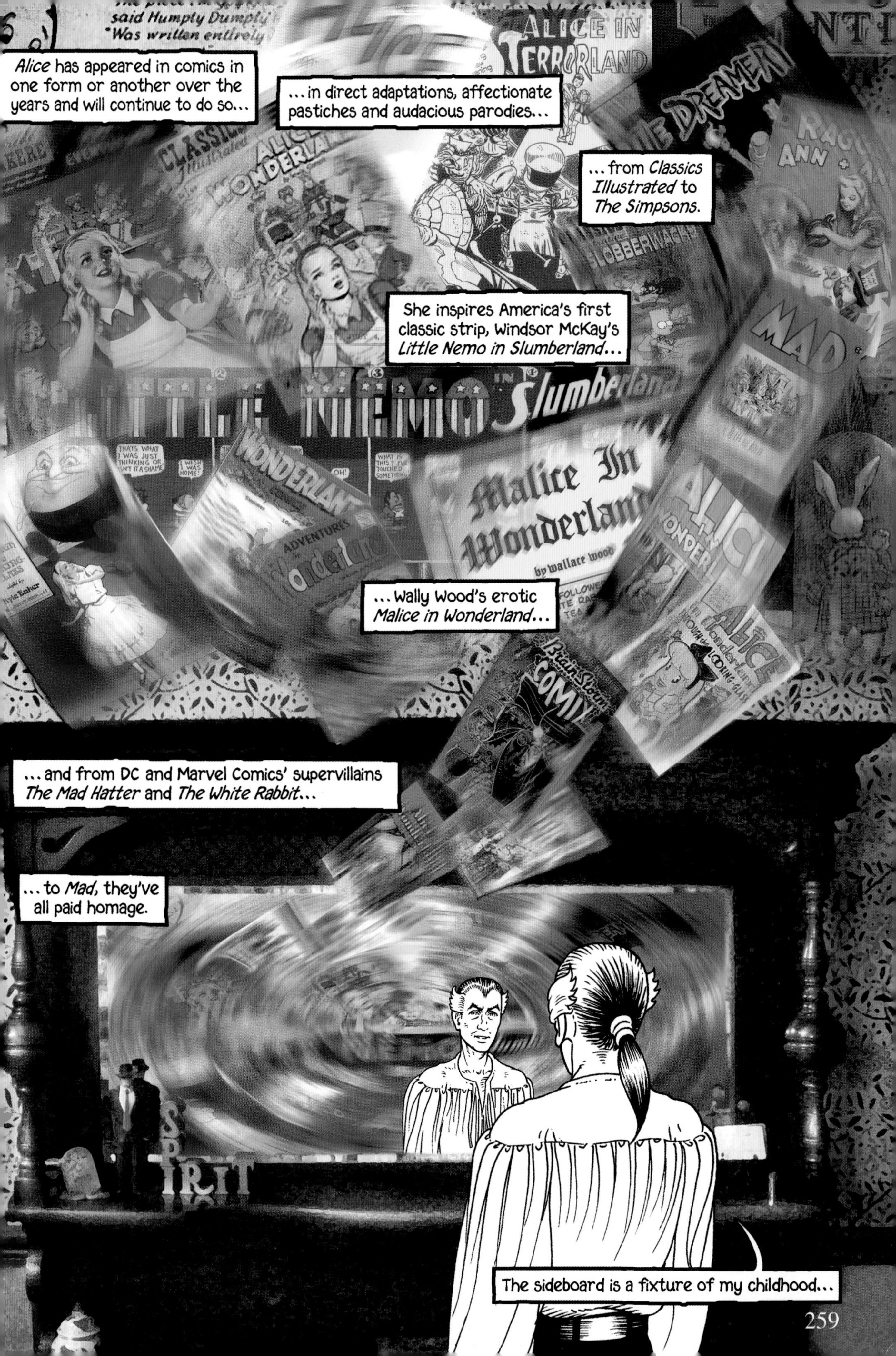
said Humpty Dumpty
"Was written entirely
Alice has appeared in comics in one form or another over the years and will continue to do so...
ALICE IN TERRORLAND
...in direct adaptations, affectionate pastiches and audacious parodies...
...from Classics Illustrated to The Simpsons.
She inspires America's first classic strip, Windsor McKay's Little Nemo in Slumberland...
Slumberland
THATS WHAT I WAS JUST THINKING OF, ISNT IT A SHAME
I WISH I WAS HOME!
WHAT IS THIS? I'VE TOUCHED SOMETHING
OH!
Malice In Wonderland
by wallace wood
...Wally Wood's erotic Malice in Wonderland...
MAD
...and from DC and Marvel Comics' supervillains The Mad Hatter and The White Rabbit...
...to Mad, they've all paid homage.
The sideboard is a fixture of my childhood...

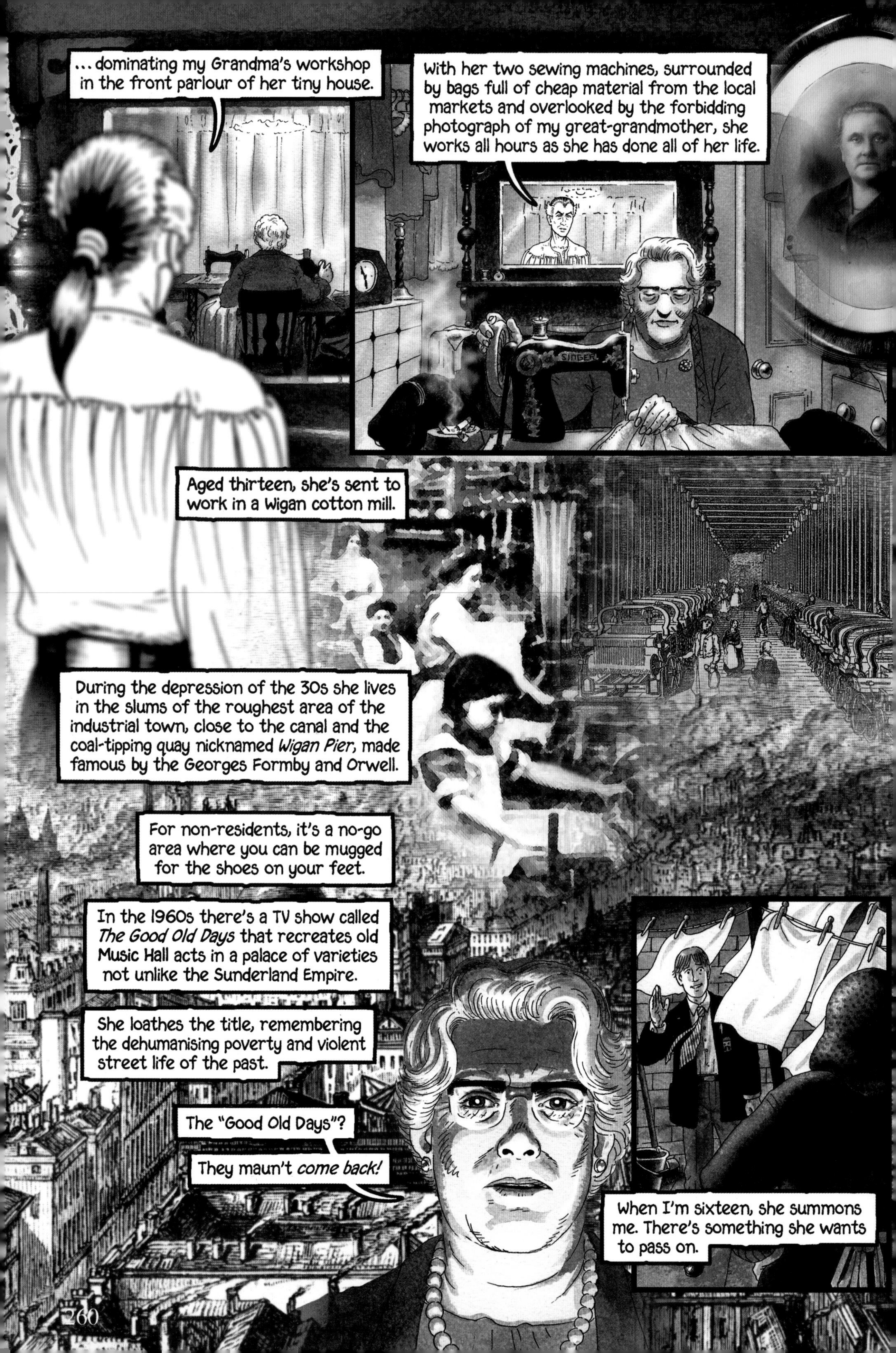
...dominating my Grandma's workshop in the front parlour of her tiny house.
With her two sewing machines, surrounded by bags full of cheap material from the local markets and overlooked by the forbidding photograph of my great-grandmother, she works all hours as she has done all of her life.
SINGER
Aged thirteen, she's sent to work in a Wigan cotton mill.
During the depression of the 30s she lives in the slums of the roughest area of the industrial town, close to the canal and the coal-tipping quay nicknamed *Wigan Pier*, made famous by the Georges Formby and Orwell.
For non-residents, it's a no-go area where you can be mugged for the shoes on your feet.
In the 1960s there's a TV show called *The Good Old Days* that recreates old Music Hall acts in a palace of varieties not unlike the Sunderland Empire.
She loathes the title, remembering the dehumanising poverty and violent street life of the past.
The "Good Old Days"?
They maun't *come back!*
When I'm sixteen, she summons me. There's something she wants to pass on.

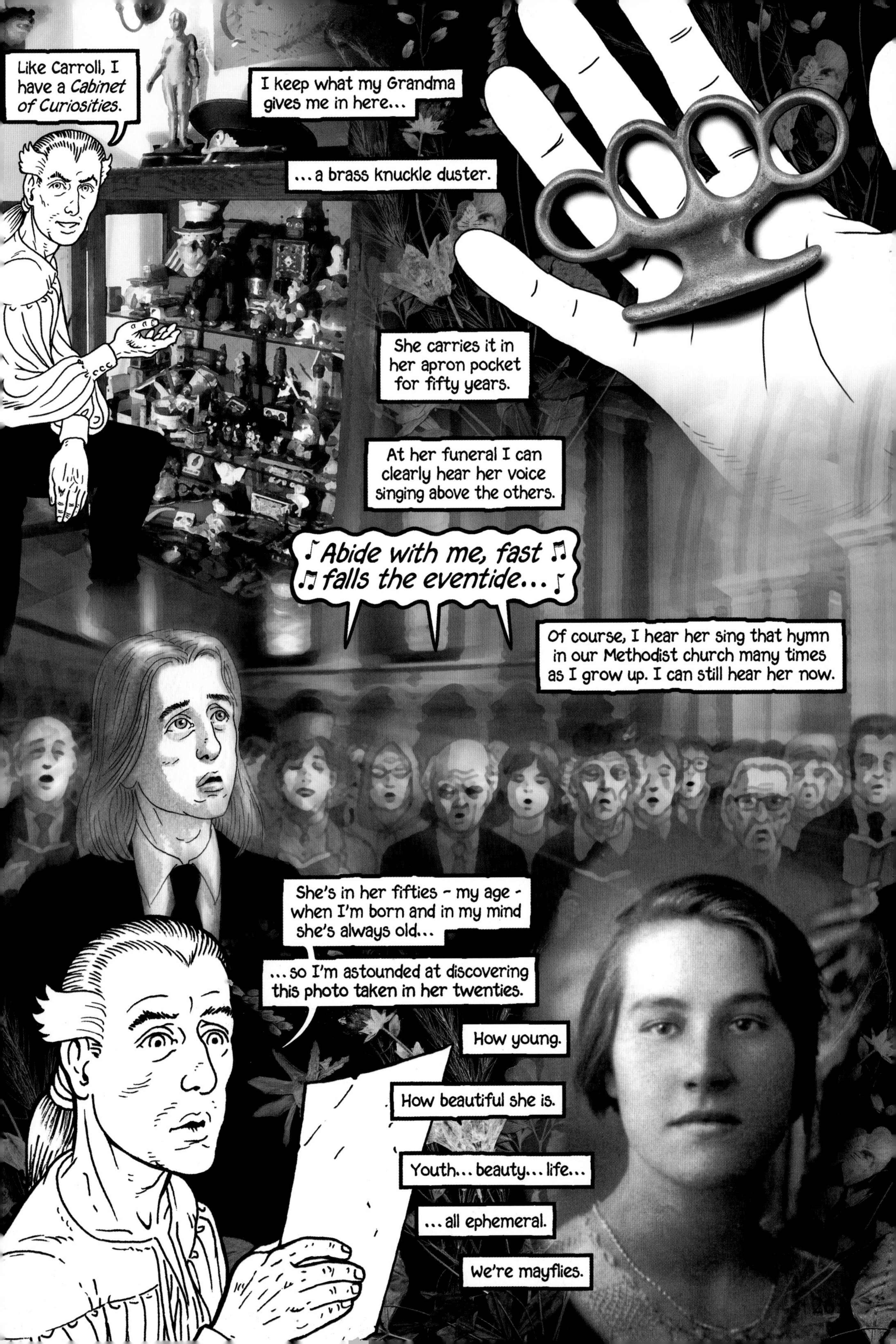

Like Carroll, I have a *Cabinet of Curiosities*.
I keep what my Grandma gives me in here...
...a brass knuckle duster.
She carries it in her apron pocket for fifty years.
At her funeral I can clearly hear her voice singing above the others.
♪ Abide with me, fast ♫ ♫ falls the eventide... ♪
Of course, I hear her sing that hymn in our Methodist church many times as I grow up. I can still hear her now.
She's in her fifties - my age - when I'm born and in my mind she's always old...
...so I'm astounded at discovering this photo taken in her twenties.
How young.
How beautiful she is.
Youth... beauty... life...
...all ephemeral.
We're mayflies.

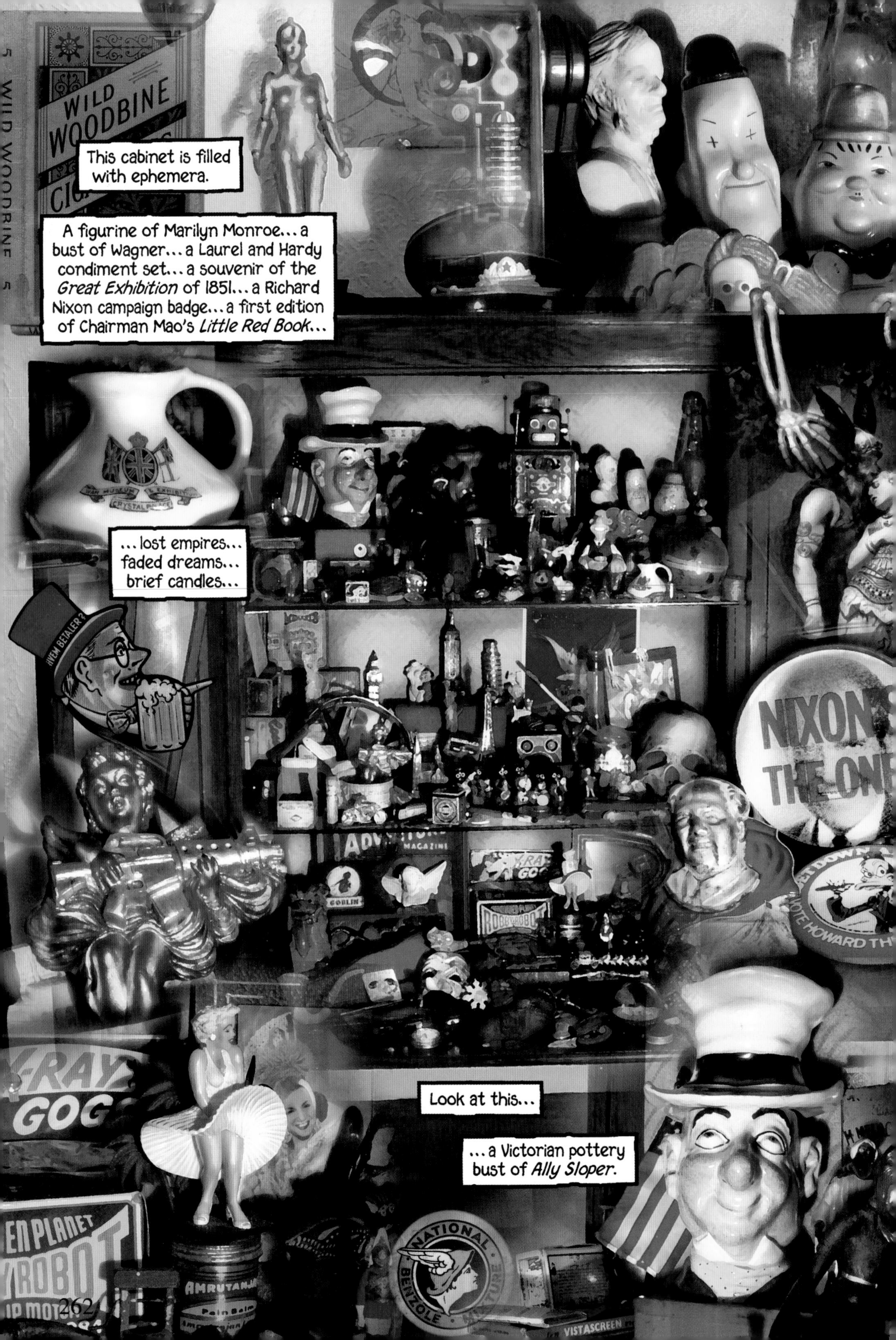
WILD WOODBINE
This cabinet is filled with ephemera.
A figurine of Marilyn Monroe... a bust of Wagner... a Laurel and Hardy condiment set... a souvenir of the *Great Exhibition* of 1851... a Richard Nixon campaign badge... a first edition of Chairman Mao's *Little Red Book*...
...lost empires... faded dreams... brief candles...
HVEM BETALER?
GOBLIN
MAGAZINE
Look at this...
...a Victorian pottery bust of *Ally Sloper*.
NATIONAL
BENZOLE
VISTASCREEN

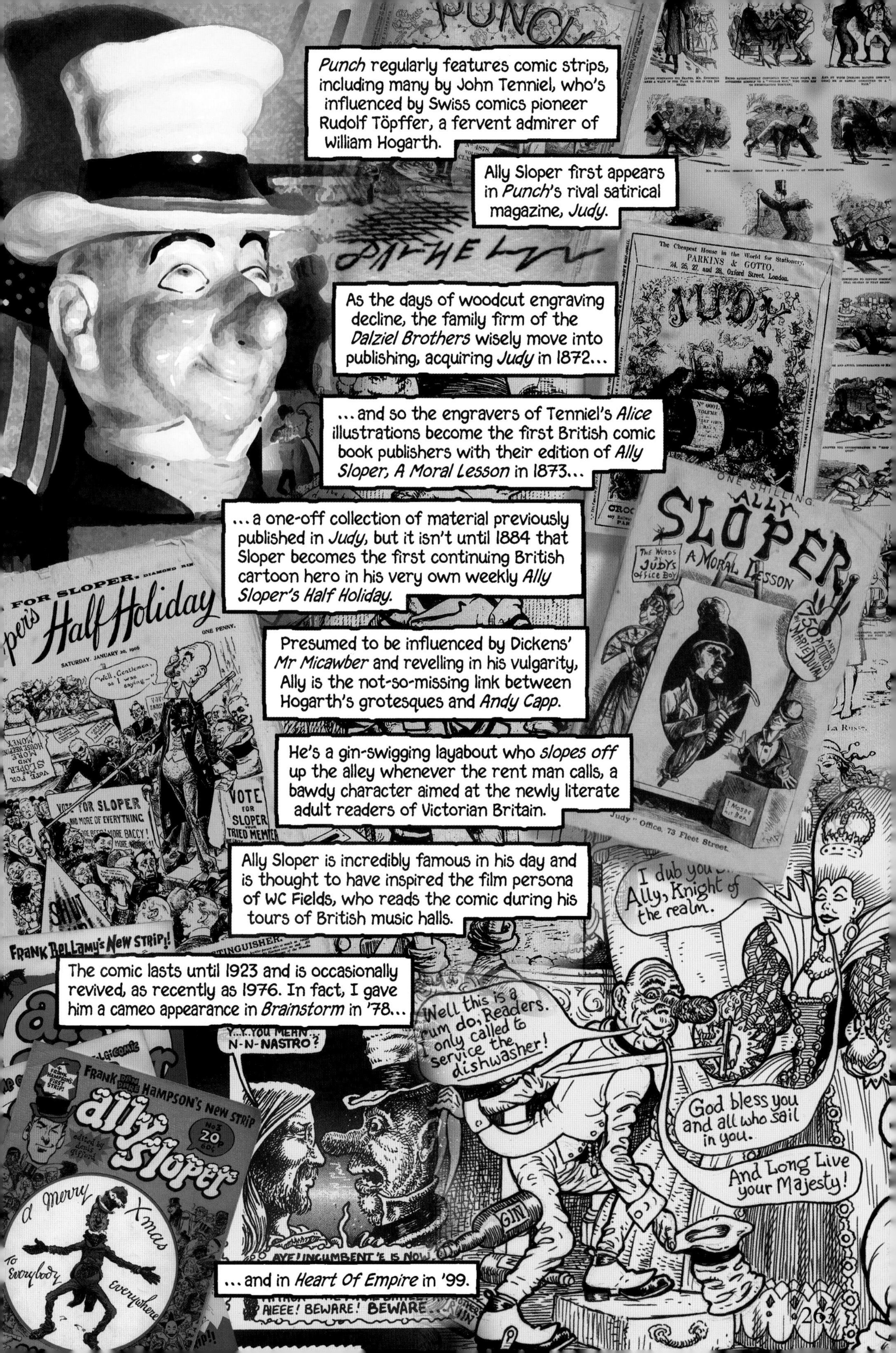
Punch regularly features comic strips, including many by John Tenniel, who's influenced by Swiss comics pioneer Rudolf Töpffer, a fervent admirer of William Hogarth.
Ally Sloper first appears in *Punch*'s rival satirical magazine, *Judy*.
The Cheapest House in the World for Stationery, PARKINS & GOTTO, 24, 25, 27, and 28, Oxford Street, London.
JUDY
As the days of woodcut engraving decline, the family firm of the *Dalziel Brothers* wisely move into publishing, acquiring *Judy* in 1872…
…and so the engravers of Tenniel's *Alice* illustrations become the first British comic book publishers with their edition of *Ally Sloper, A Moral Lesson* in 1873…
ONE SHILLING.
ALLY SLOPER
A MORAL LESSON
THE WORDS BY JUDY'S OFFICE BOY
…a one-off collection of material previously published in *Judy*, but it isn't until 1884 that Sloper becomes the first continuing British cartoon hero in his very own weekly *Ally Sloper's Half Holiday*.
FOR SLOPER.
Sloper's Half Holiday
ONE PENNY.
SATURDAY, JANUARY 20, 1906
"Well, Gentlemen, as I was saying—"
VOTE FOR SLOPER AND MORE OF EVERYTHING
VOTE FOR SLOPER YOUR TRIED MEMBER
Presumed to be influenced by Dickens' *Mr Micawber* and revelling in his vulgarity, Ally is the not-so-missing link between Hogarth's grotesques and *Andy Capp*.
He's a gin-swigging layabout who *slopes off* up the alley whenever the rent man calls, a bawdy character aimed at the newly literate adult readers of Victorian Britain.
"Judy" Office, 73 Fleet Street.
Ally Sloper is incredibly famous in his day and is thought to have inspired the film persona of WC Fields, who reads the comic during his tours of British music halls.
I dub you Sir Ally, Knight of the realm.
FRANK BELLAMY'S NEW STRIP!
The comic lasts until 1923 and is occasionally revived, as recently as 1976. In fact, I gave him a cameo appearance in *Brainstorm* in '78…
Y-Y-YOU MEAN… N-N-NASTRO?
Well this is a rum do, Readers. I only called to service the dishwasher!
FRANK HAMPSON'S NEW STRIP
ally sloper
edited by denis gifford
No 3 20p
A Merry Xmas To Everybody Everywhere
God bless you and all who sail in you.
And Long Live your Majesty!
GIN
AYE! INCUMBENT 'E IS NOW.
…and in *Heart Of Empire* in '99.
AIEEE! BEWARE! BEWARE

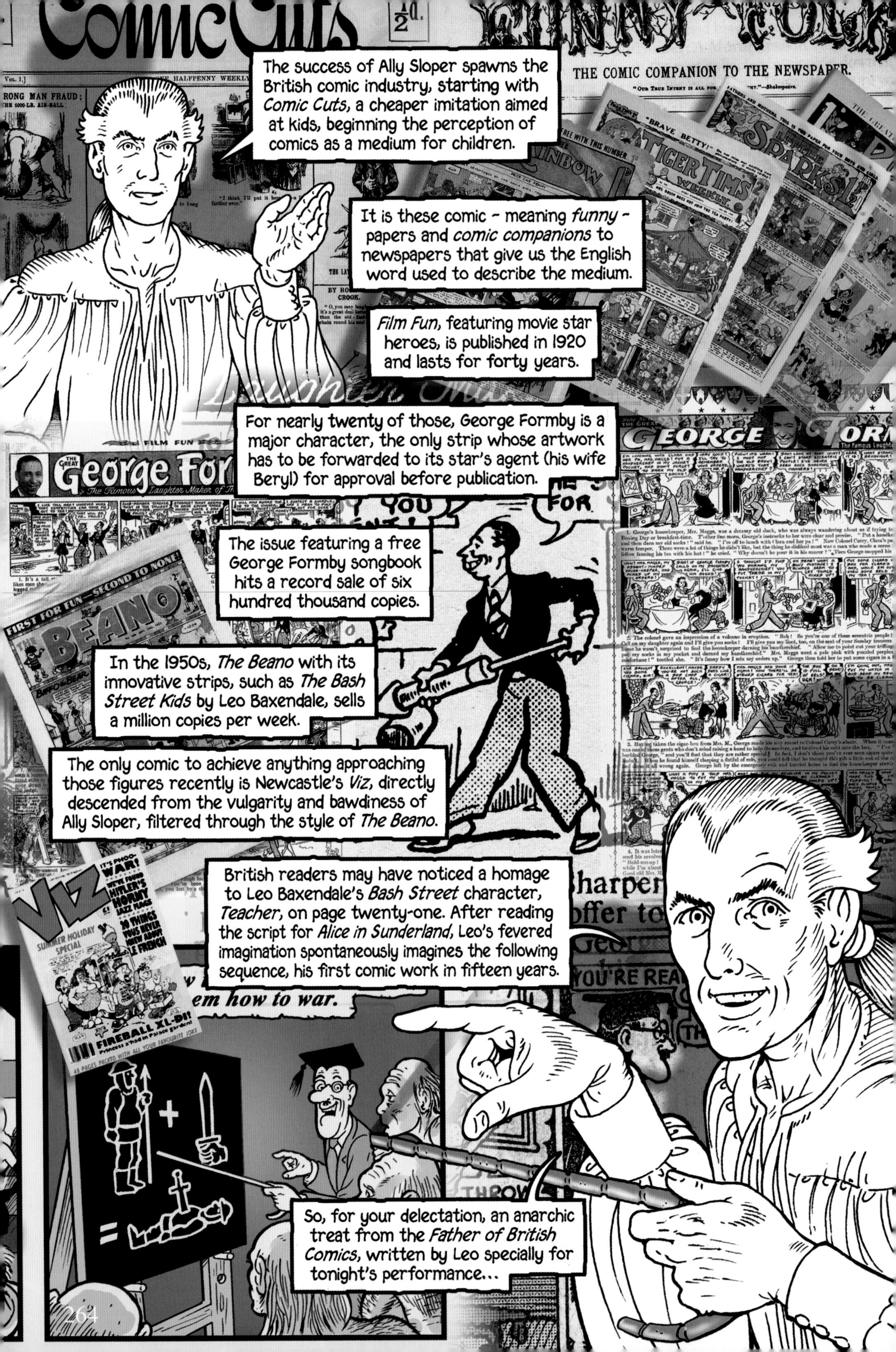
The success of Ally Sloper spawns the British comic industry, starting with *Comic Cuts*, a cheaper imitation aimed at kids, beginning the perception of comics as a medium for children.
It is these comic - meaning *funny* - papers and *comic companions* to newspapers that give us the English word used to describe the medium.
Film Fun, featuring movie star heroes, is published in 1920 and lasts for forty years.
For nearly twenty of those, George Formby is a major character, the only strip whose artwork has to be forwarded to its star's agent (his wife Beryl) for approval before publication.
The issue featuring a free George Formby songbook hits a record sale of six hundred thousand copies.
In the 1950s, *The Beano* with its innovative strips, such as *The Bash Street Kids* by Leo Baxendale, sells a million copies per week.
The only comic to achieve anything approaching those figures recently is Newcastle's *Viz*, directly descended from the vulgarity and bawdiness of Ally Sloper, filtered through the style of *The Beano*.
British readers may have noticed a homage to Leo Baxendale's *Bash Street* character, *Teacher*, on page twenty-one. After reading the script for *Alice in Sunderland*, Leo's fevered imagination spontaneously imagines the following sequence, his first comic work in fifteen years.
So, for your delectation, an anarchic treat from the *Father of British Comics*, written by Leo specially for tonight's performance...

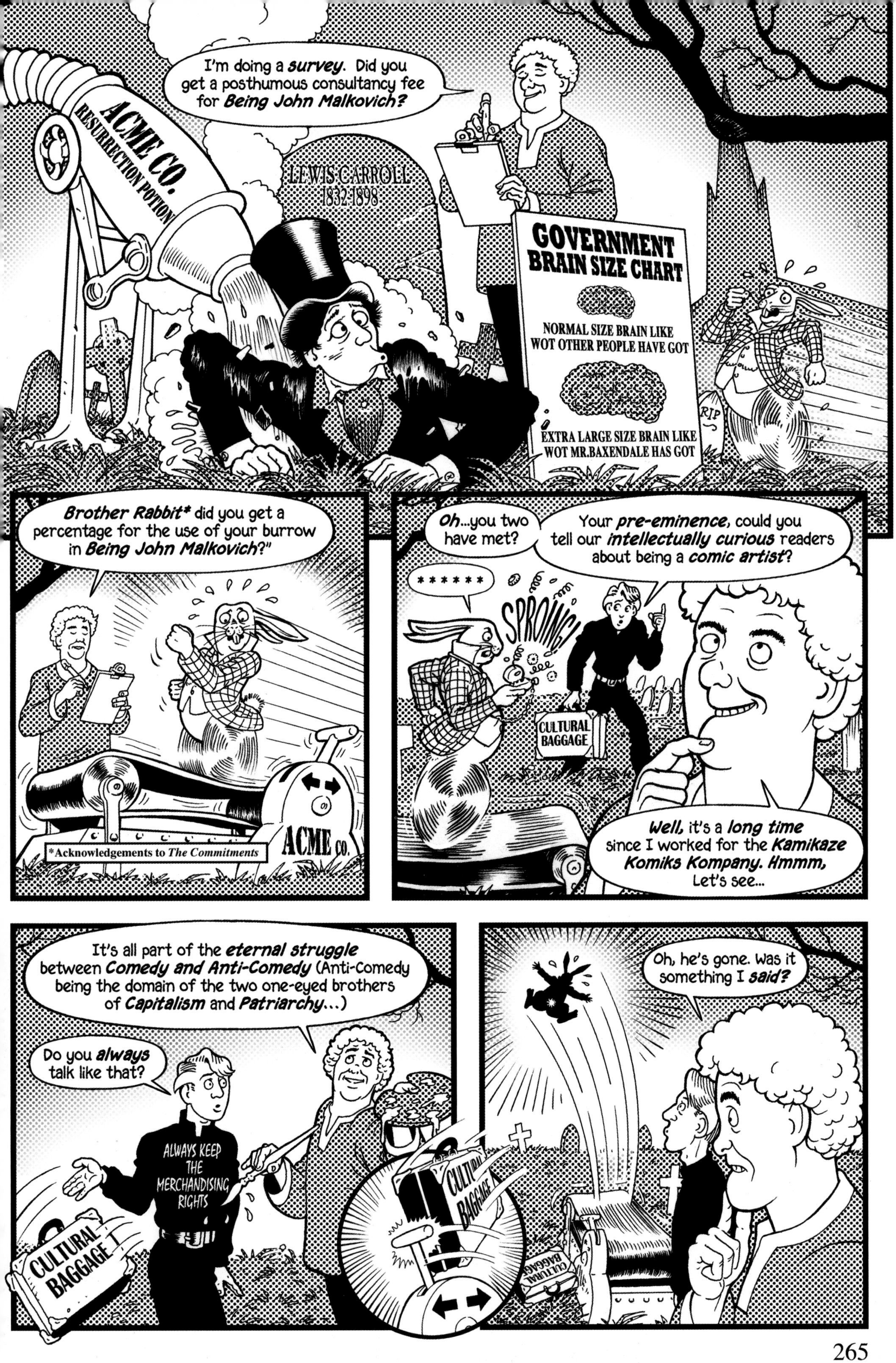
I'm doing a *survey*. Did you get a posthumous consultancy fee for *Being John Malkovich?*
ACME CO.
RESURRECTION POTION
LEWIS CARROLL
1832-1898
GOVERNMENT BRAIN SIZE CHART
NORMAL SIZE BRAIN LIKE WOT OTHER PEOPLE HAVE GOT
EXTRA LARGE SIZE BRAIN LIKE WOT MR.BAXENDALE HAS GOT
RIP
*Brother Rabbit** did you get a percentage for the use of your burrow in *Being John Malkovich*?"
*Acknowledgements to *The Commitments*
ACME CO.
Oh...you two have met?
Your *pre-eminence*, could you tell our *intellectually curious* readers about being a *comic artist*?
******
SPRONG!
CULTURAL BAGGAGE
Well, it's a *long time* since I worked for the *Kamikaze Komiks Kompany. Hmmm,* Let's see...
It's all part of the *eternal struggle* between *Comedy and Anti-Comedy* (Anti-Comedy being the domain of the two one-eyed brothers of *Capitalism* and *Patriarchy*...)
Do you *always* talk like that?
ALWAYS KEEP THE MERCHANDISING RIGHTS
CULTURAL BAGGAGE
CULTURAL BAGGAGE
Oh, he's gone. Was it something I *said?*
CULTURAL BAGGAGE

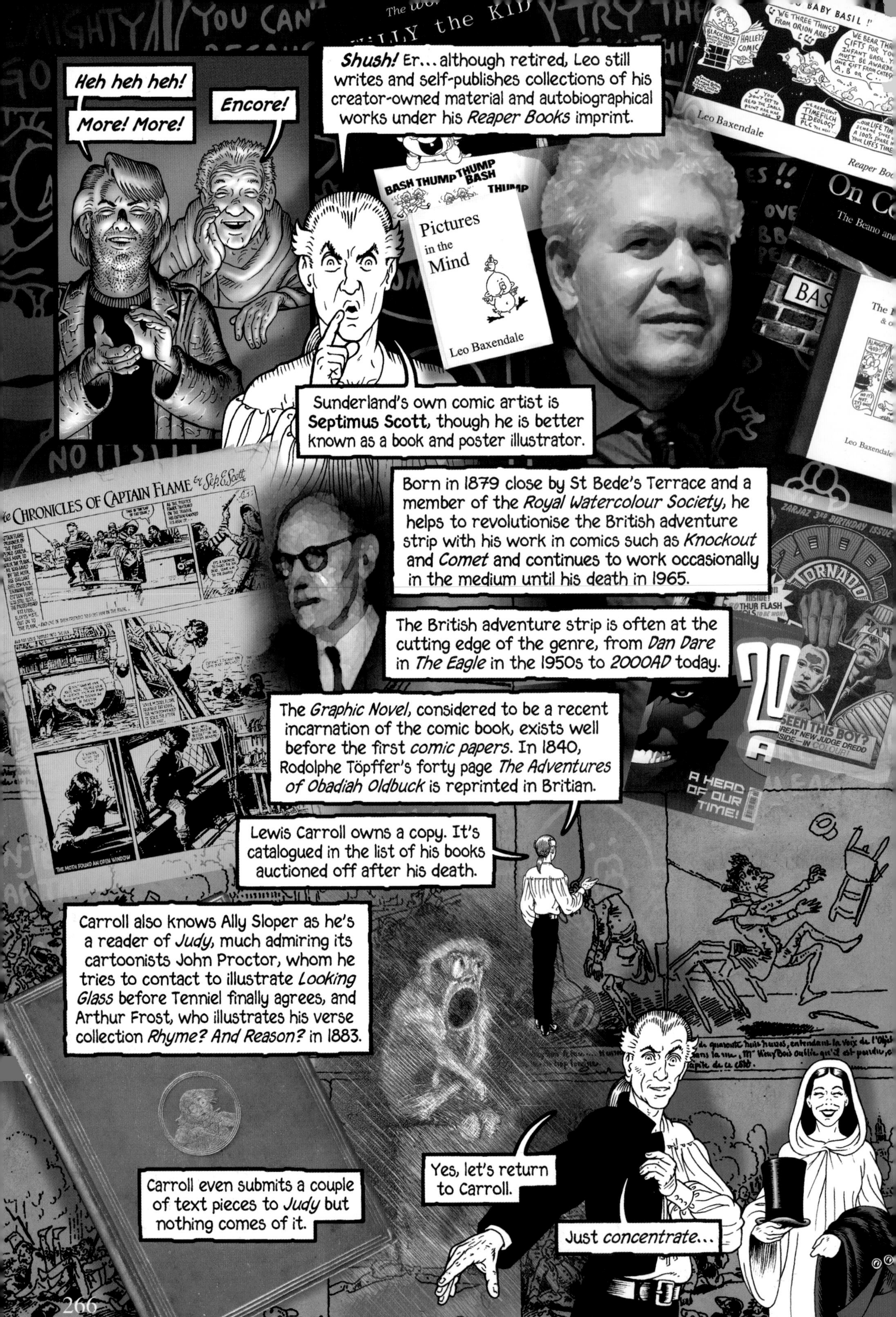

Heh heh heh!
More! More!
Encore!
Shush! Er... although retired, Leo still writes and self-publishes collections of his creator-owned material and autobiographical works under his Reaper Books imprint.
BASH THUMP THUMP BASH THUMP
Pictures in the Mind
Leo Baxendale
Leo Baxendale
Reaper Books
On C
The Beano and
Leo Baxendale
Sunderland's own comic artist is Septimus Scott, though he is better known as a book and poster illustrator.
The Chronicles of Captain Flame by Sep. E. Scott
Born in 1879 close by St Bede's Terrace and a member of the Royal Watercolour Society, he helps to revolutionise the British adventure strip with his work in comics such as Knockout and Comet and continues to work occasionally in the medium until his death in 1965.
The British adventure strip is often at the cutting edge of the genre, from Dan Dare in The Eagle in the 1950s to 2000AD today.
SEEN THIS BOY? GREAT NEW JUDGE DREDD INSIDE—IN COLOUR!
A HEAD OF OUR TIME!
The Graphic Novel, considered to be a recent incarnation of the comic book, exists well before the first comic papers. In 1840, Rodolphe Töpffer's forty page The Adventures of Obadiah Oldbuck is reprinted in Britian.
Lewis Carroll owns a copy. It's catalogued in the list of his books auctioned off after his death.
Carroll also knows Ally Sloper as he's a reader of Judy, much admiring its cartoonists John Proctor, whom he tries to contact to illustrate Looking Glass before Tenniel finally agrees, and Arthur Frost, who illustrates his verse collection Rhyme? And Reason? in 1883.
Carroll even submits a couple of text pieces to Judy but nothing comes of it.
Yes, let's return to Carroll.
Just concentrate...

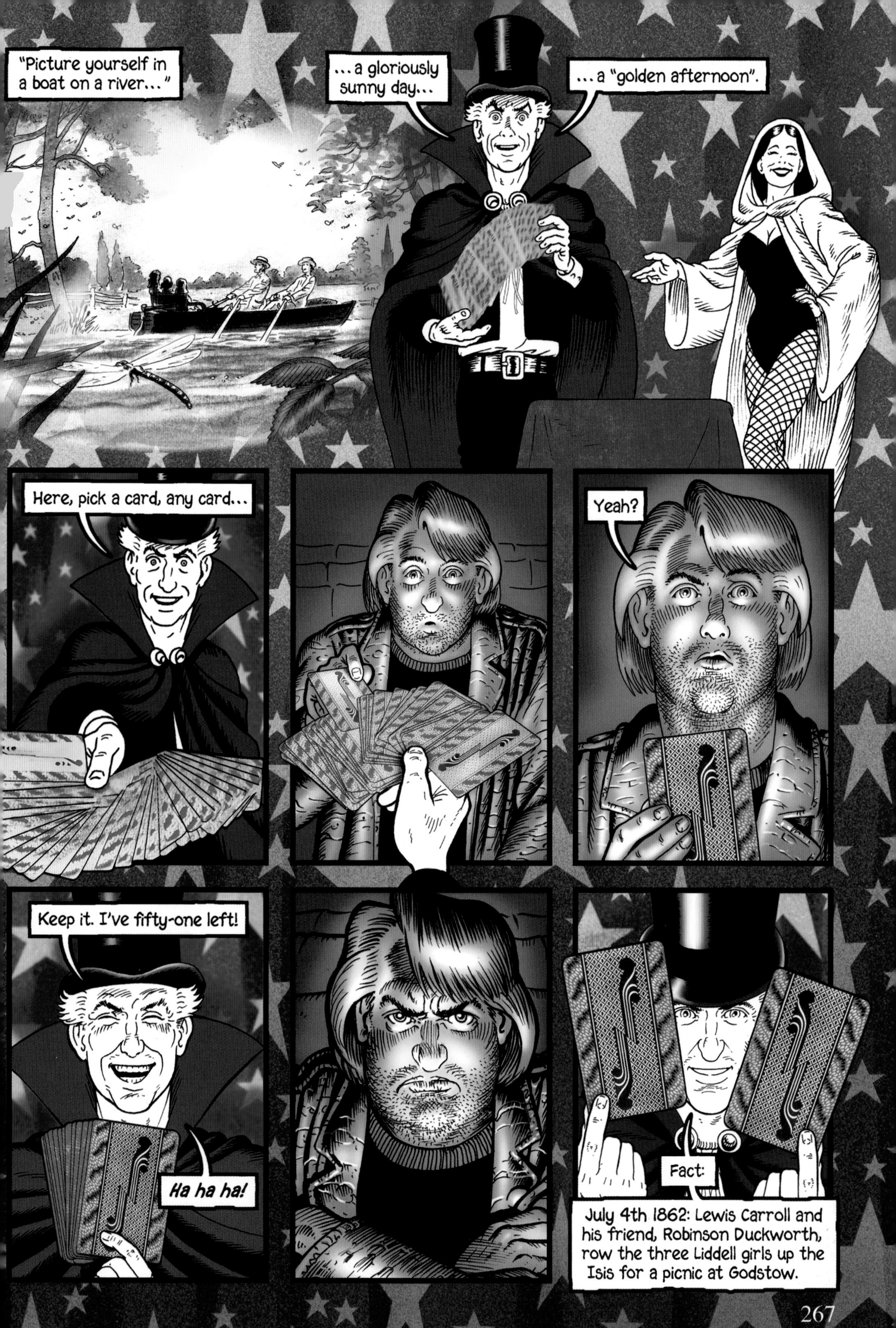
"Picture yourself in a boat on a river..."
...a gloriously sunny day...
...a "golden afternoon".
Here, pick a card, any card...
Yeah?
Keep it. I've fifty-one left!
Ha ha ha!
Fact:
July 4th 1862: Lewis Carroll and his friend, Robinson Duckworth, row the three Liddell girls up the Isis for a picnic at Godstow.

The girls demand a story. Carroll spontaneously improvises the tale of *Alice in Wonderland*. A cherished Oxford myth...

... started by Carroll himself in the opening poem of *Wonderland*, presumably to please and flatter Alice, his "favourite child-friend".

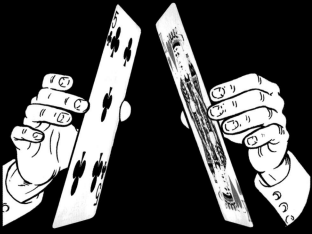

Seven years later, in its introductory poem, he describes *Looking Glass* as "the love-gift of a fairy tale". Long after his supposed banishment by Mrs Liddell, it seems that he still misses the company of Alice.

"I have not seen thy sunny face, nor heard thy silver laughter."

Did he propose marriage? In 1872, now aged twenty, she still seems to be the object of his affections, for he writes in the epilogue poem...

"Still she haunts me phantomwise, Alice moving under skies never seen by waking eyes..."

When we try to look at Carroll, we peer back in time through layers of myth.

But he's speaking here of the *fictional Alice*, not *Alice Liddell!*

In 1945, one biographer, Florence Becker Lennon, suggests the "banishment" and the marriage proposal. Now it is part of Carroll mythology and taken by many as fact.

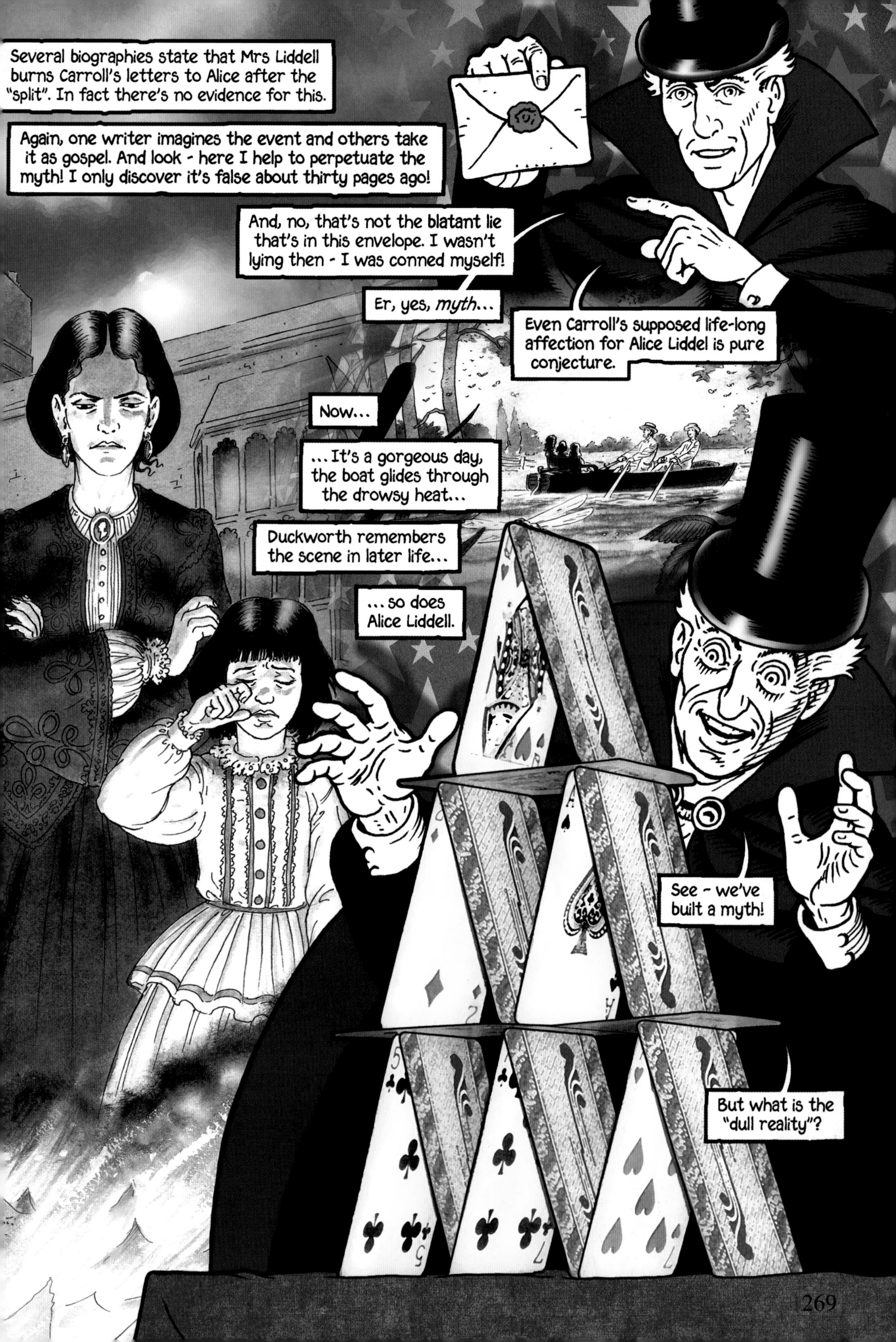
Several biographies state that Mrs Liddell burns Carroll's letters to Alice after the "split". In fact there's no evidence for this.
Again, one writer imagines the event and others take it as gospel. And look - here I help to perpetuate the myth! I only discover it's false about thirty pages ago!
And, no, that's not the blatant lie that's in this envelope. I wasn't lying then - I was conned myself!
Er, yes, *myth*...
Even Carroll's supposed life-long affection for Alice Liddel is pure conjecture.
Now...
...It's a gorgeous day, the boat glides through the drowsy heat...
Duckworth remembers the scene in later life...
...so does Alice Liddell.
See - we've built a myth!
But what is the "dull reality"?

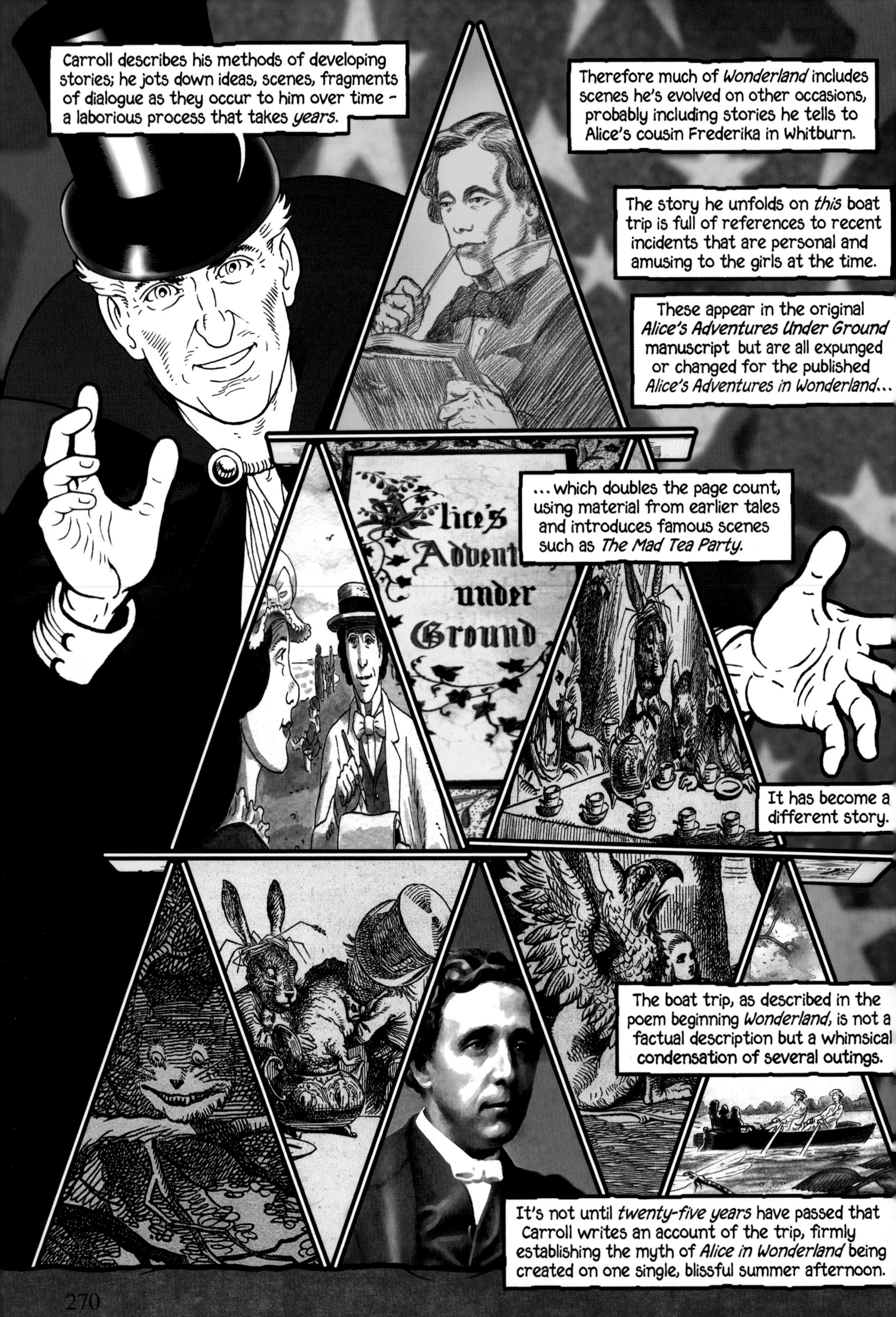

Carroll describes his methods of developing stories; he jots down ideas, scenes, fragments of dialogue as they occur to him over time - a laborious process that takes *years*.
Therefore much of *Wonderland* includes scenes he's evolved on other occasions, probably including stories he tells to Alice's cousin Frederika in Whitburn.
The story he unfolds on *this* boat trip is full of references to recent incidents that are personal and amusing to the girls at the time.
These appear in the original *Alice's Adventures Under Ground* manuscript but are all expunged or changed for the published *Alice's Adventures in Wonderland*...
Alice's Adventures under Ground
...which doubles the page count, using material from earlier tales and introduces famous scenes such as *The Mad Tea Party.*
It has become a different story.
The boat trip, as described in the poem beginning *Wonderland,* is not a factual description but a whimsical condensation of several outings.
It's not until *twenty-five years* have passed that Carroll writes an account of the trip, firmly establishing the myth of *Alice in Wonderland* being created on one single, blissful summer afternoon.

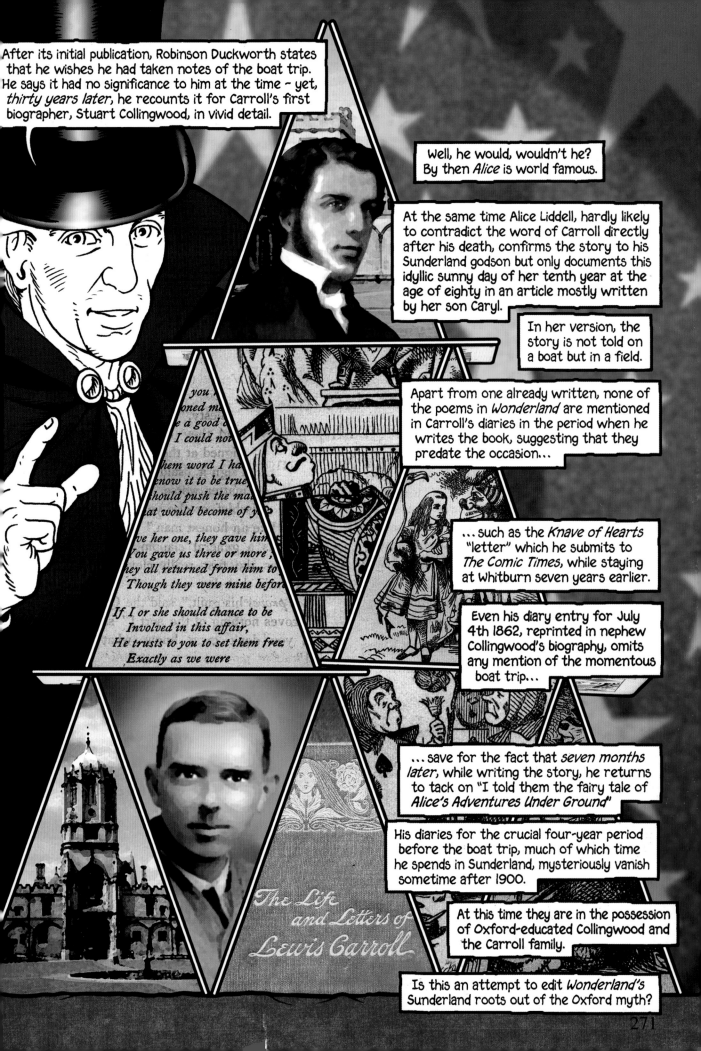

After its initial publication, Robinson Duckworth states that he wishes he had taken notes of the boat trip. He says it had no significance to him at the time ~ yet, *thirty years later*, he recounts it for Carroll's first biographer, Stuart Collingwood, in vivid detail.

Well, he would, wouldn't he? By then *Alice* is world famous.

At the same time Alice Liddell, hardly likely to contradict the word of Carroll directly after his death, confirms the story to his Sunderland godson but only documents this idyllic sunny day of her tenth year at the age of eighty in an article mostly written by her son Caryl.

In her version, the story is not told on a boat but in a field.

Apart from one already written, none of the poems in *Wonderland* are mentioned in Carroll's diaries in the period when he writes the book, suggesting that they predate the occasion...

... such as the *Knave of Hearts* "letter" which he submits to *The Comic Times*, while staying at Whitburn seven years earlier.

Even his diary entry for July 4th 1862, reprinted in nephew Collingwood's biography, omits any mention of the momentous boat trip...

... save for the fact that *seven months later*, while writing the story, he returns to tack on "I told them the fairy tale of *Alice's Adventures Under Ground*"

His diaries for the crucial four-year period before the boat trip, much of which time he spends in Sunderland, mysteriously vanish sometime after 1900.

At this time they are in the possession of Oxford-educated Collingwood and the Carroll family.

Is this an attempt to edit *Wonderland*'s Sunderland roots out of the Oxford myth?

*you ...
...oned m...
...e a good ...
I could not ...

...hem word I ha...
...now it to be true...
...hould push the ma...
...at would become of y...

...ve her one, they gave him...
You gave us three or more ...
...hey all returned from him to ...
Though they were mine befor...

If I or she should chance to be
Involved in this affair,
He trusts to you to set them free
Exactly as we were*

The Life and Letters of Lewis Carroll

271

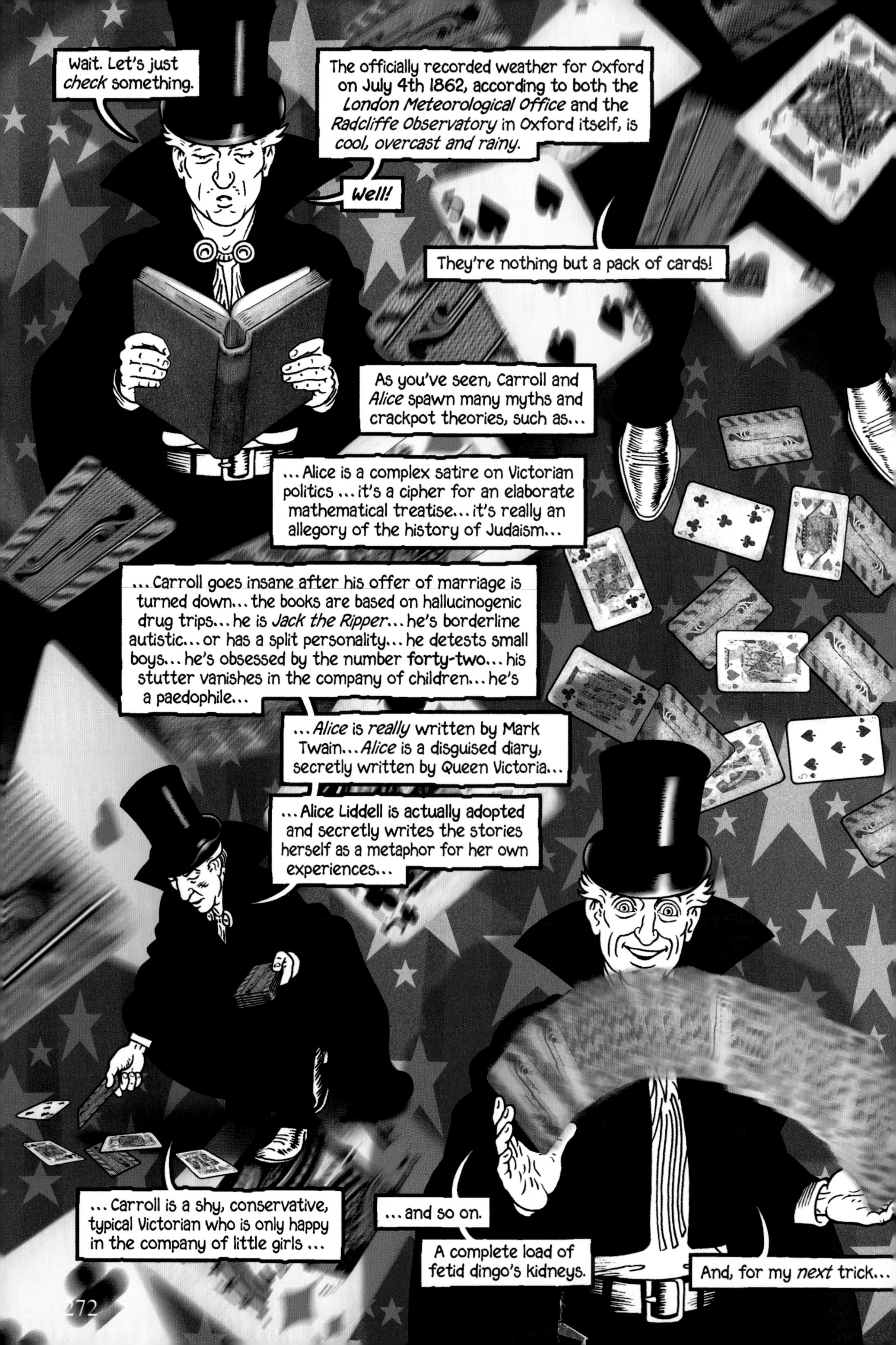
Wait. Let's just *check* something.
The officially recorded weather for Oxford on July 4th 1862, according to both the *London Meteorological Office* and the *Radcliffe Observatory* in Oxford itself, is *cool, overcast and rainy.*
Well!
They're nothing but a pack of cards!
As you've seen, Carroll and *Alice* spawn many myths and crackpot theories, such as...
...Alice is a complex satire on Victorian politics ... it's a cipher for an elaborate mathematical treatise... it's really an allegory of the history of Judaism...
...Carroll goes insane after his offer of marriage is turned down... the books are based on hallucinogenic drug trips... he is *Jack the Ripper*... he's borderline autistic... or has a split personality... he detests small boys... he's obsessed by the number forty-two... his stutter vanishes in the company of children... he's a paedophile...
...*Alice* is *really* written by Mark Twain... *Alice* is a disguised diary, secretly written by Queen Victoria...
...Alice Liddell is actually adopted and secretly writes the stories herself as a metaphor for her own experiences...
...Carroll is a shy, conservative, typical Victorian who is only happy in the company of little girls ...
...and so on.
A complete load of fetid dingo's kidneys.
And, for my *next* trick...

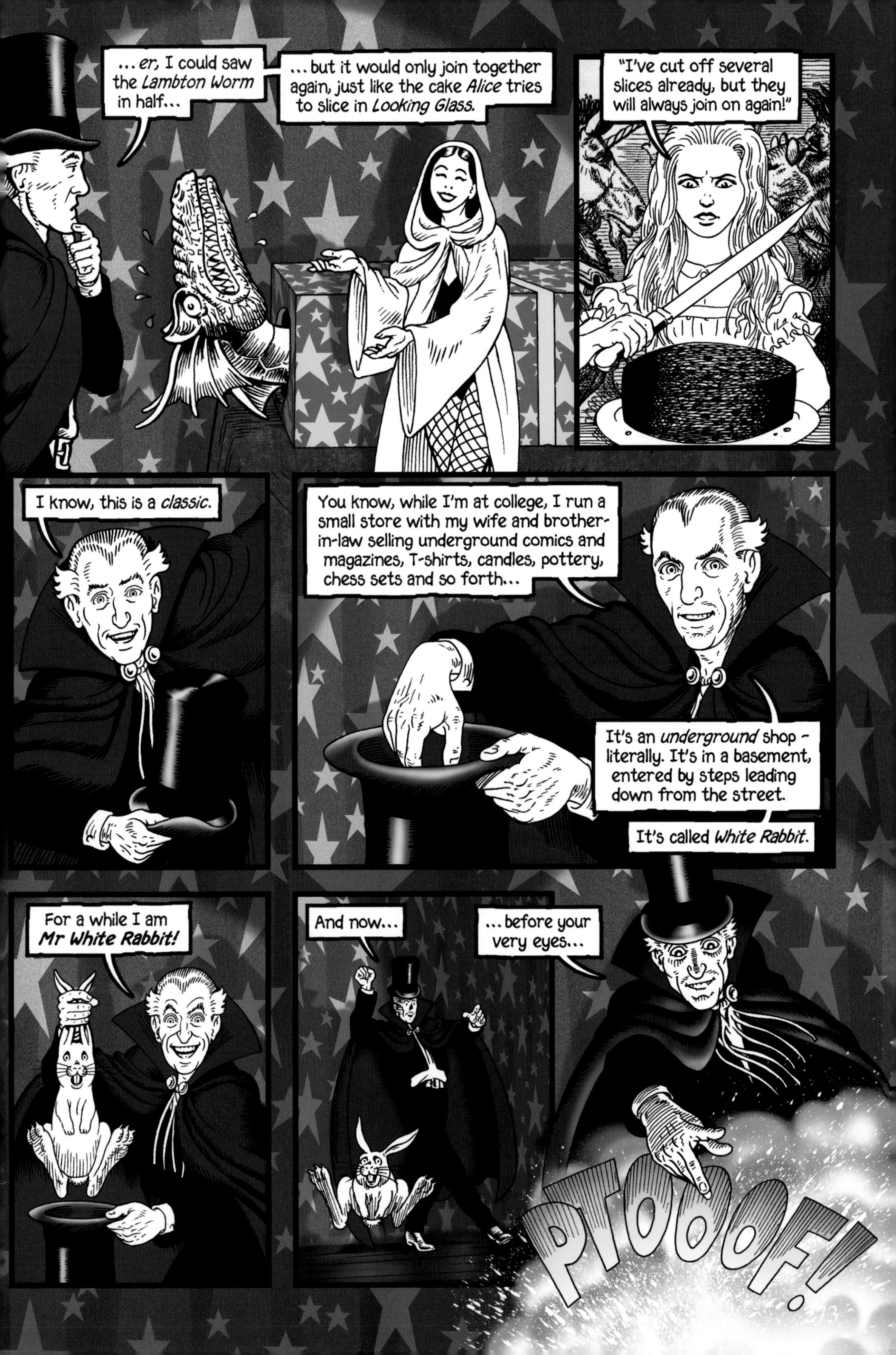

...*er*, I could saw the *Lambton Worm* in half...
...but it would only join together again, just like the cake *Alice* tries to slice in *Looking Glass*.
"I've cut off several slices already, but they will always join on again!"
I know, this is a *classic*.
You know, while I'm at college, I run a small store with my wife and brother-in-law selling underground comics and magazines, T-shirts, candles, pottery, chess sets and so forth...
It's an *underground* shop – literally. It's in a basement, entered by steps leading down from the street.
It's called *White Rabbit*.
For a while I am ***Mr White Rabbit!***
And now...
...before your very eyes...
PTOOOF!

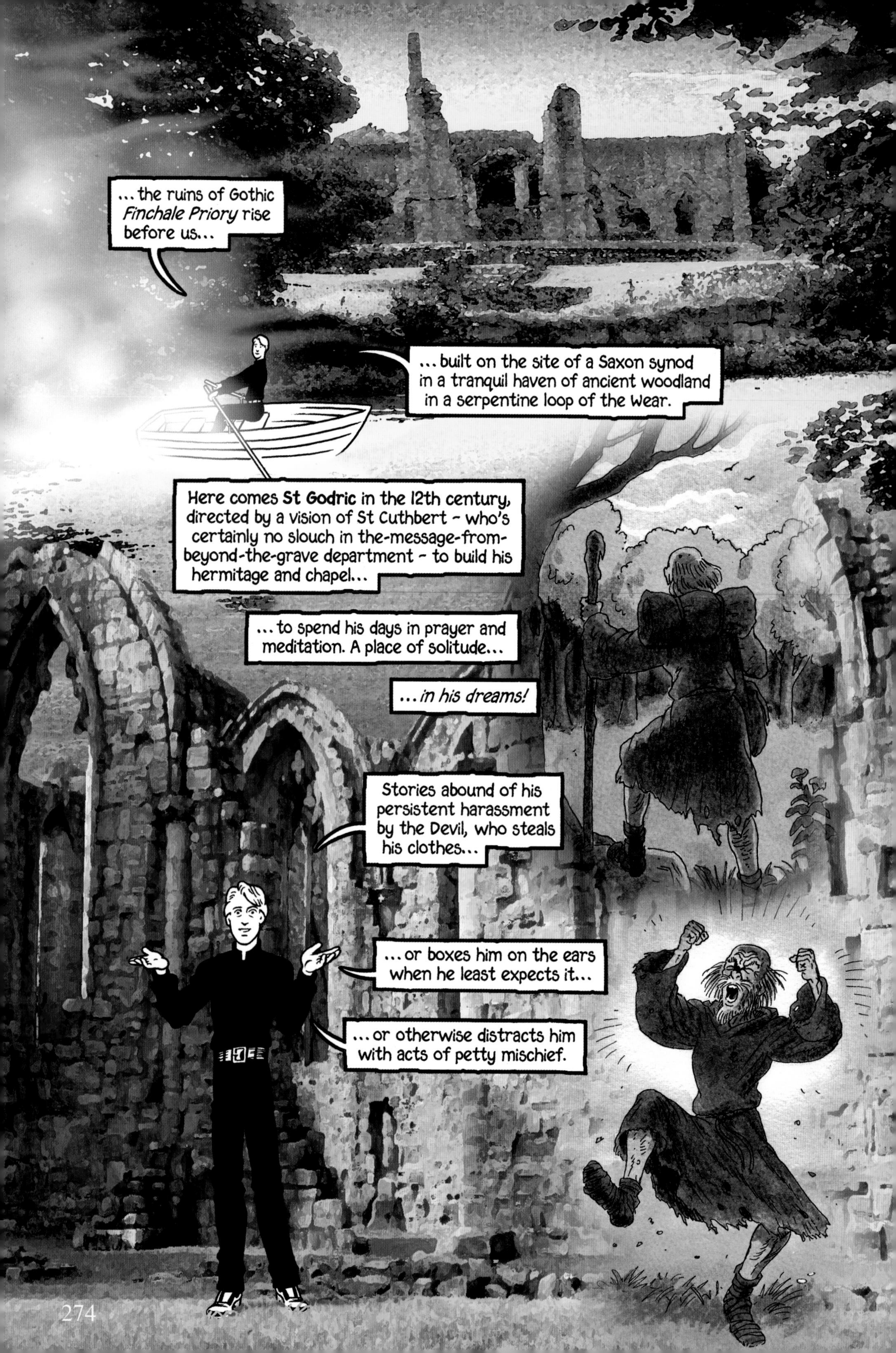
...the ruins of Gothic *Finchale Priory* rise before us...
...built on the site of a Saxon synod in a tranquil haven of ancient woodland in a serpentine loop of the Wear.
Here comes **St Godric** in the 12th century, directed by a vision of St Cuthbert - who's certainly no slouch in the-message-from-beyond-the-grave department - to build his hermitage and chapel...
...to spend his days in prayer and meditation. A place of solitude...
...*in his dreams!*
Stories abound of his persistent harassment by the Devil, who steals his clothes...
...or boxes him on the ears when he least expects it...
...or otherwise distracts him with acts of petty mischief.

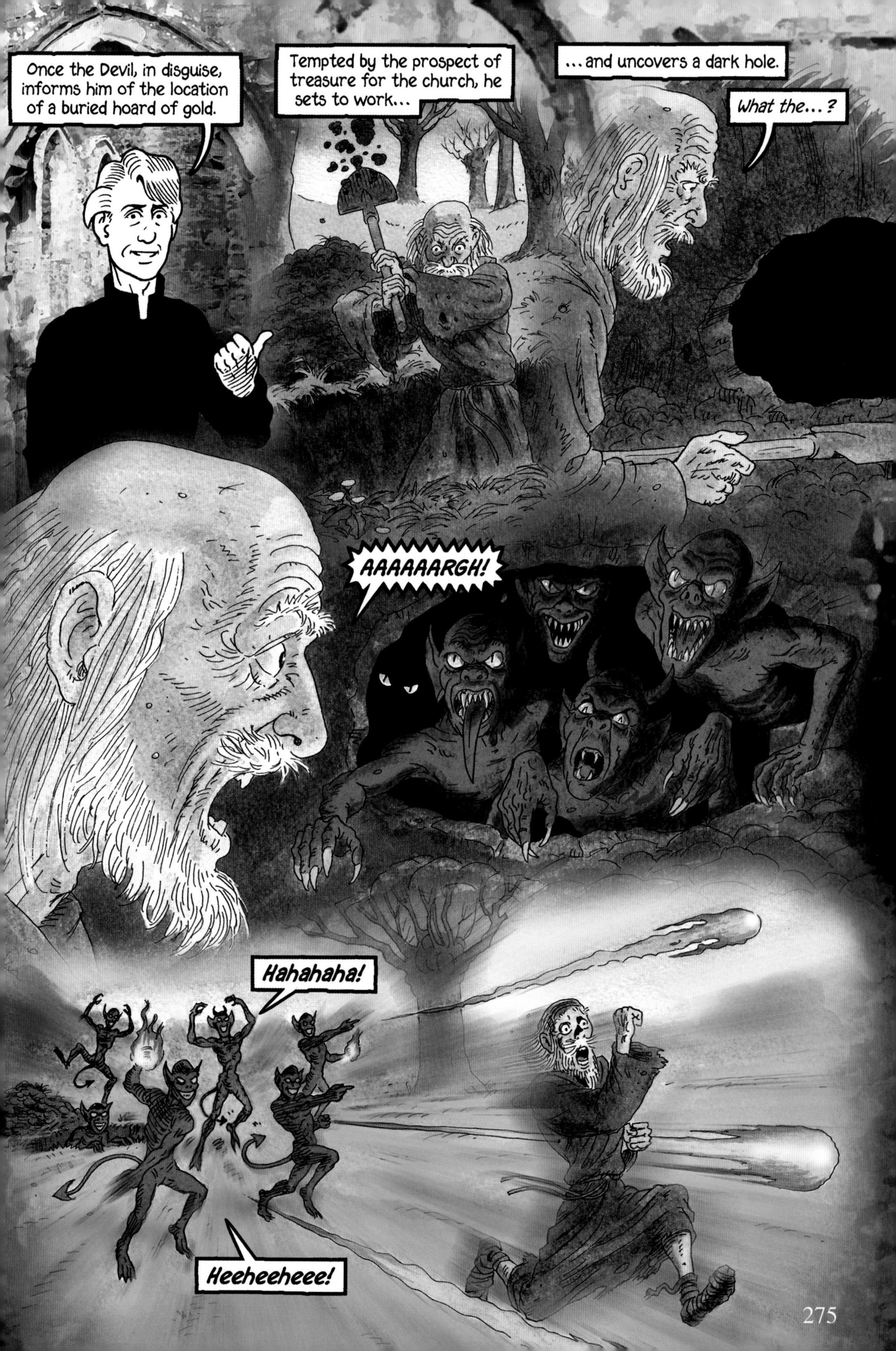
Once the Devil, in disguise, informs him of the location of a buried hoard of gold.
Tempted by the prospect of treasure for the church, he sets to work...
...and uncovers a dark hole.
What the...?
AAAAAARGH!
Hahahaha!
Heeheeheee!

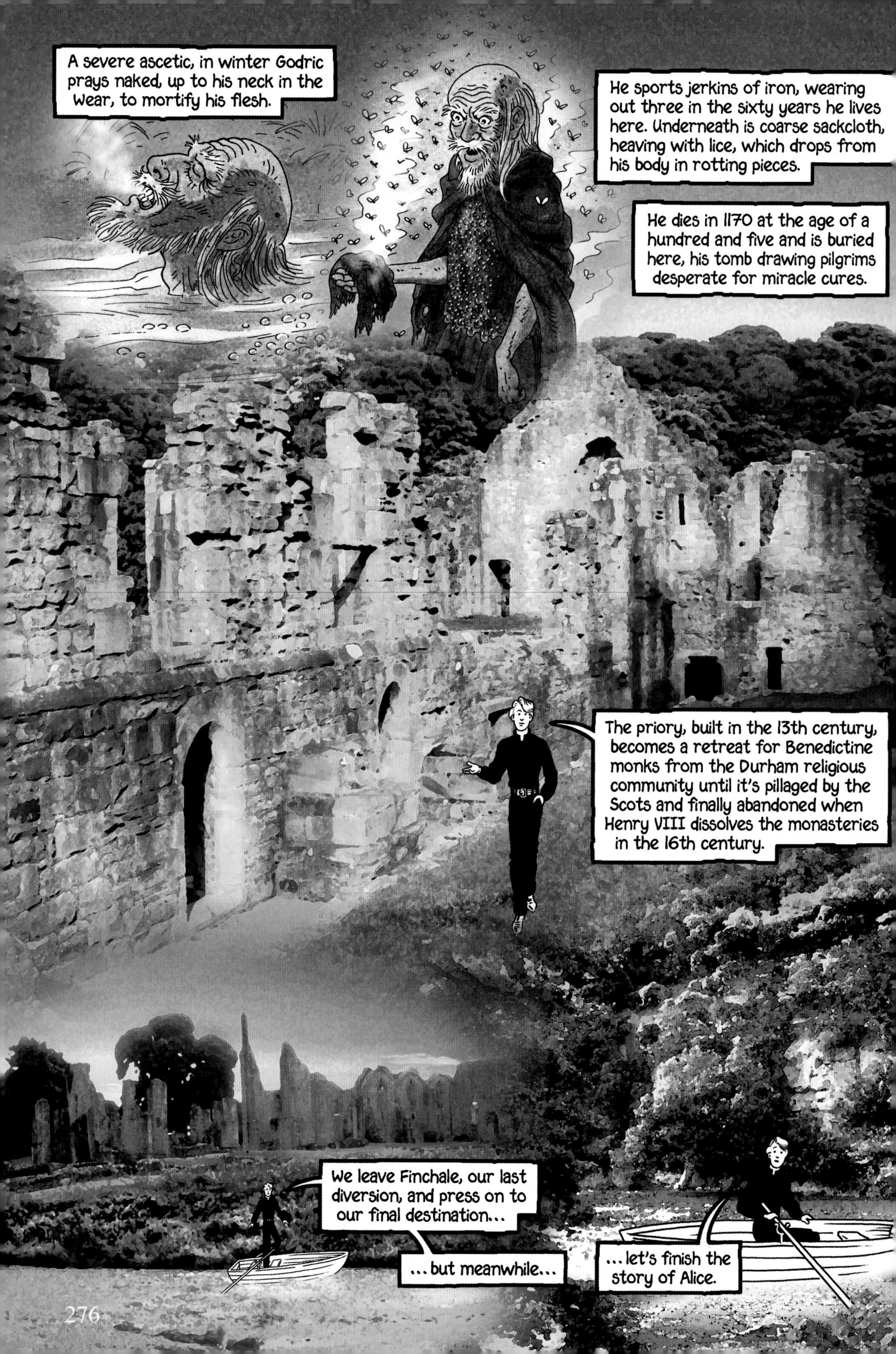

A severe ascetic, in winter Godric prays naked, up to his neck in the Wear, to mortify his flesh.
He sports jerkins of iron, wearing out three in the sixty years he lives here. Underneath is coarse sackcloth, heaving with lice, which drops from his body in rotting pieces.
He dies in 1170 at the age of a hundred and five and is buried here, his tomb drawing pilgrims desperate for miracle cures.
The priory, built in the 13th century, becomes a retreat for Benedictine monks from the Durham religious community until it's pillaged by the Scots and finally abandoned when Henry VIII dissolves the monasteries in the 16th century.
We leave Finchale, our last diversion, and press on to our final destination...
...but meanwhile...
...let's finish the story of Alice.

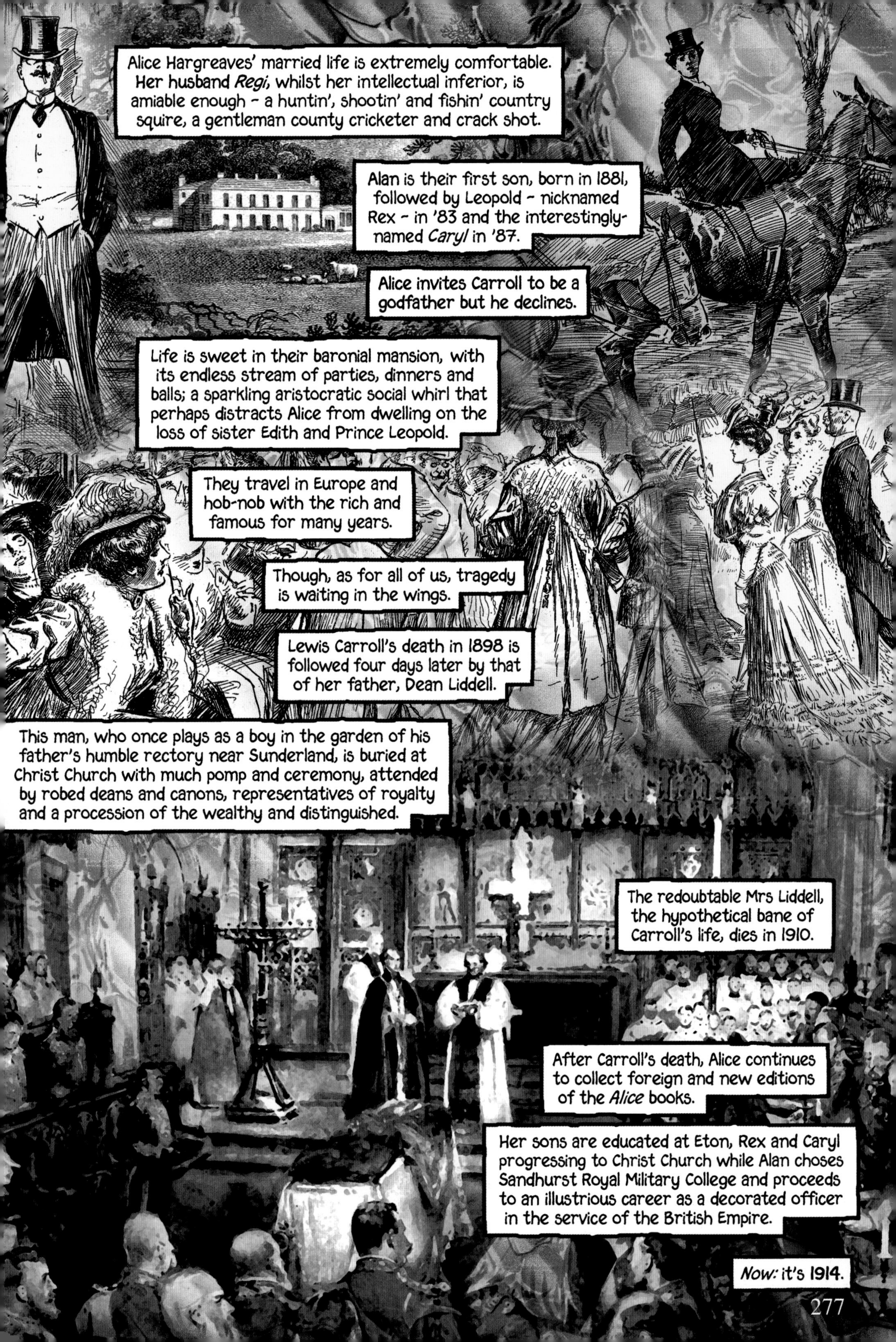
Alice Hargreaves' married life is extremely comfortable. Her husband *Regi*, whilst her intellectual inferior, is amiable enough – a huntin', shootin' and fishin' country squire, a gentleman county cricketer and crack shot.
Alan is their first son, born in 1881, followed by Leopold – nicknamed Rex – in '83 and the interestingly-named *Caryl* in '87.
Alice invites Carroll to be a godfather but he declines.
Life is sweet in their baronial mansion, with its endless stream of parties, dinners and balls; a sparkling aristocratic social whirl that perhaps distracts Alice from dwelling on the loss of sister Edith and Prince Leopold.
They travel in Europe and hob-nob with the rich and famous for many years.
Though, as for all of us, tragedy is waiting in the wings.
Lewis Carroll's death in 1898 is followed four days later by that of her father, Dean Liddell.
This man, who once plays as a boy in the garden of his father's humble rectory near Sunderland, is buried at Christ Church with much pomp and ceremony, attended by robed deans and canons, representatives of royalty and a procession of the wealthy and distinguished.
The redoubtable Mrs Liddell, the hypothetical bane of Carroll's life, dies in 1910.
After Carroll's death, Alice continues to collect foreign and new editions of the *Alice* books.
Her sons are educated at Eton, Rex and Caryl progressing to Christ Church while Alan choses Sandhurst Royal Military College and proceeds to an illustrious career as a decorated officer in the service of the British Empire.
Now: it's **1914**.

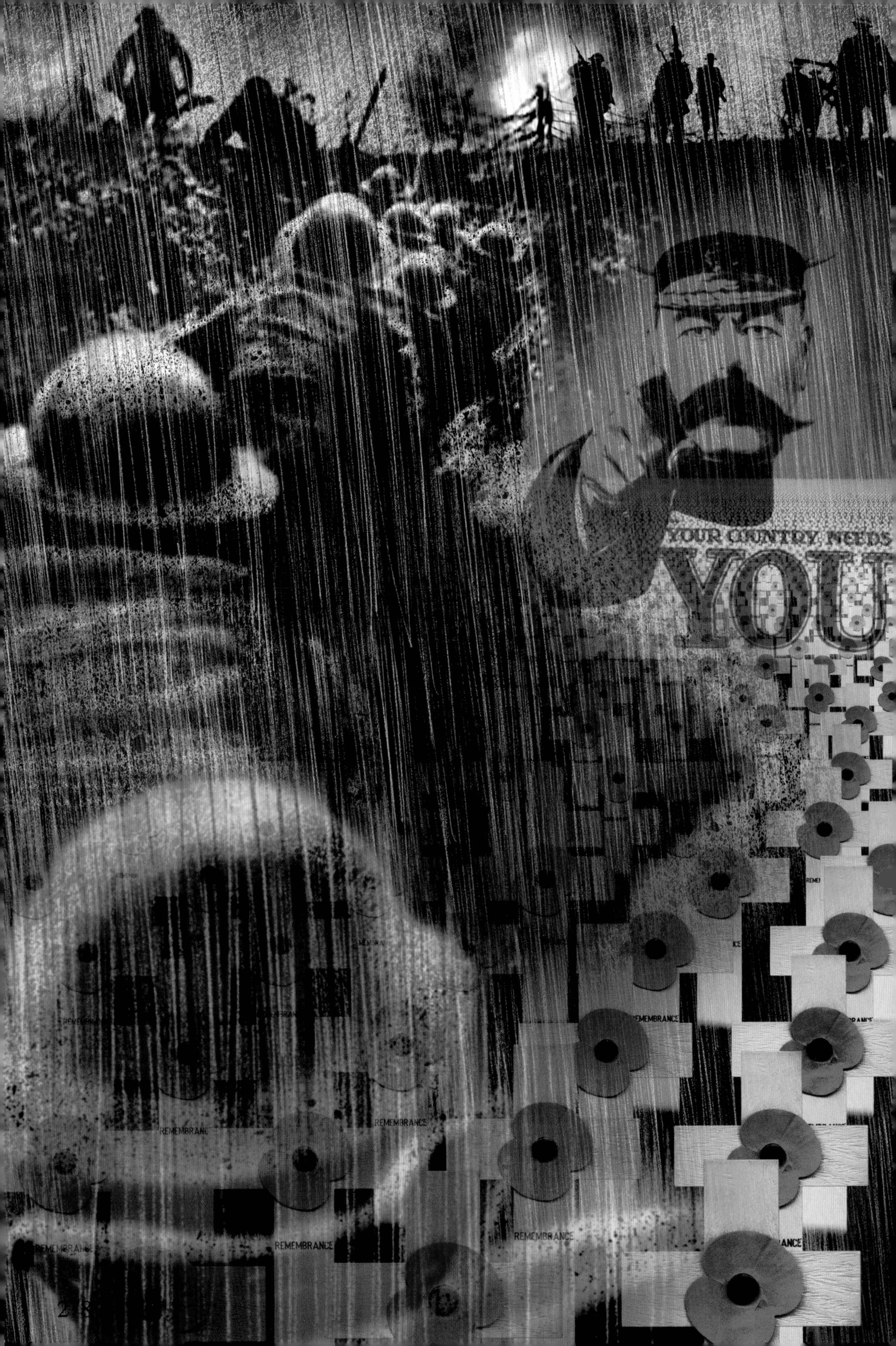
YOUR COUNTRY NEEDS
YOU
REMEMBRANCE
REMEMBRANCE
REMEMBRANCE
REMEMBRANCE
REMEMBRANCE
REMEMBRANCE
REMEMBRANCE

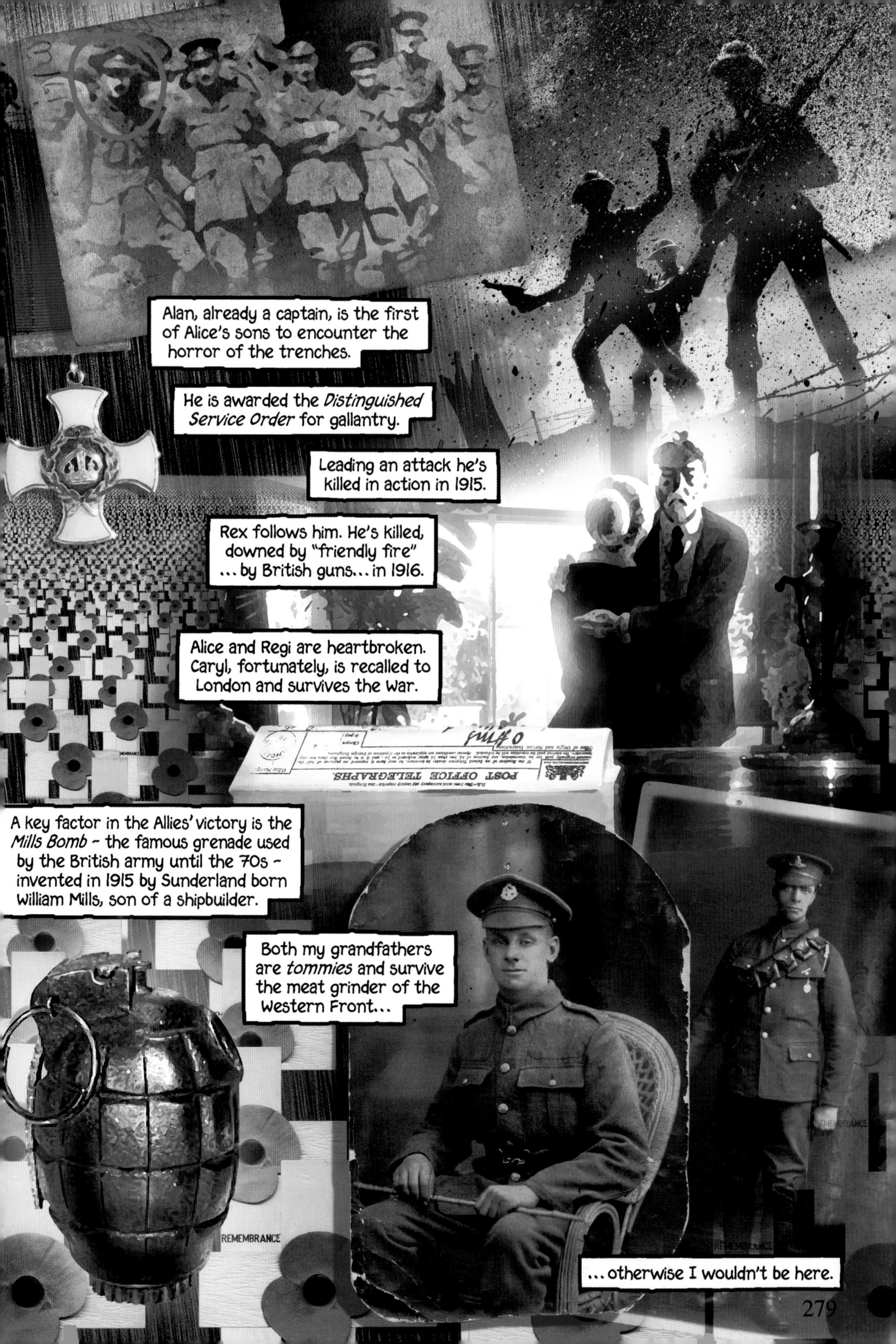
Alan, already a captain, is the first of Alice's sons to encounter the horror of the trenches.
He is awarded the *Distinguished Service Order* for gallantry.
Leading an attack he's killed in action in 1915.
Rex follows him. He's killed, downed by "friendly fire" ... by British guns... in 1916.
Alice and Regi are heartbroken. Caryl, fortunately, is recalled to London and survives the War.
POST OFFICE TELEGRAPHS.
A key factor in the Allies' victory is the *Mills Bomb* – the famous grenade used by the British army until the 70s – invented in 1915 by Sunderland born William Mills, son of a shipbuilder.
Both my grandfathers are *tommies* and survive the meat grinder of the Western Front...
REMEMBRANCE
...otherwise I wouldn't be here.

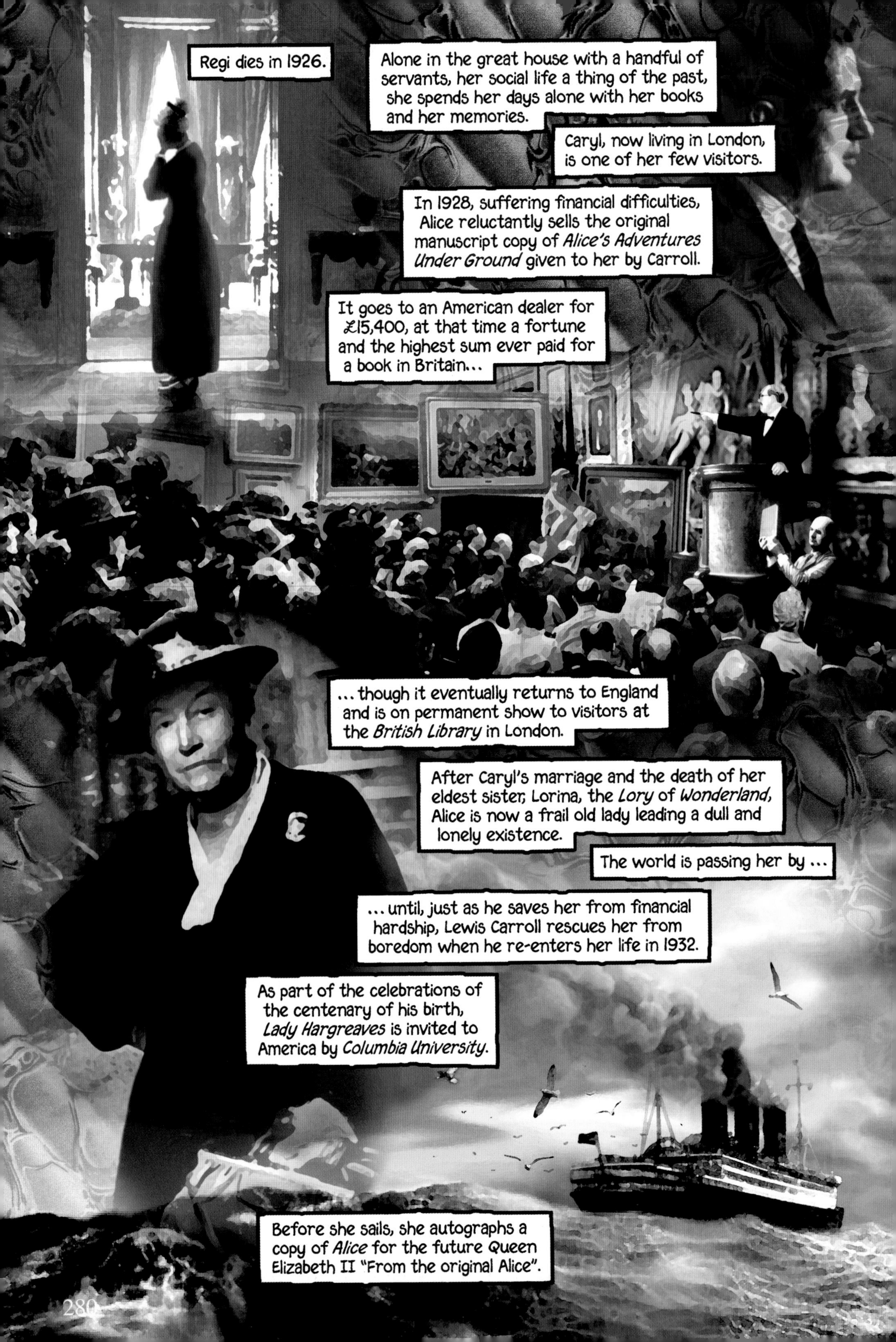
Regi dies in 1926.
Alone in the great house with a handful of servants, her social life a thing of the past, she spends her days alone with her books and her memories.
Caryl, now living in London, is one of her few visitors.
In 1928, suffering financial difficulties, Alice reluctantly sells the original manuscript copy of *Alice's Adventures Under Ground* given to her by Carroll.
It goes to an American dealer for £15,400, at that time a fortune and the highest sum ever paid for a book in Britain...
... though it eventually returns to England and is on permanent show to visitors at the *British Library* in London.
After Caryl's marriage and the death of her eldest sister, Lorina, the *Lory* of *Wonderland*, Alice is now a frail old lady leading a dull and lonely existence.
The world is passing her by ...
... until, just as he saves her from financial hardship, Lewis Carroll rescues her from boredom when he re-enters her life in 1932.
As part of the celebrations of the centenary of his birth, *Lady Hargreaves* is invited to America by *Columbia University*.
Before she sails, she autographs a copy of *Alice* for the future Queen Elizabeth II "From the original Alice".

Accompanied by Caryl and her younger sister, Rhoda, she arrives in New York and is interviewed by the press and filmed for a *Paramount* newsreel, *Alice in U.S. Land.*

She broadcasts to the people of America from her suite at *The Waldorf Astoria.*

"America and New York City are such exciting places that they take me back to *Wonderland.*"

At Columbia, she is presented with an honorary degree and, surrounded by flowers, gives her acceptance speech to a packed hall.

"I love to think... that Mr Dodgson ...*Lewis Carroll*...knows and rejoices with me."

An orchestra and chorus perform the *Alice in Wonderland* suite.

Back in Britain she opens a Lewis Carroll exhibition, a ceremony attended by Peter Davies (the "original" *Peter Pan*), the new Dean of Christ Church, authors JB Priestley, Virginia Woolf, and many other literary figures.

For *Cornhill Magazine* she co-writes with Caryl the article documenting, for the first time, her friendship with Carroll.

It's an exciting time for Alice but she is old and tires easily and is bemused by her unexpected celebrity status.

In early November 1934 she falls ill and passes into a coma, dying peacefully a few days later.

'ALICE' HERE TODAY FOR CARROLL FETE

HER BIRTH... ...ESDAY

Original of F... ...ter to Take Par...

THE TIMES

MRS. HARGREAVES

"ALICE IN WONDERLAND"

Mrs. Reginald Hargreaves, widow of Mr. Reginald Hargreaves, of Lyndhurst, the original Alice of "Alice in Wonderland," died on Thursday at her home at Westerham at the age of 82.

Alice Pleasance Liddell was the second of the three daughters of the Very Rev. H. G. Liddell, Dean of Christ Church, Oxford. It was on July 4, 1862, that Alice, then 10 years old, and her two sisters were taken on the river by Charles Lutwidge Dodgson, a mathe-... ...n of Christ Church. So hot was ...iver that day that they had to leave ...at and seek the shadow of a new-made ...yrick.

"Tell us a story," said the little girls and Mr. Dodgson began the tale which was to earn him immortality under his pen name of Lewis Carroll." In after years, when she became Mrs. Hargreaves, Alice herself wrote an account of what happened on that gorgeous afternoon

Alice Pleasance Liddell

81

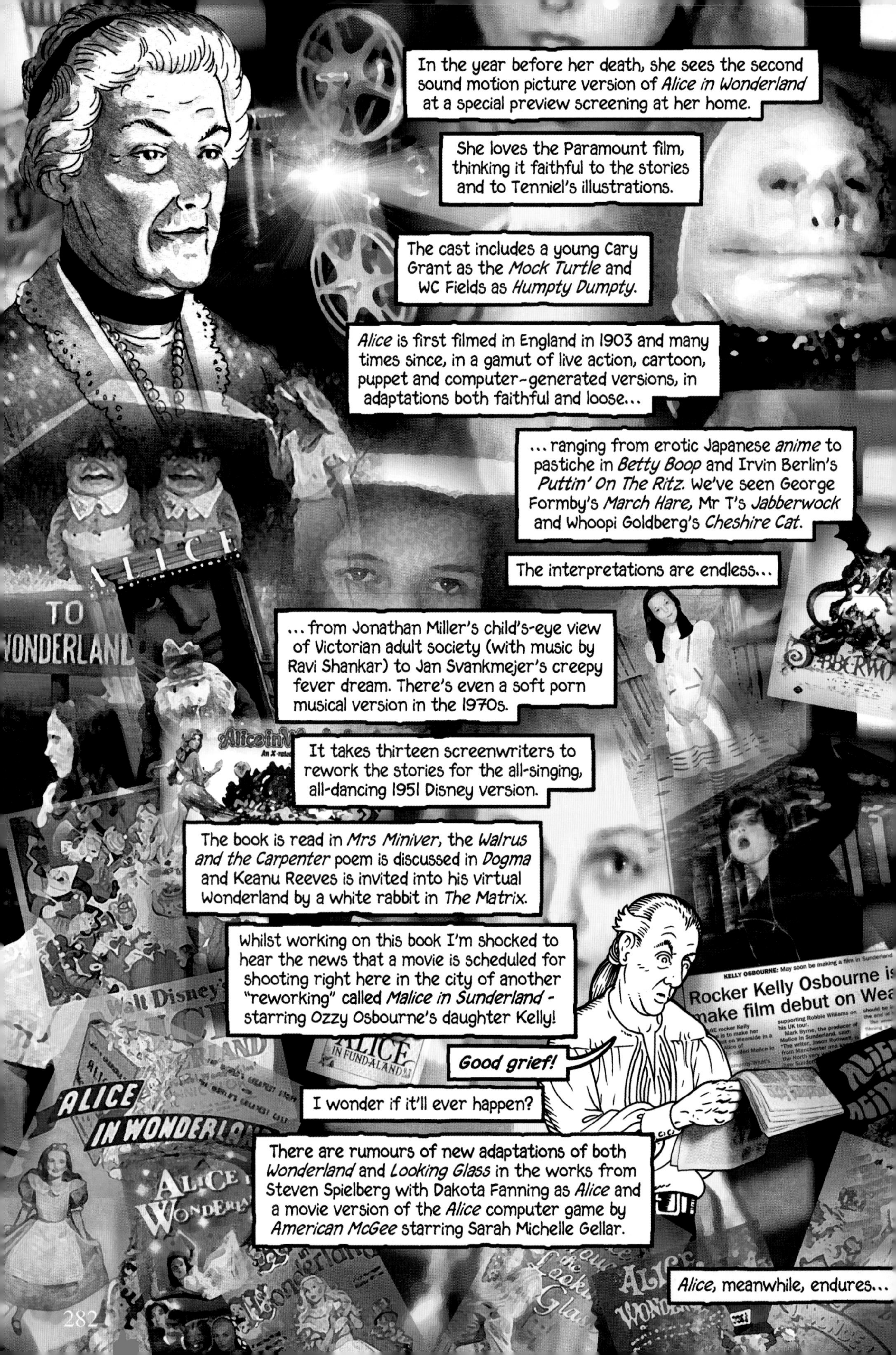
In the year before her death, she sees the second sound motion picture version of *Alice in Wonderland* at a special preview screening at her home.
She loves the Paramount film, thinking it faithful to the stories and to Tenniel's illustrations.
The cast includes a young Cary Grant as the *Mock Turtle* and WC Fields as *Humpty Dumpty*.
Alice is first filmed in England in 1903 and many times since, in a gamut of live action, cartoon, puppet and computer-generated versions, in adaptations both faithful and loose...
...ranging from erotic Japanese *anime* to pastiche in *Betty Boop* and Irvin Berlin's *Puttin' On The Ritz*. We've seen George Formby's *March Hare*, Mr T's *Jabberwock* and Whoopi Goldberg's *Cheshire Cat*.
The interpretations are endless...
...from Jonathan Miller's child's-eye view of Victorian adult society (with music by Ravi Shankar) to Jan Svankmejer's creepy fever dream. There's even a soft porn musical version in the 1970s.
It takes thirteen screenwriters to rework the stories for the all-singing, all-dancing 1951 Disney version.
The book is read in *Mrs Miniver*, the *Walrus and the Carpenter* poem is discussed in *Dogma* and Keanu Reeves is invited into his virtual Wonderland by a white rabbit in *The Matrix*.
Whilst working on this book I'm shocked to hear the news that a movie is scheduled for shooting right here in the city of another "reworking" called *Malice in Sunderland* - starring Ozzy Osbourne's daughter Kelly!
KELLY OSBOURNE: May soon be making a film in Sunderland
Good grief!
I wonder if it'll ever happen?
There are rumours of new adaptations of both *Wonderland* and *Looking Glass* in the works from Steven Spielberg with Dakota Fanning as *Alice* and a movie version of the *Alice* computer game by *American McGee* starring Sarah Michelle Gellar.
Alice, meanwhile, endures...

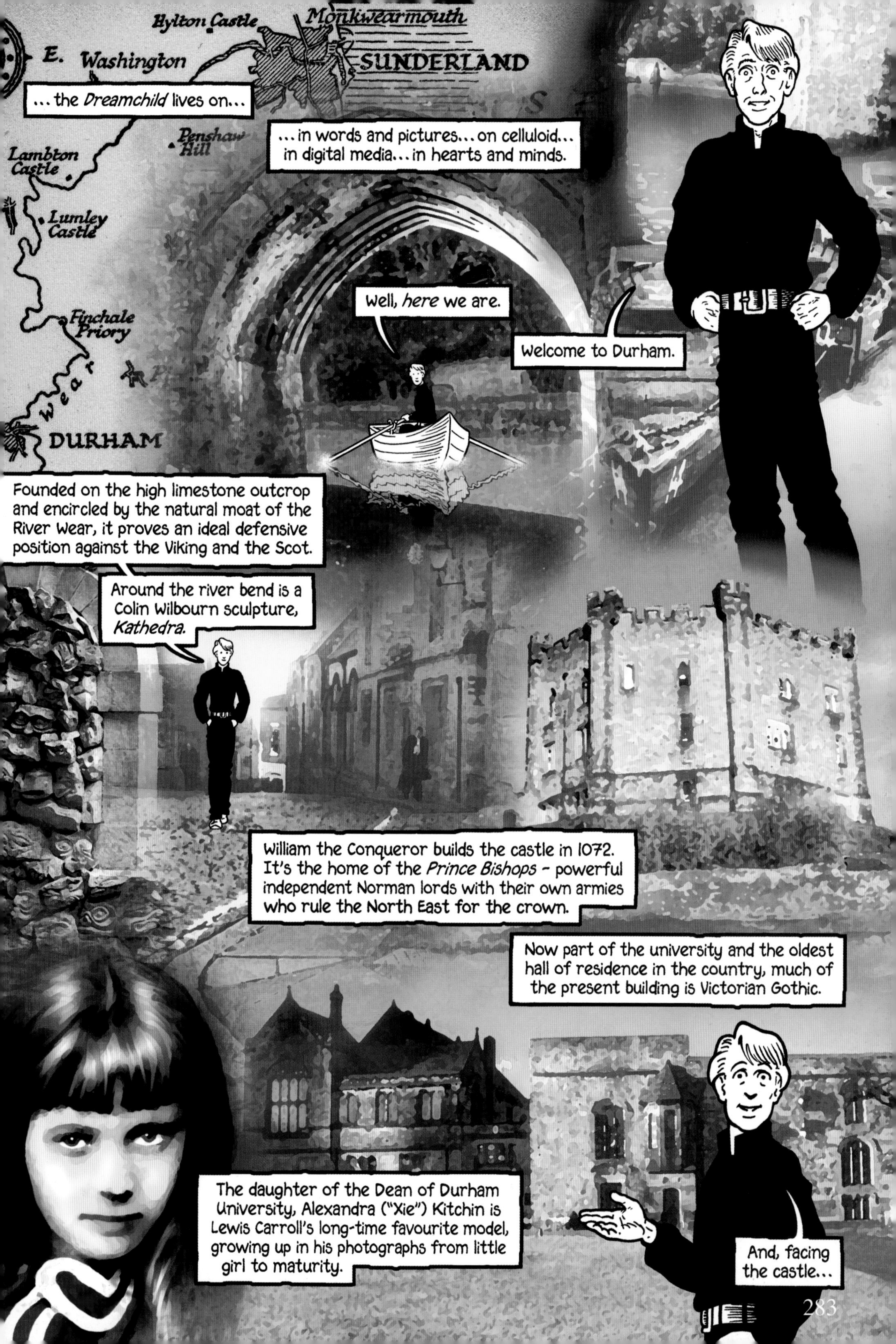

Hylton Castle
Monkwearmouth
E.
Washington
SUNDERLAND
... the *Dreamchild* lives on...
Penshaw Hill
...in words and pictures... on celluloid... in digital media... in hearts and minds.
Lambton Castle
Lumley Castle
Finchale Priory
Wear
DURHAM
Well, *here* we are.
Welcome to Durham.
Founded on the high limestone outcrop and encircled by the natural moat of the River Wear, it proves an ideal defensive position against the Viking and the Scot.
Around the river bend is a Colin Wilbourn sculpture, *Kathedra*.
William the Conqueror builds the castle in 1072. It's the home of the *Prince Bishops* – powerful independent Norman lords with their own armies who rule the North East for the crown.
Now part of the university and the oldest hall of residence in the country, much of the present building is Victorian Gothic.
The daughter of the Dean of Durham University, Alexandra ("Xie") Kitchin is Lewis Carroll's long-time favourite model, growing up in his photographs from little girl to maturity.
And, facing the castle...

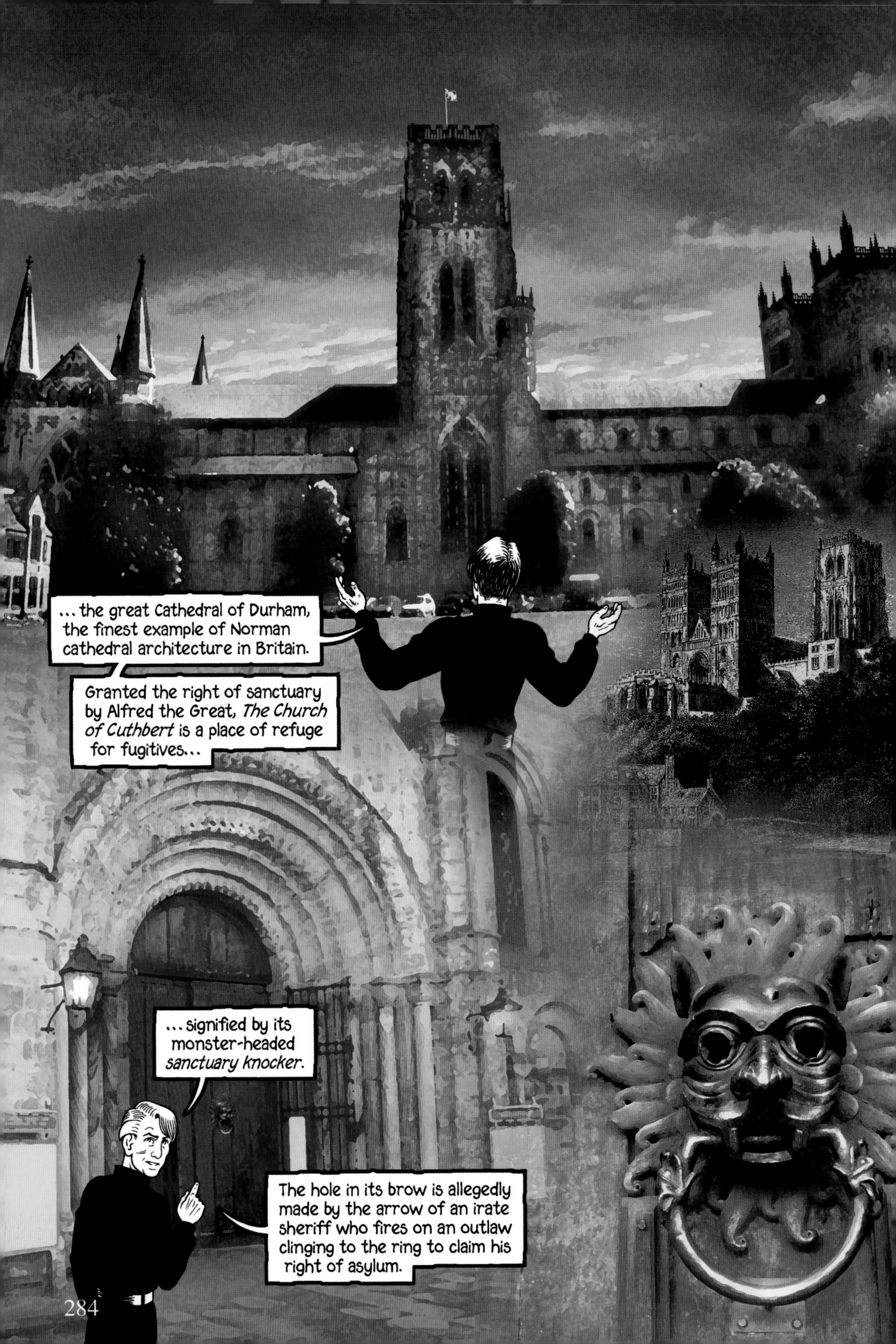

...the great Cathedral of Durham, the finest example of Norman cathedral architecture in Britain.
Granted the right of sanctuary by Alfred the Great, *The Church of Cuthbert* is a place of refuge for fugitives...
...signified by its monster-headed *sanctuary knocker*.
The hole in its brow is allegedly made by the arrow of an irate sheriff who fires on an outlaw clinging to the ring to claim his right of asylum.

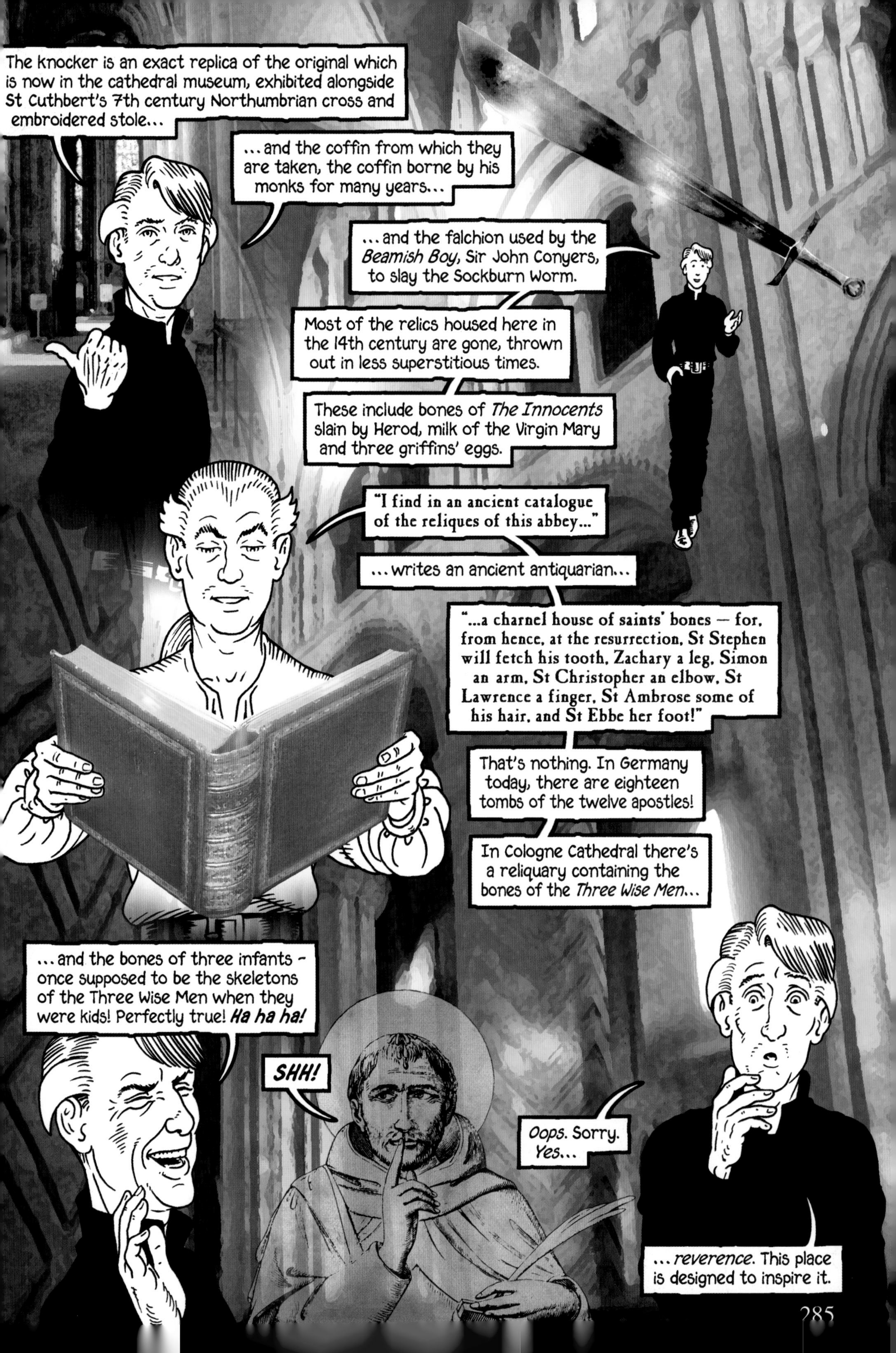
The knocker is an exact replica of the original which is now in the cathedral museum, exhibited alongside St Cuthbert's 7th century Northumbrian cross and embroidered stole...
...and the coffin from which they are taken, the coffin borne by his monks for many years...
...and the falchion used by the *Beamish Boy*, Sir John Conyers, to slay the Sockburn Worm.
Most of the relics housed here in the 14th century are gone, thrown out in less superstitious times.
These include bones of *The Innocents* slain by Herod, milk of the Virgin Mary and three griffins' eggs.
"I find in an ancient catalogue of the reliques of this abbey..."
...writes an ancient antiquarian...
"...a charnel house of saints' bones — for, from hence, at the resurrection, St Stephen will fetch his tooth, Zachary a leg, Simon an arm, St Christopher an elbow, St Lawrence a finger, St Ambrose some of his hair, and St Ebbe her foot!"
That's nothing. In Germany today, there are eighteen tombs of the twelve apostles!
In Cologne Cathedral there's a reliquary containing the bones of the *Three Wise Men*...
...and the bones of three infants - once supposed to be the skeletons of the Three Wise Men when they were kids! Perfectly true! ***Ha ha ha!***
SHH!
Oops. Sorry. *Yes*...
...*reverence*. This place is designed to inspire it.

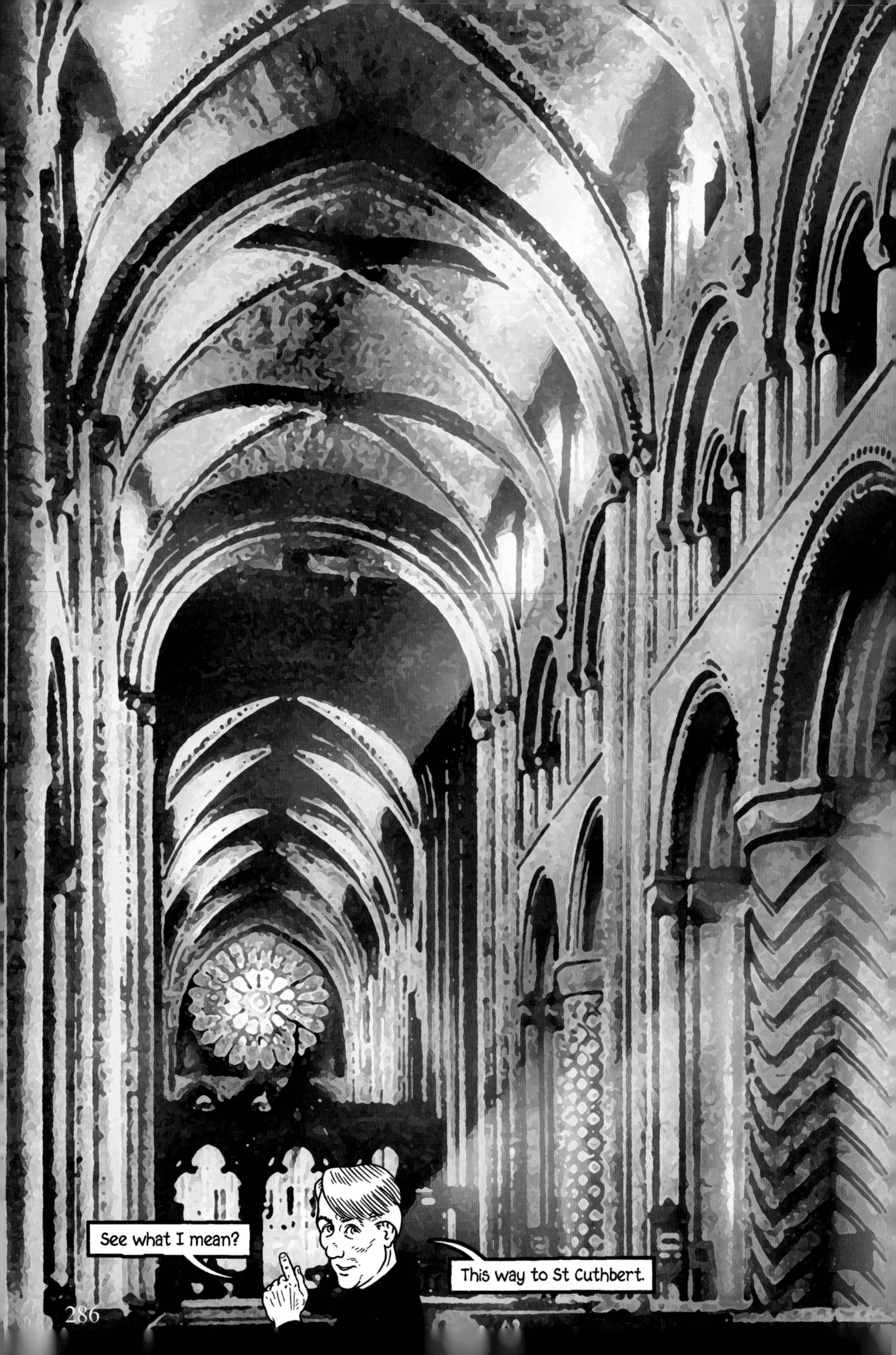
See what I mean?
This way to St Cuthbert.

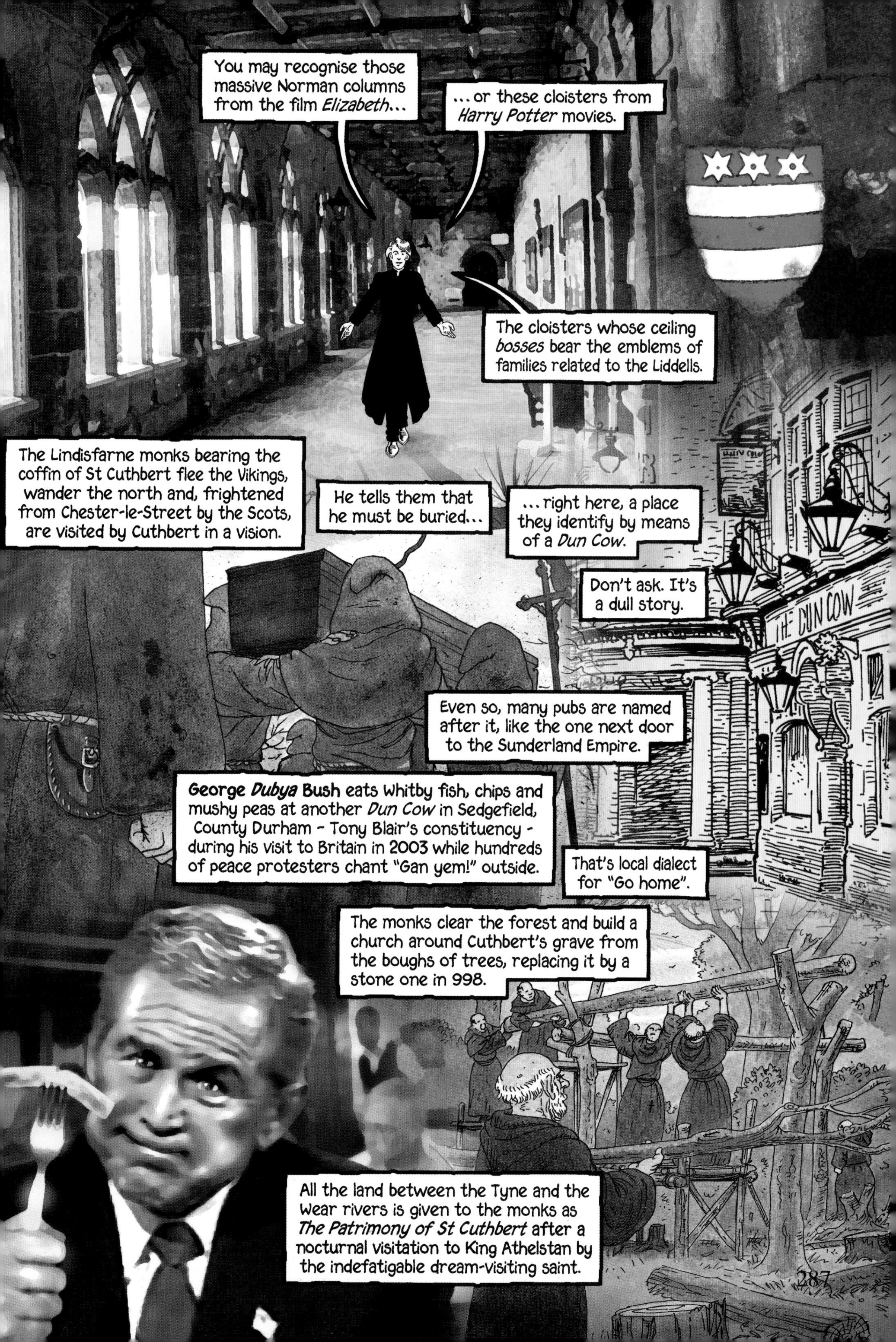
You may recognise those massive Norman columns from the film *Elizabeth*...
...or these cloisters from *Harry Potter* movies.
The cloisters whose ceiling *bosses* bear the emblems of families related to the Liddells.
The Lindisfarne monks bearing the coffin of St Cuthbert flee the Vikings, wander the north and, frightened from Chester-le-Street by the Scots, are visited by Cuthbert in a vision.
He tells them that he must be buried...
...right here, a place they identify by means of a *Dun Cow*.
Don't ask. It's a dull story.
THE DUN COW
Even so, many pubs are named after it, like the one next door to the Sunderland Empire.
George *Dubya* Bush eats Whitby fish, chips and mushy peas at another *Dun Cow* in Sedgefield, County Durham - Tony Blair's constituency - during his visit to Britain in 2003 while hundreds of peace protesters chant "Gan yem!" outside.
That's local dialect for "Go home".
The monks clear the forest and build a church around Cuthbert's grave from the boughs of trees, replacing it by a stone one in 998.
All the land between the Tyne and the Wear rivers is given to the monks as *The Patrimony of St Cuthbert* after a nocturnal visitation to King Athelstan by the indefatigable dream-visiting saint.

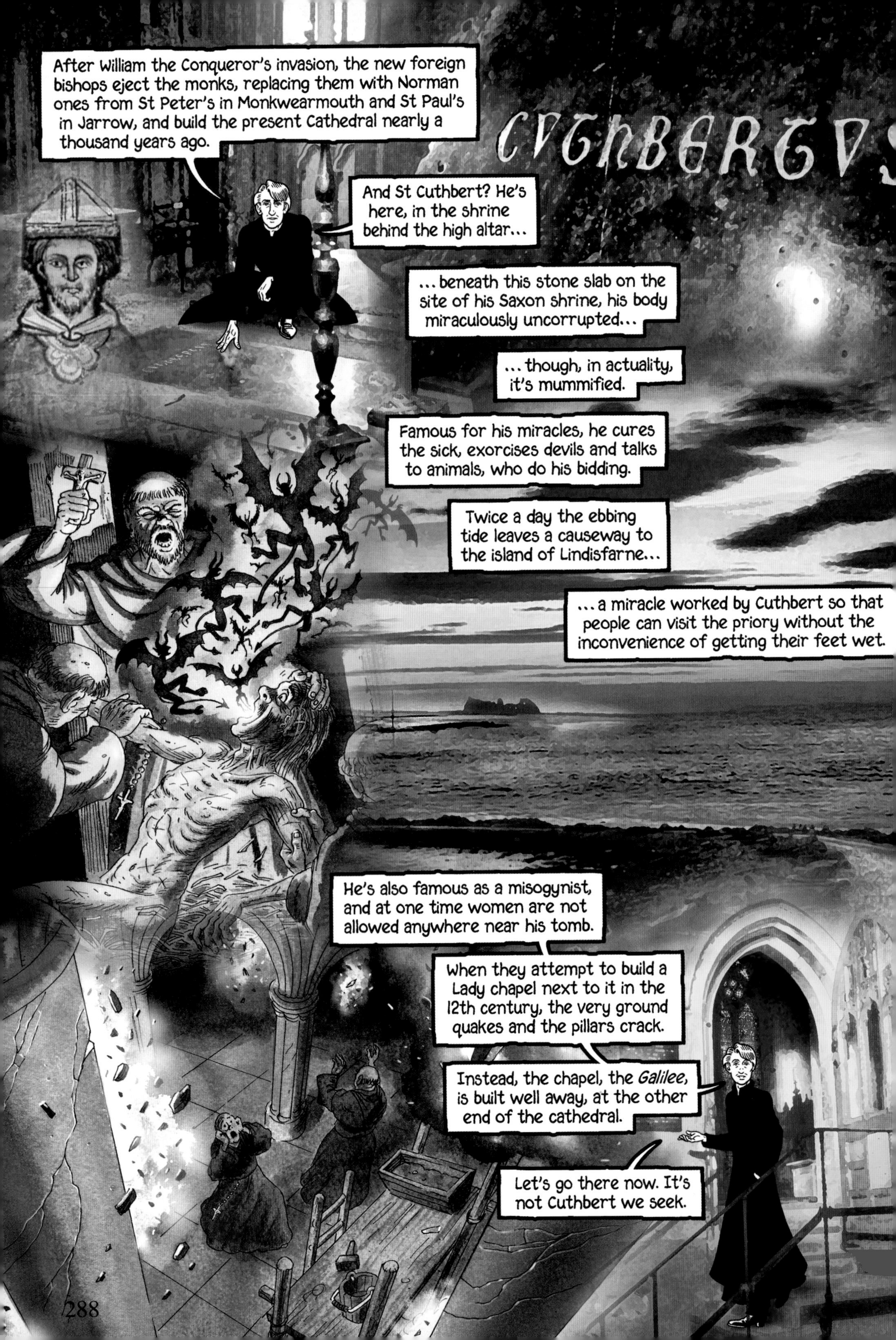
After William the Conqueror's invasion, the new foreign bishops eject the monks, replacing them with Norman ones from St Peter's in Monkwearmouth and St Paul's in Jarrow, and build the present Cathedral nearly a thousand years ago.
And St Cuthbert? He's here, in the shrine behind the high altar...
...beneath this stone slab on the site of his Saxon shrine, his body miraculously uncorrupted...
...though, in actuality, it's mummified.
Famous for his miracles, he cures the sick, exorcises devils and talks to animals, who do his bidding.
Twice a day the ebbing tide leaves a causeway to the island of Lindisfarne...
...a miracle worked by Cuthbert so that people can visit the priory without the inconvenience of getting their feet wet.
He's also famous as a misogynist, and at one time women are not allowed anywhere near his tomb.
When they attempt to build a Lady chapel next to it in the 12th century, the very ground quakes and the pillars crack.
Instead, the chapel, the *Galilee*, is built well away, at the other end of the cathedral.
Let's go there now. It's not Cuthbert we seek.

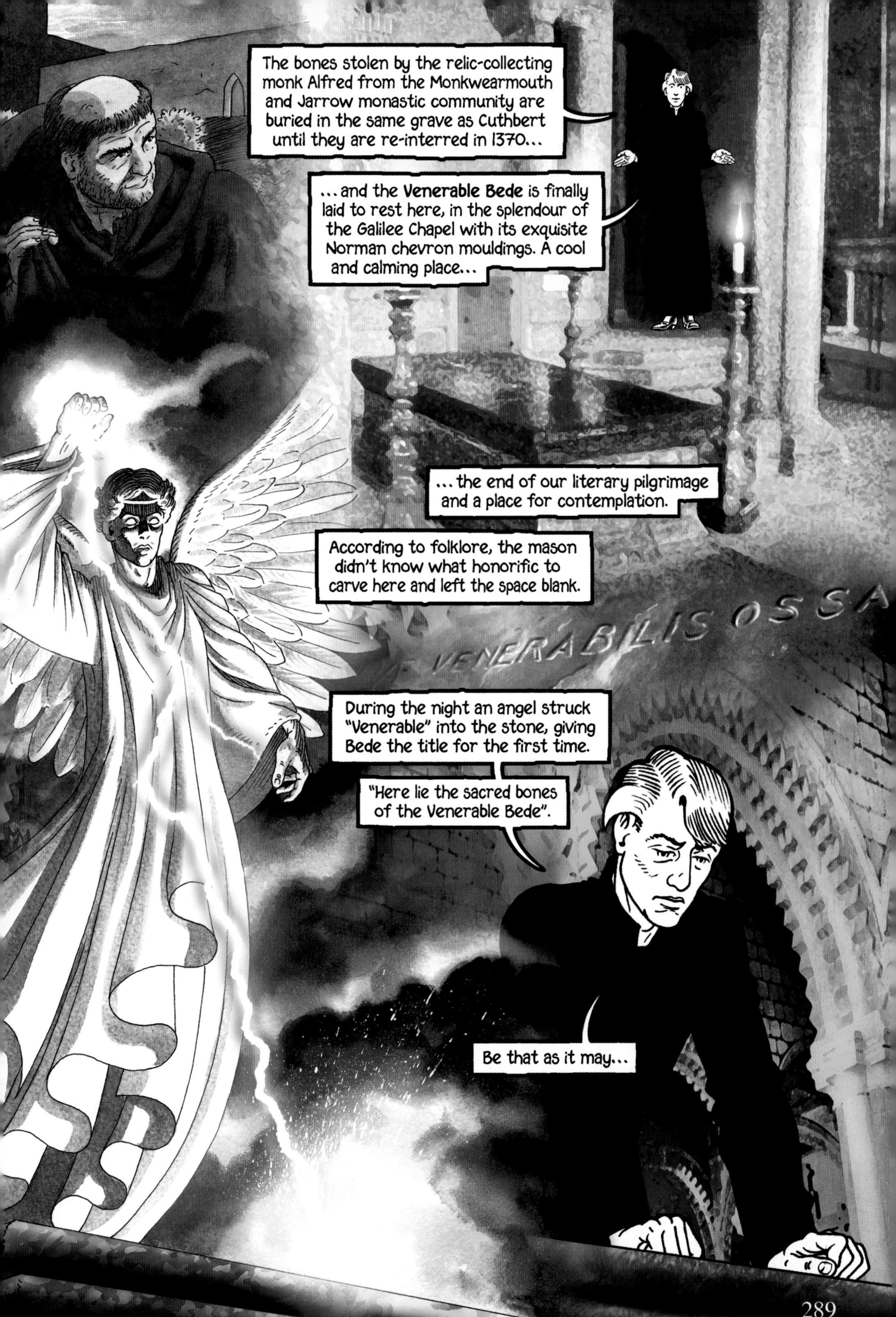
The bones stolen by the relic-collecting monk Alfred from the Monkwearmouth and Jarrow monastic community are buried in the same grave as Cuthbert until they are re-interred in 1370...
...and the **Venerable Bede** is finally laid to rest here, in the splendour of the Galilee Chapel with its exquisite Norman chevron mouldings. A cool and calming place...
...the end of our literary pilgrimage and a place for contemplation.
According to folklore, the mason didn't know what honorific to carve here and left the space blank.
VENERABILIS OSSA
During the night an angel struck "Venerable" into the stone, giving Bede the title for the first time.
"Here lie the sacred bones of the Venerable Bede".
Be that as it may...

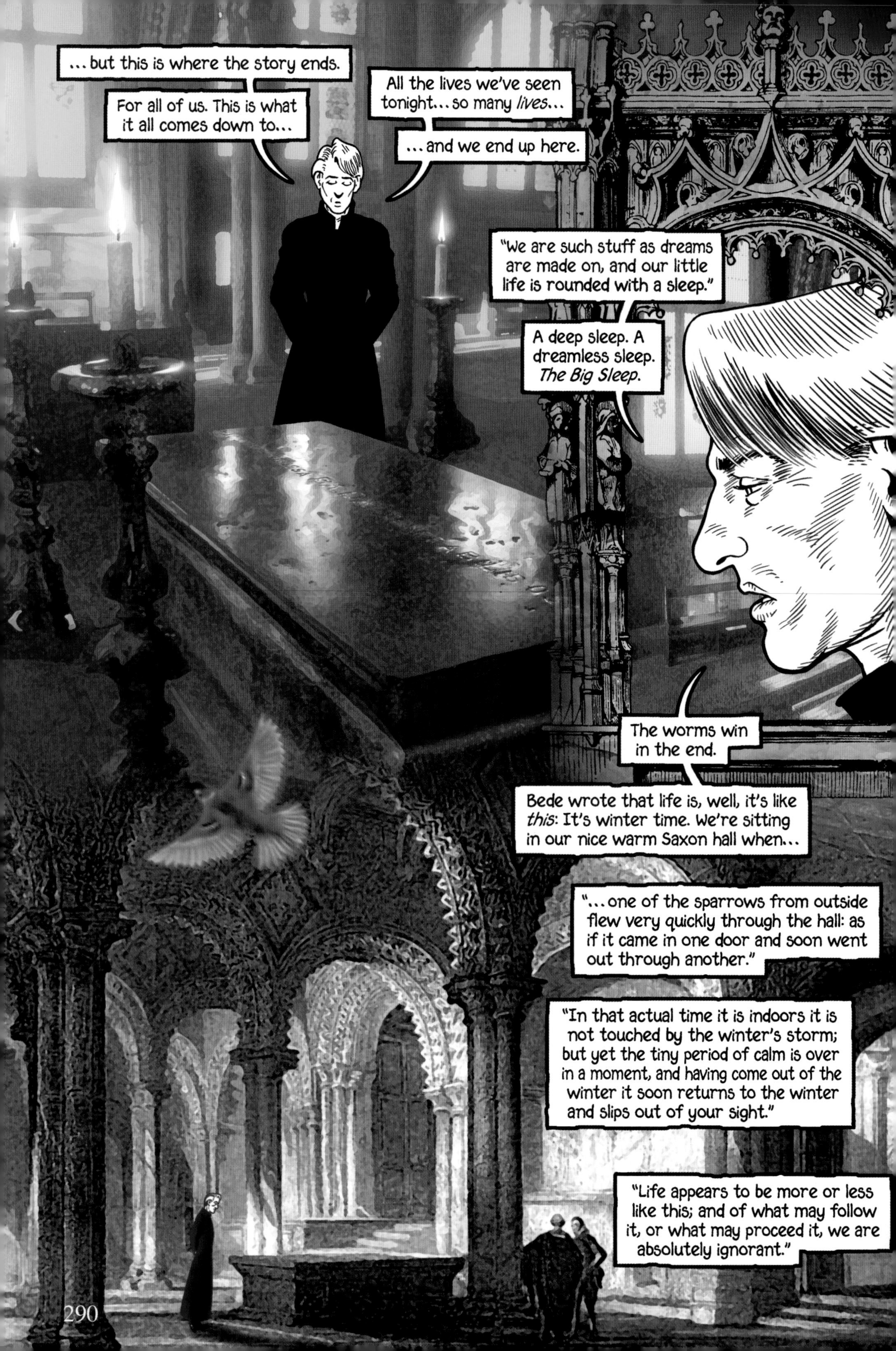

...but this is where the story ends.
For all of us. This is what it all comes down to...
All the lives we've seen tonight...so many *lives*...
...and we end up here.
"We are such stuff as dreams are made on, and our little life is rounded with a sleep."
A deep sleep. A dreamless sleep. *The Big Sleep*.
The worms win in the end.
Bede wrote that life is, well, it's like *this*: It's winter time. We're sitting in our nice warm Saxon hall when...
"...one of the sparrows from outside flew very quickly through the hall: as if it came in one door and soon went out through another."
"In that actual time it is indoors it is not touched by the winter's storm; but yet the tiny period of calm is over in a moment, and having come out of the winter it soon returns to the winter and slips out of your sight."
"Life appears to be more or less like this; and of what may follow it, or what may proceed it, we are absolutely ignorant."

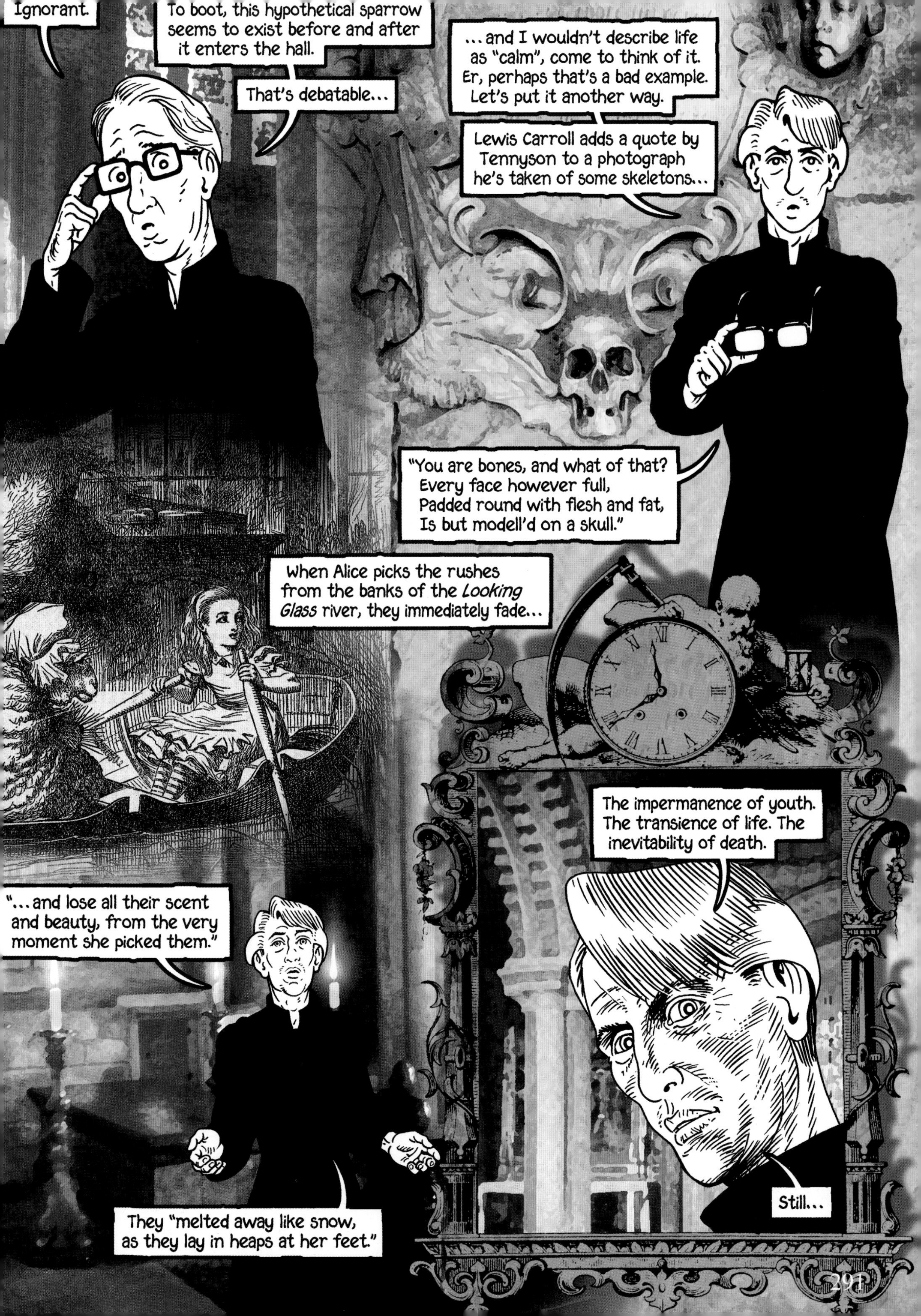

Ignorant.
To boot, this hypothetical sparrow seems to exist before and after it enters the hall.
That's debatable...
...and I wouldn't describe life as "calm", come to think of it. Er, perhaps that's a bad example. Let's put it another way.
Lewis Carroll adds a quote by Tennyson to a photograph he's taken of some skeletons...
"You are bones, and what of that? Every face however full, Padded round with flesh and fat, Is but modell'd on a skull."
When Alice picks the rushes from the banks of the *Looking Glass* river, they immediately fade...
The impermanence of youth. The transience of life. The inevitability of death.
"...and lose all their scent and beauty, from the very moment she picked them."
They "melted away like snow, as they lay in heaps at her feet."
Still...

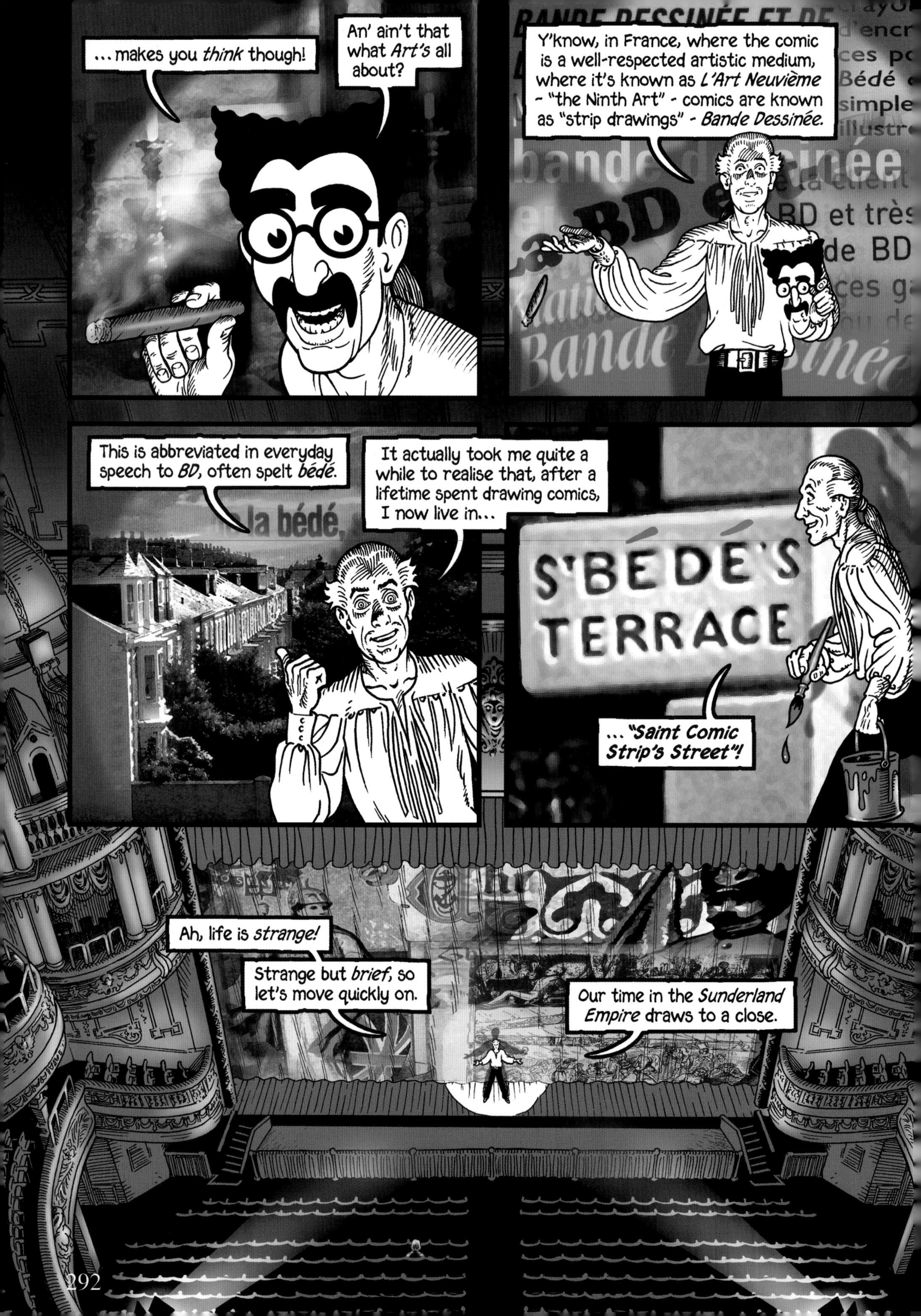
...makes you *think* though!
An' ain't that what *Art's* all about?
Y'know, in France, where the comic is a well-respected artistic medium, where it's known as *L'Art Neuvième* - "the Ninth Art" - comics are known as "strip drawings" - *Bande Dessinée.*
This is abbreviated in everyday speech to *BD*, often spelt *bédé*.
It actually took me quite a while to realise that, after a lifetime spent drawing comics, I now live in...
S'BÉDÉ'S TERRACE
...*"Saint Comic Strip's Street"*!
Ah, life is *strange!*
Strange but *brief*, so let's move quickly on.
Our time in the *Sunderland Empire* draws to a close.

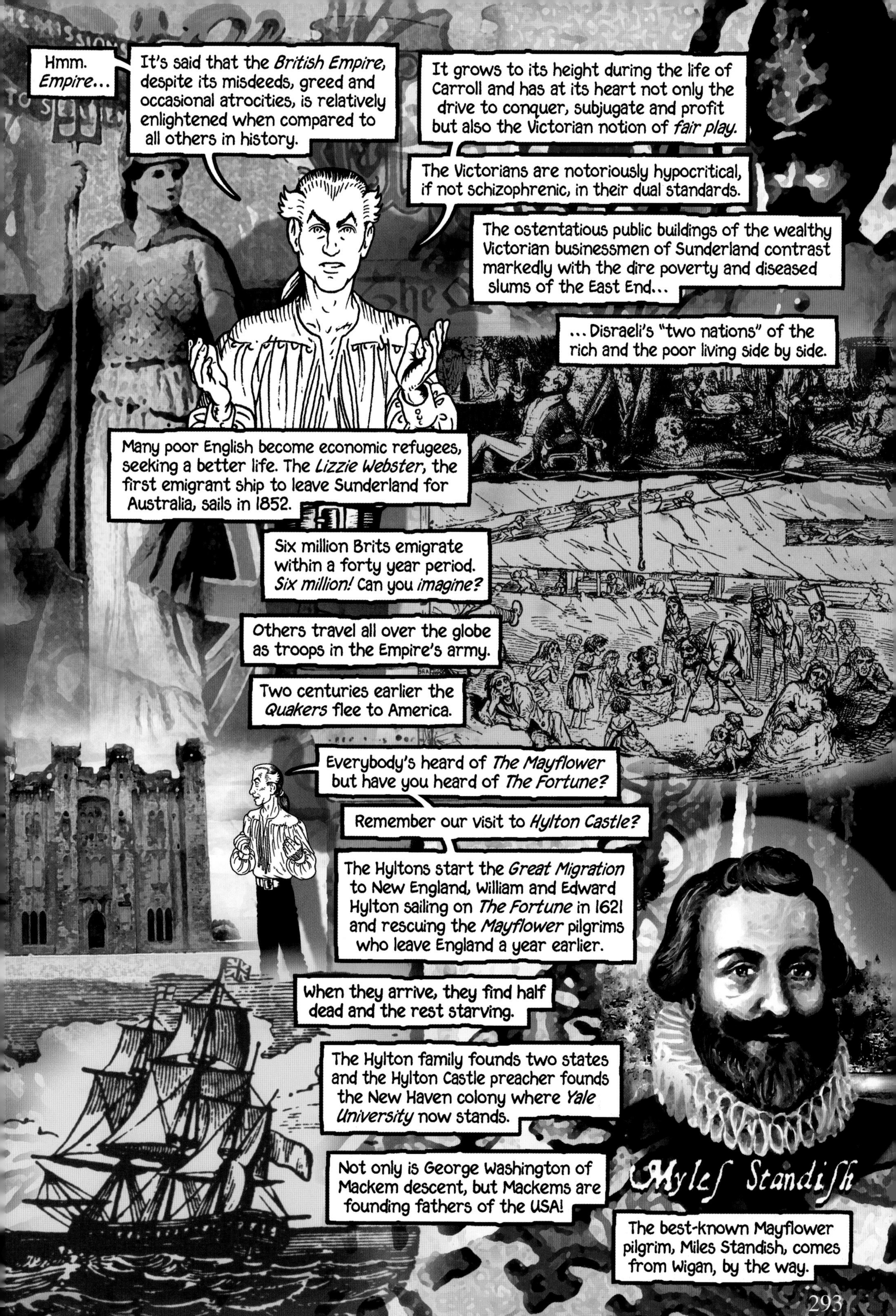

Hmm. *Empire*...
It's said that the *British Empire*, despite its misdeeds, greed and occasional atrocities, is relatively enlightened when compared to all others in history.
It grows to its height during the life of Carroll and has at its heart not only the drive to conquer, subjugate and profit but also the Victorian notion of *fair play*.
The Victorians are notoriously hypocritical, if not schizophrenic, in their dual standards.
The ostentatious public buildings of the wealthy Victorian businessmen of Sunderland contrast markedly with the dire poverty and diseased slums of the East End...
...Disraeli's "two nations" of the rich and the poor living side by side.
Many poor English become economic refugees, seeking a better life. The *Lizzie Webster*, the first emigrant ship to leave Sunderland for Australia, sails in 1852.
Six million Brits emigrate within a forty year period. *Six million!* Can you *imagine?*
Others travel all over the globe as troops in the Empire's army.
Two centuries earlier the *Quakers* flee to America.
Everybody's heard of *The Mayflower* but have you heard of *The Fortune?*
Remember our visit to *Hylton Castle?*
The Hyltons start the *Great Migration* to New England, William and Edward Hylton sailing on *The Fortune* in 1621 and rescuing the *Mayflower* pilgrims who leave England a year earlier.
When they arrive, they find half dead and the rest starving.
The Hylton family founds two states and the Hylton Castle preacher founds the New Haven colony where *Yale University* now stands.
Not only is George Washington of Mackem descent, but Mackems are founding fathers of the USA!
Myles Standish
The best-known Mayflower pilgrim, Miles Standish, comes from Wigan, by the way.

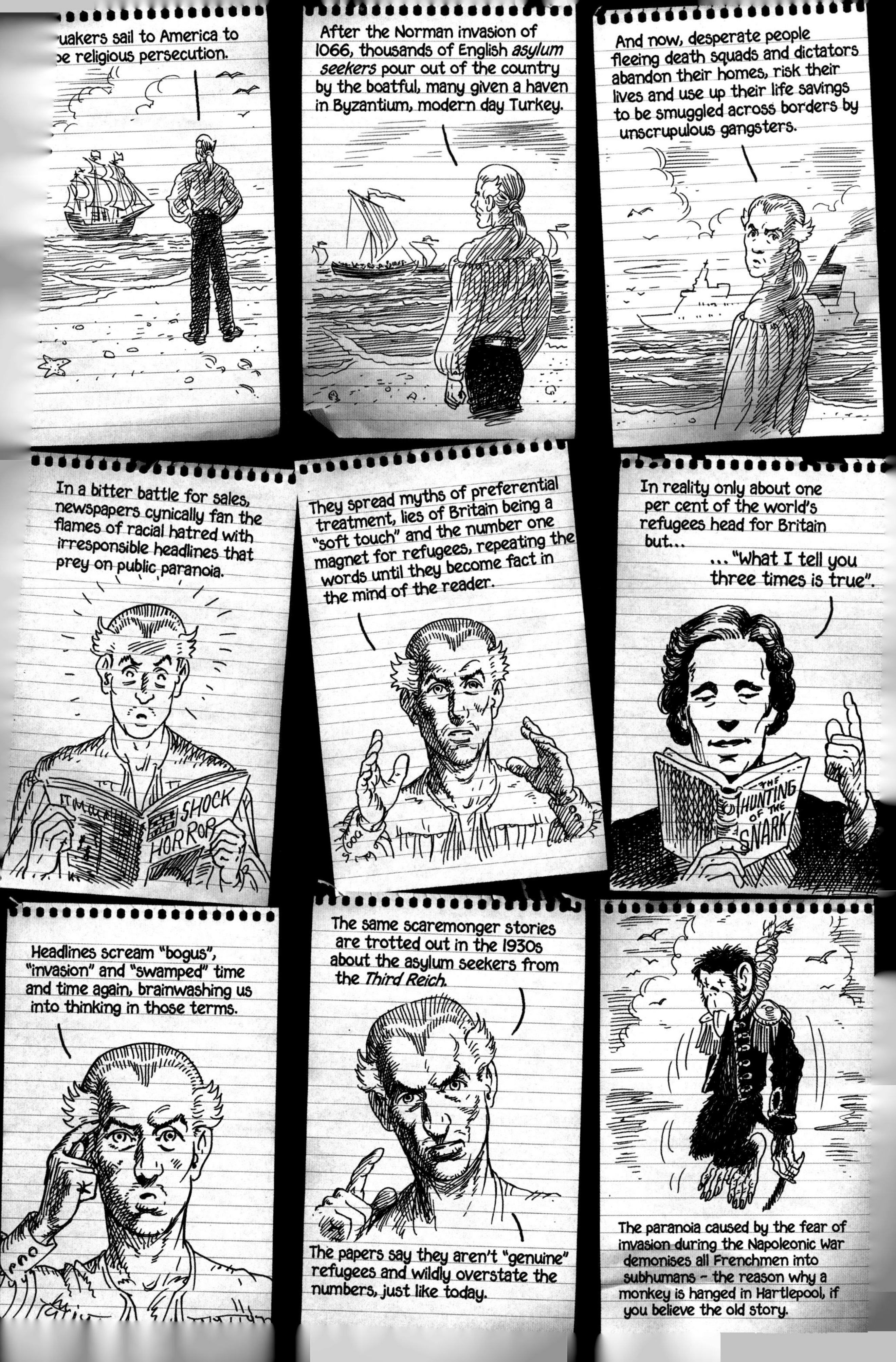
uakers sail to America to
e religious persecution.
After the Norman invasion of 1066, thousands of English *asylum seekers* pour out of the country by the boatful, many given a haven in Byzantium, modern day Turkey.
And now, desperate people fleeing death squads and dictators abandon their homes, risk their lives and use up their life savings to be smuggled across borders by unscrupulous gangsters.
In a bitter battle for sales, newspapers cynically fan the flames of racial hatred with irresponsible headlines that prey on public paranoia.
SHOCK HORROR
They spread myths of preferential treatment, lies of Britain being a "soft touch" and the number one magnet for refugees, repeating the words until they become fact in the mind of the reader.
In reality only about one per cent of the world's refugees head for Britain but...
..."What I tell you three times is true".
THE HUNTING OF THE SNARK
Headlines scream "bogus", "invasion" and "swamped" time and time again, brainwashing us into thinking in those terms.
The same scaremonger stories are trotted out in the 1930s about the asylum seekers from the *Third Reich*.
The papers say they aren't "genuine" refugees and wildly overstate the numbers, just like today.
The paranoia caused by the fear of invasion during the Napoleonic War demonises all Frenchmen into subhumans – the reason why a monkey is hanged in Hartlepool, if you believe the old story.

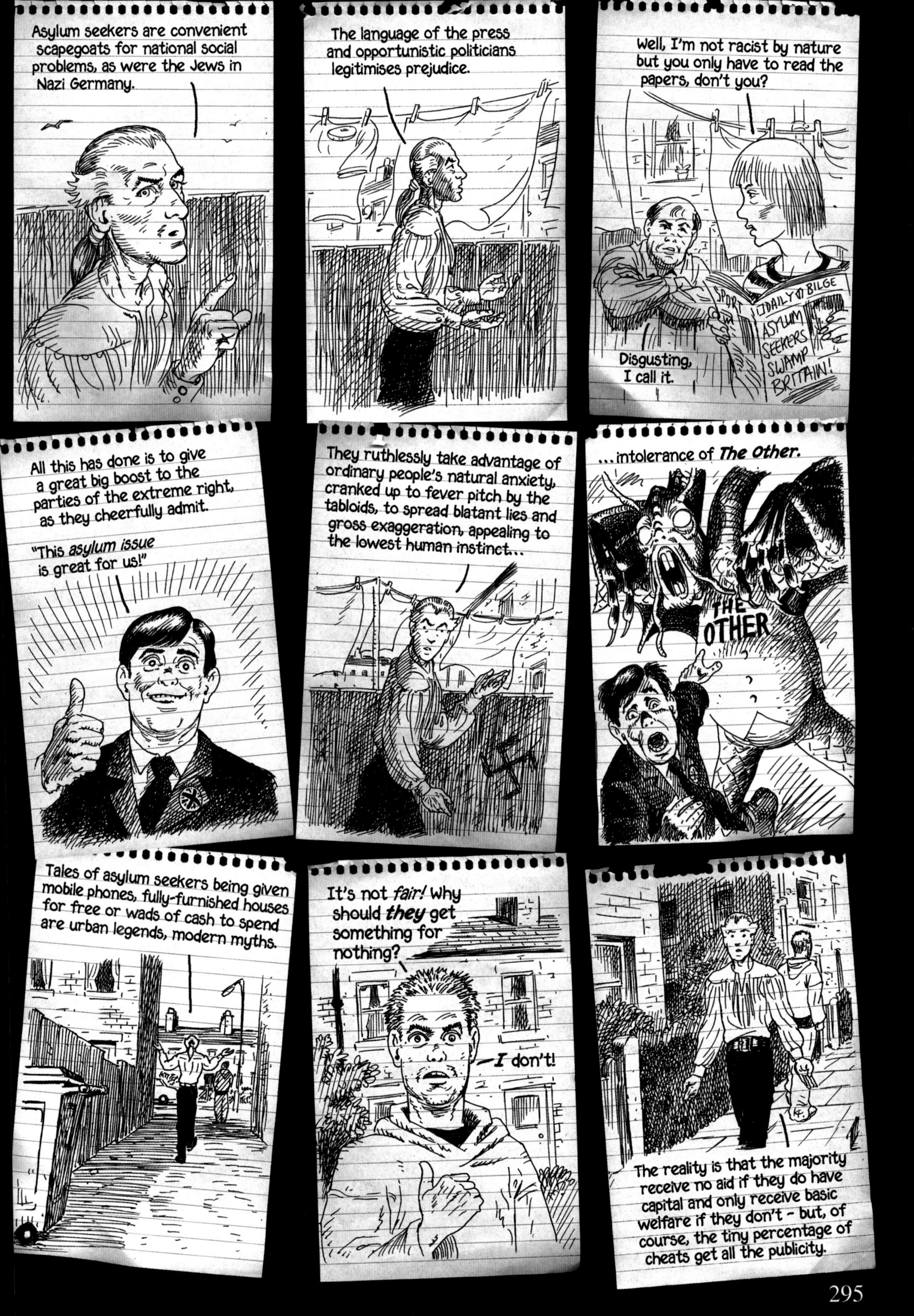

Asylum seekers are convenient scapegoats for national social problems, as were the Jews in Nazi Germany.
The language of the press and opportunistic politicians legitimises prejudice.
Well, I'm not racist by nature but you only have to read the papers, don't you?
SPORT
DAILY BILGE
ASYLUM SEEKERS SWAMP BRITAIN!
Disgusting, I call it.
All this has done is to give a great big boost to the parties of the extreme right, as they cheerfully admit.
"This *asylum issue* is great for us!"
They ruthlessly take advantage of ordinary people's natural anxiety, cranked up to fever pitch by the tabloids, to spread blatant lies and gross exaggeration, appealing to the lowest human instinct...
...intolerance of ***The Other.***
THE OTHER
Tales of asylum seekers being given mobile phones, fully-furnished houses for free or wads of cash to spend are urban legends, modern myths.
It's not *fair!* Why should ***they*** get something for nothing?
I don't!
The reality is that the majority receive no aid if they do have capital and only receive basic welfare if they don't – but, of course, the tiny percentage of cheats get all the publicity.

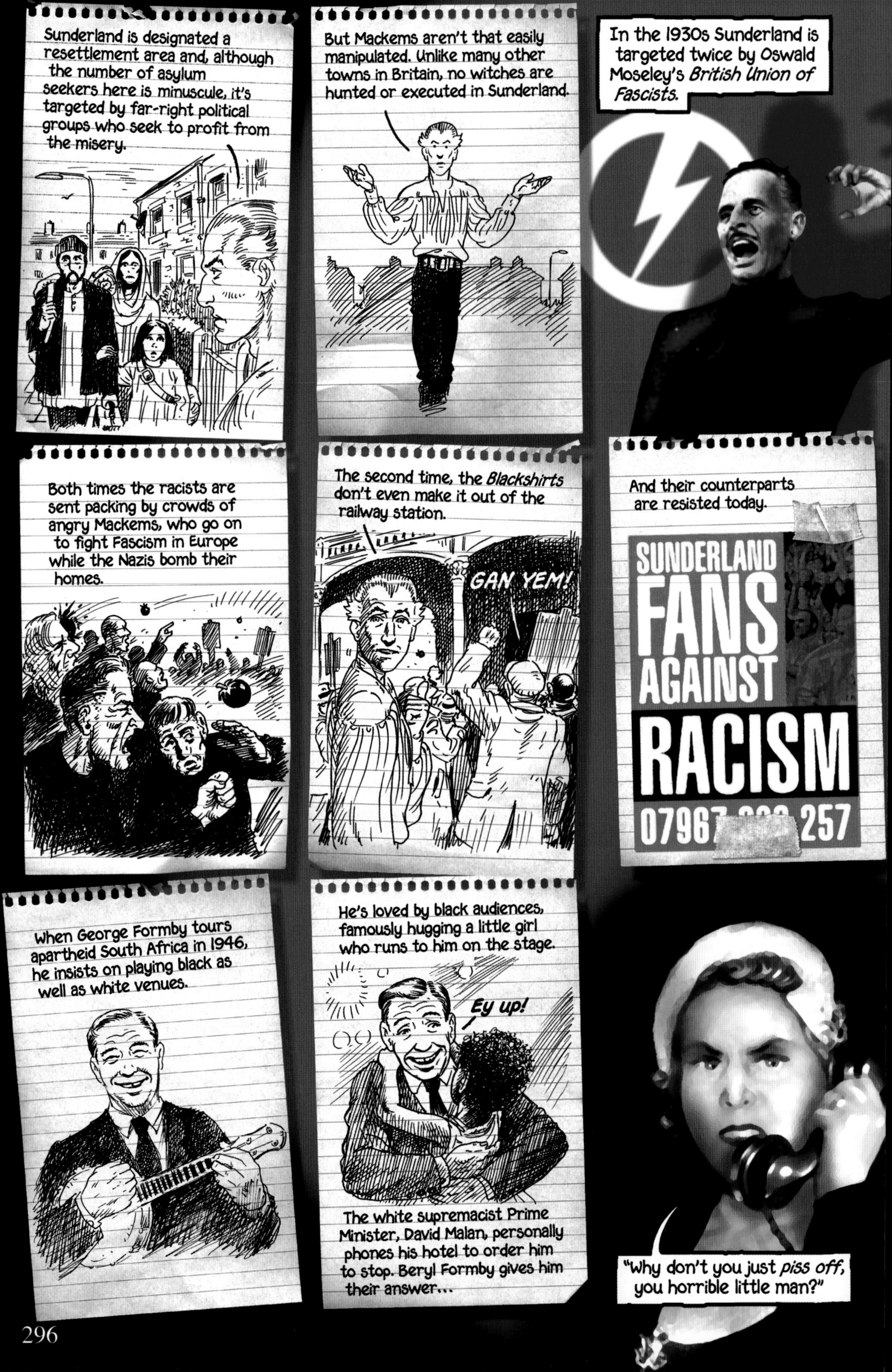

Sunderland is designated a resettlement area and, although the number of asylum seekers here is minuscule, it's targeted by far-right political groups who seek to profit from the misery.
But Mackems aren't that easily manipulated. Unlike many other towns in Britain, no witches are hunted or executed in Sunderland.
In the 1930s Sunderland is targeted twice by Oswald Moseley's *British Union of Fascists.*
Both times the racists are sent packing by crowds of angry Mackems, who go on to fight Fascism in Europe while the Nazis bomb their homes.
The second time, the *Blackshirts* don't even make it out of the railway station.
GAN YEM!
And their counterparts are resisted today.
SUNDERLAND FANS AGAINST RACISM
07967 257
When George Formby tours apartheid South Africa in 1946, he insists on playing black as well as white venues.
He's loved by black audiences, famously hugging a little girl who runs to him on the stage.
Ey up!
The white supremacist Prime Minister, David Malan, personally phones his hotel to order him to stop. Beryl Formby gives him their answer...
"Why don't you just *piss off*, you horrible little man?"

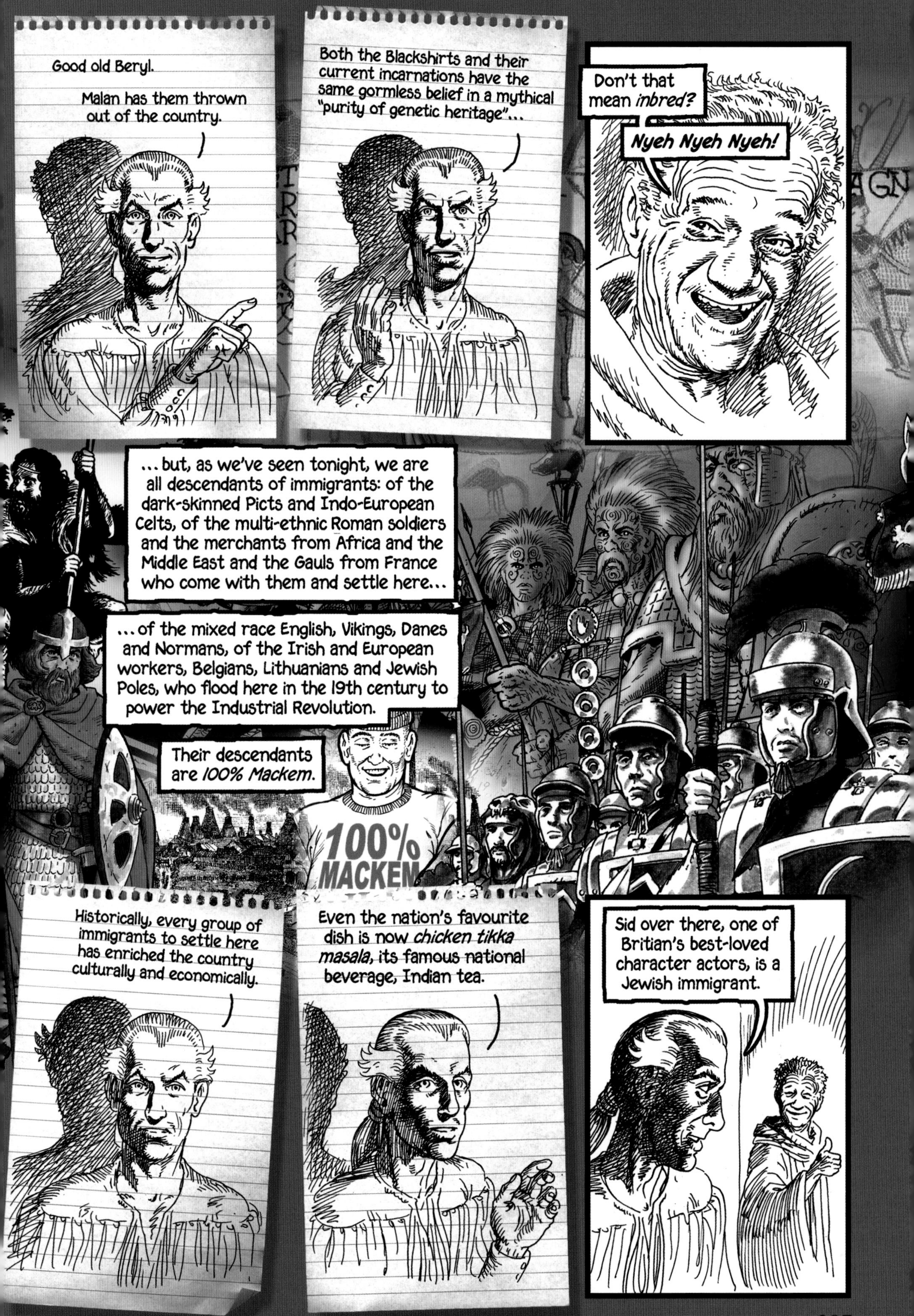
Good old Beryl.
Malan has them thrown out of the country.
Both the Blackshirts and their current incarnations have the same gormless belief in a mythical "purity of genetic heritage"...
Don't that mean *inbred?*
Nyeh Nyeh Nyeh!
... but, as we've seen tonight, we are all descendants of immigrants: of the dark-skinned Picts and Indo-European Celts, of the multi-ethnic Roman soldiers and the merchants from Africa and the Middle East and the Gauls from France who come with them and settle here...
... of the mixed race English, Vikings, Danes and Normans, of the Irish and European workers, Belgians, Lithuanians and Jewish Poles, who flood here in the 19th century to power the Industrial Revolution.
Their descendants are *100% Mackem.*
100% MACKEM
Historically, every group of immigrants to settle here has enriched the country culturally and economically.
Even the nation's favourite dish is now *chicken tikka masala*, its famous national beverage, Indian tea.
Sid over there, one of Britian's best-loved character actors, is a Jewish immigrant.

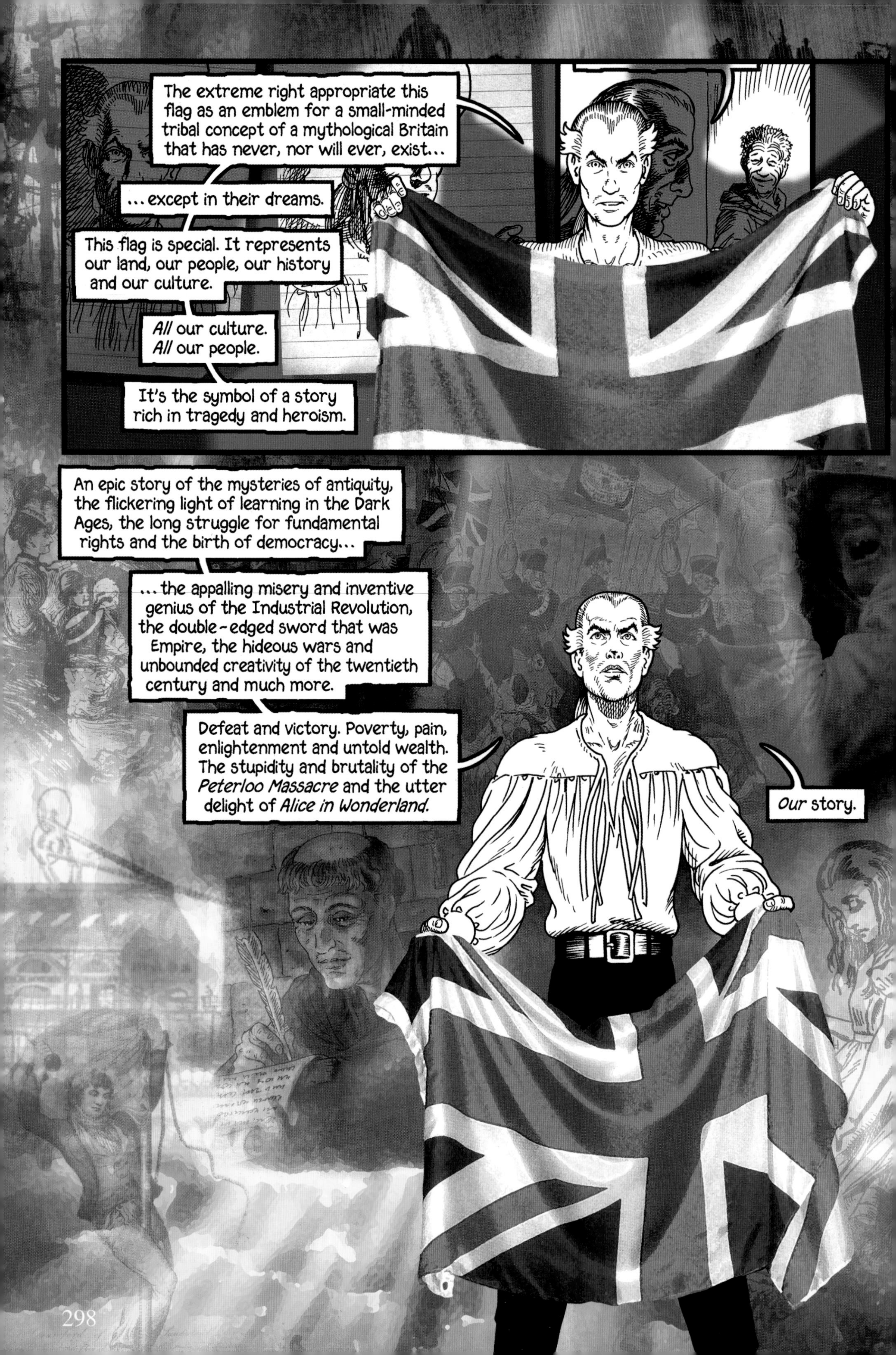
The extreme right appropriate this flag as an emblem for a small-minded tribal concept of a mythological Britain that has never, nor will ever, exist...
... except in their dreams.
This flag is special. It represents our land, our people, our history and our culture.
All our culture. *All* our people.
It's the symbol of a story rich in tragedy and heroism.
An epic story of the mysteries of antiquity, the flickering light of learning in the Dark Ages, the long struggle for fundamental rights and the birth of democracy...
... the appalling misery and inventive genius of the Industrial Revolution, the double-edged sword that was Empire, the hideous wars and unbounded creativity of the twentieth century and much more.
Defeat and victory. Poverty, pain, enlightenment and untold wealth. The stupidity and brutality of the *Peterloo Massacre* and the utter delight of *Alice in Wonderland.*
Our story.

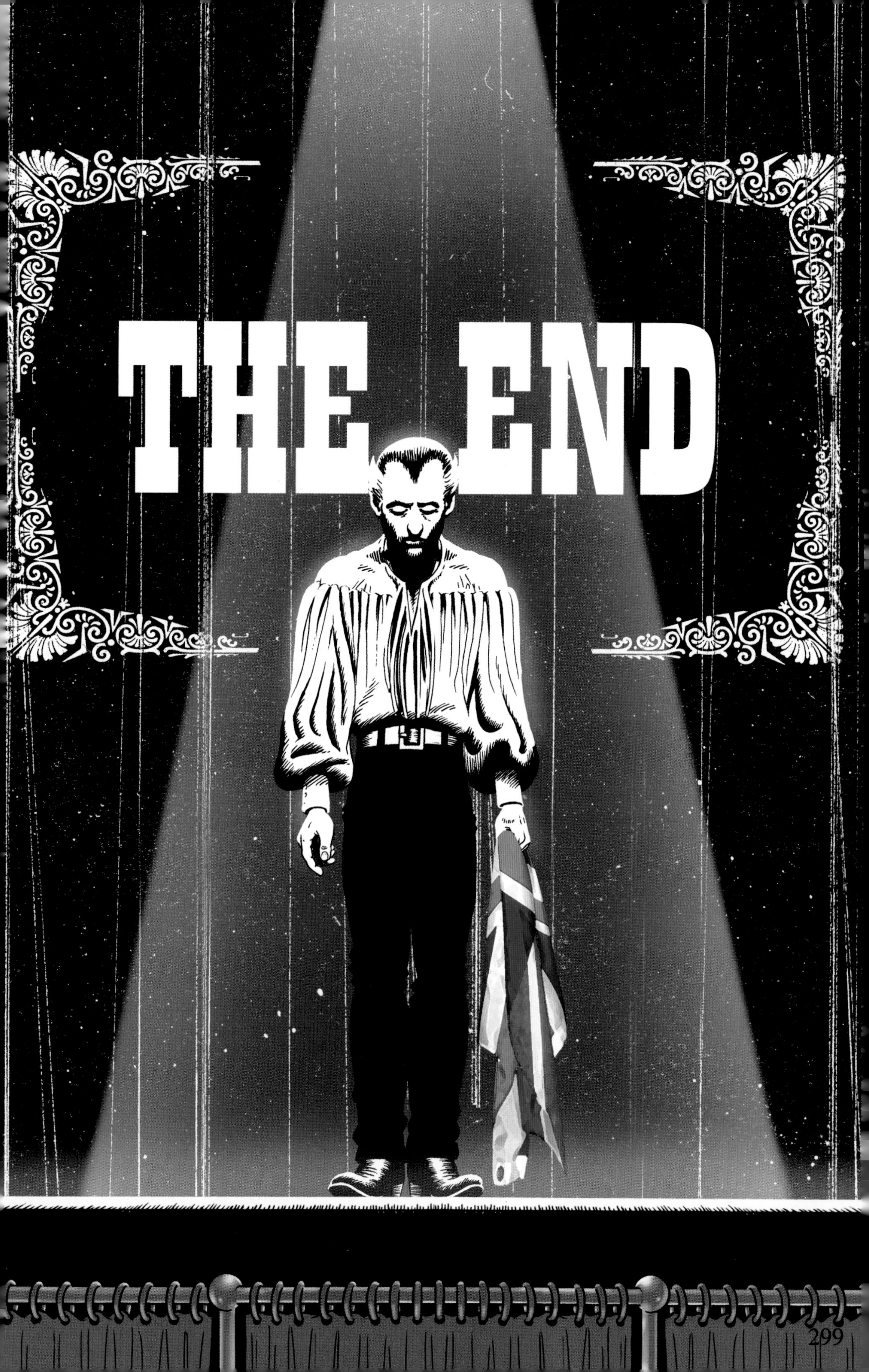
THE END

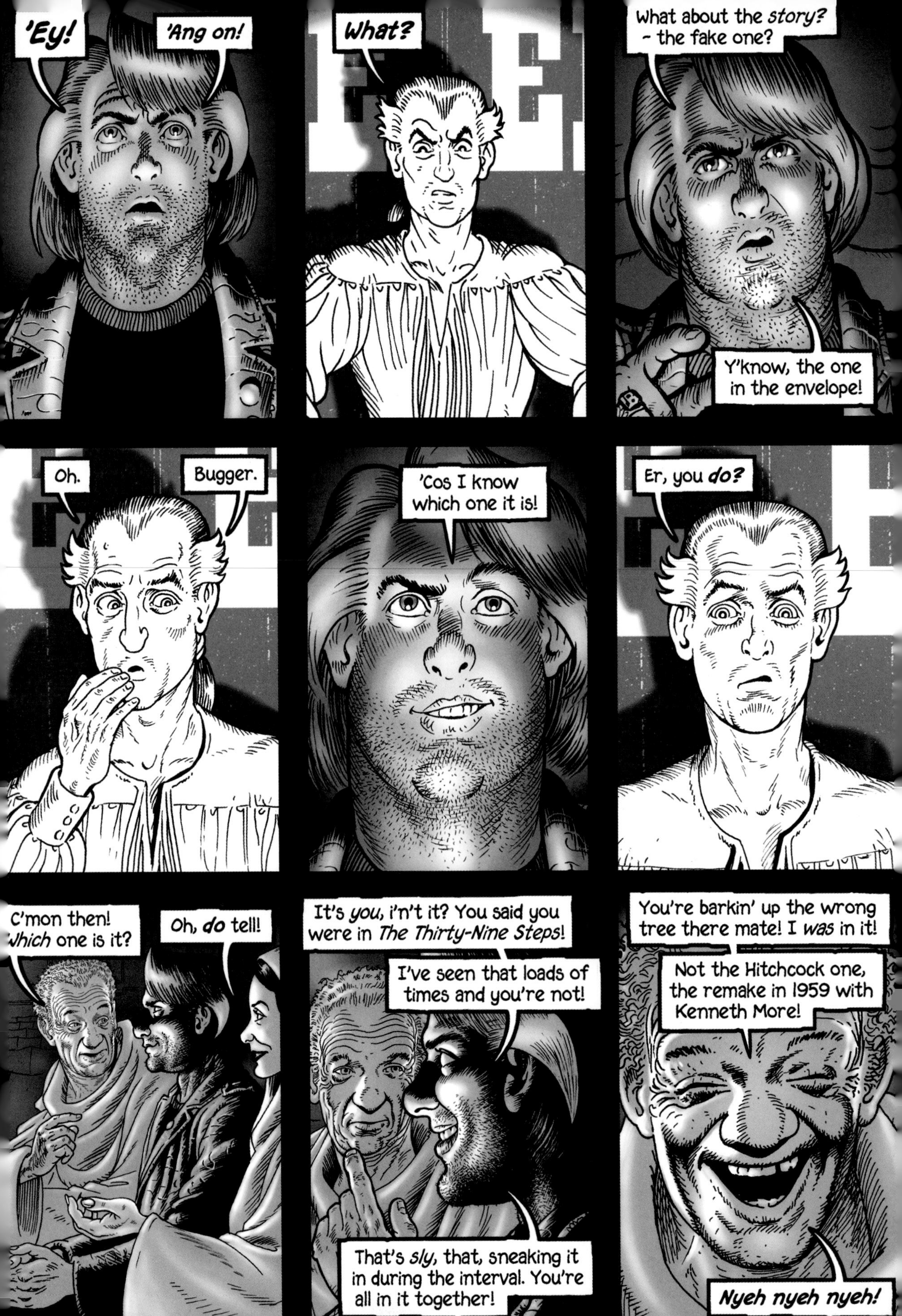
'Ey!
'Ang on!
What?
What about the *story?* – the fake one?
Y'know, the one in the envelope!
Oh.
Bugger.
'Cos I know which one it is!
Er, you *do?*
C'mon then! *Which* one is it?
Oh, *do* tell!
It's *you,* i'n't it? You said you were in *The Thirty-Nine Steps*!
I've seen that loads of times and you're not!
That's *sly,* that, sneaking it in during the interval. You're all in it together!
You're barkin' up the wrong tree there mate! I *was* in it!
Not the Hitchcock one, the remake in 1959 with Kenneth More!
Nyeh nyeh nyeh!

Oh.

Which one was it, then?

Er...*sorry.*

In all the *excitement,* I forgot to include one.

They're all *true!*

I...I *meant* to.

I just forgot.

Look - there's nothing in the envelope!

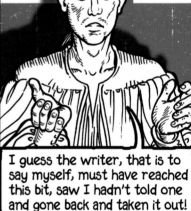

I guess the writer, that is to say myself, must have reached this bit, saw I hadn't told one and gone back and taken it out!

That doesn't make sense!

Pull the other one! What about the light bulb?

Oh, it was invented here all right.

I double and triple checked most of the stories. As far as I know, they're all *true.*

Sorry!

But stay put - I'll make it up to you...

...I'll give you an *encore.*

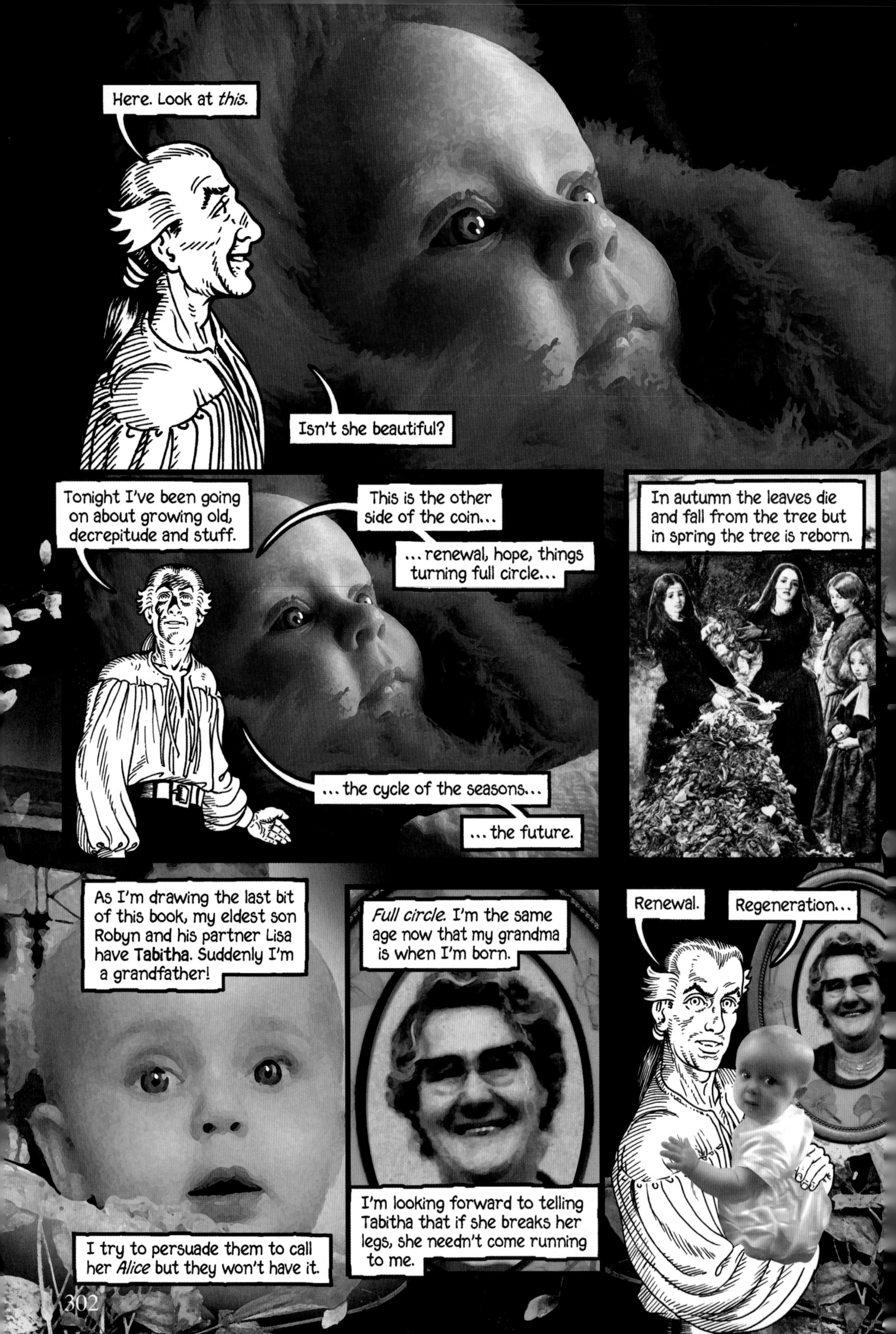
Here. Look at *this.*
Isn't she beautiful?
Tonight I've been going on about growing old, decrepitude and stuff.
This is the other side of the coin...
...renewal, hope, things turning full circle...
...the cycle of the seasons...
...the future.
In autumn the leaves die and fall from the tree but in spring the tree is reborn.
As I'm drawing the last bit of this book, my eldest son Robyn and his partner Lisa have **Tabitha**. Suddenly I'm a grandfather!
I try to persuade them to call her *Alice* but they won't have it.
Full circle. I'm the same age now that my grandma is when I'm born.
I'm looking forward to telling Tabitha that if she breaks her legs, she needn't come running to me.
Renewal.
Regeneration...

...and *that's* what's happening to Sunderland in the 21st century.

The city is reinventing itself. Old industries are replaced by new. The biggest Nissan car factory in Europe is here.

New buildings are springing up on post-industrial land.

Rival developers, each with their own vision of the Sunderland of tomorrow, are battling over the old Vaux brewery site, where once stands the Roman fort.

A large scale archaeological dig is planned while the site is empty.

The historic *Sunniside* area of the city centre has embarked upon a multi-million pound facelift...

...and the city is acknowledging its links with Lewis Carroll with the placing of a plaque to commemorate his stays in Southwick.

Yes, *change* is in the air!

marks Alice author's Wearside stay

City of Sunderland

LEWIS CARROLL

Rev. Charles Lutwidge Dodgson, pen name Lewis Carroll, author of Alice in Wonderland, stayed at Holy Trinity Rectory in 1872 and 1887 visiting his sister Mary who lived here with her husband, the Rev. Collingwood, rector of this parish.

SOUTHWICK HISTORY & PRESERVATION SOCIETY

303

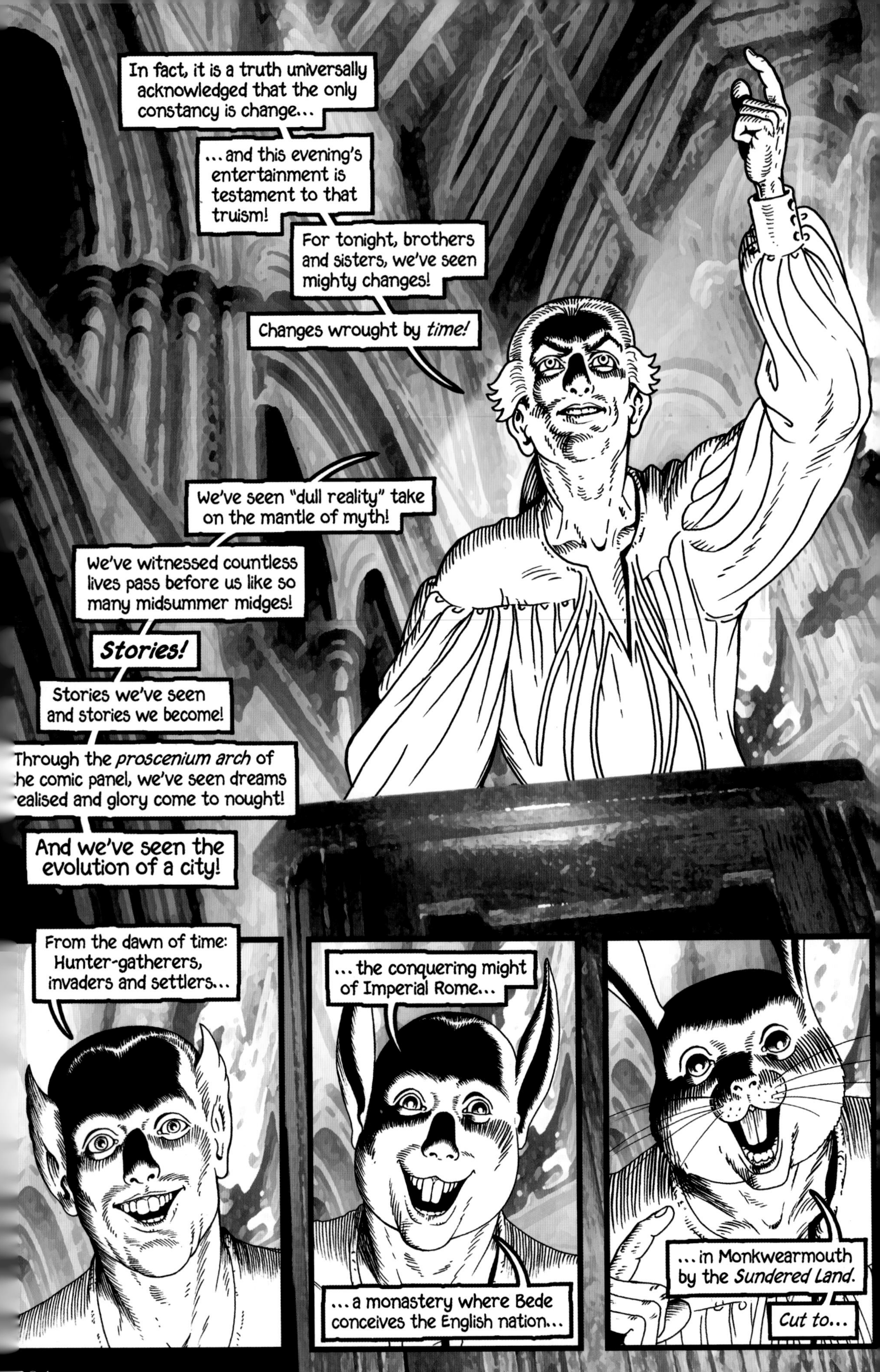
In fact, it is a truth universally acknowledged that the only constancy is change...
...and this evening's entertainment is testament to that truism!
For tonight, brothers and sisters, we've seen mighty changes!
Changes wrought by *time!*
We've seen "dull reality" take on the mantle of myth!
We've witnessed countless lives pass before us like so many midsummer midges!
Stories!
Stories we've seen and stories we become!
Through the *proscenium arch* of the comic panel, we've seen dreams realised and glory come to nought!
And we've seen the evolution of a city!
From the dawn of time: Hunter-gatherers, invaders and settlers...
...the conquering might of Imperial Rome...
...a monastery where Bede conceives the English nation...
...in Monkwearmouth by the *Sundered Land.*
Cut to...

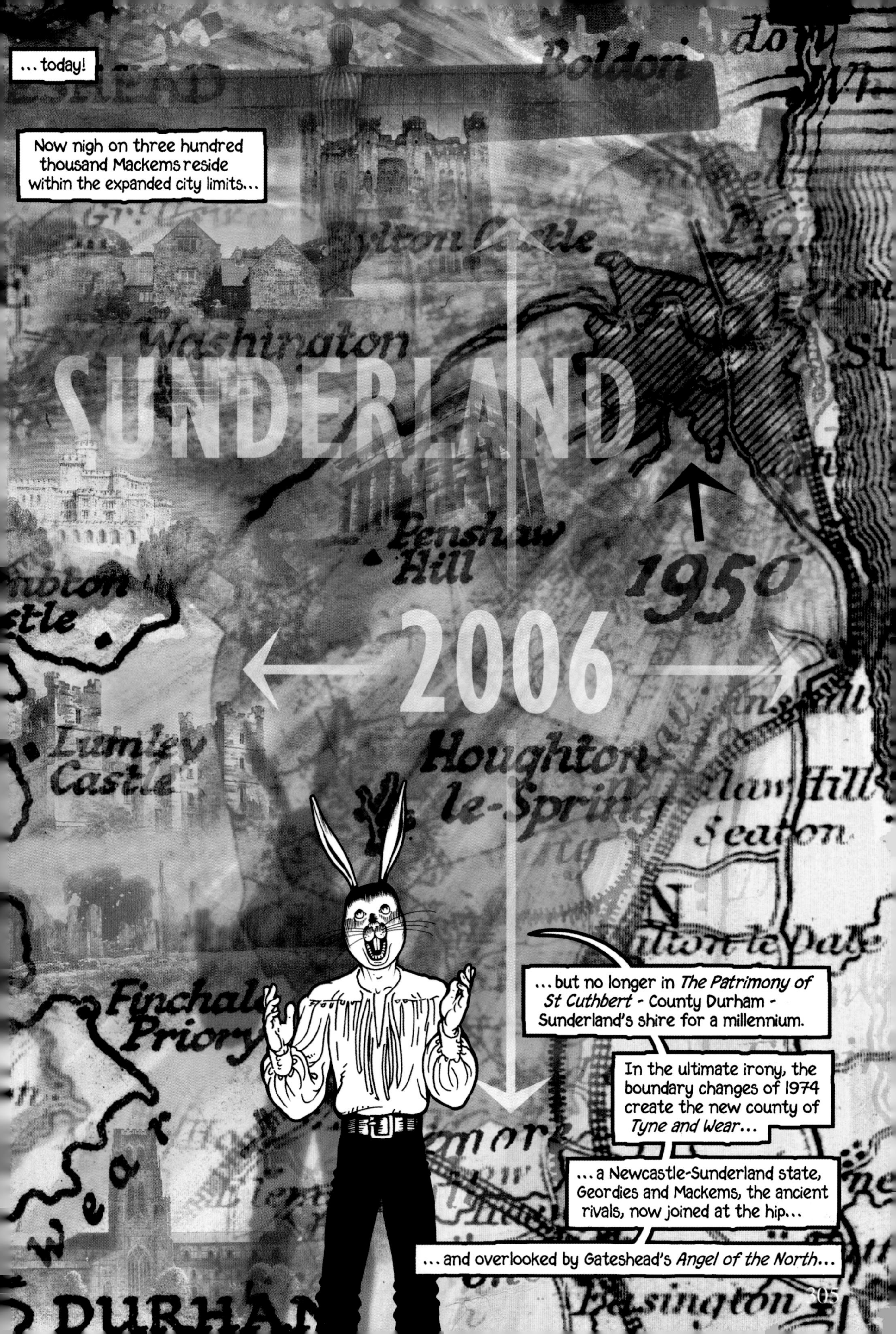

... today!
Now nigh on three hundred thousand Mackems reside within the expanded city limits...
Boldon
Washington
SUNDERLAND
Penshaw Hill
1950
2006
Lumley Castle
Houghton le-Spring
Seaton
Finchale Priory
...but no longer in *The Patrimony of St Cuthbert* - County Durham - Sunderland's shire for a millennium.
In the ultimate irony, the boundary changes of 1974 create the new county of *Tyne and Wear*...
...a Newcastle-Sunderland state, Geordies and Mackems, the ancient rivals, now joined at the hip...
...and overlooked by Gateshead's *Angel of the North*...
DURHAM

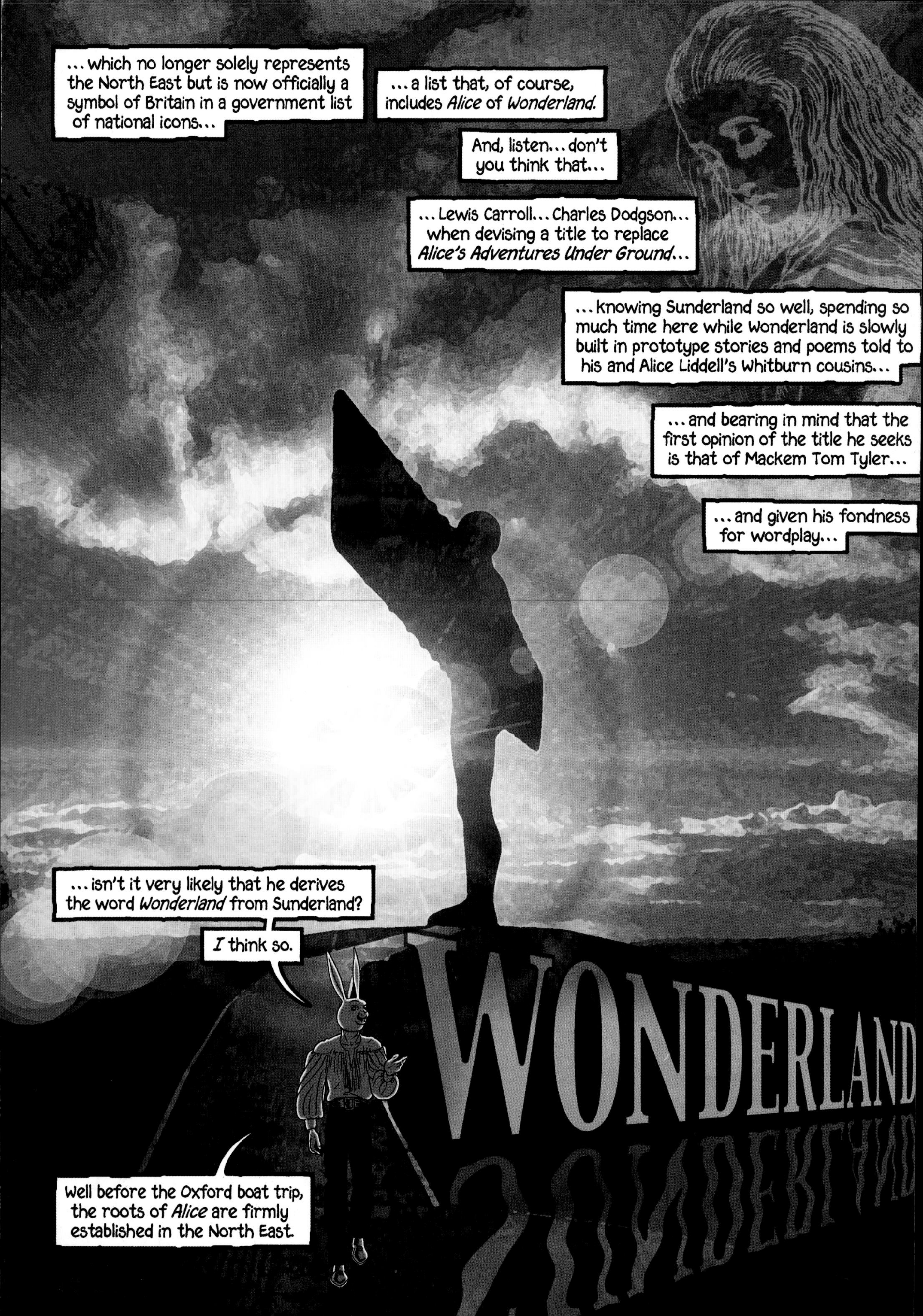
...which no longer solely represents the North East but is now officially a symbol of Britain in a government list of national icons...
...a list that, of course, includes *Alice* of *Wonderland.*
And, listen...don't you think that...
...Lewis Carroll...Charles Dodgson...when devising a title to replace *Alice's Adventures Under Ground*...
...knowing Sunderland so well, spending so much time here while Wonderland is slowly built in prototype stories and poems told to his and Alice Liddell's Whitburn cousins...
...and bearing in mind that the first opinion of the title he seeks is that of Mackem Tom Tyler...
...and given his fondness for wordplay...
...isn't it very likely that he derives the word *Wonderland* from Sunderland?
I think so.
WONDERLAND
Well before the Oxford boat trip, the roots of *Alice* are firmly established in the North East.

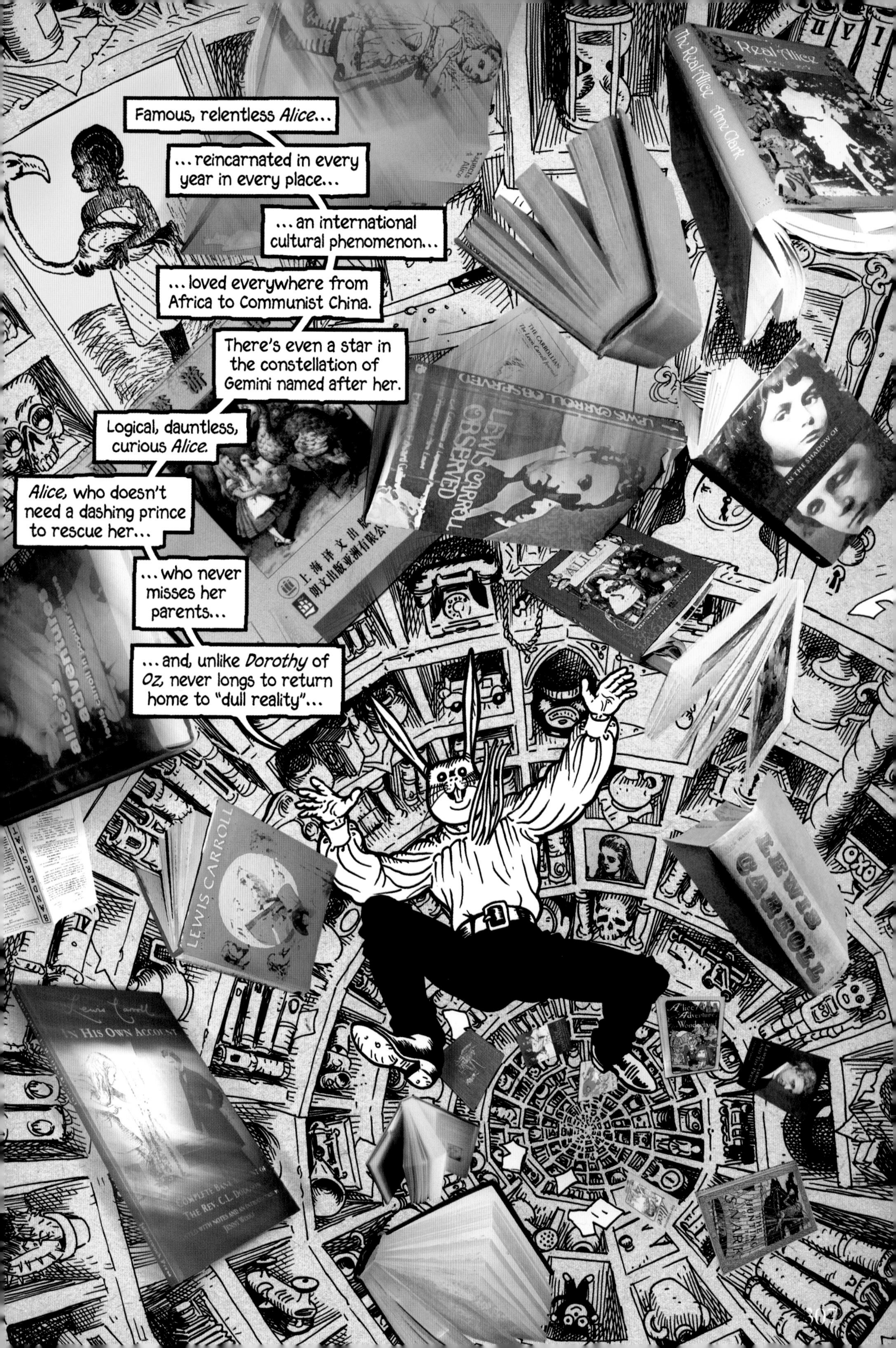
Famous, relentless *Alice*...
...reincarnated in every year in every place...
...an international cultural phenomenon...
...loved everywhere from Africa to Communist China.
There's even a star in the constellation of Gemini named after her.
Logical, dauntless, curious *Alice*.
Alice, who doesn't need a dashing prince to rescue her...
...who never misses her parents...
...and, unlike *Dorothy* of *Oz*, never longs to return home to "dull reality"...
The Real Alice
Anne Clark
Lewis Carroll Observed
In the Shadow of
Lewis Carroll
Lewis Carroll
In His Own Account
上海译文出版
朗文出版亚洲有限公司

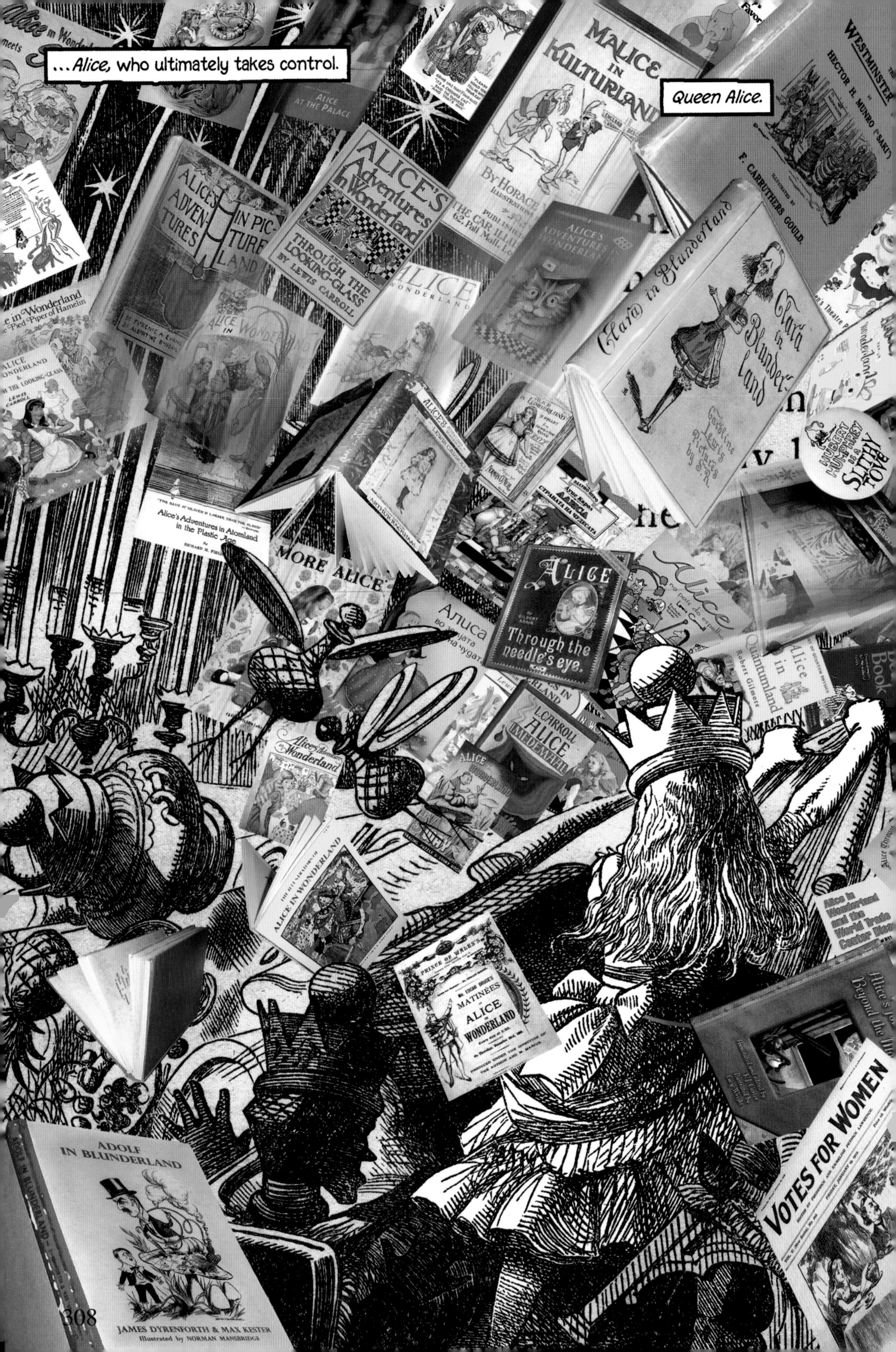
...Alice, who ultimately takes control.
Queen Alice.
MALICE IN KULTURLAND
By HORACE
WESTMINSTER
HECTOR H. MUNRO ("SAKI")
F. CARRUTHERS GOULD.
ALICE'S ADVENTURES IN PICTURE LAND
ALICE'S Adventures in Wonderland
THROUGH THE LOOKING-GLASS
BY LEWIS CARROLL
ALICE AT THE PALACE
Clara in Blunderland
Caroline Lewis
Pictures by S.R.
Alice's Adventures in Atomland in the Plastic Age
MORE ALICE
ALICE
Through the needle's eye.
Alice in Quantumland
Robert Gilmore
HUSBERY HUMPHREY IS A SLITHY TOVE
Alice in Wonderland and the World Trade Center Disaster
ALICE IN WONDERLAND
MATINÉES
ALICE IN WONDERLAND
VOTES FOR WOMEN
ADOLF IN BLUNDERLAND
JAMES DYRENFORTH & MAX KESTER
Illustrated by NORMAN MANSBRIDGE

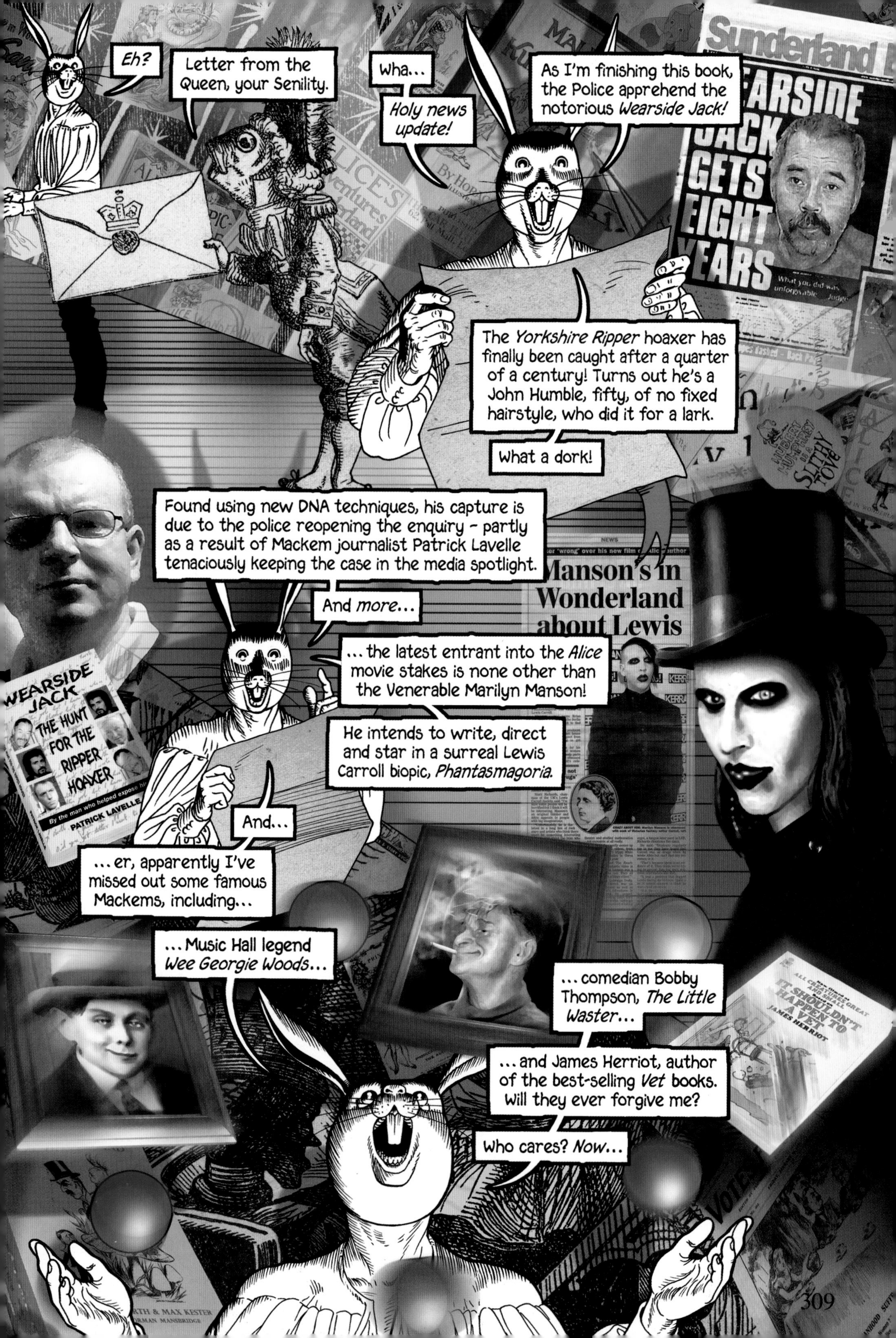
Eh?
Letter from the Queen, your Senility.
Wha...
Holy news update!
As I'm finishing this book, the Police apprehend the notorious *Wearside Jack!*
WEARSIDE JACK GETS EIGHT YEARS
The *Yorkshire Ripper* hoaxer has finally been caught after a quarter of a century! Turns out he's a John Humble, fifty, of no fixed hairstyle, who did it for a lark.
What a dork!
Found using new DNA techniques, his capture is due to the police reopening the enquiry – partly as a result of Mackem journalist Patrick Lavelle tenaciously keeping the case in the media spotlight.
And *more*...
...the latest entrant into the *Alice* movie stakes is none other than the Venerable Marilyn Manson!
He intends to write, direct and star in a surreal Lewis Carroll biopic, *Phantasmagoria.*
Manson's in Wonderland about Lewis
WEARSIDE JACK THE HUNT FOR THE RIPPER HOAXER
PATRICK LAVELLE
And...
...er, apparently I've missed out some famous Mackems, including...
...Music Hall legend *Wee Georgie Woods*...
...comedian Bobby Thompson, *The Little Waster*...
...and James Herriot, author of the best-selling *Vet* books. Will they ever forgive me?
IT SHOULDN'T HAPPEN TO A VET
JAMES HERRIOT
Who cares? *Now*...

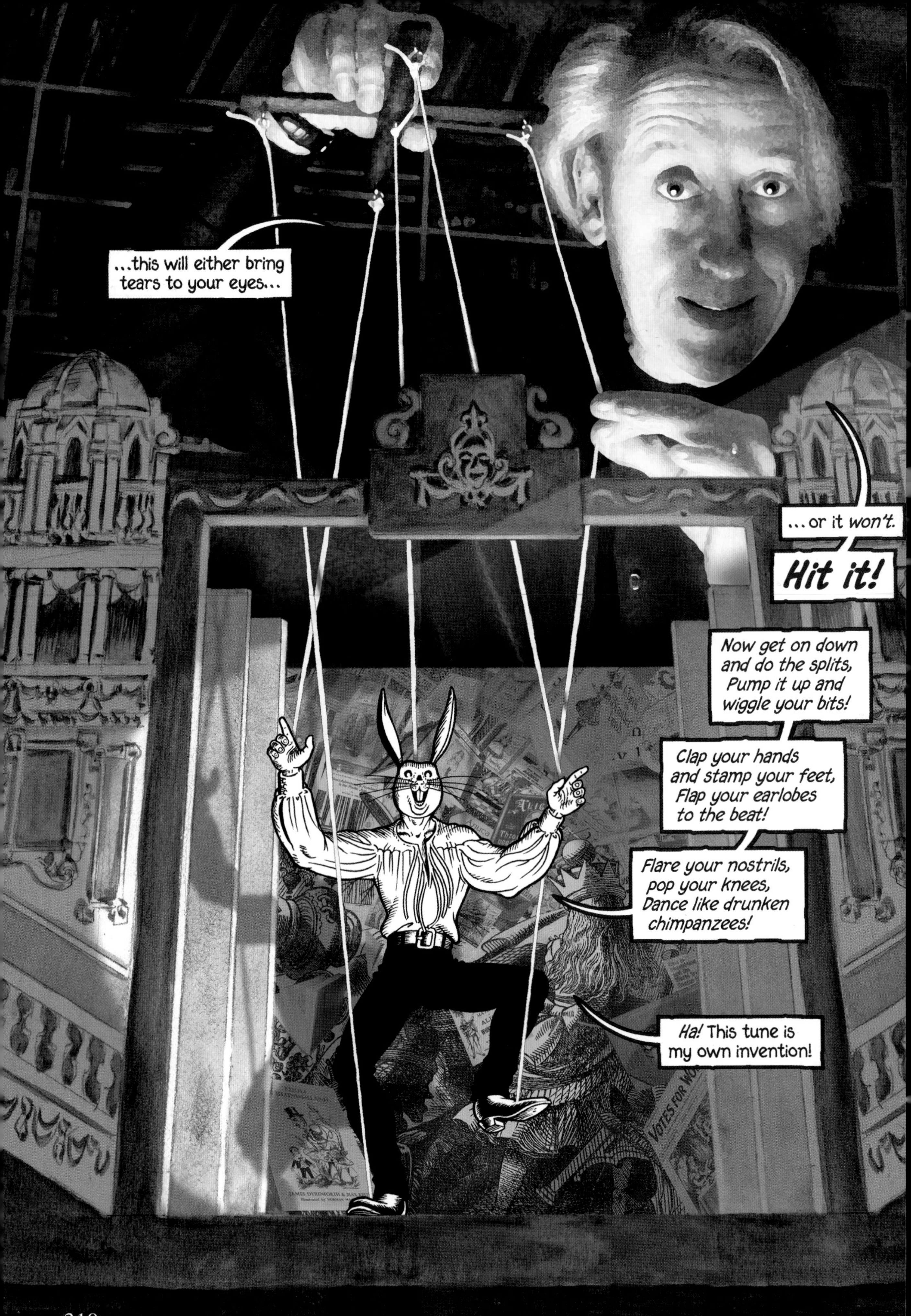
...this will either bring tears to your eyes...
...or it won't.
Hit it!
Now get on down and do the splits, Pump it up and wiggle your bits!
Clap your hands and stamp your feet, Flap your earlobes to the beat!
Flare your nostrils, pop your knees, Dance like drunken chimpanzees!
Ha! This tune is my own invention!
VOTES FOR WO

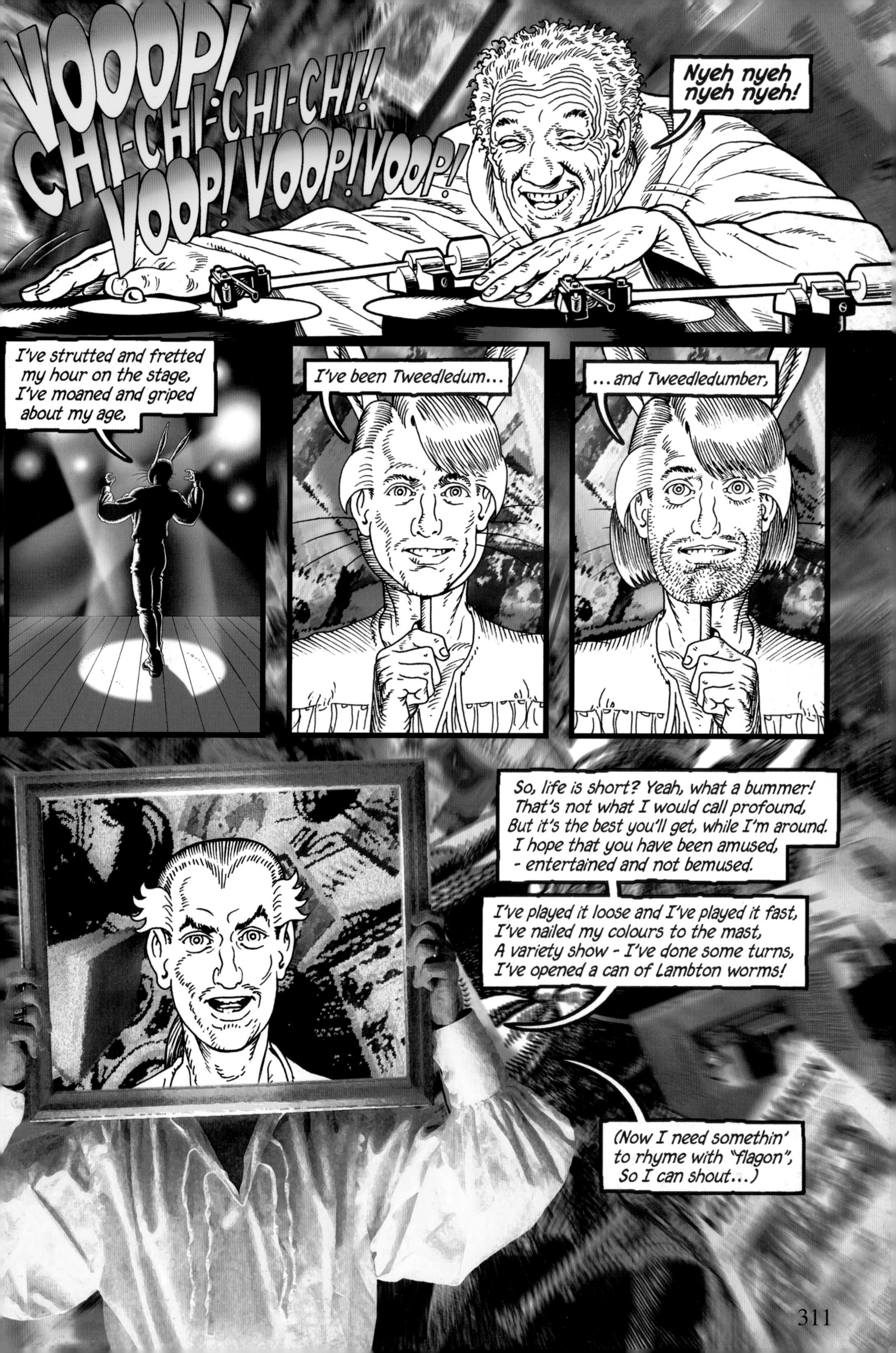
VOOOP! CHI-CHI-CHI-CHI! VOOP! VOOP! VOOP!
Nyeh nyeh nyeh nyeh!
I've strutted and fretted my hour on the stage, I've moaned and griped about my age,
I've been Tweedledum...
...and Tweedledumber,
So, life is short? Yeah, what a bummer! That's not what I would call profound, But it's the best you'll get, while I'm around. I hope that you have been amused, - entertained and not bemused.
I've played it loose and I've played it fast, I've nailed my colours to the mast, A variety show - I've done some turns, I've opened a can of Lambton worms!
(Now I need somethin' to rhyme with "flagon", So I can shout...)

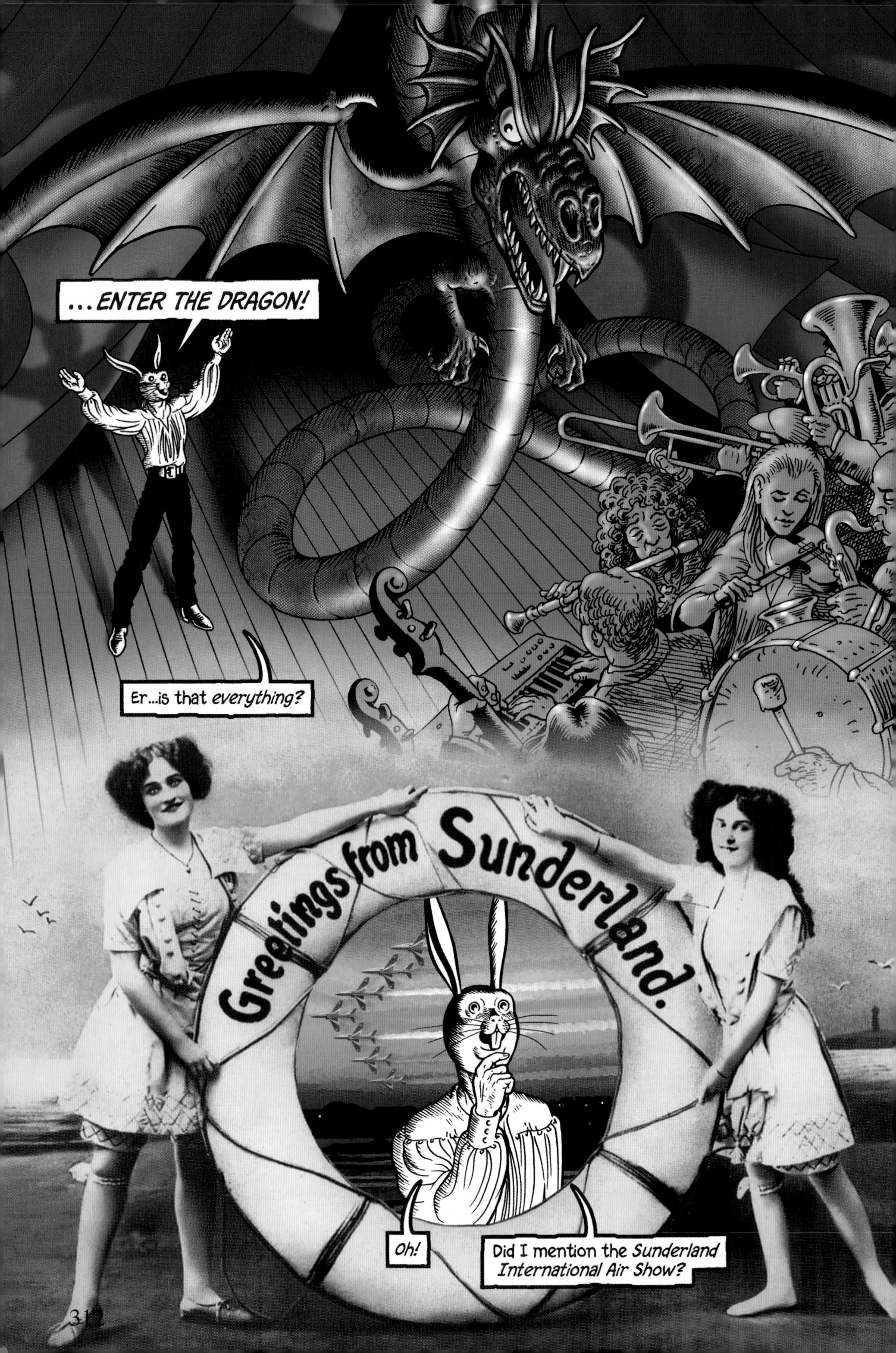

...ENTER THE DRAGON!
Er...is that *everything?*
Greetings from Sunderland.
Oh!
Did I mention the *Sunderland International Air Show?*

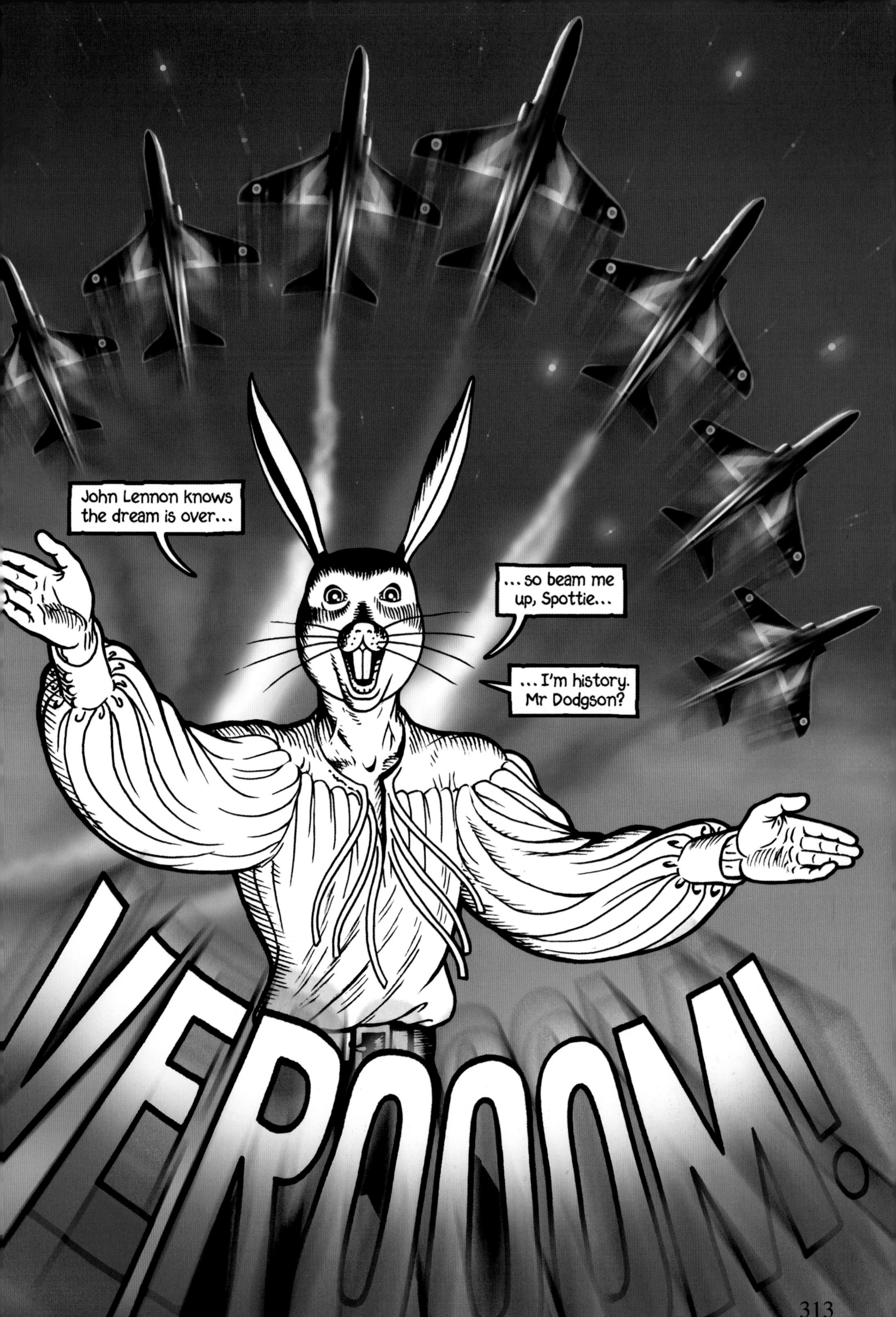
John Lennon knows the dream is over...
...so beam me up, Spottie...
...I'm history. Mr Dodgson?
VEROOOM!

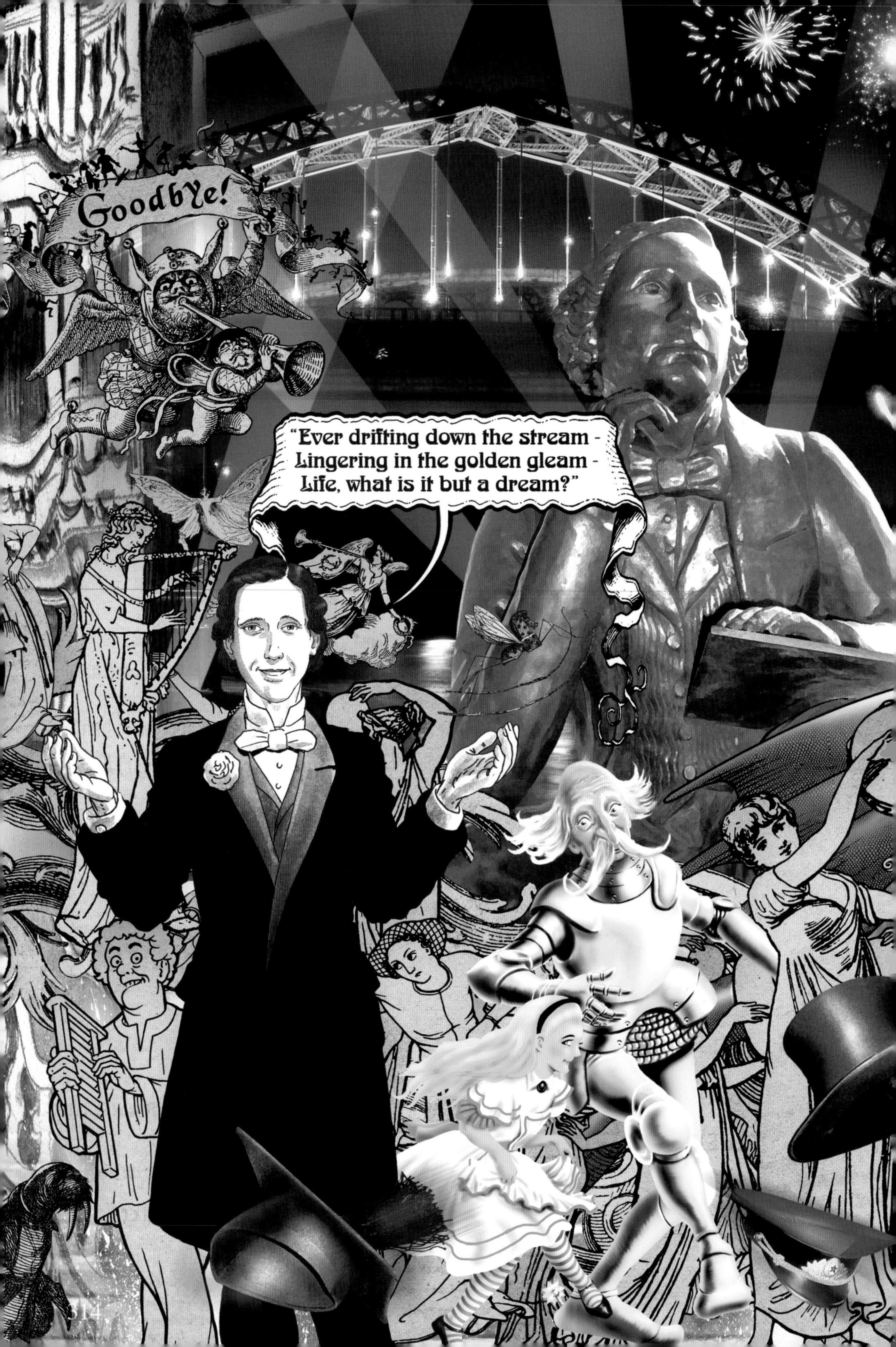
Goodbye!
"Ever drifting down the stream -
Lingering in the golden gleam -
Life, what is it but a dream?"

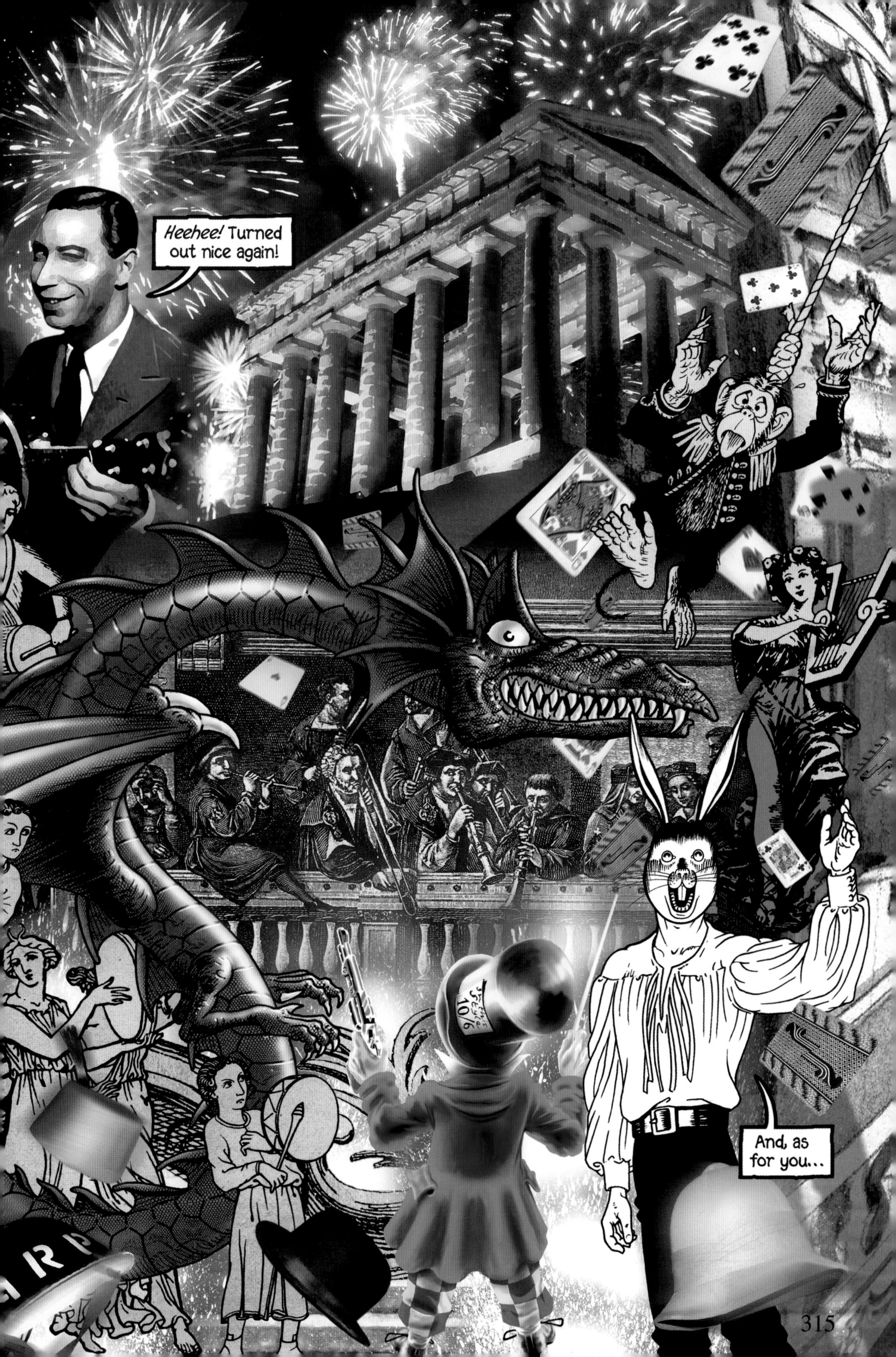
Heehee! Turned out nice again!
And, as for you...

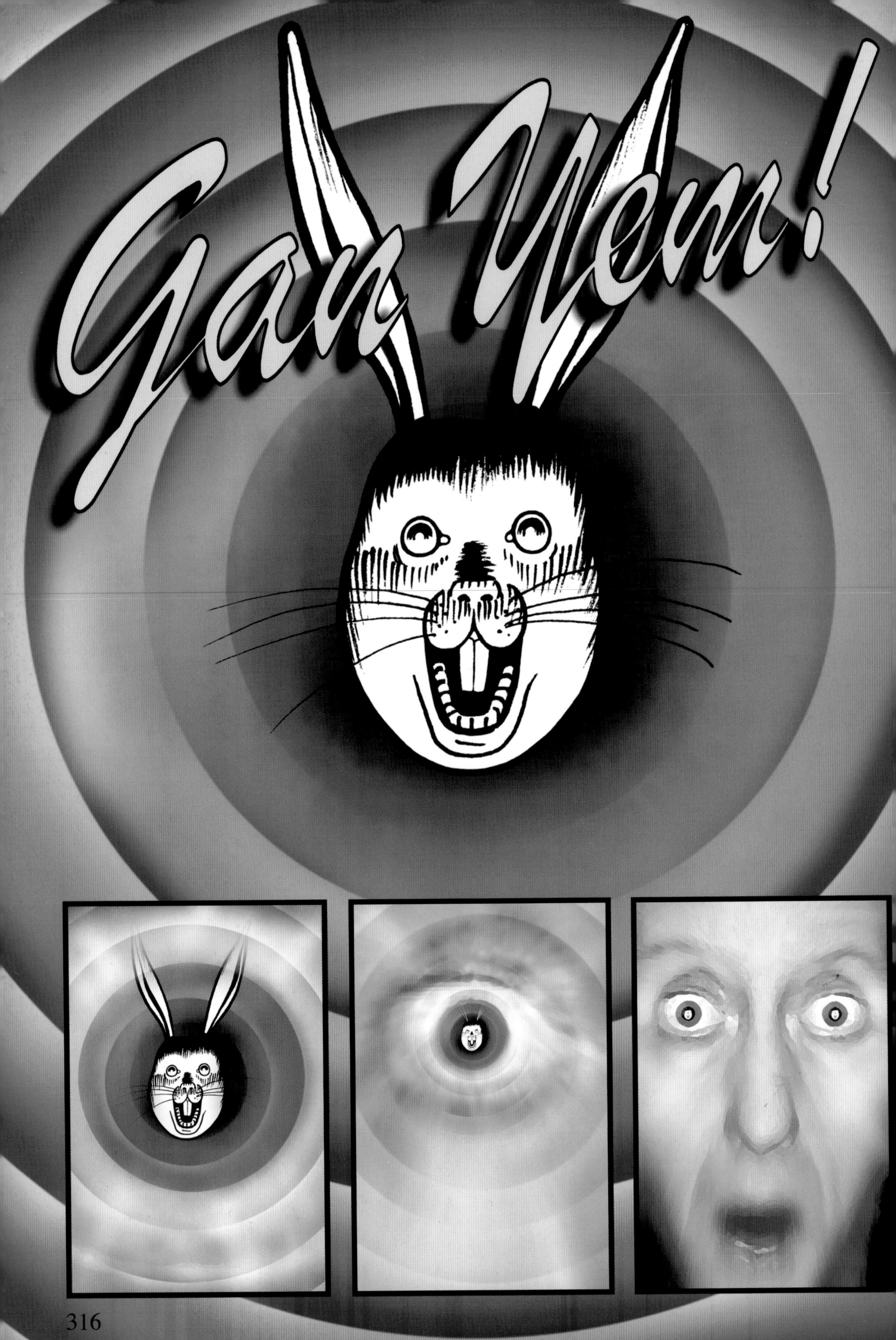
Gan Yem!

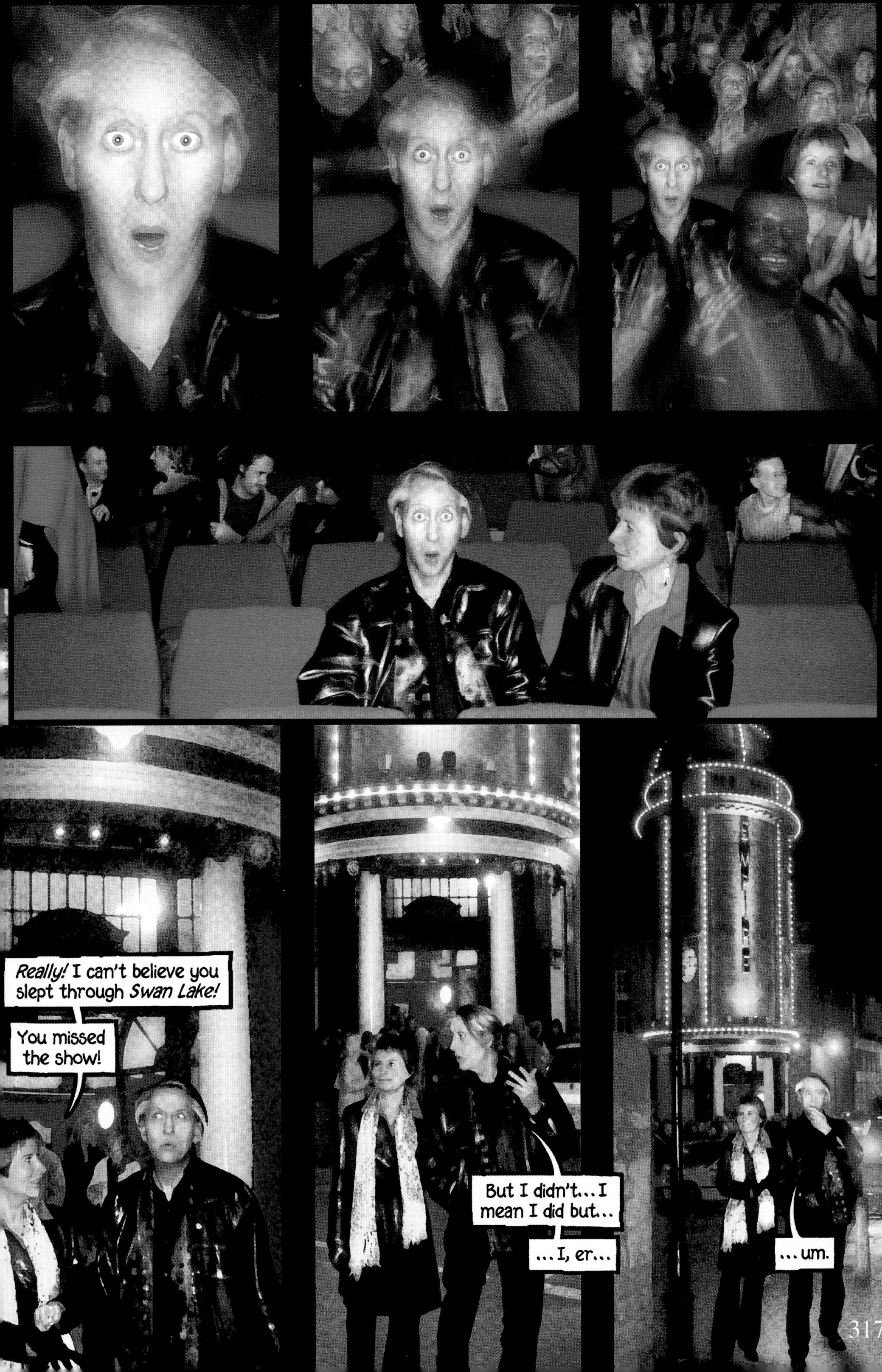
Really! I can't believe you slept through *Swan Lake!*
You missed the show!
But I didn't... I mean I did but...
...I, er...
...um.

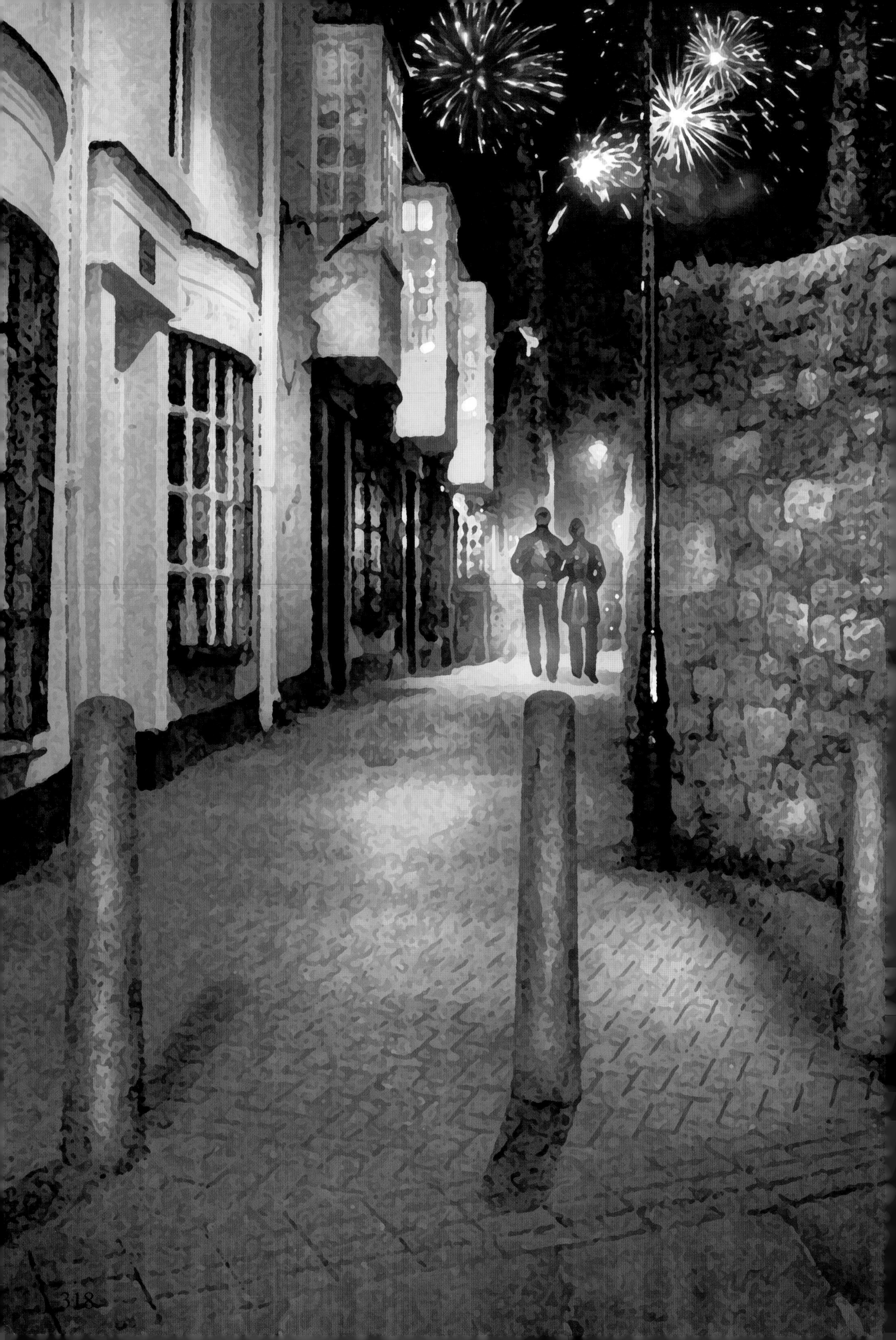

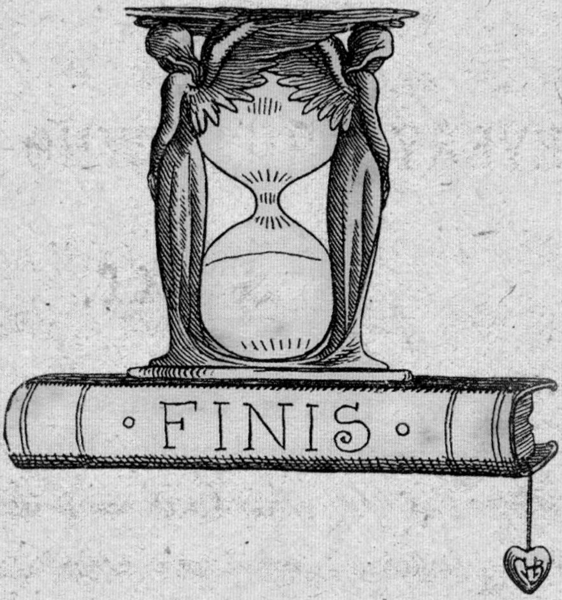
FINIS

[TURN OVER

Credits

Alice in Sunderland written, directed and produced by **Bryan Talbot**

Cover designed by Bryan Talbot & created by **Jordan Smith** (www.darkview.co.uk)

Cover model: **Kaya Anna Lawson Smith**

Page 265 Script by **Leo Baxendale** (www.reaper.co.uk)

Pages 210 – 212 Co-scripted with **Michael Bute**

Pages 95 – 108 Co-scripted with **Chaz Brenchley** & **Colin Wilbourne**

Page 30 Alice statue photograph by **Alex Simmons** (alex@teachingartists.com)

Pages 145, 229, 298 Partial photography by **Simon Bisson** & **Mary Branscombe**

Pages 215, 216, 253, 317 Partial photography by **Jordan Smith**

Pages 182, 183, 318 Photography by **Jordan Smith**

Pages 77 *The Death of Bede* by **William Bell Scott** (1811-1860). Photographed by **Simon Bisson**

Pages 228, 306 Photography by **Simon Bisson** & **Mary Branscombe** (www.sandm.com)

Page 316 *Alice & The White Knight* painted by **Davide Devereux**

Tinman font (page 193) and *Bryan Talbot* font (throughout) created by **Comicraft** (www.comicraft.com)

Headlines & pages from *The Sunderland Echo* used by kind permission of **Northeast Press**

Bayeux Tapestry images used by kind permission of **Reading Museum**

The creation of *Alice in Sunderland* was principally financed, supported and encouraged by my partner, **Dr. Mary Talbot**, whose faith in the project has never wavered. I'd also like to thank **James Owen** of *International Studio* magazine and art collector **Simon Powell** for financial support for some of the work on the book.

Practically all the research on Carroll's and the Liddell family's links to Sunderland contained herein has been done by **Michael Bute**, and *Alice in Sunderland* couldn't have existed without him. His book *A Town Like Alice's* was the starting point of my journey, and throughout the three or four years that it's taken me to complete the project, he's been a constant and encyclopaedic source on all things Carroll and all things Sunderland, often loaning me books and revealing fascinating little-known facts on these subjects, which form the body of his current PhD thesis.

This book was produced with absolutely no help whatsoever from the Newcastle-based *Arts Council England* (North East), who turned down the grant application for this Sunderland-based book.

www.bryan-talbot.com

Acknowledgements

There is a great number of people to whom I give my most sincere thanks, for this book would not have been possible without their help. This help has taken many forms, such as advising and commenting on early versions of the script, proofreading the first finished draft, tracking down articles, scanning old newspaper clippings or out of copyright illustrations, loaning me books, allowing me access to restricted buildings and posing for photographs.

I'm indebted to the Carrollian scholars Ruth Berman, Will Brooker, Michael Bute, Mark Israel, Karoline Leach, John Tufail, Edward Wakeling, Jenny Woolf, Alise G. Wagner and Keith Wright, Mark Richards of The Lewis Carroll Society and members of the Lewis Carroll email discussion group.

Of especial help locally were Ed Tutty and Dominic Stokes of the Sunderland Empire Theatre, Bill Dove, custodian of Holy Trinity Church, Sunderland, Father Geoffrey Driver of the Holy Trinity Church, Southwick, Mark Marshall of St Peter's Church, Sunderland, workers at St Andrew's Church, Roker, Darren Genson of Beamish Museum, Peter Camm and Ron Lawson of the Sunderland Antiquarian Society, River Wear Cruises Ltd., Rob Lawson and Alistair Robinson of *The Sunderland Echo*, members of *The Newcastle Regimente of Foote* (sic) of *The Sealed Knot* civil war re-enactment society, staff of *The Provincial Grand Lodge of Durham* Library and Museum and staff of the Sunderland City Library, the Sunderland Local Studies Library and Whitburn Library.

I'm very grateful to Kate John and Brendan Carr of Reading Museum for arranging permission to use their images of the Museum's replica of the Bayeux Tapestry.

Finally, many thanks to Ashraf Ismail Ahmed, John Allen-Clarke, Dr. Gail-Nina Anderson, Greg Bennett, Simon Bisley, Simon Bisson, Mary Branscombe, Leo Baxendale, Chaz Brenchley, Paul Bulmer, Kevin Cadwallender, Roger Cornwell, John Coulthart, Howard Cruse, Al Davison, Jaspinder Dhillon, Stan Evans, Glenn Fabry, George Freeman, Stephen Gallagher, Dr. Mel Gibson, Steven Grant, Paul Gravett, Steve Holland, Vijaya Iyer, Mike Kidson, Rafael Kayanan, Craig Knowles, Patrick Lavelle, John McShane, Gary Spencer Millidge, Richard and Margaret Mitchinson, Chris and Annie Moir, the Right Honourable Chris Mullin M.P. and Ngoc, Sarah and Emma Mullin, Michael Netzer, Paul Peart-Smith, David Pryke, Dr. Jean Rogers, Tom Rogers, Trina Robbins, Alex Simmons, Angela Smith, Jeff Smith, Jordan and Kaya Smith, Professor John Storey, Alwyn Talbot, May Talbot, Dr. Mary Talbot, Robyn, Lisa and Tabitha Talbot, Martin and Lisa Thomas, Pamela-Ann Walker, Ian Watson and Colin Wilbourn.

Bryan Talbot

In the interests of cleanliness, p health, and the preservation of public perty, readers are requested not to their fingers when turning over the l of books, periodicals, etc.

The corners of leaves must n turned down.

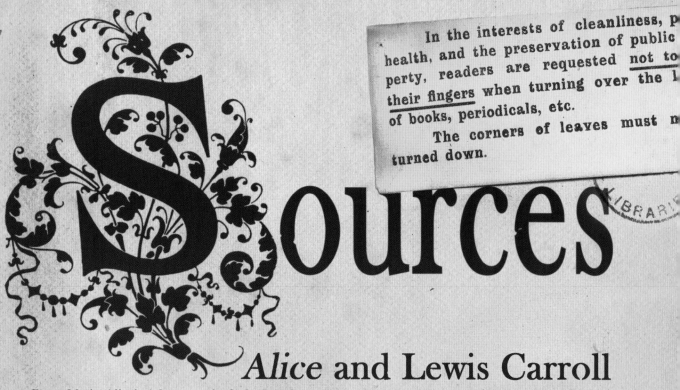

Sources

Alice and Lewis Carroll

Batey, Mavis, ***Alice's Adventures in Oxford***, Andover: Pitkin 1980

Batey, Mavis, ***The World of Alice***, Andover: Pitkin 2002

Berman, Ruth, **"Alice" as Fairytale and Non-Fairytale**, The Carrollian (magazine), The Lewis Carroll Society, Spring 2003

Björk, Christina & Erikson, Inga-Kavin, ***The Other Alice***, Stockholm: R&S Books 1993

Brooker, Will, ***Alice's Adventures: Lewis Carroll in Popular Culture***, New York: Continuum 2004

Bute, Michael, ***A Town Like Alice's***, Sunderland: Heritage Publications 1997

Carroll, Lewis, ***The Diaries of Lewis Carroll Vols 1 & 2***, (Ed.) Roger Lancelyn Green, London: Cassell & Co 1953

Carroll, Lewis, ***The Works of Lewis Carroll***, London: Paul Hamlyn 1965

Clarke Amor, Anne, ***Lewis Carroll, Child of the North***, Lewis Carroll Society 1995

Clarke, Anne, ***The Real Alice***, London: Michael Joseph Ltd. 1981

Cohen, Morton, Introduction to ***Wasp In a Wig*** by Lewis Carroll, *Telegraph Sunday Magazine* Sept 4th 1977

Dodgson, Stuart, ***The Lewis Carroll Picture Book***, London: T.Fisher Unwin 1899

Dodgson, Stuart, ***The Life and Letters of Lewis Carroll***, London: T. Fisher Unwin 1898

Engen, Rodney, ***Sir John Tenniel: Alice's White Knight***, Aldershot: Scholar Press 1991

Gardiner, Martin (ed.), ***The Annotated Alice***, London: Penguin Books 2001

Gernstein, Helmut, ***Lewis Carroll Photographer***, New York: Dover 1949

Gordon, Colin, ***Beyond the Looking Glass***, London: Hodder and Stoughton 1982

Guiliano, Edward (ed.), ***Lewis Carroll Observed***, New York: Clarkson N. Potter 1976

Jones, Jo Elwyn & Gladstone, J.Francis, ***The Alice Companion***, London: Macmillan 1998

Leach, Karoline, ***In the Shadow of the Dreamchild***, London: Peter Owen 1999

Lewis Carroll Society, **Bandersnatch** (newsletter) 2003-06

Matheson, Brenda Dane, ***Lewis Carroll Around the North***, Nordales 1974

Phillips, Robert (ed.), ***Aspects of Alice***, London: Victor Gollancz 1972

Pudney, John, ***Lewis Carroll And His World***, London: Thames and Hudson 1976

Rackin, Donald, ***Alice's Adventures in Wonderland and Through the Looking Glass: Nonsense, Sense and Meaning***, New York: Twayne Publishing 1991

Stern, Jeffrey (ed.), ***The Lewis Carroll Bibliophile***, Luton: White Stone Publishing 1997

Stoffel, Stephanie Lovett, ***Lewis Carroll and Alice***, London: Thames and Hudson 1997

Taylor, Roger & Wakeling, Edward, ***Lewis Carroll, Photographer***, Princeton Univ. Press 2002

Whitty, Joan, **The Rectory Umbrella**, Housewife (magazine), Hulton Press, July 1950

Wood, Robert, ***Victorian Delights***, London: Evans Brothers 1967

Woolf, Jenny, ***Lewis Carroll In His Own Account***, London: Jabberwocky Press 2005

Wullschläger, Jackie, ***Inventing Wonderland***, New York: Simon & Schuster 1995

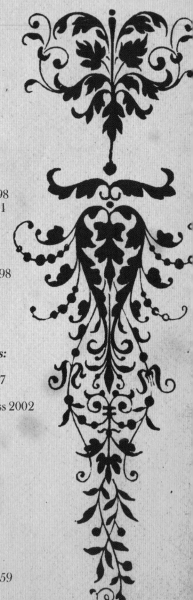

History

Ashe, Geoffrey, ***The Mythology of the British Isles***, London: Methuen 1990

Bailey, Brian, ***The Industrial Heritage of Britain***, London: Ebury Press 1982

Briggs, Asa, ***A Social History of England***, London: BCA 1994

Evans, E.J. (ed.), ***The Encyclopedia of British History***, Bath: Paragon Books 2002

Guirand, Felix (ed.), ***Larousse Encyclopaedia of Mythology***, London: Paul Hamlyn 1959

Gregg, Pauline, ***Free-born John***, London: George G. Harrap & Co. Ltd 1961

Halliday, F.E., *A Concise History of England*, London: Thames and Hudson 1966
McAleavy, Tony, *Life in a Medieval Abbey*, London: English Heritage 1996
Punch, or The London Charivari, Bound Editions, London: Punch 1870-1907
Readers' Digest, *Folklore, Myths and Legends of Britain*, London: Readers' Digest 1973
Schama, Simon, *A History of Britain*, London: BBC Worldwide 2000
Stenton, Frank (ed.), *The Bayeaux Tapestry*, London: Phaidon Press 1957

Sunderland and the North East

The Alderman (magazine), Sunderland: The Alderman 1877
Anon. (ed.), *Sketches of Public Men of the North*, Newcastle: Wllm. Gridley & Co. 1855
Appleton, Arthur, *Mary Ann Cotton*, London: Michael Joseph Ltd 1973
Arthur, T., *The Singular History of The Cauld Lad of Hilton*, York: 1858
Boyle, Maurice, *Wearside at War*, Sunderland & Hartlepool Publishing & Printing 1984
Brett, Alan, *The Amazing World of Sunderland*, Sunderland: Black Cat Publications 1994
Brockie, William, *Legends and Superstitions of the County of Durham*, Durham: Wllm. Brockie 1886
Browne, Rev. G.F., *The Venerable Bede: His Life and Writings*, London: Macmillan 1919
Cambridge, Eric, *Lindisfarne Priory and Holy Island*, London: English Heritage 1988
Colgrave, Bertram and Cramp, Rosemary, *St Peter's Church Monkwearmouth*, Sunderland: N.D.
Corfe, T., *The History of Sunderland*, Sunderland: Frank Graham 1973
Dodds, Glen Lyndon, *Historic Sites of County Durham*, Sunderland: Albion Press 1996
Dodds, Glen Lyndon, *A History of Sunderland*, Sunderland: Albion Press 2001
Fisher, T., *Picture Postcards of Old Sunderland*, Sunderland: Hendon Press 1966
Hickmore, M.A.S., *St Peter's Church Monkwearmouth*, Sunderland: N.D.
Higham, Bill, *The Castle in the Community*, Sunderland: The Friends of Hylton Dene 2005
Hill, Revd. Stuart G., *St Peter's Church and the Wearmouth-Jarrow Monastery*, Sunderland: St Peter's 2000
Hind, Albert L., *The River Wear: History and Legend of Long Ago*, Sunderland: 1979
Hind, Albert L., *The Story of the Lambton Worm*, Sunderland: 1978
Holman, Sheri, *The Dress Lodger*, New York: Ballantine Books 2000
Jessop, L. & Sinclair, N.T., *Sunderland Museum*, Newcastle: Tyne & Wear Museums 1996
Lambert, Richard, *The Railway King*, London: Allen & Unwin Ltd 1934
MacGowan, Douglas, *Burke & Hare*, Thecrimelibrary.com
MacGowan, Douglas, *Mary Anne Cotton*, Thecrimelibrary.com
MacLaren, Michael, *Jack Crawford, The Hero of Camperdown*, Sunderland: Salamander Studios 1997
Milburn, Geoffrey, *Holy Trinity Church*, Sunderland, Tyne and Wear, London: The Churches Conservation Trust 1998
Milburn, Geoffrey E. & Miller, Stuart T (ed.), *Sunderland – River, Town and People*, Sunderland Borough Council 1988
Miller, Stuart and Bell, Billy, *Sunderland in Old Photographs*, Sunderland: Sutton Publishing 1991
O'Brien, Pat, *Sunderland: The Way We Were*, Sunderland: Black Cat Publications 2001
Rhys, Ernest, *The Lambton Worm* in *Fairy Gold*, Rhys, Ernest (ed.), London: J.M. Dent & Sons Ltd. 1907
Robertson, Carol and Hall, Phil, *Millennium City: The Making of Modern Sunderland*, Sunderland: Northeast Press 2000
Robertson, Carol, *Sunderland: The Making of a 21st Century City*, City of Sunderland 2000
Robinson, Alistair, *The Sunderland Empire*, Newcastle: TUPS Books 2000
Robinson, Capt. Edward, *The Life of Jack Crawford*, Sunderland: J.D.Todd 1866
Robson, Alan, *Alan Robson's Grisly Trails and Ghostly Tales*, London: Virgin 1992
Ruttley, John, *Mowbray, The People's Park*, Sunderland: John Ruttley 2002
Screeton, Paul, *Whisht Lads and Haad Yor Gobs: The Lambton Worm and other Northumbrian Dragon Legends*, Sunderland: Northeast Press 1998
Screeton, Paul, *Who Hung the Monkey?*, Hartlepool: Printability Publishing 1991
Sharpe, Cuthbert, *The Bishopric Garland*, Durham: Nicholas & Balwin & Craddock 1834
Smith, D.W. (ed.), *Sunderland's History*, Sunderland: Sunderland Antiquarian Society 2003
Stranks, C.J., *Durham Cathedral*, Andover: Pitkin 1968
The Sunderland Echo (newspaper), Northeast Press 1999-2006
Tedder, Alan, *Ghosts, Mysteries and Legends of Sunderland*, Sunderland: Black Cat Publications 1992
Tedder, Alan, *Sunderland East End*, Sunderland: Black Cat Publications 1990
Tedder, Alan, *Sunderland East End Revisited*, Sunderland: The Peoples' Press 2000
Ward, Julie & Napthine, David (ed.), *The Likes of Us – Sunderland People Talking*, Sunderland: Wear Books 1993
Wilson, Bracey Robson, *Recollections of Sunderland in the 1820s*, Newcastle Weekly Chronicle 1881, reprinted by The Sunderland Antiquarian Society, (Ed. Peter Camm), 2004

Miscellaneous

Bindman, David, *Hogarth*, London: Thames & Hudson 1982
Fisher, John, *George Formby*, London: The Woburn Press 1975
Gifford, Denis, *The International Book of Comics*, London: WH Smith 1984
Glancey, Jonathan, *George Formby*, The Guardian (newspaper) 24 Nov 2001
Kru, Andy Konky, *Obadiah Oldbuck*, Bugpowder.com
McCloud, Scott, *Understanding Comics*, New York: Tundra 1993
Mellor, G.J., *The Northern Music Hall*, Newcastle: Frank Graham 1970
Perry, George and Aldridge, Alan, *The Penguin Book of Comics*, London: Penguin 1967
Uglow, Jenny, *Hogarth, A Life and a World*, London: Faber & Faber 1997
The Victoria and Albert Museum (ed.), *Penny Dreadfuls and Comics*, London: The Victoria and Albert Museum 1983

Bryan Talbot has written and drawn comics for thirty years, for underground publications such as *Street Comix* and *Slow Death*, magazine strips for the likes of *Ad Astra* and *Spin*, and famous titles such as *Legends of the Dark Knight, Sandman, Fables, Hellblazer*, and *Judge Dredd*. His first prose book, *The Naked Artist: Comic Book Legends* is published in June 2007 by Moonstone.

Other books by Bryan Talbot

The Adventures of Luther Arkwright
Heart of Empire: The Legacy of Luther Arkwright
The Tale of One Bad Rat
Brainstorm!

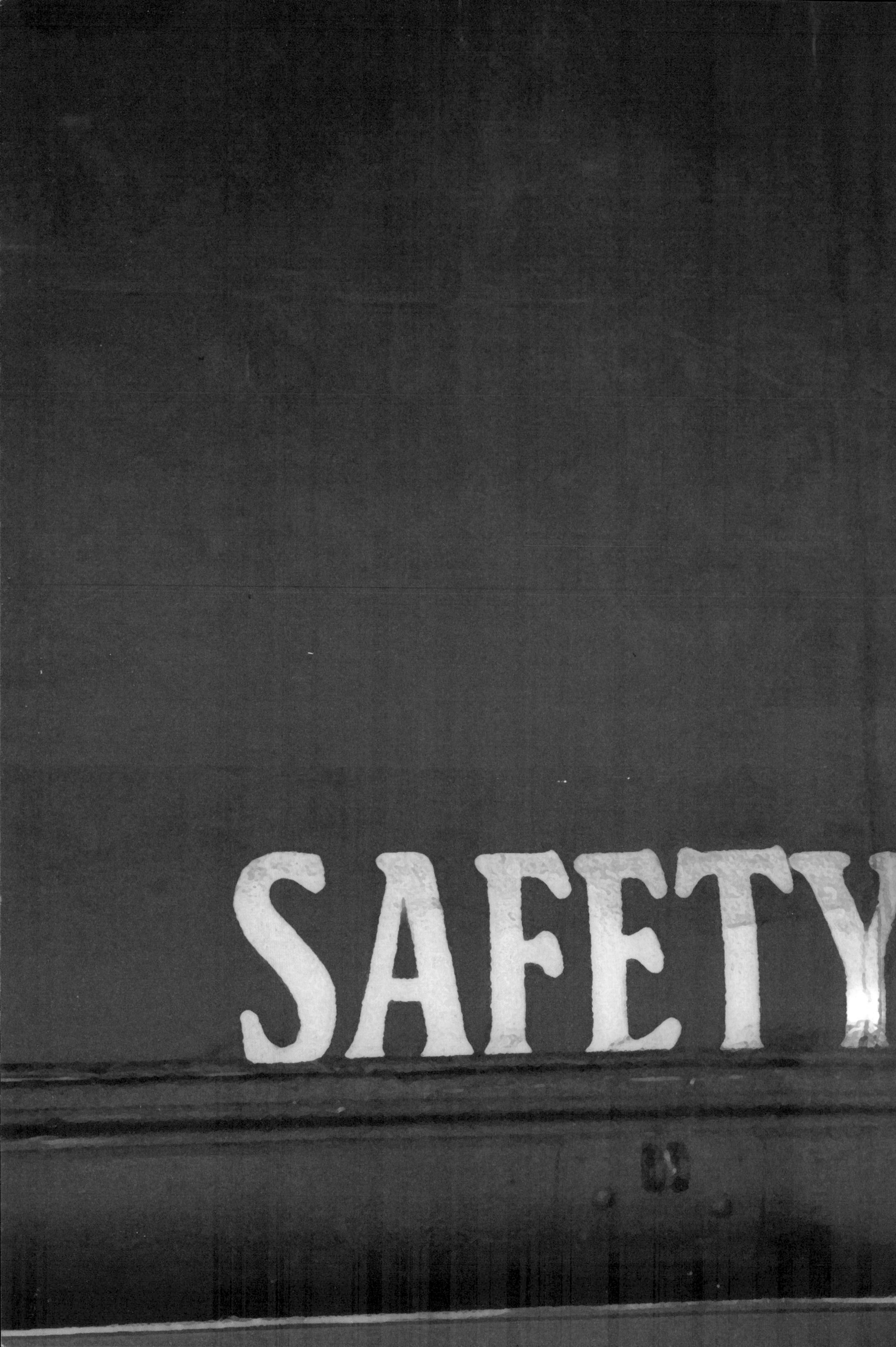
SAFETY